HUMAN NATURE, RITUAL, AND HISTORY

**STUDIES IN PHILOSOPHY
AND THE HISTORY OF PHILOSOPHY**

General Editor: Jude P. Dougherty

Studies in Philosophy
and the History of Philosophy   Volume 43

Human Nature, Ritual, and History
Studies in Xunzi and Chinese Philosophy

by Antonio S. Cua

THE CATHOLIC UNIVERSITY OF AMERICA PRESS
Washington, D.C.

Copyright © 2005
The Catholic University of America Press
All rights reserved

LIBRARY OF CONGRESS CATALOGING-IN-PUBLICATION DATA
Cua, A. S. (Antonio S.), 1932–
Human nature, ritual, and history : studies in Xunzi and Chinese philosophy /
by Antonio S. Cua.
      p. cm. — (Studies in philosophy and the history of philosophy ; 43)
Includes bibliographical references and index.
ISBN 978-0-8132-2758-0 (pbk)
    1. Xunzi, 340–245 B.C. Xunzi.   2. Philosophy, Confucian.   3. Philosophy,
Chinese—To 221 B.C.   I. Title: Studies in Xunzi and Chinese philosophy.
II. Title. III. Series.
B128.H7C82 2005
181´.112—dc22
2004002314

To Shoke-Hwee Khaw

With gratitude and affection

Contents

Preface ix
Acknowledgments xi

PART I. XUNZI'S MORAL PHILOSOPHY

1. Philosophy of Human Nature (1976) 3
2. Dimensions of *Li* (Propriety) (1978) 39
   Appendix 1—Human Relationships and the Virtues
   in the *Liji* (1979) 63
   Appendix 2—Moral Cultivation and Music in the *Liji* (1979) 68
3. Ethical Uses of the Past (1984) 73
4. The Problem of Conceptual Unity (1984) 99
5. The Unity of Virtues (1985) 121
6. The Possibility of Ethical Knowledge (1989) 138
7. The Ethical and the Religious Dimensions of
   Li (Propriety) (1999) 160
8. Ethical Significance of Shame: Insights of Aristotle
   and Xunzi (2002) 191

PART II. OTHER STUDIES IN CHINESE PHILOSOPHY

9. Practical Causation and Confucian Ethics (1974) 247
10. Moral Theory and the Quality of Life (1978) 259
11. Confucian Vision and the Human Community (1980) 281
12. Ethical Significance of Thomé H. Fang's Philosophy (1987) 292
13. Reason and Principle in Chinese Philosophy (1995) 303
14. Emergence of the History of Chinese Philosophy (1999) 317
15. *Xin* (Mind/Heart) and Moral Failure: Notes on an
    Aspect of Mencius's Moral Psychology (1999) 348

Bibliography 371
Index of Names 389
Index of Subjects 395
Glossary 401

Preface

The first part of this volume consists of a selection of eight papers written over twenty-seven years (1976–2002) on various aspects of Xunzi's moral philosophy, including the problematic character of original human nature; the moral, aesthetic, and religious dimensions of *li* (ritual); ethical uses of history; ethical knowledge; and the ethical significance of the distinction between honor and shame. Discussion of other key aspects of Xunzi's moral philosophy, especially those that pertain to the nature of ethical discourse, moral justification, and diagnosis of erroneous ethical beliefs are given in my *Ethical Argumentation: A Study in Hsün Tzu's [Xunzi's] Moral Epistemology* (1985). Notably, a number of my Confucian papers that appeared in my *Moral Vision and Tradition: Essays in Chinese Ethics* (1998) embodied insights derived from my studies of Xunzi's moral philosophy, for example, reasonable action and Confucian argumentation, morality and human nature, self-deception, the role of paradigmatic individuals in moral education, the possibility of a Confucian theory of rhetoric, and the attempt to formulate a Confucian theory of virtues.

The second part of this volume consists of papers that deal with various aspects of Chinese philosophy—the idea of *ganying* as that of practical as distinct from theoretical causation, the relevance of the Confucian conception of the unity and harmony of humanity and nature *(tianren heyi)* to ecological ethics, Confucian vision of *ren* as an ideal of extensive affection and concern for the well-being of human community, the problem of interpreting *li** (principle, pattern, reason) in Chinese philosophy, and the emergence of the history of Chinese philosophy as a transformation of the history of Chinese thought—and studies of Mencius and Thomé H. Fang.

Within each part, the essays appear in the order in which they were written. Essay 12 is a revision of a paper presented at the 1987 Conference on Fang Dongmei's Philosophy held in Taipei, and was not previously published in an English philosophy journal. Essay 10 appears here for the first time. Except for minor revisions that improve the style and clarity of presentation, and replacement of Wade-Giles by pinyin romanizations, no substantive changes have been made in any of the previously published papers. In most of the essays, however, I have included references to later writings enclosed in brackets or in new footnotes. For fuller details, see the Acknowledgments.

I am grateful to Dean Kurt Pritzl and former Dean Jude P. Dougherty for encouragement and support of my projects all through the years before my retirement as Professor Emeritus in the School of Philosophy at The Catholic University of America. Nearer home, again I am much indebted to my wife, Shoke-Hwee Khaw, and my daughter, Athene, for their affectionate concern and support. For more than forty years, Shoke-Hwee also has been a helpful discussant of most of my Confucian works in progress. I dedicate this work to her as an expression of my gratitude and affection.

NOTES ON CITATION FROM THE 'XUNZI'

In this volume, parenthetical citations of the *Xunzi [Hsün Tzu]* refer to the following: Li Disheng, *Xunzi jishi* (Taipei: Xuesheng, 1979), which was based on the standard Wang Xianqian's *Xunzi jijie;* H. H. Dubs, trans., *The Works of Hsüntze* (Taipei: Chengwen, 1966); Burton Watson, trans., *Hsün Tzu: Basic Writings* (New York: Columbia University Press, 1963); John Knoblock, *Xunzi: A Translation and Study of the Complete Works*, 3 vols. (Stanford, Calif.: Stanford University Press, 1988-94); and Wing-tsit Chan, *A Source Book in Chinese Philosophy* (Princeton, N.J.: Princeton University Press, 1963). The references are abbreviated, with "L," "D," "W," "K," and "C" indicating the works of Li, Dubs, Watson, Knoblock, and Chan, respectively, and numerals indicating their page numbers. All parenthetical citations include, first, the passage in Li, and second, the translation adopted. Additional references are given only for comparative purposes. Where only Li is cited, the translation is my own. For the convenience of readers who have other editions, all references are preceded by the titles of the essays. Asterisks indicate emendations. Transcriptions of Chinese characters with asterisks within an essay indicate homophones.

Acknowledgment of Sources of Previously Published Materials

PART I. XUNZI'S MORAL PHILOSOPHY

1. Philosophy of Human Nature
Section 1 from "The Conceptual Aspect of Hsün Tzu's Philosophy of Human Nature," *Philosophy East and West* 27, no. 4 (1977): 373–89.
Section 2 from "The Quasi-Empirical Aspect of Hsün Tzu's Philosophy of Human Nature," *Philosophy East and West* 28, no. 1 (1978): 3–19.

2. From "Dimensions of *Li* (Propriety): Reflections on an Aspect of Hsün Tzu's Ethics," *Philosophy East and West* 29, no. 4 (1979): 373–94.
Appendix 1—Human Relationships and the Virtues in the *Liji*
Appendix 2—Moral Cultivation and Music in the *Liji*
Excerpts from *"Li* and Moral Justification: A Study in the *Li Chi,"* *Philosophy East and West* 33, no. 1 (1983): 1–16.

3. From "Ethical Uses of the Past in Early Confucianism: The Case of Hsün Tzu," *Philosophy East and West* 35, no. 2 (1985): 133–56. Pinyin version in *Virtue, Nature, and Moral Agency in the Xunzi*, edited by T. C. Kline and Philip Ivanhoe (Indianapolis, Ind.: Hackett, 2000).

4. From "The Problem of Conceptual Unity in Hsün Tzu and Li Kou's Solution," *Philosophy East and West* 39, no. 2 (1989): 115–34.

5. From "Hsün Tzu and the Unity of Virtues," *Journal of Chinese Philosophy* 14, no. 4 (1987): 381–400.

6. From "The Possibility of Ethical Knowledge: Reflections on a Theme in the *Hsün Tzu.*" In Hans Lenk and Gregor Paul (eds.), *Epistemological Issues in Classical Chinese Philosophy* (Albany: State University of New York Press, 1993), 159–83.

7. From "The Ethical and the Religious Dimensions of *Li* (Rites)," *Review of Metaphysics* 55, no. 3 (2002): 501–49. A shorter version appeared in *Confucian Spirituality*, vol. 1, edited by Tu Weiming and Mary Evelyn Tucker (New York: Crossroads, 2003).

8. From "Ethical Significance of Shame: Insights of Aristotle and Xunzi," *Philosophy East and West* 53, no. 2 (2003): 147–202.

PART II. OTHER STUDIES IN CHINESE PHILOSOPHY

9. From "Practical Causation and Confucian Ethics," *Philosophy East and West* 25, no. 1 (1975): 1–10.

10. "Moral Theory and the Quality of Life," unpublished 1978 lecture.

11. From "Confucian Vision and the Human Community," *Journal of Chinese Philosophy* 11, no. 3 (1984): 226–38.

12. Revised version of "Ethical Significance of Thomé H. Fang's Philosophy." In *Philosophy of Thomé H. Fang* (Taipei: Youth Cultural Enterprise, 1989), 57–72. Not previously published in an English philosophy journal.

13. From "Reason and Principle in Chinese Philosophy." In *A Companion to World Philosophies*, edited by Eliot Deutsch and Ron Bontekoe (Oxford: Blackwell, 1997), 201–13.

14. From "Emergence of the History of Chinese Philosophy," *International Philosophical Quarterly* 45, no. 4 (2000): 441–64. Pinyin version appeared in *Comparative Approaches to Chinese Philosophy*, edited by Bo Mou (Aldershot, England and Burlington, Vermont: Ashgate, 2003), 3–30. A shorter version appeared in *One Hundred Years of Philosophy*, edited by Brian J. Shanley, O.P. (Washington, D.C.: The Catholic University of America Press, 2001), 272–98.

15. From "*Xin* (Mind/Heart) and Moral Failure: Notes on an Aspect of Mencius's Moral Psychology." In *Mencius: Contexts and Interpretations*, edited by Alan Chan (Honolulu: University of Hawaii Press, 2002), 126–50. Also in *Dao: Journal of Comparative Philosophy* 1, no. 1 (2001): 31–53.

PART I
XUNZI'S MORAL PHILOSOPHY

Essay 1
PHILOSOPHY OF HUMAN NATURE

1. THE CONCEPTUAL ASPECT

The topic of human nature has been an enduring preoccupation of major thinkers of both East and West. The underlying question pertaining to man's nature, far from being an unambiguous question, appears to be flexible and responsive enough to accommodate varying and conflicting pictures of human life as answers to a common question. We are here confronted, perhaps, with a fluid notion rather than a determinate concept that admits of a neutral and precise formulation. The various constructions of the notion reflect, as it were, different moral visions or ideals of man in relation to others and to the cosmic order.[1] In spite of the amorphous character of the question, its significance appears not to be subject to doubt. It is a question asked by human beings about themselves. In the words of a recent writer, "What is man? This is surely one of the most important questions of all. For so much else depends on our view of human nature. The meaning and purpose of human life, what we ought to do, and what we can hope to achieve—all these are fundamentally affected by whatever we think is the 'real' or the 'true' nature of man."[2] The question is a large one. And insofar as moral philosophy has a place in the inquiry, it can usefully focus on a narrower but more basic question, that is, the relation between morality and human nature. In both Eastern and Western philosophy, that is a problem that receives various formulations and solutions. This article is an experiment in comparative moral philosophy, focusing attention on Xunzi's theory of human nature. My principal aim is to offer an explication of the notions and distinctions involved in Xunzi's principal argument for

---

1. See P. F. Strawson, "Social Morality and Individual Ideal," *Philosophy* 36 (1961). For the notion of *dao* as moral vision, see my "Chinese Moral Vision, Responsive Agency, and Factual Beliefs," *Journal of Chinese Philosophy* 7, no. 1 (1980): 3–26; or *Moral Vision and Tradition: Essays in Chinese Ethics* (Washington, D.C.: The Catholic University of America Press, 1998).
2. Leslie Stevenson, *Seven Theories of Human Nature* (Oxford: Clarendon Press, 1974), 7.

the thesis that "human nature is bad." Such a study is preparatory to an examination of Xunzi's supporting arguments for his thesis and their plausibility as an answer to the problem of the relation between morality and human nature.

1.1. Methodological preliminaries

Before proceeding to the task of explication, a few methodological remarks are in order. I regard explication as an activity of conceptual analysis in the broad sense. It is primarily an activity aiming at the elucidation of notions and distinctions within the context of philosophical problems. As a philosophical activity, it is more than a mere descriptive enterprise, for to explicate a thesis is to engage in a rethinking of the problem to which the thesis may be regarded as an adequate solution.[3] For my present purpose, explication is a philosophical interpretation of a thesis in the text *Xunzi*. A plausible explication is basically a philosophical explication guided by appropriate textual materials that furnish data for elucidating philosophical problems. In this sense, explication is a philosophical reconstruction of textual materials. In what follows, I inquire into the philosophical import of Xunzi's thesis on human nature. In doing so, I have "bracketed" from my explication much of the materials pertaining to his social and political theory.[4]

Let us note at the outset that Xunzi's remark that "human nature is bad" is highly misleading. As D. C. Lau has forcefully shown, it is quite unprofitable to take the theses of Mencius and Xunzi as "being embodied in two simple assertions, viz., that human nature is good and that human nature is bad and consider them as flatly contradicting each other."[5] We should look for the grounds for these theses rather than focus upon simple remarks.[6] Along the same line, A. C. Graham observes that since many Chinese thinkers tend to use such simple formulae "only as convenient labels and pivots of debate," a question arises "whether they may have had some inkling that the formulae unduly simplify what they were trying to say." And in the case of Xunzi's remark

---

3. Admittedly these remarks are extremely sketchy. A fuller discussion and my debt to recent analytic philosophy are given in my "Reflections on Methodology in Chinese Philosophy," *International Philosophical Quarterly* 11, no. 2 (1971): 236–47. In another article, "Tasks for Confucian Ethics," *Journal of Chinese Philosophy* 6, no. 1 (1979): 55–67, the problem of explication is discussed in terms of developing a Confucian moral philosophy.

4. For a recent discussion of this aspect of Xunzi's philosophy, see Henry Rosemont, "State and Society in the *Hsün Tzu*: A Philosophical Commentary," *Monumenta Serica* 29 (1970–71): 38–78.

5. D. C. Lau, "Theories of Human Nature in *Mencius* and *Shyuntzyy*," *Bulletin of the School of Oriental and African Studies* 15 (1953): 558.

6. Ibid.

that "human nature is bad," it is quite inadequate as it stands for distinguishing his view from that of Mencius.[7] However, while acknowledging the misleading character of such simple remarks, we can profitably deal with them in relation to the notions and distinctions deployed in the arguments offered in support of these remarks. A thesis expressed in a simple remark can be illuminating, if it is seen as a compendious way of expressing a set of arguments or observations about human nature. Arguments have an essential and dual role in explicating a thesis. The obvious role concerns the inference of a thesis as a conclusion of a given set of premises. The less obvious role pertains to their function in elucidating the meaning of the thesis. The two roles of argument, I assume, cannot be separated in understanding philosophical discourse. I shall attempt to explicate Xunzi's thesis in this way, thus taking seriously the simple remark "human nature is bad" as amenable to a plausible explication.

An initial problem in explication lies in the assemblage of appropriate textual materials. The decision here is bound to be a selective one based on one's overall understanding of Xunzi. We are fortunate to have a single essay on our topic. My strategy will be to take paragraph one of Chapter 23 *(xing'e pian)* as embodying Xunzi's thesis and principal argument to be elucidated by other relevant passages in the text.[8]

In placing emphasis upon arguments in discourse, a question of proper evaluation arises. Apart from the necessity of the use of canons of logical validity, what other criteria are relevant to evaluating Xunzi's thesis? Again, we are fortunate to have Xunzi's answer without the need to appeal to external criteria. In one passage criticizing Mencius, Xunzi states:

> Those who are good at discussing matters of antiquity must support what they say with evidence from the present, and those who are good at discussing matters of Heaven *(tian)* must support what they say with evidence from the present. In any discussion, what deserves our esteem are discrimination *(bianhe)* and evidence *(fuyan)*. In so doing, one can then sit down and talk about things, propagate it and put it into practice. (*xing'e* L549, C132*)[9]

---

7. A. C. Graham, "The Background of the Mencian Theory of Human Nature," *Tsing Hua Journal of Chinese Studies*, n.s., 7, nos. 1 and 2 (1967): 258.
8. Doubts have been expressed about the authenticity of the first part of *Xing'e pian*. For my purpose, the question of authenticity need not affect our explication, since the passage in question is quite consistent with most of the remarks on human nature in other chapters of *Xunzi*. See Donald J. Munro, *The Concept of Man in Ancient China* (Stanford, Calif.: Stanford University Press, 1969), 77–78.
9. Parenthetical citations of the *Xunzi [Hsün Tzu]* in the text refer to one or more of five basic works: Li Disheng, *Xunzi jishi* (Taipei: Xuesheng, 1979), which was based on the standard Wang Xianqian's *Xunzi jijie*; H. H. Dubs, trans., *The Works of Hsüntze* (Taipei:

This passage suggests two different sets of criteria: (1) discrimination *(bianho)* and evidence *(fuyan)*, and (2) teachability and practicability. Regarding (1), it is not unreasonable to regard the notion of discrimination as inclusive of discernment of conceptual distinctions, since Xunzi is quite sensitive to confusion of terms in discourse. In the essay on rectifying names *(zhengming pian)*, the emphasis is placed on the importance of distinguishing similarities and differences between things and states of affairs in the uses of terms *(ming)*, though Xunzi is mainly interested in the accord or correspondence between distinctions and realities *(shi)* of moral conduct, that is, realities that reflect moral norms, social roles, and duties. This interest in rectifying terms *(zhengming)* is more clearly indicated in the concern with (2), the teachability and practicability of moral discourse. In a more contemporary idiom, the focus is on the action-guiding character of moral discourse. Moral discourse would be quite pointless unless its purported directives could be universally taught.[10] The practicability of moral discourse pertains especially to the necessary conditions of moral compliance, that is, to the consideration of the ability and circumstance of moral agents as relevant to fulfilling moral directives. For a full explication of Xunzi's thesis, one has to rely on the first set of requirements, that is, discrimination and evidence. In this section I shall rely mainly on discrimination as a criterion of conceptual clarity. In the next section, the requirement of evidence shall be discussed in connection with Xunzi's supporting arguments as examples of the employment of notions and distinctions explicated in this one. An adequate account of Xunzi's moral philosophy must also attend to the second set of requirements, that is, teachability and practicability. In general, I shall assume that these requirements are unproblematic, since they appear to constitute a set of minimal conditions, which any normative ethics must satisfy.[11]

Chengwen, 1966); Burton Watson, trans., *Hsün Tzu: Basic Writings* (New York: Columbia University Press, 1963), John Knoblock, *Xunzi: A Translation and Study of the Complete Works*, 3 vols. (Stanford, Calif.: Stanford University Press, 1988-94), and Wing-tsit Chan, *A Source Book in Chinese Philosophy* (Princeton, N.J.: Princeton University Press, 1963). See the preface for a full explanation of the citations.

10. For a contemporary discussion of the importance of universal teachability of moral principles, see Kurt Baier, *The Moral Point of View* (Ithaca, N.Y.: Cornell University Press, 1958), 195-200.

11. It may be noted that these requirements are *formal* rather than *material* conditions for normative ethics. The material requirements depend on the philosopher's own conception of acceptable morality. In the case of Xunzi, morality is construed in terms of *li*, or ritual rules, though the *significance* of *li* needs to be understood in terms of *ren* (benevolence), *yi* (rightness or righteousness), and other moral virtues. This theme will be taken up in the concluding section. [For a later revised and extended account of these requirements in argumentation, see my *Ethical Argumentation: A Study in Hsün Tzu's Moral Epistemology* (Honolulu: University of Hawaii Press, 1985).]

1.2. The Central Passage

With those preliminaries in mind, I shall proceed to the explication of Xunzi's thesis that "human nature is bad" by concentrating upon the following passage:

> The nature *(xing)* of man is bad *(e)*; his goodness *(shan)* is the result of activity *(wei)*. The nature of man today is such that he is born with the desire for gain *(haoli)*. If this tendency is followed, strife and rapacity will result and deference and compliance will disappear. Man is born with [the feelings of] envy and hatred of others. If these feelings are followed, injury and destruction will result and loyalty and faithfulness will disappear. Man is born with the possession of the desires *(yu)* of ears and eyes and liking *(hao)* for sound and beauty. If these desires are followed, lewdness and licentiousness will result, and the pattern and order of propriety *(li)* will disappear. Therefore, to follow man's nature and his feelings will inevitably result in strife and rapacity, combined with rebellion and disorder, and end in violence. Therefore, there must be the civilizing influence of teachers and laws and the guidance of propriety and righteousness *(yi)* and then it will result in deference and compliance, combined with pattern and order, and end in discipline. From this point of view, it is clear that the nature of man is bad and that his goodness is the result of activity. (*xing'e pian*, L538*)

1.3. The Thesis and the Principal Argument

For simplifying our task of explication of the thesis "man's nature is bad,"[12] I shall regard the principal argument as comprising the following statements to be elucidated and supported by other considerations.

P1. Man's nature today is such that he is born with a desire for gain *(haoli)*, that is, a general desire or characteristic tendency to obtain self-benefit or satisfaction of a range of desires *(yu)* (for example, sensuous desires). If these desires are followed, strife and rapacity will result, and deference and compliance, pattern and order of propriety *(li)* will disappear.

P2. Man's nature today is such that he is born with a variety of feelings *(qing)*, (e.g., envy, hate, etc.).[13] If these feelings are followed, injury and destruction will result, and all sense of loyalty and faithfulness will disappear.

---

12. Throughout this article, I shall use the expressions "human nature is bad" and "man's nature is bad" interchangeably.
13. For a discussion of the notion of *qing* (feelings), see the appendix of Graham's "The Mencian Theory of Human Nature," 259–65. [For a later discussion, see Chad Hansen, "*Qing*: Reality or Feeling," in *Encyclopedia of Chinese Philosophy*, ed. Antonio S. Cua (New York and London: Routledge, 2003).]

Conclusion: Given P1 and P2, it is clear that man's nature *(xing)* is bad *(e)*, and that his goodness *(shan)* is the result of activity *(wei)*.

Both P1 and P2 focus on consequences, or more accurately, on the consequences that ensue when desires are pursued and feelings are indulged in without regard to moral requirements. In P1 I have construed "the desire for gain" as a term referring to a characteristic tendency toward self-seeking activities in the satisfaction of a range of specific desires *(yu)* inclusive of sensuous desires, for example, "desires of ear and eye" and "the liking *(hao)* of sound and beauty." To Xunzi, there are other desires, for example, of the mouth for flavor, of the body for pleasure and comfort *(xing'e* C130, D305, W160).[14] In P2, again we focus on a range of feelings *(qing)*. Although the central passage mentioned only envy and hate, another passage explicitly points to six feelings, "love, hate, joy, anger, sorrow, and pleasure" *(zhengming* L506).[15]

Both P1 and P2 give us a characterization of man's nature *(xing)* as consisting of desires and feelings. As we shall later see, these desires and feelings are intimately connected (section 1.5). In his argument, the burden of Xunzi is to show that the actualization of desires and expression of feelings, without regard to moral requirements *(li* and *yi)*, tend toward undesirable consequences. For our purpose we may leave aside the consideration of teachers and laws *(fa)*, since our interest is in the argument as supporting a thesis in moral philosophy. We may observe here that the basic issue for Xunzi is not the possession or nonpossession of desires and feelings but the consequences from the moral point of view.[16] Thus we have in the central passage an argument that appeals to the consequences of the fulfillment and expression of desires and feelings. To characterize man's nature as "bad" is, in effect, a shorthand way of asserting the nature of these consequences. Thus, the argument is consequential in character. Feelings and desires are in themselves morally neutral. They are problematic only from the point of view of their undesirable consequences in the manner in which they tend toward certain expression and fulfillment. If this point is accepted, Xun-

---

14. This passage may appear problematic, since the "heart's desiring gain" *(xin haoli)* is characterized as being on a par with the other desires listed. My construction here is obviously a philosophical reading of *Xunzi*. Though Xunzi does not have a systematic theory of human nature inclusive of a theory of the psychology of purposive behavior, some of his remarks may be construed as providing the rudiments of such a theory.

15. Elsewhere these six feelings are called "heavenly feelings" *(tianqing)* *(tianlun* L366, D175, C118, W80).

16. "Beings that possess desires and those that do not belong to two different categories—the categories of the living and the dead. But the possession or nonpossession of desires has nothing to do with good government or bad" *(zhengming* L527, W150).

zi's thesis is not just a description of man in terms of the possession of a set of empirical properties. Empirically, man's nature consists of desires and feelings. There are, admittedly, other properties like mind and thought[17] (see *jiebi* L472ff., D187ff., W121ff.). But these other properties are not directly relevant to the argument here. However, in a sense, Xunzi is also making a *quasi-empirical* claim in his thesis that man's nature is bad. He has to show with some empirical plausibility that the indulgence in feelings and the pursuit of desires will inevitably lead to morally undesirable consequences, for example, strife and disorder. This constitutes the main burden of defending his thesis, to be examined in Part 2. In the following, I shall attend to certain distinctions that are presupposed in my construal of the central passage.

1.4. The Moral Distinction between Good (shan) and Bad (e)

In a more contemporary idiom, the principal argument discussed earlier invokes a conception of man's nature in terms of a *basic motivational structure*. This comprises his native feelings and desires. The term "structure" is used here in a loose sense of "make-up" or "arrangement" of two intimately connected components of feelings and desires. Xunzi's term for this basic motivational structure is *"qingxing"* or *"xingqing"* (emotional nature) (*xing'e* L540, W159). The purport of the principal argument is clear: Morality has a function in regulating and transforming the characteristic tendency of man's basic motivational structure. In this way, the relation between morality and human nature is an external rather than an internal one.[18] This understanding of Xunzi's principal argument rests on the distinction between good *(shan)* and bad *(e)* as a moral distinction.

Quite obviously "good" and "bad" are contrasting terms. However, Xunzi's distinction has been construed as a mere descriptive distinction. While acknowledging that good and bad are relative terms, An-

---

17. As Lau has shown, Xunzi's conception of man's nature as excluding mind *(xin)* is problematic. "There is no reason why we should not extend the name human nature to cover the capacity of invention possessed by the mind [of the sages] which is part of it" (Lau, 561). However, for Xunzi's principal thesis, all that is required is to regard the mind *(xin)* in terms of its relation to human nature, apart from moral regulation, as functioning primarily at the service of actualizing man's feelings and desires. From the moral point of view, mind, of course, has a different function, in making normative distinctions for the regulation of conduct. In this moral context, mind has a practical function quite different from that in a non-moral context. All I am suggesting here is that the issue pointed out by Lau is an arguable rather than a settled one.

18. For a later discussion of the competing views on this topic, see my "Morality and Human Nature," *Philosophy East and West* 32, no. 3 (1982): 279–94; or Essay 6 in my *Moral Vision and Tradition*.

drew Cheng states that, according to Xunzi, the word "bad" *(e)* is "used merely to describe the contemporary social conditions without any philosophical import." After invoking Xunzi's own definitions (which we shall consider shortly), Cheng goes on to say, quite correctly, that Xunzi's thesis that human nature is bad "does not mean that it is totally depraved and hopeless." What is puzzling is his explanation: "What he [Xunzi] means is simply that man has failed to adjust himself to his social environment. He conceives of evil as a moral failure instead of an innate wickedness."[19] But if evil or badness is a form of moral failure, its status implies an assessment from the moral point of view of goodness *(shan)*. Moreover, it is doubtful whether Xunzi's own definitions can be regarded as descriptive definitions without qualification. And when this qualification is made, the thesis cannot be construed as a purely descriptive thesis.

Perhaps Cheng has confused the distinction between reportive definitions and the conceptual status of moral terms. The passage at issue is the following:

All men in the world, past and present, use the term "good" *(shan)* to mean "what is upright *(zheng)*, reasonable *(li)*, and orderly *(pingzhi)*"; and use the term "bad" to mean "what is partial *(pianxian)*, rebellious *(bei)*, and disorderly *(luan)*." This is the distinction between goodness and badness. (*xing'e* L547, W162*)[20]

The distinction between good and bad is more properly construed as a distinction within moral discourse. The passage, in effect, offers us an argument from linguistic usage.[21] For the present, let us simply observe that the definitions at issue are certainly reportive rather than stipulative definitions. The appeal is made to both past and current usages of the terms "good" and "bad." Notably, within the definitions themselves,

---

19. Andrew Cheng, *Hsün Tzu's Theory of Human Nature and Its Influence on Chinese Thought* (Peking: privately published, 1928), p. 42.

20. Chan, Dubs, and Watson render this passage in various ways. My own translation is based on Watson's. However, the translations differ not in the force of the contrast between *zheng* and *pian*, nor in the contrast between *pingzhi* and *beiluan*. However we translate these terms, it appears that the contrast lies in the difference between order *(zhi)* and disorder *(luan)*. Regarding *zheng* we can read it as part of a compound term *zhengli*, and render it, as Chan and Dubs did, "true principles" or "correct principles," as contrasted with *pian* or partiality. The difference from my own translation is minor for our explication, for if the contrast is between true or correct principles and partiality, the notion of impartiality seems implicit in the notion of true principles construed as moral principles. Likewise, uprightness, in the sense of being morally honorable or respectable, also implies impartiality in some sense. As I have construed it, the distinction between good *(shan)* and bad *(e)* is a distinction in moral discourse. [For a later discussion on the status of principles in Confucian ethics, see *Moral Vision and Tradition*, Essay 13.]

21. The continuation of the passage at issue involves a fuller statement of Xunzi's argument, which I shall examine in the second part of this essay.

moral terms such as "upright" and "orderly" imply certain *standards* for assessing conduct. These standards are those that are encapsulated in the *li* or ritual rules and other virtues. If one construes the distinction as a descriptive one, a qualification needs to be made, that is, a descriptive distinction within a discourse that presupposes a moral point of view. In this way, such terms as "good" and "bad," "upright" and "partiality" may be regarded as *moral descriptions*. They have both evaluative and descriptive import. It is the evaluative point of view that governs the appropriateness of factual descriptions. Seen in this light, moral descriptions are, tautologically, descriptions from the moral point of view.[22]

Perhaps, the evaluative force of the distinction between good and bad may be further clarified if one construes Xunzi's thesis as embodying a focus on the aesthetic aspect of morality. To say "man's nature is *e*" may be regarded as a way of saying that "man's nature has a propensity to do what is inferior or ugly." And this is an elliptical expression to be expanded in terms of a point of view that contains standards for assessing what is inferior or ugly. I am not directly attributing this analysis to Xunzi, though I believe that a coherent Xunzian view can be developed to accommodate this aesthetic aspect of morality. Let us attend to an interesting passage:

Yao asked Shun, "How are the feelings (*qing*) of man?" Shun answered, "The feelings of man are far from being beautiful . . . when a man has a wife and children, his filial duty to his parents decreases; when sensual desires (*yu*) are satisfied, then faithfulness between friends decreases; when his desire for noble titles and high salary is satisfied, then his faithfulness towards his prince decreases. Man's feelings! Man's feelings are far from beautiful! Why do you ask? Only the worthy is not thus." (*xing'e pian*, L555, D314–315*)

Undoubtedly this passage has an overall emotive tone, as it expresses moral emotions. But significantly, moral emotions are not severed from either consideration of moral standards or aesthetic expression. The essay on *li (lilun pian)* quite clearly brings this point out. It does not seem unreasonable to ascribe to Xunzi the view that what is good is also beautiful and what is bad is also ugly. There is, in Xunzi's conception of *li*-morality, an explicit recognition of an intrinsic connection between morality and aesthetics. Or to borrow an expression from the eighteenth-century British moralists, a recognition of "the beauty of virtue and the deformity of vice."[23] The functions of *li*-morality are the

---

22. See Julius Kovesi, *Moral Notions* (London: Routledge and Kegan Paul, 1967), chap. 5.
23. The theme of "the beauty of virtue and the deformity of vice" is quite prominent in the writings of Shaftesbury, Francis Hutcheson, David Hume, Richard Price, and Adam Smith. See D. D. Raphael, ed., *British Moralists: 1650–1800*, 2 vols. (Oxford: Clarendon

regulation and adornment of man's basic motivational structure in terms of an ideal of moral excellence *(shan)*. Here lies the distinction between *junzi* (superior man) and *xiaoren* (small-minded man).

The distinction between good and bad may thus be elucidated in terms of the distinction between *junzi* and *xiaoren*. The latter distinction is undoubtedly a distinction within the Confucian moral discourse. Much of what Xunzi said on this topic clearly brings out the evaluative force of the distinction. Consider the following:

> The superior man *(junzi)* and the small-minded *(xiaoren)* may be the same in ability, original nature, knowledge, and capacity; they love honor and hate shame; they love what is beneficial and hate what is injurious—this is that wherein the superior and the small-minded men are alike. If, however, you compare the way *(dao)* by which they seek their goals, then they are different. *(rongru* L60, D58*)

The two types of men thus differ in the ways they pursue the means of self-satisfaction. The *junzi* is guided by moral considerations, by *ren*, *li*, and *yi*, the *xiaoren* by pure self-seeking motive. From the moral point of view, one can then say, "man by birth is certainly a small-minded man *(xiaoren)*. Without a teacher or laws and regulations, he can only think of profit" *(rongru* L65, D61). *Junzi* and *xiaoren* thus differ not in their basic motivational structure, but in the fact that the former, unlike the latter, governs his conduct by moral considerations. The title *junzi* is more an award of moral achievement than a mere descriptive title.[24]

There appear to be two different conceptions of man in Xunzi's thought. In one conception, man is to be understood in terms of his basic motivational structure. In this sense, men are alike in being actuated with the same range of feelings and desires. In another conception, man is to be characterized in terms of his capacity to make moral distinctions. In this sense, men are distinguished from animals. "Man is

---

Press, 1969). The theme suggests an area worthy of comparative exploration for a moral philosophy that recognizes the importance of the aesthetic dimension of morality. For a preliminary study, see my "Dignity of Persons and Styles of Life," *Proceedings of the American Catholic Philosophical Association* 45 (1971): 120–29. Reprinted in George F. McLean, ed., *New Dynamics in Ethical Thinking* (Lancaster, Pa.: Concorde Publishing House, 1975). [For a later study of Xunzi's view on the aesthetic aspect of *li*, see my "Dimensions of *Li* (Propriety): Reflections on an Aspect of Hsün Tzu's Ethics," *Philosophy East and West* 29, no. 4 (1979): 373–94; incorporated as Essay 2 of this volume.]

24. For a further discussion of this Confucian distinction, see my "Reflections on the Structure of Confucian Ethics," *Philosophy East and West* 21, no. 2 (1971): 125–40; and "The Concept of Paradigmatic Individuals in the Ethics of Confucius," *Inquiry* 14, nos. 1 and 2 (1971): 41–55. The latter is incorporated in chap. 4 of *Dimensions of Moral Creativity: Paradigms, Principles, and Ideals* (University Park: Pennsylvania State University Press, 1978).

not truly man more particularly in that he has two feet and no feathers, but rather in that he makes distinctions. . . . Hence the path *(dao)* of human life cannot be without distinctions; no distinction is greater than social divisions; no social division is greater than the rules for proper conduct *(li);* the rules of proper conduct are not greater than the Sage-Kings" *(feixiang pian,* L79, D71–72). In this second conception, "man" is a normative notion. Man's capacity for social organization and distinctions is characteristically his moral capacity. To regard this as an empirical matter, we need to distinguish two different sorts of facts about man. Following Searle, we may distinguish between brute and institutional facts, and reformulate Xunzi's remark on the distinction between men and animals in terms of certain institutional facts about men.[25] And these institutional facts do involve norms or rules that define and constitute the character of their activities. For Xunzi, we may also say that it is a brute fact about men that they are alike in basic motivational structure. It is an institutional fact that men are distinguished from one another in the light of their conduct as conforming or nonconforming to certain constitutive rules of proper behavior. Here again, we confront the distinction between mere factual description and moral description or description from the moral point of view. To say this, however, is not to deny that we can evaluate a moral description. After all, ethical principles are intended to serve as criteria for evaluating ordinary moral appraisals. But notably, the notions of *junzi* and *xiaoren* embody these positive and negative appraisals. The distinction here is, in general, a distinction between good and bad men from the point of view that is invested with Confucian appraisals.

1.5. Man's Basic Motivational Structure (Qingxing)

Let us now turn to the distinction between human nature *(xing)* and activity *(wei),* more particularly to the character of man's basic motivational structure. In the central passage (section 1.2 above), I have followed Wing-tsit Chan in rendering *wei* as "activity."[26] *Wei* can also be rendered as "conscious activity" (Watson), "acquired training" (Dubs), or "human artifice" (Lau). Lau has carefully examined Xunzi's defini-

---

25. See John Searle, "How to Derive 'Ought' from 'Is'" *Philosophical Review* 73 (1964): section 3.
26. As Chan notes: "According to Yang Liang, *wei* (artificial) is 'man's activity.' It means what is created by man and not a result of natural conditions. This is accepted by most commentators, including Hao Yixing, who has pointed out that in ancient times *wei* (ordinarily meaning false or artificial) and *wei* (activity) were interchangeable" (C128). Perhaps the best term for rendering *wei* is "constructive effort or activity."

tions.²⁷ The contrast between *xing* and *wei* appears to be quite clear. Lau has concisely summed up the distinction in the following way:

> Human nature *(xing)* is that which is (1) made what it is by heaven, (2) cannot be learned, (3) cannot be improved through application, and (4) is not the result of reflection by the mind; while human artifice *(wei)* is that which is (1) invented by the sages, (2) can be learned, (3) can be improved through application, and (4) is the result of reflection by the mind.²⁸

And as Graham has shown, Xunzi was the first to disentangle both the evaluative and descriptive senses of the notion of *xing*: "The course or direction of spontaneous activity and spontaneous activity itself."²⁹ Underlying the series of contrasts lies the criterion of natural spontaneity. Though the distinction *xing* and *wei* appears clear, Xunzi's definitions offer us only a formal criterion.³⁰ The thesis that human nature is bad thus depends on a further specification in terms of man's basic motivational structure *(qingxing)* as consisting of a range of feelings *(qing)* and desires *(yu)*. In section 1.3 above, I have suggested that these feelings and desires are intimately connected. It is this point that forms our immediate task. If it can be plausibly shown that Xunzi's conception of *qingxing* supports this interpretation and offers us an insight into man's nature, we are well on our way to appreciating Xunzi's conception of the relation between morality and human nature.

Before we attend to the question of connection, let us briefly consider the range of feelings.³¹ As we have previously noted (section 1.3 above), Xunzi lists six feelings, love, hate, joy, anger, sorrow, and pleasure. In the central passage (section 1.2 above), envy is also mentioned, though the word *qing* is not used. Xunzi also seems to have in mind

---

27. "What is in man but cannot be learned or worked for is his nature. What is in him and can be learned or accomplished through work is what can be achieved through activity. This is the difference between human nature *(xing)* and activity *(wei)*" (*xing'e* L541, C129, D303, W158). "That which is as it is from the time of birth is called the nature of man *(xing)*. That which is harmonious from birth, which is incapable of perceiving through the senses and of responding to stimulus spontaneously and without effort, is also called the nature *(xing)*.... When the mind conceives a thought and the body puts it into action, this is called activity *(wei)*. When the thoughts have accumulated sufficiently, the body is well trained, and then the action is carried to completion, this is also called activity *(wei)*" (*zhengming pian* L506, W139–40*).
28. Lau, "Theories of Human Nature," 559. For an illuminating account of the notion of human nature *(xing)* in Pre-Han literature, see Graham's "The Mencian Theory of Human Nature," part I. It must be mentioned here that I have profited much from reading these essays of Lau and Graham in preparing this article.
29. Graham, "The Mencian Theory of Human Nature," 264.
30. Lau, "Theories of Human Nature," 552.
31. For reasons to be given shortly, I have rendered *qing* as "feelings" throughout. *Qing* has also been rendered as "emotions," "passions," or "sentiment."

such feelings as feeling hungry, cold, tired; though, again, the word *qing* is not used (*xing'e* L542, C129, D304, W159). For clarity, the range of feelings may be said to comprise three different classes: (1) *moods* such as joy, sorrow, and pleasure (that is, in the sense of feeling pleased or happy); (2) *emotions* such as love, hate, anger, and envy; and (3) *bodily feelings* such as hunger, and so forth.[32] Common to moods, emotions, and bodily feelings may be said to be their *telic* feature. These feelings have their objects, that is, they are about something, even though at times the objects may not be clearly discerned. At times, for instance, we just feel pleased about something without knowing specifically what it is that pleases us. To say, however, that these feelings are about some objects is also to focus on the characteristic tendency displayed in the experience of these feelings. Even in the case of moods, we seem inclined to do certain things. As White points out, "To be in a certain mood is to behave and to be liable to do certain things, to be the prey of certain feelings and thoughts."[33] The same holds true for the experience of bodily feelings and emotions. In general, the experience of these feelings *inclines* us toward certain actions.

Regarding desires *(yu)*, Xunzi largely attends to those that seem to have an intimate connection with the range of feelings. When a "man is hungry he desires to eat; when he is cold he desires to be warm; when he is tired he desires to rest; he likes what is helpful and dislikes what is injurious—man is born with these ways of acting; he does not have to wait to get them" (*feixiang* L79, D71; *xing'e* L542, C129, D304, W159). We have also noted that some desires are more particularly tied to the senses, for example, a liking for beauty, sound, flavors, and so forth. I construe the range of desires as including likes and dislikes. The connection between feelings and desires is explicitly recognized in the following passage:

---

32. I have followed the classification of Alan White in regarding "feelings" as a general term to be further divided into various subclasses. We can distinguish perceptual from intellectual feelings, and these from what may be called feelings of general conditions, which, again, comprise four different sorts. "They include *bodily feelings,* such as feeling sleepy, wide awake, fidgety, hungry or seasick; *moods,* such as feeling depressed, irritable, melancholy, frivolous, jovial, or happy; *emotions,* such as feeling pity, fear, pride, admiration, anger, indignation or shame; *agitations,* such as feeling startled, shocked, excited, amazed, or flabbergasted . . . and *completions,* such as feeling fit, well, tranquil, confident, content, satisfied, bored, fed up or full" (Alan White, *The Philosophy of Mind* [New York: Random House, 1967], 116). Xunzi is mainly interested in bodily feelings, moods, and emotions. However, in general, a distinctive moral feeling, for most Chinese thinkers, pertains to completion (for example, tranquility as characteristic of the mind of the sage), though they differ in their conceptions of the nature of completion. For a discussion on this theme, see Munro, *The Concept of Man in Ancient China,* chap. 7.

33. White, *The Philosophy of Mind,* 123.

The nature of man *(xing)* is that which he receives from Heaven; his feelings *(qing)* are the constitutive elements *(zhi)* of his nature; his desires are the responses of the feelings. When a man is activated by feelings, it is impossible for him not to believe that the desires can be satisfied. The starting point of wisdom must be to consider the desires necessary and to guide them. (*zhengming* L506, D295-96*, W151-52)

This passage recognizes the distinction between feelings or emotions and desires and locates their connection in terms of desires as responses to feelings. And insofar as these feelings are regarded as natural, in the sense of their being spontaneously experienced, the desires that are connected with them are also natural. The desires thus may be regarded as natural reactive propensities of these feelings. To feel hungry is to be disposed to seek food that will satisfy the hunger. To feel love for something or someone is to be disposed to do something about our feelings. Even in the case of such moods as joy, we are disposed to do at least something in the sense of wanting to express our feelings. No doubt our feelings are typically situation-dependent, that is, the experience of them depends on our situation with respect to either our bodily conditions or external circumstances. However, doubt may be expressed if this connection between feelings and desires is construed as a necessary rather than a contingent connection. This point must be conceded. Nevertheless, it still holds in a large number of cases where we experience the connection as more than just an accidental occurrence. Even in the case of moods, such as aesthetic enjoyment, we are at times inclined to want to continue in this state. And in wanting to prolong our enjoyment, we may take steps to avoid distraction. If this point is accepted, then we may claim that, in some sense, feelings and desires are intimately connected, particularly when they are intensely experienced. And in these cases, we may say that the desires in question are responses to feelings.[34]

1.6. The Moral Point of View

In this section, I shall attend more fully to the central assumption that underlies the preceding explication. Throughout, I have invoked

---

34. For a fuller discussion on the characteristics of desires, see G. C. Field, *Moral Theory* (London: Methuen & Co., 1966), chap. 10. Incidentally, Field seems to maintain a thesis on the necessary connection between desires and feelings. According to him, "when we say that we desire a thing or want it or wish for it the essential element in the experience is a certain feeling towards the thing which we cannot define further" (117). As it turns out, what he means is that the notion of desire implies the notion of an object of desire (118). But this is simply to note the telic feature of desire, and this feature may not apply to all feelings, for example, agitations or completions. (See note 32 above.)

the notion of the moral point of view. Thus in connection with the tendency of the basic motivational structure toward strife and disorder, I have remarked that to Xunzi, the tendency toward self-benefit or satisfaction *(haoli)* inevitably leads to strife and disorder, or consequences judged to be undesirable from the moral point of view (section 3).[35] The basic motivational structure is bad from the point of view of undesirable moral consequences. What, then, is this moral point of view? More accurately, what is the Confucian point of view as understood by Xunzi? This question does not admit of a single answer. There again appear to be alternative options. When one attends to the chapter on *li*, it seems clear that whatever else Xunzi has in mind, the *li* or ritual rules occupy a central place in any account of his Confucian point of view. A coherent interpretation can thus be given by regarding *li* as a comprehensive virtue, a virtue that includes all other virtues, such as *ren* and *yi*.[36] Along this line one may even plausibly argue "that the strength of Xunzi's system lies in his insistence on the integration of economic, political, social, ethical and aesthetic behavior by means of the unifying *li*."[37] An obvious advantage of this approach lies in providing a locus of distinction between the *Analects* and *Xunzi*, for quite clearly *ren* is a central notion to Confucius, and it has its place as a moral ideal which functions as an internal criterion of morality.[38] I shall not take issue here with this approach but simply observe that, in characterizing a *li*-performance, certain distinct moral attitudes and emotions have to be stressed; and that a larger view must at least take into account the notion of *ren*. I propose that we proceed with a larger view by taking Xunzi's notion of *dao* as referring to his Confucian point of view. In the *Zhengming* chapter Xunzi explicitly offers *dao* as the standard for rectifying terms. And *dao* seems to embrace *li*, *yi*, and *ren*. Consider the following passage:

---

35. Incidentally, *xingqing* in modern Chinese can be translated as "temperament," in the sense of describing a person's characteristic manner of thinking, behavior, and reactive feelings. Xunzi's *qingsheng*, which we have called basic motivational structure, pertains more to the common rather than idiosyncratic temperament. Perhaps it is not taking too much liberty to render *qingsheng* as "natural temper," as Hume uses this term. See David Hume, *A Treatise of Human Nature*, ed. L. A. Selby-Bigge (Oxford: Clarendon Press, 1951), Book 3, part 2, section 2.

36. Homer H. Dubs, *Hsüntze: The Moulder of Ancient Confucianism* (London: Arthur Probsthain, 1927), 133. [For a critique of Dubs's view, see Essay 4 of this volume.]

37. Rosemont, "State and Society in the *Hsün Tzu*," 74.

38. Dubs, however, discerns in the thought of Confucius an unreconciled tension between *ren* and *li*, the internal and external morality (Dubs, *Hsüntze*, 129). But as I have argued elsewhere, Confucius's view is quite coherent. See my "Reflections on the Structure of Confucian Ethics," *Philosophy East and West* 21, no. 2 (1971).

The Way *(dao)* of the ancient King is the magnifying of benevolence *(ren)*. Follow the mean in acting it out. What is meant by the mean? It is the rules of proper conduct *(li)* and righteousness *(yi)*. The Way *(dao)* is not primarily the Way *(dao)* of Heaven; it is not the Way *(dao)* of the Earth; it is the Way *(dao)* men act, the Way *(dao)* the *junzi* acts. (*ruxiao* L131, D96*)[39]

Although Xunzi does not provide us with an account of the connection between *ren*, *yi*, and *li*, the passage can be construed as pointing to *ren* as a manifestation of *dao* by way of *li* and *yi*. If we regard *dao* as a vision or an ideal of moral excellence, that is, as a conception of an ideal state of affairs, it appears not implausible here to say that *dao* is to be comprehended by means of *ren*. *Ren* is more a distinctively personal virtue. As Dubs justly observes, "In Xunzi's teaching, *ren* has almost disappeared. It remains only as an attribute of the benevolent and kindly prince who seeks the welfare of his people; it has become characteristic of the Sage alone, who because of his highly developed character can rise superior to the ordinary man and can himself be the source of authority."[40] However, in saying that a man of *ren* loves others *(airen)*, there is no reason to deny that this love of others can also be a virtue of personal relations (*yibing* L328, D167, W69). The true king or the prince and the ordinary man of moral achievement differ in the degrees of their possession of *ren*, *yi*, and *li*, in their scope of exercise of these virtues. Thus a true king is said to have the loftiest *ren*, loftiest *yi*, and loftiest authority (*wangzhi* L174, W41, D130).[41] The *dao* of man at any rate is the *dao* of *junzi*, who models his conduct upon the *dao* of the sage *(shengren)*. A sage is one who founds his conduct upon *ren* and *yi* (*ruxiao* L152, D113). For Xunzi and also for Mencius, the sage is the highest personal embodiment of *ren*, *yi*, *li*, and other virtues, that is, an ideal paradigmatic individual who can function as a standard for guiding conduct. This standard-guiding function is, of course, derived from his comprehension of *dao* as *ren*, which is particularly expressed through the *li* or ritual rules.[42] In this view, both *li* and *yi* can be regarded more specially as virtues relative to conduct that is governed by constitutive

---

39. Again, "In the beginning, the ancient Kings founded their rule on benevolence *(ren)* and righteousness *(yi)*; the rules of proper conduct *(li)* controlled their goings and outgoings, their entire path" (*quanxue* L15, D38*). [Here I substitute "righteousness" for "justice" as a translation of *yi*. Righteousness is the virtue of right-doing. A just action is an instance of *yi*.]

40. Dubs, *Hsüntze*, 135.

41. Again, it is said that the *dao* of ancient kings pertains to *ren* and *yi* (*rongru* L65, D62).

42. For further discussion of this theme independently of Confucian ethics, see my "Morality and Paradigmatic Individuals," *American Philosophical Quarterly* 6, no. 4 (1969): 324–29.

rules. When *yi* is regarded as functionally equivalent to some notion of justice, what Dubs says is illuminating. "In Xunzi, *yi* is the foundation of society," and "*yi* is not definitely marked off from *li*; *li* also partook of the character of *yi* and so *li* also came to have the meaning of the recognition of the proper rights of others, perhaps with an emphasis upon the observances due to people in the way of courtesy."[43] *Yi* also has the force of doing what is right; more especially, it pertains to individual judgment of what is right in a particular circumstance.[44] But centrally, *li* figures a major role in this exercise of *yi*, and an achievement in this sense can be said to be an actualization of a virtue of righteousness.[45]

If the preceding remarks are deemed plausible, then any explication of Xunzi's moral notions must give a prominent place to *li*. If *dao* is regarded as *ren*, *ren* cannot be disassociated from *li* within the Confucian point of view. In focusing upon *li*, we view the rules of proper behavior, predominantly ritual in character, as being in some way constitutive of *ren*-achievement, or an achieved state of moral excellence. But in another way, the *li* are, from the Confucian point of view, embedded with an ideal of excellence. Collectively, the *li* may be regarded as a *moral norm* indispensable to the realization of an *ideal theme* of *ren* or *dao*. The significance of *li* thus lies in the *ren* quality of *li*-performance. The significance of *li* for *ren* lies in providing the indispensable condition for *ren*-fulfillment.[46] In this sense, the *li* are the *constitutive procedures* for the realization of *ren*. This point, incidentally, seems to be implicit in some passages in Xunzi. For instance, it is said that "when men wade across a river, they mark *(biao)* the deep places; but if the markers are not clear, those who come after will fall in. He who governs the people marks the Way *(dao)*; but if the markers are not clear, disorder will result. The *li* are the markers" (*tianlun* L379, W87*).[47] In another place, Xunzi states that

---

43. Dubs, *Hsüntze*, 157.
44. See Chung-ying Cheng, "On *yi* as a Universal Principle of Specific Application in Confucian Morality," *Philosophy East and West* 22, no. 3 (1972): 269–80; and my "Concept of Paradigmatic Individuals in the Ethics of Confucius," 43–46. [For a later analysis of the concept of *yi*, see my "Hsün Tzu and the Unity of Virtues," *Journal of Chinese Philosophy* 14, no. 4 (1987): 381–400; incorporated in this volume as Essay 5.]
45. For a later discussion of the distinction between *li* and *yi* and their connection, see "The Problem of Conceptual Unity in Hsün Tzu and Li Kou's Solution," *Philosophy East and West* 39, no. 2 (1989): 115–34; incorporated in this volume as Essay 4.
46. For the distinction between ideal theme and ideal norm, see my "Confucian Vision and Experience of the World," *Philosophy East and West* 25, no. 3 (1975): 319–33; or *Moral Vision and Tradition*, Essay 2. [More extensive discussion is found in my *Dimensions of Moral Creativity: Paradigms, Principles, and Ideals*, chap. 8.] An application of this distinction to Xunzi may be found in Steve Kensig, "Ritual versus Law in Hsün Tzu: A Discussion," *Journal of Chinese Philosophy* 3, no. 1 (1975): 57–66.
47. I have adopted this translation of Watson's because it seems to offer a plausible ground for my explication. Dubs and Chan have a different translation of *biao*, which they

the *li* and music "present us with models but no explanations *(bushuo)*" *(quanxue* L14, W20).⁴⁸ Admittedly these passages are rather meager textual support, but they do suggest a plausible explication of the Confucian point of view as a distinct moral point of view, with *dao* or *ren* as pertaining to its ideal aspect, and the *li* as furnishing the concrete loci, or more accurately, the constitutive procedures for *ren*-achievement.

More needs to be said about this explication, for, in Confucian ethics, we are confronted with a family of complex moral notions whose status and connections are not clearly mapped out by various thinkers. For our present purpose, our suggestion more especially concerns the function of this Confucian point of view with respect to Xunzi's conception of man's basic motivational structure. Our interpretation of the moral point of view furnishes us with a focal point for discussion of Xunzi's thesis and principal argument on human nature. Man's basic motivational structure is, in some sense, problematic. The function of Confucian morality, qualified in terms of the connection between *ren* and *li*, may be said to be the governance of man's basic motivational structure.

2. THE QUASI-EMPIRICAL ASPECT

In Part 1, I offer an explication of Xunzi's thesis on human nature in terms of the notions and distinctions involved in it. I have taken seriously Xunzi's own requirement of discrimination *(bienhe)*, construed as a requirement of conceptual clarity *(xing'e* L549, C132, D309, W163). I shall now turn to his requirement of evidence *(fuyan)*, in particular to

---

render as "permeate" rather than as "mark." For a coherent reconstruction of Xunzi the two renderings are not inconsistent, for the notion of *biao* may mean "display or manifest." And if *li* are regarded as contributory or constitutive rather than mere instrumental procedures for the attainment of *dao* or *ren*, the achieved state of moral excellence may be said to be permeated by a *li* or ritual character. For a further discussion of this point, see D. C. Lau, "Mencius' Use of the Method of Analogy in Argument," *Asia Major*, n.s., 10 (1963), reprinted as Appendix 5 in Lau's *Mencius* (Middlesex, England: Penguin Books, 1970), 245–46. A much fuller discussion is given in C. I. Lewis, *An Analysis of Knowledge and Valuation* (La Salle, Ill.: Open Court, 1946), chap. 16.

48. Again Dubs has a completely different translation, that is, that *li* and music "give principles and no false teaching" (D38). This rendering is an interpretation that is also consistent with Xunzi's view on *li*, for Xunzi does believe that the *li* are the true and unchanging principles (for example, *lilun pian* D254, W117). On this point, however, Xunzi's conception of *li* is problematic, for one would expect the constitutive procedures for moral achievement to vary from one culture to another. Within a culture or tradition, certain procedures may be regarded as constitutive of moral achievement, but it is purely contingent that a tradition contains only such and such procedures. No doubt Xunzi was rationalizing the Confucian tradition. However, to cast doubt upon his thesis on the unalterability of *li* is not necessarily to question his point that moral ideals require certain procedures for their realization. This insight is quite independent of his moral conservatism.

the deployment of conceptual distinctions in the context of arguments that possess empirical import. In the light of Part 1, we can reformulate Xunzi's *principal argument* for the thesis that "human nature is bad" as an argument that concerns the character of man's basic nature or basic motivational structure. Briefly stated, man's nature is bad because the characteristic tendency *(haoli)* of his basic motivational structure (for example, his desires and feelings) leads to strife and disorder, consequences which are undesirable from the moral point of view understood in terms of *ren* (benevolence) and *li* (ritual propriety) and *yi* (rightness).[49] This reformulation requires a qualification; the characteristic tendency *(haoli)* is a self-seeking tendency, an inclination or readiness of the individual to satisfy a range of his desires as responses to his feelings. This self-seeking tendency marks, however, a positive characteristic of man's basic motivational structure. Xunzi quite clearly recognizes also a negative characteristic, that is, a tendency to dislike and avoid what is injurious or harmful *(e'hai)*.[50] In effect, Xunzi recognizes both the appetitive and aversive characteristics of man's purposive behavior.[51] With this qualification in mind, we can now attend to Xunzi's supporting arguments.

2.1. A Sidelight on the Notion of Yu (Desire)

At the outset, let us take up an interesting but highly perplexing argument. The argument appears in the following passage:

> [If] a man is poor, he wants to be rich; if he is humble, he wants to be eminent. Whatever a man lacks in himself he will seek outside. But if a man is already rich, he will not want for more wealth, and if he is already eminent, he will not long for greater power. What a man already possesses in himself he will not seek it outside. From this point of view, men desire to do good precisely because their nature is bad. (*xing'e pian* L545, W161–162*)

The argument contained in this passage is said to be fallacious on the ground that "the fact that a man seeks a thing does not necessarily mean that he does not have it. For instance, when a scholar seeks learning, it doesn't mean that he is unlearned."[52] This objection is an easy way of disposing of the passage. However, if we attempt to explicate the nature of the premise, it appears to embody a conceptual point about the notion of desire independently of whether Xunzi has successfully

---

49. See section 1.6 above.
50. See, for example, *rongru* L60.
51. For an extensive empirical analysis of these characteristics, see Stephen C. Pepper, *Sources of Value* (Berkeley and Los Angeles: University of California Press, 1958).
52. Cheng, *Hsün Tzu's Theory of Human Nature*, 45.

defended his thesis that man's nature is bad. Supposing we regard the premise as asserting that the notion of man's desire logically involves the lack of the object desired. If a man thus seeks a desired object, this implicitly shows that he does not possess it by virtue of the logic of the notion of desire. Another way of saying the same thing is to say that the object desired is external to the desire itself. This gives a plausible interpretation for the remark that "what a man lacks in himself he will seek outside."

Now when a man already possesses the object, there will be no point in his seeking the object. In general, if a man desires and seeks an object x, he does not currently possess x. And this point is to be understood with the assumption that he clearly knows that the object sought for is a distinct object—an object that can be specified under a certain description. Thus, when a man clearly knows the object desired and sought for, he does not possess the object in question.

Now, if it is said that a learned man can desire and seek learning without lacking in learning, one can reply that the objection needs to spell out more fully what it is that is desired. If it were said that a scholar can desire and seek learning, one can point out that the object that he desires and seeks is more learning, and this logically implies that he does not possess what he seeks. What the scholar seeks is not learning *per se*, which he possesses, but more learning, which he clearly does not possess. Of course, one can also desire the continued possession of what one already has. The point is that if I desire and seek an object x, assuming that I clearly know x (that is, to be specifiable under a certain description), then I cannot be said to desire and seek x unless I do not possess x. But it follows also that a good man can seek and desire goodness, in the sense of more goodness, without himself lacking some degree of goodness. There are different degrees of moral goodness.

However, from the conceptual observation about the notion of desire as logically involving the lack of the object desired, Xunzi cannot establish the claim that "men desire to do good precisely because their nature is bad." The conceptual observation about the notion of desire offers no contribution to establishing his thesis that man's nature is bad. For the conceptual point, by itself, cannot serve as a criterion for determining the nature or character of the man desiring and seeking goodness. All that follows from the conceptual point is that, given a man desiring goodness, that man lacks goodness in some sense to be specified under a certain description, but this throws no light upon the character or nature of the man. For all we know, the man in question may be good, bad, or amoral. The question of the character of a man, the nature of his desires in particular circumstances, cannot be determined by purely conceptual considerations. In the passage considered, Xunzi has failed to establish his thesis.[53]

2.2. Arguments from Thought-Experiment

As noted previously, the principal argument involves both a quasi-empirical claim and a normative claim (section 1.3 above). The *quasi-empirical* claim is that man's basic motivational structure (henceforth, man's basic nature) tends inevitably toward strife and disorder, which presupposes the *normative claim* that strife and disorder are undesirable from the moral point of view. In general, Xunzi's requirement of evidence *(fuyan)*, as pertaining to an empirical claim, may be broadly construed as a thesis based on, but not derived from, certain matters of experience and observation.[54] However, there is an implicit normative claim, or moral judgment, on the outcome of the tendency of man's basic nature. Thus, the plausibility of the normative claim depends on the acceptance of the empirical claim and the moral point of view. My task here is to weave together, in an orderly fashion, the supportive arguments for these claims, leaving aside the question of vindication of the adoption of the moral point of view for discussion in the next section.

Instead of discussing all the supportive arguments found in Xunzi, I shall focus on examples as providing grounds for the plausibility of the principal argument, and thus on the acceptance of the thesis that man's (basic) nature is bad. The supportive arguments can be seen to be answers to the following question: What would the human situation be like were men to indulge in their basic nature without regard to moral requirements?[55] I suggest that we treat the interesting arguments in the

---

53. Xunzi's failure here is instructive in that his thesis on human nature cannot be used as a necessary explanation for moral desires in general.

54. As I shall discuss later, what we call the quasi-empirical claim embodies general observations about the human situation that are not directly verifiable. They are, however, supported by considerations that may be regarded as empirically plausible.

55. In dealing with Xunzi in this way, we bring him closer to some of the central concerns of Hume, Hart, and Warnock. My approach is markedly influenced by my study of and reflections upon the works of these philosophers. However, I am not here concerned with comparative matters of similarities and differences between Xunzi and these thinkers, although it is very difficult not to observe more than surface similarities between them. There appear to be *deep affinities,* say, between Hume and Xunzi, particularly in Hume's account of the origin of justice. It was an impression of these affinities that led me to explore the utility of the present approach. Hume's account, together with Hobbes's theory of human nature, has influenced Hart's doctrine of the minimal content of natural laws, and perhaps also Warnock's doctrine of the object of morality. Warnock's work particularly appears to echo, in a striking way, Xunzi's ethics of human nature. On the side of *deep differences,* in none of the Western thinkers is there a philosophical preoccupation with the role of *li* or ritual rules. In this respect, Xunzi's thought, and Confucian ethics in general, is more oriented toward offering moral solutions to concrete problems within a

Xing'e pian as answers to this question. However, one may query my use of the notion of human situation. For our present purpose, the relevant sense of "situation" is one that refers to a state of affairs in which human beings find themselves. A situation may thus be regarded as a human situation, in Dewey's words, an affair of doing, enjoying, and suffering.[56] A situation is a state of affairs in which our basic nature plays an essential role. There are situations in our experience that attain, so to speak, their natural completion: for example, cases where our desires terminate in quiescence without much effort on our part, that is, when the objects of our desires are immediately accessible or available to satisfy our desires. No problem arises in these situations. But, for the most part, human life is marked by interpersonal situations in which competing feelings and desires of different persons are involved. In marking their problematic character, we are focusing upon their interpersonal relations.

To a large extent, our notion of situation here is a moral notion.[57] To view a state of affairs as a situation, in part, reflects a moral concern, that is, a concern with the proper relation between men as actuated by their basic nature. In this way, Xunzi's normative claim is already an implicit feature of the quasi-empirical claim. Strife is a relation of conflict between men, and disorder is regarded more properly as a consequence of strife. It may be said that not all strife leads to disorder. But for Xunzi the strife at issue is to be regarded as strife outside the institu-

---

tradition. Perhaps it is in this region that one must attend seriously to Xunzi's own requirements of teachability and practicability of moral directives in the regulation of human conduct (*xing'e* L549, C132, D309, W163). The present approach, in effect, suggests an exploratory area in comparative moral philosophy. Readers interested in the suggested area of comparative exploration may consult the following works: T. Hobbes, *Leviathan*, chaps. 14 and 15; D. Hume, *Treatise of Human Nature*, Book 3, part 2; H. L. A. Hart, *The Concept of Law* (Oxford: Clarendon Press, 1961), chaps. 8 and 9; G. J. Warnock, *The Object of Morality* (London: Methuen & Co., 1971); John Rawls, *A Theory of Justice* (Cambridge, Mass.: Harvard University Press, 1971), part 1, chap. 3, section 22; R. S. Downie, *Roles and Values* (London: Methuen & Co., 1971); Thomas Aquinas, *A Treatise on Law* (Chicago: Henry Regnery, 1967); John Dewey, *Human Nature and Conduct* (New York: The Modern Library, 1930), part 3. For a brief discussion of some recent conceptions of morality, see my "Ethics, Contemporary Analytic Theories of," *New Catholic Encyclopedia*, supplementary volume 16 (1967–74): 167–69.

56. See John Dewey, *Experience and Nature* (New York: Dover Publications, 1958). For my own critical appreciation of this aspect of Dewey's thought, see my "Foundations of Dewey's Ethics and Value Theory," *Thought and Word Magazine* (Taiwan) 5, no. 4 (1967): 1–10; and "Practical Causation and Confucian Ethics," *Philosophy East and West* 25, no. 1 (1975): 1–10, or Essay 8 of this collection.

57. As Kovesi remarks, "An analysis of the notion of 'situation,' which along with other similar notions like 'predicament,' is already to some extent a moral notion.... [The] subject matter of morals is the human beings who live that moral life, that is, who are related to each other in the relevant manner. Moral notions do not evaluate the world of description but describe the world of evaluation." See Kovesi, *Moral Notions*, 119.

tional setting of rules and regulations. And in this setting, the strife itself is ungoverned by rules, and to say that it is also a state of disorder is the same as to say that it is ungoverned by rules. Ritual rules are basically procedures for guiding human activities. In the quasi-empirical claim we are dealing, so to speak, with brute facts and not institutional facts about men.[58] As far as institutional facts are concerned, the relations between human beings are, to Xunzi, social relations defined in terms of moral distinctions. A human society is in effect a moral society. Xunzi would agree that "there could not be a human society which was not also, in some sense, a moral community,"[59] though he would insist that the moral community is a community governed by rules of *li*-morality.

The notion of situation appears to be implicit in the Chinese notion of *shi* or, more accurately, *renshi*, which may be rendered as human affairs, as a sphere of actions or states of affairs amenable to human control and influence.[60] The formulation of our question in terms of the notion of human situation is thus quite appropriate to approaching Xunzi's arguments. These arguments are best construed as thought-experiments for answering our question: What would the human situation be like were men to indulge in their basic nature without regard to moral requirements? These thought-experiments may be characterized as a two-stage process: (1) a situation is imaginatively set up for consideration and reflective judgment, and (2) a justification of the reflective judgment is proffered, in terms of its empirical plausibility in the sense of its coherence with a set of current beliefs about human behavior. The normative claim is the further judgment based on the moral point of view.[61] I shall regard the arguments to be examined as having a cumulative force and as progressively elucidative of the function of the moral point of view. In other words, I have taken the liberty of utilizing, wherever relevant, the plausible aspects of one argument in the discussion of

58. See note 25 above.
59. Peter Winch, "Nature and Convention," *Proceedings of the Aristotelean Society* 60 (1959–60): 239.
60. This notion of *renshi* is often contrasted with *tian*. As Graham has forcefully shown, it is this dichotomy that created a tension within Confucian philosophy prior to Xunzi. Xunzi, however, has avoided this tension by giving a naturalistic conception to *tian*, Heaven. We may say that Xunzi, in focusing on *renshi* or human affairs, is reflecting a concern with man's basic motivational structure. (A. C. Graham, "The Background of the Mencian Theory of Human Nature," *Tsing Hua Journal of Chinese Studies*, n.s., 6, nos. 1–2 (1967): 255; see also Vincent Y. C. Shih, "Hsün Tzu's Positivism," *Tsing Hua Journal of Chinese Studies*, n.s., 4, no. 2 (1964): 162–74.)
61. I am here only noting some features of arguments from thought-experiments, generally familiar in moral philosophy. I leave open the question of their general philosophical significance. Also, the question of whether this is an adequate characterization of at least some basic features of the uses of thought-experiments is a question worthy of exploration.

other arguments. In this section, I shall deal with three arguments found in the *Xing'e pian*.

The first argument appears in the following passage:

A1. Let us suppose that there is a property to be divided among elder and younger brothers. If they follow their emotional nature (*qingxing*), loving profit (*haoli*) and seeking gain, they will quarrel and wrangle. But if they are transformed by *li* and *yi*, they will even yield to complete strangers. (*xing'e* L545, W161*)

The first argument does exhibit the two-stage process of thought-experiment. The supposition of the situation, in effect, requires us to imaginatively envisage the situation as an ordinary or relatively familiar situation in human experience. The plausibility of the argument thus, in part, depends on envisagement of a possible human situation. The reflective judgment is revealed in the latter half of the passage. Now this judgment is clearly a judgment that depends on Xunzi's moral point of view. Thus the passage displays both stages of the two-stage process.

In evaluating the argument A1, one may first query whether it is a just representation of this type of human situation, for it appears equally plausible to imagine situations of division of properties or inheritance in which the parties in question willingly accept an arrangement. But then the question arises whether the acceptance of any given arrangement can be justified without regard to moral considerations. Given the self-seeking tendency of man's basic nature, it is unlikely that an orderly situation would obtain without the parties paying regard to certain moral considerations. As a supportive consideration for the quasi-empirical claim, this argument thus clearly throws light upon the sort of situations relevant to man's basic nature, the problematic rather than determinate situations. Undoubtedly, the quasi-empirical claim embodies a contingent statement. But when one attends to problematic situations of this sort, it is not unreasonable to claim that strife and disorder will inevitably ensue from the unrestrained pursuit of men's desires in the absence of moral regulation. The inevitability at issue more directly pertains to our *confidence* that the outcome will be strife and disorder. Thus, when one reflects upon man's self-seeking tendency (*haoli*), one can properly claim that its actualization will lead to strife and disorder. More often as a matter of common experience, brothers, without regard to moral considerations, will fall into a state of disaffection, if not of vengeful response, when the outcomes of settlement of property are discrepant with their wishes.

Supposing, on the other hand, we take the imagined situation in the light of the brothers' heeding moral requirements in moderating, in particular, their demands; that is, by their consideration of *li* and *yi* we can be confident that their desires and feelings will be expressed in a manner amenable to the influence of even complete strangers. This confidence is not a confidence in a general empirical hypothesis, but a confidence founded upon our experiences of human situations in general, that is, a sort of expectation, a "belief" that carries weight and influence in our conduct in relation to other people.[62] At times this expectation is frustrated, but given our belief that morality must have a transforming influence upon our basic nature, the expectation can be regarded as reasonably justified.[63]

I believe that this argument, A1, as just elaborated, supports Xunzi's quasi-empirical claim. The reflective judgment on strife and wrangling is particularly plausible as a judgment coherent with our general beliefs about human situations of the sort envisaged. The situation of inheritance is an effective component in this argument from thought-experiment, for it is a situation of personal relation disrupted by self-seeking tendency and demands of the parties at issue. Given the acceptance of the quasi-empirical claim, we may then pronounce the judgment that disorder and strife are morally undesirable. And to accept this judgment is, in part, to appreciate a basic function of morality as establishing orderly procedures for regulating man's pursuit of desires in the context of interpersonal relations. In this respect, man's basic nature is bad from the moral point of view; his goodness owes to the transforming influence of morality.

The second argument is distinctive and strikingly modern. It deploys the moral distinction between good and bad. Given the definitions of "good" as "what is upright, reasonable, and orderly," and of "bad" as "what is partial, rebellious, and disorderly," Xunzi proposes the following challenge:

A2. Now suppose that a man's nature was in fact intrinsically upright, reasonable, and orderly—then what need would there be for sage-kings and *li*? The existence of sage-kings and *li* could certainly add nothing to the situation. (*xing'e* L547, W162*)[64]

62. It is this sort of "beliefs" which Hume is at pains to distinguish from fictions, but the important insight of Hume relevant to my present purpose is the pragmatic aspect of beliefs, that is, the beliefs that have "more weight and influence" in the governance of human actions. See Hume, *An Inquiry Concerning Human Understanding* (Indianapolis, Ind.: Bobbs-Merrill, 1955), 63.

63. The plausibility of this and other arguments, of course, assumes the point of view of a reflective agent who is committed to a morality. The case of amoralist response remains a problem that deserves a separate treatment. For an insightful discussion of this problem, see Bernard Williams, *Morality: An Introduction* (New York: Harper Torchbooks, 1972), 8–11.

64. Xunzi goes on to claim that, realizing that man's nature is bad in the sense

In this passage, we have basically a challenge. Fully expanded, by taking A1 into account, we have a challenge of this form: Given man's basic nature and its tendency toward strife and disorder, what would you say about this basic nature? Given our definitions of "good" and "bad," can we not properly say that his nature is bad? Supposing we maintain the contrary, that man's basic nature was in fact good in the sense defined, what would be the point of having morality in the first place? Morality, in this regard, would be completely useless. Here we have a sort of conceptual experiment about what we would say about an imagined situation and a challenge to rendering a reflective judgment on the function of morality.

Of course, conceptual considerations alone cannot establish Xunzi's thesis. The passage continues by proposing the following thought-experiment:

A3. Suppose we try to remove the authority of the ruler, do away with the transforming influence of *li* and *yi*, discard the rules of laws and governmental measures, do away with the restraint of punishment, and stand and see how people of the world deal with one another. In this situation, the strong would injure the weak and rob them, and many would do violence to the few and shout them down. The whole world would be in violence and disorder, and all would perish in an instant. (*xing'e* L549, W163)

Unlike A1, which focuses on a specific human situation that is familiar in common life, A3 sets up a rather extreme type of human situation not easily imaginable within the realm of human experience. It is obviously a fictional situation designed for the sole purpose of eliciting our reflective response. Though it appears to strain our imaginative capacity, it is the sort of challenge one confronts in philosophy. Xunzi's situation here is reminiscent of Hobbes's account of "the state of nature."[65] It may not be unreasonable to regard this situation as a wholesale state-of-nature situation that is completely devoid of any sort of moral and le-

---

explained, the sages of antiquity set up *li* and *yi*, laws and regulations, in order that they may transform men. And as a result of these sages' activities, a state of good order resulted and people's conduct was in accord with *li* and *yi*. I leave this problematic topic of sages' role in establishing morality for another occasion.

65. It is useful to distinguish this extreme or wholesale state-of-nature situation from those particular state-of-nature situations discussed by Singer. In the latter type of situation, moral considerations still have a role to play, though not expectably operative in all cases. It must be noted here that, unlike Hobbes, Hume, and Singer, I am not here employing this type of situation as a ground for a theoretical account of morality. My present aim is to lay bare the character of Xunzi's arguments. Quite obviously, the argument is reminiscent of Plato's myth of Gyges. And as I shall shortly note, it has a striking affinity with one argument of Hume in his utilitarian account of justice. See Marcus Singer, *Generalizations in Ethics* (New York: Alfred A. Knopf, 1961), chap. 6, section 3.

gal restraints. In our own times, we can more easily picture this situation, by way of science fiction literature, as a situation that is conceivably an outcome of total nuclear war, with massive human destruction—a situation in which some men survive as complete strangers, following their self-seeking nature without regard to other's needs, feelings, and desires. In this light, the situation envisaged in A3 is not totally remote from our possible experience. Xunzi's quasi-empirical claim thus can be rendered reasonably coherent with our general beliefs about man's basic nature in the absence of moral rules. Quite sensibly Xunzi points out that were the wholesale state-of-nature situation to obtain, men would perish. Of course, he tends to exaggerate by saying that they "would perish in an instant." But it seems clear that life cannot go on for long in this situation.[66] Contemplating the situation quite naturally yields the judgment that the situation of total chaos would be a situation undesirable from the moral point of view. In this regard man's basic nature is bad from the moral point of view.

At this point, an objection may be raised: The whole plausibility of the arguments essentially presupposes a conception of man as an egoist. The situations envisaged in the thought-experiments are biased. Some men we know do display benevolent tendencies. As Butler points out, we are not always actuated with the principle of self-love.[67] This objection, however, is irrelevant to Xunzi's thesis. The self-seeking tendency of man's basic nature does not preclude altogether a concern for others. The important point to note is that this concern is bound to be partial. And by Xunzi's definition of "bad," our basic nature is bad. We are naturally partial toward those whom we love. If we have benevolence, we are more likely to display our concern within a very limited scope. The self-seeking tendency is, in effect, a tendency toward partiality. Quite in the spirit of Xunzi, we may explain this partiality by way of Hume's observation "that in the original frame of our mind, our strongest attention is confined to ourselves; our next is extended to our relations and acquaintances; and 'tis only the weakest which reaches to strangers and indifferent person."[68] Xunzi is not condemning men for having feelings and desires (*zhengming pian* L527, W150, D249). Rather, he is concerned with the manner and means in which the desires are

---

66. In a similar spirit, Hume states: "Human nature cannot, by any means, subsist without the association of individuals; and that association never could have place were no regard paid to the laws of equity and justice. Disorder, confusion, the war of all against all are the necessary consequences of such a licentious conduct." (Hume, *An Inquiry Concerning the Principles of Morals* [Indianapolis, Ind.: Bobbs-Merrill, 1957], 34.)

67. See J. Butler, *Five Sermons* (Indianapolis, Ind.: Bobbs-Merrill, 1950).

68. Hume, *A Treatise of Human Nature*, 488.

pursued without regard to moral considerations. The state of disorder and strife envisaged is a consequence of the tendency to follow our basic nature without moral restraints. In a way, man's nature, understood in terms of his basic motivational structure, is not bad in itself, but it is bad in the way he tends to actualize this basic nature, and this from the moral point of view. Xunzi, throughout, is insistent on man as a raw material for moral transformation. Man is, like a piece of clay to be molded into a proper shape, to be transformed by *li*-morality (*xing'e* L549, W163–64). Every ordinary person in the street can become a sage. "What made the sage emperor Yu a Yu" lies in the "fact that he practiced *ren* and *yi* and abided by the proper rules and standards" (*xing'e pian* L552, W166*). A Yu is one who has been morally transformed. For as a person who habitually practices *ren* and *yi*, he has acquired morality as second nature. The basic nature remains, but it is now molded into a new and elegant form. The question, however, remains: What sorts of reasonable considerations can one offer for adopting the moral point of view? The next section will be devoted to this question.

2.3. The Aim of Morality

The question of vindicating the adoption of the moral point of view, for our purpose, is a question best answered in terms of the relation between man's basic human nature and morality, in particular, the aim of morality. Xunzi's answer is clear: Man's basic nature necessitates in some sense moral regulation. The reason lies in the observation that people's "desires are many but things are few," that is, that there is a limited amount of goods to satisfy everyone's desires. Since the resources for satisfying desires are limited, "there will inevitably be strife." And, "for the purpose of rescuing people from trouble and eliminating calamity there is no method as good as that of making social distinctions plain, and forming a social organization" (*fuguo* L195, D162).[69] To Xunzi, the social distinctions are an essential function of *li*-morality. The function of *li*-morality is to provide a regulation of the pursuit of men's desires and also to provide orderly channels for their satisfaction. For without such regulation, men's pursuit of their desires will end in strife and disorder. *Li*-morality is "to educate and nourish" man's basic nature.[70] It is thus the aim of *li*-morality to provide avenues for the satisfaction of desires in an orderly fashion. In this way, one may justly say

---

69. See also *rongru* L69, D65, and *wangzhi* L165, D137.
70. *lilun* L416, D213, W89. [For more discussion, see my "The Concept of *Li* in Confucian Moral Theory," in *Understanding the Chinese Mind: The Philosophical Roots,* ed. Robert Allinson (Hong Kong: Oxford University Press, 1989).]

that morality is a remedy for the human predicament.[71] And the adoption here involves the willingness to cooperate and to moderate the demands of our basic nature. As Lau succinctly states, Xunzi's "conception of morality [is] to enable people to reap the benefit of living in society while avoiding the accompanying evils."[72] Xunzi thus may be regarded as proposing a remedy for the human predicament beset by man's basic nature. Xunzi could agree with Hume "that if men were supplied with everything in the same abundance, or if every one had the same affection and tender regard for everyone as for himself; justice and injustice would be equally unknown among mankind."[73]

It must be admitted that Xunzi, unlike Hart, has not provided an ample analysis of the human predicament, but there is no reason why a fuller analysis cannot be accommodated within the compass of Xunzi's moral philosophy. In a way, factors such as human vulnerability, approximate equality, limited altruism, and limited resources for satisfying men's desires have been recognized in our explication. As to limited understanding and strength of will, "that is, of men's tendency to prefer immediate interests," Xunzi could simply accept this as a feature of the partiality of man's basic nature.[74] However, if Xunzi's thought has an affinity with some recent moral thinkers, his own conception of *li* as morality seems subject to doubt, for the *li* are largely a matter of rules and civility, a domain of rules of proper conduct that has been consigned by Western philosophers to the nonmoral domain. This deep difference cannot be explored here.[75] The question is a difficult one. It is not just a matter of contrast between Confucian and Western moral thinkers but of a contrast that has significance for a moral theory that recognizes the legitimate role of styles of performance and styles of

---

71. The function of ethics is "to correlate our feelings and behavior in such a way as to make the fulfillment of everyone's aims and desires as far as possible compatible" (Stephen Toulmin, *The Place of Reason in Ethics* [Cambridge: Cambridge University Press, 1950], 137). Also, "the general object of moral evaluation must be to contribute in some respects, by way of the actions of rational beings, to the amelioration of the human predicament—that is, of the conditions in which *these* rational beings find themselves" (Warnock, *The Object of Morality*, 16).

72. Lau, "Theories of Human Nature," 556.

73. Hume, *A Treatise of Human Nature*, 495.

74. Hart, chap. 9; and Warnock, chap. 2. I am not here claiming that Xunzi would maintain the same thesis as Hart's or Warnock's on the content of moral and legal rules or virtues. I am simply drawing attention to the affinity of concern and observations about man's basic nature and the circumstance that confronts him as necessitating moral regulation. The important point is to note the function of morality in relation to human nature. Xunzi's conception of *li*-morality remains a separate issue, as I have pointed out in note 55.

75. For a good treatment of this question, see Henry Rosemont, "Notes from a Confucian Perspective: Which Human Acts are Moral Acts?" *International Philosophical Quarterly* 16, no. 1 (1976): 49–61. [See also Essay 7, Conclusion.]

life.[76] Quite plainly, one cannot accept Xunzi's implausible thesis that ritual rules are unchanging and unalterable.[77] However, one can appreciate his thesis on the moral and symbolic significance of ritual performance.[78] The Confucian acceptance of *li* as a cultural tradition quite naturally raises the question of their proper role in moral theory.

Western philosophers, particularly those of a Kantian persuasion, think of moral theory as a critical enterprise rather than a rationalization of moral tradition. But if we think of tradition, in terms not only of content, but also of form, that is, as a set of standard procedures for conducting oneself, tradition seems to have a role to play not only in our practical but also our intellectual lives. Thus one may think of "the scientific tradition," not as referring "to any set of established theories, but rather to certain principles or standards which govern the procedures of scientists."[79] In this sense we can also talk of a moral tradition. It is in this spirit that I have earlier suggested that the *li* are best regarded as constitutive procedures for moral achievement (section 1.6 above). This, of course, relegates the content of Confucian *li* to the domain of cultural rather than transcultural interest. In this light, *li*-morality may be seen to be plausible, although one must insist that, contrary to Xunzi, these constitutive procedures are subject to revision in the light of moral experience. The remarks here, hopefully, serve as a tentative way of vindicating the adoption of *li*-morality.[80]

2.4. Recapitulation and Further Tasks

The explication of Xunzi's thesis on human nature has now come to an end. I have set out to take seriously Xunzi's remark that "man's nature is bad" as amenable to plausible explication. On the whole I have been guided by Xunzi's own requirements of discrimination and evidence, though these requirements are construed more liberally as re-

---

76. For tentative explorations of this region of moral experience, see my "Dignity of Persons and Styles of Life," *Proceedings of the American Catholic Philosophical Association* 45 (1971): 120–29, and "Relevance of Moral Rules and Creative Agency," *New Scholasticism* 47, no. 1 (1973): 1–21; or *Dimensions of Moral Creativity*, chaps. 6–7.

77. For example, *lilun* L441, D239, W105.

78. See, for example, A. R. Radcliff-Brown, "Taboo," in *Reader in Comparative Religion: An Anthropological Approach*, ed. W. A. Lessa and E. Z. Vogt, 2d ed. (New York: Harper & Row, 1965), 119.

79. R. W. Beardsmore, *Moral Reasoning* (London: Routledge and Kegan Paul, 1969), 63. See also Peter Winch, *Ethics and Action* (London: Routledge and Kegan Paul, 1972); D. Z. Phillips and H. O. Mounce, *Moral Practices* (London: Routledge and Kegan Paul, 1969); and Arthur E. Murphy, *The Theory of Practical Reason* (La Salle, Ill.: Open Court, 1965).

80. For a different approach, see Herbert Fingarette, *Confucius—The Secular as Sacred* (New York: Harper & Row, 1972).

quirements of conceptual clarity and empirical plausibility. The first requirement was pursued in Section 1 in the light of the notions and distinctions involved in the construal of the central passage as exemplifying what is termed the principal argument. The principal argument is further explicated in terms of a quasi-empirical claim on the self-seeking tendency of man's basic nature or motivational structure, and in terms of a normative claim that this tendency leads to morally undesirable consequences. Some supporting arguments are then examined as forms of thought-experiments, which may be regarded as empirically plausible. In this light I have construed the requirement of evidence as empirical plausibility, that is, as an accordance of our reflective judgment on the tendency of man's basic nature with a set of empirical beliefs. Xunzi's conception of morality is finally discussed in terms of the problem of vindicating adoption of *li*-morality. On the whole, I have attempted to display the coherence and plausibility of Xunzi's thesis. In doing so, however, I have ignored other aspects of Xunzi's moral philosophy. One further task pertains to a more detailed explication of the nature of *li*-morality, another to the doctrine of rectifying terms and the role of sages in the establishment of rectification of moral language. I hope to explore both these problems on another occasion. The present essay may be viewed as prolegomenon to these further tasks.[81] Below, I would like to inquire into the issue that divides Mencius and Xunzi in the light of two complementary approaches to the problem of morality and human nature.

2.5. Morality and Human Nature

In reflecting upon the issue between Xunzi and Mencius, it is difficult not to be impressed with a pair of philosophers, one "tough-minded," the other "tender-minded."[82] For different reasons, a number of scholars have pointed out that their theses (that is, that human nature is bad and that human nature is good) are consistent.[83] The issue, in part, reflects a difference in the definitions of "human nature" (*xing*),[84] for Mencius "was looking for what was distinctive while Xunzi was looking for what forms an inseparable part of it."[85] However, these

---

81. See Essay 7 of this volume for *li*, and my *Ethical Argumentation*, chap. 3, for the doctrine of rectifying terms.
82. Yu-lan Fung, *A History of Chinese Philosophy* (Princeton, N.J.: Princeton University Press, 1952), vol. 1, 281.
83. Lau, "Theories of Human Nature," 558–59; Graham, 257; Munro, *The Concept of Man in Ancient China*, 80–81.
84. Graham, 257; Lau, *Mencius*, 20–21.
85. Lau, *Mencius*, 21.

definitional differences do have conceptual and practical consequences that lead one to suspect that there is an underlying issue of philosophical significance. In this concluding part, I offer some suggestions on the philosophical import of the issue and on a way of reconciling the basic difference between Mencius and Xunzi, in the light of our explication of the latter's thesis on human nature.

There are three different ways of interpreting the issue between Mencius and Xunzi. The issue can be construed as an *empirical* one.[86] But this view commands no philosophical interest and is also quite inadequate to bring out the full import of the differences between the two philosophers. It may be suggested that the philosophical significance of the issue lies in its being a *metaphysical* one, or a conflict of metaphysical assumptions. As Dubs maintains, "We are here in the domain of what Immanuel Kant rightly called the metaphysics of ethics, not of empirical science."[87] This view, however, has its own difficulties. In the first place, it is highly dubious whether Mencius or Xunzi has any metaphysics of ethics, or "metaphysics of morals" in Kant's sense of the term. According to Kant, the metaphysics of morals is an a priori investigation of "the idea and principles of a possible pure will and not the actions and conditions of the human volition as such."[88] If either Mencius or Xunzi had a metaphysics, it cannot be construed in the Kantian sense of an a priori system of moral principles. In the second place, Xunzi clearly does not possess a metaphysical theory, unless we regard his naturalistic conception of *tian*, or Heaven, as a metaphysical conception. Even allowing that this is a plausible construction, Xunzi is insistent that the notion of *tian* has no moral implications.[89] One cannot, then, ascribe to him Kantian metaphysics of morals.

---

86. Both Wang Chong and Andrew Cheng seem to espouse this empirical view. In the case of Wang Chong, this seems explicit in his remarks that "as a matter of fact, human natural disposition is sometimes good, and sometimes bad, just as human faculties can be of a high or of a low order" and "I am decidedly of opinion that what Mencius says on the goodness of human nature, refers to people above the average, that what Sun Ching [Xunzi] says on its badness, refers to people under the average.... Bringing people back to unchanging standard and leading them into the right way, one may teach them. But this teaching alone does not exhaust human nature" (Wang Ch'ung [Wang Chong], *Lun Heng*, Part I, "On Original Nature," trans. Alfred Forke [New York: Paragon Book Gallery, 1962], 390–91). Since Andrew Cheng construed Xunzi's notion of evil as a descriptive term, I assume he would also maintain that the issue is empirical. (See Cheng, 42.) For criticisms of this empirical view, see Lau, "Theories of Human Nature" 550, 558.

87. Homer H. Dubs, "Mencius and Sün-dz [Xunzi] on Human Nature," *Philosophy East and West* 6 (1956): 213.

88. I. Kant, *Foundations of the Metaphysics of Morals* (Indianapolis, Ind.: Bobbs-Merrill, 1959), 7. See also Kant, *The Metaphysical Principles of Virtue* (Indianapolis, Ind.: Bobbs-Merrill, 1964), Introduction, section II.

89. See *tianlun pian* L362ff., C116ff., D173ff., W79ff.

A third view is to regard the issue as a normative one. Lau insightfully points out that the views of Mencius and Xunzi are "two ways of looking at morality in relation to human nature," and that "the clarification of the nature of morality carries with it also a decision as to its significance, because it seems natural to feel that morality, if it is acquired, does not possess the same significance as it would if it were part of original human nature."[90] This view does indeed offer a way of studying Mencius and Xunzi in the light of the problem of the relation between morality and human nature. In terms of our explication, I have shown that Xunzi's thesis does embrace a normative and a quasi-empirical claim. In the case of Mencius, his doctrine of four beginnings can also be regarded as a normative claim, as in part reflecting an ideal of human nature. But since they have different definitions of human nature, it seems appropriate to regard the issue as a conceptual one. One may then suggest that the issue is philosophically significant, because in dealing with the problem of morality and human nature, their conceptual differences, admittedly containing normative decisions, are cases of what may be called *conceptual reminders*. Both "human nature is good" and "human nature is bad" can thus function as conceptual reminders to be fully explicated in terms of their normative and quasi-empirical claims. As conceptual reminders, the remarks serve useful purposes. Stevenson calls these "re-emphatic definitions." The definitions in question are "usually in quasi-syntactical form, and have an effect in pointing out differences or analogies, and so an effect on interests in knowledge by making use of a temporal element of paradox of surprise." These "re-emphatic definitions" are made familiar to us in the writings of later Wittgenstein and of John Wisdom. Stevenson further notes that both persuasive and "re-emphatic" definitions may overlap.[91] And in the case of Mencius and Xunzi, it is difficult not to note the *suasive* tone of their remarks.[92] I have called their remarks "conceptual reminders" in order to focus upon their conceptual status as embodying certain normative decisions.

Conceptual reminders may be said to be *amphibious* remarks. On the

90. Lau, "Theories of Human Nature," 561.
91. Charles Stevenson, *Ethics and Language* (New Haven, Conn.: Yale University Press, 1944), 290–94. See particularly John Wisdom, *Philosophy and Psychoanalysis* (Oxford: Blackwell, 1953) and *Paradox and Discovery* (Oxford: Blackwell, 1965); Ludwig Wittgenstein, *Philosophical Investigations* (New York: Macmillan, 1969).
92. I take Mencius's remark that "human nature is good" as an adequate representation of his view. (See Graham, 258.) For the persuasive feature of Mencius's arguments, see I. A. Richards, *Mencius on the Mind* (London: Routledge and Kegan Paul, 1932), 55, and my "Reasonable Action and Confucian Argumentation," *Journal of Chinese Philosophy* 1, no. 1 (1973): 57–75, or *Moral Vision and Tradition*, Essay 1.

one hand, they serve to remind us of certain facts in contexts where we tend to overlook their relevance to discourse. On the other hand, they have a certain purport, a reason for issuing the reminder. The point of the reminder is based on the speaker's own appraisal of the facts at issue. When one looks at conceptual reminders in this way, one may say that these remarks have both descriptive and evaluative components interwoven in such a way that the one component cannot be rendered as intelligible without taking into account the other component. If Xunzi's remark that "human nature is bad" is taken in this way, given the plausibility of our explication, it is a conceptual reminder that draws our attention to certain brute facts about our basic nature, and these brute facts are seen to be significant, because morality is viewed as having a characteristic action-guiding function in the context of the human predicament, beset by conflicting desires in the circumstance of scarcity.

The remark, thus, at the same time reminds us of an aim of morality as a remedy to the human predicament. The normative point is that men must become moral agents, or men must be morally transformed to avert the disaster. The transformative significance of morality thus lies in guiding men toward a state of order and harmony. To become a moral agent is to become capable of appreciating and employing moral considerations as relevant to one's own choices in the light of his or her feelings and desires. The point of the reminder embodies an assessment of our desires as potentially productive of untoward consequences deemed undesirable from the moral point of view.

Turning to Mencius, the thesis that "human nature is good" can serve as a conceptual reminder of certain moral facts about us, facts that pertain not to our basic motivational structure, but to our moral nature, that is, to those facts that need to be considered when human beings are regarded as moral agents. As Lau points out, Mencius's thesis "amounts to no more than that human beings are moral agents, because for a man to be a moral agent is simply for him to be able to choose to do the right."[93] More fully, to be a moral agent is to be actuated by the "hearts" of compassion, shame, courtesy and modesty, and right and wrong. Significantly these four beginnings can only be plausibly construed as moral beginnings when we suppose them to flourish or develop, in the absence of external impediments, into such moral virtues as *ren, li, yi* and *zhi* (wisdom).[94] They are moral beginnings seen only from the point of view of moral virtues.

The point of this conceptual reminder embodies an assessment of

---

93. Lau, "Theories of Human Nature," 550. See also Graham, 254.
94. *Mencius*, 2A6. For the factors that contribute to moral failure, see my "*Xin* (Mind/Heart) and Moral Failure: Notes on an Aspect of Mencius's Moral Psychology," in

these moral facts as having an *ideal* import. As Mencius states: *"Ren* is man. When we speak of the two together, we have the Way *(dao)*."⁹⁵ The *dao* here is the Way of the men of *ren*. Although *ren* is often emphasized as a particular virtue, in this passage it seems to be elevated to a moral ideal that gives an import to having particular moral virtues. And when Mencius offers us what looks to be a definition of good *(shan)* as "the desirable" *(keyu)*, we may amplify his remark as "the desirable from the point of view of *ren* or a moral ideal."⁹⁶

This significantly contrasts with Xunzi's definition of "good" as "what is upright, reasonable, and orderly" (section 1.2 above). While Mencius's definition directs our attention to an ideal target of the moral life, Xunzi's definition emphasizes the necessity of procedures for ordering man's basic nature. As conceptual reminders, the definitions also encapsulate certain views of morality in relation to human nature. Xunzi's thesis is rooted in a picture of man as beset by a conflict of desires, whereas Mencius's is a picture of man as a moral agent with inherent tendencies toward the fulfillment of moral excellence. The one sees the basic task of morality as providing *conditions of restraint;* the other sees it as providing *conditions of ideal achievement.* In this way, not only are their theses consistent with one another, they are also complementary in focusing upon two aspects of moral experience. Their difference exemplifies a difference in the approach to the problem of the relation between morality and human nature. Xunzi's view is an *externalist* approach that construes the terms of the problem as logically independent but attempts to establish their connection in the light of one basic function of morality. Mencius's view is an *internalist* approach that recognizes the terms of the problem as distinct but connected; and the connection is taken as an inherent dependence of morality on human nature seen as a moral nature. The externalist and the internalist approaches may be viewed as complementary ways for understanding the nature of moral experience.⁹⁷ If we conceive of moral philosophy as inclusive of an account of all aspects of moral experience, then the problem of the relation between morality and human nature falls within its proper

---

Mencius: Contexts and Interpretations, ed. Alan Chan (Honolulu: University of Hawaii Press, 2002); Essay 15 of this volume.

95. *Mencius,* 7B16. I read the force of Mencius's remark as "to be a man of *ren* (humanity) is to be *truly* a man." What we have here appears to be a definition of moral agent and not of man in the sense of having a basic motivational structure. It must be reiterated here that I am concerned not with a textual problem but with a possible way of rendering Mencius's view amenable to a plausible explication. For a contrary view, see Munro, *The Concept of Man in Ancient China,* 72–73.

96. *Mencius,* 7B25.

97. For a later fuller discussion, see my "Morality and Human Nature," *Philosophy East and West* 32, no. 3 (1982): 279–94; or *Moral Vision and Tradition,* Essay 6.

province. In this light, a closer examination of the works of Xunzi and Mencius is philosophically important, particularly for a comparative moral philosophy of human experience.[98]

[98]. This essay contains, with minor revision, materials in "Human Nature: An Explication of a Basic Theme in Hsün Tzu's Moral Philosophy," presented before the Workshop on Classical Chinese Thought, East Asian Research Center, Harvard University, on August 5, 1976. I am grateful to Professors Henry Rosemont and Benjamin Schwartz, the directors of the workshop, for affording me an occasion for a progress report of my studies in *Hsün Tzu [Xunzi]*. I am also indebted to Professor Eliot Deutsch for helpful suggestions in preparing the final version for publication.

Essay 2

DIMENSIONS OF *LI* (PROPRIETY)

In recent years, the notion of *li* has received considerable philosophical attention.[1] Like *ren* (humanity) and *yi* (righteousness), *li* is a rich and fluid notion with a long history of evolution.[2] A Chinese brought up in Confucian morality might have acquired a fair comprehension of the uses and import of *li* in different circumstances of his life. A philosophical characterization and appreciation of the significance of this notion for contemporary moral theory and practice is a difficult task, but a welcome challenge. In general, the notion of *li* refers to a normative domain consisting of rites, ceremonies, decorum, courtesy, and civility, which may conveniently be labeled "the domain of propriety."[3] It is a domain consisting of specific requirements or rules for proper conduct for different types of occasion in personal and social intercourse. Such an explanation, while informative, gives rise to a problem of conceptual unity. For it is not evident that we are here dealing with a univocal concept. But if the notion of *li* is taken as ambiguous, the task of ex-

---

1. I have in mind the following: Herbert Fingarette, "Human Community as Holy Rite: An Interpretation of Confucius' *Analects*," *The Harvard Theological Review* 59, no. 1 (1966), incorporated in *On Responsibility* (New York: Basic Books, 1967) and substantially as Chapter I in *Confucius—The Secular as Sacred* (New York: Harper Torchbooks, 1972); Donald Munro, *The Concept of Man in Ancient China* (Stanford, Calif.: Stanford University Press, 1969); Tu Wei-ming, "The Creative Tension between *Jen* and *Li*," and "*Li* as a Process of Humanization," *Philosophy East and West* 18, nos. 1–2 (1968) and 22, no. 2 (1972); Chad Hanson, "Freedom and Moral Responsibility in Confucian Ethics," *Philosophy East and West* 22, no. 2 (1972); A. S. Cua, "Reflections on the Structure of Confucian Ethics," *Philosophy East and West* 21, no. 2 (1971), and "The Concept of Paradigmatic Individuals in the Ethics of Confucius," *Inquiry* 14 (1971). The last two papers were incorporated as chaps. 4 and 5 of Cua, *Dimensions of Moral Creativity: Paradigms, Principles, and Ideals* (University Park: Pennsylvania State University Press, 1978).

2. See Cho-yun Hsu's Foreword in Noah Edward Fehl, *Li: Rites and Propriety in Literature and Life—A Perspective for a Cultural History of Ancient China* (Hong Kong: The Chinese University of Hong Kong Press, 1971).

3. Another list is given by Dubs: "*Li* may be translated by religion, ceremony, deportment, decorum, propriety, formality, courtesy, etiquette, good form, good behaviour, good manners, or, as I prefer, the rules of proper conduct." H. H. Dubs, *Hsüntze: The Moulder of Ancient Confucianism* (London: Arthur Probsthain, 1927), 113n.

plication becomes even more difficult to execute in light of the Confucian understanding of the interconnection of *li, ren,* and *yi*. This complication moves us further away from the aim of establishing the coherence and independent plausibility of the notion of *li*.

Apart from the problem of conceptual unity, a contemporary moral philosopher may be perplexed with the recent preoccupation with *li*. For unlike ancient Confucians, recent works on *li* do not display any interest in defending a particular normative system. As Waley reminds us, "The task of the ritual theorists in the third century B.C. was to detrivialize ritual, to arrest its lapse into a domain of mere etiquette or good manners by reintegrating it into the current system of thought."[4] The task consists, in part, in defending specific rules of propriety, and, in part, in offering a general rational justification for the existence of a normative system. That the ancient philosophers were interested in the problem of rational justification of a normative system may be shown in their occasional tendency to associate the notion of *li* with its homophone *li** (reason or rationale) and *yi* (rightness or fittingness).[5] This is particularly evident in Xunzi. Thus it is their concern with this problem that commands philosophical attention, rather than their defense of specific rules of propriety.

While one may grant the philosophical importance of the problem of rational justification of a normative system, the relevance of the problem to contemporary moral philosophy may be queried. If the scope of *li* encompasses such diverse items as rites, ceremonies, good manners, and so on, it is very difficult to make any moral sense out of this list, except perhaps in the rather uninteresting sense of mores or conventional rules of behavior. The subject matter of morality, as conceived in standard Western ethical theory, does not display any concern with such a scope of *li*-conduct. In other words, one can justly suspect that *li* is not a moral notion, especially when it is viewed as independent of *ren*. To allay this suspicion, a Confucian may claim, as does Rosemont, that in Confucian ethics, there are no unique concepts of morals or moral action. *Li* is a case in point. *Li* is said to have "morals" as one of its meanings. To say that "an action is in accordance with *li* is to say that it is moral, and that it is civil, mannerly, customary, proper, and in at least one sense, religious."[6] This response to the query, apart from raising the issue of the proper interpretation of *li*, may appear to be effective in correcting a misunderstanding of Confucian ethics, but it hardly re-

---

4. Arthur Waley, *The Analects of Confucius* (New York: Random House, 1938), 57–59.
5. Mao Zishui, *Lunyu jinzhu jinyi* (Taipei: Shangwu, 1977; 1st ed. 1975), 185–87.
6. Henry Rosemont, Jr., "Notes from a Confucian Perspective: Which Human Acts Are Moral Acts?" *International Philosophical Quarterly* 16 (1976): 50.

solves the problem of conceptual unity or the problem of justification. Reminding Western readers of the peculiarity of this notion only raises the question of explication. The fact, if it be fact, that the Chinese do not have a clear demarcation between moral and nonmoral actions does not by itself establish any unitary way of dealing with the notion of *li*. One may ask, What sense of "moral" is used in Rosemont's proposed scheme for analysis? Even if one agrees that the *li*-action has always a "moral" plus meaning, the notion of "moral" here requires explication in connection with the other items given in the scheme. And if Confucian ethics is to be regarded as relevant to moral philosophy, her defender must offer some more detailed characterization of *li*, in particular its presumed importance as a component of an acceptable normative ethics. The issue here is the familiar problem of the definition of morality.[7] For as long as philosophers cling to a narrow conception of morality as referring to "something that is coordinate with, but different from, art, science, law, and convention," or in Butler's term, "the moral institution of life,"[8] they will fail to appreciate the moral import of *li*. However, if a broader conception of morality is espoused, somewhat parallel to Aristotle's, it may be quite appropriate to claim that *li* is a moral notion. And, in particular, when one attends to the desired qualities or virtues in *li*-performance, the moral significance of *li* will probably be quite readily accepted.

The task of assessing *li* as a moral notion thus depends on our understanding of the requisite qualities of the agent involved in *li*-performance. This, in turn, depends on a prior consideration of the problem of conceptual unity and its significance for moral philosophy. In this article, I center on the latter task. For explication I have chosen Xunzi as a guide, for it is Xunzi who has offered us a systematic discussion of this topic. By focusing on what I call the dimensions of *li* and their interconnection, I hope to show a way of appreciating the unity of this plurisignation.[9] Put another way, I attempt to present a partial cartography of *li* as comprising moral, aesthetic, and religious values. This exercise in axiological ethics may also be viewed as a prelude to a critical study of arguments for Confucian *li* and its contribution to the epistemology of ethics.[10] This article, I hope, will also throw some light on a

---

7. For recent works on this topic, see G. Wallace and A. D. M. Walker, eds., *The Definition of Morality* (London: Methuen & Co., 1970).
8. William K. Frankena, *Ethics*, 2nd ed. (Englewood Cliffs, N.J.: Prentice-Hall, 1973), 6.
9. See Phillip Wheelwright, *The Burning Fountain* (Bloomington: Indiana University Press, 1968), 81.
10. The term owes to J. N. Findlay, *Axiological Ethics* (New York: St. Martin's Press, 1970). For a discussion of the distinction between the cartography and the epistemology of morals, see my *Dimensions of Moral Creativity*, chap. 1, section A. [For a later study of the

basic aspect of Xunzi's moral philosophy. In this regard, it must be avowed at the outset that a fuller understanding and assessment of Xunzi's theory awaits a careful study of his conception of ethical discourse and an explication of the interconnection among *li, ren,* and *yi*.[11] In what follows, I shall treat *li* as a quasi-independent notion to be qualified in terms of such a further study.

In dealing with the problem of conceptual unity of the notion of *li* by way of its different dimensions, I shall be guided, for the most part, by Xunzi's essay on this topic. The essay on *li [lilun pian]* is important for two reasons: (1) it is a fairly coherent essay on a key Confucian notion, and (2) it presents a rational justification of *li* as a normative system, including an interesting discussion on the rites of mourning and sacrifices. If one focuses on these rites, it can be argued that Xunzi is a religious philosopher.[12] For our purpose, we shall treat this discussion as dealing with a dimension of *li*. Let me note, however, that I am using the term "dimensions of *li*" to refer to the different aspects of *li* in the light of their value-significance. Adapting a modern-looking distinction from Xunzi, I shall regard *li*, standing alone, as a generic term *(gongming)* subject to specification in context by such terms as rites, ceremonies, or manners, that is, by terms that differentiate *(bieming)* the distinct types of operative rules in particular settings or occasions for proper conduct *(zhengming* L515, W145–146). In this way, for appreciating the appropriate type of rules in a particular situation, we can

---

functions and justification of *li*, see my "The Concept of *Li* in Confucian Moral Theory," in *Understanding the Chinese Mind: The Philosophical Roots*, ed. Robert Allinson (Hong Kong: Oxford University Press, 1989); or *Moral Vision and Tradition: Essays in Chinese Ethics* (Washington, D.C.: The Catholic University of America, 1998), Essay 11.

11. In my study of Xunzi, of which this article is a partial installment, I confront the difficult conceptual problem of dealing with *li, ren, yi,* and other interdependent notions. I am now convinced that a full critical study depends on solving this conceptual problem. Consequently, my remarks on *li* are to be qualified in light of a systematic treatment of Xunzi's moral philosophy. I am not satisfied with the draft in hand. In spite of this inadequacy, the present explication has intrinsic interest as an exploration of a basic problem in axiological ethics. Also, it must be observed that my present explication is, to some extent, an ideal reconstruction of the notion of *li*. The spirit is much in line with Deutsch's remark on comparative aesthetics: "that through the study and creative reconstruction of other cultural ideas and preferences we may enrich the possibility of our understanding philosophically the nature of art and aesthetic experience" (Eliot Deutsch, *Studies in Comparative Aesthetics*, Monograph no. 2 of The Society for Asian and Comparative Philosophy [Honolulu: University of Hawaii Press, 1975]). See also Cheng Chung-ying, "Conscience, Mind and Individual in Chinese Philosophy," *Journal of Chinese Philosophy* 2, no. 2 (1974); and A. S. Cua, "Some Reflections on Methodology in Chinese Philosophy," *International Philosophical Quarterly* 11 (1971), and "Tasks of Confucian Ethics," *Journal of Chinese Philosophy* 6, no. 1 (1979). [For a later study of the problem of conceptual unity see Essay 4 of this volume.]

12. See Edward J. Machle, "Hsün Tzu As a Religious Philosopher," *Philosophy East and West* 26, no. 4 (1976).

speak of the "*li* of manners or etiquette," "the *li* of mourning," "the *li* of sacrifices," "the *li* of marriage," and more. In the generic sense, *li* pertains to a set of rules of proper conduct or to any performance that satisfies any of the specific requirements in an appropriate setting. Since there are different types of requirements, to comprehend fully a dimension of *li* is to attend to the types of situation or performance embedded with value-significance. Our discussion, however, deals only with *li* as a generic notion. I shall assume that *li*, in its generic sense, is connected with *ren*, the Confucian ideal of the good life. Consequently, a complete explication of *li* cannot be elaborated without making explicit such a connection. In discussing the dimensions of *li*, we are thus confined only to certain types of situation envisaged within the scope of *li*. To inquire into the connection between the different dimensions is to attempt to bring to light the value-connection between the different items within the scope of *li*. It cannot pretend to be a demonstration of the philosophical import of *li* as a generic notion. At most it points to a way of dealing with this larger question.

1. THE MORAL DIMENSION OF 'LI'

For locating the moral dimension, let us consider a central passage:

What is the origin of *li*? I answer that man is a creature born with desires. If his desires are not satisfied, he cannot but seek some means for satisfaction. If there are no limits or measures to govern their pursuit, contention will inevitably result. From contention comes disorder and from disorder comes poverty. The ancient Kings hated such disorder, and hence they established *li* (rules of proper conduct) and inculcated *yi* (rightness or sense of righteousness) in order to regulate men's pursuit, to educate and nourish men's desires, to provide opportunity for this seeking of satisfaction. They saw to it that desires did not overextend the means of satisfaction, and material goods did not fall short of what was desired. Thus both desires and goods were looked after and satisfied. This is the origin of *li*. (*lilun* L418, W88*, D213*)

This passage clearly reflects Xunzi's view of man's basic motivational structure, consisting of feelings and desires, which presents a problem of regulation.[13] This basic function of *li* thus directs our attention to the sort of situations that involve conflicts in man's pursuit of the means or objects for the satisfaction of desires, or, in familiar idiom, conflicts of interest. Without regulation, such situations of conflict in human inter-

13. For an attempt at a plausible explication of this thesis, see my "The Conceptual Aspect of Hsün Tzu's Philosophy of Human Nature," and its companion "The Quasi-Empirical Aspect of Hsün Tzu's Philosophy of Human Nature," *Philosophy East and West* 28, no. 1 (1978). [See Essay 1 of this volume.]

course will result in mutual injury and destruction. Contention among men is regarded here as a disvalue, and orderly conduct a value. *Li* thus embodies a value of order, more accurately, a value of social order. As a set of procedures, it is designed for restraining men's actions that affect others. In this regard, Xunzi's concern with *li* expresses a concern with what is commonly called "the moral point of view" as a point of view for adjudicating the conflict of interests.[14] The focus on *yi* or right conduct is particularly significant, for this Confucian notion implies a contrast between morality and self-interest or personal gain. As Xunzi remarked, the morally superior man *(junzi)* must be able to suppress his personal desires in favor of impartiality and rightness *(yi)* *(xiushen* L36, W32; see also *jundao* L276). Saying this, however, does not condemn desires *qua* desires, for "beings that possess desires and those that do not belong to two different categories—the categories of the living and the dead" *(zhengming* L527, W150, D294). "The possession and nonpossession of desires has nothing to do with good or had government" (ibid.). They are to be accepted as part of our native endowment.

For a reflective Confucian, to pay heed to *li* is to submit his conduct to the governance of a set of authoritative, objective, and impartial procedures, particularly in situations where his desires or interests conflict with those of others. It is, at the same time, to acknowledge the necessity of *li* as having a unifying social function. If we conceive of ethics as having the function "to correlate our feelings and behaviour in such a way as to make the fulfillment of everyone's aims and desires as far as possible compatible,"[15] we may say that *li* has a distinctive ethical or moral function. But one may object that this statement is a statement of factual or sociological description rather than a normative one.[16] This objection has no force in the present context. For Xunzi, throughout, was preoccupied with a normative problem. To regard *li* as having a unifying social function is to propose an answer to the normative problem of how one ought to govern human beings in view of their tendency toward strife or contention. The normative context marks the answer as a normative one. The indicative form of the statement that "*li* has a unifying social function" is a prescriptive, evaluative statement, that is, "We ought to regulate our conduct by *li*." The basis of this claim lies in the acceptance of the value of social order.

14. See Kurt Baier, *The Moral Point of View* (Ithaca, N.Y.: Cornell University Press, 1958).
15. Stephen Toulmin, *The Place of Reason in Ethics* (Cambridge: Cambridge University Press, 1950), 137.
16. This objection is raised against Toulmin's view. See George B. Wall, *Introduction to Ethics* (Columbus, Ohio: Charles E. Merrill Publishing Co., 1974), 174.

There is, however, a more difficult question. There are different types of social orders. What is acceptable must depend on some given standard or criterion that justifies our choice of one as morally superior to another. Can the Confucian provide an adequate answer to this question? I believe that a Confucian answer can be given, but it requires a reference to *ren*, or the ideal of humanity—a topic that goes beyond the scope of this article. Let me here just indicate a suggestion. Insofar as *li* is a set of regulative procedures, the harmony of human conduct deemed morally acceptable lies in the conception of a social order, not as an aggregative union of individuals, but as a community of members that have varying ties and relationships together with a sense of common bond. The moral value of a social order thus lies in a conception of a community of men who act on one another with mutual regard and degrees of affection appropriate to their personal relationships. Thus at the heart of a valuable social order is the ideal of *ren* as humanity. In this light, *li*, as a set of regulative procedures, is a constitutive means for the attainment of the ideal of humanity. And this is to be understood in the sense in which the *li* are more than just instruments, but a constitutive feature of *ren*-achievement. Much more is thus involved in living a morally good life than mere compliance with *li* as procedures for proper conduct. Independent of its connection with *ren*, however, one may still question whether *li* is the best means for achieving a desirable social order. What value does it have other than being a mere instrumental means, even if it can be justified in terms of efficiency? The answer to this question must await a just appreciation of other dimensions of *li*.

Let us attend to a more detailed characterization of *li* as a regulative system. In Xunzi, the envisaged social order appears to be a hierarchal structure of duties tied to one's status, position, or roles in society. We are told that when the *junzi*, or ethically superior man, has gotten his education and nourishment (through *li*) he also esteems its distinctions. Xunzi continues,

What are these distinctions? There are the distinctions of the classes of eminent and mean; there are inequalities of the senior and the younger; there is what is appropriate to those who are poor and those who are rich, to those who are important and those who are unimportant. (*lilun* L419, D214*; see also *yibing* L331)

This passage suggests that *li* is more than just a set of formal requirements. It embodies social distinctions as value-distinctions. Implied in this conception is the view that the distinctions so marked out by *li* are to be accepted by Confucian agents without any question. There appears in this view no possibility of reasonable moral judgment or evaluation of social distinctions by individual persons; consequently, it leaves no room for a conception of autonomous agency. In Dubs's words, "*li* was the expression of outer morality; it prescribed certain acts to be performed, and without giving any reason except that they must be done."[17] It may then be said that Xunzi was the best exemplar of Confucian ethics, that is, "that it was only in Xunzi that the typically Confucian principle of authority and of external morality comes to its logically preeminent place."[18] In effect, with the focus of *li* in Xunzi, we have an authoritarian rather than an individualistic ethics.

It cannot be denied that Xunzi, more than other Confucians, laid stress on *li*, and in so doing, displays an authoritarian and conservative tendency. We are told, for example, "*li* is what reason cannot alter" (*yuelun*, L463). But to lay stress on that statement without regard to Xunzi's other remarks on personal cultivation and the moral basis of social distinctions is to do a great injustice to Xunzi's ethics. While one may grant that Xunzi quite consistently emphasized the necessity of the moral authority of sage-kings, he has also given explicit recognition to the autonomous function of the mind. Says Xunzi: "The mind is the ruler of the body and the master of the spirit. It gives commands and all parts of the body obey. It itself makes choices; it itself causes action; it itself stops action" (*jiebi* L488, D269). An agent is thus conceived as an autonomous being. What subjects his conduct to *li* is in part a decision to accept *li* as a basis of conduct. The social distinctions, even if they are presumed to be value distinctions, are still subject to individual choice and judgment. And his choice, if it is moral, must be guided by a moral standard. The mere existence of a social distinction does not, therefore, confer its own moral value.[19]

We can now ask, "What then is the moral standard that underlies one's acceptance of social distinctions, say, difference in rank or riches and poverty." The answer, I believe, lies in Xunzi's distinction between two different types of honor. It is the sense of intrinsic honor that confers a moral value on a particular social distinction. Take the distinction between the eminent and the mean. This distinction pertains primarily

---

17. Dubs, *Hsüntze*, 122.
18. Ibid., 132. Note that the recent characterizations of Confucian ethics offered by Fingarette and Rosemont echo Dubs. In a different language we are told that the Chinese have no concept of moral choice, and consequently no concept of moral dilemma. I find this view extremely puzzling. I hope the observation that follows offers a partial response to what I regard as a one-sided view of Confucian ethics. (See Fingarette, *Confucius*, and Rosemont, "Notes from a Confucian Perspective.")
19. For more extensive discussion of the nature of the autonomy of agency, see my *Ethical Argumentation: A Study in Hsün Tzu's Moral Epistemology* (Honolulu: University of Hawaii Press, 1985), chap. 4.

to one's position in society. It is purely a matter of circumstance rather than moral necessity. A distinction in social rank does not necessarily imply the possession of moral merits or demerits. There is, as Xunzi observes, a distinction between intrinsic and extrinsic honor *(yirong* and *shirong)*, that is, an honor that is justly deserved on the grounds of virtues and an honor obtained by way of one's fortunate station in a particular society. "A cultivated will, many virtuous actions, brilliant thoughts belong to the honor that comes from within oneself; and this is what is meant by 'intrinsic honor *(yirong).*'" On the other hand, "high noble rank, great tribute, or emoluments, and surpassing power. ... belong to the honor that comes from without; and this is what is meant by 'extrinsic honor *(shirong)*" *(zhenglun* L410, D208).[20] There is no assurance that the two will coincide in practice. Says Xunzi, "Humanity *(ren)*, righteousness *(yi)*, and virtuous acts *(de)* are ordinarily reliable ways of managing one's life; however, it is possible that they may bring about dangerous (or unwanted) consequences" *(rongru* L60, D59*). Yet it cannot be doubted that the honor and shame one morally deserves are products of one's efforts at self-cultivation and conduct, and thus properly reflect one's virtues and vices *(quanxue* L5, D33, W17). Like Aristotle, Xunzi and other Confucians were concerned with the noble and the base in light of moral virtues and vices. He would exalt a man of *li*, not just because his outward appearance and actions conform to, say, the *li* of etiquette, but also because such a display makes manifest and glorious *(long)* his moral attainment.[21] According to Aristotle, "high-mindedness ... is the crown, as it were, of the virtues; it magnifies them and it cannot exist without them. Therefore, it is hard to be truly high-minded and, in fact, impossible without goodness and nobility."[22] So also, it is impossible to live a life of *li* without goodness and nobility.

If the foregoing remarks are deemed plausible, *li* as a set of regulative, formal procedures for conduct cannot be understood apart from

---

20. My proposed terms for *yirong* and *shirong* are not meant to be translations, though they clearly capture Xunzi's distinction. He made a similar distinction for shame: *yiru* and *shiru*. The essay on shame and honor deserves careful consideration for the explication of Confucian moral psychology, for no attention at all is given to guilt as a moral emotion or a condition of oneself. Xunzi's case is particularly interesting in that he appears to be quite clear about the distinction between moral feelings and conditions. [For a later extensive comparative study, see my "Ethical Significance of Shame: Insights of Aristotle and Xunzi," *Philosophy East and West* 53, no. 2 (2003): 147–202, incorporated as Essay 8 of this volume.]

21. A number of passages exalt *li*, while other passages exalt *ren* and *yi*. Readers may wish to consult *A Concordance to Hsün Tzu*, Harvard-Yenching Institute Sinological Index Series, supplement no. 22 (Taipei: Chinese Materials and Research Center, 1966).

22. Aristotle, *Nichomachean Ethics*, trans. Martin Ostwald (Indianapolis, Ind.: Bobbs-Merrill, 1962), 1124a.

moral virtues. *Li* is also a means to educate and nourish one's feelings and desires, because it has an intimate connection with the virtues that one wants to promote. That *li* has a moral dimension thus depends on its association with moral virtues. A *li*-performance, in this light, has moral import because it manifests the relevant moral virtue or virtues. Xunzi occasionally emphasizes such familiar Confucian virtues as filiality, loyalty, trustworthiness, sincerity, reverence, respect, modesty, integrity, courage, magnanimity, kindness, love, and extensive learning.[23] As a means to the cultivation or development of one's moral character, *li* cannot be detached from the concern with the ideal of humanity *(ren)* and righteousness *(yi)*. In one striking passage on sincerity *(cheng)*, much reminiscent of *Zhong Yong*, we find the following:

For developing the mind of the ethically superior person *(junzi)*, there is nothing better than sincerity. Preserve humanity *(ren)* only, practice righteousness *(yi)* only. With a sincere mind preserve humanity, and it will become tangibly manifested. In such manifestation, one becomes godlike *(shen)*. Being godlike one can then transform (other men). With a sincere mind practice righteousness, and there will come orderliness [and reasonableness]. With orderliness [and reasonableness] there is enlightenment *(ming)* and with enlightenment one can reform oneself. Alternately to reform oneself and to transform others is what is meant by heavenly virtue. *(tiande)* *(bugou* L47)[24]

To sum up: In terms of its basic function, *li* has a bipolar character. Negatively, as a set of procedures for regulating human intercourse, it directs attention to the problematic nature of man's basic motivational structure, that is, his natural feelings and desires, and its liability to conflict. To avoid chaos in human interaction, *li* is a set of constraints designed for resolving a conflict of desires or interests. As an educational measure, the aim of *li* is to produce a uniform pattern of behavior much in the sense in which ethologists today speak of "ritualization of behavior" in both animals and humans for the purpose of the canaliza-

---

23. See, for example, *xiushen pian, bugou pian*. Jen Chuo-hsuan rightly points out that Xunzi was concerned with morality *(daode)*, in view of his recurrent references to such moral virtues. See his "The Philosophical System of Hsün Tzu," *Zhexue lunwen ji* (Taipei: Shangwu, 1967), vol. 1. My present account of the moral dimension of *li* focuses on the neglected personal import. This is not to deny that *li* can be treated in a sociopolitical context, which is commonly stressed by writers on Xunzi, at the expense of the personal aspect. The issue here is a matter of coherent philosophical reconstruction. Different interpretations need not conflict when seen as complementary lenses for understanding Xunzi's moral philosophy. See, for example, Dubs, *Hsüntze*, and Henry Rosemont, Jr., "State and Society in the Xunzi: A Philosophical Commentary," *Monumenta Serica* 29 (1970–71).

24. This translation is adapted from Derk Bodde's with emendations. See Fung Yu-lan, *A History of Chinese Philosophy*, vol. 1 (Princeton, N.J.: Princeton University Press, 1952), 293.

tion of aggression and formation of a social bond.[25] In this sense, we may regard a *li*-performance as a ritualized behavior that satisfies its unifying social function. Positively, *li* has the function of nourishing or transforming man's basic motivational structure by way of inculcation of a regard for moral virtues and the development of moral character. A *li*-performance is here no longer a ritualized, routine behavior, but a display of moral virtue or virtues relevant to the occasion. It is a moral performance. The social order that emerges, if it does emerge, is a moral order because of the presence of moral virtues in the varying interpersonal and personal relationships among the members.[26] Society, in this light, is no longer a mere association of men, but a *moral community*.[27] And, as I have noted throughout the discussion, the positive aspect of *li* presupposes its connection with the ideal of humanity *(ren)* and *yi* (righteousness). The basic function of *li* has thus both negative and positive aspects. The two cannot be detached for a proper characterization of *li* in Xunzi's ethics.

2. THE AESTHETIC DIMENSION OF 'LI'

Scholars of Confucian ethics commonly stress the aesthetic dimension of *li*. In terms of the positive aspect of the basic function of *li*, the desired transformation, for Xunzi, is more than just a process of inculcation of moral virtues, but a sort of beautification of man's original nature. Before we attend to this beautification, let us observe that when we view moral education as excluding aesthetic concerns, the process is more accurately characterized as one that is oriented toward the formation of what may be termed second-order emotions and desires. One passage in Xunzi seems to suggest this: "A single desire which one receives from nature *(tian)* is regulated and directed by the mind in many different ways, and it is certainly difficult to identify it in terms of its original appearance" (*zhengming* L527).[28] When the natural expression of one's feeling, such as joy or sadness, love or hate, is subjected to the

---

25. K. Z. Lorenz, "Ritualization in the Psycho-social Evolution of Human Culture," in *A Discussion of Ritualization of Behaviour in Animals and Man*, Philosophical Transactions of The Royal Society of London, series B, no. 772, vol. 251, 276. It is interesting to note that Radcliff-Brown regards his own view of rituals, as having primarily a social function and symbolic import, as being anticipated by Xunzi. See A. R. Radcliff-Brown, "Taboo," in *A Reader in Comparative Religion*, ed. W. A. Lassa and E. Z. Vogt (New York: Harper and Row, 1965), 119.

26. For more discussion of human relationships and the virtues, see Appendix 1.

27. See my "Confucian Vision and the Human Community," *Journal of Chinese Philosophy* 11, no. 3 (1984): 226–38; incorporated in this volume as Essay 11.

28. My own free rendering of this difficult and perplexing passage is an attempt at a coherent reading of the Xunzi. It is substantially the same as that of Dubs and Watson

regulation and transformation of *li*, it can no longer be viewed as mere natural expression, for so regulated and transformed it acquires a significance beyond its original and spontaneous untutored expression. Likewise, the same point holds with respect to our natural desires. When our natural desires are morally transformed, they are deemed morally acceptable. And our pursuit of them is no longer a mere natural pursuit, but characteristically a moral pursuit. For the desires are now seen as mediated by a moral concern. These desires are *reflective* desires, because they have passed the test of moral approval. To pursue these second-order desires in a moral way requires an exercise of a second-order volition, that is, a second-order desire to constitute our will as a moral agent rather than an amoral agent.[29] The expression of second-order feelings and desires may, of course, appear as effortless and spontaneous as that of the first-order feelings and desires. Here the effortlessness and spontaneity is a product of self-transformation, that is, when consideration of moral virtues has become second nature. Living a moral life, in this way, requires having second-order feelings and desires. Moral feelings and desires are second-order phenomena, though not all second-order feelings and desires are moral.

Man's basic motivational structure thus furnishes the raw materials for *li*-transformation. In Xunzi's words, "The original nature of man is the beginning and material; acquired characteristics are the beautification and glorification of the original nature. Without acquired characteristics, the original nature could not become beautiful of itself. When

---

(D294, W151), though the former regards the passage as corrupt, and the latter expresses doubt about the meaning of the sentence. My reading depends on the distinction between first-order and second-order desires and emotions, a distinction implicit in Xunzi. For the moral transformation of emotions and feelings is essentially a change, not in the sense of direction alone, but in an alteration of the *form* of expression of natural emotions and means of satisfaction of material desires. It is particularly clear in the case of aesthetic transformation. One's natural desire for food, when subjected to the regard for a proper way of satisfaction, no longer appears as a mere biological drive, but as a desire invested with a regard for an elegant form of satisfaction. That this form of satisfaction is relative to culture hardly needs argument. But the transformation so effected by a particular culture may properly be said to express a particular aesthetic concern of a culture. The common stress on *li* as a humanizing or civilizing instrument cannot be denied. But the philosophical import lies in the presumed moral and aesthetic values, which properly constitute the principal dimensions of *li*. [Since the publication of this essay in 1979, I discovered the same interpretation of this problematic passage in Liang Qixiong's annotated text. Liang remarks that the contrast lies in the distinction between *tianxing yu* (desires as endowed by nature, or natural desires) and *lixing yu* (desires as guided by reason, or reflective desires). Because of this distinction, it is difficult to classify all desires in the same way. See Liang Qixiong, *Xunzi jianshi* (Taipei: Shangwu, 1978), 323.]

29. See Harry G. Frankfurt, "Freedom of the Will and the Concept of Person," *Journal of Philosophy* 68, no. 1 (1971). For a more recent discussion of man's reflective capacity to form second-order desires, see Charles Taylor, "Responsibility for Self," in *The Identities of Persons*, ed. Amelie Rorty (Berkeley and Los Angeles: University of California Press, 1976).

original nature and acquired characteristics unite in character development, then only the name of Sage becomes inseparable from that of man" (*lilun* L439, D234–235, W102). Moral virtues are acquired characteristics, that is, the dispositions to perform certain types of action in accordance with *li*-procedures. These virtues involve also the second-order moral desires and feelings. And when these are expressed in the *form* required by the appropriate *li*, they acquire an aesthetic significance. To speak of the aesthetic dimension of *li* is to focus on the intimate connection between moral and aesthetic values.

If the ideal of *ren* is to be realized by way of *li*, as constitutive procedures the *li* refine and ennoble our feelings and means of pursuing our desires. A moral action, in this light, is a beautiful performance. It is an achievement. "The learning of a *junzi* or ethically superior person is for the sake of beautifying his own person" (*quanxue*, L14, D37, W20). For Xunzi, man's basic motivational structure is "bad" in a double sense. It is "bad" because of its tendency toward chaos and destruction. It is "bad" also in the sense of its being inferior or "ugly." Without transformation by means of *li*, man can hardly be distinguished from the birds and beasts. And when he becomes good, he has become also a beautiful person. The beauty of his moral character lies in the balance between his emotions and forms. What is deemed admirable in the virtuous conduct of the superior man thus lies in the harmonious fusion of form and feelings. Such a piece of conduct complying with *li*-requirements can become a fitting object of contemplation. The spectator may take delight in contemplating the *li*-performance. So also, ideally, the *junzi* takes delight in pursuing the moral way: "The *junzi* rejoices in attaining the *dao*, while the inferior man rejoices in gratifying his desires" (*yuelun* L462).[30]

For Xunzi a *li*-performance displays a combination of three different components: (1) a characteristic *form* which exemplifies compliance with a relevant procedure; (2) an attitude or emotion which expresses the actor's feeling, deemed as something befitting the occasion; and (3) a joy or satisfaction experienced by the actor in the consummation of the act. Let us attend to the following passage:

> All *li*-performances begin in simplicity, are brought to fulfillment in elegant form *(wen)*, and end in joy. When *li*-performances have reached perfection, both the emotions and the forms embodying them are fully expressed. In the next degree, the emotions and the forms prevail by turns. And in the lowest degree everything reverts to emotion and returns to its primitive state. (*lilun* L427, W94*)

---

30. See also *ruxiao* L140, D102–3; *xing'e* L540, D302, W158.

Being a balanced integration of form, emotions, and relevant moral attitude, a *li*-performance, much like works of art, can be viewed as possessing a gestalt or organic unity. It is regarded by the Confucians as beautiful, in part because of the elegant form *(wen)*, which also expresses what may be called a cultural style of life that embodies a tradition. In this sense, in a *li*-performance, the Confucian actor may be said to integrate his action with his cultural history.[31] Apart from having a tie to a cultural tradition, a particular piece of *li*-conduct displays a "style of performance," which exemplifies a noteworthy manner of behavior. The slow and unhurried manner in which one eats one's soup, or the cautious way in which one carries oneself in executing a task, betrays a deliberate deportment without having gone through a process of deliberation or conscious reflection.[32] This style of performance does express the actor's trait, and, if it has a moral import, it is an expression of a cultivated attitude or virtuous disposition that may uniquely reveal the actor's character. In normal intercourse that observes the *li* of manners, one often also notices a feeling-tone expressive of an emotional interaction between people. This is particularly the case among people who have personal relationships—a principal focus of Confucian ethics. Thus, for a Confucian, apart from the elegant form, a *li*-performance may be said to express an emotion or possess an emotional quality, however subdued this may be because of compliance with appropriate rules of propriety. This emotional quality is at the same time viewed as a *sign* of a moral quality or virtue.

If it is proper to say, as some aestheticians have argued, that we perceive the emotional quality in some works of art,[33] it seems we can equally say that a similar quality in a *li*-performance can also be perceived. Just as I can claim that I perceive the grace of a curve in a painting, or joy in a piece of music, in much the same way I can claim that I perceive the grace or joy in a *li*-performance. The perception in question, of course, is not ordinary sense perception, but rather, in Berkeley's terms, the perception of *sign* and *thing signified*.[34] This way of look-

31. See my *Dimensions of Moral Creativity*, 62–63; also Fehl, *Li: Rites and Propriety in Literature and Life*, 3.

32. I owe the term "style of performance" and the first example to Austin. See J. L. Austin, *Philosophical Papers* (Oxford: Clarendon Press, 1961), 147. For a discussion of the relation of styles of performance and styles of life, see my *Dimensions of Moral Creativity*, chap. 7.

33. See O. K. Bowsma, "The Expression Theory of Art," in *Aesthetics and Language*, ed. W. Elton (Oxford: Blackwell, 1954); and R. W. Hepburn, "Emotions and Emotional Qualities: Some Attempts at Analysis," and Harold Osborne, "The Quality of Feeling in Art," in *Aesthetics in the Modern World*, ed. Harold Osborne (New York: Weybright and Talley, 1960).

34. For the distinction between signs and things signified, see particularly G. Berkeley,

ing at perception of personal qualities throws some light on the nature of *li*-performance. When a personal or emotional quality, with its expression in a proper form, is perceived, it is perceived as a sign of a virtue concretely embodied in action. The whole *li*-performance can be said to be beautiful in two related senses. In the first place, the elegant form is something that delights our senses. It can be contemplated with delight quite apart from the emotional quality. In the second place, when we attend to the emotion or emotional quality expressed by the action, which we perceive as a sign of a moral virtue or of a virtuous character, our mind is delighted and exalted, presuming, of course, that we are also moral agents interested in the promotion of moral virtues in general.[35] As spectators we may be mistaken about this, for the relation between sign and thing signified is a contingent relation. What we take to be a sign of a virtue, as the Confucian is well aware, may turn out to be a successful pretense rather than a genuine and sincere expression. So also the actor, however sincere in expressing his emotions, may be a victim of self-deception.[36] For this reason, Confucian moralists quite regularly stress the importance of self-examination. A reasonable and impartial review of one's conduct is an activity essential to the development of moral character and the practice of virtue.

Before we consider an example, let us observe that the relation between sign and thing signified is a *conventional* rather than a natural one. The emotional quality expressed in elegant form is perceived as a sign of a personal quality because it is conventionally so understood.

Essay Toward a New Theory of Vision, para. 65; and *Alciphron,* Seventh Dialogue, para. 14, in *The Works of George Berkeley,* 9 vols., ed. A. A. Luce and T. E. Jessop (London: Thomas Nelson & Sons, 1953). For a recent Berkeleyan account of the uses of signs, see C. M. Turbayne, *The Myth of Metaphor* (New Haven, Conn.: Yale University Press, 1962), chap. 4.

35. The following remarks on grace are owed substantially to Reid's analysis, but with an emendation in terms of conventional rather than natural signs for the personal qualities signified, as I have indicated in the preceding note. Also, I have not followed Reid in distinguishing beauty from grace. For the Confucian, and I think it is generally the case for other moralists who take the style of performance seriously, the signs of personal qualities are a matter of convention, both linguistic and nonlinguistic. The propriety of conduct is in this way entirely a matter of conventional rather than natural propriety. The ease with which we commend a graceful action reflects more our cultural upbringing than a natural response. When we vary the cultural setting, we are likely to confront a different notion of propriety. Xunzi's view that specific *li*-procedures are unchanging is subject to the same critical observation. But we can still appreciate his insight into the value-significance of *li*-procedures in general, independently of his moral and political conservatism. See Thomas Reid, *Essays on the Intellectual Powers of Man* (Cambridge, Mass.: MIT Press, 1969), 805–6.

36. For more discussion, see my "A Confucian Perspective on Self-Deception," in *Self and Deception,* ed. Roger Ames and Wimal Dissanayake (Albany: State University of New York Press, 1996), 177–99; reprinted in *Moral Vision and Tradition: Essays in Chinese Ethics,* Essay 11.

The form itself is governed by conventional rules of propriety. And since the quality is expressed in the required form, its being a sign of a virtue is also a matter of convention rather than natural necessity.[37] Supposing a Confucian expresses his delight in the graceful conduct of a hostess at a dinner party and proclaims his delight by saying that the hostess's conduct is a beautiful *li*-performance. If he were to articulate his delight, he would draw attention to her varying bodily movements, gestures, and utterances, which he perceived as signs of certain personal qualities, perhaps such qualities as integrity or dignity, kindness or love, confidence or modesty, magnanimity or largeness of mind and heart, liberality or prudent management of resources. He values such qualities because they display a moral character, and this display is viewed as being in entire accord with rules of propriety. The entire performance of the graceful hostess would be regarded as beautiful, for he is delighted not only because of the elegant formal setting, but also because he finds a concrete embodiment of laudable personal qualities which he himself would want to possess and display if he were offered an opportunity to serve in a similar capacity. Of course, he may later discover that the hostess's performance was a grand pretense. When this happens, he would withdraw his claim that the original judgment was reasonably grounded.

For the Confucians, our moral virtues attain their fruition in being fused with elegant forms. This fusion may be properly conceived as a fusion of both moral and aesthetic values. Neither the elegant form nor the attitude or emotion that embodied the moral virtue can be detached for independent description or evaluation. For the *li*-performance is a single action. This view recalls a prominent theme of the eighteenth-century British moralists in their discourse on the beauty of virtue and the deformity of vice.[38] Xunzi would be pleased with Hume's remark that the "constant habit of surveying ourselves, as it were in reflection, keeps alive all the sentiments of right and wrong, and begets in noble natures a certain reverence for themselves as well as others, which is the surest guardian of every virtue. The animal conveniences and pleasures sink gradually in their value, and every inward beauty and moral grace is studiously acquired and the mind is accomplished in every perfection,

---

37. This point is well brought out by Reid, though he would construe the sign to be natural rather than conventional as I have suggested here. See Reid, *Essays on the Intellectual Powers of Man*, 791ff.; and Peter Kevy, "The Logic of Taste," in *Thomas Reid: Critical Interpretations*, ed. S. F. Barker and T. L. Beauchamp (Philadelphia: Philosophical Monographs, 1976), especially 122.

38. For some representative selections from Shaftesbury, Hutcheson, Price, and others, see D. D. Raphael's entry in the index of *British Moralists, 1650–1800* (Oxford: Clarendon Press, 1969), vol. 2.

which can adorn or embellish a rational creature."[39] But while Hume would ground social virtues in utility, Xunzi would focus on the nonutilitarian character of moral beauty, for it is in part the elegant form that gives an aesthetic significance to virtuous conduct, not just its being admirable when we contemplate the expressed quality for its utilitarian value.

The beauty of a *li*-performance is not what is sometimes called "functional beauty," that is, a fitting means to attaining an end.[40] It is rather a means that does this but also constitutes a feature of the act that contributes to the realization of the ideal of a good life. The beauty is a quality of the gestalt, not an external instrument for achieving an end-in-view. The *li*-procedures conformed to mediate and effect the fusion of virtues and elegant form. They are also an integral part of the description of a *li*-performance, though for a non-Confucian, they may be singled out for independent description and evaluation. We may note also that much of this discussion of the beauty of virtue and the deformity of vice centers more on the emotional effects of moral actions upon the spectator rather than the perception of the emotional qualities in the actions themselves. Thus on this topic Richard Price maintained that when we pronounce an action right or wrong, we also use such words as "amiable," "odious," or "shocking." He claims that "everyone must see that these epithets denote the delight, or . . . the horror and detestation *felt* by ourselves; and consequently, signify not any real qualities or characters of actions, but the *effects* in *us,* or the particular pleasure and pain, attending the consideration of them."[41] From his deontological standpoint, these feelings are a consequence of our moral judgments. In this view, we have in a moral experience a mere conjunction of two independent elements rather than a fusion of the perceived emotion and its elegant form. In this respect, Xunzi's view is closer to appreciating the aesthetic aspect of moral experience, for the emotion perceived by a spectator is not something contingently related to the act but an integral part of the moral experience itself.

Let us return to the *li*-performance. When a person has successfully expressed his moral emotions or virtues in elegant form, he may be said

---

39. David Hume, *An Inquiry Concerning the Principles of Morals* (Indianapolis, Ind.: Bobbs-Merrill, 1957), 96.

40. See Henry David Aiken, "The Aesthetic Relevance of Artists' Intention," in *Art and Philosophy: Readings in Aesthetics,* ed. W. E. Kennick (New York: St. Martin's Press, 1964), 409. For a brief critical discussion of the ambiguity of functional theories of beauty, see Harold Osborne, *Aesthetics and Art Theory* (New York: E. P. Dutton & Co., 1970), 46–53.

41. Richard Price, *A Review of the Principal Questions in Morals* (Oxford: Clarendon Press, 1948), 57. For a discussion of this aspect of Price's theory, see my *Reason and Virtue: A Study in the Ethics of Richard Price* (Athens: Ohio University Press, 1966), chap. 5.

to have performed both a *right* and a *good* action. The rightness here refers to his compliance with the appropriate *li*-procedure, the goodness to the expression of his virtuous character. A successfully executed *li*-act can be properly regarded as a right and good act. And its goodness depends also on the elegant form. In this light, a good person is also a beautiful person. For a Confucian, it is not sufficient in a moral performance for one to be charitable, benevolent, or considerate in, say, helping a man in distress; he must also render his aid with sincerity and in seemly or well-mannered fashion. Suppose the benefactor is rude; his aid is not likely to be accepted by the needy, not just because it is an offense to the needy but also because the rude manner robs the conduct of a feature essential to its assessment.[42] This seems to be a reasonable requirement for good conduct. A good action, rendered in the spirit of sincerity and in elegant form, justly gives rise to respect and admiration. And the joy in rendering the assistance can likewise be perceived with delight by a spectator.

As Xunzi remarked: "If you are respectful in bearing and sincere in heart, if you abide by *li* and *yi* (righteousness) and are kindly to others, then you may travel all over the world and, though you may choose to live among the barbarian tribes, everyone will honor you" (*xiushen* L29, W26, D47–48). As I understand this passage, self-respect is a precondition for respect from others. The fortunate position one occupies in being a benefactor should be an occasion for the expression of self-respect, that is, for a display of one's moral achievement in the cultivation of a virtuous character. Such virtues can, of course, be exemplified in ways without regard to *li*-requirements, but a deliberate disregard of the required form betrays a deficiency in one's character development. And since the regard for *li*-requirements also expresses a respect for others appropriate to the occasion of intercourse, self-respect cannot be maintained independently of the respect for others. Furthermore, the beneficiary is also a potential subject for a personal relation. To fail to respect him is to deprive oneself of an opportunity for entering into a personal relationship. Thus one can appreciate the stress on elegant form, not just for its aesthetic value, but also for the value of personal relationship in *li*-performance.

And turning to the third feature of *li*-performance, that is, the joy the agent experienced in the consummation of his act, one can appreciate this sense of satisfaction much in the same way as one experiences satisfaction in a job well done. Thus the full context of a *li*-performance,

---

42. As Mencius points out, a wayfarer, or even a beggar, would not accept a basket of rice or a bowl of soup if it were tendered in an abusive manner, particularly when the behavior violates the requirements of *li* and *yi* (*Mencius*, 6A10).

its required form, expressed emotional qualities serving as signs of personal virtues, and the agent's joy in successfully executing the performance in accord with rules of propriety may justly be said to unveil a conception of human action as a fusion of aesthetic and moral values. The focus on joy as a consummatory emotional experience brings forth, in particular, the importance of music in human life. For Xunzi, "Music is joy, an emotion which man cannot help but feel at times. Since man cannot help but feel joy, his joy must find an outlet in voice and expression in movement.... Man must have his joy, and joy must have its expression, but if the expression is not guided by *dao* (the moral ideal), then it will inevitably become disordered" (*yuelun* L455, W112*). The unifying function of *li*, in its stress on elegant expression, promotes the experience of joy particularly in those auspicious occasions of human life in which men and women *celebrate* their social union. Music here is an important part of this joyous celebration. One can think here of community festivities, marriage ceremonials, honors convocations, graduation exercises, and presidential inaugurations as different ways of celebrating and promoting human harmony. In this light, music and *li* are two aspects of the same thing. The one embodies unvarying harmony; the other represents unalterable reason. "Music unites that which is the same; *li* distinguishes that which is different. And through the fusion of music and *li*, human heart and mind are governed" (*yuelun*, H411, W117*, D248-49).[43] In thus suggesting the fusion of moral and aesthetic values, I have no intention of claiming that Xunzi has a special contribution to aesthetic theory. Rather, I am suggesting that in his concern with elegant form, the emotions, and the virtues, some of his remarks can be construed as an interesting attempt to deal with a problem of axiological ethics, that is, an ethics that concerns itself with the relation of moral and aesthetic values. When we turn to its religious dimension, we can, perhaps, better appreciate *li* as a rich notion encapsulating what we ordinarily regard as distinct types of values.

3. THE RELIGIOUS DIMENSION OF 'LI'

In human life the experience of joy in the celebration of social union, the intermingling and confluence of moral and aesthetic values, alternates with the experience of sorrow and sadness when the loved ones take their departure. For some reflective moral agents, the human predicament is more than just a problem of conflicting interests to be

---

43. For more discussion of music and moral cultivation, see Appendix 2.

resolved, but a great perplexity to be quieted.[44] As James succinctly put it: "The fact that we can die, that we can be ill at all, is what perplexes us; the fact that we can for a moment live and are well is irrelevant to that perplexity. We need a life not correlated with death, a health not liable to illness, a kind of good that will not perish, a good in fact that flies beyond the Goods of nature."[45]

For Xunzi, the fact of human mortality is a proper concern of *li*. While the wish for continued existence beyond life cannot be fulfilled, the beginning and the end can be properly honored. He reminded his readers that the depth of the significance of *li*, its rationale, cannot be discovered through discussion of such matters as "hardness or whiteness," or "likeness and unlikeness"—a favorite topic of some Chinese logical thinkers. Nor can the deep significance of *li* be discerned by way of systematic thinking (*lilun* L428, W94–95, D224–25). Consistent with his pragmatic naturalism is his conception of heaven *(tian)* as a natural order oblivious of human joy or sufferings, or wishes and longings for gratuitous rewards and punishments, or the hope for fortune or misfortune to come by means of prayers or divination.[46] Xunzi does not take seriously the epistemic component of religious experience. Rather his interest in religious experience is moral and aesthetic, in the extension of the significance of these values. He pays homage to some customary religious practices, particularly on the *li* of mourning and sacrifices. Here we are properly concerned with religious rites. The etymology of *li* suggests its connection with sacrifices to spirits. *Shuowen*, an ancient dictionary, notes, "*li* is compliance [with rules] for serving spirits and obtaining blessings."

For Xunzi, the rites of mourning and sacrifices have a deep significance, not as an embodiment of religious beliefs, but as a profound expression of our attitude toward human life as a whole. The beginning and the end of our life may be depicted as extreme points of a line. These rites are especially important in *li*-performance, for they betray the spirit of human life itself that is lived in the intermediate regions. When we think of a person's life along a succession of stages from childhood, adolescence, adulthood, to old age, the beginning and the end occasionally cry out for attention. The *li* of mourning is an acknowledgment of the terminus of one's efforts and achievement, to be respected and venerated, not just for expressing our honor for humanity, but also

---

44. For the distinction between problems and perplexities, see *Dimensions of Moral Creativity*, 103–6.

45. William James, *The Varieties of Religious Experience* (New York: Longmans, Green and Co., 1902), 140.

46. See Xunzi's essay on Heaven *(Tianlun pian)*.

for the continuity of accomplished words and deeds. The rites are thus to be performed with sincere generosity and reverent formality. The dead have significance for the living. We honor them in rites as if they were present in order to ornament our grief; we make sacrifices to them to ornament our reverence. For Xunzi, no cognitive religious beliefs must interfere with these acts. The rites have a purely symbolic meaning; they are for the sake of unifying the beginning and the end. Said Xunzi, "In the funeral rites, one adorns the dead as though they were still living, and sends them to the grave with forms symbolic of life. They are treated as though dead, and yet as though still alive, as though gone, and yet as though still present. Beginning and end are thereby unified" (*lilun* L440, W103). In these rites we consciously engage in a pretense without self-deception in order to express our moral emotions of respect and reverence in a proper setting.

In thus focusing on the ornamenting of emotions of grief and melancholy, longing for our loved ones, the religious rites represent more an extension of the moral and the aesthetic than an autonomous domain of *li*-experience. It is an extension of a horizon for viewing life as a whole in terms of *ren*, or ideal of humanity. The *li* of mourning and sacrifices may be deemed significant because they are an articulation, in a concrete setting, of the practical and actuating force of a commitment to an ideal theme. Honoring the dead with reverence is a way of celebrating our humanity. For notably our *li*-performances here attain their distinctive character that transcends our animality. The care for the dead is in effect a care for the living human as a being endowed with an ideal import. The ideal of humanity has in this way acquired a quasi-natural habitat. Whatever virtues unfolded in this habitat may thus be seen as a partial realization of the Confucian ideal of human excellence.

If we consider the three dimensions of *li* together, *li* has an amphibious character. On the one hand, it expresses what the living regard as a morally and aesthetically desirable thing to attend to; on the other hand, it points to the world in which humans are anchored on a form of life that must, for each person, come to an end. Between the beginning and the end, we live our lives. But to be mindful of them is to appreciate the importance of our past and future. The past, in light of *li*, is no longer something fossilized and gone; we recall it, and in doing so in rites, we may be said to experience its significance in memory. It lives in our thought and action, as our beginning is a long tradition incarnate—the tradition in which human life is anchored. This feature of *li* is well brought out in Fingarette's *Confucius*. The powerful image of a sacrificial vessel of jade "in the *Analects* may in this way be viewed as the transformation of the secular into the sacred. It is a sacred not because it is useful or handsome but because it is a constitutive element in the ceremony."[47] And when the contemplation of the end of life is seen as having a prospective as well as a retrospective significance, to honor the dead is to also be mindful of the continuing responsibility of the living. While we cannot separate ourselves from the anchorage, we cannot ignore the recurrence of problems to be coped with. It is the here and now that must occupy the living. When the rites are properly performed, we take our leave and go on with our usual occupation. The symbolic significance of these rites must be taken seriously for our own sake. The instruments deployed, costumes and varying bodily motions, to a sensitive Confucian inspire awe and reverence just as they serve to express the emotions of the participants in the *li* of mourning. The sorrow and the depressing grief are not just painful emotions felt but can be experienced as emotions that express a gladness of being alive; and when it is directed to the cosmos, it may even commemorate the Confucian vision of the grand harmony of man and his world. In one edifying passage, Xunzi exalts the *li*:

> Through *li*, Heaven and earth join in harmony, the sun and the moon shine, the four seasons proceed in order, the stars and constellations march, the rivers flow, and all things flourish; men's likes and dislikes are regulated and their joys and hates made appropriate.... Through them the root and the branch are put in proper order; beginning and end are brought in concord; the most elegant forms embody all distinctions; the most penetrating insight explains all things. (*lilun* L427, W94)

In Xunzi, the moral, aesthetic, and religious dimensions of *li* are thus brought together in a vision of the good human life. The moral values occupy their preeminent place in social and personal intercourse, the aesthetic values mark their pervasive quality, and the religious celebrates the grand unity or harmony of humanity and the natural order. One finds no independent normative ethics, nor normative aesthetics, nor a philosophy of religion, but rather, with the moral alongside aesthetic and religious values, an interesting and challenging view in axiological ethics. If the foregoing discussion of this conception is deemed intelligible and plausible, it is owed to the inspiration of Xunzi in offering us a distinctive but complex notion of *li*. Xunzi thus provides an occasion for reflecting on an important problem of the interconnection between different types of values.

---

47. Fingarette, *Confucius*, 75.

CONCLUSION

In closing, let me present some reflections on two different questions. In discussing the aesthetic dimensions of *li*, I have implicitly endorsed the significance of the notion of the beauty of virtue and the deformity of vice. It may be said that the phrase "beauty of virtue" is more a figure of speech, a metaphor extremely misleading in discussing morality. It "tends to mislead us both with regard to the nature of virtue, and the motive to the practice of it," and this in two ways: "(1) it portrays the excellence of virtue without regard to its consequences, and (2) it suggests that the person who fails to perceive this excellence is in some way, blind."[48] Let us attend first to the issue of consequences. For Xunzi the issue basically pertains to the whole normative system of *li* as a set of regulative procedures. He would agree that consequences of conduct are important to human welfare. But saying this draws attention only to the rational ground of a normative system. This throws no light whatsoever on the nature of *li*-performance, which certainly displays fully the virtue and motive of the agent. Thus when one speaks of the beauty of virtue, one is not talking about the whole of the normative system, but about the particular setting in which moral virtues are expressed in elegant form. Unless one discounts elegant form, emotional quality, and delight in the consummation of an action, the full understanding of a virtuous act involves recognition of its aesthetic value. Just as much as the elegant form, the motive of the agent is a component in any characterization of a *li*-performance. If the agent is simply going through the motion, so to speak, his act cannot be properly regarded as a good act, though it may be regarded as a right act in the sense that it complies with the relevant *li*-procedure. When the agent, on the other hand, fails to conform to the required procedure, he is not held morally blameworthy; for the failure is a sign of deficiency of knowledge of propriety and not a moral failure. Thus when I endorsed the expression "beauty of virtue," I hope I have been clear about the context of its use. Whether it is a metaphor, our explication of this dimension of *li* cannot be ignored on the ground of its being a mere linguistic discomfort. As to the issue of blindness, not much can be said, except, perhaps, to remind ourselves that we differ in our sensibility in responding to the aesthetic aspect of *li*-experience, or of moral experience in general. It is possible that the uneasiness with the expression "the beauty of virtue" lies in the feeling that in using this expression one is bound to import

---

48. This is John Brown's critique of Hutcheson. See L. A. Selby-Bigge, ed., *British Moralists* (Indianapolis, Ind.: Bobbs-Merrill, 1964), vol. 2, 209–10.

values alien to moral experience. This justly raises the issue on the nature of moral experience. However, it is an issue about the proper characterization of moral experience, and not an issue in linguistic usage.

Related to the issue above, one may wonder whether my attempt at discussing the aesthetic dimension of *li* has any relevance to contemporary moral philosophy. As it stands, the discussion resolves no metaethical problems. Nor does it have any obvious bearing on normative ethical problems. But this much may be said: If one admits into one's philosophical concerns a task in understanding whatever values that are found in moral experience, the aesthetic one is liable to be present. This is, as Dewey has pointed out, one principal contribution of the Greeks and the Moral Sense School, and we may add, of Confucian ethics.[49] In the almost exclusive attention to the deontic aspect, to duties and obligations and rightness, most contemporary moral philosophers have lost sight of other aspects of moral experience, perhaps, more importantly, of the need for articulating a viable vision of the good life.[50] When Confucian *li* is considered in this way, it has much to offer. This article is another effort in a plausible explication of a main theme in Confucian ethics, particularly that of Xunzi. While it gives no complete account of *li* as a generic notion, it does point to the need of such an account, fully taking into view the Confucian ideal of *ren*, or humanity—a topic I leave for another occasion.[51]

---

49. John Dewey, *The Theory of the Moral Life* (New York: Holt, Rinehart and Winston, 1960), 130–31.

50. The one exception that I am familiar with is Kolnai. See Aurel Kolnai, "Aesthetic and Moral Experience," in *Ethics, Value, and Reality* (Indianapolis, Ind.: Hackett, 1978).

51. This essay was delivered as the Presidential Address to the Society for Asian and Comparative Philosophy at its annual meeting held in conjunction with that of the Eastern Division of the American Philosophical Association, at Washington, D.C., on December 27, 1978.

Appendix 1*
Human Relationships and the Virtues in the *Liji*

The Confucian concern with rational justification of the *li* is expressed in the concern with their significance. The possible discrepancy between understanding their significance and the actual practice of *li* is acknowledged. In the chapter on border sacrifices in the *Liji*, the writer stated: "What is esteemed in the *li*-performance is its [underlying] significance. When this is missed, the number of things and observances may [still] be exhibited" (*jiaotexing* 1:439*).¹ In other words, one can follow formal prescriptions without any idea of their underlying import.

While the *li*, as ritual propriety, place emphasis on the modality of manners and have aesthetic value owing to elegant form, the elegant form must also serve as a conventional sign for moral virtue. Given this moral background, one specific function of *li*, as I have previously indicated in "Dimensions of *Li*," involves distinctions embedded in different human relationships. The well-known Confucian doctrine of five basic human relationships cannot be properly understood independent of the associated moral virtues. In the *Liji*, this point is quite explicit:

> Kindness on the part of the father, and filial duty on that of the son; gentleness on the part of the elder brother, and obedience on the younger; righteousness on the part of the husband, and submission on that of the wife; kindness on the part of elders, and deference on that of juniors; with benevolence *(ren)* on the part of the ruler, and loyalty on that of the minister. These ten are the things which men consider being right. (*liyun* 1:379–80*)²

On this passage, most of us today would render a negative judgment, for the virtues here espoused appear to be too heavily biased toward unequal relation-

---

1. References to *Liji* are from James Legge's *The Li Ki or Collection of Treatises on the Rules of Propriety or Ceremonial Usages* [1885], 2 vols. in the series The Sacred Books of the East, ed. Max Müller (Delhi: Motilal Banarsidass, 1966). The original Chinese edition I used is Wang Mengóu's *Liji jinzhu jinyi* (Taipei: Shangwu, 1977). The citations refer to the chapter title, volume, and page number in Legge's translation. Thus, "*liyun* 1:379" refers to the *liyun* chapter in Legge, volume 1, page 379. Throughout, I retain *li* in place of Legge's translation. Asterisks indicate emendations of Legge's translation.

2. More often, Classical Confucians talked of the relationship between friends rather than that between elders and juniors, and between ruler and subjects rather than ruler and minister.

ships. But note that while the virtues are wedded to what most Confucians would view as conventional wisdom, they represent an attempt to invest *li* or ritual propriety with a moral dimension.

If we do not find such a moral justification rationally acceptable, we must at least acknowledge that rational discourse on morality, even if it quite properly takes its pride in an orientation toward atemporal truths, cannot pretend to practical relevance without embarking on a serious inquiry concerning the connection between theoretical adequacy and the concrete setting in which moral actions are performed. The practical efficacy of rationality is subject to circumstantial constraints. If rational argumentation is to have an actuating force in the moral life, it cannot be oblivious to cultural factors inherent in human relationships.[3] In this way, moral notions have their cultural roots. A Confucian philosopher would find congenial the view that "ethical concepts, no matter how detached they are felt to be in consciousness, have cultural roots and cultural functions, and their meaning is to be found in the offices they perform. And the criteria would seem to have a similar character."[4]

What perhaps underlies the difficulty of understanding and assessing Confucian ethics, apart from consideration of moral equality, is a peculiar construal of the five basic relationships as moral relationships. For the Confucian philosopher, such terms as "father," "son," "brother," "ruler," or "friends" do not merely describe natural and social relationships. They also have normative import. To discourse on the virtues associated with them is not to endow independent qualities external to the relationships, but rather, to specify the moral import inherent in the relationships. This is why Confucius and Xunzi paid great attention to the rectification of terms *(zhengming)*.[5]

In general, the statement of the five Confucian relationships (e.g., father and son, husband and wife, younger and older brother, friend and friend, ruler and subject) involves terms that have both descriptive and evaluative import; the latter is the main focal point. The uses of these terms involve the fusion, so to speak, of both the descriptive content and evaluative force in a single speech-act. "Father" and "brother" are for the Confucian not mere descriptive notions like "table" and "chair." If a father or a brother does not live up to the normative expectations implied in the uses of these terms, then he no longer deserves the name "father" or "brother." "Father" and "son," and so forth, are terms invested with moral import.

In this light the connection between the various relationships and the virtues

---

3. See my "Reasonable Action and Confucian Argumentation," *Journal of Chinese Philosophy* 1, no. 1 (1973); or *Moral Vision and Tradition: Essays in Chinese Ethics* (Washington, D.C.: The Catholic University of America Press, 1998), Essay 1.

4. May Edel and Abraham Edel, *Anthropology and Ethics* (Springfield, Ill.: Charles C. Thomas, 1959), 226.

5. For a brief discussion of this point in relation to some contemporary views, see my "Tasks of Confucian Ethics," *Journal of Chinese Philosophy* 6, no. 1 (1979). For a fuller discussion of the connection between moral attitudes and factual beliefs, see section 3 of my "Chinese Moral Vision, Responsive Agency, and Factual Beliefs," *Journal of Chinese Philosophy* 7, no. 1 (1980); or *Moral Vision and Tradition*, Essay 4.

is a noncontingent connection, though quite evidently rooted in the circumstances of the persons involved. Logical connection is not the issue here. The point is that so long as one wants to live within the relationships, he is subject to its inherent normative requirements or expectations, even if they may be felt to be burdensome and unduly restrictive of freedom of choice and action. Of course, for lack of appropriate mental or emotional capacity, a person may fail to live up to the expectations. More important, in particular circumstances, the expectations may be deemed unreasonable or morally irresponsible. This possibility is fully admitted in Confucian ethics. It is the connection of *li* with *ren* (humanity) and *yi* (righteousness) that unveils the kinds of consideration involved in *li* as a moral performance. The notion of *yi*, construed as a sense of rightness, is especially germane to carrying out one's moral responsibility. Given the unavoidable tension and problems that may arise in a personal relationship, a sense of righteousness is an essential quality in the exercise of moral agency.

Filial piety, for example, calls for nourishing the parents. This involves in part the provision of material comfort whenever possible and in part the obedience to parental wishes. The relationship, moreover, is one of reverence and love on the part of the filial son (*neize* 1:467). However, the obedience in question is not unconditional. Remonstrance with parents is just and appropriate whenever their wishes and conduct are judged to be unreasonable, unrighteous, or inhumane. Consider the following:

> If parents have faults, [the son] should with bated breath, and bland aspect, and gentle voice, admonish them. If the admonition does not take effect, he will be the more reverential and the more filial; and when they seem pleased, he will repeat the admonition. If they should be displeased with this, rather than allow them to commit an offense against anyone in the neighborhood or countryside, [the son] should strongly remonstrate. If they be angry and [more] displeased, and beat him till the blood flows, he should not presume to be angry and resentful but [still] more reverential and filial. (*neize* 1:456–457*)[6]

The genial and reverential manner of remonstration is essential to maintaining a parental relationship. This is also the case with other relationships governed by *li*. Thus the *Liji* begins with the statement: "Always and in everything let there be reverence *(jing)*" (*quli* 1:61). Notably, the different types of relationship are dominated by a concern with humility. In this way humility may be regarded as a general Confucian virtue. Given the unifying function of *li*, they are said to promote the humility *(rang)* useful for preventing occasions of strife or conflict in interpersonal intercourse (*jiyi* 2:220). Humility, however, is not incompatible with just pride in moral achievement as it is exemplified in the attainment of *ren* (humanity) and *yi* (righteousness). As Isenberg points out: "Just pride is not opposed to humility. Humility consists in knowing one's limitations as pride consists in knowing one's merits. . . . But the knowledge of both is com-

---

6. A similar point applies to the ruler-minister relationship. See, for example, *quli* 1:113, *tangong* 1:212, and the entry "Remonstrances" in Legge's Index of Subjects.

prehended in the act of knowing one's place."[7] For the Confucian agent, however, humility in serving others is incompatible with abject servility.

At this juncture, one may be justly perplexed over the significance of the Confucian doctrine of human relationships. Even if *li* is tied to moral virtues—and apart from the difficulties involved in the rational acceptance of the required virtues—human relationships appear to be completely indifferent to the rights of the individuals. Such deontic virtues—each one entailing the performance of certain duties—may be necessary in any human intercourse, but here their neglect of personal claims to a possession of the rights of individuals qua individuals raises the possibility of gross abuse of the persons involved. If Confucian ethics is to be deemed plausible for contemporary moral theory, it must in some way concede the importance of the rights of individuals apart from their special relationships to one another.[8] In general, is there a way in which the notion of individual rights can be accommodated within the Confucian scheme of human relationships without internal incoherence?

The above perplexity raises large and difficult issues for Confucian ethics. For many years I have pondered these questions, and I have no concise and completely satisfactory answers. Here I can only offer some tentative suggestions that I hope will permit me to proceed to other matters that lie at the heart of *li*. Let us observe that the Confucian relationships cannot be understood in terms of the sociological language of roles and statuses. Such language is a convenient device to use in characterizing the general function of *li*, but it can be quite misleading if the participants are regarded simply as role-players or actors concerned with "doing a good job" rather than as individuals for whom the roles and statuses have grave personal import. The relationships are personal, and are characterized by an affective bond expressed in concern, mutual care, or love—a main feature of the Confucian ideal of humanity *(ren)*. When *li* is construed in terms of the maintenance or preservation of the social structure, the roles and statuses are not simply a pattern of impersonal institutional arrangement that fatefully determines the lives of moral agents. The moral import of social institutions lies in the humane attitude of the participants engaged in personal relationships. The notion of rights does not appear significant because the relationships in the institutional setting are ideally an extension of personal ones, more particularly the familial relationship. Thus the classical Confucian often emphasized that the ruler is a parent to the people, and "regards all peoples in the world as one family" (*liyun* 1:379*).

In light of the considerations just mentioned, the notion of rights does not comfortably find a home in Confucian ethics. Given the personal nature of human relationship, to claim rights as an individual is to adopt a point of view ex-

---

7. Arnold Isenberg, "Natural Pride and Natural Shame," *Philosophy and Phenomenological Research* 10, no. 1 (1949): 7.

8. This point must be admitted by Confucian ethics. But as Hsieh reminds us, concession is not a concession of duties. For a Confucian, one cannot concede, for example, the duty to practice *ren*. See Hsieh Yu-wei, "The Status of the Individual in Chinese Ethics," in *The Chinese Mind: Essentials of Chinese Philosophy and Culture,* ed. Charles Moore (Honolulu, Hawaii: East-West Center Press, 1967), 316.

ternal to the relationship.⁹ The persons in relation need not deny the relevance of the external point of view. When the claims are made on behalf of the relationship and are reasonable and acceptable to the concerned participant, they can promote a healthier relationship. When the claims are rejected, the relationship will be strained and possibly be led to dissolution. For example, if it is gentle and affectionate, a reproach of a friend's misconduct may do much to preserve the personal relationship. But if reasonable reproach is consistently ignored, the bond of affection will inevitably be severed.

The point is that all personal relationships are amenable to qualification in terms of content and form. For the Confucian, the scope of the recommended behavior can also be enlarged as one becomes increasingly mindful of the relevance of his conduct to people who stand outside the immediate locus and focus of his personal relationships. A commitment to *ren* is a commitment to the extension of the ambience of personal relationships. There will always be lines of demarcation between personal and impersonal intercourse, and how well one removes these barriers depends much on the degree of one's commitment to *ren* and to the cultivation of moral virtues. Ritual propriety, independent of its connection with *ren* and *yi*, remains in force in the domain of impersonal relationships. In this sense, the *li* represent impersonal institutional rules. However, in this setting they cannot function effectively unless they are supplemented by legal and other forms of regulation (see *yueji* 2:93).¹⁰

---

9. For a general discussion of this point, see my *Dimensions of Moral Creativity: Paradigms, Principles, and Ideals* (University Park: Pennsylvania State University Press, 1978), 79–87. For a stimulating attempt to found the notion of rights on the model of personal relationships, see A. I. Melden, *Rights and Persons* (Berkeley: University of California Press, 1977).

10. Compare Peter K. Y. Woo, "A Metaphysical Approach to Human Rights from a Chinese Point of View," in *The Philosophy of Human Rights,* ed. Alan S. Rosenbaum (Westport, Conn.: Greenwood Press), 1980.

Appendix 2*
Moral Cultivation and Music in the *Liji*

In light of the intrinsic connection between *li* and moral virtues, it is evident that *li* has a specific function in the cultivation of personal character. In a fundamental way the cultivation consists in the direction or guidance of personal will (*yueji* 2:93), and this in turn involves a discipline of our basic motivational structure of feelings and desires. Ways of expressing our feelings and pursuing our desires are problematic because they are likely to result in conflict in the various settings of human intercourse. For example, "the small man, when poor, feels the pinch of his straitened circumstances; and when rich is liable to become proud. Under the pinch of that poverty, he may proceed to steal; and when proud, he may proceed to deeds of disorder. The *li* recognize these feelings of men, and lay down definite regulations for them to serve as dykes for the people" (*fangji* 2:284).[1] In addition to desires, six different feelings are commonly mentioned by Confucians: joy, anger, sorrow, fear, love, and hate (*liyun* 1:379).[2]

The regulation of desires and feelings, however, may lead to mere compliance with formal prescriptions devoid of moral significance. *Li* as ritual propriety alone cannot yield the desired outcome in moral cultivation. Thus regulation of feelings and desires, as Xunzi urged, cannot proceed without attention to the refinement or ennoblement of feelings and the development of second-order moral desires and emotions that comport to the ideal of humanity *(ren)* and the exercise of the sense of rightness or righteousness *(yi)*. In order to have a maximum influence in moral cultivation, *li* must pay attention to the inculcation of a concern for *ren* and *yi*.

This inculcation of moral concern is not a matter of training in ritual competence. One can acquire ritual competence as one acquires a variety of skills. While there may be ritual experts, it is doubtful whether there are moral experts, for moral concern is something one learns not from precepts alone but

---

1. As Legge points out, the character *fang* is used both as a noun, meaning "a dyke," and as a verb, "to serve as a dyke." But "a dyke has two uses: to conserve what is inside it, preventing its flowing away; and to ward off what is without, barring its entrance and encroachment" (*fangji* 2:284n). Thus the comparison of *li* with dykes also suggests the function of *li* in the conservation of those feelings and dispositions that are conducive to the acquisition of moral virtues.

2. The character *qing* is often translated as "feelings" or "emotions." But in view of the inclusion of desires in the seven *qing*, it may be better to render *qing* as "passions."

for the most part from the lives and conduct of *junzi* or paradigmatic individuals. Furthermore, the affectionate concern implicit in *ren* cannot be expressed without the sense of rightness *(yi)* coupled with knowledge and appreciation of the appropriateness of precepts to particular circumstances confronted by the moral agents. On this point, the reflective Confucian would concur with Arthur Murphy's incisive remark that "the point of moral training is to supply a starting point and to develop the concern and capacity with which we can thus go on. It is a teaching that prepares us to go beyond our instructions and to solve a problem for ourselves."[3]

In the sense of ritual propriety, *li* is properly regarded as a constitutive but insufficient means for the realization of *ren* and *yi*. As it is said, "The Way [of man], virtue, humanity, and righteousness *(yi)* cannot be carried out without *li*" (*quli* 1:63; also *liqi* 1:413–14). On the other hand, *li* is also rooted in humanity (*ren*) and righteousness (*liyun* 1:389–90). In focusing on the formal modality of action, the moral significance of *li* can easily be missed. Here the most problematic situation lies in the general function of *li*—the unification of people. In distinguishing roles and statuses, *li* too often leads to an undue suppression of morally desirable emotions, creating barriers to the promotion of human relationships as personal relationships. Instead of unifying the people, *li* as ritual propriety may even produce new conflicts between different classes in society. A government founded on *li* may in fact operate without regard to humanity and righteousness. One writer expresses this sentiment in the form of a story about Confucius:

> In passing by the side of Mount Thai, Confucius came on a woman who was wailing bitterly by a grave. The Master bowed forward to the crossbar, and hastened to her; and then sent Zilu to question her. "Your wailing," he said, "is altogether like that of one who has suffered sorrow upon sorrow." She replied, "It is so. Formerly, a tiger killed my husband's father here. My husband was also killed [by another] and now my son has died in the same way." The Master said, "Why do you not leave the place?" The answer was, "There is no oppressive government here." The Master then said [to the disciples], "Remember this, my little children. Oppressive government is more terrible than tigers." (*tangong* 1:190–91*)

---

3. Arthur E. Murphy, *The Theory of Practical Reason* (La Salle, Ill.: Open Court, 1965), 195. Confucius once said, "He who learns but does not think is lost; but he who thinks but does not learn is in danger" (*Analects* 2.15). A writer in the *Liji* also incisively reminds us that teaching involves learning. "When one learns, one knows his own deficiencies; and when he teaches, he knows the difficulties of learning. After he knows his deficiencies, one is able to turn round and examine himself; after he knows the difficulties, he is able to stimulate himself to effort. Hence it is said, 'Teaching and learning help each other'; as it is said in the Charge to Yue, 'Teaching is the half of learning'" (*xueji*, 2:82–83). For the significance of the notion of paradigmatic individuals, see my *Dimensions of Moral Creativity*, chaps. 3–5. In this article, unless otherwise indicated, all my references to the *Analects* are taken from W. T. Chan, ed. and trans., *A Source Book of Chinese Philosophy* (Princeton, N.J.: Princeton University Press, 1963).

In the realm of social intercourse, the distinction between the noble and the mean does not necessarily reflect moral distinction. Ideally all social positions of honor are open to all and are to be occupied only by morally deserving persons. In real life, this is not the case.[4] Not all persons can make use of opportunity nor succeed by way of moral efforts and deeds. Those who succeed in obtaining distinction and popular recognition may not be morally worthy. Even if they are, much of human life is subject to vagaries of fortune, and those who fail, morally or otherwise, may experience a variety of emotions that can affect virtuous behavior. Anger, contempt, frustration, envy, hatred, indignation, and especially resentment are more likely to be experienced along with demeaning emotions of shame or humiliation than with innocent contentment and self-respect. Of course, morally strong and superior individuals, such as Confucius and other paradigmatic individuals, would remain unaffected by the vicissitudes of circumstance and maintain integrity, and might even find repose in their humble station without any murmur of resentment.[5] But ordinary moral agents are at times likely to experience some of these emotions; and such reactions, though they may be quite justified in a particular situation, are not always conducive to the practice of virtue.

If *li* is connected with the ideal of humanity and righteousness in carrying out its general function of social differentiation, it will inevitably give rise to tension in human commerce—if not in conflicting courses of action, at least in the emotions we have mentioned. Taking cognizance of this problem, Xunzi argued with great persuasive force for the place of music in the moral life. In his words, "Music is the great arbiter of the world, the key to central harmony, and a necessary requirement of human emotions." In focusing on harmony, music provides for the expression of the joys inherent in different types of relationship. Special occasions must be stipulated for this purpose. *Li* and music must thus go hand in hand. More particularly,

> when music is performed in the ancestral temple of the ruler, and the ruler and his ministers, superiors and inferiors, listen to it together, there are none who are not filled with a spirit of harmonious reverence. When it is performed within the household, the father and sons, elder and younger brothers listen to it together; there are none who are not filled with a spirit of harmonious kinship. And when it is performed in the community, and old people and young together listen to it, there are none who are not filled with harmonious obedience. Hence, music brings about complete unity and induces harmony.[6]

Regardless of social distinctions, music can be enjoyed in common. And when this happens, we can think of music, quite apart from aesthetic considera-

---

4. Xunzi was quite aware of the discrepancy between the ideal and actual states of affairs. See Essays 2 and 8 of this volume.

5. Confucius once said of himself: "I do not complain against Heaven. I do not blame men" (*Analects* 14.37).

6. Burton Watson, trans., *Hsün Tzu: Basic Writings* (New York: Columbia University Press, 1963), 113–14.

tions, as having a *symbolic* value, at least in the manner in which it throws into relief the tension caused by various human relationships. While enjoying musical performances together, we become oblivious to our differences; and the demeaning and other problematic emotions associated with these differences are less likely to be experienced. And when they do occur, they will gradually disappear as we become engrossed in musical performances.

Of course, Xunzi's view cannot be accepted as adequate and effective in resolving conflicts in social intercourse. The relief provided by music is momentary rather than perduring. Further, many of the problematic emotions associated with playing our roles and duties are sometimes quite reasonably grounded. The expression of these emotions may embody substantive issues concerning the justice of social distinctions. This does not, of course, deny the importance of music in moral education. But on this topic we do not receive much light from Xunzi. While aware of the tension that arises in human relationships, Xunzi attends almost exclusively to the social aspect of music rather than to its function in harmonizing the emotions within the individual. On this theme, we find the *Liji* suggestive:[7]

> While the *li* direct men's aims, music gives harmony to their voices. All modulations of the voice arise from the mind, and the various affections of the mind are occasioned by things [external to it].... When the mind is moved to sorrow, the sound is sharp and fading away; when it is moved to pleasure, the sound is slow and gentle; when it is moved to joy, the sound is exclamatory and soon disappears; when it is moved to anger, the sound is coarse and fierce; when it is moved to reverence, the sound is straightforward, with an indication of humility; when it is moved to love, the sound is harmonious and soft. (*yueji* 2:92–93*)

In the course of an agent's engagement in role performance, an anxiety may arise in a particular situation owing to his view of conflicting obligatory requirements. The attendant feelings must find an outlet, particularly in light of the ideal of humanity, which focuses on mutual care and affection. One writer aptly observes that "similarity and union are the aim of music; difference and distinction that of *li*. From music comes mutual affection, from difference mutual respect" (*yueji* 2:98). The cooperation of *li* and music in their common task of moral cultivation must be governed by a careful attention to their due balance or proper mean, avoiding excesses that are harmful to the promotion of virtue. "Where music prevails, we find a weak coalescence; where the *li* prevail, a tendency to separation. It is the business of the two to blend people's feelings and give elegance to their outward manifestations" (*yueji* 2:98).

---

7. Fung Yu-lan points out in his *History of Chinese Philosophy* that the *Liji* (chap. 2), unlike Xunzi, definitely expresses the idea that the "the *li* serves a restraining mould, preventing conflict between the feeling of concern for one's parents, and the desire to obtain food, drink and pleasure for oneself." See Fung Yu-lan, *History of Chinese Philosophy*, vol. 1 (Princeton, N.J.: Princeton University Press, 1952), 339. In a later work, Fung explicitly draws attention to the function of music as harmonizing conflicts between classes. See *Zhongguo zhexue shi xinbian*, vol. 2 (Beijing: Renmin, 1964), 40–42.

Li as ritual propriety may prompt an exaggerated emphasis on formality and rigid uniformity of performance, thus separating or alienating people from one another. Even when its connection with the ideal of humanity is understood, ritual propriety more often has the effect of setting up a fence between people, precluding the possibility of personal relation. While some social distinctions may be both practically and morally justified in accord with our sense of righteousness, they are more often a bar rather than an inducement to the people willing and able to form personal relationships. In this context, humanity *(ren)* may be said to be akin to music, and righteousness *(yi)* to *li* (*yueji* 2:103). While music does not by itself resolve the emotional tension that arises within the individual, it promotes a mood of reflective mutual concern and mutual affection that is consonant with the desirable and meaningful moral life.

Essay 3
ETHICAL USES OF THE PAST

The ethical use of the distinction between the past *(gu)* and the present *(jin)*, of historical characters, situations, and events, is a familiar and prominent feature of early Confucianism. Henceforth, I shall refer to this feature as "the use of the historical appeal." To a Western philosopher, the use of this appeal, instead of deductive argument, is highly perplexing and problematic. For most Chinese thinkers, "philosophy meant a kind of wisdom that is necessary for the conduct of life, particularly the conduct of government," and "it sought to exercise persuasive power on princes, and . . . resorted, not to deductive reasoning, but to the exploitation of historical examples."[1] More fundamentally, it may be said that "the consideration important to the Chinese is the behavioral implications of the belief or proposition in question. What effect does adherence to the belief have on people? What implications for social action can be drawn from the statement?"[2] This account makes the use of the historical appeal readily intelligible as a vehicle for ethical instruction.[3]

---

1. Herbert Butterfield, "Historiography," in *Dictionary of the History of Ideas*, vol. 2, ed. Philip P. Wiener (New York: Charles Scribner's Sons, 1973), 480. More fully, one may contrast the social conditions of the ancient Chinese thinkers and their Greek counterparts. Unlike Greek philosophers, who lived in democratic city-states, the Chinese thinkers lived in proto-feudal states. According to Stange, given his situation, the Chinese "could not like his Greek counterpart discuss his ideas on a political situation with an assembly of men of equal rights on the same level as himself, he could only bring his thoughts to fruition in practice by gaining the ear of a prince. The democratic method of logical argumentation was not feasible in discussions with an absolute ruler, but an entirely different method, the citation of historical examples, could make a great impression. Thus it was that proof by historical examples prevailed very early in Chinese history over proof by logical argument" (quoted in Joseph Needham, *Time and the Eastern Man*, the Henry Myers Lecture, 1964 [Royal Anthropological Institute Occasional Paper, no. 21, 1965], 15).

2. Donald J. Munro, *The Concept of Man in Ancient China* (Stanford, Calif.: Stanford University Press, 1969), 55.

3. Throughout this essay, I use the term "moral" (as distinct from "non-moral") in the broad sense as inclusive of principles/rules and ideals/virtues. The term "ethical" is sometimes used interchangeably with "moral" in the broad sense. For justification of this proposal, see my "Tasks of Confucian Ethics," *Journal of Chinese Philosophy* 6, no. 1 (1979).

With such an understanding, however, the perplexity may be eased, but the problematic character of the use of the historical appeal remains. From the point of view of argumentation, it is important to know to what degree, if any, such an appeal can rationally warrant the acceptance of an ethical thesis. That is, how does one appraise the validity of the use of the historical appeal? For averting a negative judgment based on the use of the historical appeal, one should be reminded that although Confucius regarded himself as a transmitter of ancient wisdom rather than as an innovator,[4] there are still grounds to believe that his own attitude toward the past was not an uncritical one. Moreover, his attitude seemed to have been flexible and was reflected in his conception of paradigmatic individuals—who were cherished for their ability to deal with changing circumstances.[5] In support of the former claim, one may cite this remark of Confucius: "I am able to discourse on the *li* (rules of proper conduct) of Hsia (Xia), but the state of Ch'i (Qi) does not furnish sufficient evidence. I am able to discourse on the *li* of Yin, but the state of Sung (Song) does not furnish sufficient supporting evidence. This is because there are not enough records of men of erudition. Otherwise I would be able to support what I say with evidence."[6] For his belief in flexibility as a virtue, we may recall this saying: "I have no preconceptions about the permissible and the impermissible."[7] Also it is reported that "there were four things the Master refused to have anything to do with: he refused to entertain conjectures or to insist on certainty; he refused to be inflexible or to be egotistical."[8]

The foregoing remarks from the *Analects* suggest that, had Confucius reflected upon the value of the historical appeal, he would have maintained that its proper use depends on a careful attention to evidence and to ethical considerations relevant to issues that arise out of changing circumstances.[9] Thus qualified, the use of the historical appeal cannot be considered merely as an "argument from authority," or an ap-

---

4. D. C. Lau, trans., *Confucius: The Analects* (Middlesex, England: Penguin Books, 1979), 7.1. Unless indicated otherwise, all citations of the *Analects* refer to Lau's translation.

5. For fuller discussion of the notion of paradigmatic individuals, see my *Dimensions of Moral Creativity: Paradigms, Principles, and Ideals* (University Park: Pennsylvania State University Press, 1978), chaps. 3 and 5. See also *Mencius*, 5B1.

6. *Analects* 3.9.   7. Ibid., 18.8.
8. Ibid., 9.4.

9. For other relevant remarks of Confucius, see *Analects* 2.11, 2.15, and 13.5. On Confucius's attitude toward antiquity, Ames justly said that he "tempers this respect for antiquity with the practical consideration that this inherited knowledge must be made relevant to prevailing circumstances," though it is misleading to claim, as Ames does, that Confucius has a philosophy of history. See Roger Ames, *The Art of Rulership: A Study in Ancient Chinese Political Thought* (Honolulu: University of Hawaii Press, 1983), 5.

peal to historical sanctions for backing one's ethical conviction. Nor can it be characterized as an "argument from historical examples" if this phrase is intended to convey the idea that its use constitutes a sufficient condition for warranting conclusions in ethical discourse.

The foregoing reminder of Confucius's attitude toward the past, while useful as a caveat against hasty judgment based on the Confucian use of the historical appeal, does not by itself contribute to an answer to the question concerning the validity of such an appeal. However, a just discussion of this question depends on a prior inquiry into its role in exemplary Confucian discourse. The works of Xunzi provide us with a good case study.[10] In Xunzi, one finds an extensive use of the historical appeal in contexts that are often illuminating. His philosophical essays, on the whole, evince a respect for argumentation as a disciplined, rather than a haphazard, form of discourse.[11] On this basis, a serious student may concur with Dubs's observation: "While there may not be the vividness of illustration and brilliance of exposition found in Mencius, yet there is a cogency of argument, a closeness of reasoning, and an analytic power which shows a mind of the first order."[12] Of greater significance, as I have shown elsewhere,[13] the works of Xunzi furnished us excellent materials for a coherent explication of a complex and distinctive Confucian conception of ethical argumentation. Among other things, this conception stresses the desirable qualities of participation, rational and empirical standards of competence, and compliance with

---

10. For quick identification of a number of passages containing the historical appeal, I have sometimes referred to *A Concordance to Hsün Tzu*, Harvard-Yenching Institute Sinological Index Series, supplement no. 22 (Taipei: Chinese Materials and Research Center, 1966); hereafter cited as *Concordance*. For a detailed discussion of textual problems, see Yang Yunru, *Xunzi yanjiu* (Taipei: Shangwu, 1974), chap. 1. [For a later, more extensive discussion, see John Knoblock, *Xunzi: A Translation and Study of the Complete Works*, vol. 1 (Stanford, Calif.: Stanford University Press, 1989), and my review essay in *Philosophy East and West* 41, no. 2 (1991): 215–27.]

11. I have in mind the essays cited in the preceding note.

12. It must be admitted, as Dubs points out, that Xunzi's style is "terse and sententious." This style often creates problems for systematic presentation of his theses in standard Western philosophical form. For example, see my "The Conceptual Aspect of Xunzi's Philosophy of Human Nature," *Philosophy East and West* 27, no. 4 (October 1977). [Incorporated as Part 1 of Essay 1 in this collection.] For similar appreciations of Xunzi's philosophical stature, see Fung Yu-lan, *A History of Chinese Philosophy*, vol. 1 (Princeton, N.J.: Princeton University Press, 1952), 280; E. R. Hughes, *Chinese Philosophy in the Classical Times* (New York: E. P. Dutton, 1942), 226; Frederick Mote, *Intellectual Foundations of China* (New York: Alfred A. Knopf, 1971), 61; Liu Wu-chi, *A Short History of Confucian Philosophy* (New York: Delta Books, 1955), 65; and H. G. Creel, *Chinese Thought from Confucius to Mao Tse-tung* (Chicago: University of Chicago Press, 1953), 115–16.

13. A partial profile of argumentation is given in my "Hsün Tzu's Theory of Argumentation: A Reconstruction," *Review of Metaphysics* 36, no. 4 (1983): 867–92. For a full explication of this profile, see my *Ethical Argumentation: A Study in Hsün Tzu's Moral Epistemology* (Honolulu: University of Hawaii Press, 1985).

these standards in dealing with difficulties that may arise in the course of argumentation.[14] When Confucian argumentation is construed as a reason-giving activity engaged in by concerned and responsible persons for the exposition and defense of ethical claims, the use of the historical appeal, particularly in different phases of discourse, may be seen to be quite valuable, not as a form of argument, but as an instrument serving a variety of legitimate purposes. Xunzi was the case in point. In what follows, I shall present a critical sketch of four different functions of the historical appeal: pedagogical, rhetorical, elucidative, and evaluative. It is hoped that this discussion will pave the way toward a general appraisal of the Confucian use of the historical appeal.[15]

In charting the principal functions of the historical appeal in Xunzi, I shall confine my attention to two different types of cases: (1) those in which a sharp ethical distinction is drawn between items (for example, between the past *(gu)* and the present *(jin)* or between contrasting types of characters); and (2) those in which some sort of affinity is stressed between distinct items. I shall also attend to Xunzi's extensive use of the notion of former kings *(xianwang)*, which is sometimes contrasted with that of later kings *(houwang)*. This approach is quite consonant with Xunzi's conception of *dao* (the way) as the unifying perspective implicit in his notion of *daoguan* (the thread of *dao*) or *tonglei* (the unity of classes).[16] More formally, my approach may be characterized by way of Xunzi's distinction between generic *(gongming)* and specific terms *(bieming)*.[17] Regarding "the historical appeal" as a generic term, its various functions constitute different ways of specifying its significance. The names for these functions are thus specific terms relative to "the historical appeal" as a generic term. However, the distinction between generic and specific terms is a relative rather than an absolute distinction. A

---

14. This last topic, followed by others, such as the nature of ethical reasoning, the uses of definition, and diagnosis of erroneous ethical beliefs, is extensively discussed in chap. 2 of my *Ethical Argumentation*. [For an emphasis on the rhetorical character of ethical argumentation, see my "The Possibility of a Confucian Theory of Rhetoric," in *Moral Vision and Tradition: Essays in Chinese Ethics*, (Washington, D.C.: The Catholic University of America Press, 1998).]

15. An adequate appraisal of the value of the historical appeal, I believe, depends on considerations that are functionally equivalent to the elements of the profile elaborated in my *Ethical Argumentation*. Seen in light of that book, my present aim is quite limited, being an exercise in application of the Confucian conception of ethical argumentation. Thus I have often made use of materials from the book without explicit reference.

16. For *daoguan* ("the tread of *dao*"), see *tianlun* L379, D183–84, W87. For *tonglei* ("unity of classes"), see *fei shi'er zi* L100; *ruxiao* L149 and 157, D112 and 117–18; *jiebi* L498, D276–77, W136; and *xing'e* L555, D315, W168–69. For an incisive discussion of the notion of *tonglei*, see Wei Zhengtong, *Xunzi yu gudai zhexue* (Taipei: Shangwu, 1974), chap. 1. See also Cua, *Ethical Argumentation*, chap. 2, section 2.8.

17. See *zhengming* L575–76, W143–44, D286.

term like *li* (rules of proper conduct), for example, may be viewed as a generic term subject to specification in terms of rules of etiquette or religious rites; yet in relation to *dao* as a generic term, *li* is a specific term among others like *ren* (benevolence) and *yi* (rightness).[18] For my present purpose, I shall set aside the question concerning the degree of generality or specificity of the functions of the historical appeal. In distinguishing these functions I do not intend to suggest a categorial distinction, for in many contexts these functions overlap. Our classification is given only for convenience of explication. In the final analysis, the functions of the historical appeal, in light of *dao* as a unifying perspective, are but aspects of one thing. To borrow a famous saying of Cheng Yi, "Substance and function come from the same source *(tiyong yiyuan)*, and there is no gap between the manifest and the hidden."[19]

1. THE PEDAGOGICAL FUNCTION

An obvious characteristic of most Confucian writings in general, and of Xunzi in particular, is an overriding concern for moral education. Against the background of this concern, the historical appeal may be said to have a pedagogical function. In *Xunzi*, one finds extensive reference to sage rulers such as Yao, Shun, and Yu, and to virtuous rulers such as Tang, Wen, and Wu in contradistinction to Jie and Zhou.[20] This extensive use of historical characters suggests that the appeal is used to promote educational objectives. Before pursuing this suggestion, however, I will preface it with some remarks on Xunzi's conception of moral education.

---

18. Throughout this paper, I focus on *dao* as an ideal way of life, rather than *dao* of heaven or earth. An explicit passage runs: "The *dao* of the former kings is the magnifying of *ren*. Follow the mean *(zhong)* in acting it out. What is meant by the mean? It is *li* and *yi*. *Dao* is not primarily the *dao* of heaven *(tian)*; it is not the *dao* of earth; it is the *dao* man acts; the *dao* the superior man acts" *(ruxiao* L131, D96*). For discussion of *li* (rules of proper conduct) as a generic term, see my "Dimensions of *Li* (Propriety): Reflections on An Aspect of Hsün Tzu's Ethics," *Philosophy East and West* 29, no. 4 (October 1979), incorporated in this volume as Essay 2. For the relation between *li* and *dao*, see Cua, "Conceptual Aspect," 383–85, and Cua, *Ethical Argumentation,* chap. 4, section 4.4.

19. Or more perspicuously, Wang Yang-ming's comment on Cheng Yi's saying: "When we speak of substance as substance, function is already involved in it, and when we speak of function as function, substance is already involved in it" (Wang Yang-ming, *Instructions for Practical Living and Other Neo-Confucian Writings,* trans. Wing-tsit Chan (New York: Columbia University Press, 1963), 69. For Cheng Yi's remark, see Wing-tsit Chan, trans. and ed., *A Source Book in Chinese Philosophy* (Princeton, N.J.: Princeton University Press, 1963), 570. [For more discussion of the *ti-yong* distinction, see my "On the Ethical Significance of *Ti-Yong* Distinction," *Journal of Chinese Philosophy* 29, no. 2 (2002): 163–70.]

20. See, for example, *bugou* L52, and *rongru* L65, D62–63 passim. As Watson points out, "Xunzi frequently harks back to the golden ages of the past—the reigns of sage rulers Yao, Shun, Yü, King T'ang of the Shang dynasty, and King Wen and Wu of the Chou—as

For Xunzi, the primary aim of moral education is the transformation of man's native but problematic motivational structure (for example, feelings and desires) by way of knowledge of standards of goodness or excellence (for example, *ren* and *yi*) and rules of proper conduct *(li)*.[21] One learns for the sake of doing; knowing the right and the good is for the sake of acting in accord with such knowledge. Learning, however, is not equivalent to the mere acquisition of knowledge but more essentially requires understanding and insight. In Xunzi's words,

> Not having learned it [for example, *dao*] is not as good as having learned it; having learned it is not as good as having seen it carried out; having seen it carried out is not as good as understanding it; understanding it is not as good as doing it. The utmost attainment of learning lies in moral performance,[22] and that is its end and goal. He who can carry it out must possess an insight [into the nature of *dao*]. If he has such an insight *(ming)*, he is a sage. The sage founds his conduct upon *ren* and *yi;* he accurately distinguishes right from wrong; he makes his speech and action correspond to each other, not varying the least bit—there is no other reason for that than because he simply carries it out. (*ruxiao* L152, D113*)

Thus the ultimate objective of moral learning is to become a sage, one who has "a keen insight *(ming)* which never fails" into the rationale of *dao* and its import for dealing with different sorts *(lei)* of human situation.[23] *Dao,* as the ideal way of life, is an object of knowledge, and thus learning this way of life consists essentially in comprehending its rationale.[24] "The man who is good at learning is one who can exhaust the rationales of things *(jin qi li)*" *(dalüe* L623).[25]

For Xunzi, the basic philosophical issue in moral education pertains to the rational coordination of the intellectual and volitional activities of the mind *(xin)* by means of the *dao.* Given the autonomy of man's

---

examples of such periods of ideal peace and order" (W5–6). While Xunzi accepted much of the traditional account of Chinese history, he is quite aware of the issue of evidence. See *feixiang* L82–83, D74–75; *xing'e* L549, D309, W163.

21. For an explication of the problematic character of man's basic nature, see Cua, "Conceptual Aspect." For a clearer and more plausible articulation of the connection between moral knowledge and action, see my *The Unity of Knowledge and Action: A Study in Wang Yang-ming's Moral Psychology* (Honolulu: University of Hawaii Press, 1982).

22. In *zhengming* L506, *xing* (moral conduct) is defined as "action that is performed for the sake of righteousness *(yi)*."

23. *Quanxue* L10, D36, W19, and *xiushen* L33, W30. For stress on comprehending the rationales of changing circumstances in terms of a unifying perspective, see *dalüe* L617.

24. As Xunzi remarks, if a person's "words are reasonable, you may discuss with him the *li* (rationale) of *dao*" (*quanxue* L17, W21*).

25. For the *junzi,* or ethically superior person, completeness and purity are basic values. For this reason, says Xunzi, "he reads and listens to explanations in order to penetrate the Way *(dao),* ponders in order to make it part of himself, and shuns those who impede it in order to sustain and nourish it" (*quanxue* L19, W22).

mind, he can choose to accept or reject its guidance. "It is the nature of the mind that no prohibition may be placed upon its selections" (*jiebi* L488, W129, D269), but if it is directed by reason (*li*) and nourished with clarity, and not perturbed by extraneous matters, "it will be capable of determining right and wrong and of resolving doubts" (*jiebi* L490, W131, D271).[26]

In the essay entitled "Encouraging Learning" (*quanxue pian*), Xunzi points out that learning is an unceasing process of accumulation (*ji*) of goodness, knowledge, and practical understanding. "If a superior man (*junzi*) studies widely and daily engages in self-examination, his intellect will become enlightened and his conduct be without fault" (*quanxue* L2, W14*, D31). The subject matter of moral education consists of the classics, which were considered by Xunzi to embody in different ways the concrete significance of *dao*. Practical understanding thus involves an appreciation of this concrete significance. For example, "The *Odes* give expression to the will (*zhi*) or determination [to realize *dao*]; the *History* to its significance in human affairs; the *Li* (Rules of Propriety) to its significance in conduct; the *Music* to its significance in promoting harmony; and the *Spring* and *Autumn* to its subtleties" (*ruxiao* L143, D104*).[27] It is important to note, however, that these classics are not self-explanatory. Therefore, the guidance of perceptive teachers is essential. As Xunzi emphatically states: "The *Li* and Music present us with models, but no explanations; the Odes and the History deal with ancient matters and are not always pertinent; the Spring and Autumn annals are terse and cannot be quickly understood" (*quanxue* L14, W20, D38). The point, for our present purpose, is that intellectual and practical understanding of the classics go hand in hand. In the ideal situation, moral teachers are those who, in addition to commanding extensive knowledge, are honorable and clearheaded in explaining the meanings and the concrete significance of the classics. More fundamentally, they must conduct their discourse coherently and with detailed insight into the rationales that underlie different sorts of human affairs (*zhiwei erlun*), exemplifying the enlightened intellect of the *junzi* (*zhishi*, L308).[28] Similarly, an accomplished learner or scholar must show not only a single-minded dedication to *ren* and *yi* but also an enlightened knowledge concerning different kinds of human relationships. As Xunzi says, "If a man does not comprehend the unifying significance of different kinds of human relationships and make himself one with *ren* and *yi*

---

26. For further discussion, see Cua, *Ethical Argumentation*, chap. 4, sections 4.1–4.2.
27. For a different passage of similar purport, see *quanxue* L10, D36–37, W19–20.
28. In this passage (*zhishi* L308), other qualifications for moral teachers are also mentioned, for example, sternness, trustworthiness, and awe-inspiringness.

he does not deserve to be called a good scholar" (*quanxue* L18, W22*, D40). Since *dao* provides the unifying perspective, there is a constant need to study and ponder its significance in the process of self-cultivation and experience. Moral learning culminates in the attainment of what Xunzi terms "completeness *(quan)* and purity *(cui)*," that is, a thorough understanding of *dao* and a state of moral integrity *(decao)*. As a consequence, one can deploy a resolute will in coping with moral perplexities or exercise one's sense of what is right in responding to changing circumstances *(yiyi bianying)*.[29]

The preceding observations of Xunzi's theory of moral education focused on some key elements such as the acquisition of knowledge and critical reflection upon its actuating import in moral life. Given this context, one can readily appreciate the extensive use of the historical appeal for pedagogical purposes. In general, the success of moral education lies in the effective inculcation of the importance of standards and rules of proper conduct, the development of moral dispositions, desires, and abilities for coping with the changing circumstances of personal life. Thus, counsels and admonitions, along with encouragement, exaltation, and edification, may at times occupy the center of attention in ethical discourse. Given the appropriate setting, the historical appeal may serve any of these purposes. In general, Xunzi's uses of the historical appeal, in the form of citation of contrasting historical characters, were intended to encourage the adoption of appropriate models for emulation and discourage the imitation of contrary models of evil or depravity. In effect, then, the reader is confronted with a contrast between exemplary moral achievement and moral failure. The historical appeal is a way of presenting "object lessons" in moral learning and conduct. If this suggestion is to be taken seriously, however, it must be qualified by attending to those cases where the affinity between contrasting characters is stressed in terms of their similar capacities for moral achievement. Consider this passage:

Every ordinary person has characteristics in common with others. When hungry he desires to eat; when cold he desires to be warm at rest; he is fond of what is beneficial and detests what is harmful—these are native characteristics men have in common and do not depend on learning. In these respects, Yu and Jie were alike. The eyes distinguish white and black, beautiful and ugly; the ears distinguish clear and confused tones and sounds. . . . In these respects also, men normally have the same capacity for discerning distinctions. It does not depend

29. See *quanxue* L19, W22, D40–41; *ruxiao* L143, D104; *buguo* L43; and *zhishi* L306. For rendering *decao* as moral integrity, I follow Mei. See Y. P. Mei, "Hsün Tzu's Theory of Education with An English Translation of the Hsün Tzu, Chapter I, An Exhortation to Learning," *Tsing Hua Journal of Chinese Studies*, n.s., 2, no. 2 (1961): 375.

on learning, and Yu and Jie alike possessed it. Anyone can be a Yao or a Yu; he can become a Jie or a Zhi. . . . What he becomes depends on how he manages his life through the accumulation *(ji)* of careful choices and rejections and habitual practices *(zhucuo xisu)*. . . . To be a Yao or a Yu ordinarily brings tranquility and honor; to be a Jie or a Zhi ordinarily brings danger and shame. . . . But most men are the latter and few are the former. Why is this the case? Because their natures are low. Yao and Yu were not born great. They became what they were because of their success in moral transformation, that is, they had exerted their utmost effort in cultivating their capacity for great moral achievement. (*rongru* L64–65, D60–61*)[30]

In this passage, the use of contrasting historical characters, Yu versus Jie, has less to do with presenting "object lessons" than with objects for moral choice. This use is even more important in that it provides reminders in a twofold sense. On the one hand, there is a reminder of one's basic capacity for moral achievement and hence the importance of self-cultivation. Instead of historical characters, the distinction between the past *(gu)* and the present *(jin)* is used; for example, "In the past *(gu)* men studied for the sake of self-improvement, today *(jin)* men study to impress others."[31] The *junzi* studies in order to ennoble himself, the *xiaoren* (small-minded man) studies in order to win attention from others" (*quanxue* L14, W20*). In a similar fashion Xunzi utilizes the notion of former kings: "If you want to become like the former kings *(xianwang)* and seek out *ren* and *yi*, the *li* is the very road by which you must travel" (*quanxue* L15, W21*, D38).

On the other hand, within the context of argumentation, we are reminded that self-cultivation and acting in accord with standards and rules of proper conduct are in the *true interest* of the individual, since they give rise to such desirable consequences as tranquility and honor rather than danger and shame. Of course, one is given no guarantee that they will in fact occur; however, in the course of ordinary life, such an expectation is quite reasonable given wise and informed deliberation *(zhilü)*. After all, we engage in ethical deliberation in order to cope with changing circumstances and to resolve perplexities (*jundao* L284). In its reminding function, the historical appeal, with respect to the individual's true interest, has no special connection with historical beliefs concerning the existence of specific historical personages, events, or states

---

30. For similar passages involving contrast between Yu and Jie, see *feixiang* L79, D71, and *xing'e* L550, W164–65, D310–11. For the notion of proper objects of the senses, see *tianlun* L366, D175–76, W80–81; *zhengming* L513, D284–85, W142. For a discussion of the general capacity for making distinctions, see Cua, "Hsün Tzu's Theory of Argumentation," 886–91.

31. As Watson points out, this is actually a quotation from the *Analects* 14.25 (W20, note).

of affairs. It is an *implicit* appeal to prudence or the desirability of reflection. It could be characterized as a form of thought-experiment: "If one reflects seriously on the desirable consequences of adopting and acting in accord with standards and rules of proper conduct, he would discover where his true interest lies."[32] The historical appeal, in the context of the desirability of reflection, while valuable, is dispensable in ethical discourse. What is crucial in effective teaching procedure is the appeal to the reflective desirability of accepting and cultivating virtuous dispositions and the desire to act with due consideration for *ren, li,* and *yi,* and other associated standards of excellence. In his essay on self-cultivation, we find such an appeal devoid of the use of historical characters:

If a person is respectful in his bearing, loyal and sincere, abides by *li* and *yi* and is actuated by affection and *ren,* he may travel all over the world. Even though he may choose to live among the barbarian tribes, people would not fail to honor him. (*xiushen* L29, D47–48*, W27*)[33]

In sum, the pedagogical use of the historical appeal points not only to models who are worthy or unworthy of emulation, but more significantly to models functioning as reminders in moral learning and conduct that appeal especially to what is deemed in the real interests of the learner. Notably, gentle suasion rather than coercion is involved, as the individual still retains the freedom to accept or reject it. This constitutes the argumentative value of the pedagogical function of the historical appeal rather than the mere exhibition of moral exemplars. The latter's effectiveness lies primarily in the appeal to paradigmatic individuals *(junzi).*[34] In Xunzi, as in the *Analects,* one finds a recurrent contrast between the *junzi* or ethically superior man and the *xiaoren* or small minded man.[35] At any rate, the ultimate value of the historical appeal in pedagogical contexts lies in the effectiveness of the appeal to reflective desires and emotions, rather than to the ability to follow deductive arguments.[36]

32. In Xunzi, such thought-experiments are, I believe, plausibly deployed in supporting his famous thesis on the problematic character or badness of man's basic nature. See my "The Quasi-Empirical Aspect of Hsün Tzu's Philosophy of Human Nature," *Philosophy East and West* 28, no. 1 (1978), or Part 2 of Essay 1 in this volume. For the general form of appeal to reflective desirability in the vindication of the Confucian vision of *dao,* see Cua, *Unity of Knowledge and Action,* 79–100.
33. For the importance of developing second-order reflective desires, see Cua, "Dimensions of *Li,*" 380–81.
34. For a discussion of the role of this and other appeals in argumentation, see my "Reasonable Action and Confucian Argumentation," *Journal of Chinese Philosophy* 1, no. 1 (1973).
35. I have discussed this notion of paradigmatic individuals in Cua, *Dimensions of Moral Creativity,* chaps. 3 and 5.
36. With some qualification in terms of the role of reflection, Xunzi would concur with this assessment by Hume of sentiment in ethical discourse:

2. THE RHETORICAL FUNCTION

Were one preoccupied solely with the arguments Xunzi offered in support of his ethical theses, the use of the historical appeal would have merely stylistic interest. As Watson recently maintained: Unlike Zhuangzi, for whom historical anecdotes constitute a form of argument, for Mozi, Mencius, and Xunzi, the historical anecdotes "serve effectively to vary the tone and pace of discourse. . . . But such anecdotes, lively as they may be, represent no more than ornaments to the argument, momentary detours from the expository highroad."[37] I must confess that until I was engaged in this study, I accepted this view without much qualm throughout more than a decade of preoccupation with Xunzi's ethical theory. This conception of the value of the historical appeal relegates its function to an accessory role, but in reflecting upon its value in ethical argumentation, one sees that it can be quite important, not in proffering or arguing for the acceptability of a thesis, but in responding to a recurrent problem of regress in argumentation.[38] As a recent writer on informal logic justly points out, "The answer to this ancient problem depends upon an obvious fact. The activity of arguing or presenting proofs depends upon a shared set of beliefs and upon a certain amount of trust. When I present reasons, I try to cite these beliefs—things that will not be challenged. Beyond this, I expect people to believe me when I cite information that only I possess."[39] Obviously, the historical appeal

---

The end of all moral speculations is to teach us our duty, and, by proper representations of the deformity of vice and beauty of virtue, beget correspondent habits, and engage us to avoid the one, and embrace the other. But is this ever to be expected from inferences and conclusions of the understanding, which of themselves have no hold of the affections or set in motion the active powers of men? They discover truths. But where the truths which they discover are indifferent and beget no desire or aversion, they can have no influence on conduct and behavior. What is honorable, what is fair, what is becoming, what is noble, what is generous takes possession of the heart and animates us to embrace and maintain it.

See David Hume, *An Inquiry Concerning the Principles of Morals* (Indianapolis, Ind.: Bobbs-Merrill, 1957), 5–6.

37. Burton Watson's Foreword in *Experimental Essays on Chuang Tzu*, ed. Victor H. Mair (Honolulu: University of Hawaii Press, 1983). It must be noted that Mozi explicitly espouses the appeal to the deeds of the sage kings of antiquity as one of the three criteria for the acceptability of theories—a thesis explicitly rejected by Xunzi. See Watson, trans., *Mo Tzu: Basic Writings* (New York: Columbia University Press, 1963), 118; and *xing'e* L549, W163, D309. I shall later consider Xunzi's view in connection with the evaluative function of the historical appeal.

38. Arguably, the infinite regress argument is valuable in philosophical discourse because of its function as a reminder, rather than as an argument that validates a philosophical thesis. See John Passmore, *Philosophical Reasoning* (London: Gerald Duckworth, 1961), chap. 2.

39. Robert J. Fogelin, *Understanding Arguments: An Introduction to Informal Logic* (New York: Harcourt Brace Jovanovich, 1978), 41.

functions as a technique for *assuring* the audience that the thesis maintained is consonant with shared historical beliefs and obviates having to state reasons for their support. It also constitutes a technique of *discounting* alternative views, shifting the burden of proof to a possible adversary.[40] These uses, of course, are subject to further challenge, for the rational acceptability of the thesis and an assurance that the thesis is not a mere imaginative contrivance to avoid questioning.

In Xunzi, we sometimes find a historical idiom that suggests such an interpretation: "from the ancient times to the present" *(zigu jijin)*. For example: "It is possible to have good laws and still have disorder in the state. But to have a *junzi* acting as a ruler and disorder in the state—from the ancient times to the present I have never heard of such a thing" *(wangzhi* L163, W35*).[41] An interesting passage involving historical characters may be cited for closer examination:

> In ancient times there were officials who were warped by obsession. Tang Yang and Xiqi are examples. Tang Yang was obsessed by the desire for power and drove Master Dai from the state; Xiqi was obsessed with a desire for the throne and succeeded in casting suspicion upon Shensheng. Tang Yang was executed in Sun; Xiqi was executed in *Jin*. One of them drove a worthy minister into exile; the other cast suspicion upon his brother. They ended by being executed and did not know that this was the misfortune which comes from obsession and closed mind. Is it possible that a man whose conduct is motivated by greed, treason, and struggle for power can be freed from the danger of shame and destruction? From ancient times to the present *(zigu jijin)*, there has never been such a case. *(jiebi* L477, W124*, D262-263*)[42]

This passage, along with several others involving historical characters and incidents, occurs in Xunzi's essay on dispelling obsession or obscurations *(bi)*. To expedite the discussion of this passage, something must be said about Xunzi's doctrine of the origin of erroneous beliefs.[43] In terms of his ethical conception of *dao* as a unifying perspective, a partial grasp of its fundamental rationale *(dali)* and significance has a serious repercussion upon conduct *(jiebi* L472, W121, D159). More generally, the human mind is liable to be obscured *(bi)* by failure to appreciate the

---

40. Ibid., 41–43.
41. For a similar passage, see *zhishi* L304. Also, *A Concordance to Hsün Tzu* lists the following relevant occurrences of *zigu jijin*: 23/8/70, 26/9/24, 49/12/116, 79/21/18, 53/14/22, and 79/21/18. My following observations also apply to such expressions as "from the ancient times to the present, it has always been the same" *(gujin yiye)*. See *Concordance*: 58/15/112, 59/16/19, 68/18/71, and 91/24/20.
42. The translation of the last two sentences is my own, with the deletion of *gu* (hence) in order to bring out the rhetorical force of the historical idiom. For informative notes on the historical characters and incidents, see W124n.
43. For a fuller treatment of Xunzi's doctrine of erroneous beliefs, see Cua, *Ethical Argumentation*, chap. 4.

situation because it is partial to one side of a distinction. Clarity of mind is essential to comprehension of a situation as a whole. *Bi* (obscuration) is Xunzi's metaphor for factors that obstruct the mind's cognitive task. Among the distinctions that are potential sources of *bi* are desire and aversion, past *(gu)* and present *(jin)*, and distant and immediate consequences of actions *(yuanjin)*. How can one be impartial, then, in order to avoid that *bi* which may result in harmful conduct? Earlier, we focused on the role of informed deliberation *(zhilü)* with respect to the consequences of a contemplated course of action. Informed deliberation must be impartial, particularly in weighing *(quan)* desires and aversions in terms of harmful and beneficial consequences *(bugou* L54).[44]

Since the passage offers an illustration of Xunzi's doctrine of *bi*, the historical characters and incidents are used for the exposition of a thesis and constitute the *elucidative* use of the historical appeal. As we have indicated earlier, the historical appeal can have more than one function in the same context. For our immediate purpose, the passage provides an example of the failure to exercise impartiality in weighing the consequences of actions, because their minds were obscured and they could not see where their true interests were. This recalls one function of the pedagogical use of the historical appeal. Here the appeal to reflective desirability is explicit rather than implicit.

In focusing on the rhetorical function of the locution "from ancient times to the present" *(zigu jijin)*, the use of historical characters and incidents presupposes a background of shared historical knowledge or beliefs about the past. Given this background, the locution can be considered as an argumentative technique for issuing assurance and discounting possible objections. Its rhetorical force is obvious, as it is usually preceded by a rhetorical question. The locution is functionally equivalent to such English phrases as "it is certain that," "it is indisputable," and so forth, and occurs at the end, marking a completion of a train of thought. Thus it can be construed as an emphatic terminating linguistic expression which serves as a reminder of the significance of historical knowledge.

Only a historian can judge whether or not Xunzi is correct in presuming common historical knowledge. The presumption seems legitimate when viewed as a personal testimony of Xunzi's own historical beliefs. Belief in the testimony of others is a necessary condition of communication. As Austin points out:

Believing in other persons, in authority and testimony is an essential part of the act of communicating, an act which we constantly perform. It is as much an irre-

44. See note 33 above.

ducible part of our experience as, say, giving promises, or playing competitive games, or even sensing colored patches. We can state certain advantages of such performances, and we can elaborate rules of a kind for their "rational" conduct (as the Law Courts and historians and psychologists work out the rules for accepting testimony). But there is no "justification" for our doing them as such.[45]

In this light, we can also appreciate the propriety of the use of historical characters and the function of Xunzi's use of the expression "from ancient times to the present" *(zigu jijin)*. Of course, Xunzi's historical beliefs may well be mistaken, but this is an issue that can only be settled by historians of Chinese antiquity. Much of Confucian argumentation makes use of the presumption of the truth of historical beliefs, which is a plausible presumption in Rescher's sense, where the plausibility of a thesis is not a matter of probability or falsification, but depends on how well it fits in with a conceptual scheme that contains established, operative standards for argumentation. A thesis that employs a plausible presumption can be defeated in context, but it can be warranted so long as there exist no contraindications in common experience.[46]

From a standpoint external to Confucian discourse, the rhetorical function of the historical appeal possesses primarily a psychological value in ethical discourse. We have here an instrument of persuasion, akin to a conjoint use of "persuasive definitions" and "re-emphatic definitions," where the reasons have only a psychological, rather than a logical, connection with the thesis proffered.[47] In the context of Xunzi's rhetorical use of the historical appeal, this interpretation is acceptable only when it is qualified by an acknowledgment of the force of plausible presumptions. At the same time, however, one must also admit that the rhetorical function of the historical appeal pertains primarily to the techniques rather than to the substance of argumentation. Its value belongs to the art of discourse and can neither be regarded as an acceptable substitute for the necessity of arguments nor forestall disputes as to the soundness or validity of arguments. In actuality Xunzi rarely employs the historical idiom. Our excursion to the rhetorical use is interesting mainly for revealing the plausible presumption involved in some of the uses of historical appeal.

---

45. J. L. Austin, "Other Minds," in *Philosophical Papers* (Oxford: Oxford University Press, 1961), 83.

46. See Nicholas Rescher, *Dialectics* (Albany: State University of New York Press, 1977), 38; and *Skepticism* (Totowa, N.J.: Rowan and Littlefield, 1980), chap. 7.

47. C. L. Stevenson, *Ethics and Language* (New Haven, Conn.: Yale University Press, 1944), 290–94.

Ethical Uses of the Past 87

Before I turn to the elucidative and evaluative uses of the historical appeal, I would like to sketch that aspect of Xunzi's conception of argumentation which governs my interpretation and analysis. Apart from various rational and empirical standards of competence, Xunzi also focuses on what may be termed phases of argumentation, which are centrally concerned with ways of resolving difficulties that may arise in the course of communication.[48] Xunzi is aware throughout that the activity of argumentation is not a facile proceeding. At any moment in discourse, reasonable questions can arise with respect to the clarity of theses and to the reasons offered in their behalf. To these questions, proper answers must be given so that the relevant standard of competence can be satisfied. The four different phases of argumentation are described below:

When the actualities *(shi)* referred to by our terms are not understood, one must fix their references *(ming)*. When the fixing of references is not understood, one must secure concurrence in linguistic understanding *(qi)*. When one fails to achieve this concurrence, one must resort to explanation *(shuo)*. When such an explanation fails, one must embark upon a course of justification *(bian)*. (*zhengming* L521)[49]

Another way to characterize these four phases of argumentation is to view them as four different kinds of speech acts, namely, fixing reference, matching linguistic understanding, explaining, and justifying. The first is necessary whenever the speaker's referential use of terms fails to secure the understanding of his audience due to their ambiguity or vagueness. To fix the reference of a term clearly is to make more precise the use of the term. To assume this responsibility in the context of discourse exhibits the speaker's willingness to engage in successful communication. In cases where there is a failure to understand the fixed reference of terms, the speaker must make an attempt to match his linguistic understanding with that of his audience. Here the concern is not with reference as such, but with the common understanding of the referential function of terms in a particular context. Obviously, at this point in the discourse, questions and answers will be exchanged in an effort by concerned and responsible participants to promote successful communication.

But the matching of linguistic understanding with respect to the ref-

48. The following remarks are mostly taken from the preliminary summary of a lengthy treatment of phases of argumentation in chaps. 2 and 3 of my *Ethical Argumentation*.
49. This translation is my own. A full justification for this rendering is given in the work cited in the preceding note. For Watson's and Dubs's translations, see W147 and D290.

erential function of terms may still fail to bring about successful communication. In such cases, explanations must be given as to why the speaker chose such and such a term in this particular context. Here definitions explaining the uses of terms as well as examples of proper use and the description of the situation may help in satisfying the query. Sometimes the giving of such explanatory reasons may not suffice to produce understanding, for in addition to a comprehension of explanation, there must also be an acceptance of the thesis as warranted by appropriate reasons. In this sense, even if one succeeds in explaining one's position in discourse, one must engage in a process of justification, for without such an attempt, one can hardly be said to be engaged in argumentation or to have expended effort in trying to satisfy the standards of competence.

3. THE ELUCIDATIVE FUNCTION

The elucidative and evaluative functions of the historical appeal belong to the explanatory and justificatory phases of discourse. Compared to Xunzi's extensive use of *wei* (say/call),[50] these functions are quite restrictive. Nevertheless, they are valuable in the exposition and defense of ethical theses. Unlike the pedagogical and rhetorical function, the elucidative one has a direct, argumentative force. It makes explicit the ethical criteria for appraising character and/or clarifies the general thesis that underlies the ethical distinction at issue. The following example explicates Xunzi's thesis on the importance of impartiality in the weighing of the possible consequences of pursuing certain desires.

> Impartiality gives rise to enlightenment, partiality to obscuration [of the mind]; uprightness and honesty give rise to success, deception and hypocrisy to obstacles; sincerity and trustworthiness give rise to marvelous actions *(shen)*, false pride to perplexity. A superior man is cautious about the casual relation among these six matters, and they are the basis for distinguishing Yu and Jie. (*bugou* L52)[51]

Xunzi goes on to explain his thesis that what presumably distinguishes Yu and Jie lies in part in the method of weighing desirable against undesirable consequences, that is, in a clarity of mind versus a mind obscured *(bi)* by an unthoughtful preoccupation with impulses and desires

---

50. In the *Xunzi*, there are around four hundred occurrences of *wei* in such constructions as *sowei, kewei, zhiwei,* and *weizhi* that can be construed as quasi-definitional formulas. An extensive analysis of these constructions is given in chap. 3 of my *Ethical Argumentation*.

51. For passages of similar purport but pertaining to other fundamental theses, for example, king *(wang)* versus hegemon *(ba)*, see *wangzhi* L168–72, W37–42, D126–30; *wang-ba* L230–33.

without taking into consideration their possible averse consequences. Xunzi rightly points out that human beings generally suffer because they are afflicted with partiality.

When they see something they want, they do not carefully consider whether or not it will lead to something that they detest; when they see something beneficial, they do not consider carefully whether or not it will lead to something harmful. In this way, any action that they perform is bound to entrap them [in their impulses and desires] and to bring about shame. This is the predicament that besets us all—the harm that ensues from the partial view of things *(pianshang zhi huan)*. (*bugou* L53)

In the preceding example, the use of historical characters appears to have both conceptual and pragmatic significance. In general, clarity in conceptual distinction as well as in the articulation of ethical criteria for *distinguishing* character-types or different grades of moral attainment is a recurrent preoccupation with Xunzi. Much of his effort is devoted to the elucidation of his general notions of the sage *(sheng)*, the superior man *(junzi)*, and the scholar *(shi)*. On occasion, however, more specific criteria are proposed for grading characters in terms of one virtue. One interesting passage on different grades of loyalty *(zhong)* uses historical characters to illustrate how the criteria set forth may be satisfied.

Loyalty of the highest sort consists in the exercise of virtue *(de)* to protect and transform the ruler. Loyalty of the intermediate sort consists in the exercise of virtue to harmonize and assist the ruler in his undertakings. Loyalty of the lowest sort consists in the use of what is right as a basis for remonstrating the ruler's wrong conduct but arousing his anger. . . . If one serves his ruler as the Duke of Zhou served King Cheng, he can be said to exemplify loyalty of the highest sort. If one serves his ruler as Guan Zhong served Duke Huan (of Qi), he can be said to exemplify loyalty of the intermediate sort. If one serves his ruler as Zi Xu served Fu Cha (of Wu), he can be said to exemplify loyalty of the lowest sort. (*chendao* L297)

Theoretically one can achieve clarity when expounding theses by using purely hypothetical examples, but the use of historical characters in ethical discourse has a dual pragmatic significance in guiding judgment and conduct. First, it shows how an ethical thesis may be applied in practice. Secondly, the historical figures illustrate and embody what otherwise would be an abstract ethical conception. The former enhances one's understanding of the empirical possibility of application, the latter mediates between the ethical thesis as an ideal and the actual world.[52] The historical characters here function as mediating rather

---

52. I owe this conception of mediation to Paul Dietrichson's interpretation of Kant's notion of a typic of the moral law. See Dietrichson, "Kant's Criteria of Universalizability,"

than instantiating terms.[53] Obviously, then, the elucidative function of the historical appeal has an important role to play in the explanatory phase of argumentative discourse.

4. THE EVALUATIVE FUNCTION

Inherent in the use of historical characters for elucidating and demonstrating the applicability of an ethical thesis is the implicit claim that human history is the proper subject of ethical appraisal. However, this claim is explicit in the evaluative use of the historical appeal. For Xunzi, "*dao* is the proper standard for judging the past as well as the present *(gujin zhi zhengquan)*" (*zhengming* L506, W153*). Earlier, in connection with Xunzi's conception of moral education (section 1 above), I pointed out that becoming a sage was the ultimate end of learning. When a person becomes a sage, he possesses not only a knowledge of the rationale of *dao*, but also of its significance as a unifying perspective for viewing different sorts of human relationships and affairs, particularly in all matters pertaining to *ren*, *li*, and *yi*. In light of his knowledge of the unity of different kinds of things *(tonglei)*, his discourse is both reasonable and coherent (*xing'e* L555, W168–69, D315). Moreover, in discourse, he does not engage in any prior deliberation or planning (*feixiang*, L89). With this knowledge, the sage can deal with the present through the past *(yigu chijin)* or with the past through the present *(yijin chigu)*.[54] In the words of Xunzi,

> The sage considers himself a measure for appraising things. Hence, by means of [his knowledge of] men in the present, he can judge men in the past. By means of [his knowledge of] conditions of the present, he can judge conditions of the past. By means of [his knowledge of] different kinds of things *(lei)*, he can determine the kinds to which things belong. By means of speech, he can assess accomplishments. By means of *dao*, he can command a comprehensive view of things. The same standard applies to both the past and the present. So long as different kinds of things are not confused, although they might have persisted for a long time, the rationales [underlying their respective classifications] remain the same *(suijiu tongli)*. (*feixiang*, L83)

---

in *Kant: Foundations of the Metaphysics of Morals: Text and Critical Essays*, ed. Robert Paul Wolff (Indianapolis, Ind.: Bobbs-Merrill, 1969).

53. Such a mediation, of course, may be accomplished by the use of fictional rather than historical characters, as in the case of Classical Daoism. See my "Opposites as Complements: Reflections on the Significance of *Tao*," *Philosophy East and West* 31, no. 2 (1981), or *Moral Vision and Tradition*, Essay 5.

54. The expression *yigu chijin* occurs in *ruxiao* L149, D111–12, where a similar point is made.

Unlike the sage, the superior man *(junzi)* has no such comprehensive and systematic knowledge. While he is aware that *dao* is the ultimate standard for thought and action (as a committed agent), he cannot claim to understand how it guides action without first expending effort in intelligent and informed reflection. Similarly in discourse, we would expect a reasonable and conscientious person to engage in inquiry and deliberation before pronouncing any ethical judgment *(feixiang,* L89).[55] As Xunzi succinctly states, "In argumentative discourse, one must give an exhaustive account of one's reasons *(bian ze jingu)*" *(zhengming* L521, W147–48, D291). Of special interest to moral philosophy is the kind of reasoning involved in judging the present through the past *(yigu chijin)* as distinct from judging the past through the present *(yijin chigu).* The distinction is not based on logical structure but has to do with two different kinds of ethical justification.[56]

For purposes of discussion, I shall use the term "retrospective" to refer to the use of the appeal to the past for judging the present *(yigu chijin),* and "prospective" to indicate its converse *(yijin chigu).*[57] In the context of argumentation, Xunzi's expression *yigu chijin* can be perspicuously rendered as "to use one's knowledge of or beliefs about the past in order to maintain a view about the present." Xunzi is clearly recommending the adoption of a standpoint based on historical knowledge or beliefs for the purpose of maintaining or assessing the adequacy of current beliefs. Both the retrospective and prospective uses of the historical appeal are essentially *critical,* and can be used either in the positive defense of one's thesis or in the negative evaluation of another's thesis or both. In Xunzi, the retrospective use is far more frequent and wide-ranging than the prospective one. In attacking the current pervasive view that physiognomy can foretell fortune and misfortune as well as indicate human character, Xunzi uses examples of historical characters to show that a man's fortune or misfortune has no necessary connection with his height or weight and handsomeness or ugliness. Rather the crux of the matter lies in the way in which the man employs his mind and his method of choice *(zeshu).* "When a person's method is upright and his mind follows it without reservation, although his physiognomy be repulsive, yet if his mind and method of choice are directed toward the attainment of moral excellence *(shan),*

---

55. See also *jiebi* L498, W136, D276–77; and *bugou* L50.

56. Again, the explication that follows is an application of a highly condensed account of Xunzi's conception of ethical justification based on a reconstruction of extant materials given in Cua, *Ethical Argumentation,* chaps. 2 and 3.

57. For an elaboration of this distinction, see my "Introduction," *Dimensions of Moral Creativity.*

his physiognomy will not hinder him from being a *junzi*" (*feixiang* L73, D67*).[58]

In discussing the retrospective use of the historical appeal, however, I shall focus on the following passage, which illustrates more clearly the kind of justification involved in the defense of an ethical thesis as a response to challenge.

> Chen Xiao said to Xunzi, "When you talk about the use of arms, you always insist on *ren* (benevolence) and *yi* (rightness) as the basis of justification *(ben)*. A man of *ren* loves others; a man of *yi* does what is right and reasonable *(xunli)*. Why, then, would they have any recourse to arms in the first place? Those who take up arms do so only in order to contend with others and seize some spoil!"
>
> Xunzi replied, "This is not something that you would understand. The man of *ren* indeed loves others, and because he loves others, he hates what brings harm to others. The man of *yi* indeed does what is right and reasonable, and for that reason he hates those that lead others astray. He takes up arms in order to put an end to violence and to do away harm, not in order to contend with others for spoil. Therefore, where the soldiers of the man of *ren* encamp they command a godlike respect; and where they pass, they transform the people. They are like the seasonable rain in whose falling all men rejoiced. Thus Yao attacked Huan Dou, Shun attacked the rulers of the Miao, Yu attacked Gong Gong, Tang attacked the ruler of Xia, King Wen attacked Chong, and King Wu attacked Zhou. These four emperors and two kings all marched through the world with their soldiers of *ren* and *yi*. Those nearby were won by their goodness, and those far off were filled with longing by their virtue. They did not stain their swords with blood, and yet near and far alike submitted; their virtue flourished in the center and spread to the four quarters." (*yibing* L328, W69–70*)

Although Xunzi considers *dao* to be the ultimate standard for all ethical judgment, justification of an ethical view or judgment appeals to one or more of its basic specifications, that is, to *ren, yi,* or *li,* more often to the conjoined appeal to *li* and *yi*. In the present case, Xunzi appeals to *ren* and *yi* as a justification for the permissibility of the use of arms. The appeal consists essentially in invoking certain established or accepted applications of ethical notions attested to by the historical incidents presumed to be matters of common knowledge. In the present instance, the appeal does involve plausible presumptions discussed earlier (section 2 above). One distinctive feature of the retrospective use of the historical appeal, however, may be said to be *standard-invoking*, as contrasted with the *standard-setting* aspect of the

---

58. Lengthy examples are noteworthy in such essays as *wangzhi* (Regulations of Kings), *yibing* (Discussion on Military Affairs), and *zhenglun* (Correction of Errors). I have chosen for discussion one passage, among many others, from *yibing*. But notably, Xunzi sometimes explicitly states the distinction between the past *(gu)* and the present *(jin)* in the retrospective sense. See, for example, *fei shi'er zi* L105; *fuguo* L202–6; *jundao* L278–80.

elucidative use.[59] In effect, it constitutes an appeal to an established framework with its operative criteria or standards for justification of ethical judgments. Of course, one can always raise external questions about an established practice, but a discussion of this question, as important as it is to moral epistemology, goes beyond the scope of this paper.[60]

From a view internal to the practice of ethical justification, the invocation of accepted standards of conduct and their applications amounts to an appeal to rules. Perhaps, for this reason, Xunzi often couples *li* (rules of proper conduct) and *yi* (rightness) in order to emphasize that the rules of proper conduct are the right sort of rules to employ in justifying one's ethical judgments with regard to conduct. In the context of argumentation, such an appeal to established rules is legitimate unless it can be shown that what is at issue falls outside their purview. These practice rules, to borrow a term from Rawls, are authoritative in that they command obedience irrespective of one's wishes or desires, for they have been, explicitly or tacitly, acknowledged to be legitimate constraints upon one's freedom of thought, speech, and action.[61] It is in this light that one can appreciate Xunzi's insistence on the key role of learning the classics, particularly the ones pertaining to history and the rules of proper conduct *(li)*. Mastering ethical justification is thus learning how to apply established standards of conduct, and must rely on teachers who possess extensive knowledge of the existing ethical framework and its history of application. Thus an uninformed moral agent must rely on those who have the expertise in and knowledge of an ethical practice and its history. Retrospective use of the historical appeal is thus *conservative*, in that it attempts to preserve the continuity of an eth-

---

59. This distinction is indebted to Urmson but is perhaps employed in a context that may be alien to his intent. Also, while the distinction is important in elucidating some aspect of Xunzi's ethical theory, as Urmson points out, the distinction may be blurred in practice, especially in situations "where standards are gradually evolved and gradually changed." I believe that Xunzi was quite sensitive to this issue of changing and evolving standards, as shown, for example, in his insistence on distinguishing different grades of Confucians in his essay on the merits of *Ru* or Confucians *(Ruxiao pian)*. This effort may be regarded as a response to the shifting and changing conception of being *Ru* in his own times. And it may be quite properly construed as an effort directed to standard-setting guided by the ideal of *dao*. See J. O. Urmson, *The Emotive Theory of Ethics* (London: Hutcheson University Library, 1968), chap. 6.

60. My defense of Xunzi's view of ethical justification is found in the first three sections of chap. 3 in *Ethical Argumentation*.

61. This feature of Xunzi's ethics is the basis of some scholars' complaint about his authoritarianism. If I have not been mistaken in my presentation thus far, this complaint is more a Western "democratic" reaction than one based in the works of Xunzi. See, for example, Dubs, *Hsüntze: The Moulder of Ancient Confucianism* (London: Arthur Probsthain, 1927), 109 passim; and H. G. Creel, *Chinese Thought from Confucius to Mao Tse Tung* (Chicago: University of Chicago Press, 1953), 133. [For the notion of practice as contrasted with summary rules, see John Rawls, "Two Concepts of Rules," *Philosophical Review* 64 (1955).]

ical practice. If the appeal is deemed problematic, the relevant inquiry is more a search of the historical memory than an exploration of new avenues for resolving ethical problems. The historical memory, however, is not always reliable and often requires ethical interpretation. It is for this reason that the retrospective use of the historical appeal in problematic cases cannot offer a sufficient basis for ascertaining the adequacy of ethical judgments. Its value for argumentation lies primarily in its focus on the importance of complying with the normal practice of ethical justification.

The prospective use of the historical appeal reverses the standpoint of the retrospective one. Human history is seen as subject matter rather than as a basis for ethical judgment. In adopting this standpoint, one can no longer avail oneself of the presumption of the truth of historical beliefs without critical examination, nor can one presume the existence of shared historical knowledge. The key issue here lies in the present evidential grounding of ethical claims. Xunzi is emphatic concerning this requirement: "Those who are good at discussing matters pertaining to the past (*gu*) must support their claims by an appeal to matters pertaining to the present (*jin*). . . . In any discussion, what deserves our esteem are clarity in conceptual distinction, consistency and coherence (*bianhe*), and accord with evidence (*fuyan*)" (*xing'e* L549). Also, Xunzi is quite sensitive to the difficulty of acquiring accurate information about the past, although he does not doubt that such a difficulty could not arise for a sage who possesses comprehensive knowledge of things. His own answer to this difficulty, however, poses a problem for the coherent interpretation of a central thesis in his political philosophy, namely, that an ethically responsible ruler must follow the sage kings (*fa shengwang*) or former kings (*fa xianwang*) who embodied *dao*, or *ren*, *li*, and *yi*.[62] In response to the question as to which specific *li* to follow among the existing diversity of *li* (rules of proper conduct) among the sage kings, Xunzi avers,

> When the rules of proper conduct (*li*) are preserved too long, they are lost. There are officials to preserve the arts and rules of proper conduct; but if preserved to a great age, they become negligent [in recording their significance]. Hence, it is said that if one wants to see the footprints of (the *dao* of) the sage kings, then look where they are most clear, that is to say, at the later kings (*houwang*). Hence, it is said that if you wish to know a thousand years, then consider today. . . . By the present you can understand the past, by means of the one, you can deal with diversity; by the subtle you can understand the clear—this saying expresses what I mean. (*feixiang* L80, D72–73*)[63]

---

62. For identification of relevant passages on "following the former kings," see *Concordance*, 14/5/40, 24/8/97, 15/6/8, 15/6/10, and 24/8/91.

63. See also *ruxiao* L158, D118.

Xunzi goes on to point out, "The longer things have been handed down, the more sketchy they are; the more recent they are, the more detailed they are" (*feixiang* L83, D74-75*).⁶⁴

This passage seems to confuse the distinction between the earlier and later kings with the distinction between the past and the present. The former pertains to the historic past rather than a distinction between past and present. Such a passage also seems to contradict Xunzi's recurrent emphasis on following the former kings (*fa xianwang*). One way to resolve this problem is to suggest that when Xunzi uses the notion of former kings (*xianwang*), it is functionally equivalent to that of sage kings. When "former kings" occurs singly, it is basically to be construed as a generic term (*gongming*) for which the distinction between earlier and later kings are proper specifications (*bieming*). Further, where Xunzi uses the notion of later kings (*houwang*), what he means to emphasize is the importance of the critical consideration of evidence in assessing any claim about historic events or states of affairs. As for following the sage kings, Xunzi is clear that the following (*fa*) at issue is not a matter of imitation, but a matter of doing what is required by *ren*, *yi*, or *li*, given critical reflection on the significance of these requirements. "If a person wants to discuss following the sage kings (*fa shengwang*), he must know what they valued. If he uses *yi* to regulate all his undertakings, then he may know what is truly beneficial to the state. If he wants to discuss what they valued, then he must know why they engaged in self-cultivation" (*junzi* L565). However one resolves the issue of coherent interpretation, Xunzi is clear in his insistence on the need for evidential support in making ethical judgments about the past. For my immediate purpose this is an important feature of the prospective use of the historical appeal. Before I elaborate this and other features, let me turn briefly to Xunzi's own prospective use of the historical appeal.

For the most part, Xunzi's prospective use of the historical appeal takes the form of ethical explanations of historical events, that is, historical explanations involving the use of ethical notions. For example, in attacking the view that Jie and Zhou were the legitimate rulers of the empire, and that Tang and Wu rebelled and usurped the throne by force, Xunzi points out, among other things, that:

Tang and Wu did not capture the empire; they cultivated the *dao;* they practiced *yi* (rightness); they rigorously promoted common benefits and did away with common sources of harm; and so the whole world professed allegiance. Jie and

---

64. Or more generally, "In discussing small and intricate matters, one must exercise care in inquiry. When the clues for dealing with them are seen, one can then deal with them with understanding and appreciate the rationales (*li*) underlying the fundamental distinctions involved" (*feixiang* L89).

Zhou did not abandon the whole world; they perverted the virtues of Yu and Tang; they confused the distinction between rules of proper conduct *(li)* and righteousness *(yi);* their bestial actions heaped up misfortune for them, completed their evil destiny, and the whole world dismissed them. (*zhenglun* L388, D190–91*)[65]

As I understand it, the historical explanations proffered are essentially ethical judgments or verdicts about historical events rather than attempts at objective historical explanations. Although I am in no position to decide the truth of Xunzi's historical accounts, I assume that given his own requirement of accord with evidence, Xunzi must have had some factual basis for his claims. At issue is the question of historical objectivity when ethical or value judgments enter into the historian's causal explanation or characterization of action. It is not possible to pursue this problem in the philosophy of history in this paper. However, on behalf of Xunzi, one may point out that, although his ethical explanation of history is reminiscent of the Chinese praise-and-blame theory of history, there is no evidence to suggest that he holds such a theory in its naive form. He does offer ethical judgments of history, but the crux of the matter is whether these judgments would then influence his account of ancient Chinese history, if he were writing a historical account thereof. Given his requirement of accord with evidence, it is not likely that he would have allowed himself to distort evidence to support his ethical theses.[66] Needless to say, Xunzi is a moral philosopher and not a historian. Thus my main interest here lies in explicating the prospective use of the historical appeal and its argumentative value, rather than es-

---

65. According to traditional Chinese history, Tang was the first ruler of the Shang dynasty; Wu, founder of the Western Zhou dynasty, who defeated Zhou, the last ruler of the Shang dynasty. Jie was the last ruler of Xia, and Yu established the Xia dynasty (see note 30 above). For other examples, see *wangba* L251, and *chendao* L292 passim.

66. Arguably, as Dray points out, the notion of history is a quasi-evaluative notion, for the notion pertains not just to the past, but to the significant past. And the issue of the praise and blame theory of history is incisively stated by Max Fisch:

> The historian is not blamed for praising or blaming, and praised for doing neither, but blamed if antecedent judgments of value blind him to contrary evidence, and praised if his selection and treatment of evidence is clearly not unbalanced by the desires to support judgments formed in advance of the search for evidence.... The historian of art is a critic of art, the historian of science a critic of science, and similarly the historian of economic, social, and political institutions is a critic of those institutions. Objectivity is not the absence of criticism, but unreserved submission to further criticism, complete openness, withholding nothing from judgment.

This notion of objectivity is present in Xunzi's requirement of impartiality in argumentation. See William H. Dray, *Philosophy of History* (Englewood Cliffs, N.J.: Prentice-Hall, 1964), 28 and 40–55. See also William H. Dray, *Perspective on History* (London: Routledge and Kegan Paul, 1980), 42–46. For Xunzi's view, see Cua, "Hsün Tzu's Theory of Argumentation," 873–75.

tablishing the accuracy and legitimacy of ethical explanations of history as a thesis in the philosophy of history. More specifically, I am interested in the form of ethical justification that contrasts it with the retrospective use of the historical appeal.

Returning to the form of ethical justification, let us recall the passage which expresses Xunzi's view in response to the question concerning the diversity of *li* (rules of proper conduct). In his response, Xunzi speaks of the "footprints" or "traces" of the *dao* of the sage kings (*feixiang* L83, D74–75). This metaphor of footprints indicates that in problematic cases of ethical judgment, evidence is a product of the reconstruction of the past application of *dao* in light of what a reflective person deems to be an *acceptable* application on the basis of his present knowledge about the past. Evidence is factual information that is present-at-hand, rather than something which is presumed. For the realization of the practical import of ethical notions or their applicability to the issue at hand requires the addition of imaginative reconstruction. The prospective use of the historical appeal, unlike the retrospective one, does not rely on an established practice of ethical justification, but rather on the *acceptability* of one's ethical judgments about the past, that is, on the strength of one's reasons supported by argument and relevant matters of fact. While the retrospective use of the historical appeal is conservative, the prospective use implies a creative form of ethical judgment, though essentially contestable, in response to exigent and changing circumstances. Its argumentative value lies in laying the ground for a possible reasonable acceptance rather than invoking the support of an established framework of ethical justification. This interpretation is plausibly suggested in Xunzi's remark:

> Where there are established rules of conduct *(fa)*, comply with them. Where there are no such rules, act in the spirit of analogy *(lei)*. Know the branches through the root, the right from the left. In general, the hundred human affairs have their different rationales *(li)*, yet they all abide by the same *dao*. (*dalüe* L617)[67]

Finally, in view of Xunzi's conception of the holistic character of *dao* as a unifying perspective, both the retrospective and prospective, as well as the pedagogical and rhetorical, uses of the historical appeal are liable to abuse, for the distinction between the past and the present is a potential source of erroneous ethical beliefs (section 2 above). In this essay, I have merely offered a sketch of the various functions of the historical appeal. I hope this discussion of an aspect of Xunzi's thought

---

67. See also *wangzhi* L163, D123, W35.

provides some materials which might aid in a general evaluation of the Confucian use of history and promote an understanding of some aspects of ethical discourse which may be relevant to contemporary moral philosophy.[68]

68. This paper was presented at the joint meetings of the Society for Asian and Comparative Studies and the Association for Asian Studies, Washington, D.C., March 25, 1984.

Essay 4
THE PROBLEM OF CONCEPTUAL UNITY

It is reported that Confucius once said to Zengzi, "My way has one thread that runs through it *(Wudao yi yi guanzhi)*."[1] The "way" *(dao)* here, it is widely acknowledged, refers to Confucius's teachings. Zengzi construed this *dao* to consist of *zhong* (conscientiousness) and *shu* (consideration for others). There are at least two reasons for not accepting Zengzi's interpretation as a guide to Confucius's intention. In the first place, the interpretation, as it stands, is uninformative. We are not told anything about the object or goal of *zhong*. While it is unproblematic to construe *shu* as pertaining to the adoption of an other-regarding attitude, it is not clear what sort of standard is at issue. In the second place, if *shu* is defined as "using oneself as a measure,"[2] then according to another remark of Confucius, it is a method of realizing *ren* (humanity): "To be able to judge others by what is near to ourselves may be called the method of realizing humanity *(ren)*."[3] It is plausible to maintain that *ren* is the "one thread" of Confucius's *dao*.[4] However, to the same question on *ren*, Confucius gave different answers to different pupils. For example, to Zigong, it is *shu;* to Fan Chi, it is the love of others; and to Yan

---

1. *Analects (Lunyu)*, 4.15. Unless otherwise specified, all translations from the *Analects* are taken from Wing-tsit Chan, trans., *A Source Book in Chinese Philosophy* (Princeton, N.J.: Princeton University Press, 1963). Asterisks indicate minor emendations.
2. D. C. Lau, trans., *Confucius: The Analects* (Middlesex, England: Penguin Books, 1979), Introduction, 16 n.
3. *Analects* 6.28.
4. The basis for this claim is this remark of Confucius: "If a superior man *(junzi)* departs from humanity *(ren)*, how can he fulfill that name? A superior man never abandons humanity even for the lapse of a single meal. In moments of haste, he acts according to it. In times of difficulty or confusion, he acts according to it" (*Analects* 4:5). It must be noted that Zengzi's interpretation, if taken as a heuristic assumption for a philosophical elaboration of the importance of *zhong* and *shu,* can be quite incisive in contrast with certain views in contemporary moral philosophy. See Herbert Fingarette, "Following the 'One Thread' of the *Analects*," *Journal of the American Academy of Religion* 47, no. 35 (1979); and A. S. Cua, "Confucian Vision and Human Community," *Journal of Chinese Philosophy* 11, no. 3 (1984), or Essay 11 of this volume. For a plausible interpretation of the "one thread" as *ren*, see Xu Fuguan, *Zhongguo sixiang shi lunji* (Taipei: Xuesheng, 1975), 226–34.

Yuan, it is self-discipline and compliance with *li* (ritual rules).[5] One way of easing this perplexity is to point out that Confucius adapted his teaching to the ability of his students *(yincai shijiao)*, or to the needs of his students in terms of helping them to rectify defects or weaknesses of character, rather than imparting theses or doctrines that claim the allegiance of all reasonable persons.

This common observation, however, does not resolve the problem of coherence in the *Analects*. Toward the solution of this problem, one may draw attention to the conversational tradition in Chinese thought,[6] and attempt to characterize the logico-semantical aspects of Confucius's general remarks in particular contexts. In this manner, it is possible to mark the salient features of Confucian as distinct from Zen and Socratic dialogues.[7] While this approach may throw some light on the conversational form of the *Analects*, it does not by itself contribute to the problem of the coherence of Confucius's vision of *dao* as the good life consisting in the attainment of a variety of human excellences or virtues, more centrally of *ren*, *li*, and *yi* (rightness).[8] In the *Analects*, *ren*, *li*, and *yi* are recurrent and central aretaic notions (that is, notions of virtue). In addition, there are many others like trustworthiness, uprightness, courage, wisdom, tolerance, and so forth.[9] The *Analects* thus presents a complex ethical vocabulary and a problem of conceptual unity, that is, the connection or interdependence of central aretaic notions *(ren, li, and yi)*. For philosophical reconstruction, one can take either *ren* or *li* as the key aretaic term and explain the other aretaic notions by way of a holistic or subsumptive approach. The holistic approach proceeds by regarding, say, *ren*, as the key aretaic notion that has its specifications in all other aretaic terms. In this conception, all virtues are, so to speak, pervaded by *ren*, much like a gestalt in relation to its interrelated or interdependent components. The subsumptive approach may take either *ren* or *li* (ritual rules) as a notion of inclusive virtue, or as a class term

---

5. *Analects* 15.24; 12.22; and 12.1.
6. Donald Holzman, "The Conversational Tradition in Chinese Philosophy," *Philosophy East and West* 6, no. 3 (1956).
7. A. S. Cua, "The Logic of Confucian Dialogues," in *Studies in Philosophy and the History of Philosophy*, ed. J. K. Ryan (Washington, D.C.: The Catholic University of America Press, 1969), vol. 4; and "Uses of Dialogues and Moral Understanding," *Journal of Chinese Philosophy* 2, no. 1 (1975).
8. For plausible arguments for the centrality of *ren*, *li*, and *yi*, along with *dao* and *de* (virtue), see Chen Daqi, *Kongzi xueshuo* (Taipei: Zhengzhong, 1976; 1st ed., 1964), 93–152.
9. In addition to *ren*, *li*, and *yi*, Chen discussed twenty-two other aretaic notions. More recently, some thirty-four aretaic notions are claimed to be important topics in the *Analects*. See Chen, *Kongzi xueshuo*; and Ye Jinggui, *Kongzi de daode zhexue* (Taipei: Zhengzhong, 1977), 15.

that contains subclasses as its members. The main idea of the subsumptive approach is the notion of classification. On this approach, the key aretaic term functions as a basis for classifying all aretaic notions.[10]

In dealing with the problem of the unity of the central aretaic notions in the *Analects* (henceforth, the problem of conceptual unity), one would expect some assistance from Xunzi, not for an adequate interpretation of the *Analects*, but for a plausible development of classical Confucianism.[11] In the first place, apart from the general appreciation of Xunzi as a systematic Confucian, Xunzi often insists on rational coherence in both ethical thought and discourse. Notably Xunzi's expression "the thread of *dao (daoguan)*" is an ellipsis of Confucius's "My way has one thread that runs through it" *(Wudao yi yi guanzhi)*.[12] Xunzi's preferred term is *tong* (unity) or *tonglei* (unity of kinds),[13] which, on closer examination, is a requirement of argumentative competence, along with requirements of conceptual clarity and accord with linguistic practices and experience *(bianhe, fuyan)*.[14] In Xunzi's judgment, although Mencius followed the *dao* of the former kings, he had only a sketchy

---

10. Chen Daqi incisively employs this holistic conception that focuses on *ren* in his *Kongzi xueshuo*. Fingarette takes *li* as the highest aretaic notion for dealing with *ren*, but he neglects to discuss *yi*. The construal of *ren* as an inclusive virtue suggests a subsumptive conception. It is interesting to note that no scholar considers *yi* the highest aretaic notion, though such a reconstruction can be plausibly pursued. My own approach is closer to Chen's holism but focuses on the unity of embodiment of the virtues in paradigmatic individuals or *junzi*. See Herbert Fingarette, *Confucius—The Secular as Sacred* (New York: Harper and Row, 1971), 22–24; Wing-tsit Chan, "The Evolution of the Concept *Jen*," *Philosophy East and West* 4, no. 4 (1955); A. S. Cua, *Dimensions of Moral Creativity: Paradigms, Principles, and Ideals* (University Park: Pennsylvania State University Press, 1978), chaps. 4–5.

11. For convenience of reference to *Xunzi*, I have throughout referred to Xunzi as the author of his work, well aware of the problem of authorship. My interest lies primarily in the coherence of basic philosophical views expressed in such essays as *tianlun, jiebi, zhengming, fuguo, zhenglun, and xing'e*. The problem of textual authenticity does not affect the issue of philosophical explication. For quick identification of passages, I have sometimes referred to *A Concordance to Hsün Tzu*, Harvard-Yenching Institute Sinological Index Series, supplement no. 22 (Taipei: Chinese Materials and Research Center, 1966); hereafter cited as *Concordance*. For a detailed discussion of textual problems, see Yang Yunru, *Xunzi yanjiu* (Taipei: Shangwu, 1974), chap. 1. [For a later, more extended discussion, see John Knoblock, *Xunzi: A Translation and Study of the Complete Works*, vol. 1 (Stanford, Calif.: Stanford University Press, 1989), and my review essay in *Philosophy East and West* 41, no. 2 (1991): 215–27.]

12. *tianlun* L377, D183–84, W87.

13. *fei shi'er zi* L100; *ruxiao* L149, 157; D112, 117–18; *jiebi* L498, D276–77; *xing'e* L555, D315, W168–69. For a good discussion of the notion of *tonglei*, see Mou Zongsan, *Xunzi dalüe* (Taipei: Zhongyang wenwu gongying she, 1953), and Wei Zhengtong, *Xunzi yu gudai zhexue* (Taipei: Shangwu, 1974; 1st ed., 1966), chap. 1. See also A. S. Cua, *Ethical Argumentation: A Study in Hsün Tzu's Moral Epistemology* (Honolulu: University of Hawaii Press, 1985), chap. 2.

14. Ultimately these requirements may be broadly construed as requirements of reason and experience. See Cua, *Ethical Argumentation*, chap. 1, or "Hsün Tzu's Theory of Argumentation: A Reconstruction," *Review of Metaphysics* 36, no. 4 (1983).

conception but no real understanding of its underlying unity *(buzhi qi-tong).*[15]

Although Xunzi makes extensive use of quasi-definitional formulas involving *wei* (say/call) in explaining the meanings of a variety of terms,[16] he does not pay much attention to the central aretaic terms *(ren, yi,* and *li).* Except for a couple of terse remarks on *ren* and *yi* which appear to have an explanatory force *(yibing* L328, W69, D167), on the whole he probably presumes that these terms have established meanings familiar to the readers. If we grant this presumption as reasonable,[17] we still do not find any clear guide to Xunzi's own response to the problem of conceptual unity, that is, the connection of *ren, yi,* and *li.*[18] This problem presents a task for reconstruction. It is an important task, because a coherent and plausible explication of Xunzi's ethical theory ultimately depends on an adequate solution to the problem of conceptual unity.

Moreover, there is a special problem of co-occurrence of *li* and *yi* in many passages in his works—a problem that creates an obstacle to any attempt at coherent reconstruction of Xunzi's conception of the nature of conceptual unity. What I have in mind are numerous cases where the expression *"li yi"* occurs as a pair. Following Xunzi's own distinction between a single term *(danming)* and a compound term *(jianming),* that is, a term with more than one Chinese character *(zhengming* L515, W143, D285), one may wonder whether the co-occurrence of *li* and *yi* can be read as a compound term *(jianming)* or as a conjunction of single terms *(danming),* since we find many instances of independent occurrence of *li* without *yi.* Conversely,[19] it seems quite proper to regard the co-occurrence of *li* and *yi* as a conjunction of two single terms *(danming).*[20]

---

15. *fei shi'er zi* L98. For Xunzi, following the *dao* of former kings *(fa xianwang)* is not blind compliance but a critical reflection on its rationale *(li).* For a brief discussion, see A. S. Cua, "Ethical Uses of History in Early Confucianism: The Case of Hsün Tzu," *Philosophy East and West* 35, no. 2 (1985); incorporated in this volume as Essay 3. See also *zidao* L651.

16. For an extensive discussion of the notion of *wei,* see Cua, *Ethical Argumentation,* chap. 3.

17. This presumption is plausible particularly in the light of his requirement of accord with linguistic practices and his use of this requirement in criticizing Mencius's doctrine of the inherent goodness of human nature *(xing'e* L547, W162, D307). See my "Hsün Tzu's Theory of Argumentation," 879–80.

18. The connection, I believe, is implicit in instances where the central aretaic notions occur in the same sentence or context. For example, *quanxue* L15, D38, W21; and *ruxiao* L131, D96.

19. For example, *quanxue* L10; *zhishi* L307; *bugou* L43; *rongru* L60; and *wangba* L238.

20. The decision concerning this problem of the co-occurrence of *li* and *yi* is reflected in the difference between Dubs's and Watson's translations. Dubs's, and later Chan's, translation is based on the reading of co-occurrence as a conjunction of single terms, Watson's on reading it as a compound term. For an example, among many, see *xing'e* L538, D301, W157; and Chan, *A Source Book in Chinese Philosophy,* 128. It is interesting to note

If this reading is followed, there is still a question concerning the proper interpretation of this conjunction. Different answers have been proposed, some of them are reminiscent of the holistic and subsumptive approaches to the problem of conceptual unity in the *Analects*.

In this essay, I offer a preliminary exploration of this problem. Section 1 is devoted to a critical appreciation of four different responses to the co-occurrence of *li* and *yi* as a conjunction of distinct notions and to the problem of conceptual unity. Section 2 makes a brief excursion into Li Gou's conception of *li*, which is a distinctive and original development of a key aspect of Xunzi's ethical theory, and anticipates in a brilliant way the subsumptive interpretation discussed in section 1.

1. FOUR PROPOSALS

In this section, I consider four different proposals for dealing with the problem of the co-occurrence of *li* and *yi* as a conjunction of single terms *(danming)* found in the works of Chen Daqi, Wei Zhengtong, Zhou Shaoxian, and Homer Dubs.[21] Both Dubs and Zhou also attend to the role of *ren*, thus addressing the more general problem of conceptual unity. For the purpose of assessing these contributions, we need to assume that, for Xunzi, the basic Confucian terms *(ren, li,* and *yi)* have established meanings.[22] While it is doubtful that any scholarly consensus can be achieved on the issue of definition, it seems unproblematic, though lacking in solid textual support, to maintain that these terms, with a minimum of interpretation, function much like the use of focal notions for conveying distinct, though not unrelated, centers of ethical con-

---

that cases of the co-occurrence of *ren* and *yi* quite rightly do not call for such a decision. I suspect that the reading of the co-occurrence of *li* and *yi* as a compound term is based on the subsumptive conception of *li*, much akin to that of Li Gou, and actually suggested by some passages in *Xunzi*. However, even if this reading has textual support, this construal of the co-occurrence of *li* and *yi* in effect cancels out the ethical force of *yi*, as in Watson's rendering in terms of "ritual principles." In this case, *yi* no longer functions as an aretaic term. It is *li* that carries, so to speak, the ethical weight. So construed, all cases of co-occurrence have no relevance to the problem of conceptual unity. On the other hand, in treating co-occurrence as a conjunction of single terms, we are treating them as independent aretaic notions. Also this procedure seems amply justified by numerous independent occurrences of *yi*. For the role of selective decision in explication, see Cua, "Some Reflections on Methodology in Chinese Philosophy," *International Philosophical Quarterly* 11, no. 2 (1971); and "Tasks of Confucian Ethics," *Journal of Chinese Philosophy* 6, no. 1 (1979).

21. Chen Daqi, *Xunzi xueshuo* (Taipei: Zhongyang wenwu gongying she, 1954); Wei Zhengtong, *Xunzi yu gudai zhexue;* Homer H. Dubs, *Hsüntze: The Moulder of Ancient Confucianism* (London: Arthur Probsthain, 1927); and Zhou Shaoxian, *Xunzi yaoyi* (Taipei: Sanmin, 1976).

22. It is significant that Xunzi occasionally used *li* and *yi* as a basis for explaining the meaning of other terms, e.g., "good order" *(zhi)* and "chaos" *(luan)* *(bugou* L45). See also note 17 above.

cern.²³ *Ren* typically focuses, as in the *Analects* (12:22), on the love and care for one's fellows *(yibing* L328, W69, D167) and *li* on ritual code *(lixian),* which is essentially a set of formal prescriptions or procedures for characterizing proper behavior *(quanxue* L15, W21, D38–39).²⁴ As for *yi,* we have this brief statement: "The man of *yi* follows reason" *(yizhe xunli)* *(yibing* L328, W69*). Obviously, an interpolation is in order. I suggest that the focus pertains primarily to the exercise of reason in arriving at a sound judgment on the right or appropriate thing to do in a particular situation. This suggestion is well supported by Xunzi's remark that if one "guides the mind with reason and nourishes it with clarity, and does not allow extraneous matters to upset it, then it will be capable of determining right and wrong and of resolving doubts" *(jiebi* L490, W131*). Thus, Xunzi's brief statement on *yi (yizhe xunli)* can freely be rendered as "The man of *yi* follows what is right and reasonable," that is, conducts himself in accord with his reasoned judgment of what is right and appropriate.²⁵ Given this interpretation, Xunzi's emphasis on *yi* as the means of responding to changing circumstances *(yiyi bianying)* is readily intelligible *(bugou* L43, *zhishi* L306). For, as he points out, wise and informed deliberation *(zhilü)* is essential to resolving perplexities that arise out of changing circumstances *(jundao* L284).²⁶ Implied in such a deliberation is the requirement of impartiality *(gong),* particularly in not allowing self-interest to interfere with the exercise of *yi.* In Xunzi's succinct words, "From impartiality comes enlightenment *(gong sheng ming);* from partiality comes obscuration *(pian sheng an)" (bugou* L52).²⁷

Given the foregoing assumption on *ren, li,* and *yi* as focal notions that mark out distinct centers of ethical interest and activity,²⁸ we can now

23. For the use of what I call focal notions for understanding some aspects of ethical experience and activity, see Cua, *Dimensions of Moral Creativity,* chap. 1.

24. This usage of ritual has an established sanction, as indicated in the *Oxford Dictionary of the English Language.* For a discussion in connection with the *Li Chi [Liji],* see A. S. Cua, "*Li* and Moral Justification: A Study in the *Li Chi,*" *Philosophy East and West* 33, no. 1 (1983).

25. "Moral conduct *(xing)*" is defined as "that which is in accord with *yi (zhengyi)."* See *zhengming* L506, W140*. For *yi* as appropriateness, see *Zhong Yong [The Doctrine of the Mean],* in Chan, *A Source Book in Chinese Philosophy,* section 20.

26. For an extensive discussion of the role of deliberation in Hsün Tzu's doctrine of moral justification, see Cua, *Ethical Argumentation,* chap. 2.

27. This contrast between *yi* and self-interest is evident in the *Analects* 4:16. But in coupling *yi* with *gong* (impartiality) in many passages, Xunzi brings out more clearly the distinction between what is public and what is private. Thus, the exercise of *yi* has nothing to do with prudence, but with issues of personal conduct that affect others. Consequently, impartiality is required in attending to issues of moral perplexity.

28. These concerns are evident in the themes of some of Xunzi's essays. For example, there is the concern for *ren* in the form of enriching people's welfare in *fugou pian; li* in *lilun pian;* and *yi* in the form of honor and shame, in *rongru pian* and part of *zhenglun pian.* It must be noted that in construing *ren, li,* and *yi* as focal notions, I leave open the

better appreciate their aretaic character, that is, as terms for expressing distinct human excellences.[29] *Ren* is the virtue of benevolence implying an affectionate concern for the well-being of others. *Li* is the virtue of rule-compliance or rule-responsibility, and *yi* the virtue of sound judgment. In Aristotelian language, *ren* and *li* are moral virtues, and *yi* an intellectual virtue, not unlike Aristotle's *phronesis* or practical wisdom.[30] The problem of conceptual unity is a problem of philosophical reconstruction of the relation between these foci of ethical concern.

The works of Xunzi, because of the absence of a definitive guide, present various options for such a reconstruction. The views discussed below represent possible options and contain important insights that contribute to an understanding of certain aspects of Xunzi's ethical thought, not only in terms of textual interpretation, but also in indicating directions in which Xunzi's ethical theory may plausibly be developed.[31] For convenience of reference, I shall assign these labels to the views to be discussed: functional equivalence, delimitation, subsumption, and completion. I shall also use the term holism as interchangeable with the completion thesis.[32] The first two theses pertain primarily

---

question of how such notions may be amplified by further theoretical elaboration. The career of *ren* in the history of Chinese thought is instructive, as incisively demonstrated by Professor Chan's well-known study. The notion of *li*, at least up to the Warring States period, as Hu Shi pointed out, had also undergone a conceptual evolution. The notion of *yi*, to my knowledge, had not the same fortune of similar development. Arguably, if Confucian ethics today is to cope with changing circumstances, as Xunzi believed it should, these central notions must respond to issues of cultural change that arise out of intercultural contacts. See W. T. Chan, "The Evolution of the Concept *Jen*," and "Chinese and Western Interpretations of *Jen* (Humanity)," *Journal of Chinese Philosophy* 2, no. 2 (1975): 107–29; and Cua, "*Li* and Moral Justification." [Later analysis of *yi* is given in Essays 5 and 6 of this volume. For the problem of intercultural conflict, see *Moral Vision and Tradition*, Essay 14.]

29. In Rescher's felicitous term, "aristic values." For a critical appreciation of Rescher's view from the point of view of critical Confucian ethics, see A. S. Cua, "Ideals and Values: A Study in Rescher's Moral Vision," in *Praxis and Reason: Studies in the Philosophy of Nicholas Rescher*, ed. Robert Almeder (Lanham, Md.: University Press of America, 1982).

30. It is significant that Xunzi, after remarking on man's ability to acquire knowledge, defines wisdom (*zhi*) as "knowledge that harmonizes with the requirements of practical life (*zhi you sohe*)" (*zhengming* L506; cf. D282 and W140). For Aristotle, see *Nicomachean Ethics*, Book 6, 1141b–1143b.

31. I believe that Xunzi would have approved of this spirit of critical appreciation of scholarship. On the discourse of the superior man (*junzi*), he says: "With a benevolent mind (*renxsin*) he explains his ideas to others, with a receptive mind (*xuexin*) he listens to their words, and with an impartial mind (*gongxin*) he makes his judgment. . . . He honors what is fair and upright and despises meanness and wrangling" (*zhengming* L524, W148–49*). For a general discussion of the desirable qualities of participants in discourse, see Chen, *Xunzi xueshuo*, chap. 6; and Cua, *Ethical Argumentation*, chap. 1.

32. Both the subsumption and the completion theses may be metaphorically characterized as *containment* views. They differ in the conception of the nature of containment as categorial or noncategorial. I shall say more about this distinction toward the end of this article.

to the special problem of the co-occurrence of *li* and *yi* as distinct terms, the last two to the larger problem of conceptual unity.

1.1 Functional Equivalence

After a fairly detailed and incisive discussion of the wide-ranging scope of *li* (which embraces not only matters pertaining to government and law, but also to self-cultivation, thought, speech, and action), Chen addresses the problem of the co-occurrence of *li* and *yi*. The question is: Wherein lies the similarity or difference between these two notions? Chen suggests that when we attend to their functions, *li* and *yi* are equivalent. Consider, for example, these two passages: (1) "*Yi* is for the sake of restraining men from evil conduct and from association with wicked men.... Within, it regulates the man himself; and without, it regulates [his conduct in relation to] myriad things" (*qiangguo* L358, D171*). (2) "The various instruments of measurement are standards for things; the *li* are the standards for laws and regulations. The instruments of measurement determine quantity; the *li* fix the various kinds of human relationship" (*zhishi*, L307). Chen goes on to point out that both *li* and *yi* are concerned with distinction *(fen)*.[33] Evidently, for Xunzi, *li* and *yi* have the same regulative function, that is, the same purpose in indicating standards for proper conduct. Chen justly observes that from the fact that two terms are used to perform the same function, one cannot logically conclude that they have the same referent, that is, that they refer to the same actuality *(shi)*. For it is possible that two distinct terms are used to refer to different actualities. However, "since *li* and *yi* have the same function, from the functional point of view, there is no need to draw any fine distinction between them."[34]

From the pragmatic point of view, Chen's approach to the problem of the co-occurrence of *li* and *yi* is sound. Extensive evidence can be marshaled, as Chen has done, to support the functional-equivalence thesis. Both *li* and *yi* have the same objective in distinguishing right and wrong conduct, as Chen has forcefully shown in his discussion of Xunzi's conception of *dao*.[35] However, the problem of the co-occurrence of *li* and *yi* is a theoretical or conceptual problem. Even if these terms are

---

33. The relevant passages cited by Chen are *feixiang* L80, D71; and *wangzhi* L180, D136, W45.

34. Chen, *Xunzi xueshuo*, 144. It is indeed puzzling, given his sound observation, that Chen goes on to say that whether *li* is used singly or in conjunction with *yi*, it is unnecessary to infer that they have different meanings. This thesis seems to confuse functional equivalence, which is a question of pragmatics, with the semantic question concerning *li* and *yi*.

35. Ibid., 70.

functionally equivalent, there is still a need to account for their occurrence as distinct notions, at least an attempt along the lines of the one Chen has made in connection with the *Analects*.³⁶ The functional equivalence thesis cannot thus be viewed as a contribution to the issue of semantic equivalence, nor to the issue of extensional equivalence. For even if *li* and *yi*, for the sake of argument, are semantically equivalent, that is, if they have the same meaning, the question is entirely open, as Chen has acknowledged, whether or not they coincide in reference. There are grounds to think that they do not. As we have seen, it is significant that *yi* has a direct connection with the exercise of reason *(yizhe xunli)*. *Li*, on the contrary, does not have such a direct connection. Although for Xunzi the *li*, along with *ren* and *yi*, have rationales that can be known and practiced *(xing'e* L552, W166*, D312), he is also clear that the *li* present us only with "models but no explanations" *(quanxue* L14, W20, D18; *dalüe* L603). For this reason, Xunzi plausibly compares *li* with precise instruments of measurement, as Chen has noted in proposing his functional-equivalence thesis.

Thus, quite unlike *yi*, the *li* simply indicate distinctions without explanation or justification. Although the *li*, for Xunzi, are the basis of laws, like laws in general they depend on paradigmatic individuals or *junzi* (who embody *ren* and *yi*) to carry them out *(jundao* L263). Notably, Xunzi distinguishes between the numerousness of laws *(fa zhi shu)* and their underlying significance *(fa zhi yi)*. Just as it is possible to master the wide-ranging scope of law without understanding *(jundao* L264), one can also master all ritual rules without understanding their underlying significance.³⁷ Thus Xunzi insists that one must not only learn the *li*, but also ponder the rationale for their existence *(lilun*, L428–29; W94–95; D224–25).

1.2 Delimitation

Wei agrees with Chen that "both *li* and *yi* have the same function." Wei goes further in maintaining that in many passages where *li* or *yi* occurs singly, one can be substituted for the other without affecting the meaning of the passage. This support of Chen, however, misses the insight of the functional-equivalence thesis. For the issue of interchangeability of *li* and *yi* in interpretation has no direct relevance to the issue of the co-occurrence of *li* and *yi* as a conjunction of single terms *(danming)*. The real issue, as Wei properly notes, is to render intelligible

---

36. See Chen, *Kongzi xueshuo*.
37. Elsewhere Chen appeals to this distinction in analyzing different questions concerning *li*. See Chen Daqi, *Ming-li luncong* (Taipei: Zhengzhong, 1960), 216–20.

Xunzi's occasional insistence on the "unity of *li* and *yi*" *(li yi zhi tong)*. The co-occurrence of *li* and *yi* poses an obstacle to explicating this unity in a coherent way. On this difficulty, Wei proposes what I call the delimitation thesis.

According to Wei, in coupling *li* with *yi*, it is the desire of Xunzi "to use *yi* to prescribe or fix the boundary (or the scope) of *li*."[38] In general, when we find *yi* in *Xunzi*, these occurrences of *yi* belong to what is "objectively significant." Says Wei, "Xunzi uses the objective significance of *yi* in order to specify the *li* which he honors." Consequently, when Xunzi speaks of the "unity of *li* and *yi*," the *li* represent something objective. Moreover, Xunzi also wants to use *"li* to complete the manifestation of *yi.*"[39] Wei also draws our attention to cases in which *li* is often used in the same context where *fa* (law) occurs, in order to emphasize the objective, as contrasted with the subjective, point of view stressed by Mencius.

Wei has indeed offered us a challenging view. The stress on the unity of *li* and *yi (li yi zhi tong)* clearly points to a conceptual distinction and connection. In this manner, it paves the way for the formulation of the completion thesis. Of more immediate interest, his point that *li* and *yi* are mutually dependent notions does clearly indicate that we are dealing with two distinct notions. The problem of the co-occurrence of *li* and *yi* is basically a problem of appreciating Xunzi's recurrent concern with objective standards and problems that arise out of man's commerce with an external world of nature and society. Unfortunately, we find in Wei no elaboration of the delimitation thesis. In the first place, it is unclear how *yi* is supposed to fix the boundary of *li*, or how *li* is supposed "to complete it." By merely pointing to the "objective significance of *yi*," we get no guide to locating this significance. Moreover, it can equally be said that the *li*, quite independent of the problem of co-occurrence, also have an "objective significance," if this term is used to refer to the concern with objective standards of conduct. So construed, Wei's thesis is no more plausible than the functional-equivalence thesis.

In the second place, if we grant that both *li* and *yi* have objective significance, and, if I am correct in regarding them as distinct focal notions, that is, if they have distinct ethical foci, they consequently differ in what may be termed the direction of semantic stress. Thus, while both *li* and *yi* can be regarded as referring to something objectively significant (that is, to objective requirements external to the individual), they differ, so to speak, in their vectorial character. Otherwise, *li* and *yi*

---

38. Wei, *Xunzi yu gudai zhexue*, 7.
39. Ibid., 7–8.

The Problem of Conceptual Unity 109

would be extensionally equivalent, that is, have the same referent. *Li* focuses on a set of ritual rules; *yi* on what is right and reasonable. The objectivity of *li* lies in the existence of a set of established standards of conduct; the objectivity of *yi*, however, lies in the impartiality *(gong)* of reasoned judgment and conduct. The former sort of objectivity has no connection with *yi* as involving impartiality.[40] In other words, Wei's delimitation thesis, without further elaboration and argument, does not help us in understanding *li* and *yi* as distinct aretaic notions, although one must admit that his delimitation thesis justly points to the intimate connection between *li* and *yi*, and to the completion thesis.[41]

1.3 Subsumption

For a philosophical scholar inclined toward logical empiricism, the subsumption thesis represents a viable approach. The initial attraction lies in its merit of simplicity, in the possibility of *reducing* all sentences involving aretaic terms into one that contains the key aretaic term. In this way the subsumption thesis provides a perspective for dealing with a variety of apparently unconnected remarks of Xunzi. This approach seems justified in terms of the logical significance of Xunzi's essay on rectifying terms *(zhengming pian)*. Some scholars claimed that in Xunzi one finds the distinction of deductive, inductive, and analogical inferences. As I have shown elsewhere, this claim has meager textual support. It is more a product of logical speculation than systematic reconstruction. More plausible is the attribution to Xunzi of a kind of doctrine of informal logic that focuses on standards of competence in ethical argumentation rather than on the validity of arguments proffered in support of ethical judgments.[42]

It is difficult to find a well-articulated subsumption thesis. Such a thesis, however, is suggested by Dubs.[43] In concluding his chapter on *ren*

---

40. In raising my difficulties, I follow Wei's use of the term "objective" as contrasted with "subjective." While there are difficulties in explicating this distinction, Wei's use does serve to bring out the sorts of issues involved in his delimitation view.

41. Curiously, in his appreciative essay on Li Gou, Wei suggests the subsumption thesis. See Wei Zhengtong, *Zhongguo zhexue sixiang pipan* (Taipei: Buffalo Book, 1981), 174; and Wei, *Zhongguo zhexue sixiang shih* (Taipei: Dalin, 1980), vol. 2, 994.

42. See Cua, *Ethical Argumentation*. For ascription to Xunzi of different types of inference, see, e.g., Chen, *Xunzi xueshuo*, 96–99; Zhou, *Xunzi yaoyi*, 178; You You, *Zhongguo mingxue* (Taipei: Zhengzhong, 1959), 41–42; Wang Tianji, *Zhongguo luoqi sixiang shi* (Shanghai: Renwen, 1979), 152–53; and Xia Zhentao, *Lun Xunzi de zhexue sixiang* (Shanghai: Renwen, 1979), 216–17.

43. See also Henry Rosemont, "State and Society in the *Hsün Tzu*: A Philosophical Commentary," *Monumenta Serica* 29 (1970–71): 74; and also Wei, *Zhongguo zhexue sixiang shih*, vol. 2, 994.

and *li*, Dubs says, "*Li* for Hsüntze [Xunzi] embraces the whole of virtue and of all metaphysical principles. Other ethical or metaphysical concepts are but expressions of one aspect of *Li*. Yet he does not usually use this word in this broad sense, but in a more restricted one, and puts another ethical concept with it to complete its meaning [*ren* or *yi*]." Of greater relevance to our problem of conceptual unity, Dubs maintains: "*Li* is the chief virtue, and really the whole of virtue. Frequently in his writings he combines another with it to emphasize one aspect of the whole; usually, it is *Li* and *Yi*, or *Li* and music, sometimes *Li* alone; but *Li* is so developed that *it includes within itself the constituent elements of . . . other virtues.*"[44]

I shall not here inquire into the complex question whether Dubs is correct in claiming that *li* includes ethical as well as metaphysical principles, except by remarking that a plausible alternative interpretation is available without recourse to the notion of principle and metaphysical considerations.[45] My concern is Dubs's subsumption thesis that *li*, presumably in some broad rather than narrow sense, "includes within itself the constituent elements of . . . other virtues." For proper assessment, let me first inquire whether there is ground for the distinction between broad and narrow senses of terms in the *Xunzi*. On this question, we do find what appears to be a relevant distinction between two kinds of terms: *gongming* and *bieming*. Dubs himself does not invoke this distinction, but the plausibility of his subsumption thesis may be said to be grounded in an interpretation of such a distinction. As we shall later see, Li Gou's formulation of a version of the subsumption thesis explicitly rests on an interpretation of Xunzi's distinction.

Let me consider the passage on *gongming* and *bieming* in the light of Dubs's translation, which clearly offers a possible basis for Dubs's own distinction between the broad and narrow senses of *li*. Dubs's translation runs:

44. Dubs, *Hsüntze*, 154, 133; emphasis added.
45. See A. S. Cua, "Dimensions of *Li:* Reflections on an Aspect of Hsün Tzu's Ethics," *Philosophy East and West* 29, no. 4 (1979). I cannot forbear to observe that there is difficulty in accepting Dubs's thesis that "moral concepts are *ipso facto* metaphysical concepts, and vice versa." The only passage Dubs invoked is this: "*Li* is that whereby Heaven and Earth unite . . . whereby the stars move in their course, whereby all things prosper, whereby love and hatred are tempered" (Dubs, *Hsüntze*, 52, Dubs's ellipses). This passage, I believe, can be construed as exaltation to *li*, a way in which Xunzi expresses his respect for *li* as a ritual code. In Xunzi's term, it is a way of expressing *longli*. We sometimes find passages involving *tian* (Heaven), suggesting some notion of the will of Heaven that contradicts Xunzi's naturalistic view on *tian* in his essay of *tian (tianlun pian)* (for example, *xing'e* L550, D311, W165). These passages, from the point of view of coherent explication, are best construed, like the one of *li*, as emotive rather than cognitive expressions. For other interpretations, see Liang Ch'i-hsiung [Liang Qixiong], "A Descriptive Review of Hsün Tzu's

For although all things are manifold, there are times when we wish to speak of them all, so we call them "things." "Things" is the most general term *(gongming)*. We press on *(tui)* and generalize *(gong)* and generalize still more; then only we stop. There are times when we wish to speak of one aspect *(pian)*,[46] so we may say "birds and beasts." "Birds and beasts" is the greatest classifying term *(bieming)*. We press on *(tui)* and classify *(bie)*; we classify and classify still more, until there is no more classification to be made, and then we stop. (*zhengming* L515–16, D286)

Evidently Dubs's translation of Xunzi's distinction is an interpretation that implicitly presupposes the truth of certain assumptions. By rendering *gongming* as "general term" and *bieming* as "classifying term," it is assumed that both *gongming* and *bieming* are class terms. So construed, the relation between *gongming* and *bieming* is arguably subsumptive, that is, we have an example of class inclusion. In other words, *gongming*, as a class term, has a number of *bieming* as subclasses. The truth of this assumption of class inclusion cannot be denied without denying that both *gongming* and *bieming* are class terms. I accept this assumption as plausible, since the alternative to this interpretation would render the whole passage obscure. There is, however, a question on Dubs's rendering of *gongming* as general term and *bieming* as classifying term. For this further assumes that Xunzi, in the present passage, is expounding a view on classification and generalization. And from this reading, it is easy to ascribe to Xunzi the distinction between deduction and induction as suggested by some recent writers.[47] This assumption, however, depends on the proper construal of *gong, tui,* and *bie*. There is ground to think that Dubs's translation of these terms rests on dubious and implausible assumptions. However, there is a prior issue on the subject matter of this passage. The solution of this issue, I believe, provides us a way of understanding *gong, tui,* and *bie*.

As I read the passage, I take what Xunzi says to be concerned with neither generalization nor classification, but with the *formation* of class terms. In the abstract, one relation between class terms may be viewed as class inclusion. But this has no relevance to the problem of the formation of class terms. In the passage preceding the present one, Xunzi points out that terms are formed on the basis of observation of similarities and differences. Things that are similar, after comparison and selective decision, are *grouped* together. *Gong*, in the verbal sense in our passage, suggests grouping things into kinds *(lei)*, not generalizing. Thus, a

---

Thought," *Chinese Studies in Philosophy* 6, no. 1 (1974): 15–16. [For a later discussion of *tian*, see Essay 6 of this volume.]

46. Read *pian* for *bian*.

47. See note 42 above, and Li Disheng's annotation, L517.

gongming may be rendered as a *generic term* rather than a general term. For a *bieming*, being a class term, is also a general term. The distinction between *gongming* and *bieming*, in my judgment, is a distinction between two kinds of general or class terms, and not between general and classifying terms. A generic term, much like a generic drug, is a term descriptive of a kind or group as a whole. Thus, the formation of a *gongming* is an outcome of the activity of grouping things together. *Bie*, in the verbal sense in our passage, refers to the activity of making distinctions or distinguishing between things. As for *bieming*, we may thus render it as a *specific term* in contrast with *gongming* as a generic term. A *bieming* may be said to be an outcome of the activity of specification, since specification involves making clear distinction of details or ingredients of a thing at issue. In the formation of *gongming*, one attends to *similarities* between actualities *(shi);* in the formation of *bieming*, one attends to the *differences* between actualities.

Xunzi describes both the activities of grouping and distinguishing as *tui*. *Tui*, in a literary sense, is "to push or to extend." According to our passage, when one pushes upward, one gets a *gongming;* when one pushes downward, one gets a *bieming*. There are thus two different sorts of *tui*, which, in conceptual analysis, may be called "semantic ascent" and "semantic descent."[48] A *gongming* may thus be alternatively described as a term that is produced by semantic ascent, a *bieming*, a term that is produced by semantic descent. Whether we embark upon semantic ascent or descent, as Xunzi explicitly states, depends on what we wish to accomplish. The distinction between *gongming* and *bieming* (henceforth, generic and specific terms) is thus a distinction relative to purposes and does not rest on any theory concerning the intrinsic character of terms or essential attributes of things. Xunzi, as is well known, is a conventionalist with respect to terms. In his words, "terms in themselves have no intrinsic appropriateness. It is agreement that determines their actuality. When the agreement is settled and customary practice developed, then they may be said to possess actuality" (*zhengming* L521, W147*). To employ a contemporary terminology: Both generic and specific terms are, for Xunzi, nominal rather than natural-kind terms.[49]

We can also render *tui* in the sense of semantic extension, that is, as pertaining to the scope of application of terms. The difference between generic and specific terms may thus be described as a difference in the broader or narrower scope of application of terms. Watson's translation

---

48. I borrow the term "semantic ascent" from Quine without attributing to him my interpretation; "semantic descent" is of my own coinage.

49. See Stephen P. Schwartz, ed., *Naming, Necessity, and Natural Kinds* (Ithaca, N.Y.: Cornell University Press, 1977), Introduction, 39.

of our passage, I believe, is based on this plausible interpretation (*zhengming* L515–16, W143–44). Since the extension of the scope of application of a term depends on one's current purpose, it is this purpose, informed by empirical observation and decision, that provides the rationale. As Xunzi reminds us, "A man who is good at learning is one who exhausts the rationales of things" (*jin qi li*) (*dalüe* L623).

If the foregoing interpretation of *gongming* and *bieming* as generic and specific terms is deemed acceptable and plausible, it is a viable alternative to Dubs's general and classifying terms. Thus Xunzi's distinction does not provide a firm ground for the formulation of Dubs's subsumption thesis. Even if we follow Dubs's distinction between general and classifying terms, it is doubtful that one can distinguish the broad from the narrow sense of *li* without an explicit stipulation that Li Gou provides concerning the broad sense of *li*. Supposing that we follow Dubs in saying that *li* in the broad sense "includes within itself the constituent elements of . . . other virtues," then we may justly presume that *li* is a class term which contains subclasses such as *ren* and *yi*. But Dubs offers us no evidence or explanation of the sense in which *ren* and *yi* are subclasses of *li*. However, in the same passage, Dubs also suggests that his view has to do with *aspects* of *li*. If this is so, we have a version of the completion thesis; but this would be incompatible with his claim that *li* is "the chief virtue." For "chief virtue" suggests that other virtues are subordinated to *li* in perhaps some hierarchical fashion. Dubs's claim that *li*, in the broad sense, "includes" all other virtues may be taken in this subsumptive fashion, but I am far from certain that this is his considered view. For when he turns to the problem of the co-occurrence of *li* and *yi*, what he says, presumably on *li* in the narrow sense, is this: ". . . in Hsüntze's [Xunzi's] teaching *Yi* is not definitely marked off from *Li*; *Li* also partook of the character of *Yi*."[50] But then we are not told what *li* is in the narrow sense, as what *li* is in the broad sense. One also wonders: Assuming that there is such a distinction between two senses of *li*, does *li* in the broad sense "include" *li* in the narrow sense? What is this "inclusion" anyway? Obviously, it cannot be class inclusion. I find, therefore, that Dubs's solution to the problem of conceptual unity is extremely tenuous, mainly for lack of a clear explanation of the distinction he uses, and the vagueness of his various remarks relevant to our problem. Nevertheless, some version of a subsumption thesis is suggested. But as compared with Li Gou's, this version is highly implausible, as we shall see in section 2.

50. Dubs, *Hsüntze*, 157.

1.4 Completion

Wei, as we have seen, has suggested a holistic approach in his remark that *li* "completes the manifestation of *yi*," but his discussion is devoted to the problem of the co-occurrence of *li* and *yi* and not to the problem of conceptual unity. Dubs makes a similar suggestion: that *li*, in the restricted sense, is completed by other terms. The completion thesis, roughly, may be described as the thesis that *ren*, *li*, and *yi* are, in some sense to be elaborated, interdependent notions. Again, like the subsumption thesis, it is difficult to find an articulate exposition. We have more of a *suggestion* than an elaboration in Zhou's brief remarks. According to Zhou, "*ren* is the foundation *(ben)* of various virtues. *Yi* is the means to the practice of *ren*, and *li* is the means to the practice of *yi*." Put differently, "*Ren* is the foundation *(ben)* of *yi*, and *yi* is the foundation of *li*."[51] Without further explanation, Zhou cites a number of passages in support of his two statements. But these statements do not appear to have identical import.

The first statement pertains to means-end relation, the second to "the foundation of foundations," suggesting more a subsumption than a completion thesis. Since he offers neither elaboration nor argument, it is difficult to conjecture what he has in mind. However, his first statement can be construed along the holistic line if we regard the means at issue in the *constitutive* rather than in the instrumental sense.[52] Given *dao* as the ideal of a good human life on the whole, *ren*, *li*, and *yi* are the constitutive means to its actualization. In other words, the actualization of *dao* requires the co-satisfaction of the requirements expressed in *ren*, *li*, and *yi*. Since these three focal notions pertain to different foci of ethical interest, we may also say that the actualization of *dao* requires a *coordination* of three equally important centers of ethical interest. The connection between these foci is one of *interdependence* rather than subordination. Thus, in the ideal case, *ren*, *li*, and *yi* are mutually support-

---

51. Zhou, *Xunzi yaoyi*, 65.

52. The terms in this distinction are Lau's. While this distinction is introduced by Lau to explicate Mencius's notion of *dao*, I believe that it also applies to Xunzi. Actually, Lau's distinction, except for terminological difference, seems akin to a distinction familiar in contemporary ethical theory: *contributory and instrumental values*, incisively discussed by Lewis. I prefer Lau's term, but I shall also use the latter term to explicate the notion of constitutive means. This use of Lau's terminology does not commit me to his further claim that in some sense all constitutive means are unique, or to his analysis of Mencius's argument relative to, say, the famous case of the drowning sister-in-law—a topic discussed without the use of Lau's distinction in my *Dimensions of Moral Creativity*, chap. 5. For Lau, see Appendix 5 in D. C. Lau, *Mencius: Translated with an Introduction* (Middlesex, England: Penguin Books, 1970), 245; and C. I. Lewis, *An Analysis of Knowledge and Valuation* (La Salle, Ill.: Open Court, 1946), chap. 16.

ive and adherent to the same ideal *(dao)*. When *dao* is in fact realized, *ren, li,* and *yi* would be deemed constituents of this condition of achievement. This may be said to be a retrospective view of moral achievement. When, on the other hand, one attends to the prospect of *dao*-realization, then *ren, li,* and *yi* would be regarded as complementary foci and means to *dao* as the end-in-view. In this way, we can state the completion thesis as follows: *Ren, li,* and *yi* are complementary foci of human interest directed toward *dao*-realization. The problem of conceptual unity is thus ultimately a problem of systematically explicating the nature of the interdependence of these aretaic notions in a way that admits of theoretical assessment. That these notions are interdependent is clear in the following passage, which Zhou partially cites in support of his view:

Ren is love. . . . *Yi* is accord with reason *(yi li ye)*. . . . The *li* are rules and regulations. . . . If one extends benevolent affection *(tui'en)* without reason, one cannot realize the objective of *ren*. If one follows reason without regard to rules and regulation, one cannot realize the objective of *yi*. If one has a clear understanding of rules and regulations but is unable to act in harmony with others, he cannot realize the objective of *li*. When one's inner harmony is not expressed, he cannot realize the objective of music. Hence, it is said, "*ren, li, yi* and music, in terms of their destination, constitute a unity." A *junzi* abides by *ren* and acts in accord with *yi* before he considers himself to have fulfilled the requirement of *ren;* he acts in accord with *yi* with due regard to *li* before he considers himself to have fulfilled the requirements of *yi;* he regulates his conduct by *li* and returns to the foundation [that is, *ren* and *yi*] before he considers himself to have fulfilled the requirements of *li*. When a person has a clear comprehension of the interconnection among these three things [that is, *ren, yi,* and *li*], he can then be considered to be a man of *dao*. (*dalüe* L605–6)

This passage clearly points to *ren, li,* and *yi* as interdependent aretaic notions, that is, that each of these notions cannot be rendered intelligible without involving the others.

Summing up, the four theses examined in this section have their respective contribution to make to the problem of conceptual unity. The functional-equivalence thesis justly draws our attention to the common aim of *li* and *yi*. The delimitation thesis is valuable in suggesting an important insight for further inquiry. The co-occurrence of *li* and *yi* can be viewed as having a twofold significance: that the *li*, as a set of formal prescriptions, are the *right sort of rules* for governing human conduct, and that the *right application* of these rules depends on reasonable men sensitive to the changing circumstances of human life. The latter point may well be intended by Wei when he insists that *yi* fixes the scope of the application of *li*. As for the subsumption thesis, I have expressed my great reservation, but the possibility of a viable version like that of Li Gou—to be examined next—offers a great challenge. On the whole, I am inclined toward some version of the completion thesis. But the plausibility of such a completion thesis depends on systematic exposition.[53]

2. LI GOU'S SUBSUMPTION THESIS

The problem of conceptual unity in Xunzi, as we have seen, can be resolved on internal grounds along the holistic line. The completion thesis, I believe, can be plausibly developed quite in the spirit of classical Confucian ethics. Such a problem, from our perspective today, is a serious one for any Confucian philosopher. When we turn back to Li Gou (1009–1059), we can appreciate even better the task of developing a coherent response to the problem. In attending to his conception of *li*, we find a challenging version of a subsumption thesis and speculate the reason for the neglect of his thought by subsequent philosophers, particularly by Song and Ming Confucians. The subsumption thesis of Li Gou is incompatible with their holistic vision of *dao* or *ren*. Whether or not this speculation is sound is a question that can be explored in intellectual history. My aim in this section centers primarily on Li Gou as a respondent to Xunzi's problem, rather than on his status within the history of Chinese thought.[54]

Of special interest is the probability of Xunzi's influence on Li Gou's formulation of the subsumption thesis.[55] As a matter of fact, Li Gou's essay on *li (lilun)* can be read as a critical commentary on an important as-

---

53. A sketch of a systematic approach along holistic lines is given in the concluding section of my *Ethical Argumentation*. In this approach, *dao* is viewed as a generic term, and *ren*, *li*, and *yi* as specific terms. Since the completion of *Ethical Argumentation* in 1982, I have discovered Li Gou with a great deal of surprise and admiration. For Li Gou made use of a similar distinction from *Xunzi*, i.e., *gongming* and *bieming* (generic and specific terms), in developing a challenging version of the subsumption thesis. Thus, the present essay is a preliminary exploration of the problem of conceptual unity toward a systematic exposition of my own version of the completion thesis. [For a later discussion of this thesis in Confucian ethics general, see *Moral Vision and Tradition*, Essay 12, or "Confucian Philosophy, Chinese," in *Routledge Encyclopedia of Philosophy* (London: Routledge, 1999).

54. For a high valuation of Li Gou's status, see Hu Shi, "Ji Li Gou de xueshuo," in *Hu Shi wencun*, vol. 2 (Taipei: Yuandong, n.d.), 28; Wei, *Zhongguo zhexue sixiang pipan*, 167. But for a lower and just valuation, see Shan-yuan Hsieh, *The Life and Thought of Li Kou, 1009–1059* (San Francisco: Chinese Materials Center, 1979), 205–11.

55. The titles of some essays of Li Gou remind us of those of Xunzi, e.g., *lilun*, *fuguo ce*, and *qiangbing*. For an examination of similarity of content, see Hsieh, *Li Kou*, 84–85 n. My references to Li Gou's seven essays on *li* are taken from *Li Taibo xiansheng quanji* (Taipei: Wenhai, 1971), vol. 1, Quan [Book] 1. Citation in the text of this paper will follow the page numbers in this volume.

pect of Xunzi's ethical theory.[56] His formulation of the subsumption thesis, in my view, represents an interpretation of Xunzi's distinction between *gongming* (generic terms) and *bieming* (specific terms), though he uses the term *zongming* (collective term) rather than *gongming*. This terminological substitution reflects, as I shall argue, a change in theoretical orientation rather than a mere linguistic innovation. And significantly, for Li Gou, *li* is the key notion in Confucian ethics. The following account focuses on his subsumption thesis rather than on its detailed elaboration.

According to Li Gou, "*li* is an abstract label *(xucheng)*; it is the collective term *(zongming)* of all laws and institutions *(fazhi)*" (*lilun*, 192). Since all laws and institutions involve rules, we may understand Li Gou's succinct statement as a statement on the *rule-like* character of all ethical standards. If this interpretation is plausible, we have here a conception of *li* as a focal notion that attends exclusively to all rules governing conduct, *except* that now in Li Gou, a focal notion is transformed into one that has a *nuclear sense* that can be used as a basis for explication of aretaic notions.[57] Li Gou attends to five such aretaic notions. In his view, *li* as a collective term has four *bieming* and three branches *(zhi)*. The *bieming* of *li* are *ren*, *yi*, wisdom, and trustworthiness *(xin)*; the three branches are music, government, and punishment (*lilun*, 174). For explication, I shall retain "specific term" for *bieming*. Before we attend to Li Gou's explanation of these specific terms of *li*, let us consider the relation between Xunzi's distinction between generic and specific terms *(gongming* and *bieming)* and Li Gou's distinction between collective *(zongming)* and specific terms *(bieming)*.

Earlier in this article, we saw that Xunzi's distinction was entirely relative to current purposes (section 1.3 above). There is no suggestion that his distinction is to be taken as a categorial distinction or theoretical dichotomy. In fact, a term may be generic with respect to another term and yet can function as a specific term relative to still another term. Thus, the distinction is relative to the purpose occasioned by the need to group or to specify. Li Gou's distinction, on the contrary, is a categorial distinction that serves a theoretical purpose. His distinction, if accepted by Confucian thinkers, does offer a systematic way of organizing the complex ethical vocabulary inherited from the *Analects*. Of course, Xunzi's distinction can be employed in a theoretical way, as I have attempted to do in my explication of the different dimensions of *li*

---

56. See Wei, *Zhongguo zhexue sixiang pipan*, 168; and Wei, *Zhongguo zhexue sixiang shi*, vol. 2, 984–96.
57. See J. L. Austin, "The Meaning of a Word," in *Philosophical Papers* (Oxford: Oxford University Press, 1961), 39.

and ethical argumentation.[58] Perhaps, for this reason, Li Gou needs to substitute the collective term *(zongming)* for Xunzi's generic term *(gongming)*. But his retention of the specific term *(bieming)* raises a question on the relation between collective and specific terms. In particular, one can justly query the sense in which *ren, yi*, wisdom, and trustworthiness are said to be specific terms of *li*.

Li Gou offers us this explanation: Within *li* there are certain matters that can be designated by specific terms. *Ren*, as a specific term, stands for "gentleness, sincerity, and extensive love"; *yi* for "decisive judgment *(duanjue)* that is appropriate (to the situation at hand)"; "wisdom" for "the clarity of thought *(shuda)*[59] and the ability to make plans"; and "trustworthiness" for "firm and unchanging adherence (to one's commitment and duties)" *(lilun* 177). This explanation of specific terms is not very clear, but it can be explicated in this way. The specific terms constitute specifications of the different objects *(wu)* or the purposes and intentions that underlie the system of laws and regulations promulgated in the three branches (that is, music, government, and punishment). Conversely, the significance of these objects cannot be appreciated without the existence of laws and regulations *(fazhi)*. In Li Gou's words, "without these objects *(wu)*, we cannot understand the existence of laws and regulations. [Likewise,] without these laws and regulations, one cannot understand [the significance of] *ren, yi*, wisdom, and trustworthiness" *(lilun,* 197). In *li*, there is a mutual dependency relation between its specific terms and the three branches of music, government, and punishment.

Li Gou's conception of the dependency of laws and regulations on the specific terms or objects of *li* is quite in line with the spirit of Confucian ethics. For I understand this conception to embody the idea that the existence of any system of rules requires justification, at least in terms of the ethical notions of *ren* and *yi*. Li Gou's conception of *ren* as embracing extensive love is a familiar Confucian theme, if it is construed as involving distinction in various human relationships *(lilun,* 176). However, in conceiving the dependence of *ren* and *yi* on laws and regulations, Li Gou has radically departed from classical Confucian ethics and from the later development of Song and Ming Confucianism. For in conceiving this dependence, apart from the elevation of *li* into a key notion, an acceptance of Li Gou's theory in effect amounts to the acceptance of some version of the subsumption thesis—a thesis that

58. See "Dimensions of *Li*" and *Ethical Argumentation*. It must be noted that although I have used Xunzi's distinction in my philosophical reconstruction of his ethical theory, I have not used the distinction in the categorial fashion evident in Li Gou's own distinction.

59. I read *shuda* in the sense of *shutong*, i.e., perspicuity.

is congenial to the rule theories of ethics in Western moral philosophy, particularly to rule-utilitarianism.

Li Gou seems to accept without question the classical Confucian vocabulary that focuses on five main aretaic notions *(ren, yi, li, zhi,* and *xin)*. However, in conceiving these notions to be rule-governed, Li Gou is urging that four of these notions can in some sense be *subsumed* under *li*. But in this subsumption the notion of *li* as a collective term no longer depends on *ren* or *yi*, as we have earlier seen in discussing the completion thesis (section 1.4 above). Moreover, in Li Gou, this subsumption does not take the hierarchical route, as suggested by Dubs (section 1.3 above). Rather, we have a kind of reductionism, as I have characterized the subsumption thesis. For his conception of the dependence of *ren* and *yi* on laws and regulations amounts to a reductionist claim: that any expression of *ren* and *yi* must be governed by rules. Formally, Li Gou's thesis may be stated thus: Aretaic sentences are intelligible if, and only if, they can be explicated in sentences that involve the use of the notion of rule. This thesis is reductionist in the sense of logical empiricism. In the material mode of speech, we may say that any virtue or virtuous disposition cannot be considered to be ethically significant, unless it is manifested in a manner that signifies rule compliance.

If I have not misunderstood Li Gou's conception of *li* as a collective term *(zongming)* for laws and regulations, his conception cannot be acceptable to Xunzi, and more importantly to his younger contemporaries like Cheng Hao and Cheng Yi, and later to Zhu Xi. For an acceptance of Li Gou's subsumption thesis would require the rejection of their holistic vision.[60] In relation to Xunzi, as we have seen in section 1.3 above, the subsumption thesis cannot be considered to be a viable interpretation. But in Li Gou's version, we have a challenging formulation of a subsumption thesis that threatens to undermine the standard Confucian preoccupation with the development of moral character that focuses on personal effort and merits rather than on rule responsibility. Were Li Gou's conception of *li* as a collective term accepted by Confucians, it would involve a radical transformation of an ethics of virtues into an ethics of rules or principles. From the point of view of plausible explication of Confucian moral philosophy, Li Gou's version of the sub-

---

60. For this holistic vision, see Cua, "Practical Causation and Confucian Ethics" and "Confucian Vision and Experience of the World," in *Philosophy East and West* 25, no. 1 and no. 3 (1975); "Chinese Moral Vision, Responsive Agency, and Factual Beliefs," *Journal of Chinese Philosophy* 7, no. 1 (1980); and "Harmony and the Neo-Confucian Sage," *Philosophical Inquiry: An International Quarterly* 5, nos. 2–3 (1983). For the first essay, see Essay 9 of this volume. For the last three essays, see *Moral Vision and Tradition,* Essays 2, 4, and 7.

sumption thesis has great merit in presenting a challenge to anyone inclined toward the holistic vision of either Zhu Xi or Wang Yangming, which clearly suggests different versions of the completion thesis.[61] The critical development of Confucian ethical thought must involve a careful discussion of the issues that divide Li Gou's subsumption thesis and the various versions of completion thesis, including the one that I have proposed for Xunzi.[62]

61. See A. S. Cua, *The Unity of Knowledge and Action: A Study in Wang Yang-ming's Moral Psychology* (Honolulu: University Press of Hawaii, 1982), chap. 4.
62. Early versions of this paper were presented at the Columbia University Seminar in Neo-Confucian Studies, April 5, 1984, and at the First World Congress in Chinese Philosophy, Taipei, Taiwan, August 20–25, 1984.

Essay 5
THE UNITY OF VIRTUES

One major legacy of the *Lunyu (The Analects)* is a complex ethical vocabulary for the assessment of personal character and conduct. In addition to terms for central notions of virtue *(de)*, i.e., *ren* (humanity), *li* (propriety), and *yi* (rightness), the vocabulary contains a large number of terms for particular virtues, such as filiality, trustworthiness, loyalty, considerateness, uprightness, courage, respectfulness, friendliness, and integrity. While it appears unproblematic to construe terms for particular virtues as varying expressions, in appropriate contexts, of the concern for *ren*, *li*, and *yi*, there is a problem of the conceptual unity of these central notions of virtue. For dealing with this problem in the *Lunyu*, we are indebted to the works of Chen Daqi. Chen's rigorous and systematic study is perhaps the most brilliant and comprehensive reconstruction of the teaching of Confucius.[1] However, as his own extensive writings on Xunzi and Mencius have shown,[2] such a reconstruction, without modification, cannot be considered an adequate account of the subsequent employment of these central notions in the history of Confucian thought.[3] Moreover, from the point of view of the critical development of Confucian ethics as an autonomous ethics of virtue, Xunzi provides us

---

1. See Chen Daqi, *Kongzi xueshuo* (Taipei: Zhengzhong, 1977, 1st ed. 1964). Also worthy of attention are Chen's earlier and later works such as *Kongzi xueshuo lunji* (Taipei: Zhengzhong, 1958); *Qianjian ji* (Taipei: Zhonghua, 1968); *Kongzi yanlun guantong ji* (Taipei: Shangwu, 1982); along with his more general work *Pingfan de daode guan* (Taipei: Zhonghua, 1977, 2nd ed.); and articles reprinted in Chen Daqi et al., *Kongzi sixiang yanjiu lunji*, vol. 2 (Taipei: Liming, 1983). For an informative account of Chen Daqi's contributions to Chinese philosophy, see Vincent Shen, "Chen Daqi (Ch'en Ta-ch'i)," in *Encyclopedia of Chinese Philosophy*, ed. Antonio S. Cua (New York and London: Routledge, 2003).

2. Chen Daqi, *Xunzi xueshuo* (Taipei: Zhonghua wenhua she, 1954); *Mengzi daijie lu* (Taipei: Shangwu, 1980); and articles reprinted in Hua Zhonglin et al., *Rujia sixiang yanjiu lunji*, vol. 2 (Taipei: Li-ming, 1983). Like the ones cited in the preceding note, these works deserve attention for the insights they offer to plausible explication.

3. For *ren*, see W. T. Chan, "The Evolution of the Confucian Concept *Jen*," *Philosophy East and West* 4, no. 4 (1955), and "Chinese and Western Interpretations of *Jen* (Humanity)," *Journal of Chinese Philosophy* 2, no. 2 (1975).

a better source for reconstruction. There is, in Xunzi, an explicit concern with rational coherence in ethical discourse, in particular an emphasis on the unity of *ren, li,* and *yi*. Also, with respect to his conception of the unity of these basic notions, different interpretations have been proposed, indicating possible lines of approach to our problem.

In a recent paper, I examined four different interpretations, including one proposed by Chen Daqi, and argued for the plausibility of what I called the completion thesis.[4] This thesis maintains that *ren, li,* and *yi* are distinct but interdependent notions. I suggested that for systematic explication, due attention must be paid to the challenge of some version of the subsumption thesis akin to that of Li Gou. This thesis maintains that *li* is the key notion that, in some sense, contains *ren* and *yi* as components. In my book on Xunzi's moral epistemology, I gave a brief sketch of the completion thesis based on Xunzi's distinction between generic and specific terms *(gongming* and *bieming)*.[5] According to this view, *dao* (i.e., *dao* of man as contrasted with the *dao* of Heaven *[tian])*,[6] the telos of ethical argumentation, is a generic term for the notion of the good human life that has its fundamentally distinct but connected specification in *ren, li,* and *yi*. In this paper, I offer a partial explication of this thesis. After a characterization of the thesis by focusing on the holistic character of *dao,* with *ren, li,* and *yi* as expressive of its distinctive and connected aspects (section 1), I propose a scheme for the analysis of *yi* in order to elucidate further the distinction and connection between *li* and *yi* (section 2) and conclude with some remarks on two important problems that deserve further exploration (section 3).

1. THE THREAD OF 'DAO'

The key to the explication of the completion thesis lies in Xunzi's notion of *dao*. While Xunzi sometimes uses *dao* in a value-neutral sense, describing, say, the different ways of life of the people, on the whole, it is used in the evaluative sense, conveying the notion of an ideal way of life, a standard governing thought, decision, and action.[7] In his words,

---

4. A. S. Cua, "The Problem of Conceptual Unity in Hsün Tzu and Li Kou's Solution," Proceedings of the First World Conference in Chinese Philosophy, *Bulletin of The Chinese Philosophical Association,* vol. 3 (1985): 469–95; or *Philosophy East and West* 39, no. 2 (1989): 115–34 [incorporated as Essay 4 in this volume].

5. A. S. Cua, *Ethical Argumentation: A Study in Hsün Tzu's Moral Epistemology* (Honolulu: University of Hawaii Press, 1985), 160–63. For the distinction between generic and specific terms, see 44–47 and 76–79.

6. See *ruxiao* L131, D96.

7. For parallel distinction and a good discussion of relevant passages, see Chen, *Xunzi xueshuo,* 68–69.

"*dao* is the proper standard *(zhengquan)* for past and present. He who deviates from *dao* does not understand wherein fortune and misfortune lie" (*zhengming* L531, W153*, D297).[8] As an ideal way of life, *dao* provides a unifying perspective for evaluating human life as a whole. In this sense, *dao* is basically a holistic notion. It has many aspects, but an exclusive attention to one aspect may lead to an obscuration *(bi)* of other aspects, thus producing different sorts of delusion *(huo)*.[9] Accordingly, a *junzi* or morally superior person "knows that what lacks completeness *(quan)* and purity *(cui)* does not deserve commendation *(mei)*. For this reason, he studies the classics in order to discern the thread *(guan)* that runs through them, and engages in reflection in order to comprehend *(tong)* their significance" (*quanxue* L19, W22*). This thread is the thread of *dao (daoguan)*. Understanding this thread consists in having an insight into the interconnection of rationales *(li)* that underlie the diversity of changing circumstances. Says Xunzi, "If a person does not know this thread, he will not be able to respond to changing circumstances of human life" (*tianlun* L379).[10] This notion of *daoguan* quite naturally gives rise to the query on the nature of *dao* and its constitutive elements.

For probing this question, let us consider the following passage, which occurs in a context critical of various philosophers:[11]

Each of these doctrines expresses only one aspect of *dao*. *Dao* embodies constancy *(chang)* and embraces all changes *(bian)*.[12] One cannot adequately characterize its nature by merely attending to one aspect. (*jiebi* L478)[13]

For elucidating the thread of *dao*, we focus on the aspect of *chang* (constancy) as contrasted with *bian* (changes). The contrast between *chang* and *bian*, in Neo-Confucian terminology, represents a contrast between *dao*'s intrinsic nature *(ti)* and its function *(yong)*.[14] The contrast, as Chen

---

8. See also *zhengming* L521, W147, D290; and *jiebi* L482, W127, D266. For *dao* as the standard of ethical discourse, particularly for explanation and justification, see my *Ethical Argumentation*, 51–61.

9. For further discussion, see my *Ethical Argumentation*, 61–65, 143–59.

10. *Bu zhi guan, bu zhi yingbian.* Cf. W87, D183.

11. For example, Mozi is said to exaggerate the importance of utility without understanding the beauty of forms, and Zhuangzi exaggerates the importance of Heaven without understanding human beings. For Xunzi, the minds of those philosophers are obscured *(bi)* or beclouded by exclusive preoccupation with one aspect of *dao* without understanding *dao* as a holistic concept. For further discussion, see *Ethical Argumentation*, 143–59.

12. The original text runs: *"Fu dao zhe tichang er jinbian."*

13. This is an interpretive translation. I have construed *yu* (corner) as referring to an aspect of *dao*. Cf. W126, D265.

14. For further discussion, see my "On the Ethical Significance of *Ti-Yong* Distinction," *Journal of Chinese Philosophy* 29, no. 2 (2002): 163–70.

points out, may be elaborated by three related pairs of distinctions: (1) determinate and indeterminate, (2) enduring and occasional or familiar and unfamiliar, and (3) unity and diversity.[15] *Dao* as a unifying perspective pertains to the first item of the pair, i.e., to *chang* and its function in relation to *bian*. The basic distinction may be theoretically formulated as a distinction between a stable core of ideas or notions and its function in relation to changing circumstances. In this manner, we can paraphrase Xunzi's characterization: "*Dao* embodies a systemic core of notions that can respond to changing circumstances." Or more formally, *dao* is a generic term *(gongming)* that has a number of specifications *(bieming)*. The thread of *dao* points to the interconnection among these specifications.

Given the foregoing we may restate the completion thesis on the unity of virtues: *Ren, li,* and *yi* comprise the systemic core of *dao*. Without this systemic core of notions for specifying its concrete significance, *dao* would be merely an empty and abstract concept.[16] The completeness *(quan)* desired by *junzi* or an ethically superior person is the thread of *dao*. In support for this thesis, we can appeal to the following passage.

> *Ren* is expressed in love ... *Yi* is accord with reason *(li)* ... *Li* is regulation ... If one extends affection without regard to reason, he cannot realize the objective of *ren*. If one acts in accord with reason without paying heed to the requirements of *li*, he cannot realize the objective of *yi*. If one has a clear understanding of regulation, but is unable to act in harmony with others he cannot realize the objective of *li*. ... When a person has a clear comprehension of the interconnection *(tong)* among these three things (i.e., *ren, li, yi*), he can then be considered to be a man of *dao*. (*dalüe* L605–6)[17]

This passage is also important in providing the ground for maintaining that *ren, li,* and *yi* are distinct notions, though, as we shall see in section 2, the connection between *li* and *yi* is far from perspicuous, particularly in light of numerous cases of co-occurrence of *li* and *yi* in Xunzi. For explicating this distinction, let us attend to the question concerning the kind of notions at issue. In the absence of explicit definitions for necessary and/or sufficient conditions for the application of these terms, it is best to construe *ren, li,* and *yi* as focal notions used for conveying dis-

---

15. See Chen's article in Chen et al., *Kongzi sixiang yanjiu lunji*, 33–36.
16. This point is well brought out in Zhou Hongran's *"Yi zhi biaoxian neirong ji qi shijian," Annals of Philosophy* 3 (1965), 148.
17. For some other passages that support the completion thesis, see *A Concordance to Hsün Tzu*, Harvard-Yenching Institute Sinological Index Series, supplement no. 22 (Taipei: Chinese Materials and Research Center, 1966), 3/1/37, 20/8/23, and 45/12/29. Although Xunzi often speaks of the unity of *li* and *yi*, he sometimes stresses the unity of *ren* and *yi*. See, for example, *Concordance*, 8/3/37 and 11/4/55.

tinct, though not unconnected, centers of ethical concern.[18] As a specific term *(bieming)* of *dao, ren* focuses on the love and care for the wellbeing of one's fellows.[19] Xunzi is mainly preoccupied with human welfare, that is, with material resources indispensable to the satisfaction of man's needs.[20] In this positive sense, *ren* is active benevolence. For Xunzi, any good government must enrich the lives of the people *(yumin)* in providing abundant resources for the satisfaction of human needs and desires.[21] Aside from the active promotion of benefits, a man of *ren* is concerned with the prevention of harm. Because of his love for others, a *ren*-person hates to see them as victims of harm *(yibing* L308, W69, D167). In an emphatic tone, Xunzi remarks that a man of *ren* "will not engage in any wrongful conduct *(buyi)*, kill an innocent person, in order to gain allegiance of the whole world" *(wangba* L230).

Unlike *ren*, which focuses on benefit and harm, *li* stresses regulation, i.e., the governance of conduct by rules. In this basic sense, *li* is a set of formal prescriptions, or in Dubs's felicitous term, rules of proper conduct. Because of its predominantly ritual character, *li* can be rendered as ritual rules.[22] As rules of proper conduct, the *li* represent the tradition of ritual code *(lixian)* and delineate quite precisely how one ought to behave on different occasions of human life *(quanxue* L15, W21, D38–39). Thus Xunzi compares the *li* to weights and measures, e.g., to scale, plumb line, T-square, and compass *(wangba* L239).[23] However, the *li* are simply the "markers" of *dao (tianlun* L379, W87),[24] and "state the rules to be followed without explanation" *(quanxue* L14, W20, D38).[25]

The distinction between *ren* and *li*, as specific terms *(bieming)* of *dao*,

---

18. This is the suggestion given in my paper "The Problem of Conceptual Unity in Hsün Tzu and Li Kou's Solution," *Philosophy East and West* 39, no. 2 (1989), or Essay 4 of this volume.

19. See also *yibing* L328, W69, D167.

20. For an incisive discussion of welfare and its limitations, see Nicholas Rescher, *Welfare: The Social Issues in Philosophical Perspective* (Pittsburgh, Pa.: University of Pittsburgh Press, 1972).

21. This is the principal reason for Xunzi's unpopular thesis that man's nature is originally bad. For an explication and defense of this thesis, see A. S. Cua, "The Conceptual Aspect of Hsün Tzu's Philosophy of Human Nature" and "The Quasi-Empirical Aspect of Hsün Tzu's Philosophy of Human Nature," *Philosophy East and West* 27, no. 4 (1977), and 28, no. 1 (1978). [See parts 1 and 2 of Essay 1 in this volume.] For concern with human welfare, see particularly *fuguo pian*.

22. For a more extensive discussion of *li*, see A. S. Cua, "Dimensions of *Li* (Propriety): Reflections on an Aspect of Hsün Tzu's Ethics," *Philosophy East and West* 29, no. 4 (1979), or Essay 2 in this volume; and "*Li* and Moral Justification," *Philosophy East and West* 33, no. 1 (1983), the basis for the appendices to Essay 2 in this volume.

23. See *wangba* L239; *zhishi* L309; and *lilun* L428–29, D224–25, W95.

24. See also *dalüe* L603.

25. See *bugou* L43, *zhishi* L306. For the role of *yi* in ethical justification, see my *Ethical Argumentation*, 65–69 and 78–86.

can thus be regarded as a distinction between ethical motivation and the respect for customary morality. It is *ren* that renders intelligible the respect for the authoritative import of conventional requirements of good behavior. But this respect for customary morality must be rationally determined. In focusing on *yi* as accord with reason, we can properly construe *yi* as a mediating term between *ren* and *li*, though *yi* is also an element of the systemic core of *dao*, that is, the intrinsic nature of *chang* (constancy). But unlike *ren* and *li*, *yi* is a Janus-notion. Relative to *chang*, in the sense of what is familiar, enduring, and determinate, *yi* pertains to the duties that must be performed in normal situations of human relationship and the division of labor in different occupations *(fen)*. But, unlike *ren* and *li*, *yi* is essentially tied to the exercise of reason in coping with the changing circumstances of human life, i.e., to *bian* or the changing aspect of *dao*. Put differently, *ren* and *li*, as specifications *(bieming)* of the concrete significance of *dao* pertain primarily to normal or familiar situations of human intercourse, whereas *yi* focuses primarily on the exercise our rational capacity to deal with the abnormal or exigent situations of human life.[26] Thus Xunzi insists that we must "use *yi* to cope with the changes" *(yiyi bianying)*. In this primary sense, *yi* addresses our sense of what is reasonable and appropriate to particular circumstances.[27]

2. ANALYSIS OF 'YI'

Because of the large number of co-occurrences of *li* and *yi* without a conjunctive particle in Xunzi, scholars have disputed their proper interpretation. The issue is important not only to textual interpretation, but also to a coherent explication of Confucian ethics. In a former paper, I criticized a number of interpretations based on textual materials, but I failed to provide an adequate solution to this issue.[28] This section offers a tentative scheme for the analysis of the complex notion of *yi*, with a bidirectional focus on the constant *(chang)* and the changing *(bian)* aspects of *dao*. The scheme for analysis of *yi* is intended as a conceptual experiment. The question at issue pertains to *li* and *yi* as distinct but interdependent notions.

For *yi* as a distinct ethical notion, I propose the following scheme for explication:[29]

---

26. For the significance of this distinction, see my *Dimensions of Moral Creativity*, chaps. 5 and 6, and *The Unity of Knowledge and Action: A Study in Wang Yang-ming's Moral Psychology* (Honolulu: University of Hawaii Press, 1982), chap. 3.
27. Cf. Chen et al., *Kongzi sixiang yanjiu lunji*, 27–45.
28. See essay cited in note 4 above.
29. This scheme for the analysis of *yi* is an attempt to shape the notion of *yi*. No claim

S_1 Rightness, right action, duty or oughtness.

S_2 Righteousness.

S_3 Reasoned or correct judgment on what is right and appropriate.

S_4 Sense of moral distinction, i.e., between right and wrong actions, or moral sense.

In contemporary idiom, *yi* as an ethical notion can be explicated as (S_1) a deontic, (S_2) an aretaic, (S_3) an epistemic, or (S_4) a psychological term. Thus *yi* as a distinct notion is a plurisign adaptable to a range of meaning or significance in various contexts of discourse.[30] For a fuller explication, I propose the following:

S_1 An action is right if

a. it conforms to the requirement of an established rule, or

b. it conforms to the agent's judgment of what is appropriate or fitting to the requirement of the situation at hand.[31]

S_2 A person is *righteous* if he is conscientious in performing the right action as indicated in S_1.

S_3 A person's *judgment* concerning what is right (S_1) is correct (i.e., has a reasoned justification) if

a. it can be shown to be a correct judgment of the relevance of an established rule to his action (S_{1a}), or

b. it can be shown to be consonant with other ethical values, which, in the situation, are considered to be relevant and not open to question (S_{1b}).

S_4 A person possesses a moral sense if

a. he appreciates the distinction between right and wrong (moral distinction), or

b. he is actuated by a sense of duty as pertaining to what he ought or ought not to do in a particular situation which he confronts.

With the foregoing scheme, let us first take up the question of *li* and *yi* as distinct notions. We may proceed by inquiring into the respect in which they differ. In other words, let us focus on each sense of *yi* and see what can be plausibly said about *li* and *yi* as distinct notions.

---

is made to textual fidelity, although the scheme is a product of my reflection on different uses of *yi* in *Xunzi*.

30. See Philip Wheelwright, *The Burning Fountain: A Study in the Language of Symbolism* (Bloomington: Indiana University Press, 1968).

31. See paper cited in note 4 above.

Both *li* and *yi*, in general, may be said to have the same objective in ensuring the performance of right conduct. This is the strength of Chen Daqi's functional equivalence thesis.[32] Thus with respect to S_1, S_{1a} can be said to be functionally equivalent to *li*, since the *li* collectively represent the established rules for proper conduct. Along with *li* Xunzi often stresses laws *(fa)*, rules, and regulations. But for him, the *li* collectively constitute the foundation for all rule-like requirements *(quanxue* L10, W19, D37). According to S_{1a}, a right action is one that accords with an established rule, and this rule may be said to be a part of *li*. But this leaves open the possibility of action in accord with S_{1b}, that is, to the case of right conduct that falls outside the scope of *li*. I have suggested that this may well be the strength of Wei Zhengtong's delimitation thesis, in that *yi* in the sense of S_{1b} fixes the boundary or the scope of *li* in particular situations, which are deemed to be exigent rather than normal.[33] Xunzi recognizes the real possibility of this sort of situation, as is evident in his remark, "Where there are established rules of conduct *(fa)*, comply with them. Where there are no such rules, act in the spirit of analogy *(lei)*" *(wangzhi* L163, W35*). Thus the *li* cannot deal with situations envisaged by S_{1b}. Our scheme suggests that *li* and *yi* can be properly distinguished along the line indicated by the distinction between S_{1a} and S_{1b}.

Alternatively, the distinction, as I have pointed out in an earlier paper on conceptual unity, depicts a difference in the direction of focus. *Li* is rule-oriented and *yi* situation-oriented. Thus even if an action is right by merely conforming to a rule of *li*, such a description already presupposes that the rule in question is relevant to the action in a particular situation. Now S_{1b} clearly points out that the action in a particular situation may be judged by the agent to be outside the operative scope of *li*. This judgment, of course, has to be justified as required by S_3. Both S_{1a} and S_{1b} are thus related to S_3, which, as we have seen in section 1 above, is the distinctive function of *yi*. Let me briefly look at S_2.

I have construed S_2 as dependent on S_1 for explication, which in turn depends on S_3. The focus of S_2 is on *yi* as a virtue, a desirable character trait or virtuous disposition. Like Confucius and Mencius, Xunzi often contrasts *yi* with the concern for personal gain or profit. To be a man of *yi* in S_2 is to display a conscientious regard for moral distinctions (S_4) in considering one's desires. In this sense, *yi* is an aretaic term. *Li* can also be construed as an aretaic term referring to the virtue of rule-responsibility or compliance, i.e., to the disposition to conform to estab-

---

32. Ibid.
33. Ibid.

lished requirements. But basically *li* is a first-order virtue, whereas *yi* is a second-order virtue. As Frankena points out, "Besides first order virtues such as these (e.g., honesty, fidelity, benevolence, and justice), there are certain other moral virtues that ought also to be cultivated, which are in a way more abstract and general and may be called second order virtues. Conscientiousness is such a virtue; it is not limited to a certain sector of the moral life, as gratitude and honesty are, but as a virtue covering the whole of the moral life."[34] Along with conscientiousness, Xunzi also emphasizes the virtues of integrity, moral courage, circumspection, informed and wise deliberation, etc.—a common theme in both Confucian and Western ethical theories. It is important to note, however, that *yi* as a virtue implicitly presupposes the quality of impartiality, as we shall see in connection with S_3.

Yi in S_2 embodies the contrast between morality and egoism. Though this contrast may also be said to be present in *li*, *li* focuses for the most part on conventional standards, *yi* on the enduring disposition throughout the whole of the moral life. *Li* puts a premium on compliance with established standards; *yi* on the detachment from the standpoint of personal desires in conscientious inquiry into what a particular situation requires, i.e., on situational appropriateness. As Xunzi reminds his readers, "a clear system of rules and regulations, weights and measures, exist for the sake of proper employment; they are not conventions to be tied down to" (*jundao* L286). *Li* and *yi* in S_2 are thus distinct notions. For compliance with *li* may be based on consideration of personal gain rather than on the conscientious regard for right actions. But equally, it is possible to perform a conscientious action devoid of a reasoned judgment of appropriateness in a particular situation. Thus *yi* in S_2 requires the substantive support of *yi* in S_3.

Let us now turn to S_3, which lies at the heart of *yi* as a distinct ethical notion. It is essentially the notion of reasoned or correct judgment or ruling. In S_{3a}, *yi* pertains to the judgment of the relevance of a rule to a particular situation, in S_{3b}, to the judgment that appeals to the relevance of other ethical notions. Within Confucian ethics, such notions as *ren*, in the sense of benevolence, may be deemed operative in particular cases. If we construe *li* broadly as having an inclusive range of value significance, all these notions may be considered as *li*-dependent. But the notion of *li* so construed would be a set of ideal-embedded rules rather than a mere set of established rules. However, *li* in the primary regulative sense, which is our principal concern in this paper, depends on *yi*

---

34. William K. Frankena, *Ethics,* 2nd ed. (Englewood Cliffs, N.J.: Prentice-Hall, 1973), 46.

for assessing the relevance of rules to particular cases. *Yi* in the distinctive sense of S_3, as a focus on reasoned judgment, is essentially an epistemic notion, thus involving explanation and justification of ethical judgments.[35]

Again, *yi* in S_4 cannot be equated with *li* in the regulative sense. Moral sense is essentially a cognitive appreciation of moral distinction (S_{4a}) and more specially a sense of duty (S_{4b}). One can perform a *li*-action without appreciating its rationale, and *yi* as cognitive appreciation of ethical distinctions presupposes the capacity to form reasoned judgment (*yi* in S_3) or to engage in informed deliberation *(zhilü)*—a theme that pervades Xunzi's concern with reasoned response to changing circumstances *(yiyi bianying)* *(jundao* L284). Our analytic scheme for the analysis of *yi* in relation to *li* thus provides us a way for locating *li* and *yi* as distinct ethical notions.

The foregoing remarks, however, focus on the distinction between *li* and *yi*. While we acknowledge that in terms of S_{1a}, both *li* and *yi* are functionally equivalent, it is also important to inquire into their connection. As specific terms for the elaboration of *dao* as a generic term, both *li* and *yi* are partners in the same enterprise of morality. I have suggested that they are focal or complementary notions in understanding the Confucian ideal of human excellence *(dao)*. Generally, within Confucian ethical theory, the distinction between notions is important only because some connection can be made out in appropriate contexts of discourse.

Let us now go through the various senses of *yi* and exhibit, if possible, connection between *li* and *yi*. With respect to S_{1a}, we may construe the connection in terms of the priority of *li* over *yi*, for S_{1a} clearly implies such a thesis, that is, we have the need to appeal to our own judgment of the appropriate thing to do in a particular situation only when *li*, as embodying the established rules, in some sense fails to guide us in resolving our problem, when *li* is considered but deemed inoperative or inapplicable to a case at hand. As Xunzi points out, "Just as weights and measures are the standard for things, the *li* are the standard for rules and regulations. Weights and measures establish quantity; the *li* fix the different sorts of human relationship" *(zhishi* L307). The *li* always, in the first instance, provide ethical considerations as reasons for action, though in a particular situation, they may not furnish sufficient guidance. In the sense of *li* as the first consideration, *yi* is thus dependent on *li*.

However, in another sense *yi* in S_3 is prior to *li*. For in S_{3a}, *yi* in the sense of reasoned judgment on the relevance of a rule to a particular case is presupposed by any application of *li*. For Xunzi, just as there are

---

35. For further discussion, see my *Ethical Argumentation*, 8–11.

no rules or laws that can establish their own efficacy without men to carry them out, there are no classes *(lei)* that contain their own rules for application (*jundao* L263). Thus *yi* in S_{3a} can claim a priority in determining the relevance of rules to particular cases. If the *li* are deemed applicable to particular cases, they must be judged to be the right sort of rule. In S_{3b}, this claim of priority of *yi* over *li* is even more obvious, for *li* has to be declared as irrelevant to exigent situations. Thus while the *li* always present a claim to attention in ethical thinking, it is *yi* in S_3 that decisively establishes their relevance or irrelevance. The same sort of priority may be said of *yi* in S_2 as a second-order virtue, for acting ethically requires not only attention to rules (S_{1a}) but also a disposition to do the right thing in a particular situation, which calls for a judgment of appropriateness (S_{2b}), and in turn, requires reasoned justification. Moreover, as we have earlier observed, acting in terms of a virtuous disposition is quite different from mere rule-responsibility, for this implies the willingness to forgo one's personal interests for the sake of the requirement of righteousness. As Xunzi puts it, "A *junzi* (ethically superior person) must be able to overcome his private desires in favor of public interest and rightness" (*xiushen* L36, W32*).

When we turn to *yi* in S_4, the appreciation of moral distinctions and sense of duty, we can again claim the priority of *yi* over *li*. The former (S_{4a}) implies, in particular, that one possesses an enlightened understanding of the significance of *li*. In Xunzi's words, "A *junzi* engages in extensive learning and daily examines himself, so that his understanding will be enlightened and his conduct be without fault" (*quanxue* L2, W15*). And this enlightened understanding essentially involves an appreciation of the rationale of *li* and related matters, i.e., its connection with other moral values (S_{3b}). We may thus conclude that, with the exception of *yi* in S_{1a}, which is functionally equivalent to *li*, in all other cases *yi* is prior to *li* in moral thought and action.

However, this claim of priority of *yi* over *li* is not an absolute claim. For if it were to be a claim to absolute priority, it might misleadingly suggest that *li* could be ignored when one judged that a particular rule is irrelevant to an exigent circumstance. After all, given the functional equivalence of *li* and *yi* (S_{1a}) in some contexts, both have the same objective in governing conduct. Given *yi* in S_3, for instance, *li* may again become relevant in communicating our reasoned judgments to others as they affect the well-being of others *(ren)*. In so doing, *li*, in the form of rules of civility, need to be attended to for they are an essential requirement for participation in ethical argumentation.[36] Thus the ques-

36. Ibid.

tion of priority regarding *li* and *yi* is not one of an absolute or abstract statement of priority, but a contextual question to be answered in dealing with the normal and changing circumstances of human life. In this light, while *li* and *yi* are distinct focal notions, in context, they may be mutually dependent for understanding their actuating import for moral conduct. In this way, we may regard *li* and *yi* as partners in the same human enterprise.

3. WISDOM AND THE DYNAMICS OF THE VIRTUES

In the foregoing sections I have given a partial explication of the completion thesis on the unity of virtues. As a formulation of a major aspect of a critical Confucian moral theory, the account presents a highly abstract and static conception. There remain, among others, two related questions that deserve further inquiry. The first pertains to the noticeable neglect of wisdom *(zhi)*, which is commonly acknowledged as a basic Confucian virtue. The second, more importantly, pertains to the explanation of the dynamic character of the unity of virtues, particularly in light of the Confucian doctrine of the unity of knowledge and action.[37]

Relative to the first question, we may recall Xunzi's conception of wisdom *(zhi)* as consisting in knowledge that is harmonious with experience *(zhengming* L506).[38] This experience pertains to matters in normal and changing circumstances of human life. It is the exercise of *yi* that enables us to cope with changing circumstances *(yiyi bianying)*. The outcome of this exercise, having paid heed to the requirements of *ren* and *li*, represents an item to be cherished as a part of wisdom. Thus Xunzi often stresses the importance of the accumulation *(ji)* of goodness.[39] In this manner, we may conceive of wisdom primarily as a repository of insights derived from the proper exercise of *yi* in exigent situations—a conception that is reminiscent of Zhu Xi's, that is, wisdom as *shoulian* or gathering of the fruits of ethical activities. In itself wisdom is not a virtue in the same sense as *ren*, *yi* and *li* are virtues. Its status is derived from the movement of *ren*, *yi*, and *li;* thus the crucial importance of our second question concerning the dynamic character of the unity of virtues.

The conception of wisdom as a repository of insights seems to be implicit in Zhu Xi's conception of wisdom as that which is "hidden and stored" *(zhicang)*. As Takehiko points out, this is one of the neglected and important themes in Zhu Xi scholarship:

---

37. See my *The Unity of Knowledge and Action*.
38. *"Zhi you sohe weizhi zhi."* Cf. D282, W140.
39. See, for example, *quanxue* L7, W18, D34.

Zhu Xi's idea of wisdom as hidden and stored is a comprehensive synthesis not only of ideas on it before the Qin period (221–206 B.C.) and those handed down through the Han and the Tang periods, but also of the opinions of Northern Song Confucian scholars in regard to wisdom. His "wisdom," which is based on realization through personal experience, should be differentiated from the literal and philological interpretations of the Han and Tang scholars. By rejecting the Buddhist and the Daoist ideas of wisdom, Zhu Xi raised the traditional understanding of wisdom to a higher level.[40]

Below, I present a personal reading of Zhu Xi's conception of wisdom by pondering the parallels he draws between the four attributes of Heaven and Earth and the four seasons, and the latter with the four cardinal virtues, as stated in his classic essay entitled "A Treatise on *Ren*":

The moral qualities *[de]* of Heaven and Earth are four: origination *[yuan]*, flourish *[heng]*, advantage *[li]*, and firmness *[zhen]*. And the principle of origination unites and controls them all. In their operation they constitute the course of the four seasons, and the vital force of spring permeates them all. Therefore in the mind of man there are also four moral qualities—namely, *ren*, righteousness *[yi]*, propriety *[li]*, and wisdom *[zhi]*—and *ren* embraces them all.[41]

Consider the analogy of the four seasons and the four cardinal virtues. Were we to take Zhu Xi's passage as stating a correspondence thesis, from our perspective today the analogy would be nothing but a fanciful speculation, a thesis with no empirical support. On the other hand, if we take the analogy, not as a thesis with factual grounding, but as an expression of the symbolic significance of the seasonal analogy, it is suggestive of valuable insights concerning the nature of wisdom and the dynamic relation of the four cardinal virtues. This reading presupposes the analogy between the four attributes or virtues *(de)* of Heaven and Earth and the four seasons. Our symbolic interpretation is plausible, since Zhu Xi's attribution of the four attributes of Heaven and Earth are indebted to the commentary of the first and second hexagrams of the *Yijing*, which was an attempt to give a symbolic representation of the

---

40. Takehiko's paper provides a valuable account of the sources of Zhu Xi's conception. See Okada Takehiko, "Chu Hsi and Wisdom as Hidden and Stored," in *Chu Hsi and Neo-Confucianism*, ed. Wing-tsit Chan (Honolulu: University of Hawaii Press, 1986), 200. The emphasis on personal experience for acquiring wisdom recalls an important feature of Zhu Xi's conception of interpreting the classics. As Yü Ying-shih has shown, for Zhu Xi the interpretive process must culminate in a stage in which the reader can reanimate a text in such a manner that it becomes an integral part of the reader's life (Yü Ying-shih, "Morality and Knowledge in Chu Hsi's Philosophical System," in *Chu Hsi and Neo-Confucianism*, 238–39). Note that pinyin romanization replaced Wade-Giles's in my quotation.

41. W. T. Chan, *A Source Book in Chinese Philosophy* (Princeton, N.J.: Princeton University Press, 1963), 593–94. For original text, see *Zhuzi Daquan* (Taipei: Zhonghua, 1970), vol. 8, chap. 67:20.

hexagrams *qian* (Heaven) and *kun* (Earth). Derivatively, the four seasons are the symbolic representation of the concrete significance of the abstract ideas of the four Confucian cardinal virtues. Notably, a symbolic representation of an abstract, general idea is a device for providing an example of concrete specification of the practical significance of the idea in actual human life. In this light, the seasonal analogy is insightful, expressing Zhu Xi's notion of wisdom and an elucidation of a possible relation of the four cardinal virtues.[42]

Recall Cheng Yi's metaphor "*ren* is seed." *Ren* conveys the requisite ethical motivation and creative vitality, the source or beginning of the ethical life dedicated to the realization of *dao*. The cultivation of *ren* requires a period for "planting" the seeds or ethical education, providing the *yuan* (origination) of the ethical life. Metaphorically, this is the spring of ethical life. Again, recall Confucius's notion of *ren* as extensive love and Wang Yang-ming's vision of the universe as a moral community.[43] For ordinary intelligent people, without some concrete example of how this ideal may be realized, it will appear merely as a speculative idea. This is perhaps the basis for Mencius's doctrine of the four *xin* (heart/mind), especially when the *xin* of commiseration is conceived as the first beginning, because the inculcation of compassion provides the material for developing the virtue of *ren*. Absent the sensitivity to the suffering of one's fellows, it is not possible to acquire the virtue of *ren*. Appreciating Mencius's doctrine of the four *xin* as the seeds for the four cardinal virtues does not imply an acceptance of his thesis on the inherent goodness of human nature.[44] Ideally a *ren*-person will not confine his benevolence to his family, society, or state. He or she will enlarge the scope of affectionate concern for humanity whenever possible, and ultimately, for all things in the world.

The efforts to realize *ren* depend on *yi* (S_3)—the agent's reasoned judgment of what one ought to do in a particular, uncertain situation. It is, so to speak, the "summer" of the ethical life, a time in which *ren* develops or flourishes *(heng)*. There are times in one's life when the intense preoccupation with self-interest renders the commitment to *ren* a side issue. Also, the concern with self-interest often conflicts with one's

---

42. See my "Opposites as Complements: Reflections on the Significance of *Tao*," *Philosophy East and West* 31, no. 2, (1981): 123–40; or *Moral Vision and Tradition: Essays in Chinese Ethics* (Washington, D.C.: The Catholic University of America Press, 1998), Essay 5.

43. See my "Between Commitment and Realization: Wang Yang-ming's Vision of the Universe as a Moral Community," *Philosophy East and West* 43, no. 4 (1993): 611–49; or *Moral Vision and Tradition*, Essay 9.

44. *Mengzi*, 2A6. For my view on the dispute between Xunzi and Mencius on human nature, see my "The Quasi-Empirical Aspect of Hsün Tzu's Philosophy of Human Nature, *Philosophy East and West* 28, no. 1 (1978): 373–89; or part 2 of Essay 1 in this volume.

sense of rightness *(yi)*. The cultivation of the ethical motivation for attainment of *ren* depends on the exercise of *yi*. Given the interdependence of *ren* and *yi*, the attainment of *ren* presupposes that the pursuit of *ren* pays due attention to particular circumstances. This, in turn, presupposes that the agent has sufficient self-discipline *(geji)*, the ability to control his or her desires or passions. This is perhaps the force of Confucius's conception that self-mastery is a constitutive means for the realization of *ren*.[45] As Confucius reminds his pupils, the *junzi* regards *yi* as indispensable to the ethical life.[46] The "summer" is, so to speak, the maturation of the activity of *ren*, which entails the successful exercise of *yi* in coping with changing, exigent circumstances of human life.

Autumn is, so to speak, a time of maturity, a season for gathering the crops and fruits of moral experiences, owing to the exercise of *yi* or *quan* (moral discretion) in exigent circumstances. For the most part, these experiences consist of unrelated particular judgments, which need to be put in some systematic order, i.e., in the form of *li* or rules of proper conduct. The *li* represent a codification of the products of the exercise of *yi*. Moreover, from the point of view of tradition, the *li* have a supportive function, enabling individuals to satisfy their desires within the boundary of propriety. In Xunzi's words, "the *li* provide satisfaction of desires" *(geren zhi qiu) (lilun* L417). Since the *li* are a code of proper conduct, it is expected that the exercise of *yi* will also be involved in the process of codification. For reasoned value judgment is required to decide what is to be rightly included in a coherent code. When such a code has been followed over a few generations, it acquires a *de jure* status and constitutes the established tradition of proper behavior.[47] In Rawls's term, the *li* are originally summary rules or generalizations of ethical experiences, though in the course of time, because of general acceptance and/or blind conformity, they become practice rules.[48]

Instead of discarding the uncodifiable cases, they are to be preserved or stored, say, as a savings account in a bank. Selective, reasoned judgment is involved in the process. At the same time, the deposit requires attention as to its possible future use. In this light, wisdom is the ability to make use of the depository of moral insights derived from the exercise of *yi*, those ethical experiences that cannot be codified in terms of *li*. It is important that the storehouse be located in a firm *(chen)* or rock solid place.

An ethical life devoted to the pursuit of *dao* requires vigilance even in

---

45. *Analects* 12.1.
46. Ibid., 17.23.
47. For the Confucian idea of tradition, see *Moral Vision and Tradition*, Essay 12.
48. John Rawls, "Two Concepts of Rules," *Philosophical Review* 64 (1955).

times of tranquility. These are the occasions indispensable for contemplating the significance of the uncodified ethical experiences. Here is perhaps the import of Zhu Xi's analogy of wisdom *(zhi)* and winter. Metaphorically, winter is the time for the acquisition of wisdom, for gathering the fruits of ethical experience, a time for contemplating the prospective import of the temporal upshot of moral experience. The practical efficacy in employing wisdom lies in the agent's ability to make intelligent use of the gathering *(shoulian)* or depository of insights derived from the exercises of *ren*, *li*, and *yi*, the basic interdependent virtues of the tradition. In this light, wisdom *(zhi)* is a virtue of sagacity, a second-order virtue like *yi*, which, as Zhu Xi has shown, is implicit in the intelligent exercise of moral discretion *(quan)* in dealing with changing circumstances of human life.[49] A Confucian sage, the idealized perfect person possessing wisdom, without any thought or deliberation, would simply respond to things as they come. In the words of Xunzi: "The sage considers himself a measure *[du]* or standard for appraising things. Hence, by means of his [knowledge of] men in the present, he can judge those of the past . . . By means of *dao* he can command a comprehensive view of all things." But for ordinary agents, the realistic hope is to become a *junzi*, a paradigmatic individual who must engage in deliberation, especially in coping with changing circumstances.[50]

If the above reading of Zhu Xi's correlativity thesis is plausible, we may regard the seasons as expressive symbols of the Confucian vision of *dao*. These symbols suggest ways of thinking about the dynamic connection of *ren*, *yi*, and *li* as specifications *(bieming)* of the concrete significance of *dao*. An important task is the detailed specification of these basic notions in terms of the notions of particular virtues mentioned at the beginning of this paper. I hope this progress report of my study of the unity of virtues offers some ideas for further exploration. In prosecuting this task, let us be mindful that the Confucian *dao* as the unifying perspective of the ethical life can be construed in different and complementary ways. The basic virtues have the claim to a preeminent position, for they are the characteristic concern of committed ethical persons, the paradigmatic individuals *(junzi)* who seek to realize *dao* in human life.[51] As Confucius points out, only dedicated human beings can bring about the realization of the diverse, extensive, and concrete significance of *dao*.[52] The significance of *dao*, as Wang Yangming re-

---

49. "*Quan*: Moral Discretion," in *Encyclopedia of Chinese Philosophy*.
50. See *feixiang* L82. For further discussion, see my *Ethical Argumentation*, 64–69.
51. See my *Dimensions of Moral Creativity*, chaps. 2 and 4.
52. See *Analects* 15.29.

minds us, cannot be exhausted with any finality *(dao wu zhongqion)*.[53] Thus, a commitment to the pursuit of *dao* is a commitment to expansive vision encompassing humanity, nature, and the universe.[54]

53. Wang Yang-ming, *Instructions for Practical Living and Other Neo-Confucian Writings*, trans. Wing-tsit Chan (New York: Columbia University Press, 1963), section 64.

54. An early version of this paper was presented as the Presidential Address, International Society for Chinese Philosophy, State University of New York at Stony Brook, July 15, 1985.

Essay 6

THE POSSIBILITY OF ETHICAL KNOWLEDGE

This essay is an inquiry into the nature and possibility of knowing *dao* in the *Xunzi*. First, I offer a reconstruction of Xunzi's conception of *dao* as the object of ideal ethical knowledge, and on this basis sketch a Confucian thesis on ethical judgments, for convenience labeled "practical coherentism" (section 1). This thesis is elaborated by way of focusing on the role of mind *(xin)*, that is to say, the nature and method of deliberation requisite to the formation of sound ethical judgments (section 2). I conclude this study with suggestions for dealing with some problems in developing and defending practical coherentism (section 3).

1. 'DAO' AS THE OBJECT OF ETHICAL KNOWLEDGE

For an explication of *dao* as the object of ideal ethical knowledge *(zhi)* in the *Xunzi*, I shall make use of Xunzi's distinction between generic and specific terms *(gongming* and *bieming)*.[1] To a large extent, we may employ the recent, functionally analogous distinction of concept and conception.[2] A generic term is a formal, general, abstract term amenable to specific uses in different contexts of discourse. These uses in theoretical or practical contexts may be said to be specific terms in the sense that they specify the significance of the use of the generic term adapted to the current purpose of discourse.[3] Alternatively, we

---

1. This distinction is employed in my *Ethical Argumentation: A Study in Hsün Tzu's Moral Epistemology* (Honolulu: University of Hawaii Press, 1985), 121–25.

2. For the distinction between concept and conceptions, see John Rawls, *A Theory of Justice* (Cambridge, Mass.: Harvard University Press, 1971), 5–9; Robin Attfield, "On Being Human," *Inquiry* 14 (1974): 175–76; suggested by H. L. A. Hart in *The Concept of Law* (Oxford: Clarendon Press, 1961), 15. For recent use and elaboration, see Ronald Dworkin, *Law's Empire* (Cambridge, Mass.: Harvard University Press, 1986), 71–72; and Gerald Dworkin, *The Theory and Practice of Autonomy* (Cambridge: Cambridge University Press, 1988), 9–10.

3. As Chen Daqi remarks, this distinction between *gongming* and *bieming* is a relative

may say that there are various degrees or levels of abstraction or specification in the use of generic terms. Thus a generic term in one context may function as a specific term in another context, whenever the current purpose requires such further specification. In the language of concept and conception, a generic term designates a concept that can be used in developing various conceptions.

In ancient Chinese thought, *dao* is a term of art, in the Greek sense of *techne*, used by different schools *(jia)* for propounding competing solutions to the common problem of ordering the state and personal life.[4] In the *Xunzi*, *dao* is often used as a generic term *(gongming)* for a holistic ethical vision, the ideal standard of thought, speech, and action.[5] *Dao* may be elucidated by way of focusing on two sets of specific terms *(bieming)*, pertaining respectively to the subject matter and the epistemic character of coherence. *Dao* may be characterized in terms of *ren* (benevolence), *li* (ritual propriety), and *yi* (rightness). Consider the following:

The *dao* of the former [sage] kings is the magnificent display of *ren (ren zhi long ye)*, for they follow what is fitting and appropriate *(zhong)*. What is meant by the fitting and the appropriate? It is *li* and *yi*. The *dao* is neither the *dao* of Heaven nor the *dao* of the Earth. It is the *dao* humans [should] use as a guide to conduct, the *dao* the superior man *(junzi)* follows. *(ruxiao* L131)[6]

---

distinction rather than an exclusive disjunction. However, it is important not to construe the distinction in terms of class inclusion as Chen does. See Chen Daqi, *Xunzi xueshuo* (Taipei: Zhonghua wenhua she, 1954), 125–26.

4. As Graham succinctly states, "The crucial question for all of them is not the Western philosopher's question 'What is the truth?' but 'where is the Way *[dao]?*', the way to order the state and conduct personal life" (A. C. Graham, *Disputers of the Tao: Philosophical Arguments in Ancient China* [La Salle, Ill.: Open Court, 1989], 3. But this central concern cannot be construed as a lack of interest in factual truth. Graham offers an instructive sinological treatment of this issue in Appendix 2 of the work cited. At any rate, the concern with factual truth *(fuyan)* is quite evident in Xunzi as one standard of argumentative competence and is implicit in his essay on the correct or proper use of terms *(zhengming pian)*. The same interest is present in the Later Mohist's concern with procedure for consistent description. Indeed, as we shall see in section 2 of this essay, it is very difficult to explicate some uses of *zhi* without employing the notion of factual truth. For further discussion on Xunzi, see Cua, *Ethical Argumentation*, esp. 30–36; for the Later Mohists, see A. C. Graham, *Later Mohist Logic, Ethics and Science* (Hong Kong: The Chinese University of Hong Kong Press, 1978), 35–44 and 348. Cf. Donald Munro, *The Concept of Man in Ancient China* (Stanford, Calif.: Stanford University Press, 1969), and *The Concept of Man in Contemporary China* (Ann Arbor: University of Michigan Press, 1977); David L. Hall and Roger T. Ames, *Thinking Through Confucius* (Albany: State University of New York Press, 1987), 298–99.

5. To my knowledge, Chen Daqi was the first to propose *dao* as a generic term *(gongming)* with specific terms *(bieming): tong, lei,* and *ren*. My own reconstruction given in this essay is different, but indebted to his examination of the uses of *dao*. See Chen, *Xunzi xueshuo*, chap. 5, esp. 70–79. For a couple of explicit passages on *dao* as the standard of conduct, see *zhengming* L521, 531; D290, 297; W147, 153.

6. This interpretive reading takes *zhong* (the center) as the central, fitting, and appropriate *telos* of human life. The emendation in terms of "should" follows Liang's gloss: "*Dao*

This passage suggests that *ren, li,* and *yi* comprise the subject matter of *dao,* that is, the general, fundamental, ethical significance of *dao* is to be construed in such specific terms. It is plausible to maintain that these basic terms are interdependent and constitute a coherent, normative framework in Confucian ethics. They function as focal notions for conveying distinct but convergent centers of ethical concern, though Xunzi, for the most part, stresses *li* and *yi*.[7]

Setting aside the issue of conceptual unity or interdependence of *ren, li,* and *yi,* it seems unproblematic to ascribe to Xunzi a coherent or holistic conception of *dao* in ethical discourse.[8] This conception is especially evident in Xunzi's criticism of philosophers for grasping only one aspect of *dao* and neglecting others.[9] Apart from its subject matter, however, it is unclear how his notion of coherence is to be explicated. For this purpose, we may construe *dao* as having *daoguan, liguan,* or *tonglei* as specific terms.[10] The first two terms occur in this passage:

What remains unchanged throughout the times of the Hundred Kings is worthy to be considered *daoguan*. To their rise and fall, respond with *guan*. [Thus,] there is no confusion in *liguan*. If one does not know *guan*, one will not know how to respond to changing circumstances. (*tianlun* L379)[11]

The use of *guan,* I presume, is metaphorical, as is familiar to the students of the *Lunyu* (*The Analects*) (4.15). Literally, a *guan* is "a thread for stringing holed, copper coins."[12] Implicit in the metaphorical use of *guan* in our passage is an analogy between a thread or string for holed,

---

is for the sake of human conduct." While it is the *dao* the *junzi* follows, ordinary humans are generally unable to do so. My reading is partly indebted to Wang Zhonglin. See Liang Qixiong, *Xunzi jianshi,* 4th ed. (Taipei: Shangwu, 1978), 79; Wang Zhonglin, *Xinyi Xunzi duben* (Taipei: San Min, 1977), 133. For other relevant passages, see *ruxiao* L152, 149; D113, 111; *dalüe* L605–6.

7. A preliminary sketch and argument for this thesis was presented in *Ethical Argumentation,* 160–63. A subsequent elaboration and critique of competing views and a detailed discussion of *li* and *yi* are given in Essays 4 and 5 of this volume. [A more comprehensive discussion is given in my *Moral Vision and Tradition: Essays in Chinese Ethics* (Washington, D.C.: The Catholic University of America Press, 1998), Essay 13.] For a general discussion of the significance of focal notions in ethics, see my *Dimensions of Moral Creativity: Paradigms, Principles, and Ideals* (University Park: Pennsylvania State University Press, 1978), chap. 1.

8. For an instructive discussion accompanied by a Marxist critique, see Feng Youlan (Fung Yu-lan), *Zhongguo zhexue shi xinpian* (Beijing: Jen-min, 1964), chap. 16, esp. 556–62.

9. See *tianlun* L381, D184–85, W87–88; and *jiebi* L478, D263–64, W125–26.

10. For more discussion of *tonglei* as expressing the ideal of rational coherence in ethical argumentation, see my *Ethical Argumentation,* 61–65. Here I focus principally on the metaphor of *guan*.

11. Cf. D183, W87.

12. Liang Shiqiu, *A New Practical Chinese-English Dictionary* (Taipei: Far East, 1972).

copper coins and a "thread" as a characteristic of an ideal, intellectual activity or discourse.[13]

Preliminary to elucidating the problem of interpreting the metaphorical use of *guan* in our passage, let us note that similarity claims are generally useful, because they are informative and help us to solve "the infallibility problem."[14] As Fogelin points out, comparisons "help us to make connection when there is no direct way of saying what the connection is. Metaphors extend this capacity by allowing us to make connection even when no straightforward comparison is available."[15] In our passage, *guan* is a connection metaphor, presenting us with a challenge in constructive interpretation. As evident in its use in an important remark on "completeness" *(quan)* of learning, *guan* is properly construed in the sense of coherent, comprehensive understanding.

The *junzi* knows that what lacks completeness *(quan)* and purity *(cui)* does not deserve commendation *(mei)*. Thus he reads and listens to explanations [of the Classics] in order to *guan* through their meaning, reflects on them in order to achieve *tong*. (*quaxue* L19)

Following Yang Liang, we may read *guan* in terms of *guanchuan*, that is, "to penetrate fully their meaning."[16] However, in the light of the role of reflection *(sisuo)* and comprehensive understanding *(tong)* as the objective of learning, we may read *guan* by way of the homophone *(guanchuan*)*, that is, "to piece together, interconnect, or interrelate."[17] *Guan*, in the verbal use, pertains to engaging in an intellectual performance directed not only to the understanding of the meanings of the classics, but also their interconnection.

Perhaps it is not too fanciful to view the foregoing passage as a *locus classicus* for the common use of *guantong* among Chinese philosophers as expressing the idea of coherent, comprehensive understanding or of a mastery of a subject, involving an insight into the interconnection of the detailed items of learning and reflection. Indeed, one recent commentator explicitly glosses *guan* as *guantong*.[18] Chen Daqi, followed by Li Disheng, also uses *guantong* to explain Xunzi's holistic conception of

---

13. The following remarks on *guan* are indebted to and inspired by Fogelin's theory of figurative comparisons. I have found his work particularly helpful, quite apart from the plausibility of his defense of the Aristotelian conception of metaphors as elliptical similes. See Robert J. Fogelin, *Figuratively Speaking* (New Haven, Conn.: Yale University Press, 1988).
14. Ibid., chap. 6, esp. 78–80.
15. Ibid., 92.
16. Yang Liang, *Xunzi* (Taipei: Zhonghua, 1976), *juan* 1:6A.
17. Lin Yutang, *Chinese-English Dictionary of Modern Usage* (Hong Kong: Chinese University of Hong Kong Press, 1972).
18. Wang Zhonglin, 62.

dao.[19] Regardless of the plausibility of our speculation on the above passage as an authoritative source for the use of *guantong* in the *Xunzi*, significantly *tong* is frequently coupled with *ming* (clarity, insight) in the same passage.[20] On this basis, *guan* is plausibly read as *guantong* and construed as a characteristic activity of a *junzi* or person of extensive learning and insight,[21] and in its perfect exercise, a characteristic of a sage *(shengren)* who has a keen, inexhaustible, unfailing insight into the interconnection of all relevant matters (*feixiang* L82, D74, K1:207).

Returning to our earlier passage (*tianlun* L379), we can now quite properly consider *daoguan* and *liguan* as specific terms of *dao*. The former pertains to the nature of *dao* as a conception of a whole made up of interconnected "parts," the latter points to these "parts" as consisting of *li** (rationales). Arguably, *tonglei* serves better as a specific term of *dao*, that is, the unity of rationales that underlie different kinds of things or ideas. For Xunzi, it is the sage or the Great Confucian *(da Ru)* who possesses comprehensive knowledge and insight into all kinds of things *(zhitong tonglei)*.[22] A *junzi*, however, is one who aspires to this knowledge. Informed by his sense of rightness, he can, though with no assurance of success, like the sage engage in *guan* in responding to all changing circumstances.[23] In sum, we may regard *daoguan*, *liguan*, and *tonglei* as alternative specific terms of *dao*, though *tonglei* seems to be a clearer term for articulating the holistic character of *dao*.[24]

If the foregoing account is acceptable, a question naturally arises concerning the nature of the coherent knowledge of *dao*. Our account suggests that such a knowledge is systemic, that is, that it is a whole consisting of interrelated constituents, much akin to Butler's notion of a system or Moore's notion of organic unity.[25] When we ask about these

---

19. Chen, *Xunzi xueshuo*, 78–79; and Li, L379–80n. See also Tang Junyi, *Zhongguo zhexue yuanlun, yuandao pian* (Taipei: Xuesheng, 1978), 453.

20. See also *A Concordance to Hsün Tzu*, Harvard-Yenching Institute Sinological Index Series, supplement no. 22 (Taipei: Chinese Materials and Research Center, 1966), 7/3/17, 7/3/18, 10/4/38, 25/8/111, 25/8/122, 55/15/57, 59/16/28, and 89/23/29.

21. *quanxue* L2, D31, W15, K135.

22. *xiushen* L33, D51, W30, K156.

23. Chen Daqi and Mou Zongsan are perhaps the first commentators to stress *tonglei* as a key concept in the *Xunzi*. See Chen, *Xunzi xueshuo*; and Mou, *Ming Chia yu Xunzi* (Taipei: Xuesheng, 1979). For some subsequent discussions, see Wei Zhengtong, *Xunzi yu gudai zhexue* (Taipei: Shangwu, 1974), chap. 1; Zeng Chunhai, "Xunzi sixiang zhong de 'tong lei' yu 'li fa'," *Fu Jen Philosophical Studies* 13 (1981); and Cai Renhou, *Kong Meng Xun zhexue* (Taipei: Xuesheng, 1984), 461–66. For more discussion of the distinction between *junzi* and the sage, and the notion of *tonglei* as the ideal of rational coherence in ethical argumentation, see my *Ethical Argumentation*, 61–65. For some relevant passages, see *Concordance*, 55/15/57, 16/6/14, 22/8/63, 24/8/99, 25/8/122, 82/21/83, 90/23/79.

24. Cf. Chen, *Xunzi xueshuo*, 78–79; and Li Disheng, *Xunzi jishi*, 379n.

25. Joseph Butler, *Five Sermons* (Indianapolis, Ind.: Bobbs-Merrill, 1950), 7–9; G. E.

constituents from the theoretical point of view, we are bound to be disappointed. Perhaps, as Graham maintains, for Xunzi, as for the Sophists and the later Mohists, "intelligence is what Anglo-Saxons call 'common sense,' the sort which values a synthesizing grasp of how things hang together above analysis, and which prefers not to push analysis farther than is needed to resolve issues arising in controversy."[26] Were one to follow Graham, except for Graham's argumentative orientation, Xunzi's notion of *dao* would be similar to Wang Yang-ming's, that is, the conception of *dao* as "an ideal attitude or a perspective for organizing or unifying the diverse and conflicting elements of moral experience."[27] This view is indeed implicit in our understanding of *daoguan* as a unifying perspective.

However, at issue is whether Xunzi can criticize other philosophers for exaggerating the importance of some aspects of *dao* at the expense of others. The critique carries a burden of showing, in light of *tonglei*, that these other aspects are interconnected in some ways, but Xunzi's critique is much too concise to be informative. His general position is clear: "Each of these doctrines expresses only one aspect of *dao. Dao* embodies constancy *(chang)* and embraces all changes. One cannot characterize its nature by merely attending to one aspect" (*jiepi* L478). Various philosophers are criticized, for example, in terms of such coupling notions as utility and cultural refinement, law and the role of worthy men, power or political purchase and the role of knowledge. In each case, the second of the pair is said to be neglected, and the first exaggerated. The first in the pair is considered by these philosophers to be the exclusive significance of *dao*. Notably, we are provided with no systematic information on the connection between the notions within each pair, nor connection, if any, among the pairs themselves.[28] However, inspired by Xunzi, a Confucian philosopher today may engage in theory construction and, at the same time, pay heed to the importance of conceptual analysis in the light of *dao* as a holistic conception. She can agree with Thomé Fang that "it is only the use of deep and thoroughgoing analysis that can assist us, through our reflective intuition, in grasping the holistic meaning, value, and reality of the universe."[29]

Moore, *Principia Ethica* (Cambridge: Cambridge University Press, 1969, 1st ed., 1903), 183–87.

26. Graham, *Disputers of Tao*, 254.

27. See my *The Unity of Knowledge and Action: A Study in Wang Yang-ming's Moral Psychology* (Honolulu: University Press of Hawaii, 1982), 52.

28. The philosophers criticized here are Mozi, Shenzi, and Shen Pu-hai. For an instructive exposition, see Fung, *Zhongguo zhexue shi xinpian*, 556–62. See also Chen Daqi's paper in Chen Daqi et al., *Kongzi sixiang yanjiu lunji*, vol. 2 (Taipei: Liming, 1983).

29. Thomé H. Fang, *Yuanshi Rujia Daojia zhexue* (Taipei: Liming, 1983), 19 (my trans-

Being deprived of Xunzi's exposition concerning *tonglei*, the systemic relation between normative judgments or propositions, it is perhaps best to construe *dao* as a sort of Kantian "regulative principle" or ideal, unifying perspective, primarily oriented toward practical rather than theoretical interest. Much in the spirit of Xunzi, one may propose *practical coherentism* as a thesis for consideration in moral epistemology.[30] In this view, the knowledge of *dao* or *tonglei* does not represent sagely knowledge, contrary to Xunzi's claim. While it does not deny the philosophical significance of theory construction, it does insist that any proposed theory has at most the status of plausible presumption concerning its claim to adequacy, defeasible in the light of further inquiry.[31] Confucian ethics, in this conception, is "practical," that is, it stresses the primacy of practice. Normative requirements of conduct are minimal requirements and the adequacy test of normative theory lies in part in accounting for these requirements as being capable of compliance in everyday life. Moreover, an account of these requirements must reflect a coherent understanding of social practices, embracing customs, conventions, and acknowledged, permissible forms of conduct. Thus, for the Confucian, in normal circumstances the *li*, as an embodiment of a tradition though subject to revision, justly lay claim to the most important component of ethical consideration. In exigent or changing circumstances, the *li* may well be problematic in providing guidance.[32]

More fundamentally, the *dao*-perspective is *conservative*, in the sense that it is oriented toward a critical conservation of the values of a living ethical tradition, informed by the historical knowledge of a common culture as embodied in the Confucian classics. Also, the perspective is conservative in that *dao*, specified in terms of the *li*, conserve those nat-

---

lation). For tentative efforts in line with Fang's suggestion, see Cua, "The Concept of *Li* in Confucian Moral Theory," in *Understanding the Chinese Mind: The Philosophical Roots*, ed. Robert E. Allinson (Hong Kong: Oxford University Press, 1989); and "Ethical Significance of Thomé H. Fang's Philosophy," Essay 12 in this volume.

30. "Practical coherentism" is intended as a compendious term for the remarks that follow. Were it not for Copp's critique of what he calls "conservative coherentism," a label for the Rawlsian view of Daniels, I would have employed this term instead. For the Rawlsian view, unlike that of the Confucian theorist and MacIntyre, does not take seriously the notion of a living tradition. See David Copp and David Zimmerman, eds., *Morality, Reason, and Truth* (Totowa, N.J.: Rowman and Allanheld, 1985), chap. 5; and Alasdair MacIntyre, *After Virtue* (Notre Dame, Ind.: University of Notre Dame Press, 1981), and *Whose Justice? Which Rationality?* (Notre Dame, Ind.: University of Notre Dame Press, 1988). For more discussion, particularly in relation to MacIntyre's conception of a living tradition, see my "The Idea of Confucian Tradition," *Review of Metaphysics* 45, no. 4 (1992): 803–40; or *Moral Vision and Tradition*, Essay 12.

31. For the notion of plausible presumption, see Nicholas Rescher, *Dialectics* (Albany: State University of New York Press, 1977), 38.

32. For more discussion on this theme and its general significance, see my *Dimensions of Moral Creativity*, chaps. 4–5.

ural feelings and dispositions that are deemed conducive to the acquisition and promotion of the virtues. Both these senses of "conservative" are present in the use of *fang* in a chapter *(fangji)* in the *Liji*. There it is said that Confucius compared the *dao* to dykes *(fang)* for the sake of providing guidance in rectifying the deficiency of the usual standards of conduct followed by ordinary people. For this reason, "the *junzi* uses the *li* as a dyke to conserve virtues *(fangde)*, punishment as a dyke against licentiousness, and prescriptions as a dyke against evil desires."[33] As Legge comments, the character *fang* is used in this chapter both as a noun, meaning "a dyke," and as a verb "to serve as a dyke." A dyke has two uses: "to conserve what is inside it, preventing its flowing away, and to ward off what is without, barring its entrance and encroachment."[34]

For a practical coherentist, any claim to ethical knowledge based on *dao* as a unifying perspective must have a historical dimension. As Mou Zongsan insightfully points out, "Xunzi is fond of speaking of *tonglei*. Its fundamental spirit revolves around a culture with a long history. For this reason, he stresses first the agglomeration of the laws and institutions of the Hundred Kings, and on this basis, he speaks of the unity of *li* and *yi (li yi zhi tong)*."[35] It is quite in accord with this spirit that Xunzi, on one occasion, criticizes Mencius for his partial conformity to the spirit of the Former Kings without understanding their underlying unity *(fei shi'er zi)*.[36] In other words, ethical claims have their roots in the historical past of a common culture or ethical tradition. Conceived as a living tradition, these claims cannot be considered absolute, for there are other competing claims to interpreting the living significance of a tradition, essentially contestable claims to a coherent understanding of the present significance of a historical culture.[37]

In general, a practical coherentist would consider any claim to "doctrinal purity," even if it is espoused with ethical integrity, to be "facially invalid," to borrow the language of the U.S. Supreme Court. For such a claim shows a lack of serious regard for the role of argumentation in interpreting the significance of an ethical tradition. It shows a lack of ap-

33. This translation follows Wang Mengou's reading. See Wang Mengou, *Liji jinzhu jinyi*, vol. 2 (Taipei: Shangwu, 1977), 673. For more discussion of the *Liji*, see my *"Li* and Moral Justification: A Study in the *Li Chi,"* Philosophy East and West 33, no. 1 (1983): 1–16. For an alternative reading, see James Legge's translation, *The Li Ki or Collection of Treatises on the Rules of Propriety or Ceremonial Usages,* in The Sacred Books of the East, ed. Max Müller (Delhi: Motilal Banarsidass, 1966), vol. 2, 284.
34. Ibid., 284n.
35. Mou, *Xunzi dalüe* (my translation); reprinted in Mou, *Ming Chia yu Xunzi*, 200.
36. Ibid. For similar interpretation with extensive discussion, see Tang, esp. chap. 14. For Mou's citation, see *fei shi'er zi* L98.
37. For an extensive discussion of the interpretive character of the Confucian tradition as a living tradition, see *Moral Vision and Tradition*, Essay 12.

preciation for the need of concerned and responsible participants to engage in argumentation as a shared enterprise, in order to arrive at a reasoned view of the significance of the tradition's past in meeting present as well as future problems and perplexities. As Xunzi explicitly reminds his readers, argumentation, as involving explanation and justification, is the means of delineating the *dao*.[38] The Neo-Confucian conception of *daotong*, elaborated by Zhu Xi, arguably is not a conception of scholastic orthodoxy, but that of recovery or reconstitution of the *dao* of Confucian tradition.[39] The very idea of the Confucian tradition as a living tradition is hardly plausible without an acknowledgment of the value of different or competing interpretations of its practical significance. A Confucian practical coherentist would endorse Pelikan's succinct remark: "Tradition is the living faith of the dead, traditionalism is the dead faith of the living."[40]

Closer to home, consistent with Xunzi's complaint against non-Confucian philosophers for their blindness to other aspects of *dao*, he would recall Mencius's warning against stubborn adherence to any one doctrine, even if it is a moderate position between extremes. Says Mencius, "Holding on to the middle is closer to being right, but to do this without weighing circumstances *(quan*)* is no different from holding to one extreme. The reason for disliking those who hold to one extreme is that they cripple the Way *(dao)*. One thing is singled out to the neglect of a hundred others."[41]

---

38. See *zhengming* L521, D290, W147. For more discussion on explanation and justification as two phases of argumentation, see my *Ethical Argumentation*, 51–101.

39. See Wm. Theodore de Bary, *The Liberal Tradition in China* (Hong Kong and New York: Chinese University of Hong Kong Press, 1983); and Tu Wei-ming, "Reconstituting the Confucian Tradition," in *Humanity and Self-Cultivation: Essays in Confucian Thought* (Berkeley, Calif.: Asian Humanities Press, 1979).

40. Jaroslav Pelikan, *The Vindication of Tradition* (New Haven, Conn.: Yale University Press, 1984), 65.

41. *Mencius*, 7A26, D.C. Lau's translation in *Mencius* (Middlesex, England: Penguin Books, 1970), with minor emendation on **quan* as "weighing of circumstances" instead of "the proper measure." As Graham justly points out, "one has the impression that Xunzi is one of those whose thought thrives on controversy and who, without ever acknowledging it, are continually learning from those they criticize." Of course, we have no evidence that Xunzi has any direct knowledge of Mencius's thought as we can cull it from the extant text. One is especially puzzled by his attribution of the doctrine of five processes *(wu-xing)* to the followers of Zisi and Mencius. Moreover, as we shall shortly see, Xunzi's own conception of ethical deliberation essentially makes use of the same conception of *quan**. See Graham, *Disputers of Tao*, 236. For a discussion of the background of Xunzi's attribution, see John Knoblock, *Xunzi: A Translation and Study of the Complete Works*, vols. 1–3 (Stanford, Calif.: Stanford University Press, 1988, 1990, 1994), 1: 215–19. For a discussion of Mencius's conception of *quan* (ch'üan)* in relation to the doctrine of rules and exceptions, see my *Dimensions of Moral Creativity*, 72–76. More detailed and instructive discussion is given in Chen Daqi, *Mengzi de mingli sixiang ji qi bianshuo shikuang* (Taipei: Shangwu, 1974), chap. 2.

With a focus on the merits of particular cases, a Confucian practical coherentist may be called a contextualist, though she is not a theoretician constructing a "world hypothesis" or categorial system. Her use of *daoguan* is more a metaphor for a basic, practical orientation than a root-metaphor in Pepper's sense.[42] While informed by a sense of historical continuity of an established tradition, in the final analysis the realization of *dao*, specified in terms of *ren* and *li*, is a matter of the exercise of *yi* in analogical projection of ethical experiences *(yiyi bianying)*.[43] Any claim to interpreting the significance of the tradition, however plausible in its appeal to historical continuity, must be cognizant of the value of disagreement or controversy, not only as a valuable resource for preserving the vitality of the tradition, but also, even more important, as a capital asset for reasoned assessment of protests against "the tyranny of tradition" and for uncovering wayward and pathological tendencies among adherents of the tradition. As Pelikan points out, "Like any growth, development [of a living tradition] may be healthy or it may be malignant; discerning the difference between these two kinds of growth requires constant research into the pathology of traditions. But it is healthy development that keeps a tradition both out of the cancer ward and out of the fossil museum."[44]

In sum, in the light of Xunzi's holistic conception of *dao*, a practical coherentist would regard ethical judgments as primarily interpretive judgments concerning the living significance of an established tradition. Such judgments, *prima facie*, deserve attention, because they reflect knowledge of the tradition informed by a coherent conception of its subject matter, in particular, knowledge of "institutional facts" as these reflect existing normative requirements of proper behavior.[45] In the end, all ethical judgments, as well as their prospective significance, are subject to reconsideration in the context of problematic particular circumstances, even when they are well grounded in a comprehensive historical understanding.

---

42. Stephen C. Pepper, *World Hypotheses* (Berkeley: University of California Press, 1948) or "Metaphor in Philosophy," in *Dictionary of the History of Ideas* (New York: Charles Scribner's Sons, 1973), vol. 3; and Cua, "Basic Metaphors and the Emergence of Root Metaphors," *Journal of Mind and Behavior* 3, no. 3 (1982):251–58.

43. For the role of analogical projection in ethical deliberation, see my *Ethical Argumentation*, chap. 2, esp. 78–87.

44. Pelikan, *The Vindication of Tradition*, 60.

45. John R. Searle, "How to Derive 'Ought' from 'Is'," *Philosophical Review* 73, no. 1 (1964): 43–58.

2. DELIBERATION AND THE PROBLEM OF CHOICE

Like Mencius and Song-Ming Confucians, Xunzi believes that every person is capable of becoming a sage. Given the fact that *ren, yi,* rules and standards of proper conduct have their rationales *(li*)* that can be known and practiced, we are quite justified in ascribing to every person a capacity to understand as well as to comply with these requirements (*xing'e* L552). Of course, the actualization of this capacity depends on learning and reflection, single-mindedness and resolute will to pursue *dao,* in addition to mature and careful inquiry. When such efforts are extended over a long period of time, along with ceaseless accumulation of good deeds, "everyone can attain the state of *shenming* (daemonic and clear-seeing) and form a triad with Heaven and Earth *(can tiandi).* For the sage is one who has attained to the state by accumulated efforts" (*xing'e* D313*, W167*). However, Xunzi is well aware that such a conception, proffered in abstract discourse, carries no implication for its possible realization in the actual world. In principle, everyone can become a sage; in practice, primarily because of lack of will and sustained effort in the pursuit of *dao,* not everyone can in fact become a sage. Differently put, what is admissible *(ke)* as a thesis concerning sagely potentiality has no necessary connection with the claim to empirical capability *(neng).* The implausibility of the latter claim casts no light on the acceptability of the former, for the two theses represent answers to two distinct issues, calling for quite different kinds of evaluation.[46]

46. The remarks in this paragraph, excepting the quotation, are an interpretive restatement of Xunzi's view. My reading of *ke* as what is admissible in discourse, as contrasted with *neng* as what is actually possible, is consistent with Graham's explanation of this term in the later Mohist treatises (A. C. Graham, *Later Mohist Logic, Ethics and Science* [Hong Kong: Chinese University of Hong Kong Press, 1978], 552); also with Graham's recent explanation of Xunzi's use as a distinction between "the possibility and the capability." Says Graham, "The word used to pronounce something physically possible is *ke* 'admissible' (morally and logically) with which we are already familiar in argumentation; an affirmation pronounced *ke* is valid, an action or process merely possible" (Graham, *Disputers of the Tao,* 249). My own reading, however, is less committed to "moral possibility," for I take Xunzi, in the present passage, to be concerned with a sort of conceptual distinction close to that of logical and empirical or technological possibility, though *ke* here is more than a matter of logical possibility, for his thesis is proffered as plausible, i.e., as a claim to acceptability in discourse. As we shall see shortly, *ke* is also used in the sense of "approve" without any moral connotation (*jiebi* L482). My reading is thus closer to Watson's distinction between "theoretical and actual capability" (W167) than to Dubs's "ability and possibility" (D313–24). For the rendering of *shenming* as "daemonic and clear-seeing"—a "superlative insight of the sages," see Graham, *Disputers of the Tao,* 101, 252, and explanatory entries on *shen* and *shenming* in the Subject Index. For more detailed and informative discussion, see Knoblock's glossary in *Xunzi,* 252–55. [For a later discussion of *shenming* in the light of the religious dimensions of *li,* see my "The Ethical and the Religious Dimensions *Li,*" *Review of Metaphysics* 55:3 (2002): 501–49; incorporated as Essay 7 of this volume.]

Xunzi's skepticism over the latter claim is implicit in his conception of the exercise of political authority. While such an exercise requires justification in terms of knowledge of *dao* and *de* (virtue/moral power), an enlightened ruler would not attempt to offer such a justification to ordinary people. Reminiscent of Confucius's remark,[47] Xunzi says that "it is easy to unify the people by means of the way, though one cannot share with them the reasons [that underlie the exercise of authority]" (*zhengming* L520).[48] In the first place, it is difficult for ordinary people to appreciate the need for expertise in governance.[49] In the second place, the knowledge of *dao*, as knowledge of *tonglei*, requires coherent and comprehensive understanding of a living tradition, which is an outcome of imaginative reconstruction of the past applications of *dao* of the sage kings as embodied in existing historical materials, and an outcome of interpretation of their significance for dealing with present problems and perplexities.[50] And this achievement is possible because of reliable evidential grounding and successful participation in explanatory and justificatory discourse—a concern, for the most part, falling outside the purview of ordinary people (*zhengming* L521, D290, W147).[51]

More fundamentally, the human mind *(xin)*, apart from its intellectu-

47. *Lunyu* 8:9. See also *faxing* L657.
48. Cf. D289, W146.
49. In defense of Xunzi's notion of political expertise, Dubs justly points out that at issue is the distinction between "the logic of tradition" (traditionalism) and "the logic of knowledge." "The logic of tradition is 'what is, is right,' but what *Hsüntze [Xunzi]* said was, 'What the expert says, is right.' Do we not in actual practice to-day depend upon authority in most matters? . . . The logic of knowledge to-day is, 'If you can satisfy the conditions of knowledge, you may know; but if you cannot, you must take the authority of the man who has satisfied the conditions'" (H. H. Dubs, *Hsüntze: The Moulder of Ancient Confucianism* [Taipei: Chengwen, 1966], 100).
50. For further discussion, see my *Ethical Argumentation*, 63–69; and "Ethical Uses of History in Early Confucianism: The Case of Hsün Tzu," *Philosophy East and West* 35, no. 2 (1985): 133–56; or Essay 3 in this volume.
51. The theme of imaginative reconstruction of the significance of *dao* in the past for the present seems to be the point of Xunzi's remark that "justification *(bian)* and explanation *(shuo)* are the means by which the mind *(xin)* forms an image *(xiang)* of the *dao*" (*zhengming* L521). I construe *xiang*, which also can be used to refer to elephants, as the imaginative reconstruction elucidated by Han Feizi in his commentary on the *Laozi*. "Men rarely see living elephants *(xiang)*. As they come by the skeleton of a dead elephant, they imagine its living according to its features. Therefore it comes to pass that whatever people use for imagining the real is called 'image' *(xiang)*." See W. K. Liao, trans., *The Complete Works of Han Fei Tzu* (London: Arthur Probsthain, 1959), 1:193; Chen Qiyou, *Han Feizi jishi* (Taipei: World Publishing Co. 1963), 1:368. For a similar interpretation of this use of *xiang* in the *Yijing* in reconstructing the notion of *zhi* in the *Lunyu*, see Roger Ames, "Meaning as Imaging: Prolegomena to a Confucian Epistemology," in *Culture and Modernity: East-West Philosophical Perspectives*, ed. Eliot Deutsch (Honolulu: University of Hawaii Press, 1991). For further discussion of "accord with evidence" *(fuyan)* as a standard of argumentative competence as well as explanation and justification, see my *Ethical Argumentation*, 30–36 and 51–86.

al function, has also a volitional function or a power of self-determination.[52] Of its own volition, it approves, rejects, chooses, decides, and initiates actions. "It accepts what it approves, and refuses what it disapproves. Hence, we may say that its basic state, with respect to choice *(ze)*, is not subject to any constraints; inevitably, the choice will express its own nature" (*jiebi* L488).[53] Thus, even if the mind *(xin)* possesses the knowledge of *dao*, there is no assurance that it will assent to its guidance, for "the mind *(xin)* must first know *dao (zhidao)* before it can approve of *dao (kedao)*, and it must first approve of *dao* before it can abide by *dao* and desist from doing what is contrary to *dao*" (*jiebi* L482, W127*).

Suppose an agent endorses practical coherentism, that is, he knows and adopts *dao* as an ideal, unifying perspective, how is he to apply or specify its significance in dealing with the problem of choice *(ze)* in particular situations? The answer lies in the guidance of *li**. Says Xunzi, "If one guides the mind *(xin)* by *li** and nourishes it with clarity and does not allow any extrinsic things to upset it, then it is quite capable of determining right and wrong and resolving doubts" (*jiebi* L490, W131*).[54]

52. In *Ethical Argumentation*, I used the term "mind" rather than "heart" in discussing Xunzi's conception of *xin* as a general psychological term referring to mental activities and processes, in contrast to feelings, desires, and sensations. Attention was centered on the intellectual and volitional functions of *xin*, and their contrast with *shen* or bodily movements. My use of "mind" was not intended to suggest that *xin* has its seat in the brain. For as Graham justly reminds us, *xin* refers to "the heart," an organ of thought, approval, and disapproval. "Thinking is not in traditional China located in the brain" (Graham, *Disputers of the Tao*, 24). However, it is significant that Xunzi's use of *xin* as the controller of the body and the knowing agent does anticipate the use of *xin* in Song Confucianism. While the term "mind" may not be a good translation of *xin* in classical Chinese thought, it seems to me an appropriate term to use, especially in contrasting *xin* and *shen*, which are quite naturally used in translating modern Chinese usage. Also, it is difficult to avoid the use of the term "mind," especially when one is interested in a constructive interpretation of Xunzi's conception of *xin*, however rudimentary, as an ancient Chinese contribution to the philosophy of mind and moral epistemology. In the remarks that follow, I use "mind" without claiming accuracy of translation of *xin*, primarily for focusing on the nature of deliberation. Readers uncomfortable with such a procedure can always substitute *xin* for "mind" without, I believe, affecting the plausibility of my exposition. For more discussion of the nature of *xin*, its problems, and diagnosis of erroneous beliefs, see *Ethical Argumentation*, chap. 4. For examples of the use of "mind" in discussing *xin*, see Dubs, *Hsüntze*, and Lee H. Yearley, "Hsün Tzu on the Mind: His Attempted Synthesis of Confucianism and Taoism," *Journal of Asian Studies* 36, no. 3 (1980).

53. Xunzi's conception of the autonomy of mind *(xin)* is a conception of precondition of agency rather than a moral ideal. A similar idea may be expressed by use of the term "autarchy" or "procedural independence." For the former, see Stanley Benn, "Freedom, Autonomy and the Concept of a Person," *Proceedings of the Aristotelean Society*, 76 (1976): 109–30; for the latter, see G. Dworkin, *The Theory and Practice of Autonomy*, 18.

54. As some scholars have observed, notably Wei and Cai, unlike Mencius, Xunzi's conception of autonomy of *xin* mainly focuses upon intelligence or its knowing ability, as is evident in such remarks as *"xin* is the ruler of the body and master of daemonic and clear-seeing *(shenming),"* "*xin* is the lord or controller *(tianjun)* of senses," and *"xin* as the supervisor of *(gongcai)* of *dao."* This conception, as I have pointed out elsewhere, poses a

An examination of Xunzi's uses of *li**, in terms of their epistemic import, discloses that it is a notion functionally equivalent to "*reason* in the general sense of capacity for rational thought or the power to acquire intellectual knowledge."[55] Given Xunzi's primarily practical orientation, we may say that *li** expresses a notion of practical reason. The problem of choice can thus be said to be a problem of reasoned choice, an outcome of the exercise of practical reason. It is important to inquire into the nature of thinking involved. For this purpose, let us attend to Xunzi's conception of *zhilü*, which may be rendered as "wise and informed deliberation."[56]

Zhilü performs two different but related functions: (1) the resolution of perplexities concerning right or wrong conduct that arise in present, particular situations, and (2) preparation for a response to changing circumstances (*jundao* L284). For an elucidation of its nature and method, let us consider the component characters, *zhi* and *lü*, focusing primarily on their epistemic import.[57] *Lü* may be rendered as "thought, reflection, careful consideration, or deliberation." Xunzi's definition explicitly connects it with choice or selection *(ze)*: "the love, hate, pleasure, anger, sorrow, and joy in our original nature *(xing)* are called feel-

---

problem of unity of mind, that is, "a problem of coordinating the intellectual and volitional functions of the mind by way of an ethical ideal of *dao*" (*Ethical Argumentation*, 141). See Wei, *Xunzi yu gudai zhexue*, 127–31; Cai, *Kong Meng Xun zhexue*, 410–13; and *Ethical Argumentation*, 138–42. For relevant passages on the autonomy of *xin*, see *Concordance*, 62/17/12, 78/21/4, 80/21/32, 83/22/19-20, 84/22/40, 84/22/41, and 85/22/60.

55. This is a compendious statement of my reconstruction of Xunzi's uses of li*. See *Ethical Argumentation*, 20–30.

56. The following explication of *zhilü* is in part indebted to Chen Daqi. Chen's introductory remark, however, is a bit misleading: "*Dao* is the ultimate standard for thought, speech and action. Justification or argumentation *(bian)* and explanation *(shuo)* must accord with *dao*. Also, the distinctive human ability to discriminate *(*bian)* must accord with our sense of rightness *(yi)*. If one seeks to satisfy the standard of *dao*, one must acquire the knowledge of *dao*. Thus, acquiring the knowledge of *dao* is actually the fundamental task. But what we rely on for knowing *dao* is *zhilü*" (Chen, *Xunzi xueshuo*, 100). Chen's exposition actually considers discrimination *(bian)*, study or probing *(sisu)*, and comprehension or understanding *(lijie)* as factors involved in *zhilü*, rather than independent epistemic activities.

57. My discussion of *zhi* is highly tentative and pretends to being no more than a suggestive conceptual map for some of its epistemic uses. The *Concordance* lists, for example, 433 occurrences of *zhi*. An adequate treatment of *zhi* must provide a conceptual framework for all these uses. This is a topic worthy of further exploration, as it is indispensable to a comprehensive study of Xunzi's moral epistemology and psychology. As we shall note shortly, some of Xunzi's uses of *zhi* recall those in the *Analects* (*Lunyu*) and may also be important to examine with care, particularly in the light of the recent works of Hall and Ames. See note 51 above and Roger T. Ames, "Confucius and the Ontology of Knowing," in *Interpreting Across Boundaries: New Essays in Comparative Philosophy*, ed. Gerald James Larson and Eliot Deutsch (Princeton, N.J.: Princeton University Press, 1988), 265–79; and David L. Hall and Roger T. Ames, *Thinking Through Confucius* (Albany: State University of New York Press, 1987), chap. I, section 4.

ings *(qing)*. When these feelings arise and the mind *(xin)* makes a selection, this is called *lü*" *(zhengming* L506, D281*, W12). Since our original nature *(xing)*, in the sense of motivational structure, also comprises desires and aversions, which are natural responses to feelings, *lü* is properly considered to have its principal function in the choice of the desires. This interpretation is suggested by the following passage:

> The nature *(xing)* of man is what he receives from Heaven; his feelings *(qing)* are constitutive of his nature; his desires are the responses to these feelings.... Although a person cannot completely satisfy all his desires, he can come close to satisfying them, and although he cannot do away with all desires, by means of *lü*, he can regulate his pursuit.... The man of *dao* will advance his pursuit when he can and will regulate his pursuit when he cannot satisfy his desires. *(zhengming* L529, D295*, W152*)

Note that the regulation of the pursuit of desires by means of *lü* (henceforth, deliberation) entails a choice *(ze)* or decision on which occurrent desire is to be preferred as the end of action. However, given that a person is a self-determining agent, deliberation can be viewed as aiming at the formation of second-order or reflective desires.[58] For a natural desire, if directed by the mind *(xin)* and in accordance with reason, can be transformed into reflective desires in such a way that it is difficult to identify and distinguish it from the class *(lei)* of natural desires *(zhengming* L527, D294, W151).[59] In the light of commitment to *dao*, ethical autonomy is the ideal autonomy of will as constituted by second-order desires, the product of deliberation.

For performing the dual task of *zhilü*, the agent must adopt a method for evaluating or weighing *(quan*)* the relative merits and demerits of desires and aversions, as well as alternative options in terms of their beneficial and harmful consequences. Guided by *dao* as a holistic perspective, the proper method is *jianquan*, that is, thoughtful consideration of all relevant factors before arriving at a decision.[60] In Xunzi's

---

58. For more discussion of this passage in terms of Frankfurt's distinction between first-order and second-order desires, see my "Dimensions of *Li* (Propriety): Reflections on an Aspect of Hsün Tzu's Ethics," *Philosophy East and West* 29, no. 4 (1979), 380–81, or Essay 2 of this volume; Harry Frankfurt, "Freedom of the Will and the Concept of Person," *Journal of Philosophy* 68, no. 1 (1971), reprinted in *The Importance of What We Care About* (Cambridge: Cambridge University Press, 1988). Similar distinction is given in Liang Qixiong, *Xunzi jianshi*, 323. For other relevant passages on the connection between *lü* (deliberation) and choice, see *Concordance*, 10/4/32, 8/3/46–48, 10/4/32, 12/5/3, 47/12/74 and 61/18/63.

59. For further discussion of *xing* or motivational structure, see Essay 1 of this volume.

60. For emphasis on proper method in evaluating the mind *(xin)*, see *feixiang* L73, D66, K202; on method and standards of competence, see *Ethical Argumentation*, chap. 1. For the notion of desire as an outcome of weighing harm and benefit in the later Mohists, see Graham, *Later Mohist Logic, Ethics and Science*, A84, EC8.

words, "when one sees something desirable, he must carefully consider *(lü)* whether or not it will lead to a detestable consequence; when he sees something beneficial, he must carefully consider *(lü)* whether or not it will lead to a harmful consequence. All these consequences must be weighed together *(jianquan)* and taken into account in any mature plan before one determines which desire or aversion, choice or rejection is to be preferred" *(bugou* L53).[61]

Deliberation, in its inception, addresses a current perplexity. Its primary concern is the immediate consequence of pursuing occurrent desires. But the present situation, in posing a problem of choice, may well be an exigent situation, i.e., a novel circumstance in which past experience does not provide sufficient guidance. Also, it may be one in which the decision to be made is a plan of action. In this case, the agent cannot be content with a mere examination of the immediate consequences of the contemplated actions, for she must attend to distant consequences, in Xunzi's words, "consider the long view of things and think of their consequences *(changlü guhou)*" *(rongru* L68–69, K193–94). In this case, the dual task of *zhilü* represents a single process of thought.[62] Nevertheless, the focus is the present problem of choice. Like most judicial decisions in the Anglo-American higher court, observant of the doctrine of precedent, the current decision settles a case at hand, but at the same time projects its significance for like cases in the future.

Implicit in the foregoing characterization of *zhilü* is cost-benefit analysis, but significantly such a deliberation must be guided by *dao*, specifiable in terms of *ren*, *li* (ritual rules), and *yi* (rightness), especially *yi*, since it is through the use of *yi* that one responds to changing circumstances *(bugou* L43, K175–76; *zhishi* L306).[63] It is interesting to note that, focusing on the present, the object of deliberation may be said, à la Dewey, to be a *unified preference*. Says Dewey, "Choice is not the emergence of preference out of indifference. It is the emergence of a unified preference out of competing preferences."[64] Two passages on

---

61. Daniel Dahlstrom, "The *Tao* of Ethical Argumentation," *Journal of Chinese Philosophy* 14, no. 4 (1987): 475–85; and Cua, "Some Aspects of Ethical Argumentation: A Reply to Daniel Dahlstrom and John Marshall," *Journal of Chinese Philosophy* 14, no. 4 (1987): 501–16.

62. For this consequentialist theme in Xunzi's conception of deliberation, see also *Concordance*, 15/5/59–60, 19/7/27, 55/15/53, and 87/23/24. Cf. *Lunyu* 15:12.

63. Also the understanding of the classics. For an explicit passage, see *rongru* L68–69, K193–94. For the contrast between *yi* and concern for personal interests or desires, see especially *xiushen* L36, D53, W32, K158.

64. John Dewey, *Human Nature and Conduct* (New York: Modern Library, 1922), 193. Dewey's view is also reminiscent of Aristotle's account of deliberation, though Dewey may question Aristotle's conception of the end as the object of wish and confine it merely to a

the *li* (ritual rules), taken together, suggest Xunzi's concern with unity. In the essay on the *li*, Xunzi points out that "the *li* has a profound rationale *(li*)*" and "he who dwells in *li* and can ponder it well *(sisuo)* may be said to be capable of engaging in deliberation *(lü)*" (*lilun* L428, W95*, D224). The reflection at issue pertains not only to understanding the purposes of *li*, but also their justification.[65] The other passage I have in mind is this: "In summary, of all the methods of controlling the vital breath *(qi)* and nourishing the mind *(xin)*, none is more direct than proceeding according to the *li*, none more essential than obtaining a good teacher, and none more intelligent than *unifying one's likes*" (*xiushen* L27, K1:154).[66] My emphasis is Knoblock's rendering of *yi*, meaning oneness or unity. At any rate, the stress on *yi* or unity, especially as a characteristic of clarity of mind indispensable to *zhilü*, is a recurrent theme in the *Xunzi*.[67]

For deliberation *(lü)* to be adequate in resolving the problem of choice, it must be qualified by *zhi*. As a component of *zhilü*, I suggest that *zhi* be construed as "wise and well-informed." To elaborate its nature, let us consider *zhi* as a cognitive term with a range of uses that corresponds somewhat to that of "know" or "knowledge." Implicit in Xunzi's definition of *zhi*, as Liang Qixiong points out, is a distinction between the natural ability to know *(benneng zhi zhi)* and its achievement *(chenggong zhi zhi)*. "That in man by which he knows *(zhi)* is called *zhi;* the *zhi* that corresponds *(he)* to actuality is called wisdom *(zhi*)*" (*zhengming* L506, D282*, W140).[68] For present purposes, we may regard the

---

consideration of means. My own reading of Xunzi is closer to Dewey, since both preconceived end and means are objects of deliberation. Moreover, for Xunzi deliberation may also be characterized as "a dramatic rehearsal (in imagination) of various competing lines of action . . . an experiment in finding out what various lines of possible action are really like." And given its focus on the present, "deliberation is not calculation of indeterminate future results" (ibid., 190, 207). Of course, Dewey, unlike Xunzi, has no conception of sagely insight. For Aristotle, see *Nicomachean Ethics*, Book III, 1112a–13a.

65. See my "The Concept of *Li* in Confucian Moral Theory."

66. This is Knoblock's translation with my emphasis added, except that I retain *li* rather than Knoblock's "ritual principles," which, in my view, is highly problematic. See, for example, my "The Concept of *Li* in Confucian Moral Theory," or *Moral Vision and Tradition*, Essay 13.

67. More generally, Xunzi points out, in dealing with different kinds of things, one's mind should not be divided. For this reason, "the wise person *(zhizhe)* selects one thing and unifies his actions about it" (*jiebi* L488, W130, D270). And one who is wholeheartedly devoted to *dao (jingyi daozhe)*, unlike a specialist, will adopt an inclusive, unified approach *(jianwu)* in dealing with matters of all sorts. (See *jiebi* L490, D270, W130). For samples of relevant passages on unity, see *Concordance*, 16/6/14, 35/10/32, 40/11/64, 80/21/35, 80/21/41, 80/21/52, and 83/22/9.

68. The text is difficult to translate without using "know" for *zhi*. The passage runs: "*soyi zhi zhi cai ren zhe weizhi zhi. Zhi you sohe weizhi zhi*.*" I follow Liang in construing this passage as a distinction between *zhi* as a capacity to know in its first occurrence, and *zhi* as an accomplishment in the second occurrence. This distinction is reminiscent of Gilbert

range of achievement to comprise two broad types of knowledge: perceptual and ethical knowledge. In both types of knowledge, discrimination *(bian)* is involved. The content of perceptual knowledge is provided by the data of the five senses. Each sense has its proper object; for example, the eye can distinguish differences in "shape, color, or marking," the ear can distinguish differences in "tone, timbre, pitch, or modulation." While each sense has its proper object, it cannot provide any classification *(lei)* of, say, the different types of color or tone. Strictly speaking, perceptual knowledge is possible because the mind *(xin)* possesses *zhengzhi*, i.e., the ability to identify and reidentify the sense content as belonging to different sorts, as well as to synthesize these data and explain the grounds of perceptual judgments *(zhengming* L513, D285, W142–43).

Since explanation is a phase of argumentation, it must satisfy certain standards. In general, according to Xunzi, "before one can profitably engage in any discussion, there must first be established, just, and proper standards. Without such standards, right and wrong *(shifei)* cannot be distinguished and dispute cannot be settled" *(zhenglun* L410, D207–8*).[69] Among the standards of competence, accord with evidence *(fuyan)* is crucial to determining the reliability of perceptual judgments.[70] Equally important, especially in the case of direct perception, there must be evidence that the claimant possesses a clear and settled state of mind. Says Xunzi, "In general, when doubts arise in the course of observing things, and one's mind is unsettled *(buding)*, then one's perception of the external things will become unclear. When our thoughts *(lü)* are unclear, one cannot be in a position to determine whether a thing is so or is not so *(ranfou)*" *(jiebi* L495).[71] Xunzi goes on

---

Ryle's distinction between "know" as a capacity word and as an achievement word, in *The Concept of Mind* (New York: Barnes and Noble, 1949). Note that Liang's annotated edition of the *Xunzi*, which I consulted, contains a preface dated 1934. Note also that my rendering of *sohe* as "corresponding to actuality" is based on my understanding of Xunzi's doctrine of rectifying terms *(zhengming)*, given in *Ethical Argumentation*, chap. 3. Also, *zhi* and *zhi**, as homophones, are often used interchangeably. See the *Concordance* list for *zhi** and *zhilü*. For a distinction similar to Liang's, see Chen, *Xunzi xueshuo*, 34; Wang Zhonglin, *Xinyi Xunzi doupen*, 337.

69. For the distinction between *shi/fei* (right/wrong, correct/incorrect), see *Concordance*, 3/1/47, 3/1/48, 4/2/12, 9/4/17, 10/4/40, 15/6/1, 21/8/42, 24/8/103, 26/9/7, 39/11/40, 51/13/47, 59/16/29, 68/18/74, 69/18/102, 69/18/104, 82/21/85, 82/21/86, 82/21/87, and 99/27/82.

70. Because of his primary ethical concern, Xunzi does not provide us with an elaborate theory of perception. For the most part, his remarks seem to be confined to direct rather than indirect perception. For a discussion of the problem and solution regarding *zhengzhi* and the general standards of argumentative competence, see my *Ethical Argumentation*, chap. 1, esp. 31–36.

71. This is a revised translation of the one given in my *Ethical Argumentation* (140), and partly indebted to Dubs and Watson (D274, W132).

to cite and explain numerous examples of perceptual deceptions. For example, how darkness can distort vision, as in the case of a man walking in darkness, mistaking a stone for a tiger; or how excessive consumption of wine can impair our normal vision, as in the case of a drunkard who stoops to go through a city gate, mistaking its height. Apart from these cases of illusion, Xunzi also discusses cases of delusion, e.g., double image, mirror reflection, and the blind man's mistaken judgment concerning the existence or nonexistence of stars. What he says about the blind is particularly instructive.[72]

When a blind man looks up at the sky and declares that he sees no stars, men do not use his declaration to decide whether stars really exist or not, for they know that his faculties are impaired. Anyone who would actually base his judgments upon such evidence would be the biggest fool in the world. Such a fool in his judgments uses what is already doubtful to try to settle further doubts, and hence his judgments are never accurate. And if his judgments are never accurate, how can he hope to escape error? (*jiebi* L496, W134)

In the light of Xunzi's discussion of perceptual delusion, it is plausible to ascribe to him the notion of standard observer, though we do not find much textual material for reconstructing a Confucian theory of perception.

As in the case of perceptual knowledge, ethical knowledge involves knowledge of facts and thus also requires *fuyan*, that is, evidential judgments concerning matters of fact. As suggested earlier (section 1 above), ethical judgments are interpretive judgments informed by an ideal, unifying perspective. Reliable claims to ethical knowledge must be supported by accurate information concerning the *li* (rules of proper conduct) or institutional facts. This accounts for one frequent use of *zhi*, in the sense of acquisition of information or knowledge of right and wrong *(shifei)* and of the noble and the base *(guijian)*. However, the use of *zhi* in *zhidao* (knowing *dao*) also involves knowledge in the sense of acknowledgment, that is, an assent to *dao*; as well as the sense of *zhi* as realization, that is, the successful effort to make *dao* an actual object of deliberation. If we make the distinction between *zhi* as a task word and *zhi* as an achievement word, implicit, for example, in Wang Yangming's doctrine of the unity of knowledge and action *(zhixing heyi)*, then *zhi* in *zhidao* may be construed as embracing the distinction between prospective and retrospective knowledge.

---

72. Other examples pertain to perceptual relativity, e.g., how distance can obscure the actual size of objects, how height can distort the actual dimension of objects. It is disappointing that Xunzi does not pursue the issues involved in analyzing different sorts of perceptual deception. For the distinction between illusions and delusions, see J. L. Austin, *Sense and Sensibilia* (Oxford: Clarendon Press, 1962), Lecture III.

In terms of *zhidao*, the definition of *zhi**, cited earlier as "the *zhi* that corresponds to actuality," can now be understood as *zhi* in the sense of retrospective knowledge, an achievement of the effort to realize *dao* in the actual world. Since *zhi** and *zhi* are often used interchangeably in the classical literature, *zhi* can be properly rendered as "wisdom." The *zhi* in *zhilü* may thus be construed as "wise and well-informed," embracing both prospective and retrospective knowledge of *dao*.[73] Sound ethical judgments responsive to the problem of choice in *zhilü* are not only *well-informed*, as they are grounded in available factual knowledge of the living, historical tradition. They are also *wise* in the sense of being prudent, since they reflect a reasoned assessment of desires and aversions, as well as of competing options in the light of their beneficial and harmful consequences. Such wisdom, as an achievement of *zhi* or retrospective knowledge, may be viewed as a depository of ethical judgments and insights derived from the exercise of *yi* in deliberation *(lü)* on coping with changing circumstances in human life. Much in the spirit of Xunzi, this is the suggestion in Zhu Xi's notion of wisdom *(zhi*)* as *shoulian*, the gathering of the fruits of reflective ethical activities.[74] As earlier indicated in our sketch of practical coherentism, ethical judgments are essentially contestable, interpretive rather than absolute judgments. Nor are they universal and necessary in the Kantian sense, as Cai Renhou justly observes concerning Xunzi's conception of the knowing mind *(renshi xin)*.[75]

Like perceptual judgments, ethical judgments are *fallible*, for in the ideal case, they are judgments rendered, *all things considered*, as the best solutions to the problems of choice. Factors germane to deliberation may well be neglected or mistakenly consigned to irrelevance. And

73. Hall and Ames (in *Thinking Through Confucius*, chap. I, section 4) focus primarily on the use of *zhi* in both the prospective and retrospective senses of ethical knowledge in the *Analects (Lunyu)*. Such knowledge, however, also involves use of *zhi* in the sense of acquiring information, and is implicit in the use of *zhi* as "to realize." A cursory reading of *A Concordance to the Analects* (Harvard-Yenching Institute Sinological Index Series, supplement no. 16 [Taipei: Chinese Materials and Research Aids Service Center, 1972]) also discloses uses of *zhi* in the senses of acknowledgment, understanding or appreciation, and knowing-how. For the informational sense, see, for example, 2.11, 2.23, 5.9, 7.31; for the sense of understanding and appreciation, see, for example, 2.4, 4.14, 11.12; for knowing-how, 12.22. No doubt, these sample uses of *zhi* are subject to interpretation. In the case of Xunzi, readers may want to test my tentative proposal in this paragraph. (See note 68 above.) For Wang Yangming's distinction, see my *The Unity of Knowledge and Action*, chap. 1.

74. For more discussion, see Essay 5 in this volume. For discussion of *li* as a depository of insights, see D. C. Lau, trans., *Confucius: The Analects* (Middlesex, England: Penguin Books, 1979), 21–23. For different uses of the notion of intuition in ethical theory, see my *Reason and Virtue: A Study in the Ethics of Richard Price* (Athens: Ohio University Press, 1966), Appendix.

75. See note 54 above.

more importantly, as Xunzi urges, the agent may not possess the clarity of mind *(xin)* indispensable to wise and well-informed deliberation *(zhilü)*. Given the autonomy of mind *(xin)*, even if the agent has access to knowledge of *dao* adequate to resolving the problem of choice, he may willfully act in a manner contrary to *dao*, perhaps owing to a lack of genuine and wholehearted commitment to realizing *dao*, or to the weakness of will. More likely, the agent's mind, though guided by practical reason, is beset with preconceptions of good and evil or of right and wrong, as well as unexamined prejudices. Xunzi's technical term for these liabilities is *bi*, a condition of the mind cluttered up with extraneous preconceptions and preferences—a common affliction of humanity. This is a theme I have examined elsewhere.[76] For present purposes, let us briefly remark that "the problem of *bi* is the problem of replacing bad habits [of mind] with good and flexible ones.... The freedom from *bi* is an ethical transformation of the basic autonomy of mind, through reflection and self-cultivation, into moral autonomy—Xunzi's ideal of moral agency."[77]

Ethical judgments, as implicit throughout our discussion of *zhilü*, are not only liable to errors, but also *revisable* in the light of our historical understanding of an ethical tradition and its prospective significance. In this respect, even if the mind *(xin)* is completely free from *bi*, its ethical judgments have only the status of plausible presumptions. They are to be qualified in such terms as "adequate insofar as our experience goes." Nevertheless, given the conception of wisdom *(zhi*)* as a depository of insights, they may be viewed as "intuitions." And to the extent such wisdom provides sufficient guidance to resolving the problem of choice, *zhilü* will appear to be a facile proceeding. Nevertheless, our intuitions will always be the starting point in *zhilü*, as an articulation of wisdom even if in the end they may be deemed inadequate to resolving the problem of choice.

Our foregoing sketch of practical coherentism is highly incomplete. For further elaboration, what is required is some account of the nature of justification of ethical judgments and the types of reasoning involved. Perhaps even more important from the point of view of contemporary moral philosophy, what is lacking is an account of the role of transcultural principles, especially in the context of reasoned adjudication of competing judgments grounded in alternative, tradition-oriented, coherent, ethical perspectives of the good human life as a whole. Tentative explorations of these topics are found elsewhere.[78] In the final

---

76. *Ethical Argumentation*, 138–45.   77. Ibid., 145.
78. See *Moral Vision and Tradition*, Essay 14.

analysis, the basic question for a contemporary Confucian philosopher concerns the possibility of developing a systematic Confucian ethical theory.[79] This is an open question amenable to quite different philosophical treatment. Here, for the limited purpose of this essay, I offer a mere sketch of practical coherentism as one viable approach to this difficult and challenging task.

79. Ibid., Essays 12–14.

Essay 7

THE ETHICAL AND THE RELIGIOUS DIMENSIONS OF *LI* (PROPRIETY)

This essay presents a Confucian perspective on *li*. My main concern is the question, how can a Confucian moral philosopher move from the ethical to the religious dimension of *li*? The first section provides an analysis of the scope, evolution, and functions of *li*. The second section deals with the inner aspect of the foundation of conduct, the motivational aspect of *li*-performance. The third section discusses the outer aspect of the foundation of *li*, focusing on Xunzi's vision of the triad of *tian*, earth, and humanity *(can tiandi)*, an interpretation of his use of *tian, shen,* and *shenming* as expressing a respect for established linguistic, religious practice without an endorsement of associated popular religious beliefs. This interpretation leaves open the question of the validity of reasoned religious beliefs, while presuming the religious dimension of *li* as an extension of Confucian ethics.[1] The final section centers on the ethical significance of the *li* of mourning and sacrifice and concludes with some remarks on the transformative significance of the religious dimension of *li*.

1. AN ANALYSIS OF 'LI'

For more than two millennia, traditional Chinese moral life and thought have been much preoccupied with *li* as a means for the realization of the Confucian ideal of *dao* (Way) or human excellence *(shan)*. Implicit in this notion of *li* is an idea of rule-governed conduct. A rough indication of its scope may be gathered from a list of possible translations. Depending on the context of Confucian discourse, *li* can be trans-

---

[1]. For an extensive discussion of Confucian ethics, its tradition-orientation, basic conceptual framework focusing on *ren, yi,* and *li* as interdependent notions, and principles for intercultural adjudication, see A. S. Cua, *Moral Vision and Tradition: Essays in Chinese Ethics* (Washington, D.C.: The Catholic University of America Press, 1998), Essays 12–14.

lated as "religious rites, ceremony, deportment, decorum, propriety, formality, politeness, courtesy, etiquette, good form, good behavior, [or] good manners."[2] For convenience of reference it is sometimes desirable to use such terms as "propriety," "rules of propriety," or "rules of proper conduct."[3] For marking the pervasive feature of the members of this list, one might propose such terms as "rites/rituals," "ritual propriety," or "ritual rules," especially if we think of "rites" in the broad sense as inclusive of any established practice or set of action-guides that stresses formal procedures for proper behavior. However, without explicit explanation, this usage is likely to be misleading, particularly in view of the different connotations of the term. For this reason, I shall retain the transliteration *li* in this essay and adopt Xunzi's distinction between generic *(gongming)* and specific terms *(bieming)*. A generic term is a formal, general, abstract term amenable to specification by other terms in different contexts of discourse. These terms, used in practical or theoretical contexts, may be said to be specific terms in the sense that they specify the significance of the use of a generic term adapted to a current purpose of discourse. *Li* will be used as a generic notion subject to specification in context by such locutions as "the *li* of *x*" where *x* may mean "mourning," "sacrifices," "marriage," "manners," etc.[4] In this sense, law, morality, religion, and other social institutions, insofar as they require compliance with formal procedures, may be said to be concerned with ritual propriety. However, as a term for compendious description of the scope of *li*, "ritual propriety" or the like presupposes some understanding of the connection of *li* with other cardinal notions of Confucian ethics. Although we occasionally refer to the dependence of the ethical significance of *li* on *ren* (benevolence, humanity), and *yi* (rightness, righteousness), for present purposes, we assume their conceptual connection without elaboration.[5]

Our explication of *li* is based mainly on the works of Xunzi and *Liji (Record of Li)*.[6] The *Liji* is one of the three extant ancient texts on *li*:

---

2. Homer H. Dubs, *Hsüntze: The Moulder of Ancient Confucianism* (London: Arthur Probsthain, 1927), 113n. Here, I replace Dubs's "religion" with "religious rites." In this essay, "rites" and "rituals" are used interchangeably.

3. See *Chinese Classics*, trans. James Legge, vol. 1 (Oxford: Clarendon Press, 1893), and *The Works of Hsüntze*, trans. Homer H. Dubs (Taipei: Chengwen, 1966).

4. For further discussion, see Cua, *Ethical Argumentation: A Study in Hsün Tzu's Moral Epistemology* (Honolulu: University of Hawaii Press, 1985), 6 passim.

5. In this essay, parenthetical expressions of transcription function primarily as focal indicators of meanings of terms and for facility in distinguishing homophones. For the connection of *li*, *ren*, and *yi*, see *Moral Vision and Tradition*, Essay 13.

6. The *Liji* is one of the five basic Confucian classics, compiled probably in the first century B.C. Many chapters reflect the influence and further development of Xunzi's ethics. Reference to *Liji* is Legge's translation in *The Li Ki or Collection of Treatises on the*

Zhouli, Yili, and *Liji. Zhouli* deals with Zhou organization and institutions, *Yili* with codes of social conduct. The *Liji* mainly "deals with the meaning and significance of organization and institutions as well as with rules of social life and certain related academic matters."⁷ The extensive scope of *li* is indicated by the title of Legge's translation: "Collection of Treatises on the Rules of Propriety or Ceremonial Usages."

1.1 The Scope and the Evolution of Li

In the *Liji*, we find a wide scope of *li*, ranging from the *li* governing special occasions, such as mourning, sacrifices, marriage, and communal festivities, to the more ordinary occasions relating to conduct toward ruler, parents, elders, teachers, and guests. Different classifications are possible. Zhu Xi points to five different sorts of concerns exemplified in the *li:* family, communities, study, states, and dynasties. More modern but misleading classification can be offered in terms of law, religion, military matters, politics, and ethics.⁸

For elucidating the concept *li*, let us briefly consider its conceptual evolution. Following Hu Shi (1891–1962), we may regard the wide-ranging scope as exemplifying three different strata in the conceptual evolution of *li*.⁹ The basic meaning of *li* lies in the idea of rule. (In this sense, Dubs's rendering of *li* as "rules of proper conduct" is perhaps the best.) The evolution of *li* refers to its increasing extension. The earliest use, as far as scholars are able to ascertain, pertains to religious rites. The etymology of *li* suggests its connection with sacrifices to spirits. *Shuowen*, an ancient dictionary, notes that *li* is "compliance [with rules] for serving spirits *(shen)* and obtaining blessings."¹⁰

In the second stage, *li* becomes a comprehensive notion embracing

---

Rules of Propriety or Ceremonial Usages [1885], 2 vols. in The Sacred Books of the East, ed. Max Müller (Delhi: Motilal Banarsidass, 1966). The original Chinese edition I used is Wang Meng'ou's *Liji jinzhu jinyi* (Taipei: Shangwu, 1977). A similar device is used for citation from the *Xunzi*. Transcriptions are inserted in the translations to indicate my interpretive reading of Chinese characters and for subsequent comment.

7. Kao Ming (Gao Ming), "Chu Hsi and the Discipline of Propriety," in *Chu Hsi and Neo-Confucianism*, ed. Wing-tsit Chan (Honolulu: University of Hawaii Press, 1981), 313.
8. See Joken Kato, "The Meaning of Li," *Philosophical Studies of Japan* 4 (1963).
9. The following discussion of the conceptual evolution of *li* owes largely to Hu Shih, *Zhongguo zhexue shi dagang*, Part I (Taipei: Shangwu, 1947), 134–43. My use of Hu Shi is independent of his apparent claim to providing an historical account, for, as Kato points out, it is not plausible to regard the original meaning of *li* as pertaining exclusively to religious rites. "The religious rites go back to the oldest antiquity when they were not something different from [those of] everyday life." However, Kato does not deny that the Confucians in the classics made a distinction between religious and ethical rules, as suggested by Hu Shih. Kato is more interested in the anthropological than the philosophical significance of *li*. See Kato, 82.
10. Duan Yucai, *Shuowen jiezi zhu* (Shanghai: Shanghai guji publisher, 1980).

all social habits and customs acknowledged and accepted as a set of action-guiding rules. In this sense, the scope of *li* is coextensive with that of tradition comprising established conventions, that is, customs and usages deemed as a coherent set of precedents. *Li* is what distinguishes human beings from animals (*quli*, Legge, 1:64–65).

The third stage in the evolution of *li* is connected with the notions of right (*yi*) and reason (*li**). In this sense, any rule that is right and reasonable can be accepted as an exemplary rule of conduct. Rules can be constructed or revised, and thus are not exclusively determined by old customs and usages.[11] As one writer remarked: "The *li* are [the prescriptions of] reason. . . . The superior man (*junzi*) makes no movement without [a ground of] reason" (*zhongni yanqu*, Legge, 2:275). Another emphatic passage maintains that "[the rules of] *li* are the embodied expression of what is right (*yi*). If an observance stands the test of being judged by the standard of what is right (*yi*), although it may not have been among the usages of the ancient kings, it may be adopted on the ground of its being right" (*liyun*, Legge, 1:390). It is quite evident that the *Liji*, like *Xunzi*, was concerned with the problem of ethical justification. As Waley reminds us, "The task of the ritual theorists in the third century B.C. was to detrivialize ritual, to arrest its lapse into a domain of mere etiquette or good manners by reintegrating it into the current system of thought."[12] The task consists, in part, in defending specific rules of propriety, and, in part, in offering reasoned justification for the existence of an established normative system. This concern of ancient Confucians is shown in their occasional tendency to associate *li* with its homophone *li** (reason or rationale) and *yi* (rightness or fittingness).[13] The notion of *yi*, in part, is an attempt to provide a rationale for the acceptance of *li*. *Yi* focuses principally on what is right or fitting. Since what is right and reasonable depends primarily on judgment, *yi* may be understood as reasoned judgment concerning the right thing to do, more especially in particular exigencies. In two respects, acceptability of *li* depends on *yi*: (1) *yi* determines whether specific rules of *li* are the right sort of rules to regulate different types of conduct, and (2) the application of *li* requires *yi*, in the sense of reasoned judgment for their application to particular cases. Thus any established system of *li* is subject to

11. Hu Shi, 137–38.
12. Arthur Waley, *The Analects of Confucius* (New York: Random House, 1938), 59.
13. Mao Zishui, *Lunyu jinzhu jinyi* (Taipei: Shangwu, 1975), 185–87. For a general explication of *li** (reason, principle), see Cua "Reason and Principle in Chinese Philosophy," in *A Companion to World Philosophies,* ed. Eliot Deutsch and Ron Bontekoe (Oxford: Blackwell, 1997); incorporated in this volume as Essay 13. For the uses of *li** in Xunzi and Wang Yangming, see Cua, *Ethical Argumentation,* and *The Unity of Knowledge and Action* (Honolulu: University of Hawaii Press, 1982).

a *yi*-evaluation, given the conceptual connection of *li* and *yi*.[14] For explicating the rationale of *li (lizhili)*, we attend to overlapping questions concerning the significance *(lizhiyi)* and foundation of *li (lizhiben)*.[15]

1.2 The Significance of Li (lizhiyi)

In his essay on *li*, Xunzi points out that the rationale of *li* (lizhili)* is truly profound *(lilun* L428, W93). One must not confuse questions concerning the plurality or numerousness of *li (lizhishu)* and their underlying significance *(lizhiyi)*. The *li* or rules of proper conduct provide models without explanation *(quanxue* L14, W20). For a *junzi* or paradigmatic individual, moral learning must culminate in the state of integrity or "completeness and purity" *(quancui)*. And the achievement of integrity depends on efforts to attain *guantong*, i.e., to gain a comprehensive understanding of the meaning and practical import of the texts *(quanxue* L19, W 22).[16] We find similar emphasis on the significance of *li* in the *Liji*. In the chapter on border sacrifices, the writer stated that "what is esteemed in the *li*-performance is its [underlying] significance. When this is missed, the number of things and observances may [still] be exhibited" *(jiaote xing*, Legge, 1:439*).

For appreciating the significance of *li (lizhiyi)*, it is instructive to consider its principal functions by pondering on Xunzi's remark on the origin of *li*.

What is the origin of *li*? I answer that men are born with desires. If their desires are not satisfied, they cannot but seek means for satisfaction. If there are no limits or measures to govern their pursuit, contention will inevitably result. From contention comes disorder and from disorder comes poverty. The ancient Kings hated such disorder, and hence they established *li* (rules of proper con-

---

14. Cua, *Moral Vision and Tradition*, 277–87.
15. This scheme of analysis is partially indebted to Chen Daqi, *Mingli luncong* (Taipei: Zhengzhong, 1957). In his essay "*Li zhi fenshi* (An Analysis of *Li*)," Chen distinguishes three layers of *li*, ranging from the superficial to the profound: (1) the outer layer or the numerousness of *li (lizhishu)*, (2) the middle layer or significance of *li (lizhiyi)*, and (3) the inner layer or foundation of *li (lizhiben)*, which stresses the appropriate attitude in human intercourse. We leave aside the complex question of justification of *li (li zhi lizheng)*. (See Cua, *Moral Vision and Tradition*, Essay 13, 296–302.) An additional, more practical question may be raised on the efficacy or application of *li (li zhi gongxiao)*. The present explication of *li* is an abbreviated and modified scheme given in Cua, "The Concept of *Li* in Confucian Moral Theory," in *Understanding the Chinese Mind: The Philosophical Roots*, ed. Robert E. Allinson (Hong Kong: Oxford University Press, 1989); and elaborated in Cua, *Moral Vision and Tradition*.
16. For a discussion of *quantong* as a characteristic of ethical knowledge, see "The Possibility of Ethical Knowledge," in *Epistemological Issues in Ancient Chinese Philosophy*, ed. Hans Lenk and Gregor Paul (Albany: State University of New York Press, 1993), incorporated in this volume as Essay 6.

duct) and inculcated *yi* (sense of rightness) in order to make distinctions *(fen)* and draw the boundaries of responsibility for regulating men's pursuit, to educate and nourish *(yang)* men's desires, to provide opportunity for their satisfaction *(geiren zhi qiu)*. They saw to it that desires did not overextend the means of satisfaction, and material goods did not fall short of what was desired. Thus, both desires and goods mutually support each other. This is the origin of *li*. (*lilun* L417, W88*)

a. Delimiting Function. The foregoing passage gives a clear statement of the *li*'s main objective or primary function to prevent social disorder. For Xunzi, social disorder is an inevitable result of humans' conflicting pursuit of things to satisfy their desires. Elsewhere he reminds his readers that the scarcity of resources to satisfy everyone's desires would inevitably lead to contention *(zheng)* or conflict. As a set of rules for proper conduct, *li* has a delimiting function that defines the limits of individual pursuit of self-interest as well as boundaries of ethical responsibility. In this respect, the rules of *li* are functionally analogous to those of negative moral injunctions against killing, lying, stealing, etc. We must also note that for Xunzi, there is also a complementary positive objective in *li*-regulation, that is, the rules of *li* are necessary to human life in society and community. For this reason, cooperation through division of labor and observance of social or class distinctions *(fen)* are required for an orderly, harmonious social life.

For Xunzi, the most important social distinctions are the distinctions of the eminent and the mean, the elder and the younger, rich and poor, important and unimportant members of society. These distinctions represent different sorts of responsibilities. From the sociological point of view, the *li* are concerned with the maintenance of social structure as a harmonious pattern of roles and statuses.[17] Much in the spirit of Xunzi, one writer in the *Liji* remarks, "It is by the *li* that what is doubtful is displayed, and what is minute is distinguished, that they may serve as dykes for the people. Thus it is that there are grades of the noble and the mean, the distinctions of dress, the different places at court; and so the people [are taught to] give place to one another" (*fangji*, Legge, 2:285; also 1:63). Again, it is said: "It is by the universal application of the *li* that the lot and duty [of different classes] are fixed" (*Liyun*, Legge, 1:378). For the ruler, the *li* are an important instrument of social and political control, but notably, the social distinctions are valued not only because of their traditional backing but also because of their display of

---

17. In sociological terms, *li* may be regarded as a structure in Robert Merton's sense: "the pattern arrangements of role-sets, status-sets, and status-sequences." See Victor Turner, *Dramas, Fields, and Metaphors* (Ithaca, N.Y.: Cornell University Press, 1974), 237, 284.

personal moral merits. The significance of *li* as a tradition thus lies in its implicit critical moral acceptance.

b. Supportive Function. The idea of *li* as dykes for conserving virtues provides us a way to appreciate the supportive function. Recall Xunzi's remark on the origin of *li:* The rules of *li* also provide satisfaction of desires within the boundary of proper conduct. Within this boundary of proper conduct, expression of feelings and desires must be recognized. In Xunzi's words, the *li* must provide for opportunity for their satisfaction *(geiren zhi qiu)*. Thus, in addition to the delimiting function, the *li* have a supportive function, that is, they provide conditions or opportunities for satisfaction of desires within the prescribed limits of action. The *junzi* or ethically paradigmatic individuals are the same as the small-minded persons with respect to their nature *(xing)* and capacities *(cai)* for acquiring knowledge and action.

When hungry, they desire food, when cold, they desire to be warm; when exhausted from toil, they desire rest; and they all desire benefit and hate harm. Such is the nature that men are born possessing. They do not have to await development before they become so. (*rongru* L64, K1:191)

In an important sense, the supportive function of *li* acknowledges the integrity of our natural desires. So long as they are satisfied within the bounds of propriety, we accept them for what they are whether reasonable or unreasonable, wise or foolish, good or bad. The main supportive function of *li* is the redirection of the course of individual self-seeking activities, not the suppression of motivating desires. This is the *sublimating* function of *li.* Just as the delimiting function of *li* is functionally analogous to that of negative moral injunctions or criminal law, their supportive function may be compared with that of procedural law, which contains rules that enable us to carry out our wishes and desires, for example, the law of wills and contracts. Like these procedural rules, the *li* contribute to the fulfillment of desires without pronouncing value judgments. More importantly, the *li* also have an educational and nourishing function *(yang)* in encouraging learning and cultivation of personal character, the subjects of the first two essays in the *Xunzi.* To be a human being, in the ethical rather than the biological sense, is to aspire to become an ethically responsible scholar or official *(shi)*, a paradigmatic ethical person *(junzi)*, or a sage *(sheng).*

More generally, in ordinary human intercourse, we can appreciate the supportive function of *li* by pondering the significance of the *li* of civility. Many of the *li* of civility facilitate human intercourse, especially among strangers. The *li* of civility are especially important in discursive or argumentative context, for their supportive function reminds the parties in conflict that there must be agreeable procedures for resolving conflict before they deal with substantive matters at issue.[18] A Confucian philosopher, while aware of the possibility of mere observance of *li* without appropriate regard for *ren* and *yi*, will not altogether reject their ethical value, because conformity to the *li* of manners and civility is an example of regard for the necessity of *li* as having an *enabling* function in promoting easy, effortless, smooth conditions for human interaction.

c. The Ennobling Function. The focus on the ennobling function of *li* is a distinctive feature of Confucian ethics and traditional Chinese culture. The keynote of the ennobling function is "cultural refinement," the education and nourishment *(yang)* of emotions or their transformation in accord with the spirit of *ren* and *yi*. The characteristic concern with the form of proper behavior is still present. However, the form stressed is not just a matter of fitting into an established social structure or set of distinctions, nor is it a matter of methodical procedure that facilitates the satisfaction of the agent's desires and wishes; rather, it involves the elegant form *(wen)* for the expression of ethical character. A *li*-performance is not just an exhibition of an empty form; for the *junzi* complies with *li* in order "to give proper and elegant expression to his feelings" (*Zengzi wen*, Legge, 1:331). In other words, the ennobling function of *li* is directed primarily to the development of commendable or beautiful virtues *(meide)*. The beauty *(mei)* of the expression of an ethical character lies in the balance between emotions and form. What is deemed admirable in the virtuous conduct of an ethically superior person *(junzi)* is the harmonious fusion of elegant form and feelings *(lilun* L430, W96).[19]

Notably for Xunzi, the desired transformation of the original, problematic human nature *(xing)* is not just an outcome of a process of inculcation of moral virtues, principally directed to conflict-resolution, but also a beautification of man's original nature. As Xunzi put it:

Original human nature *(xing)* provides raw material, and constructive human effort *(wei)* is responsible for the glorification and flourishing of elegant form and orderly expression. Without constructive human effort, original human nature cannot beautify itself *(zimei)*. Only when original human nature and constructive effort are harmoniously united in character and conduct can the person be designated a sage and the task of unifying the world be accomplished. (*lilun*, L439, W102*)

---

18. *Moral Vision and Tradition,* Essay 13.
19. For a discussion of the aesthetic aspect of li-performance, see section 2 of Essay 2, "The Dimensions of *Li*," in this volume.

In this light the *li*-performance culminates in the experience of joy. In Xunzi's words: "All rites *(li)* begin in simplicity, are perfected in elegant form *(wen)*, and end in producing joy" *(lilun,* L427, W94*).

With the ennobling function of *li* in mind, we can appreciate some scholars' preference for "noble person" as a translation of *junzi* (Giles, Fingarette, Schwartz). Divested of its aristocratic connotation, a noble person is an ethically superior person or paradigmatic individual whose life and conduct exemplify *meide* or virtues in a very high degree, embodying particularly the concern for *ren* and *yi*. As we shall see in section 3, respect for traditional *li* or rites of mourning and sacrifices is in part an expression of the concern with *ren* and *yi*, because such practices exemplify the regard for the Confucian *dao* or ideal of humanity.

2. THE FOUNDATION OF 'LI (LIZHIBEN)': THE INNER ASPECT

For a contemporary Confucian moral philosopher, there are questions concerning the foundation of a person's commitment to the practice of *li*, especially to *li*'s ennobling function, i.e., to *ren* and *yi*. Our question of foundation *(ben)* inquires, so to speak, into the supporting edifice that provides the actuating force to the commitment to the practice of *li*. We may approach this question by distinguishing the inner *(nei)* and outer *(wai)* aspects of the foundation of *li*, deemed as the anchorage of the agent's serious commitment to the Confucian *dao* or ideal of human excellence *(shan)*. In the language of *Daxue (The Great Learning)*, such a person has attained *cheng* (sincerity) and is free from self-deception, that is, he or she has attained, in Zhu Xi's words, the state of "truthfulness, genuineness, and freedom from falsity" *(zhenshi wuwang)*.[20] Whereas the inner aspect of the *li*-performance pertains to *cheng* (sincerity), embracing a variety of moral attitudes, dispositions, and emotions, the outer aspect pertains to the underlying Confucian vision of the unity and harmony of humanity and *tian* (Heaven, Nature) and its implication for concern for the well-being of all things in the universe.[21] Differently put, the inner aspect pertains to the psychology of *li*-performance, the outer aspect to the committed person's ultimate

---

20. Zhu Xi, *Sishu jizhu* [Collected Commentaries on the Four Books] (Hong Kong: Taiping, 1980), 19. For a different translation of *chengyi* as "making the will sincere" instead of "making one's thought sincere," see Wing-tsit Chan, trans., *A Source Book in Chinese Philosophy* (Princeton, N.J.: Princeton University Press, 1963), 89. For more discussion of *chengyi*, see Cua, *Moral Vision and Tradition*, Essay 11. Note that the inner aspect of the foundation of *li* may also be elaborated along the line suggested in the notion of *cheng* (sincerity) in the *Doctrine of the Mean*.

21. Cua, *Moral Vision and Tradition*, Essays 2 and 7.

concern, to his/her understanding of the *dao* as a moral vision with cosmic significance. As we shall later see, the outer aspect of the foundation of *li* provides a transition to Confucian spirituality or the religious dimension of *li*.

Let us first consider the inner aspect of a *li*-performance conformable, say, to a *li* of civility, manners, or deportment. The *li* of manners and deportment are those formal prescriptions governing ordinary incidents of life, e.g., greetings, bowing, handshakes, smiling on appropriate occasions, decency in speech and appearance, etc. In this context, respectfulness *(gong)* and reverence *(jing)* are essential to the *li*-performance. More generally, the person must express *cheng* (sincerity). In one striking passage in the *Xunzi*, much reminiscent of *Zhong Yong (Doctrine of the Mean)*, we find the following: "For nourishing *(yang)* the mind of *junzi* (paradigmatic individual), there is nothing better than sincerity *(cheng)*. For attaining sincerity there is no other concern than to abide by *ren* and to practice *yi*" *(bugou* L47).[22] Recall Mencius's saying, "Benevolence *(ren)* is man's peaceful abode and rightness *(yi)* his proper path."[23]

Thus the *cheng* (sincerity) of a *li*-performance presupposes a concern with *ren* and *yi*. In the light of *ren*, the agent, apart from attention to *wen* or cultural refinement, must also have an affectionate concern for the well-being of the fellows of the community. And this concern involves *zhong* and *shu*, i.e., doing one's best to realize one's ethical commitment to the practice of *ren* and consideration of others' desires and thought,[24] presupposing *yi* as the ethical standard for the evaluation of conduct in an appropriate context of action.[25] Confucius's idea of *shu*, i.e., "Do not impose on others what you yourself do not desire" *(Analects* 15.24), may be construed as a counsel of *humility* and *modesty*. While humility is compatible with just pride, it is a desirable moral attitude, because one's claim to knowledge about what is good for oneself and another must be proportional to accessible information and experience. While such knowledge may provide grounds for a claim for its significance for future conduct, reasonable persons would avow their sense of fallibility or humility. Sagacious or judicious judgments will also be informed by a sense of timeliness *(shi)*, that is, an adaptation to the current situation in order to achieve equilibrium and an adjustment to varying, changing circumstances through the exercise of one's sense of rightness *(yi)*.

Further, for the *ren*-person, humility is a desirable ethical attribute,

---

22. Cf. Knoblock 1:177.
23. D. C. Lau, trans., *Mencius* (Middlesex, England: Penguin Books, 1970), 4A10.
24. *Analects* 4.15, 15.24.
25. Cua, "Confucian Vision and the Human Community," *Journal of Chinese Philosophy* 11, no. 3 (1984), 226–38, incorporated in this volume as Essay 11.

because no human possesses the knowledge of all possible, appropriate specifications of the significance of the good for individual human life. As a result, one's understanding and concrete specification of the ideal of the good human life will be always made from a limited and partial perspective. When *shu* is positively construed, while it is compatible with just pride in ethical attainment, it is best construed as a counsel of modesty, which stresses the importance of making reasonable or moderate claims on others. One ordinary sense of "reasonable" indicates that a reasonable person will refrain from making excessive or extravagant demands on others.[26]

More fundamentally, in the light of Confucian *dao* or *ren* as an ideal theme of the good *(shan)*, one must be modest in imposing wishes and desires upon others. A person committed to *ren* and *yi*, actuated by modesty or moderation, will be concerned with the mean *(zhong)* between excess and deficiency. Such a concern, however, presupposes that the agent exercises moral discretion *(quan)*. As Mencius reminds us, "Holding on to the middle *[zhong]* is closer to being right, but to do this without moral discretion *[quan]* is no different from holding to one extreme. The reason for disliking those who hold to one extreme is that they cripple the Way. One thing is singled out to the neglect of a hundred others."[27]

Expression of concern for *ren* and *yi* requires, to borrow Hume's words, a delicacy of taste, sensitivity not only to *wen*, the elegant form of conduct, but also to others' "prosperity and adversity, obligations and injuries."[28] Again, recall Mencius's notion of commiseration as a beginning or seed of *ren* and a *ren*-person as one who has a *xin* (heart/mind) that is sensitive to the suffering of others *(Mencius*, 2A.6) and a sense of shame as a seed of the virtue of *yi*. On the latter, Xunzi would add that just as it is important to distinguish between intrinsic honor or honor justly deserved *(yirong)* and extrinsic honor or honor derived from a person's circumstance *(shirong)*, one must also distinguish shame justly deserved *(yiru)* and shame derived from a person's circumstance *(shiru)*. The honor and shame justly deserved are conditions of character for which one is ethically responsible. The shame justly deserved is thus the agent's responsibility, because the person has deliberately engaged in ethically wrong conduct, e.g., conduct that is wayward and abandoned, reckless, arrogant and cruel, oppressive and rapacious *(zhenglun*, L410–11, K3:46).

26. See Cua, *The Unity of Knowledge and Action*, chap. 4.
27. Lau, trans., *Mencius*, 7A26*.
28. David Hume, "Of the Delicacy of Taste and Passion," in *Essays: Moral, Political and Literary* (Oxford: Oxford University Press, 1963), 4.

There is no assurance that intrinsic and extrinsic honor will coincide in practice. "Abiding by benevolence *(ren)* and acting in accord with one's sense of what is right *(yi)* and virtuous acts *(de)* are ordinarily reliable ways of managing one's life; however, it is possible that they may bring about dangerous (or unwanted) consequences" *(rongru,* L60, K1:189). Yet it cannot be doubted that the honor and shame one morally deserves are products of one's own intentional acts and thus properly reflect one's virtues and vices *(quanxue,* L5, W17). Implicit in both Mencius's and Xunzi's conception of shame is something like the distinction between social and ethical standards.[29] Like Aristotle, Classical Confucians were concerned with the noble and the base in the light of moral virtues and vices. Xunzi, in particular, would exalt a man of *li,* not just because his outward appearance and actions conform to *li,* but also because such a display makes manifest and glorious *(long)* his moral attainment.[30]

Before turning to the outer aspect of the foundation of *li,* let us briefly note that the range of attitudes, dispositions, and emotions involved in the inner aspect are complex, and often associated with the names of virtues. The *Analects* provides an ample vocabulary of ordinary ethical virtues amenable to interpretation and reinterpretation of their significance. One thinks of generic terms designating particular virtues such as filiality, courage, loyalty, fidelity, yielding to elders or superiors, uprightness, circumspection, and accommodation.[31] Different times and circumstances of the Confucian agents would yield different interpretations. Moreover, these terms refer to dependent virtues, for their ethical significance depends on concern for the cardinal virtues such as *ren* and *yi.* Positive attitudes toward these cardinal and dependent virtues are considered praiseworthy, just as negative attitudes toward the same virtues are disapproved by the Confucians. Expressions of emotions such as joy and sorrow, anger and resentment, as well as desires and aversions, must observe the relevant *li* with due regard to *ren* and *yi.* Ethical attitudes, dispositions, and emotions are for the most part the outcome of education. The *junzi* or paradigmatic individuals, persons whose lives exemplify a high degree of ethical attainment, play an important role in ethical education.[32]

---

29. Kwong-loi Shun, *Mencius and Early Chinese Thought* (Stanford, Calif.: Stanford University Press, 1997), 58–63. For more discussion of shame, see Cua, "Ethical Significance of Shame," *Philosophy East and West* 53, no. 2 (2003), reprinted in this volume as Essay 8.
30. For the extensive occurrence of *long* in connection with *li* or *li* and *yi,* see *A Concordance to Hsün Tzu,* Harvard-Yenching Institute Sinological Index Series, supplement no. 22 (Taipei: Chinese Materials and Research Center, 1966), 5/82270.
31. See Chen Daqi, *Kongzi xueshuo* (Taipei: Zhengzhong, 1976).
32. Cua, *Moral Vision and Tradition,* Essay 8.

Perhaps a bit stringent for people today, a Confucian would agree with Xunzi that such learning ceases only at death *(quanxue pian)*. Nevertheless, while moral learning is a heavy burden *(Analects* 7:7), it is not a process devoid of joy. Confucius once said of himself that his life is "so full of joy that he forgets his worries" *(Analects* 7:19). On another occasion, perhaps in a light-hearted mood, Confucius said that a *ren*-person would find joy in mountains and have a long life. The *ren* person, inspired by the ideal of *ren*, delights in mountains because his or her life is distinguished by an inspiration derived from the commitment to *ren* as the highest ideal of the good human life as a whole *(shan)*. In this sense, symbolically we may compare *ren*'s value height to the height of the mountains. And a person's *ren*-achievement, because of unwavering commitment and integrity, may be said to be still and firm as the mountains. But the idea that the *ren*-person is long-lived cannot be literally construed; for Confucius, a paradigmatic individual *(junzi)*, if the situation demands, "would sacrifice his life for the sake of *ren*" *(Analects* 15.9). The "long life" should be construed as "lifelong" commitment to the ethical vision and/or the enduring character of *ren*-achievement. Perhaps, for this reason, Qian Mu, an eminent Confucian scholar, points out that this dialogue implicitly appeals to the Confucian ideal of *tianren heyi*, the unity and harmony of humans and Heaven *(tian)*.[33] When we turn to the outer aspect of the foundation of *li*, the relevance of this Confucian vision will become manifest.

3. FOUNDATION OF 'LI (LIZHIBEN)': THE OUTER ASPECT

One way to approach the religious dimension of *li* is to discuss the outer aspect of the foundation of *li*, which is intrinsically connected with the inner aspect. Because of the intricate complexity of scholarship on the religious or spiritual aspect of Classical Confucianism, it is difficult for a Confucian moral philosopher to present a definitive interpretation of the outer aspect of the foundation of *li (lizhiben)*. Perhaps, the reason lies in the essentially contestable and vague concepts such as "religion" and "spirituality" in contemporary Confucian and comparative Chinese and Western philosophy. If we think of such terms as somewhat descriptive of a person's "ultimate commitment," then for a Confucian, particularly for a Neo-Confucian like Cheng Hao and Wang Yangming, commitment to *ren* may be so characterized, because the Confucian *ren*, by virtue of the indefinite and inexhaustible extension of affectionate

---

33. Qian Mu, *Sishu duben*, 2 vols. (Taipei: Liming, 1992), 2:165.

Ethical and the Religious Dimensions of Li *(Propriety)* 173

concern for all things, envisages the attainment of an exalted and jubilant state in which one would "form one body with all things without differentiation."³⁴ Chinese scholars commonly call this Confucian vision *tianren heyi*, the ideal of the unity and harmony of humanity and Heaven *(tian)*. More commonly in the Classical texts, we find the notion of *can tiandi*, humans "forming a triad with Heaven and earth."

Because of this vision, Xunzi exalts *(long)* the *li* as "joining Heaven and Earth in harmony" (*lilun* L427, W94). He is emphatic, however, that the profound rationale of *li (lizhili)* cannot be captured by the practitioners of the School of Names (Mingjia), arguing over such topics as "hardness and whiteness," "similarity and difference," nor by "uncouth and inane theories of the system-makers," nor by "the violent and arrogant ways of those who despise customs and consider themselves to be above other men" (*lilun* L429, W94–95). Xunzi continues:

> He who dwells in *li* and can ponder it well may be said to know how to think; he who dwells in *li* and does not change his ways may be said to be steadfast, and in addition has a true love for *li*—he is a sage. Heaven is the acme of loftiness, earth the acme of depth, the boundless the acme of breadth, and the sage the acme of the Way. Therefore, the scholar studies to become a sage; he does not study merely to become one of the people without direction. (*lilun* L429, W94–95*)

As a preliminary to understanding Xunzi's ideal of *can tiandi*, let us mention the different conceptions of the relation of *tian* and *ren* (humanity). In ancient China we find three different conceptions, embodying different ideals of the good human life. First, we find the idea of *tianren ganying*, the vision of mutual interplay of *tian* and humans exemplified in *Mozi;* secondly, the Daoist vision of *yinren ziran* embodied in *Laozi* and *Zhuangzi*, the vision of humans' harmony with the natural order of events oblivious of human desires and ethical concerns; and thirdly, the more influential Confucian (Mencian) vision of *tianren hede* in the *Works of Mencius*, the vision of achieving unity and harmony of *tian* and humans through the perfection of ethical character and virtues. The fourth vision is exemplified in Xunzi's vision of *tiansheng rencheng*, the vision that *tian* provides materials for humans to complete their proper tasks, through the exercise of their native capacities.³⁵

---

34. Cua, *Moral Vision and Tradition*, Essay 7.
35. For a good, informative account of the topic of the relation of *tian* and humans, see Yang Huijie, *Tianren guanxi lun* (Taipei: Dalin, 1981).

3.1 Tian *as Nature*

At the outset of Xunsi's essay on *tian*, we find a sharp distinction between *tian* and humans *(tianren zhi fen)*. *Tian* is the domain of *chang*, constancy or regularities of natural occurrences. For the most part, human fortune and misfortune depend on human efforts. As long as one follows the *dao* with single-mindedness, *tian* cannot bring misfortune. Says Xunzi,

> To bring completion without acting, to obtain without seeking—this is the work of *tian*. Thus, although the sage has deep understanding, he does not attempt to exercise it upon the work of *tian;* though he has great talent, he does not attempt to apply it to the work of *tian;* though he has keen perception, he does not attempt to use it on the work of *tian*. Hence, he does not compete against *tian*'s work. *Tian* has its seasons, earth has its riches, and man has his government. Hence man may form a triad *(can)* with the other two. But if he sets aside that which allows him to form a triad with the other two and longs for what they have, then he is deluded. (*tianlun* L362, W79-80*)

The above citation is Watson's translation except for substituting *tian* for "Heaven," a common rendering of *tian*. One may question the adequacy of this translation in the *Xunzi*, for unlike that in Confucius and Mencius, *tian* in most of Xunzi's uses, especially in our citation, is best rendered as "Nature" or "nature" in the sense of *tian* as "the objective . . . operation of certain processes and principles of Nature."[36] On the other hand, rendering *tian* as "Nature" or "nature" often leads to implausible interpretive theses ascribed to Xunzi.[37] While we cannot settle the interpretive issues here, "nature" seems a useful term for capturing Xunzi's conception of *tian*, if we attend to its divergence of opposites.[38] For *tian*, like *dao*, in Chinese philosophy, is a generic term *(gongming)* adaptable to different uses by different schools of thought.[39]

---

36. Knoblock, 3:7.
37. Edward J. Machle, *Nature and Heaven in the Xunzi: A Study of the Tian Lun* (Albany: State University of New York Press, 1993).
38. J. L. Austin, "A Plea for Excuses," in *Philosophical Papers* (Oxford: Clarendon Press, 1961), 139–40.
39. *Tian* may be said to be a "plurisign" or term suggesting varieties of uses and interpretations (Philip Wheelwright, *The Burning Fountain: A Study of Language and Symbolism*, new and revised edition [Bloomington: Indiana University Press, 1968]) or a systematically ambiguous expression (Gilbert Ryle, "Systematically Misleading Expressions," in *Logic and Language*, 1st ser., ed. A. G. N. Flew [Oxford: Blackwell, 1951]). Disambiguation depends on the context of use. For this reason, unless clear explanations are provided, it is best to retain the transliteration *tian*. The explanatory remarks are partially indebted to Hume. In Appendix III, entitled "Further Considerations Regarding Justice," to the Second Inquiry, Hume complains about the "looseness" of the term "natural" in speaking of "natural justice." In a note, he points out that there are three uses of "natural": "Natural may be opposed, either to what is *unusual, miraculous,* or *artificial*" (David Hume, *An*

For rendering *tian* as "nature" or "natural," some explanatory addenda are in order.

First, *tian* as nature is *chang*, the domain of regularities, i.e., our normal, usual, or customary experience of events or states of affairs. In practical planning and deliberation, we rely on such experience in expecting occurrence or recurrence of events and states of affairs. For Xunzi, this domain of natural phenomena must not be confused with that of *wei* or the *artificial*, that is, events and phenomena that occur as a result of constructive human efforts. This distinction is explicit in Xunzi's essay on *xing* (human nature), where he maintains that it is a mistake to attribute goodness to original human nature *(xing)*, for human goodness or excellence *(shan)* is a product of *wei*. Attainment of *shan* is an outcome of *wei* or constructive human activity in molding *xing*, the basic and problematic motivational structure of humans, into an ethically acceptable and beautiful nature. Of course, when a cultivated person achieves goodness, his or her virtues of integrity *(quan)* and purity *(cui)* will become second nature. Human nature is a raw material much like a potter's clay or a carpenter's wood for making pots and utensils. Says Xunzi, "A potter may mold clay and produce an earthen pot, but surely molding pots out of clay is not a part of the potter's human nature. A carpenter may carve wood and produce a utensil, but surely carving utensils out of wood is not a part of the carpenter's human nature. The sage stands in relation to *li* as the potter to the things he molds and produces" (*xing'e* L550, W164*).

Second, *tian*, as the domain of *chang* or natural regularities, does not preclude apparent anomalies such as falling stars and eclipses, which are viewed by ordinary folks as terrifying events or phenomena *(kong)*, as objects of fear and anxiety, because of the superstitious belief that these occurrences portend misfortune. For Xunzi, these strange, abnormal, and uncanny occurrences are proper objects of wonder or awe rather than fear.

> The sun and moon are subject to eclipses, wind and rain do not always come at the proper season, and strange stars occasionally appear. There has never been an age that was without such occurrences. If the ruler is enlightened and his government just, then there is no harm done even if they occur at the same time. But if the ruler is benighted and his government ill-run, then it will be no benefit to him even if they never occur at all. (*tianlun* L373, W83–84)

The proper objects of fear are such human portents as poor harvest, evil government that loses the support of the people, neglect of the

---

Inquiry Concerning the Principles of Morals [Indianapolis, Ind.: Bobbs-Merrill, 1957], 124).
For Xunzi, as we shall see shortly, *tian* may also comprise unusual and strange events.

fields, and starvation of the people. These are calamities due to human actions rather than natural causes (*tianlun* L373, 84–85).[40]

While Xunzi clearly rejects superstitious beliefs concerning apparent anomalies of *tian* as objects of fear, it is difficult to interpret with confidence his view that they are the proper objects of wonder or awe. Perhaps his view is that these are marvelous events that require no explanation, because they have no relevance to human well-being. It is also possible that Xunzi has a special regard for the belief that the anomalies exemplify "the uncanny and the supernatural" as awesome events, for he does not deny significance to all omens. "He makes a clear distinction between those who presage human misfortune, and hence are to be held in awe, and those which do not, and may only be deemed wield (*guai*)."[41]

Notably, some seemingly unusual or rare occurrences are often viewed by common people as *miraculous* and as having potential beneficial or harmful effects on human welfare. For people who believe in the efficacy of magical practices, certain humans possess magical power. While Xunzi considered the belief superstitious, on par with belief in physiognomy (*feixiang*, L73–91), he did not condemn these practices.

> You pray for rain and it rains. Why? For no particular reason, I say. It is just as though you had not prayed for rain and it rained anyway. When the sun or moon are eclipsed, you try to save them; a drought occurs and you pray for rain; you consult the art of divination before making a decision on some important matter. But it is not as though you could hope to accomplish anything by such ceremonies. They are done merely for the sake of *wen*. The *junzi* (ethically superior person) regards them as matters of *wen*, but the common people regard them as matters of *shen*. He who considers them as matters of *wen* is fortunate; he who considers them as matters of *shen* is unfortunate. (*tianlun* L376, W85*)

Recall *wen*, the beauty or elegant form of behavior, pertains to matters of cultural refinement. *Wen* is the way of honoring the cultural roots of our existence and reasonableness is familiarity with usages of *li* (*lilun* L424, W92–93). In this passage, the belief that *shen* is responsible for rain is considered to be unworthy of acceptance, yet Xunzi does not condemn the rain sacrifice. Why? Perhaps, when we turn to Xunzi's re-

---

40. While insisting that scarcity of goods to satisfy all humans' desires renders problematic cooperative social life, an argument for his thesis that "man's nature is bad," Xunzi also thinks that the problem of economic scarcity is often a result of mismanagement of existing natural resources. Thus Mozi's advocacy of economy of expenditure and attack on the Confucian stress on the importance of *li* and music are misfired and misguided. See *Fuguo* L195, K2:126–29; and Essay 1 of this volume. For a more general discussion on the ethical significance of scarcity, see Vivian Charles Walsh, *Scarcity and Evil* (Englewood Cliffs, N.J.: Prentice-Hall, 1961).

41. Machle, *Nature and Heaven in the Xunzi*, 117.

mark on the three bases *(ben)* for the practice of *li*, another expression of *can tiandi*, a plausible explanation is available.

The *Li* have three bases: *Tian* and earth are the basis of life, the ancestors are the basis of the family, and rulers and teachers are the basis of order. If there were no *tian* or earth, how could men be born? If there were no ancestors, how would the family come into being? If there were no rulers or teachers, how would order be brought about? If even one of these were lacking, there would be no peace and security for people *(an)*. Hence, *li* serves Heaven *(tian)* above and earth below, honors the ancestors, and exalts *(long)* rulers and teachers. These are the three bases of *li*. (*lilun* L421–22, W91*)

This passage suggests that peace and security *(an)* are primary considerations in the enforcement of the *li*, regardless of their reasoned explanation and justification. This concern with people's peace and security reflects the commitment to *ren*, an affectionate concern for the well-being of one's fellows in the community. Says Xunzi, "A *ren* person loves others. He loves others and thus hates what injures others" (*yibing* L328, W69*). But a *ren* person must respect others regardless of their capabilities or his own desire for association (*chendao* L298).[42] For securing peace and security, the ruler and the well-informed Confucian elites must not interfere with people's religious beliefs, regardless of their reasonableness. For Xunzi, human mind *(xin)* has a volitional function that may counteract its intellectual function. Given its autonomy, *xin* can act on its own will without regard to reason. And without the guidance of reason, it is bound to lead to delusion.[43] Yet, regarding the efficacy of the *li*, the ruler or responsible authority cannot ignore or legislate against ordinary people's religious beliefs, even if they are deemed unreasonable. It is not the business of those in government or ethical persons of the community to insure that ordinary people hold reasonable religious beliefs. To borrow William James's term, respect for people's "will to believe" is essential to the preservation of a harmonious social and political order. Perhaps this concern with the efficacy of the enforcement of the *li* is implied in this passage: "The [efficacy of] *li* relies on conformity to human *xin* (heart and mind) as foundation. Hence, even if there were no *li* in the *Classic of Li*, so long as they accord with *xin*, they may be considered as part of *li*" (*dalue* L605).

Moreover, recall our earlier discussion of *shu* as embracing modesty and humility. Having no infallible knowledge of the good *(shan)*, the *junzi* or ethically superior persons, without compromising their intellectual integrity, would refrain from condemning religious beliefs, which

---

42. For a *ren*-person's love of others, see also *Analects* 14.42.
43. Cua, *Ethical Argumentation*, chap. 4.

they consider ill-founded or superstitious. They would adhere to their conviction that the rain sacrifice is a matter of *wen,* a cultural embellishment. The associated popular belief in magic has no positive ethical significance, since it does not contribute to the realization of the Confucian vision of the unity of *tian,* earth, and humanity *(can tiandi).* Unless the practice of superstitious beliefs is deemed pernicious to preserving the ethical order of the community, the practice may be condoned without endorsement. Perhaps Xunzi's attitude may be characterized by Berkeley's epigram: "We ought think with the learned, and speak with the vulgar."[44] Admittedly some of Xunzi's uses of *shen* indicate approval of some religious beliefs, though we cannot be certain of his definitive views. Let us consider a couple of passages using *shen* and binomial *shenming.*

3.2 Shen *and* Shenming

Xunzi gives two explanations of the meaning of *shen.* We find the first and primary definition in his essay on *tian.* For convenience of reference, let us call this definition D1. This passage involving *shen* pertains to natural regularities of *tian,* the transformative process of *yin* and *yang:*

> Although we do not see the process, we can observe the results. All people understand that the process has reached completion, but none understand the formless or unobservable factors underlying the process. For this reason, it is properly called the accomplishment of *tian.* Only the sage does not seek to understand *tian.* (*tianlun* L65, W80*)

In this passage, *shen* pertains to the unobservable and inexplicable thing that underlies the process. This use of *shen* recalls the succinct remark in the *Yijing:* "The unfathomable *yinyang* process is what is meant by *shen.*"[45] This use of *shen* seems to imply the existence of a supernatural or transcendental entity at the base of natural processes. Thus *shen* is often translated as "spirit" or "god," as this is a common use in ancient literature. This use is exemplified in our earlier citation of the passage on the rain sacrifice. Here, our question does not concern the propriety of translation, but about the interpretation of *shen* as referring to a special superhuman being. For Xunzi, the question concerning the exis-

---

44. A remark, according to Jessop, quoted from the sixteenth-century Italian Augustinus Niphus. See George Berkeley, *A Treatise Concerning the Principles of Human Knowledge,* para. 51, in *The Works of George Berkeley,* 9 vols., ed. A. A. Luce and T. E. Jessop (London: Thomas Nelson & Sons, 1953).

45. Nan Huaijin and Xu Qinding, *Zhou Li jinzhu jinyi* (Taipei: Shangwu, 1976), 372.

tence and nature of such a being has no special relevance to resolving human problems, thus the sage-aspiring person will not seek knowledge of *tian*. Because of his pragmatic attitude toward metaphysical or ontological discourse, Xunzi discourages inquiring into the inexplicable factors that underlie natural processes, though, as we have seen earlier, he appreciates wonder or awe as a fitting response to strange and uncanny phenomena.

A secondary definition of *shen* (D2) pertains to ascription of ethical excellence or goodness to ideal persons. "To be wholly good and fully self-disciplined is called *shen*" (*ruxiao* L141). In both D1 and D2 Xunzi makes use of the quasi-definitional locution *zhiwei* in two different ways. D1, where *zhiwei* is a component of *fushi zhiwei*, provides both the necessary and sufficient conditions for the proper use of *shen*. D2, on the other hand, provides only the necessary condition.[46] Divested of ontological interpretation, anything that satisfies the definition D1 must be considered as something mysterious and incomprehensible. I suspect that Xunzi is offering a demythologized conception of *shen* that echoes the one given in the *Yijing*. D2, however, seems to be an explanation of the use of *shen* as a metaphor, while conveying the sense of the mysterious and the inexplicable. The context in which *shen* occurs in D2 is concerned with characterizing the sage as one whose Way of life and thought proceeds from Oneness, i.e., the person who resolutely holds fast to *shen*. This use of *shen* is plausibly a metaphor implying an analogy with *shen* in the sense of D1, as in the expression *rushen* that occurs in three passages that deal with good and well-ordered government.

Let us look at one passage involving *rushen*. In this instance, the discussion pertains to how an enlightened ruler *(mingjun)* unifies and guides the people by the Way *(dao)*, makes clear the ethical teachings and the use of punishment to forbid evils. Thus, says Xunzi, "his people are transformed by the Way as though his actions were those of a *shen*."[47] Here *shen* can be properly rendered as "spirit" or "god." In effect, Xunzi is saying that what an enlightened ruler accomplishes through *dao* is much like *(ru)* a *shen*. Much like the *yinyang* process, there is something mysterious and inexplicable as indicated by Xunzi's remark that precedes his discussion: "It is easy to unify the people by means of the Way, though the ruler could not make them understand

---

46. For a study of Xunzi's definitional locutions such as *zhiwei* and *weizhi*, see Cua, *Ethical Argumentation*, chap. 3.

47. Alternative translations somewhat differ from mine, though the import is similar. For examples, Watson renders *rushen* as "as though by supernatural power" (W146), Knoblock as "as if by magic" (K3:132), and Dubs "as by magic" (D288). For the two other examples involving *rushen*, see *Concordance*, 84/22/35 and 91/24/12.

all the reasons for things" (*ruxiao* L141, D289*). This remark recalls Confucius's: "The common people can be made to follow a path but not to understand it."⁴⁸

Let us turn to the second occurrence of *rushen*. Again, the context is good order, where Xunzi insists that a good ruler must be "sincere and trustworthy as though he were a *shen*" (*zhishi* L305). In the third occurrence, Xunzi maintains that in the good government by enlightened or sage kings of antiquity, we would learn that, among other things, punishments and penalties are rare, decrees and regulations are clearly promulgated, and "the transformations and reforms are like those of a *shen*" (*junzi* L563–64; K3:166). In all these examples, *shen* can be rendered as "a spirit" or "a god." Our explanation of the first occurrence of *rushen* also applies to the second and third occurrence.

First, let us note that the use of *shen* according to D2 implies a positive, normative judgment, expressing both approval and commendation. If we consider this use as metaphorical, then as in the case of D1 ontological interpretation is irrelevant. At the heart of this use is an analogy between one thing and another. For instance, the expression "He is a *shen*" is essentially a collapsed simile "He is like a *shen*."⁴⁹ Here *shen* is a metaphor in that it is a term that applies to something to which it is not literally applicable in order to suggest a resemblance to *shen* in the primary sense of D1, a metaphorical extension of D1.

For dealing with Xunzi's conception of *shenming*, let us look at an interesting passage where we find a connection between *cheng* (sincerity), *ming* (insight, clarity), and *shen*.

> For nourishing *(yang)* the mind of *junzi* (paradigmatic individual), there is nothing better than sincerity *(cheng)*. For attaining sincerity there is no other concern than to abide by *ren* and to practice *yi*. When his mind *(xin)* has attained *cheng* and abided by *ren*, his *cheng* will become manifest. In this way, he becomes a *shen* and is capable of transforming things *(hua)*. When his mind is sincere *(cheng)* and he acts according to his sense of rightness *(yi)*, he becomes reasonable *(li*)*. When his mind is reasonable, it is in the state of *ming*. Consequently, he [can adapt himself] to changing circumstances. *(bugou* L47)⁵⁰

In this passage, construing *shen* as a metaphor, an ellipsis of *rushen*, we can render it as "godlike." Remarkably the passage recalls the similar idea of the connection of *cheng* and *ming* and the vision of the triad of *tian*, earth, and humanity *(can tiandi)* in the *Zhong Yong*, where we find

48. *Analects* 8.9 (Lau's translation).
49. For an elaboration and defense of this Aristotelian view of "metaphors as elliptical similes," see Robert J. Fogelin, *Figuratively Speaking* (New Haven, Conn.: Yale University Press, 1988). See also Aristotle, *On Rhetoric*, Book 3, chap. 2, 1404b–05a.
50. Cf. Knoblock, 1: 177–78.

Ethical and the Religious Dimensions of Li (Propriety)

the view that truly sincere *(cheng)* persons who possess *ming* can develop themselves as well as others and "can then assist in the transforming and nourishing processes of Heaven *(tian)* and Earth, [and] can thus form a trinity with Heaven and Earth *[can tiandi]*."[51] More importantly, as Xunzi goes on to point out, although the sages are wise, without *cheng* they cannot transform the multitude *(bugou* L47). Implicit is the notion of the sage *(shengren)* as one who embodies the confluence of *cheng* and *ming*.

For elucidating the notion of *ming*, let us remark on an ambiguity. In the context of the connection of *ming* and *cheng*, *ming* seems to refer to an achievement. In this sense, *ming* may be rendered as "insight" or "enlightenment"—an achievement arrived at through assiduous efforts to pursue *dao* through moral learning and practice in conjunction with constant self-cultivation. These are the themes in Xunzi's first two essays, entitled "Encouraging Learning *(Quanxue pian)*" and "Self-Cultivation *(Xiushen pian)*." In both essays, sagehood is viewed as the ultimate end of learning. Like Mencius, Xunzi is confident that all human beings, regardless of their economic, political, or ethical standing in society are capable of becoming sages. In another sense, *ming* is an achievement of clarity of mind, rather than an achievement of insight. After we consider a passage on *shenming*, we will attend to this sense of *ming* as a precondition of insight in connection with Xunzi's notion of *da qingming*.

Let us turn to a passage involving *shenming* in the context of Xunzi's claim that all ordinary persons are capable of becoming sages—a view shared by Mencius and Song-Ming Confucians. According to Xunzi, all ordinary persons have a native capability to understand the rationales *(li*)* of *ren, yi,* and rules and regulations. If they devote themselves with single-mindedness to moral learning and contemplate the significance of *ren, yi,* and rules and regulations, persevere over a long period of time, through unceasing effort to accumulate good deeds, "they can acquire a comprehensive *shenming (tong yu shenming)* into the inner significance of things and form a triad with *tian* and earth *(can tiandi).* Thus the sage is one who has attained the highest state through the accumulation of good deeds" *(xing'e* L552, W167*). Again, here we find another use of *ming* as an achievement of insight. In effect, the sage is one who possesses a sort of insight that befits a "god or spirit *(shen).*" *Ming* in the sense of "insight" is an achievement, an outcome of persistent effort at moral learning. However, from the epistemic point of view, there is a more fundamental sense of *ming* as "clarity," which refers to a precondition for attaining *ming* in the sense of "insight" or "enlightenment."

---

51. Chan, *Source Book,* 107–8.

In the essay on dispelling *bi* (obscuration, blindness of the mind), Xunzi maintains that unless the mind is in the state of *ming* (clarity), it is liable to suffer from *bi* or cognitive blindness. Earlier we referred to this passage for Xunzi's conception of the autonomy of human mind without considering the full context involving the use of *shenming*. The passage runs: "The mind *(xin)* is the ruler of the body and *shenming zhi zhu*" *(jiebi* L488). We find different English translations for *"shenming zhi zhu,"* e.g., "the master of godlike intelligence" (Watson), "the master of the daemonic-and-clear-seeing" (Graham), "the master of spiritual intelligence" (Knoblock), and "the host to such a divine manifestation" (Machle).[52] It is difficult to resolve the issue here.[53] I propose, as a minimal interpretation, perhaps acceptable to these translators, that we regard *shenming* here in the light of the connection between *shen* and *ming*. Interpreting *shen* as "godlike" and *ming* as "insight" gives us a reading of *shenming* as a special characteristic of the sage, an interpretation closer to Graham and Knoblock, with an additional appreciation of Machle's rendering of *zhu* as "host."[54] Construing *shen* in *shenming* as "godlike," we have the sense of insight *(ming)* that befits a god or spirit *(shen)*, a rare and extraordinary human achievement. In this light, it is also acceptable to render *shenming* as "spiritual insight," which suggests an affinity to Descartes's notion of *intuitus*,[55] although for Xunzi *shenming* is more a form of wisdom or perspicacity—a product of cultivation, accumulation of goodness, and evidential learning *(chengzhi)*,

---

52. See Watson, W139; A. C. Graham, *Disputers of the Tao: Philosophical Argument in Ancient China* (La Salle, Ill.: Open Court, 1989), 252; Knoblock K3: 105; Edward J. Machle, "The Mind and the *'Shen-ming'* in Hsün Tzu," *Journal of Chinese Philosophy* 19 (1992): 383.

53. Below, my interpretation of *shenming* differs from Machle's, although I accept his construal of *zhu* as "host." Machle plausibly claims that Xunzi's uses of *shenming* convey a numinous or spiritual quality, for given that *shenming* is the quality of the sage's insight or enlightenment, it may be said to have a spiritual quality, "spiritual" in the sense of "the sacred," of something that is worthy of veneration or reverence. As we have indicated earlier in connection with the inner aspect of the foundation of *li*, reverence is a required attitude for *li*-performance. When we turn to another passage on *shenming*, we will bring out Machle's alternative reading and its value. My own interpretation differs from Machle's in that I propose a minimal interpretation based on Xunzi's appropriation of Zhuangzi's use of *ming*, without Machle's confident attribution to Xunzi's belief about the existence and nature of the *shen* or *shenming* when these terms are construed as referring to ontological entities. In the next section, we will say something more about the Confucian perspective on this issue.

54. Machle also objected to the translation of *er* as "and," presumably because these writers regard "and" as a coordinative conjunction. But "and" can also be used with the force of a consequence or conditional result, for example, "He felt tired and decided to stay home." It is possible that Machle is right that *er* conveys this special sense of "and," though I find the use of "and" in translation is perfectly acceptable if proper explanation is given.

55. Harold H. Joachim, *Descartes's Rules for the Direction of the Mind* (London: George Allen & Unwin, 1957), 25 and following.

rather than an a priori intuition or way of knowledge. In the essay on encouraging learning, Xunzi remarks that "if a *junzi* engages in extensive learning and daily examines himself, his wisdom will become clear *(ming)* and conduct be without fault" *(quanxue* L2, W15*). However, more accomplished is the sage who possesses an understanding *(zhi)* of the holistic character of *dao*. A doctrine of the *dao* based on a limited perspective, raising for attention "one corner" of *dao*, is insufficient to capture its intrinsic holistic nature *(jiebi* L478, W126; *tianlun* L381, W87). Because of this understanding of "the thread of *dao (daoquan),*" without deliberation or planning, the sage can respond appropriately to changes as they come.[56] The understanding *(zhi)* is an insight into the interconnection of things rather than factual knowledge. Unlike a truth claim, the sage's insight is akin to keen appreciation or perception of the significance of the interconnection of facts that sheds light on human problems.[57] Succinctly put, a sage has "a keen insight which never fails" *(xiushen* L33, W30).

If the foregoing remarks on *shenming* are considered adequate for understanding Xunzi's use of *shenming*, we can also appreciate Machle's translation of *zhu* as "the host," rather than the common translation "the master," thus rendering the phrase on the mind *(xin)* as "the host of *shenming.*" For insight *(ming)* arrived at through a long process of learning and self-cultivation, including constant self-examination, is something that one acquires, not as a result of thinking or inference, but a consummation and reward of a lifelong effort in pursuing *daoquan* or a holistic understanding of *dao* and *liquan*, the "thread that runs through the rationales of things." The sage is a recipient of *shenming*. Something echoing this interpretation of *shenming* may be found in Zhu Xi's conception of *qiongli*, i.e., exhaustive investigation of the rationales *(li*)* of things. Zhu Xi writes, "The first step in the education of the adult is to instruct the learner, in regard to all things in the world, to proceed from what knowledge he has of their rationales *(li*)*, and investigate further until he reaches the limit. After exerting himself in this way for a long time, he will one day achieve a wide and far-reaching penetration *(quantong).*"[58] Understanding the living significance of classical texts is an occurrence, something that happens independently of one's efforts, though efforts are the prerequisites for this experience. Insight is a prize of these efforts at learning, not a realization of an end-in-view. Recall our earlier emphasis on effort to *quantong* as essential to

56. Cua, *Ethical Argumentation*, 31–35, 61–65.
57. Cua, *Moral Vision and Tradition*, 95–99.
58. *Great Learning*, chap. 5; Chan, *Source Book,* 89*; Zhu Xi, *Sishu jizju* (Hong Kong: Taiping, 1980), 5.

the *junzi*'s or paradigmatic individual's attainment of moral integrity, i.e., to gain a comprehensive understanding of the meaning and practical import of the classical texts (*quanxue* L19).

As regards Xunzi's uses of *shen* and *shenming*, whatever translation one adopts, e.g., "spirit," "god," "godlike," "godliness," absent our knowledge of his view on the nature and existence of *shen* and *shenming*, I sometimes wonder whether Xunzi's attitude of wonder or awe toward *shen* as the unfathomable that underlies the *yinyang* process reflects the attitude of a conservative, linguistic revisionist as suggested in his essay on "rectifying terms or names" (*zhengming pian*). There he points out that it is the task of a sage king to preserve old terms and create new ones, as they are needed. To do so, he would have to consider three questions: "Why terms are needed? What is the basis for distinguishing similarities and differences between things, and the essential standard in regulation?" (*zhengming* L510, W141*). The essential standard governing the uses of terms lies in abiding by appropriate conventions, for "terms have no intrinsic appropriateness. It is agreement that determines their actuality or concrete application *(shi)*" (*zhengming* L616, W144*).[59]

Moreover, for Xunzi, respect for linguistic practices is an important criterion for successful communication. Would Xunzi similarly regard his own use of *shen* and *shenming* as an example of respect for the linguistic practice of his time? An affirmative answer to this question would ascribe to Xunzi the thesis that the established usages of *shen* and *shenming* are acceptable independently of their associated religious beliefs, superstitions as well as doctrines concerning their metaphysical or ontological status. Of course, this established linguistic practice provides a language for honoring and glorifying *shen* and *shenming*, indirectly exemplifying our pivotal ethical concerns in the light of *dao*. This interpretation has a partial support in Xunzi's uses of *long* (magnifying, glorifying, exalting) in connection with *ren, li,* and *yi*.[60] In this regard we find an interesting analogue in Hobbes's view on the language of Christianity, namely, that the use of "the Spirit of God" does not imply an understanding of "*what he is,* but only that *he is;* and therefore the Attributes we give him, [that he is omnipotent, benevolent, and wise,] are not to tell one another, *what he is,* but only *that he is* nor to signifie our opinion of his Nature, but our desire to honour him with such names as we conceive most honorable amongst ourselves."[61] I also wonder whether Xun-

---

59. *Moral Vision and Tradition*, 95–99.
60. A significant number of occurrences of *long* involve *li* alone, *li* and *yi*, and *ren*. For example, see *Concordance*, 3/1/36, 3/1/39, 20/8/11, 24/8/91, 43/11/136, 46/12/57, 54/15/22, 58/16/4, 64/17/43, and 72/19/39.
61. Thomas Hobbes, *Leviathan* (Oxford: Clarendon Press, 1952), 304.

zi would also endorse Hobbes's saying: "Words are wise men's counters; they do reckon by them; but they are the money of fools."[62]

4. THE RELIGIOUS DIMENSION OF 'LI'

For Xunzi, the practice of religious rites of his times, the *li* of mourning and sacrifice, has a profound significance for a good human life, not because of its association with specific religious beliefs, say, concerning the existence of the spirits of the dead, but because of ordinary, human longing for a long life and reverence for the dead, especially their beloved. His attitude echoes Confucius's and an earlier view of immortality *(shi er buxiu)*, that immortality pertains to "establishing virtues *(lide)*, establishing accomplishments *(ligong)*, and establishing words *(liyan)*."[63] However, the fact of human mortality is a proper concern of *li*. While the wish for continued existence after death cannot be fulfilled, the beginning and the end can be properly honored. All human beings encounter the beginning of life and death as boundary situations. The religious rites for mourning and sacrifice provide occasions for honoring our roots, a symbolic expression of our reverence for human life. These rites deal with our conception of our own boundary situations, birth, marriage, and death.

Austin once remarked: "A word never—well, hardly ever—shakes off from its etymology and its formation. In spite of all changes in and extensions of and additions to its meaning, and indeed rather pervading and governing these, there will persist the old idea."[64] As noted earlier in section 1, the etymology of *li* suggests its connection with sacrifices to spirits. The common translation of *li* as "rites" or "ritual" thus recalls the early Pre-Confucian use of *li* in religious context. In the last section, especially in connection with *shen* and *shenming*, we occasionally noted the associated beliefs in the existence of gods and their influence in human life. This feature is also prominent in some essays in the *Liji*. Xunzi's view somewhat echoes Confucius's. Confucius seems to have an insouciant attitude toward the existence of spirits and the relevance of belief in an afterlife, though sometimes he appealed to Heaven *(tian)* as a quasi-purposive, religious being. We find, for instance, the following:

The Master said, "There is no one who understands me." Zigong said, "How is it that there is no one who understands you?" The Master said, "I do not complain

---

62. Hobbes, 29; C. M. Turbayne, *The Myth of Metaphor* (New Haven, Conn.: Yale University Press, 1962), 101.
63. Chan, *Source Book,* 13.
64. Austin, "A Plea for Excuses," 149.

against Heaven *(tian)*, nor do I blame men. In my studies, I start from below and get through to what is up above. If I am understood at all, it is, perhaps, by Heaven *(tian)*."[65]

But, at another time, when he was asked about wisdom *(zhi)*, Confucius said that one must serve the people with a sense of what is right and appropriate *(yi)*, and respect the ghosts and spirits *(guishen)*, but keep them at a distance.[66] Confucius approved of the *li* of mourning and sacrifices largely because of his adoption of the Zhou tradition as an ethical guide to communal intercourse, not because of the specific associated religious beliefs about the existence of ghosts and spirits.

Notably, Confucius seems to have an "as if" attitude toward the existence of the dead as objects of sacrifice,[67] and stresses the importance of reverence in sacrifice and sorrow in mourning.[68] In the *Liji*, it is said that King Wen "in sacrificing, served the dead as if he were serving the living" *(jiyi* 2:608, Legge 2:212). We find a similar attitude in Xunzi: "The funeral rites have no other purpose than to clarify the rationales *(li)* of life and death, to send the dead person away with grief and reverence, and to lay him at the ground" *(lilun* L441, W105*). In sacrificial rites, "one serves the dead as though they were living, the departed as though present, giving body to the bodiless and thus fulfill the proper form of *li*" *(lilun* L451, W111*). Moreover, appropriate expression of emotions is essential. Says Xunzi, "The sacrificial rites originate in the emotions of remembrance and longing for the dead. Everyone is at times visited by sudden feelings of depression and melancholy longing. . . . [These rites] express the highest degree of loyalty, love and reverence, and embody what is finest in ritual conduct and formal bearing" *(lilun* L450–51, W109–11). For Xunzi, it is especially important for participants in a *li*-performance to aim at the "middle state," i.e., between excessive emphasis on formality and the inordinate expression of emotions *(lilun* L430, W96).

More succinctly, "one serves the dead as though they were living, the departed as though present—an appearance without reality yet sufficient to fulfill the requirements of elegant form."[69] This view suggests that religious rites have a significance as an extension of the moral and aesthetic dimension of *li*—an idea echoed by this passage in the *Liji:* "In

---

65. *Analects* 14.3 (Lau's translation).   66. *Analects* 6.22.
67. *Analects* 3.12.   68. *Analects* 19.1.
69. My remarks here on religious rites supplement section 3 of my "Dimensions of *Li*" (Essay 2 of this volume). For a fuller treatment, see Tang Junyi's incisive discussion of the *Liji* in vol. 2 of his *Zhongguo zhexue yuanlun: yuandao pian* (Taipei: Xuesheng, 1978). A more general discussion is given in Tang's *Zhongguo renwen jingshen zhi fazhan* (Taipei: Xuesheng, 1978).

dealing with the dead, if we treat them as if they were entirely dead, that would show a want of affection; or if we treat them as if they were entirely alive that would show a want of wisdom" (*tangong* 1:148). Reverence or awe is required in all ritual performances. Awe, however, is not incompatible with wondering about the existence of the objects of religious rites. As Wheelwright notes: "Awe is ambivalent emotion, compounded of wonder and humility; the wonder keeps the emotion alive and the mind open, while humility restrains the wonder from slipping into idle curiosity."[70] However, if one allows the wondering to take the form of ontological speculation, the emotion of awe or reverence would fade away, and the ritual performance would appear a mere formality divested of any moral and aesthetic significance.

Though coherent and plausible, this elucidation of the Confucian attitude toward religious rites does not fully account for certain peculiar features of the *Liji*. Because of its dominant emphasis on the moral and aesthetic import of all types of *li*, it is accepted as a Confucian canon. But some chapters on mourning and sacrifices display a sense of supplication implying a belief in the existence of spiritual beings (for example, *jiyi*, Legge 2:220–21). And others reflect a confidence in the ultimate grounding of all the *li* in some inarticulate form of cosmology. One reads, for example,

Music is [an echo of] the harmony between heaven and earth; the *li* reflect the orderly distinctions [in the operations of] heaven and earth. From that harmony all things receive their being; to those orderly distinctions they owe the differences between them. Music has its origin from heaven; the *li* take their form from the appearances of the earth. If the imitation of those appearances were carried to excess, confusion [of the *li*] would appear; if the framing of music were carried to excess, it would be too vehement. Let there be an intelligent understanding of the nature and interaction of [heaven and earth], and there will be ability to practice well both the *li* and music. (*yueji* 2:100–101).[71]

Furthermore, a reader may be puzzled by the liberality of the *Liji* in acknowledging all sorts of spiritual beings as objects of sacrifice. Apart from those of ancestors and parents, we find reference to the spirits of heaven and earth, sun and moon, and other material objects. One way to deal with these problematic features in the *Liji* is simply an outright admission that religious rites, in addition to their basic moral and aesthetic import, have a cosmological dimension, and this dimension is amenable to metaphysical speculations. I cannot pursue the philosophi-

---

70. Philip Wheelwright, *Metaphor and Reality* (Bloomington: Indiana University Press, 1968), 47.
71. This passage is a partial echo of Xunzi's remark (*yuelun* L463, W117).

cal issue here, but will offer some suggestions for further exploration.

The standard Confucian conception can accept such a cosmological extension without internal incoherence and without being burdened with the ontological issue. The basis for such an extension lies in *ren* or the ideal of humanity. This orientation toward mutual care and the bond between all human beings is inherently extensible to embrace other creatures and inanimate things and objects of remembrance and longing as well. *Ren* may thus be viewed as an idea of unbounded extensive affection. To be a man of *ren* or to be committed to *ren* is to will sincerely and actively the enlargement of one's scope of affection in all forms of human relationships. The joy experienced in the pursuit of *ren*, however transitory, can take on a quality of diffusion characteristic of many of our emotional experiences. In general, the joy or "pleasure that suffuses a consummatory act or gratuitous satisfaction tends to spread out over neighboring and similar object and acts."[72] An experience of *ren* is an experience of a diffusive affection. And reflection on this character of *ren* experience can yield a vision of cosmic harmony—a prominent theme in the Confucian classic on the mean *(Zhong Yong)* and in the works of the Neo-Confucians, for example, Cheng Hao and Wang Yangming.[73] The cosmological passages in the *Liji*, in this light, are more profitably construed as exaltations to this Confucian vision rather than an embodiment of an ethical cosmology.[74]

CONCLUSION

For a contemporary Confucian philosopher, an appreciation of the religious dimension of *li*, the *li* of mourning and sacrifices, does not depend on inquiry into their metaphysical or ontological significance. Tang Junyi points out that the significance of sacrifices to spiritual beings *(guishen)* does not depend on any ontological view on their independent and external existence, but on our *ren*-capacity to *guantong*, that is, to permeate or penetrate through all existent things.[75] Spiritual beings may be said to exist only insofar as they are the objects of this

---

72. Stephen C. Pepper, *Sources of Value* (Berkeley: University of California Press, 1958), 246.

73. For an elaboration of this Confucian vision of the harmony of man and nature, see Cua, *Moral Vision and Tradition*, Essays 2, 4, 7, and 9; and *The Unity of Knowledge and Action*, chap. 4.

74. Chinese religious practices are generally coupled with a belief in the existence of spirits and spiritual worlds—a belief that is viewed as a necessary supplement to, rather than determinative of, the nature of human life. For an interesting anthropological study, see Francis L. K. Hsu, *Under the Ancestors' Shadow* (New York: Doubleday Anchor, 1967), particularly chap. 6.

75. Tang, *Zhongguo renwen jingshen zhi fazhan*, 141.

penetrating process—they "exist" as objects of our emotions or thought, expressive of our moral attitudes. In the ontological sense, they need not exist, for we have no knowledge of their nature independent of our emotions or thought. In the spirit of Xunzi, we may regard these entities as our own creations *(wei)*; they exist as supervenient qualities of our reflective ethical experience, the resultant attributes of the expression of our ethical emotions or thought in the context of religious observances.[76] In this sense, the religious dimension of *li*, like its aesthetic dimension, is an extension of its primary ethical dimension, and may properly be considered as a constitutive feature of the Confucian ethical life. Differently put, ideally, in the growth of the ethical experience of a committed Confucian agent, religious quality may become a salient feature of his or her life. Xunzi's endorsement of the uses of *shen* and *shenming* in his own thought, aside from his respect for established linguistic practices, possibly reflects his appreciation of the transformative character of religious beliefs, insofar as they are consistent with *ren*, *yi*, and *li*.

In light of the Confucian vision of the unity and harmony of *tian* and humanity, especially in Cheng Hao and Wang Yangming, this ideal of the good human life encompasses all living and nonliving things. Although this ideal is a wish rather than an object of reasoned deliberation, it may be considered a religious ideal, for a person seriously committed to *ren* will regard all things as "one body." In the words of Wang Yangming,

> The great man regards Heaven, Earth, and the myriad things as one body *(yiti)*. He sees *(shi)* the world as one family and the country as one person. . . . Forming one body with Heaven, Earth, and the myriad things is true not only of the great man. Even the mind *(xin)* of the small man is no different. Only he makes it small. Therefore, when he sees a child about to fall into a well, he cannot help a feeling of alarm and commiseration. This shows that his humanity *(ren)* forms one body with the child. Again, when he observes the pitiful cries and frightened appearance of the birds and animals about to be slaughtered, he cannot help feeling an "inability to bear" their suffering. This shows that his humanity forms one body with birds and animals.[77]

Wang goes on to point out that a man of *ren* also forms "one body" with plants, stones, tiles, mountains, and rivers. In this version of the Confucian vision of *can tiandi*, the unity and harmony of humanity and all things becomes an ethical ideal that provides a cosmic perspective. In

---

76. W. D. Ross, *The Right and the Good* (Oxford: Clarendon Press, 1930), chap. 2.
77. Wang Yang-ming, *Instructions for Practical Living and Other Neo-Confucian Writings*, trans. W. T. Chan (New York: Columbia University Press, 1963), 272.

Tu Weiming's words, it is an "anthropocosmic" vision, where the human "self" is the center of all human and nonhuman relationships.[78] If the primary function of the language of religious beliefs is an expression of religious commitment or of the "will to belief," this Confucian vision may properly be regarded as a religious vision, presupposing the Confucian ethical ideal of the good human life as a whole, variously termed as *dao, ren, tianren heyi,* or *can tiandi.* For a committed agent, this vision may provide a motivating force in self-transformation, since the vision answers to vital personal perplexities that resist problematic formulation.[79] In this way, we can have an open, ethical vista that embraces and preserves the integrity of religious beliefs without prejudging their reasoned justification, thus leaving open a serious inquiry into the possibility of Confucian philosophy of religion and comparative religion.[80]

78. Tu Weiming, *Centrality and Commonality* (Albany: State University of New York Press, 1989).
79. See Cua, *Dimensions of Moral Creativity,* chap. 8.
80. An early version of this essay was presented at the International Conference on Ritual and Philosophy of China, International Institute for Asian Studies, Leiden University, May 27–28, 1999.

Essay 8
ETHICAL SIGNIFICANCE OF SHAME: INSIGHTS OF ARISTOTLE AND XUNZI

1. INTRODUCTION

1.1

The principal aim of this paper is to offer a constructive interpretation of the Confucian conception of shame. We focus on Xunzi's discussion as the *locus classicus* of the Confucian conception of shame as contrasted with honor. In order to show Xunzi's conception as an articulation and development of the more inchoate attitudes of Confucius and Mencius, we make an excursion to *Lunyu* and *Mengzi*. Aristotle's conception of shame is used as a sort of catalyst, an opening for appreciating Xunzi's complementary insights. Notably, some scholars of Xunzi regard his achievement as comparable to that of Aristotle. Homer H. Dubs remarks: "Although Hsüntze [Xunzi] lacked the interest in metaphysics and science that distinguished the Stagirite, yet he had a capacity for rounding out and systematizing the Confucian philosophy, which until his time had been mostly a set of authoritarian deliverances, that shows him akin to his Greek contemporary. His, too, was an interest in psychology, in the analysis of experience, and above all a synthetic power that reveals a truly great man. To the Confucian philosophy he gave a systematic theoretical foundation that served it in good stead until imperial authority established it as authoritarian."[1] Notably, Dubs is right to reject the common ascription to Xunzi of the label of authoritarian moralist, who espouses a social and political hierarchy of ranks and values. Careful studies of various philosophical aspects of Xunzi's thought concur with Dubs's assessment, e.g., Xunzi's insights on

---

1. H. H. Dubs, *Hsüntze [Xunzi]: The Moulder of Ancient Confucianism* (London: Arthur Probsthain, 1927), xix; see also John Knoblock, *Xunzi: A Translation and Study of the Complete Works,* vol. 1 (Stanford, Calif.: Stanford University Press, 1988), vii.

human nature, proper conduct, moral knowledge, deliberation, and ethical uses of history and argumentation.[2]

1.2

For both Aristotle and Xunzi, shame is not a moral virtue. Its importance has to do chiefly with the connection with the ideal of *eudaemonia* or *dao* or *ren* (humanity, benevolence) as a life of moral virtue. In other words, the ethical significance of shame is derived from the ethical concept of virtue. For one who takes seriously any version of an ethics of virtue, the concept of shame deserves attention.

As a preliminary, adopting Xunzi's distinction between generic *(gongming)* and specific *(bieming)* terms,[3] we take the term "shame" to be a generic term for a family of specific terms such as "disgrace," "humiliation," "chagrin," "embarrassment," "ignominy." A generic term is a formal, general, or abstract term amenable to specification by other terms in different discursive contexts. These terms, used in practical or theoretical contexts, may be said to be specific terms in the sense that they specify the significance of the use of a generic term adapted to a current purpose of discourse.[4]

Notably, lexical definitions of "shame" make use of one or more of these specific terms, e.g., "disgrace," "humiliation," or "dishonor"—the opposite of "honor." In the *Oxford English Dictionary Online*,[5] for instance, we find these two entries for "shame": (1a) "The painful emotion arising from the consciousness of something dishonouring, ridiculous, or indecorous in one's own conduct or circumstances (or in those

---

2. See A. S. Cua, *Ethical Argumentation: A Study in Hsün Tzu's Moral Epistemology* (Honolulu: University of Hawaii Press, 1985); and Essays 1, 2, 3, 6, and 7 of this volume.

3. For a discussion of Xunzi's distinction between *gongming* and *bieming* in the *Zhengming pian* L515, see Cua, *Ethical Argumentation*, 29, passim; and A. S. Cua, *Moral Vision and Tradition: Essays in Chinese Ethics* (Washington, D.C.: The Catholic University of America Press, 1998), Essay 10.

4. Note that this is a relative distinction, for one can talk about the levels of abstractness or concreteness relative to the context of practical discourse, thus the distinction does not correspond to Aristotle's notion of genus and species. The contemporary counterpart of this distinction is concept and conception. See, for example, H. L. A. Hart, *The Concept of Law* (Oxford: Clarendon Press, 1961), 156; John Rawls, *A Theory of Justice* (Cambridge, Mass.: Harvard University Press, 1971), 5–9; Robin Attfield, "On Being Human," *Inquiry* 14 (1974): 175–76; Ronald Dworkin, *Law's Empire* (Cambridge, Mass.: Harvard University Press, 1986), 71–72.

5. More succinctly in the *New Shorter Oxford English Dictionary* (1997), we find these two entries for "shame": (1a) "The feeling of humiliation or distress arising from the consciousness of something dishonourable or ridiculous in one's own or another's behaviour or circumstances, or from a situation offensive to one's own or another's sense of propriety or decency," and (2a) "Disgrace, loss of esteem or reputation; an instance of this." (The electronic version used is 1.0.03, ©1996, Oxford University Press.)

of others whose honour or disgrace one regards as one's own), or of being in a situation which offends one's sense of modesty or decency" and (3a) "Disgrace, ignominy, loss of esteem or reputation." In some widely used dictionaries, these specific terms are commonly given as synonyms of "shame." In another electronic dictionary, we find the following synonyms of "shame": "Disgrace, discredit, disesteem, dishonor, disrepute, ignominy, infamy, obloquy, odium, opprobrium."[6] The synonyms are obviously intended as usable approximations, as a resource for a writer's judgment of appropriate contextual and stylistic concerns. More informative about the difference in the family of specific terms for "shame" as a generic term is this list: "embarrassment, mortification, humiliation, chagrin," which presumably "designate different kinds or degrees of painful feeling caused by injury to one's pride or self-respect."[7] Understandably, "honor" is missing from the list of antonyms, i.e., "pride, self-esteem, self-respect." If we regard the specific terms for "shame" as possible ways of characterizing the degrees of intensity in the experience or feeling of shame, these terms may also be considered as terms for variants of shame feeling.[8]

1.3

For distinguishing the different qualities or kinds of shame experience, some writers seem to use "shame" as a generic term in hyphenated expressions such as "propriety-shame," "honor-shame," "worth-shame;"[9] or "disgrace-shame," "discretion-shame," and "humiliation-

---

6. For "related words," we have "chagrin, embarrassment; guilt, mortification, self-reproach, self-reproof"; for contrasted words, "pride, self-admiration, self-love, self-respect." (*Merriam-Webster's Collegiate English Dictionary*, electronic version 1.1 [1994–95].)

7. *Random House Webster's Unabridged Electronic Dictionary* (CD-ROM version 2.0 for Windows 3.1/95) gives the following: "—Syn. 1. SHAME, EMBARRASSMENT, MORTIFICATION, HUMILIATION, CHAGRIN designate different kinds or degrees of painful feeling caused by injury to one's pride or self-respect. SHAME is a painful feeling caused by the consciousness or exposure of unworthy or indecent conduct or circumstances: *One feels shame at being caught in a lie.* It is similar to guilt in the nature and origin of the feeling. EMBARRASSMENT usually refers to a feeling less painful than that of SHAME, one associated with less serious situations, often of a social nature: *embarrassment over breaking a teacup at a party.* MORTIFICATION is a more painful feeling, akin to SHAME but also more likely to arise from specifically social circumstances: *his mortification at being singled out for rebuke.* HUMILIATION is mortification at being humbled in the estimation of others: *Being ignored gives one a sense of humiliation.* CHAGRIN is humiliation mingled with vexation or anger: *She felt chagrin at her failure to remember her promise.*"

8. For a discussion of the lexical meanings of such terms as a prelude to a working concept of shame in connection with neurosis, see Helen B. Lewis, *Shame and Guilt in Neurosis* (New York: International Universities Press, 1971).

9. John, Kekes, "Shame and Moral Progress," *Midwest Studies in Philosophy* 13 (1988): 287–90.

shame."[10] Note that these expressions function as binomials that convey different conceptions of shame. As we shall see later, this is the case with Xunzi's distinction between two types of shame *(ru), shi-ru* and *yi-ru*.[11] In some cases, for distinguishing the quality of a particular shame experience from disgrace, an alternative to using a binomial such as "disgrace-shame" is to use "shame" as a specific term, in a narrow sense, as distinct from the use of "shame" as a generic term. The distinction between generic and specific terms is somewhat parallel to the distinction between the broad and the narrow senses of "good" in ethical analysis. In Confucian ethics, if we regard *ren* as functionally analogous to "good," we can also distinguish *ren* in a similar way.[12] To my knowledge, the best example is Zhu Xi's uses of *ren* in his essay on *ren (Renshuo)*. *Ren* is said to embrace the four moral qualities in the mind of man, that is, *ren* (humanity, benevolence), *yi* (rightness, righteousness), *li* (propriety, rites), and *zhi* (wisdom). In the generic sense *ren* is said to be constitutive of *dao*, "which consists of the fact that the mind of Heaven and Earth to produce things is present in everything."[13]

For present purposes, "shame" is used as a generic term for discussing Greek and Chinese/Confucian conceptions in Aristotle and Xunzi. Our interest lies in the ethical significance of shame experience and not in the phenomenology, sociology, and psychology of shame. In what follows, we rely on the lexical meanings of "shame" and use it as a translation for both Greek and Chinese terms. The spirit of this accords with that of Bernard Williams's philosophical study of shame in Ancient Greek literature. Says Williams, "In this discussion, I have been using the English word 'shame' in two ways. It has translated certain Greek words, in particular *aidōs*. It has also its usual modern meaning" (presumably the understanding provided by our lexical guide). In this way, we hope to acquire some insights into the rationales of the ethical significance of shame.[14]

10. Carl D. Schneider, *Shame, Exposure, & Privacy* (Boston: Beacon Press, 1977), chap. 3. An alternative to this hyphenation device is to discuss the difference between "shame" and related terms such as "humiliation" and "embarrassment," especially to point to their difference in ethical significance. See Gabriele Taylor, *Pride, Shame, and Guilt: Emotions of Self-Assessment* (Oxford: Clarendon Press, 1985), chap 3. Our distinction between "shame" as a generic and as a specific term leaves open the question of phenomenology, psychology, and/or ethical significance.

11. For indicating a combination of Chinese characters for special attention, I use the device of hyphenation as in the Wade-Giles romanization. In other cases, I follow the standard pinyin romanization.

12. Wing-tsit Chan, trans., *A Source Book in Chinese Philosophy* (Princeton, N.J.: Princeton University Press, 1963); A. S. Cua, *Dimensions of Moral Creativity: Paradigms, Principles, and Ideals* (University Park: Pennsylvania State University Press, 1978), chap 3.

13. Chan, *Source Book*, 594. For more discussion, see Cua, *Moral Vision and Tradition*, Essay 13.

14. Williams continues: "I have been able to use it in both these ways without falling

2. ARISTOTLE AND THE EARLY GREEK TRADITION

2.1

The concern with honor and shame is very much evident at the time of Plato and Aristotle. The role of shame as a sanction for conduct is functionally analogous to that of conscience. According to K. J. Dover:

[w]here a modern speaker would probably make some reference to good or bad conscience the Athenians tended to use expression such as "be seen to . . .", "be regarded as . . ." [And] these expressions were also used where we would refer neither to conscience nor to reputation, so that an Athenian's "I wanted to be regarded as honest" is equivalent to our "I wanted to be honest". In such cases there was no intention, of course, of drawing a distinction between disguise and reality; it was rather that goodness divorced from a reputation of goodness was of limited interest.

The desires for honor and the aversion to shame are important motives for conforming to social expectations of proper behavior, e.g., expectations of one's family, friends, as well as fellow-citizens. Generally, "the hope for praise is a major incentive to virtue and the fear of reproach a major deterrent to wrongdoing."[15]

Alasdair MacIntyre maintains that in the Heroic Societies the standards of conduct are entirely dependent on the acceptance of a moral tradition and there is no external point of view for evaluation:

The heroes in the *Iliad* do not find it difficult to know what they owe one another: they feel *aidōs*—a proper sense of shame—when confronted with the possibility of wrongdoing. . . . Honor is conferred by one's peers and without honor a man is without worth. The heroes do not possess a vocabulary that enables them to evaluate, from the outside, their own culture and society. Instead, evaluative expressions they have are interdefinable and explainable only in terms of one another.[16]

---

apart, and this shows something significant. What we have discovered about the Greeks' understanding of these reactions, that they can transcend both an assertive egoism and a conventional concern for public opinion, applies equally well to what we recognise in our own world as shame. If it were not so, the translation could not have delivered so much that is familiar to us from our acquaintance with what we call 'shame'" (Bernard Williams, *Shame and Necessity* [Berkeley: University of California Press, 1993], 88). In Aristotle, other terms for "shame" are *aidōs* and *aischunē*, in *Nichomachean Ethics* and the latter in the extensive discussion in *Rhetoric*.

15. K. J. Dover, *Greek Popular Morality in the Time of Plato and Aristotle* (Berkeley: University of California Press, 1974), 226–28.

16. Alasdair MacIntyre, *After Virtue* (Notre Dame, Ind.: University of Notre Dame Press, 1984), 125.

For appreciating the role of shame in the Heroic Societies, we must consider what is involved in the experience of shame. In Williams's instructive study, a person who experiences shame in the early Greek society is aware of being exposed inappropriately to the "eyes of others," i.e., to the wrong people at the wrong time. The natural reaction is to hide or cover oneself. Moreover, shame becomes a sanction or motive of action when the agent is fearful of what other people will say about his actions.[17] Also, there is *nemesis* as a reaction.

The reaction in Homer to someone who has done something that shame should have prevented is *nemesis*, a reaction that can be understood, according to context, as ranging from shock, contempt, and malice to righteous rage and indignation . . . but it is natural, and indeed basic to the operation of these feelings, that *nemesis* and *aidōs* itself, can appear on both sides of a social relation. People have at once a sense of their honour and a respect for other people's honour; they can feel indignation or other forms of anger when honour is violated, in their own case or someone else's. These are shared sentiments with similar objects, and they serve to bind people together in a community of feeling.[18]

2.2

The common Greek concern with honor and shame provides the setting for Aristotle's discussion. In *Nichomachean Ethics*, honor as the end of political life is rejected as a "superficial" answer to the inquiry concerning the highest good or the best human life, for the bestowal of honor seems to depend on others rather than the recipient's real merits. Furthermore, those who pursue honor want to confirm their own worth, and, at any rate, "they seek to be honored by sensible men and by those who know them, and they want to be honored on the basis of their virtue or excellence" (NE 1095b22–1096a3).[19]

However, in characterizing high-mindedness or magnanimity *(megalopsychia)* as the crown of virtues, Aristotle gives special notice of the honor deserved. The high-minded men are concerned with honor, for honor is the greatest of the external goods that they deserve as a reward for their achievement (NE 1123a34–1124a).[20] The honor that the high-

17. Williams, 78–79.
18. MacIntyre, 80.
19. Unless otherwise indicated, Ostwald's translation of the *Nichomachean Ethics* is the source of the citations. See Aristotle, *Nicomachean Ethics*, trans. Martin Ostwald (Indianapolis, Ind.: Bobbs-Merrill, 1962), hereafter cited as NE.
20. "If a high-minded man thinks he deserves great things and actually deserves great things, especially the greatest, there will be one matter that will be his major concern. 'Desert' is a relative term that refers to external goods; and as the greatest external good, we may posit that which we pay as a tribute to the gods, for which eminent people strive most, and which is the prize for the noblest achievements. Honor fits that description, for

minded men deserve, however, is intrinsically connected with virtues of character, goodness and nobility. Says Aristotle, high-mindedness "is the crown, as it were, of the virtues: it magnifies them and it cannot exist without them. Therefore, it is hard to be truly high-minded and, in fact, impossible without goodness and nobility" (NE 1124a1–4).

2.3

In the *Rhetoric*, Aristotle stresses even more perspicuously the value assigned to honor and its connection with nobility.[21] First, Aristotle points to honor as a constituent of happiness, along with "good birth, plenty of friends, good friends, wealth, good children, plenty of children, a happy old age, also such bodily excellences as health, beauty, strength, large stature, athletic powers, together with fame, honour, good luck, and virtue" (RH 1360b). Second, the internal good of possessing virtue is inseparable from nobility. For virtue and vice, the noble and the base are the proper objects of praise and blame: "The Noble is that which is both desirable for its own sake and also worthy of praise; or that which is both good and pleasant because good. If this is the true definition of the Noble, it follows that virtue must be noble, since it is both a good thing and also praiseworthy" (RH 1366a). And the opposites of honor are shameful actions. Among other things, noble actions are those performed for the sake of honor only. Also, all actions done for the sake of others, for their benefit and not for the sake of one's profit, are good deeds. "And the opposites are those things of which men feel ashamed, for men are ashamed of saying, doing, or intending to do shameful things" (RH 1367a).

2.4

What, then, is shame? Aristotle gives more ample discussion in the *Rhetoric* than in the *Nichomachean Ethics*.[22] Let us first consider the brief

---

it is the greatest of external goods. Consequently, it is a matter of honor and dishonor that a high-minded man has a right attitude. It is an obvious fact, and need not be argued, that the high-minded are concerned with honor. For they regard themselves as worthy of honor above all else, but of the honor they deserve" (NE 1123a17–24).

21. Unless indicated otherwise, the source of citations is Rhys Roberts's translation of *Rhetorica* in *The Works of Aristotle*, vol. 11 (Oxford: Clarendon Press, 1952), hereafter cited as RH.

22. As we shall see later, the difference in treatment lies in the difference between two notions of shame: *aidōs* and *aischunē*. The former stresses shame, or sense of shame, as a restraining factor in moral conduct; the latter focuses on shame as an emotion that arises out of misdeeds. *Aischunē* "describes what is base or worthy of shame as opposed to the sense of shame. It is the exact opposite of *kalos* or 'noble.'" I owe this note to my colleague

discussion in the latter, Chapter 4.9. For Aristotle, shame is not a virtue, for it resembles an emotion more than a characteristic. Moreover, its value is confined to youth rather than to other stages of life. "In fact, shame is not a mark of a decent man at all, since it is a consequence of base actions." Shame is "felt for voluntary actions, and no decent man will ever voluntarily do what is base" (NE 1128b10–35). This remark seems to contradict another in a chapter on courage, i.e., that a sense of shame is a characteristic of a decent man. Says Aristotle, "There are some evils, such as disrepute, which are proper and right for him [the courageous man] to fear: a man who fears disrepute is decent and has a sense of shame, a man who does not fear is shameless" (NE 1115a12–15).

2.5

In the light of our concern with the ethical significance of shame, one way to resolve the apparent difficulty is to distinguish, as Aristotle does in *Rhetoric*, two time dimensions of shame with respect to the past and the future, the *retrospective* and the *prospective* senses of "shame."[23] It

---

Bradley Lewis's response to my 12 March 2001 e-mail inquiry on the Greek terms for "shame." For sense of shame, Aristotle also uses *aischron*, as in his discussion of qualities similar to courage, such as the case of the courage of the citizen soldiers, exemplified in Diomedes and Hector: "This kind of courage bears the closest resemblance to the one we described earlier, for it is motivated by virtue, that is, by a sense of shame *(aischron)* and by the desire for a noble object (to wit, honor) and the avoidance of reproach as something base" (NE 1116a15–30).

23. This interpretation is similar to Irwin's note on NE 1128b30, where Aristotle maintains that shame is "irrelevant to virtues": "The assumed situation that would warrant shame is so far from anything that the virtuous person would do that it is pointless for him to acquire the tendency to be ashamed in that situation. 1124b10 is not an exception to Aristotle's claim here, since it is not concerned with base actions. Aristotle is concerned here with *retrospective* shame at actions we have done, and reasonably enough, denies it to the virtuous person. He does not consider the *anticipatory* shame of 1115a16, where I am properly ashamed of the possibility of doing a wrong action. He need not be rejecting that type of shame, since it will apparently be a motive for the virtuous person (though not one of his virtues)." (Terrence Irwin, trans., *Nicomachean Ethics* [Indianapolis, Ind.: Hackett, 1985], 330–31). My interpretation, however, differs from Irwin's, perhaps only in emphasis. More generally, for the importance of the distinction between prospective and retrospective shame, see N. Rotenstreich, "On Shame," *Review of Metaphysics* 19, no. 1 (1965): 59–60. For the idea of the prospective sense of shame, see Williams, 79. The distinction between the prospective and the retrospective sense of "shame" seems to be implicit in the distinction between *honte* and *pudeur* in French, as stated by Riezler. *"Pudeur* is shame felt before, and warning against, an action. *Honte* is felt after an action. . . . Before an action endangers the thing in the making, the bashful will timidly hesitate and resist—the case of *pudeur;* after an act that harms, hurts, or soils, shame will burn in the memory—the case of *honte."* Schneider cites this passage for discussing his distinction between "two faces of shame," i.e. "shame as discretion" and "disgrace-shame" (Schneider, 19ff.). See Kurt Riezler, *Man: Mutable and Immutable* (New York: Henry Regnery, 1951), 227.

is important to note that prospective shame, or the sense of shame, much like conscience, serves as a private, internal monitor and not merely a judge of moral conduct.[24]

2.6

Let us now turn to a fuller discussion of shame in Aristotle's *Rhetoric*. For Aristotle rhetoric is a study of the modes of reasoned persuasion. It is a kind of "offshoot of ethical and political studies" and may be defined as "the faculty of observing in any case the available means of persuasion." Aristotle's analysis of the modes of persuasion consists of *ethos, logos,* and *pathos* (RH 1355b–1356a).[25] *Ethos* pertains to the speaker's personal character, i.e., "good sense, good moral character, and good will" (RH 1355b). *Logos* focuses on "proofs" or lines of reasoning exemplified in enthymenes and "rhetorical induction," i.e., arguments from examples or case-by-case reasoning. *Pathos*, on the other hand, centers on the appeal to the audience's emotions, "putting the audience into a certain frame of mind" (RH 1356a). *Ethos, logos,* and *pathos* are "integral components of rhetoric and addressed to the whole man."[26] In other words, rhetorical discourse is a reasoned, persuasive ethical discourse, involving a particular rather than a universal audience.[27]

On Epideictic rhetoric or oratory, Aristotle discusses "the virtues and the concept of *to kalon,* the 'honorable,' 'fine,' or 'noble,' and to a less-

---

24. We find a perspicuous statement on the ethical importance of this idea in Kant's statement in his pre-critical period. In commenting on the moral sympathy of the good-hearted person in the suffering or distress of another, Kant says: "But, since this moral sympathy is none the less not yet enough to incite the sluggish human nature to activities for the common good, providence has given us a certain delicate feeling which can arouse us to make opposition against the coarser self-interest and against vulgar sensuality. This is the *sense of honor* and its consequence *shame*." See Paul Arthur Schilpp, *Kant's Pre-Critical Ethics,* 2nd ed. (Evanston, Ill.: Northwestern University Press, 1960), 54. On conscience as an internal monitor, Ryle remarks: "My application of a principle to me can take the form of doing what I should. In this sense conscience is never merely a verdict-passing faculty, it is a conduct-regulating faculty" (Gilbert Ryle, "Conscience and Moral Convictions," *Analysis* 7, no. 2 [1940], reprinted in *Philosophy and Analysis,* ed. Margaret MacDonald [Oxford: Blackwell, 1954], 160).

25. For an employment of Aristotle's tripartite scheme in constructing a Confucian theory of rhetoric, see my "The Possibility of a Confucian Theory of Rhetoric" in *Moral Vision and Tradition*.

26. William M. Grimaldi, *Studies in the Philosophy of Aristotle's Rhetoric* (Wiesbaden: Franz Steiner Verlag, 1972), 16–17.

27. "We must also take into account the nature of our particular audience when making a speech of praise; for as Socrates used to say, it is not difficult to praise the Athenians to an Athenian audience" (RH 1367b). For the distinction between universal and particular audience, see Chaim Perelman and Anna Olbrechts-Tyteca, *The New Rhetoric: A Treatise on Argumentation,* trans. John Wilkinson and Purcell Weaver (Notre Dame, Ind.: Notre Dame University Press, 1969).

er extent its opposite, the 'shameful' ... as the bases for praise and blame."[28] Aristotle is emphatic that nobility and goodness and virtues are inseparable: "The Noble *(kalon)* is that which is both desirable for its own sake and also worthy of praise; or that which is both good *(agathon)* and pleasant because good. If this is the true definition of the Noble, it follows that virtue must be noble, since it is both a good thing and also praiseworthy" (RH 1366a). The virtues mentioned receive more extensive treatment in the *Nichomachean Ethics*, e.g., justice, courage, liberality, magnanimity, and *phronesis* (RH 1366b).

Because *ethos* is an integral component of rhetoric, *pathos* or the appeal to the emotions of the audience will involve ethical considerations, in particular, goodwill and friendliness of disposition. The emotions are feelings that affect judgment and are attended by pain or pleasure (RH 1378a). Emotions are "temporary states of mind—not attributes of character or natural desires—and arise in large part from perception of what is publicly due to or from oneself at a given time."[29] Some of the emotions Aristotle discusses are anger, fear, and shame, as well as their opposites, calmness, confidence, shamelessness.[30] A tripartite scheme is proposed for the analysis of emotions. Consider, for instance, the emotion of anger: "we must discover (1) the state of mind of angry people, (2) who the people are with whom they usually get angry, and (3) on what grounds they get angry with them. It is not enough to know one or two of these points; unless we know all three, we shall be unable to arouse anger in any one" (RH 1338a24–31).

2.7

Aristotle states that "shame may be defined as pain or disturbance in regard to bad things, whether present, past, or future, which seem likely to involve us in discredit; and shamelessness as contempt or indifference in regard to the same bad things" (RH 1383b15–19). According to Aristotle's tripartite scheme, understanding shame involves the following: (1) shame as a feeling of pain or uneasiness (2) that arises out of one's consciousness of having done bad things, evils, or misdeeds—the grounds for experiencing shame, and (3) the "conditions" that occasion the shame experience or "the eyes of others." These others are

---

28. George A. Kennedy, trans., *Aristotle on Rhetoric: A Theory of Civic Discourse: Newly Translated with Introduction, Notes, and Appendices* (New York: Oxford University Press, 1991), 79.

29. Ibid., 123–24.

30. Other emotions discussed are kindness and unkindness, pity, indignation, envy, and emulation.

those (a) whom we admire, (b) who admire us, (c) by whom we wish to be admired, or (d) from whom we desire some service that we shall not obtain if we forfeit their good opinion.

2.8

As a mental state shame is one of pain or uneasiness arising out of the agents' consciousness of having done bad things or evils that they think are disgraceful to themselves or to those they care for, evils that are "due to moral badness." Aristotle's examples are evil or morally bad actions that are hurtful to others due to cowardice, injustice, licentiousness, meanness, and flattery (RH 1383b). Here the pain or uneasiness is the moral agent's acknowledgment of having done the bad or evil thing. In this respect shame experience is ethically significant because it is an expression of an aspect of moral consciousness. Presumably the agent is a moral person who cares for his/her development of moral virtues and acknowledges responsibility and failure to live up to the ideal.[31] For moral conduct and misconduct reflect the virtuous agent's character, knowledge of what he or she is doing, and the nature of the choice (NE 1105a27–35). Thus, for the moral agent, the shame experience has ethical significance, because it is an avowal of responsibility of a personal character fault. To some contemporary moral philosophers, this feature of shame has no necessary connection with character fault and/or one's attitude toward personal relationships or tradition.[32] To Aristotle and Xunzi, on the contrary, this view seems plausible only because it ignores the social, interpersonal context of human interactions.

---

31. This point seems implicit in Aristotle's discussion. One may elaborate its significance as one that gives rise to a search for one's identity, or as contrasted with guilt, shame is a failure to live up to one's moral ideal—"failure to achieve an ideal [or] perfection." For the former view, see Helen Merrell Lynd, *On Shame and the Search for Identity* (New York: Harcourt, Brace, & World, 1958); for the latter, see Herbert Morris, *On Guilt and Innocence: Essays in Legal Philosophy and Moral Psychology* (Berkeley: University of California Press, 1976), 61. As we shall see, for a Confucian, some of these attempts implausibly dissociate the agent's ideal from the ideal of moral tradition. For more extensive discussion on self-identification and accountability, see Rotenstreich, 80–86.

32. Morris, 61. Helen Lynd makes a similar claim as a tentative hypothesis: "Aspects of the phenomenon of shame can be understood only with reference to transcultural values" (Lynd, 35–36). How can such a thesis be supported without a careful comparative and critical study of moral traditions? The complex question involved cannot be settled without such an inquiry, especially one that is concerned with the philosophical bases of moral traditions. For a tradition-oriented attempt to formulate reasonable principles for resolving intercultural ethical conflict, see the last essay in my *Moral Tradition and Vision*.

2.9

In understanding shame, we must attend to the "conditions under which we feel shame," which pertain to the social, interpersonal context of human relationships. We care for the opinions of others, especially those whose opinions are in some ways important to our sense of self-worth. And shame is more intensely experienced when our conduct is more open or observable before "the eyes of others." Aristotle cites the proverb "Shame dwells in the eyes" (RH 1384b).

> Now since shame is a mental picture of disgrace, in which we shrink from the disgrace itself and not from its consequences, and we only care what opinion is held of us because of the people who form that opinion, it follows that the people before whom we feel shame are those whose opinion of us matters to us. Such persons are: those who admire us, those whom we admire, those by whom we wished to be admired, those with whom we are competing, and those whose opinion of us we respect. . . . We respect, as true, the views of sensible people, such as our elders and those who have been well educated. And we feel shame about a thing if it is done openly, before all men's eyes. (RH 1384a25–36)

We may restate Aristotle's view by saying that the experience of shame cannot be understood without appreciating the agent's regard for the opinions of significant others, which implicitly entail acceptance of certain standards for interpersonal relationship. The significant others are those persons for whom the agent has special concern as regards personal and/or intimate relationships. And these persons have great influence on the agent's behavior and self-esteem, or more generally, those persons who greatly affect or influence the agent's thoughts and feelings. Significant others are an aspect of shame experience, perhaps because they are people we take as models or who "take us as their models" (RH 1385a). It is quite possible that the audience of significant others is a by-product of the agent's imaginative idealization of others' personal merits or virtues. Says Aristotle, "We can always idealize any given man by drawing on the virtues akin to his actual qualities; thus we may say that the passionate and excitable man is 'outspoken'; or that the arrogant man is 'superb' or 'impressive'" (RH 1367a35–40).[33]

---

33. As Williams remarks, "Even if shame and its motivations always involve in some way or other an idea of the gaze of another, it is important that for many of its operations the imagined gaze of an imagined other will do" (Williams, 82). For more discussion on the role of an imagined audience in shame experience, see Taylor, 57–60.

2.10

Given the assumption of personal and interpersonal contexts of human interaction, we can readily appreciate Aristotle's analysis of the role of the opinions of significant others in shame experience, especially when these significant others provide a model for the agent as well as the agent himself serving as a model to significant others. Both the agent and his significant others may function as models for imitation. These models function more like "standards of aspiration" for moral achievement. This view seems to be the main focus in the *Rhetoric*. However, there is another way, perhaps even more important, in which persons may serve as standards for others without providing any specific opinions, or action-guides, say, in the form of precepts or principles. Although these persons are sometimes regarded as "models of emulation," they are best understood as paradigmatic individuals who serve as "standards of inspiration" or "beacons of orientation," persons who inspire a moral agent's endeavor toward pursuit of excellence.[34] The idea of paradigmatic individuals seems implicit in Aristotle's notion of *spoudaios* ("a man of high moral standards") in *Nichomachean Ethics*. Martin Ostwald remarks, *spoudaios* is "literally, 'serious man,' whom Aristotle frequently invokes for purposes similar to those which make modern laws invoke the 'reasonable man.' However, Aristotle's stress is less on the reasonableness of the man under particular circumstances than on a person who has a sense of the importance of living his life well and of fulfilling his function in society in accordance with the highest stan-

---

34. For the first notion, see Donald J. Munro, *The Concept of Man in Ancient China* (Stanford, Calif.: Stanford University Press, 1969), 114; for the second, see Morris, 60–62. As I stated in "Competence, Concern, and the Role of Paradigmatic Individuals *(Chün-tzu)* in Moral Education," *Philosophy East and West* 42, no. 2 (1992): "In moral instruction or training, paradigmatic individuals may quite properly play the role of models for imitation or emulation by providing standards of aspiration or examples of competence to be attained. In the inculcation of *jen [ren]* or moral concern, they serve as standards of inspiration by providing a point of orientation rather than specific targets of achievement. The notion of imitation seems out of place in characterizing this function, for it may misleadingly suggest an 'unthinking imitation of the lives and conduct of certain individuals without regard to moral criteria.' With proper qualification, allowing for creativity, however, the use of the notion of imitation in the sense of *mimesis* may be acceptable. As Tatarkiewicz points out, 'In early Greece, *mimesis* signified imitation, but in the sense in which the term is applied to acting and not to copying.' As this process of *mimesis* involves imaginative experiments in 'acting like the person who has such a character,' it is best to use Collingwood's notion of *re-enactment* rather than imitation. In 'acting like' a paradigmatic individual in a particular situation, the agent is trying to re-enact the *spirit* in which he or she acts, and this involves imaginatively rethinking the concrete significance of moral concern in the present. The moral agent is much like Collingwood's historian, re-enacting in 'the historian's mind of the thought whose history he is studying.'" (For a revised version, see Essay 8 in *Moral Vision and Tradition*.)

dards."[35] Arguably, Aristotle's *spoudaios* is functionally analogous to the Confucian notion of *junzi* or paradigmatic individuals.[36]

2.11

Since rhetorical discourse aims at the persuasion of a particular audience, concern with the role of significant others in shame experience raises the question of the nature and ethical justification of the presumed social standards of the relevant groups involved. From the standpoint of social psychology, one explanatory hypothesis points out that the varying standards of significant others belong to different groups and their overlapping applications represent interpretations of more general established standards of the society, which are the outcome of the degrees of internalization of what G. H. Mead calls the "generalized other," i.e., "the attitude of the whole community."[37] Shame construed as a kind of social or cultural sanction is particularly amenable to this explanation. However, the significant others whose standards a person has internalized are not simply those who represent neighbors. As Williams points out, "The other may be identified in ethical terms. [The other] is conceived as one whose reactions I would respect; equally, he is conceived as someone who would respect those same reactions if they were appropriately directed to him."[38] The deeper question on the standards internalized pertains to the ethical justification of one's concern with significant others and the related societal, tradition-oriented standards. Aristotle's *Nichomachean Ethics* may be interpreted as an attempt to provide a nontraditional theory. This is an important issue for Aristotelian scholarship. For moral philosophy appreciative of moral traditions, the more important question lies in understanding the nature of moral tradition and the more general problem of morality and self-interest. On this question, Classical Confucian thinkers, especially Xunzi, I think, have important contributions to make, especially in their conception of honor and shame.

35. See Ostwald's translation of the *Nicomachean Ethics*, 314.
36. See my *Dimensions of Moral Creativity*, 45–46. For more discussion on paradigmatic individuals, see chaps. 3–5. For their role in moral education, see Essay 8 cited above. For an earlier suggestion on the comparison of *spoudaios* with *junzi*, see Lionel Giles, *The Sayings of Confucius* (London: John Murray, 1907), 52n; and Max Hamburger, "Aristotle and Confucius: A Study in Comparative Philosophy," *Philosophy* 31 (1956): 355.
37. G. H. Mead, *Mind, Self, and Society* (Chicago: University of Chicago Press, 1952), 154.
38. Williams continues: "The internalised other is indeed abstracted and generalised and idealised, but he is potentially somebody rather than nobody, and somebody other than me. He can provide the focus of real social expectations, of how shall I live if I act in one way rather than another, of how my actions and reactions will alter my relations to the world about me" (84).

3. XUNZI AND HIS PREDECESSORS

3.1

Earlier (1.2 above), adopting Xunzi's distinction between generic and specific terms *(gongming* and *bieming)*, I proposed to use the English term "shame" as a generic term for a family of specific terms, such as "disgrace" and "humiliation." Similar linguistic observation applies to the Chinese language. Notably, as in the familiar dictionaries of English, Chinese terms that can be translated as "shame" in appropriate contexts seem to indicate differences in the nature of the shame experience. A translator of Classical Confucian literature such as the *Analects, Mencius,* or *Xunzi* has different options for rendering *chi, xiu,* and *ru* as "shame," "disgrace," or "dishonor."

As noted earlier (1.3 above), we find an analogous device in some contemporary English writers on shame, where the difference in the degrees and kinds of shame experience is indicated by hyphenation, e.g., "disgrace-shame," "humiliation-shame."

The functional equivalence of this hyphenation device is the use of binomial terms in modern Chinese. Unlike modern Chinese, literary or Classical Chinese consists largely of one-character terms, which presents a problem of disambiguation that challenges the reader's interpretation. To solve this problem, we find a helpful distinction between *dan-ming* and *jian-ming* in the *Xunzi*. A *dan-ming* is a single term or word that has only one character or graph, and *jian-ming* are compound terms or terms that consist of more than one character, such as binomials. According to Xunzi, in fixing reference for terms *(ming)*, things that are similar should have the same term; and things that are different should have different terms. "In cases where a *dan-ming* is adequate to express one's intention, use a *dan-ming*. In a situation where a *dan-ming* is inadequate to express one's intention, use a *jian-ming* instead" (*zhengming* L515).[39] Note that the terms *dan-ming* and *jian-ming* are binomials, representing two kinds of *ming*.

Modern Chinese lexicographers often use *jian-ming* or binomials to explain *dan-ming*. In a recent fairly large dictionary, *Xinbian Zhongguo cidian*, explanations of these terms for "shame," *chi, xiu,* and *ru*, make use of binomials that involve one another.[40] The nominal use of *chi* is explained as *xiu-kui,* and the verbal use as *wu-ru*. The nominal use of *xiu* is explained as *chi-ru* and the example is *xiu-chi*. And when we turn

---

39. For more discussion, see Cua, *Ethical Argumentation*, 44–45.
40. Xue Songliu, chief editor, *Xinbian Zhongguo cidian*, rev. ed. (Taipei: Da Zhongguo guoshu, 1998).

to the verbal use of *ru,* we have *qi-wu* and the example is *wu-ru.* The adjectival use of *ru* is explained as *xiu-chi* and the example is *chi-ru.*[41]

Xunzi's distinction between *dan-ming* and *jian-ming* is also useful for dealing with the problem of disambiguation of *dan-ming,* which significantly affects interpretation and/or translation. A case in point in the *Xunzi* is what may be called the problem of co-occurrence, i.e., when two *dan-ming* or single-character terms occur side by side. A crucial example is the co-occurrence of "*li yi*" that presents a challenge to interpretation and/or translation. If the co-occurrence is construed as a conjunction of *dan-ming* or single-character terms, that is, "*li* and *yi,*" one obtains a translation that indicates the conjunction, for example, "propriety and righteousness."[42] But if the co-occurrence is read as a *jian-ming* or binomial, one may use "ritual principles."[43] In that context, Xunzi's question concerns the explanation of the origin of "*li yi,*" given his thesis that man's nature is bad (*xing'e pian,* Book 23). Reading "*li yi*" as a *jian-ming,* one may even use two English binomials for translation, for example, "ritual principles [for *li*] and moral duty [for *yi*]."[44]

3.2

Before we take up Xunzi's conception of shame and honor, let us consider some earlier Confucian uses of the Chinese characters for "shame," i.e., *chi, xiu,* and *ru* in the *Lunyu (Analects)* and *Mengzi (Works of Mencius).*[45] This brief excursion provides a support of my reconstruction of Xunzi's theory of the ethical significance of shame, focusing on *ru,* as a systematic development of the insights of Confucius's notion of *chi* and Mencius's conception of *xiu* as a component of *xiuwu zhi xin,* the root of the virtue of *yi.*

41. Xue's dictionary consists of 2,001 pages. I use lexical definitions of our three key terms for shame to illustrate my point about the use of binomials and the circularity of the definitions, perhaps because they are interdependent in their definitional function in particular contexts of discourse. Interdependent definitional function of the three terms *chi, xiu,* and *ru* is clear in an older comprehensive dictionary of the Chinese language. In *Zhongwen da cidian* (The Encyclopedic Dictionary of Chinese Language), for *chi,* the first entry cites *Shuowen* is *ru,* for the entry *ru,* we have *chi,* and the relevant entry #6 for *xiu* is *ru.* As for binomials, *xiu-chi,* we have *xiu-kui,* and for *xiu-ru,* we have *xiu-chi.*

42. Chan, *Source Book,* 130.

43. Burton Watson, trans., *Hsün Tzu: Basic Writings* (New York: Columbia University, 1963), 160.

44. Knoblock, *Xunzi,* K3:153. For a study of the problem of co-occurrence and different interpretive theses in Chinese Xunzi scholarship, see Essay 4 in this volume.

45. Shun's recent survey of the relevant Pre-Confucian uses for elucidating Mencius's notion of *xiuwu zhi xin* as the seed or root of *yi* renders *ru* as "disgrace" and *chi* as "regard as below oneself," and *xiu* as a focus "more on the badness or the low standing of oneself in, or as likely to ensue from, the thing that occasions *hsiu.*" See Kwong-loi Shun, *Mencius and Early Chinese Thought* (Stanford, Calif.: Stanford University Press, 1997), 58–59. My

3.3

One apparent puzzle in the *Lunyu* is the absence of concern for honor *(rong)* among the sayings attributed to Confucius. One plausible explanation is that Confucius wanted to revise the established norms for honor or reputation in the light of his vision of *ren* as an affectionate concern for the well-being of one's fellows in the community. Moreover, the established norms for personal conduct and institutions that embodied the *li* (rites or rules of proper behavior) require ethical justification in the light of *ren* and *yi*.[46] Differently put, in Confucius's view, the established conventions concerning good behavior as requiring courtesy, deference, deportment, and ceremonies have no ethical significance unless they are justifiable in the light of *ren* and *yi*. His preoccupation with established *li* displays a critical attitude toward the established tradition of *li* with a view to conserving the best elements in the spirit of *ren* and *yi*. This attitude toward the wisdom of the past may be gathered from his remarks: "I transmit but do not innovate. I am truthful to what I say and devoted to antiquity" (*Lunyu* 7.1 [Lau 1979]).[47] Elsewhere he remarks that one is worthy of being called a moral teacher only if he can review what he has learned as a basis for acquiring new information (*Lunyu* 2.11). Reviewing the old, however, involves reflective efforts to

---

own reading of *Lunyu* and *Mengzi* somewhat complements Shun's. Since Shun does not deal with *Lunyu* or give an analysis of Xunzi's uses, except in relevant places, I make no reference to his view in expounding my thesis below. Note also that the lexica of Classical Chinese I consulted are not very helpful, except indicating again that we are dealing with functionally interdefinable terms. Xu Shen's *Shuowen jiezi*, published in the Han dynasty, explains *chi* as *ru*, and *ru* as *chi*. *Xiu* in the sense of shame is not found. Weigel's *Chinese Characters* restates *Shuowen* entries on *chi* and *ru*. Karlgren's lexicon gives us this: *xiu*—shame; *chi*—shame, disgrace; and *ru*—disgrace, condescend; and notes that the explanation of the graph is uncertain. For a recent lexicon of Chinese graphs that incorporates *Shuowen* and various philological annotations, see Zhang Xuan, *Wenzi xingyi liu-bian shidian* (Taipei: Xinan,1980). Zhang's lexicon gives helpful comparative tables of correspondence with Karlgren's two works as well as comparative tables for *Pinyin* and Wade-Giles romanizations. See Bernard Karlgren, *Grammata Serica* (Taipei: Chengwen, 1966), first published in the *Bulletin of the Museum of Far Eastern Antiquities* (Stockholm), no. 12; and Karlgren, *Analytic Dictionary of Chinese and Sino-Japanese* (Taipei: Chengwen, 1975). For Xu Xin, see Duan Yucai, *Shuowen jiezi zhu* (Shanghai: Guji, 1981).

46. As Waley reminds us, with respect to *li* the *junzi* or paradigmatic individuals are not specialists. "But it was with the relation of ritual as a whole to morality and not with the details of etiquette and precedence that the early Confucians were chiefly concerned. Master Tseng [Zeng], indeed, even goes as far as to say that the ordering of ritual vessels is a matter for special officers put in charge of them, and does not fall within the *chün-tzu*'s [*junzi*'s] proper sphere" (Arthur Waley, trans., *The Analects of Confucius* [New York: Random House, 1938], 68–69).

47. Unless indicated otherwise, translation of the *Lunyu* is my own. Adoption of other translations is indicated by the names of the authors following the section reference; see D. C. Lau, *Confucius: The Analects* (Middlesex, England: Penguin Books, 1979). An asterisk indicates emendation of translation.

reanimate an existing tradition, that is, to reinvent or renovate the tradition.[48] More generally, moral learning requires reflective thought. Says Confucius, "If one learns from others but does not think, one will be bewildered. If, on the other hand, one thinks but does not learn from others, one will be in peril" (*Lunyu* 2.15 [Lau 1979]).

Confucius's depreciation of honor is perhaps best explained by his attitude toward its association with *gui* (honors, high station, rank), which may be acquired through unethical means. Says Confucius:

Riches and honors *(gui)* are what men desire. If they cannot be obtained in the proper way, I would not hold on to them. Poverty and meanness *(jian)* are what men dislike. If they cannot be avoided in the proper way, they should not be avoided. If a *junzi* abandons *ren*, how can he fulfill the requirements of that name? The *junzi* does not, even for the space of a single meal, act contrary to *ren*. In moments of haste, he cleaves to it. In seasons of danger, he cleaves to it. (*Lunyu* 4.5 [Legge 1893*])[49]

Another saying of Confucius brings out the importance of *yi* as a standard for wealth and honors:

With coarse rice to eat, with water to drink, and my bended arm for a pillow, I have still joy in the midst of these things. Riches and honors *(gui)* acquired through wrong and improper means *(buyi)* are to me as a floating cloud. (*Lunyu* 7.15 [Legge*])[50]

Like Aristotle, Confucius questions the value of honors conferred according to established standards. Again, as in Aristotle (2.3 above), when honor is seen as connected with virtues and nobility, the concern is deemed ethically acceptable when they exemplify the virtues of *ren, yi,* and *li*. As we shall see shortly, *yi* provides the ethical standard of justification for the acquisition of honors, as it provides a standard for right and reasonable conduct.[51] When honors *(gui)* are so acquired, they may also be considered noble, especially as they conform to the appropriate *li*, given the concern with the ennobling function of *li*.[52]

Indeed, a *junzi* is supposed to be an embodiment of virtues such as *ren, yi,* and *li*,[53] as well as nobility. For this reason, with proper qualification, *junzi* may be rendered as "noble man," particularly when we think

---

48. On this point, Waley's translation of 7.11 is perhaps the best: "The Master said, He who by reanimating the old can gain knowledge of the new."
49. James Legge, trans., *The Chinese Classics*, vol. 1 (Oxford: Clarendon Press, 1893).
50. Another remark on reputation is revealing: "I am not distressed about men's not knowing me; I worry about my own want of ability" (14.30). See also 1.2.
51. See Cua, *Moral Vision and Tradition*, Essay 13, and Essay 5 in this volume.
52. Ibid., Essay 12.
53. *Dimensions of Moral Creativity*, chap. 4.

of *junzi* as the functional analogue of Aristotle's *spoudaios* (2.10 above). In 1907 Lionel Giles, while agreeing with James Legge that *junzi* literarily means "princely man," thinks that Legge's "superior man" is a misleading translation. For a remark in *Lunyu* 1:2, we have this rendering from Giles: "The Master said: Is he not a princely man *[junzi]*—he who is never vexed that others know him not?" A long and significant note follows Giles's translation:

> This is the much discussed *chün tzu [junzi]*, an expression of which the stereotyped English equivalent is "the superior man." But in this there is, unhappily, a tinge of blended superciliousness and irony absolutely foreign to the native phrase, which in my opinion makes it unsuitable. "Princely man" is as nearly as possible a literal translation, and sometimes, as we shall see, it actually means "prince." But in the majority of cases the connotation of rank or authority is certainly not explicit, and as a general rendering I have preferred "the higher type of man," "the nobler sort of man," or sometimes more simply as "the good man." Perhaps the nearest approximation in any European language is to be found in the Greek *ho kalos kagathos*, because that implies high mental and moral qualities combined with all the outward bearing of a gentleman. Compare also with Aristotle's *ho spoudaios* who is however more abstract and ideal.[54]

3.4

When we look at some of the uses of *chi* in the *Lunyu*, we see that hardly any emphasis is put on the feeling of shame; presumably this feeling is an unreliable guide to moral conduct. *Chi*, in the sense of "sense of shame," as an internal monitor (2.5 above), implying the satisfaction of requisite ethical standards, seems to be Confucius's main concern. Let us consider some passages.

> The Master said, "If in government you depend upon laws and enforce the laws by meting out punishments, you may keep the people from wrongdoing, but they will lose the sense of shame *(chi)*. If, on the other hand, in government you depend on virtues and maintain order by encouraging the rites *(li)* the people will have a sense of shame for wrongdoing, and, moreover, will emulate what is good." (*Lunyu* 2.3 [Ku, 1984])[55]

In this remark, *chi* expresses the idea of self-regard, concern with conduct that is deemed by the agent "as something that is beneath oneself

---

54. Giles, 52n. It is better to use the transliteration *junzi* than the translations offered by various writers. For a critical appreciation of various translations such as "superior man," "gentleman," "noble man," see *"Junzi (Chün-tzu): The Moral Person"* in the *Encyclopedia of Chinese Philosophy*, ed. Antonio S. Cua (London and New York: Routledge, 2003).

55. Ku Hung-ming, trans., *The Analects* (Taipei: Xinsheng Daily News, 1984). For translation of *chi* as "sense of shame" in this remark (*Lunyu* 2.3), see Legge, Chan, and Lau.

or lowers one's standing." Unlike *ru*, "*chi* involves a more reflective concern with the self."[56] Concern with *chi* is a concern with self-respect, as Waley's obviously interpretive translation shows.[57] However, the focus on *li* may suggest that *li* is the exclusive standard for the ethical significance of the sense of shame. Consider Fingarette's interpretation of *chi:*

> If we are unaware of the crucial differences in perspective, these texts on *ch'ih* [*chi*] lend themselves easily to an assimilation of Confucian "shame" with Western "guilt." Yet the differences are crucial with respect to the issues that concern us here. Although *ch'ih* [*chi*] is definitely a moral concept and designates a moral condition or response, the moral relation to which it corresponds is that of a person to his status and role as defined by *li*. *Ch'ih* looks "outward," not "inward." It is a matter of the spoken but empty word, of the immorally gained material possessions, of the excessive in appearance and in conduct. It is not as guilt a matter of inward state, of repugnance at inner corruption, of self-denigration, of the sense that one is a person, and independently of one's public status and repute, mean or reprehensible.
>
> It would be a basic error, however, to assume that shame is concerned with "mere appearances" rather than moral realities. The Confucian concept of shame is a genuinely moral concept, but it is oriented to morality as centering in *li*, traditionally ceremonially defined social comportment, rather than to an inner core of one's being, "the self."[58]

3.5

Fingarette's interpretation of the uses of *chi* is highly problematic. First, he is too facile in comparing Confucius's view with the Western concept of guilt. He does not tell us what that "Western" concept is that he has in mind. Earlier, in criticizing translators who render *xing* as punishment, Fingarette has in mind the association of punishment with guilt as "peculiar to Graeco-Hebraic-Christian tradition"—"Punishment is an appropriate moral response to prior guilty wrongdoing by a morally responsible agent."[59] Fingarette also contrasts Confucius's attitude to-

---

56. Shun continues, "Such a concern is arguably present in the *Lun-yü*, in a way not in the *Mo-tzu*—although both texts contain certain occurrences of 'wu' and 'ju/ru,' the former but not the latter contains occurrences of 'chih/chi'" (Shun, 59). My analysis in terms of *chi* as "sense of shame" provides an argument for Shun's suggestion.

57. It is interesting to note that Waley's translation renders *chi* as "self-respect": "The Master said, Govern the people by regulations, keep order among them by chastisement, and they will flee from you, and lose all self-respect. Govern them by moral force *(de)*, keep order among them by ritual and they will keep their self-respect and come to you of their own accord" (Waley, 88).

58. Herbert Fingarette, *Confucius—The Secular as Sacred* (New York: Harper Torchbooks, 1972), 30.

59. Ibid., 26.

ward punishment with the "legalists," presumably Han Fei. Let us leave aside this issue, since Confucius has a rather negative attitude toward the judicial system.⁶⁰ Were Fingarette to compare Confucius's attitude toward *chi* with his notion of honors and ranks *(gui)*, he would have arrived at a different interpretation. For it is a more illuminating contrast than that between shame and guilt, a distinction more appropriate to the sociological study of Chinese folk religion and its contrast with the conception of the Confucian "elites."⁶¹

Second, because of his eagerness to expound the *Lunyu* as embodying Confucius's vision of *li* as "holy rite" or the conception of "the secular as sacred," Fingarette tends to belittle the ethical importance of other concepts such as *yi* and the role of judgment in interpreting some passages involving *chi* as well as *ru*. An alternative reading casts serious doubt on his claim that Confucius's conception of shame is "oriented to morality as centering in *li*, traditionally ceremonially defined social comportment."⁶²

Consider this saying: "A *junzi* is ashamed *(chi)* to let his words outrun his deeds" (*Lunyu* 14.29 [Waley, 1938]). This translation seems to convey a descriptive characteristic of a *junzi*. However, if we consider the *force* of Confucius's remark, we will have a different translation: "A *junzi* would be ashamed to let his words outrun his deeds."⁶³ Note the implicit normative judgment that an ethical person must expend effort to secure the harmony of words and actions—a central theme in Confucius's

---

60. Says Confucius, "In hearing litigations, I am no different from any other men. But if you insist on a difference, it is, perhaps, that I try to get the party not to resort to litigation in the first place" (*Lunyu* 12.13 [Lau 1979]).

61. See Wolfram Eberhard, *Guilt and Sin in Traditional China* (Berkeley: University of California Press, 1967). Fingarette's approach to the *Lunyu* represents a popular, external perspective on Classical Chinese philosophy. My own approach is based on an internal perspective, that is, I seek to understand Chinese philosophy by using Chinese conceptual resources as a first consideration, before employing Western conceptions as a basis for contrast. For a discussion of these two approaches, see my "Problems of Chinese Moral Philosophy," *Journal of Chinese Philosophy* 27, no. 3 (2000): 269–85. As regards Eberhard's contrast between guilt and sin in Chinese folk religions and the Confucian conception of shame, it is a puzzle that no reference was made to the Confucian classics, say, the Four Books, or to the later work. The same remark applies to Ng's paper on shame. Her characterization of *junzi*, for example, shows no attempt to appeal to textual support. See Margaret Ng, "Shame as a Moral Sanction," *Journal of Chinese Philosophy* 8, no. 1 (1981).

62. I leave aside the issue of the "self," which I discussed in my "A Confucian Perspective on Self-Deception" in *Self and Deception*, ed. Roger Ames and Wimal Dissanayake (Albany: State University of New York Press, 1996), or *Moral Vision and Tradition*, Essay 11.

63. This translation is Ku's, with my substitution of *junzi* for "gentleman." Ku's numbering is 14.28. Though not using *chi*, 14.21 expresses a similar point: "He who speaks without modesty *(zuo)* will find it difficult to make his words good" (*Lunyu* 14.20 [Legge 1893]). *Zuo* can also be rendered as "to be ashamed" or "to feel ashamed," as in *zuoyi*.

conception of *junzi*.⁶⁴ At issue here is the virtue of *xin* or trustworthiness. When asked about the exaltation of virtue *(de)*, Confucius replied, "Take as fundamental guides doing your best for others and being trustworthy in what you say *(zhu zhongxin)*, and move yourself to where the rightness is, then you will be exalting virtue" (*Lunyu* 12.10 [Lau, 1979]*). For another saying involving *chi:* "The Master said, In antiquity men were loath to speak. This was because they counted it *shameful (chi)* if their person failed to keep up with their words" (*Lunyu* 4.22 [Lau, 1979]). In other words, an action that fails to fulfill one's words was considered by the ancient to be a shameful deed. Indeed a *ren*-person is watchful in his speech (*Lunyu* 12.3), lest his action fail to conform to his words. In the ideal situation, there is a perfect match between words and deeds. This is an expression of Confucius's concern with a basic aspect of the ethics of speech. Arguably, the *li*, as rules of civility, are important to Confucian ethical argumentation only as providing the style and not the substance of discourse.⁶⁵ *Li* as formal rules for proper behavior cannot provide substantive ethical content without an implicit appeal to *ren* and *yi*.

3.6

Because of the importance of trustworthiness, especially in keeping one's word, Confucius is suspicious of clever talkers. We have a revealing report of Confucius's own attitude to the effect that he would be ashamed *(chi)* of clever talk, ingratiating appearance, and servility in expressing respect (*Lunyu* 5.25).⁶⁶ Indeed, for Confucius, clever words and ingratiating appearance are seldom associated with *ren* (*Lunyu* 1.3). And whether one's actions correspond with one's words is a question that cannot be decided by *li* as a set of formal rules for proper behavior. Only when the agent exercises his sense of *yi* can he secure the proper match; there is no assurance of success of his efforts. And diversities of circumstances call for varying judgments. For this reason, Confucius says of the *junzi* that he "considers *yi* to be the foundation of the moral life, carries it out according to the rules of proper conduct *(li)*, expresses his concern with modesty, and brings it into completion by being trustworthy in words" (*Lunyu* 15.17). In dealing with things and affairs of the world, a *junzi* maintains a neutral posture, i.e., "in his judgment

---

64. For more discussion, see my "The Concept of Paradigmatic Individuals in the Ethics of Confucius," *Inquiry* 14 (1971): 41–55; or *Dimensions of Moral Creativity*, chap. 5.

65. See my *Ethical Argumentation*, chap. 1.

66. For more discussion of Confucius's attitude toward the ethics of speech, see my *Dimensions of Moral Creativity*, chap. 4.

of the world, he has no predilections nor prejudice; he is on the side of what is right *(yi)*" (*Lunyu* 4.10 [Ku, 1986]). This characterization of *junzi* echoes Confucius's autobiographical remark: "I have no preconceptions about the permissible and the impermissible" (*Lunyu* 18.8 [Lau, 1979]).[67]

3.7

A few passages give examples of shameful conduct implying ethical judgment of *yi*. For negative judgment, we have the example of Confucius's view that a determined scholar who aspires to realize *dao* and yet is ashamed of poor food and bad clothes is unworthy of being a partner in discourse (*Lunyu* 4.9). For an example of positive judgment, we have Confucius's advice that one should not be ashamed of learning from a person of a lower station in life (*Lunyu* 5.15). Notably, preserving the attitude of neutrality and impartiality bespeaks the freedom of judgment of what is right and fitting *(yi)* in a particular situation. As Xunzi later put it, *yi* must also be used for dealing with changing circumstances of human life *(yiyi bianying)*.[68]

Remarks such as *Lunyu* 4.10, 4.22, and 9.26 about being ashamed of poor clothing, about thinking only of salary while serving either a good or bad government (*Lunyu* 14.1), and more generally about poverty and mean conditions in a well-governed state (*Lunyu* 8.13), pragmatically imply negative ethical and value judgments. But these judgments are not to be construed as a wholesale rejection of the value of external, material goods. The key issue here pertains to the priority of consideration of *yi* over *li**, i.e., personal gain, benefit, profit, advantage, or more generally, self-interest.[69] Like Aristotle, Confucius thinks that a good human life of well-being requires external goods, "for it is impossible or at

---

67. Given the following discussion on the role of *yi* in the moral life, it is most difficult to accept Fingarette's thesis that for Confucius, "the moral task is to make a proper classification, to locate an act within the scheme of *li*" (Fingarette, 22). I wonder, to borrow Xunzi's words, whether Fingarette's mind is so preoccupied with *li* that he consequently fails to properly understand *yi* (*Bi yili er buzhi yi*). For a discussion of Xunzi's conception of *bi*, see Cua, *Ethical Argumentation*, chap. 4; and Essay 6 in this volume. Graham's attempt at a partial defense of Fingarette's thesis that Confucius lacks the "full" concepts of choice and responsibility, and his classification of all Chinese philosophies by way of a "quasi-syllogism" raise important issues on the study of Ancient Chinese philosophy. I hope to deal with the issues on another occasion. (See A. C. Graham, *Disputers of the Tao: Philosophical Argument in Ancient China* [LaSalle, Ill.: Open Court, 1989], 26–30 and Appendix 1.) My own view of the notion of *yi* in Confucian ethics as part of a fundamental conceptual framework is given in Essay 13 of *Moral Vision and Tradition*.

68. See *bugou* L43 and *zhishi* L306.

69. Henceforth, I shall use such words as personal gain, benefit, profit, advantage, or more generally, self-interest, interchangeably for the notion of *li**.

least not easy to perform noble actions if one lacks the wherewithal" (NE 1099a). For Confucius, the difficulty arises in cases where there is a conflict between our desire for doing the right thing *(yi)* and desire for personal gain or benefit. Here we have the familiar problem of the conflict of morality and advantage. Since external goods are required for living a life of *ren* and conformity with *li* or rules of proper behavior, concern for *li** or self-interest without regard for *yi* is liable to bring undesirable consequences. Says Confucius, "When one is guided by *li** in one's own actions, one will incur much ill will" (*Lunyu* 4.12 [Lau 1979]). More importantly, for a man of consummate virtue *(chengren)*, when seeing that there is *li** or advantage to be gained, he thinks of *yi* or the right thing to do *(jiande siyi)* (*Lunyu* 16.10).[70] At any rate, unlike a small-minded fellow *(xiaoren)* who is conversant with *li** or profit, a *junzi* understands what constitutes *yi* or right conduct (*Lunyu* 4.16). As we shall see later, this theme on the relation between *yi* and *li** in the *Xunzi* is much more explicit.

3.8

The foregoing discussion presents a reconstruction of the remarks on *chi* attributed to Confucius in the *Lunyu*. There we find a conception of shame that places its ethical significance in the form of shame as sense of shame, an internal, ethical monitor of conduct.[71] In other words, the emphasis is placed on the prospective significance of shame as in Aristotle's ethics (2.5 above). For the proper exercise of the sense of shame, the agent must be ready to correct moral faults *(gaiguo)*. Says Confucius, "Failure to cultivate virtue, failure to probe more deeply into what I have learned, inability to move toward what is right *(yi)* when I have heard it, and inability to correct my faults: these are the things which cause me concern" (*Lunyu* 7.3). Faults are defects of character that require rectification or reformation. More fundamentally, the rare ability to engage in self-reproach *(zisong)* is presupposed whenever the agent is aware of such faults (*Lunyu* 5.27). However, self-reproach would be pointless, unless the agent engaged in self-examination *(zix-*

---

70. The same expression, *jiande siyi*, in connection with scholars *(shi)* also occurs in *Lunyu* 19.1. For informative surveys of the problem of the relation of *yi* and *li**, see Zhengtong Wei, *Zhongguo zhexue cidian* (Taipei: Dalin, 1980); and *Zhongguo zhexue cidian daquan* (Taipei: Shuiniu, 1983).

71. In the *Lunyu*, in addition to *chi*, there are other specific terms for shame such as *ru* and *xiu*. But these terms do not occur in direct discourse in the remarks attributed to Confucius. In the cases of the occurrence of *ru*, they are commonly, and I think properly, rendered as "disgrace." The ethical significance of *ru* will be discussed when I deal with Xunzi's conception after Mencius's.

ing). If self-examination discloses nothing for self-reproach, the person may indeed be said to be free from worries and fears (*Lunyu* 12.4). In relation to others Confucius says, "When you meet a character of moral worth *(xian),* you should think of emulating him; when you meet a morally unworthy character *(buxian),* you should turn inwards and examine yourselves *(zixing)*" (*Lunyu* 4.17).[72]

Also, our conduct is publicly observable; for this reason our self-examination must effect a self-transformation and result in proper conduct in the future. As Zigong remarks: "The *junzi*'s errors are like the eclipse of the sun and the moon in that when he errs the whole world sees him doing so and when he reforms the whole world looks up to him" (*Lunyu* 19.21 [Lau 1979]). The eclipse metaphor recalls the Greek "eyes of the others" metaphor (2.1, 2.9 above). More explicit about public observation and the difficulty of hiding misconduct from others (2.1 above) is the comment on sincerity of thought *(chengyi)* in the *Daxue (Great Learning):*

What is meant by "making the thoughts sincere" *(cheng qi yi)?* One must not allow self-deception, as when we detest a bad smell or as when we love a beautiful color. This is what is called self-respect *(ziqian).*[73] Therefore, the *junzi* will always be watchful when he is alone. When the small-minded man is alone and at leisure, there is no limit to which he does not go in his evil thoughts. Only when he sees a *junzi* does he then disguise himself, concealing his evil thoughts and displaying his goodness. But what is the use? For other people see him as if they see his lungs and livers. This is what is meant by the saying that what is true in a man's heart will be shown in outward appearance. Therefore the superior man must be watchful when he is alone. Zengzi said, "What ten eyes are beholding and what ten hands are pointing to—isn't it frightening?" Wealth makes a house shining and virtue *[de]* makes a person shining. The mind is broad and the body at ease. Therefore, the *junzi* always makes his thought or will sincere.[74]

Conduct that is deemed shameful and requires reform implies a normative judgment in accord with *yi* (rightness), as distinct from the agent's concern for *li** or personal gain. A concern for *chi* is a self-regarding concern that does not exclude that of *li** or personal advantage so long as *li** does not violate the *yi* requirement. If we conceive of the moral

---

72. In the *Lunyu,* Zengzi, a prominent disciple of Confucius, stresses daily self-examination: "Every day I examine myself on three counts. In what I have undertaken on another's behalf, have I failed to do my best? In dealing with my friends, have I failed to be trustworthy in what I say? Have I passed on to others anything that I have not tried out myself?" (*Lunyu* 1.4 [Lau 1979]).

73. Reading of *ziqian* as *zizun* (self-respect) follows Zehou Zhao, *Daxue yanjiu* (Taipei: Zhonghua, 1972).

74. Chan, *Source Book,* 89–90*. For more discussion, see my "A Confucian Perspective on Self-Deception," or Essay 11 in *Moral Vision and Tradition.*

point of view as a court of appeal for resolving conflict of interests, *yi* may be said to represent the Confucian moral point of view.[75]

3.9

Let us now turn to *Mengzi*.[76] As compared to Confucius's conception of shame *(chi)* in the *Analects*, Mencius's conception differs somewhat but supplements it in at least two important ways. Unlike Confucius (3.5 above), Mencius is very much concerned with honor *(rong)* and his conception of shame *(xiu)* brings into prominence the role of *yi* in his theory of the *xin* as the seat of the beginnings of the four cardinal virtues *(siduan)*, i.e., *ren, yi, li,* and *zhi* (practical wisdom). The *xiu* in *xiuwu zhixin* is said to be the beginning of the virtue *yi*, which focuses on feeling, though invested with a cognitive content.[77]

For Mencius, a life devoted to *ren*, to the ideal of affectionate concern for one's fellows, will bring honor *(rong)*. A life of malevolence *(buren)*, on the other hand, will bring nothing but shame or disgrace *(ru)*. Says Mencius, "People who dwell in malevolence while disliking disgrace *(ru)* are like those who are content to dwell in a low-lying place while disliking dampness. If one dislikes disgrace, one's best course of action is to honor virtue *(guide)* and to respect virtuous scholars" (*Mengzi* 2A4*). More forcefully, Mencius points out:

Benevolence *(ren)* is the high honour bestowed by Heaven and the peaceful abode of men.[78] Not to be benevolent when nothing stands in the way is to show a lack of wisdom. A man neither benevolent nor wise, devoid of respect for rules of proper conduct *(li)* and for rightness *(yi)*, is a slave. A slave ashamed of *(chi)* serving is like a maker of bows ashamed of making bows, or maker of arrows ashamed of making arrows. If one is ashamed *(chi)*, there is no better remedy than to practice benevolence *(ren)*. Benevolence is like archery: an archer makes sure his stance is correct before letting fly the arrow, and if he fails to hit

---

75. See my *Dimensions of Moral Creativity*, 67–68.
76. Unless indicated otherwise, translations are adopted from D. C. Lau, *Mencius* (Middlesex, England: Penguin Books, 1970). Asterisks indicate emendations.
77. For a discussion supporting this interpretation, see my "*Xin* and Moral Failure: Notes on an Aspect of Mencius's Moral Psychology," in *Mencius: Contexts and Interpretations*, ed. Alan Chan (Honolulu: University of Hawaii Press, 2002); incorporated in this volume as Essay 15.
78. Elsewhere, Mencius says: "It is not worth the trouble to talk to a man who has no respect for himself *(zibao)*, and it is not worth the trouble to make a common effort with a man who abandons himself *(ziqi)* [in pursuing the *dao*]. The former has no respect for *li* or rules of proper conduct and *yi* (rightness); the latter says, 'I do not think that I am capable of abiding by *ren* or following *yi*.' *Ren* is man's peaceful abode and *yi* is his proper path. It is indeed lamentable for anyone not to live in his peaceful abode and not to follow his proper path" (*Mengzi* 4A10*).

the mark, he does not hold it against the victor. He simply seeks the cause within himself. (*Mengzi* 2A7*)[79]

In this passage, we see the ideal of *ren* as a peaceful abode, and its connection with *yi* and *li*. Concern for avoidance of shameful conduct is best remedied by the practice of *ren*, involving *li* and *yi*. And failure in realizing *ren* requires self-examination—echoing a familiar theme in *Lunyu* (3.6 above). Presupposed is that the agent has the sense of shame and a commitment to *ren*. The archer analogy implies an audience or observer of an agent's actions—again reverberating a theme in the *Lunyu* (3.8 above). Mencius would even go further in reminding us that a shameful person cannot hide his misconduct, especially if it is revelatory of his character. Says Mencius, "There is in man nothing more ingenuous than the pupils of his eyes. They cannot conceal his wickedness. When he is upright within his own breast, a man's pupils are clear and bright; when he is not, they are clouded and murky. How can a man conceal his true character if you listen to his words and observe the pupils of his eyes?" (*Mengzi* 4A15)

For Mencius *ren* is one's peaceful abode, and *yi* is the road to *ren*. "To dwell in benevolence *(ren)* and follow rightness *(yi)* constitute the sum total of the business of a great man" (*Mengzi* 7A33). However, doing what is right *(yi)* involves the exercise of discretion *(qian)* with sensitivity to timing *(shi)*. Both Yangzi and Mozi fail to appreciate discretion. Says Mencius:

Yang Tzu [Yangzi] chooses egoism. Even if he could benefit the whole world by pulling out one hair, he would not do it. Mo Tzu [Mozi] advocates love without discrimination *(jianai)*. If by shaving his head and showing his heels he could benefit the whole world, he would do it. Tzu-mo [Zimo] holds on to the middle halfway between the two extremes. Holding on to the middle is closer to being right, but to do this without exercising discretion *(zhizhong wuquan)* is not different from holding to one extreme. The reason for disliking those who hold on to one extreme is that they cripple the Way *(dao)*. One thing is singled out to the neglect of a hundred others. (*Mengzi* 7A26*)[80]

---

79. Elsewhere, Mencius is emphatic: "A man cannot be without a sense of shame *(chi)*, for the shame of being without a sense of shame is shamelessness indeed" (7A6).
80. Mencius emphasizes *quan* in the hypothetical case of saving one's sister-in-law from drowning (4A17). For further discussion, see my *Dimensions of Moral Creativity*, 72–76. For a general discussion of the notion of *quan* in Confucian ethics, see my "The Idea of Confucian Tradition," *Review of Metaphysics* 45, no. 4 (1992); incorporated as Essay 12 in *Moral Vision and Tradition*. For an insightful discussion of Mencius's notion of "not holding to a particular thing *(buzhiyi)*," see Chen Daqi, *Mengzi de mingli sixiang ji qi bianshuo shikuang* (Taipei: Shangwu, 1968), chap. 2.

The exercise of *quan* must be informed by a sense of timing *(shi)*. Notably, perhaps because of Confucius's neutrality or open-mindedness (3.5 above), Mencius regards Confucius as "the sage of timeliness *(sheng zhi shizhe)*" (5B1) who acted "according to circumstances" *(Mengzi* 2A1).

3.10

Again echoing *Lunyu*, Mencius stresses the importance of self-respect in pursuing *dao*. Following Confucius, Mencius draws a fairly sharp contrast between *yi* (rightness) and *li** (profit or personal gain) *(Mengzi* 1A1). For Mencius, an agent's lack of *hengxin*, the constant or persevering *xin*, may well be a result of preoccupation with personal gain without attending to the relevance of *yi* as a basis for assessment, or the exercise of *quan*, particularly when the situation is one that promises personal gain. Alternatively, lack of *hengxin* is a failure to appreciate *xin* as a weighing standard for determining the ethically proper course of action and the failure may also be a consequence of the corruption of moral integrity. Mencius stresses the ethical integrity of the sages: "The conduct of the sages is not always the same. Some live in retirement, others enter the world; some withdraw, others stay on; but it all comes to keeping their integrity intact *(guijie qishen)*" *(Mengzi* 5A7). Indeed, integrity is not limited to the sages. No self-respecting villager, for instance, would sell himself into slavery "in order to help one's prince towards achievement" *(Mengzi* 5A9). More important, a wayfarer, or even a beggar, would not accept a basket of rice or a bowl of soup if it were tendered in an abusive manner, particularly when the behavior violates the requirements of *li* and *yi* *(Mengzi* 6A10).

Ordinarily, failure to preserve one's ethical integrity is a failure of *cheng* (being true to oneself). Says Mencius, "Being true *(cheng)* is the Way of Heaven; to reflect upon this is the Way of man. There has never been a man totally true to himself who fails to move others. On the other hand, one who is not true to himself can never hope to move others" *(Mengzi* 4A12). The utmost development of *xin (jinxin)* presupposes knowing one's nature *(xing)* and self-respect. Notably, ethical integrity has no special connection with Fingarette's *li*—"traditionally ceremonially defined social comportment" (3.4 above).

3.11

As a background for understanding *xiuwu zhi xin* as the wellspring of *yi*, let us look briefly at Mencius's notion of *xin* as the seat of the four cardinal virtues *(Mengzi* 2A6). The *siduan* or "four beginnings" are (1) the *xin* of compassion *(ceyin zhi xin)*, (2) the *xin* of *xiuwu*, (3) the *xin* of courtesy and modesty *(cirang zhi xin)*, and (4) the *xin* of right and wrong *(shifei zhi xin)*. If we regard the *siduan* as sentiments that have both emotive and cognitive import, we can then say that *xin*, while expressive of a feeling, has also a cognitive aspect, thus the appropriateness of rendering *xin* as "heart and mind." This notion of sentiment captures the sense of Butler's apt characterization of "a moral faculty" as "a sentiment of the understanding or perception of the heart."[81] More importantly, implicit in the notion of sentiment is prereflective judgment that the deed performed or to be performed is deemed to be something evil or bad. Plausibly, these sentiments embody *prereflective* judgments subject to reasoned revision.[82]

More formally, the *xin* of compassion, for instance, is expressed as a *qing* (feeling, passion), which pragmatically implies an epistemic attitude, i.e., belief, thought, or judgment.[83] Thus, the *xin* of compassion involves the following: (a) a feeling of alarm and distress, (b) an implicit belief, thought, or judgment that one ought to help the person in distress, and (c) a disposition to act accordingly. Since the *siduan*, the germs of virtue, are spontaneously expressed, these epistemic attitudes are subject to reasoned evaluation. I take this to be the purport of Mencius's remark that reason and rightness *(liyi)* are common to all *xin*.[84]

Analogously, we may say that the *xin* of *xiuwu* involves the following: (a) a feeling of shame, (b) implicit belief, thought, or judgment that one ought to refrain from performing bad or evil deeds, (c) and a disposition to act accordingly. *Xiuwu zhi xin* may be elucidated as having inner and outer aspects. The inner aspect pertains to feeling ashamed

---

81. Says Butler in "A Dissertation Upon the Nature of Virtue": "It is manifest great part of common language, and of common behavior over the world, is formed upon the supposition of such a moral faculty, whether called conscience, moral reason, moral sense, or divine reason; whether considered as a *sentiment of the understanding or perception of the heart*, or, which seems the truth, as including both." See Joseph Butler, *Five Sermons* (Indianapolis, Ind.: Bobbs-Merrill, 1950), 82, my emphasis.

82. For explanation and justification of this interpretation of Mencius's conception of *xin*, see Essay 15 in this volume.

83. In Xunzi, we find a sharper distinction between *xin* and *qing* (passions, feelings). *Xin* has a primary cognitive function that is distinct from *qing*. When this function is guided by *li* (reason), *xin* can provide a reliable ethical guide to the expression of *qing*. This notion of *xin* is best rendered as "mind" in the sense of the mental capacity of remembering, thinking, judging, and reasoning, rather than a sort of mental feeling or affection as seems to be implicit in Mencius's doctrine of *siduan*. It must be noted that Xunzi's conception of *xin* also embraces a volitional function, which may counter its intellectual or cognitive function, resulting in different sorts of cognitive delusion *(huo)*. However, when it approves of *dao* and is guided by reason, *xin* can provide a reliable ethical guide to conduct. For a fuller discussion, see my *Ethical Argumentation*, chap. 4; and Essay 6 in this volume.

84. For elaboration, see paper cited in note 77.

of one's own bad conduct, and the outer aspect to *wu* or dislike of other people's bad conduct.⁸⁵ This explanation of *xiuwu* is based on Zhu Xi's comment: "*Xiu* refers to the *xiu* of one's own wrongdoing; *wu* to the dislike *(wu)* of others' bad deeds."⁸⁶

According to Shun, contrary to Zhu Xi's interpretation of *wu* as directed to the bad deeds of others, *wu* can also be directed to one's own badness. However, there is an "element of truth" in Zhu Xi's interpretation: "Even *wu* can be directed at one's own actions or things that happen to oneself, the attitude involved in *wu* when so directed is like the attitude one has toward what one dislikes in others. This is unlike the attitudes occasioned by *xiu* and *ch'ih [chi]*, which cannot be directed at what one dislikes in another person unless the other person stands in some special relation to oneself."⁸⁷ However, if we make clear the presupposition of the Confucian doctrine of human relationships *(lun)*, which Mencius accepts,⁸⁸ involved are significant others that stand "in some special relation to oneself" (2.9 above).

3.12

Mencius's conception of shame articulates the connection between *xiuwu zhi xin* or the sense of shame and *yi* implicit in the *Lunyu*, though *xiu* is used rather than *chi*. Perhaps *xiu* conveys more clearly the emotive or affective aspect of *xin* than *chi* does.⁸⁹ In distinguishing the different groundings of the virtues of *yi* and *li*, Mencius develops the distinction between *yi* and *li* in the *Lunyu*, by giving them different groundings in

---

85. This explanation of *xiuwu* is based on Xue's dictionary as an elucidation of Mencius's claim that if a person is devoid of *xiuwu zhi xin*, he or she is not human *(wu xiuwu zhi xin fei ren ye)*.

86. Zhu Xi, *Zhuzi yulei* (Taipei: Zhengzhong, 1962), chap. 53, 4:1286.

87. Shun, 60.

88. See, for example, Mencius's remark in *Mengzi* 4B19: "Slight is the difference between man and brutes. The common man loses his distinguishing feature, while the *junzi* retains it. Shun understood the ways of things and had a keen insight into human relationships. These relationships have their foundation in *ren* and their practice in *yi*. It is not because of these relationships that we proceed towards *ren* and *yi*" (*Mengzi* 4B19*). Emendation of the last two sentences adopted in part from Dobson's translation of *"youren yixing, fei ren xingyi ye."* See W. A. C. H. Dobson, *Mencius: A New Translation arranged and annotated for the General Reader* (Toronto, Ontario: University of Toronto Press, 1963), 141.

89. On the basis of his survey of early uses of *chi* and *xiu* in early texts such as *Zuozhuan*, Shun thinks that these texts suggest that *"ch'ih (chi)* is probably focused more on the thing that reflects badly on oneself and involves a resolution to distance oneself from or remedy the situation. . . . Hsiu (xiu), on the other hand, is focused more on the badness or the low standing of oneself as reflected in, or as likely to ensue from, the thing that occasions *hsiu*" (Shun, 59). It is unclear to me how this difference throws light on Mencius's use of *xiu* as a component of *xiuwu zhi xin*. What requires explication is the use of *xiu* as connected with *yi*. If we construe *xiuwu zhi xin* as *xiuchi zhi xin* (sense of shame) as in modern Chinese, then the difference between *xiu* as a component of *xiuwu zhi xin*

xin as the seat of the virtues, thus anticipating our more recent concern with the problem of the connection between the form and content of morality. The *li* are the rules of proper conduct, more accurately, formal prescriptions for proper behavior. Mencius wisely connects shame *(xiu)* with what is right *(yi)*, rather than with *li*, for fundamentally right conduct in a particular situation cannot always be determined by compliance with formal rules of proper behavior, although, in a normal situation, it is acceptable to follow *li*, presuming that the *li* in question does not violate the spirit of *ren* and *yi*. On the question of the relation of *yi* to profit or personal gain *(li*)*, Mencius concurs with Confucius (3.7 above), though he conjoins *ren* and *yi* as having a priority over personal gain *(Mengzi* 1A1). However, in a dilemma that involves the ultimate choice between *yi* and life, Mencius would choose *yi* rather than life, reminiscent of Confucius's remark that a scholar with a firm purpose or a *ren*-person would sacrifice his life for the sake of fulfilling *ren* (*Lunyu* 15.9).

As Confucius and Mencius are well aware, ordinary persons who are committed to *ren* and *yi* are much less steadfast. Mencius, in particular, points out that ordinary people with a *xin* devoted to *ren* and *yi* must be supported by constant means. In his words: "Only a *junzi* can have a constant heart *(hengxin)* in spite of a lack of constant means of support. The people, on the other hand, will not have constant hearts if they are without constant means. Lacking constant hearts, they will go astray and fall into excesses, stopping at nothing" (*Mengzi* 1A7). A *ren* government such as King Wen's did not extend punishment to the wife and children of the offender. "Old men without wives, old women without husbands, old people without children, young children without fathers—these four types of people are the most destitute and have no one to turn for help. Whenever King Wen put benevolent measures into effect, he always gave them first consideration" (*Mengzi* 1A5). Admittedly, it is often through hardship and suffering that people "acquire virtue, wisdom, talent, and brilliance" (*Mengzi* 7A18).[90] Along the same line, Xunzi's conception of kingly government also calls for providing support, especially for the incapacitated such as the dumb, deaf, crippled, dwarf, one-armed and one-legged people. However, these people must not be left idle. All recipients of government welfare should be assigned tasks they are capable of performing.[91] On this measure a Confucian today

---

and *chi* is that the latter, unlike the former as used in the passages in the *Lunyu* we have considered, brings out the emotive aspect of shame.

90. Following Shi, I read *zhi* as *caizhi*, i.e. "brilliance" in the sense of "exceptional ability." See Shi Ciyun, *Mengzi jinzhu jinyi* (Taipei: Shangwu, 1974).

91. *Wanzhi pian*, Book 8, Watson, 34n.

will be gratified to see a modern actualization of an aspect of the vision of *ren* government in recent American programs of workfare, i.e., requiring unemployed men and women on welfare to work in return for welfare payments, e.g., doing community work or attending training courses.

3.13

Like Confucius and Mencius, Xunzi emphasizes the ethical standard of *yi* for the judgment of conduct involved in shame experience; but, unlike Mencius, Xunzi does not connect shame with *xin*. More importantly Xunzi assigns a greater role to the desire for honor and aversion to shame in the moral life and gives special attention to the moral condition of the agent—a feature that has an affinity to a characteristic feature of Aristotle's ethics. Moreover, for Xunzi, the idea of ethical shame or disgrace *(ru)* cannot be rendered intelligible without seeing its connection with honor as an ethical concept. As Shun justly remarks, "The *ju [ru]* one suffers is not just something that one dislikes; it reflects adversely on oneself and results in lowering one's standing [in the community]."[92] The idea of *ru* thus conveys dishonor or disgrace, i.e., a loss of respect from others. Differently put, the concepts of honor and shame are wedded to each other, partners in the same domain of moral discourse. This is not the case for Aristotle, although honor is tied to nobility and virtue (2.2 and 2.3 above). This lack of interest in contrasting shame with honor is perhaps the result of Aristotle's rhetorical orientation toward the *pathos* of the audience of significant others or "the eyes of others" (2.9). In a way, Confucius and Mencius, as our discussion has shown, would acknowledge the audience of significant others, because of the publicly observable aspects of moral conduct (3.8 and 3.9 above). Xunzi would agree but would add that the opinions of significant others must be subject to the more fundamental ethical question of justification.[93] Below we focus on these distinctive contributions of Xunzi to assessing the ethical significance of shame experience. However, essential

92. Shun, 58.
93. The main sources for our discussion of Xunzi's conception of the ethical significance of shame are his essay entitled "On Honor and Shame" (*Rongru pian*, Book 4) and relevant passages from *Zhenglun pian*, Book 18. Reference to Xunzi is based on Li Disheng, *Xunzi jishi* (Taipei: Xuesheng, 1979), which is an annotated edition of Wang Xianqian's *Xunzi jijie*, hereafter cited by way of the title of Xunzi's essay. Aside from the works mentioned, my own reading and translation benefit much from the annotations of Liang, Xiong, Yang, and the Beijing University Philosophy Department. See Liang Qixiong, *Xunzi jianshi* (Taipei: Shangwu, 1978); Xiong Gongzhe, *Xunzi jinzhu jinyi* (Taipei: Shangwu, 1975); Yang Liang, *Xunzi* (Taipei: Zhonghua, 1976); and Beijing University Philosophy Department, *Xunzi xinzhu* (Taipei: Liren, 1983).

is a preliminary understanding of Xunzi's distinction between honor and shame and its significance for considered judgment and choice.

3.14

For Xunzi, just as all kinds of things that appear have their sources, the honor *(rong)* and shame *(ru)* that come to a man reflect his virtues. If one is lazy or neglectful of caring for one's own person, he can expect calamity and misfortune. Evil and corruption in oneself invite the enmity of others. "So there are words that invite disaster and actions that summon shame. A *junzi* is cautious about where he takes his stand" (*quanxue* L5, W17*).

Xunzi explains the basic distinction between honor *(rong)* and shame *(ru)* and its importance in connection with the usual conditions of being peaceful or uneasy, beneficial or injurious *(anwei li*hai zhi changti)*.[94] For convenience of explication, we divide the passage into two sections, A and B.

A. Individuals who think of what is right *(yi)* before personal gain *(li*)* are honorable *(rong)*; and those who think of personal gain before what is right *(yi)* are shameful. Honorable persons are ordinarily successful *(changtong)* in life; and shameful ones are ordinarily failures *(changqiong)*. The successful ones ordinarily dominate others, the failures usually submit to control by others. Herein lies the basic distinction between honor and shame.

B. Upright and honest individuals ordinarily *(chang)* have peace of mind and acquire benefits; dissolute and ruthless persons ordinarily acquire danger and

---

94. I read *changti* as *tongchang de qingkuang*, that is, the normal or ordinary condition. The Beijing Philosophy Department gives a similar explanation of *changti*: *tongchang de qingxing*, i.e., "common situation or circumstance." For a different rendering of *changti* as "invariable condition," see Knoblock, 3:14. This is a possible reading, since *chang* may also means "constant" or "invariable." However, the subsequent occurrence of *chang* in the passages (labeled A and B) to be examined means "ordinary, normal, or usual." I do not think that in A and B Xunzi is claiming a necessary connection between the antecedents and consequents, for, as we shall see, he subsequently clearly states that a life of *ren* and *yi* and virtuous conduct are not necessarily free from danger (*rongru* L61). In the case of Xunzi's view of *tian* (Heaven, Nature), he explicitly states that "the course of *tian* is *chang* (*tianxing youchang)*." Here *chang* may be rendered as "constant," as Knoblock does (*tianlun pian*, Book 17, K3:14). But as Xunzi points out, what is *chang* may well co-exist with strange occurrences. This use of *chang*, when rendered as "constant" does admit of exceptions or irregularities. We do not have direct textual evidence for construing Xunzi's view on *tian* as comprising natural necessities, especially in the light of his admission that there are inexplicable occurrences that are mysterious or matters of *shen*. For explaining *shen*, Li cites a passage from the *Yijing*: "The unfathomable *yinyang* process is what is meant by *shen*" (*Xici chuan*). (See Nan Huaijin and Xu Qinting, *Zhouyi jinzhu jinyi* [Taipei: Shangwu, 1979], 372.) For more discussion of *shen* and *shenming* (godlike insight), see my "The Ethical and the Religious Dimensions of *Li* (Rites)," *Review of Metaphysics* 55, no. 3 (2002): 501–49; incorporated as Essay 7 in this volume.

harm. Individuals who have peace of mind and possess benefits are usually joyous and calm; those who are exposed to danger and harm are ordinarily sorrowful and apprehensive. Those who are joyous and calm ordinarily have long lives; those who are exposed to harm and danger usually die young. [Generally speaking,] these are the conditions of being peaceful or uneasy, beneficial or injurious *(anwei li*hai zhi changti)*. (*Rongru pian* L60, D55–56*)

3.15

Passage A states the Confucian moral point of view in the *Lunyu* (3.7 above), contrasting *yi* and *li** (personal gain, profit, benefit)—the moral and prudential points of view—not as a dichotomy, but as a subject of potential conflict to be resolved by *yi* in the event of conflict between *yi* and *li**. Mencius's contribution makes explicit the connection of shame with *yi* or rightness (3.12 above), and not with *li* or rules of proper conduct. While Xunzi stresses the importance of *li* (ritual propriety) throughout his essays, passage A commands attention for two different reasons. It provides grounds for rejecting the common interpretation of Xunzi as a proponent of *li* as an inclusive virtue. More importantly, from the standpoint of ethical theory, the argument proffered for the desirability of honor and the undesirability of shame as ways of life is basically a prudential argument.

Homer Dubs, an eminent scholar and pioneer translator of the *Xunzi*, is a proponent of the interpretation of *li* as an inclusive virtue, well aware of the distinction of *ren*, *li*, and *yi*. According to Dubs:

> *Li* is the chief virtue, and really the whole of virtue, including every other. Frequently in his writings he combines another with it to emphasize one aspect of the whole; usually, it is *Li* and *Yi*, or *Li* and music, sometimes *Li* alone; but *Li* is so developed that it includes within itself the constituent elements of these other virtues too.[95]

Even in the brilliant analytical commentary of Chen Daqi, we find a more plausible, but equally misleading interpretation that *li* and *yi* are functionally equivalent.[96] The difficulty of accepting Dubs's view is this:

---

95. Dubs, *Hsüntze*, 133. These remarks also apply to the claim that for Xunzi, "*Li* is said to have 'morals' as one of its meanings. To say that an action is in accordance with *li* is to say that it is moral, and that it is civil, mannerly, customary, proper, and in at least one sense, religious." See Henry Rosemont, Jr., "Notes from a Confucian Perspective: Which Human Acts Are Moral Acts?" *International Philosophical Quarterly* 16, no. 1 (1976): 50. But this interpretation overlooks the role of *yi*, especially in the contrast of *yi* and *li** (personal gain) crucial to understanding the Confucian conception of morality. Incidentally, Dubs's thesis would be a sound interpretation of Li Gou's theory of *li*. See my paper cited in the next note.

96. Chen, *Xunzi xueshuo*, 144. For a critical discussion of Chen's view and others on

If we associate shame with the violation of *li* rather than *yi*, we would have to overlook the views of Confucius and Mencius. Also, if *li* is a set of formal prescriptions for proper behavior, then it make no sense to attribute ethical significance to the feeling of shame occasioned, say, by an infringement of a formal rule of propriety. Even if the shame experienced by the agent is more than a mild form of embarrassment caused by a breach of, say, a *li* of etiquette, an observer's disapproval or critical judgment of this violation cannot be reasonably accepted as an ethical or moral judgment. As Waley has noted, the early Confucians were concerned with the problem of justifying the established system of *li*.[97] Arguably, on my reconstruction, Xunzi's solution is to invest the notion of *li* with *yi*, showing in effect that the formal rules of propriety must be the right sort of rules. It follows that a mere violation of a rule of proper conduct cannot be regarded as ethically blamable unless the judgment can be shown to have a basis in the rightness *(yi)* of the rule both in formulation and its appropriate application to a particular case.[98] Moreover, in the case of shame, Xunzi clearly states that *ren* is also involved (*rongru pian* L61). We shall take up this passage shortly.

3.16

Let us inquire further into the significance of passage A. As we have remarked, Xunzi is presenting a decision problem to his readers. Presumed is the presence of highly literate and intelligent readers concerned with making a deliberate, judicious choice between two competing ways of life, of honor and shame. In effect, Xunzi confronts his reader with the question: "Were you fully cognizant of the expected consequences in the ordinary course of events of honorable and shameful ways of life, after deliberation *(lü)*, would you choose the former and reject the latter, or conversely?" Passage A goes on to present two opposing arguments for the consequences of choosing the way of honor or the way of shame. Before we examine these arguments, let us step back a bit and say something about Xunzi's underlying conception of *xin* as a seat of thought and volition (volition in the sense of the capacity to make conscious choices and decisions).[99]

---

the problem of co-occurrence of *li* and *yi*, see my "The Problem of Conceptual Unity in Hsün Tzu and Li Kou's Solution," *Philosophy East and West* 39, no. 2 (1989): 115–34; incorporated in this volume as Essay 4.

97. Lau, *Analects*, 57–59.

98. See my "Hsün Tzu and the Unity of Virtues," *Journal of Chinese Philosophy* 14, no. 4 (1987): 381–400; incorporated in this volume as Essay 5.

99. For more discussion of this aspect of Xunzi's thought, see my *Ethical Argumentation*, chap. 4.

Unlike Mencius, Xunzi ascribes to *xin* not only a capacity for thought and deliberation, but also a capacity to approve or disapprove, and crucially, of *dao* as the ultimate end of human life. To borrow Thomas Reid's terms, Xunzi thinks that all human beings possess intellectual and active powers. Significantly, these powers may be exercised even to the extent of rejecting Xunzi's holistic vision of *dao*, comprising the Confucian cardinal aretaic notions of *ren*, *li*, and *yi*. Says Xunzi: "This is the salient feature of *xin (xinrung)*: Its choices are not subject to any external control. Inevitably it manifests its own choices" (*jiebi pian* L488). For *xin* to approve or disapprove of *dao* as the ideal balance or weighing standard *(heng)* for all thought and action, *xin* must first understand *dao*. And for *xin* to understand *dao*, it must attain the state of great purity and clarity *(da qingming)*. (See *jiebi* L482.) Furthermore, the clear mind must also be guided by reason *(li)* in order to resolve perplexities about right and wrong in particular cases.[100]

3.17

Given the autonomy of mind, in passage A Xunzi presents the problem of choice in a pair of chain arguments: a form of argument consisting of a series of premises arranged so that the predicate of each premise forms the subject of the next. If we rewrite both passages (A and B) as a pair of a series of conditional propositions, connecting the antecedents and the consequents, then we will have valid arguments, i.e., substitution instances of hypothetical syllogism in propositional logic.[101] For passage A we have the following, preceded by a statement of the choice: "Individuals who consider what is right *(yi)* before personal gain *(li*)* are honorable *(rong)*; and those who consider personal gain before what is right *(yi)* are shameful."

A1. If you choose the honorable way of life, you will lead a successful life. If you are successful, you will dominate others. (Suppressed Conclusion: Therefore, if you choose the way of honor, you will dominate others.)

On the other hand,

A2. If you choose the shameful way of life, you will lead a life of failure. If you lead a life of failure, others will control you. (Suppressed Conclusion: Therefore, if you choose the shameful way of life, others will control you.)

---

100. Says Xunzi, "If you guide it [the mind] with reason *[li]*, nourish it with clarity, and do not allow external objects to unbalance it, then it will be capable of determining right and wrong and of resolving doubts" (*jiebi pian* L490, W131).

101. The valid argument form is "$[(p \to q) \& (q \to r)] \to (p \to r)$."

In effect, Xunzi presents a decision problem for the thoughtful reader, for the choice between A1 and A2. Note, however, his use of *chang*, which we render as "ordinarily," implicitly conveys such qualification as "generally speaking," "as a general rule," or "what is true for the most part," which we spell out in brackets in the last line of passage B. Although these contrastive arguments A1 and A2 are formally valid, a question arises with respect to the soundness of the alleged connection between the antecedents and consequents. Qualified by "generally speaking," the presumed connection between antecedents and consequents is quite weak. Thus, with respect to the soundness of the argument A1 or A2, it is as strong as its weakest link.

The content of passage B would be more persuasive, if we reconstruct Xunzi's argument as a form of coordinative argument, wherein desirable goods and their opposites are presented as independent supporting considerations for choosing the life of honor as one characterized by uprightness and honesty.[102] The honorable way of life is preferable to the shameful way of life, because it is likely to bring about a number of benefits to the agent, for instance, peace of mind, joy, and long life. These are particular goods independent of their actual or possible connection, but viewed together, they support the choice of honor as a way of life. Of course, presupposed is that the agent would consider peace of mind, joy, and long life desirable conditions of life. Even if one of the goods is not realized, still the realization of the others may offer comfort to the agent, rather than any of the opposites in choosing shame as a way of life.

Worthy of note is that passage B presents the problem of choice between honor and shame as the ideal way of life in the light of benefit or harm *(lihai)* to the agent. And since a good human life is a life in a community of *ren* or mutual love and concern,[103] that means that an agent's final decision in favor of honor will have an impact upon his well-being as well as the well-being of fellow members of his community. At issue then is a prudential choice between personal goods and public goods or common good. Xunzi is confident that if the agent were committed to the priority of *yi* over personal gain, he would choose the way of honor rather than the way of shame, because it promises benefits to the agent and the community. Although defeasible, Xunzi's plausible pre-

---

102. For an elaboration and justification of the coordinative form of argument, see my *Ethical Argumentation*, chap. 3 (3.1–3.3); and *Moral Vision and Tradition*, Essay 10.

103. For examples of *ren* as embracing love or affectionate concern, see *Lunyu* 12.23; *Mengzi* 2A6; and *Xunzi, Yibing pian* L326. For more discussion, see my "Confucian Vision and the Human Community," *Journal of Chinese Philosophy* 11, no. 3 (1984): 226–38; incorporated as Essay 11 in this volume.

sumption may well hold for people of his times and not ours. The ethical issue presented is important today, because the choice has significant consequences for the agent's self-regarding and other-regarding interest or common good. Of course, an amoralist would be quite unmoved by Xunzi's arguments, since he may be a gambler hoping to satisfy as many desires as possible regardless of whether the members of his community call him a shameful or dishonorable person. The amoralist has neither a sense of honor nor a sense of shame. Thus the decision problem offered by Xunzi would be quite meaningless to the amoralist.

3.18

These passages, A and B, make explicit the distinction between rightness *(yi)* and benefit, personal gain, or profit *(li*)* as the criterion for honor and shame. What is depicted is Xunzi's view of the human condition in his times and of his conception of viable alternatives for the agent's choice between contrasting ways of life. Choosing a life of honor instead of a life of shame would constitute a commitment to moral agency dedicated, as Xunzi points out elsewhere, to the pursuit of the ideal of *dao* comprising interconnected concerns for *ren, yi,* and *li.*[104] Significantly the consequences of the agent's choice would determine his or her moral condition, or moral health or sickness, so to speak.

Thus, for Xunzi, a decision to adopt the *dao* as the guiding ideal of the good human life as a whole crucially involves the weighing of benefits and harms. In fact, Xunzi explicitly recommends the prudential method of choice or, in his words, a balancing scale *(quan)* for evaluating or weighing *(yuwu qushe zhi quan)* the relative merits and demerits of desires and aversions, as well as alternative options in terms of their beneficial and harmful consequences.

C. When one sees something desirable, one must deliberate *(lü)* whether or not it will lead to undesirable consequences. When one sees something beneficial, one must deliberate whether or not it will lead to harm. All these consequences must be weighed together *(jianquan)* and taken into account in any mature plan before one arrives at a decision concerning desires and aversions, and choices and rejections. If a person follows this weighing method, usually *(chang)* he will avoid errors and entrapment in harm's way.

---

104. For a discussion of this notion of *dao,* see my *Ethical Argumentation,* 160–63; and Essay 5 in this volume. More generally for the vision of *dao* in Confucian and Neo-Confucian ethics, see my *Moral Vision and Tradition,* Essays 2, 7, 9, and 13.

D. Generally humans suffer, because they tend toward partiality *(pian)* and the harms that result therefrom. When they see something desirable, they do not deliberate *(lü)* whether or not it will lead to something detestable. When they see something beneficial, they do not deliberate whether or not it will lead to something harmful. In this manner, any action they perform is bound to entrap them and to bring about shame *(ru)*. This is the predicament that besets us all—the harm that ensues from partiality *(pian)*. (*bugou pian* L53)

In passage C, we have in effect a strikingly modern conception of cost-benefit analysis for dealing with desires and aversions or preferences.[105] At issue is the need to strike a balance between competing considerations in order to arrive at a sound judgment or decision. A sound decision to pursue one's desire and aversion must be an outcome of *lü*, i.e., careful consideration of a matter at hand. Our rendering of *lü* as "deliberate" in passages C and D is a felicitous one, for the word "deliberate" is "derived from Latin *deliberare*, literally 'to weigh carefully,' which in turn is derived from *librare* 'to weigh,' from *libra* 'balance' (source of English level and equilibrium)."[106] *Lü* is a reflective activity of *xin* that makes a selection *(ze)* among the aroused feelings *(qing)* of our nature *(xing)*, feelings such as likes and dislikes, delight and anger, sorrow and joy. "When the mind *(xin)* can put its *lü* into action, this is called constructive activity *(wei)*" (*zhengming* L506, W139–40*).[107] However, since desires are responses to the feelings when they are aroused,[108] *lü* or deliberation makes a choice as indicated in the passages C and D.

3.19

Passage D goes on to explain our failure in arriving at a reasonable judgment or decision as a failure in *pian* or partiality. In other words, a reasonable judgment on the choice or rejection of an agent's desires or

---

105. For this consequentialist theme in Xunzi's conception of deliberation, see also *A Concordance to Hsün Tzu*, Harvard-Yenching Institute Sinological Index Series, supplement no. 22 (Taipei: Chinese Materials and Research Center, 1966), 15/5/59–60, 19/7/27, 55/15/53, and 87/23/24. Cf. *Lunyu* 15:12.
106. From *Encarta World Dictionary of English* (New York: St. Martin's Press, 2001). A similar explanation is given in *Concise Oxford Dictionary of the English Language*.
107. This summary statement of Xunzi's conception of *lü* is based on the following definitions: "The likes and dislikes, delight and anger, sorrow and joys of our nature *(xing)* are called feeling *(qing)*. When the feelings are aroused and the mind *(xin)* makes a choice from among them, this is called *lü*. When the mind can put its *lü* into action, this is called constructive activity *(wei)*" (*zhengming* L506, W139–40*).
108. "The nature of man *(xing)* is that which he receives from Heaven; his feelings are the constitutive elements *(zhi)* of his nature; his desires are the responses of the feelings. When a man is activated by feelings, he would pursue the desires that he thinks can be satisfied. This is the inevitable human situation *(qing)*. The starting point of wisdom must be to consider which desires are satisfiable and to guide them" (*zhengming* L529).

aversions must at least satisfy the requirement of impartiality. Also, the decision must have evidential grounding.[109] Elsewhere, Xunzi calls this *zhilü*, wise and well-informed deliberation—a process necessary to cope with changing circumstances and resolve doubts on issues of right and wrong conduct and/or the best thing to do in a situation at hand (*jundao* L284). When the outcome of deliberation accords with the reality of the situation, it may be called "wise and well-informed deliberation *(zhilü)*."[110] Notably Xunzi attributes to *xin* a confirmatory function with respect to claims of knowledge *(zhengzhi)*. Consequently, adequate evidential grounding of decision or judgment is required for reasonable, deliberate assessment of the options for choice.[111]

With regard to the requirement of impartiality, Xunzi's remark in the preceding passage D is worthy of attention. "From impartiality comes clear understanding and insight *(gong sheng ming)*; from partiality comes obscurity and darkness *(pian sheng an)*" *(bugou* L52). Xunzi says of the discourse of the scholar and the *junzi*: "With a humane mind *(renxin)*, he explains his ideas to others, with a receptive mind *(xuexin)*, he listens to their words, and with an impartial mind *(gongxin)* he makes his judgment" *(zhengming* L524, W148*).[112]

Notwithstanding our willingness to adhere to the standard of *gong* or impartiality, all humans are predisposed to be *pian* or partial in two different but connected ways.[113] We can be partial in favoring our own desires or interests *(siyu)* in cases where public interest has a right claim to consideration. In Xunzi's words, a *junzi* "is able to let rightful public in-

---

109. For more discussion of evidential grounding, see my *Ethical Argumentation*, chap. 2.

110. This interpretation is in part based on Xunzi's definitions of *zhi* and *zhi**. Below is a free translation: "*Zhi* is the capacity for knowing, and *zhi** is the knowledge obtained that has appropriate application which accords with the reality of the situation" *(zhengming pian* L502). As Long points out, these definitions probably reflect the influence of the definitions of *zhi* and *zhi** in the Later Mohist text, *Mozi, Jingshang pian*. See Long Yuchun, *Xunzi lunji* (Taipei: Xuesheng, 1987), 164. For the Mohist text, translation, and notes, along with Xunzi's definitions, see A. C. Graham, *Later Mohist Logic, Ethics and Science* (Hong Kong and London: Chinese University Press and University of London, 1978), 266–69. For more discussion of *zhilü*, see my "The Possibility of Ethical Knowledge: Reflections on a Theme in the *Hsün Tzu*," in *Epistemological Issues in Ancient Chinese Philosophy*, ed. Hans Lenk and Gregor Paul (Albany: State University of New York Press, 1993); incorporated in this volume as Essay 6.

111. See my *Ethical Argumentation*, 30–36.

112. Xunzi continues: "He is not moved by the censure or praise of the mob; he does not try to bewitch the ears and eyes of his observers; he does not cringe before the power and authority of eminent men.... He honors what is fair and upright and despises meanness and wrangling" *(zhengming* L524, W148).

113. The following remarks owe much to Daniel Dahlstrom's critical discussion of my *Ethical Argumentation*. See Daniel Dahlstrom, "The *Tao* of Ethical Argumentation," *Journal of Chinese Philosophy* 14, no. 4 (1987).

terest overcome his private desires *(yi gongyi sheng siyu)*" *(xiushen* L36). Note that *pian* in this sense refers to predilections, propensities, or more generally to unexamined preferences rather than deliberate prejudices. Perspicacity is required for careful deliberation. As we have earlier indicated, one function of *lü* or deliberation is to resolve perplexities concerning the best thing to do under the circumstances, for example, careful thought on a projected plan of action in terms of avoidance of risks that may result in harm and/or overestimating available resources for satisfying our desires. Thus, *pian* as partiality in this sense is always subject to reasoned evaluation.

3.20

The sense of *pian* as a predisposition to favor one's own interest rather than the public interest perhaps reflects a more fundamental, cognitive predisposition. Humans are liable to *pian*, in the sense of a partial grasp of the whole. In weighing the competing claims of desires, ordinary persons tend to follow their unexamined preferences without having an understanding of the situation as a whole, particularly in the light of the holistic perspective of *dao*. In Xunzi's words:

> What remains unchanged throughout the times of the Hundred Kings is worthy to be considered as the connecting thread of *dao (daoguan)*. To their rise and fall, respond with this connecting thread *(guan)*. If you apply the connecting thread with reason *(liguan)*, there will be no disorder. If you do not know the fundamental spirit of this connecting thread, you will not know how to respond to changing circumstances. (*tianlun* L379, K3:21*)[114]

This sense of *pian* or cognitive partiality, mistaking parts for the whole, is a common affliction of humanity. In Xunzi's language, we are victims of *bi*. Because of *bi*, we have a tendency to construe partial aspects of things and situations as a characteristic of a whole. In the case of discourse about the *dao* as an ideal of the good human life, we are liable to see its partial aspects and think that we understand its holistic nature, and thus fail to comprehend its overall rationale *(dali)* (*jiebi* L472). The worst victims of *bi* are philosophers, e.g., Laozi, Mozi, and Songzi. These philosophers have grounds for espousing their theses, thus their theses appear quite plausible *(qiyen zhi chengli)* (*fei shi'erzi pian* L93–96). Put differently, from perspectival points of view, what they advocate is reasonable. Yet they have only a partial understanding of aspects of *dao* and fail to comprehend the other aspects. Says Xunzi:

---

114. For the interpretation of *daoguan* and *liguan* as expressing the idea of rational coherence, see my *Ethical Argumentation*, 61–65.

The myriad things are only one corner of *dao*. One thing is only one corner of *dao*. The fools consider only one corner of one thing, and think that they understand *dao*. . . . Laozi sees the benefit of yielding, but not the benefit of advancing. Mozi sees the benefit of equality, but not the benefit of disproportionate treatment. Songzi sees the benefit of having few desires, but not the benefit of having many desires. (*tianlun* L381)

Xunzi's point is that, depending on particular situations, yielding to or getting ahead of others, equality or differential treatment of people, satisfying a few or many desires are valuable items for deliberation concerning a matter at hand. To seize upon one of these values and represent it as an all-or-nothing value in every problematic situation is to set up a misguided theory. Xunzi thus criticizes presumably influential philosophers of his time, that they appreciate only one aspect and do not appreciate the other aspect of *dao*.[115] They are victims of *bi*.

Yang Liang's gloss on *bi* is this: "The man beset by *bi* is one who is unable to see through things clearly. His view is impeded by one corner as if there were things that hindered his vision."[116] A *bi*, literally, is "a screen, shelter, or cover." *Bi* is Xunzi's metaphor for obscuration or darkening of the mind *(xin)*. In this condition the mind is obstructed in its proper functioning, e.g., thinking, remembering, imagining, and judging. In short, a *bi* is any sort of factor that obstructs the mind's cognitive task. When the mind is in the state of *bi*, reason is, so to speak, not operating properly. The opposite of *bi* is clarity of mind. Says Xunzi, "If you guide it [the mind] with reason *(li)*, nourish it with clarity, and do not allow external objects to unbalance it, then it will be capable of determining right and wrong and of resolving doubts" (*jiebi* L499, W131). In this light, *bi* can also be rendered as "blindness," as Knoblock does (K3:88ff.). As Watson notes, Xunzi's use of *bi* refers to "a clouding or darkening of the faculties or the understanding, and Hsün Tzu [Xunzi] plays on the image of light and darkness throughout the chapter [*Jiebi pian*, Book 21]" (Watson, 121n).

There are many sources of *bi* that impede the understanding of particular situations as wholes and/or *dao* as a holistic ideal of human life. Xunzi's examples are pairs of opposites: desire and aversion, beginning and end of affairs, distance and nearness, the depth and shallowness of knowledge, past and present. Generally the differences among the myriad things are potential sources of *bi* that afflict common humanity (*jiebi* L474). Since the state of *bi* is contrary to reason *(li)*, we may regard that state as one of irrational preoccupation with one side of the

---

115. See Liang, 232.
116. Yang Liang, 1976, Book 15a.

distinction at the expense of careful consideration of the other, an example of aspect obsession. Well aware of the distinction between desire and aversion, a person may pursue his current desire without attending to its possible unwanted consequences. That person's mind may be said to be in the state of *bi*.

More generally, humans suffer because of their concern for the acquisition of benefit and the avoidance of harm. As indicated in passage D (3.18 above), when they see something beneficial, they do not consider carefully *(lü)* whether it may lead to harmful consequences. However, even if consequences are considered, the person may fail to attend to distant consequences *(yuan)* and simply focus upon near or immediate ones *(jin)*, well aware of the relevance of the distinction at issue. Conversely, a person may be preoccupied with distant consequences without attending to immediate ones that may well bring disaster. This is the sense in which nearness and distance *(yuanjin)* can be a source of *bi*. Xunzi cites examples of ancient rulers preoccupied with their concubines and ancient subjects preoccupied with the acquisition of power. Thus "their minds become deluded *(huo)* and their actions were thrown into confusion" *(jiebi* L474, W122). Similarly, on matters of life and death, a person may be a victim of *bi* because of his inordinate attention to one without regard to the other. So also as regards the present *(jin*)* and past *(gu)*,[117] and the depth *(bo)* and shallowness *(qian)* of knowledge.

These sources of *bi* influence our choice between alternatives of honor or shame as the best way of life. A reasonable deliberation *(lü)* will attend to the weight of alternatives in the light of the holistic ideal of *dao* as well as size up the current situation as a whole, i.e., have a firm grasp of the reality of the situation according to the best available evidence.

For present purposes, the most important source of aspect-obsession is the depth and shallowness of knowledge. While attentive to, say, near and distant consequences of action, well-educated persons or academics may engage in an inordinate quest for depth of knowledge or erudition and ordinary people may be quite content with inadequate shallow knowledge to deal with practical problems. Both are liable to *bi*. While a reasonable deliberation must be well-informed, the knowledge it seeks must not be too deep, or too shallow. The quest for relevant information for deliberation must be practical and reasonable, appropriate to dealing with a problem at hand, not an academic, intellectual exercise, which is likely to lead to abulia or inability to act decisively. Also, the knowledge or information sought in deliberation must not be hasty and

---

117. For reasonable uses of the past or tradition, see my "Ethical Uses of History in Early Confucianism: The Case of Hsün Tzu," *Philosophy East and West* 35, no. 2 (1985): 133–56, incorporated in this volume as Essay 3.

too limited for making a reasonable decision, when there is opportunity to engage in more extensive investigation. In Xunzi's words, we must engage in "extensive deliberation in guarding against untoward consequences *(changlü guhou)*" (*rongru* L68).

For Xunzi the best counsel for those agents who tend to seek profound knowledge in deliberation is to soften their minds with mild sincerity. Among other things, the method for regulating our temperament *(qi)* and nourishing the mind *(xin)* is this: "If your temperament is too strong and stubborn, soften it with harmony. If your search for informed deliberation is too deep and penetrating, unify it with mild sincerity" (see *xiushen* L27, W26*). Shallow deliberation is also liable to *bi*. So also the *bi* that arises out of excessive preoccupation with the immediate or distant consequences of projected action. *Bi* is what afflicts common humanity, because the human mind *(xin)*, without guidance of *reason*, is susceptible to the governance of unexamined impulses, desires, and aversions. Xunzi would agree with Dewey that deliberation must be a reasonable process that unifies competing preferences and eventuates in a choice that resolves a problematic situation. But unlike Dewey, he sees the end of deliberation as a step to the realization of *dao*, and not "growth" in learned abilities to resolve problems that arise from indeterminate situations. For *dao* is an ideal weighing standard for resolving perplexities of moral choice, and not an ideal for the unending process of transforming indeterminate, problematic situations into determinate and unified ones.[118]

Perhaps more surprising is the resemblance of Xunzi's view on deliberation to Aristotle's. For Aristotle, as for Xunzi, we deliberate only about things that are subject to what we, as active agents, can bring about,[119] and which "hold good as a general rule, but whose outcomes are unpredictable and in cases in which an indeterminate element is involved" (NE 1112a–b). Xunzi would concur with Aristotle's view that ethics must be content "with a rough and general sketch: when the basis of a discussion consists of matters that hold good only as a general rule, but not always, the conclusions reached must be of the same order. The

---

118. For Dewey, the choice as the outcome of deliberation "is not the emergence of preferences out of indifference. It is the emergence of preference out of competing preferences." Moreover, choice may be reasonable or unreasonable. Reasonableness is "a quality of an effective relationship among desires rather than a thing opposed to desire. It signifies the order, perspective, proportion which is achieved, during deliberation, out of diversity of earlier incompatible preferences." See John Dewey, *Human Nature and Conduct* (New York: The Modern Library, 1922), 193–94.

119. For the Confucian notion of practical causation, see my "Practical Causation and Confucian Ethics," *Philosophy East and West* 25, no. 1 (1975): 1–10; incorporated as Essay 9 of this volume.

various points made must be received in the same spirit" (NE 1094b). Xunzi's notion of wise and well-informed deliberation also recalls Aristotle's conception of practical wisdom *(phronesis)* as "excellence in deliberation," i.e., as "correctness in assessing what is beneficial, i.e., correctness in assessing the goal, the manner, and the time" (NE 1142b).

3.21

The problem of choice regarding honor and shame can also be viewed as a problem of moral commitment and self-transformation, i.e., as a choice between the ways of life of *junzi* or paradigmatic individuals or of *xiaoren*, the small-minded persons. Says Xunzi:

In natural talent, inborn nature, capacity for acquiring knowledge and understanding, the *junzi* and the small-minded persons *(xiaoren)*, they are one and the same. Both prefer honor and despise shame; both prefer what is beneficial and despise what is harmful. However, if we consider the way they pursue their goals, they differ markedly. The small-minded man is strong at boasting, yet wants others to believe in him; he enthusiastically engages in deception, yet wants others to have affection for him. He behaves like an animal, yet wants others to think well of him. When he deliberates on something, it is difficult for others to understand [his intentions]. When he acts on something, it is difficult to make it secure. When he tries to sustain something, he has difficulty in establishing it. In the end he is certain to fail to obtain what he loves and is sure to encounter what he hates. (*rongru* L60–61, K1: 191*)

A *junzi* would find such behavior of *xiaoren* abhorrent. Generally, the difference between *junzi* and *xiaoren* may be explained by their difference in accumulation of their ways of managing things and the influence of habits and customs. More fundamentally, with respect to shame, a *junzi*, unlike *xiaoren*, abides by *ren* and *yi*. Normally, we can expect that such a life will be peaceful and secure, but we have no assurance that this way of life will always and necessarily be free from danger and harm. Likewise, the way of life of *xiaoren*, as it involves foul, unrestrained, and thievish behavior, is normally expected to be dangerous and harmful, but we have no assurance that this way of life will be necessarily insecure.[120]

120. This is a paraphrase of *rongru* L61. For translations, see Dubs 59–60, Knoblock 1:191. It is interesting to note that *li* (ritual propriety) is not mentioned at all. The point is that in the context of shame and honor, *li* has no significant role to play. But generally, Xunzi considers the observance of *li* as the best means of self-cultivation, especially in regulating one's *qi* or temperament and in cultivating the mind (*xiushen* L27). However, the *li* and music provide only models but no explanation *(liyue fa er bu shuo)*. And if one wants to seek the *dao* of the former kings, the *li* provide "the very road which you must travel" (*Quanxue* L14–15; W20–21).

If a person chooses *dao* as the best way and guide to life, his commitment must be *cheng*, i.e., a truthful, honest, sincere, genuine, or wholehearted commitment, rather than a halfhearted commitment. According to Xunzi, for the *junzi*, commitment to *dao* requires sustained effort in learning and self-cultivation. For nourishing the mind *(yangxin)* of the *junzi*, there is nothing better than *cheng*. Having attained the utmost *cheng*, he will have no other concern than to abide by *ren* and to practice *yi (shouren xingyi)*. "If the mind is truthful *(cheng)* and abides by *ren*, it will manifest itself. In this way, the mind will achieve godlike insight,[121] and, as a consequence, can transform the world. If the mind is *cheng* and practices *yi*, the rationale *(li)* of things and affairs will become clear. With such a clarity of mind, one can transform all things" *(bugou* L47).

3.22

As we have seen earlier (3.13 above), for Xunzi the ethical significance of shame cannot be rendered intelligible without its contrast with honor. Moreover, as ethical concepts, both honor and shame depend on the moral distinction between *yi* (rightness) and *li** (profit or benefit). Not only moral agents who live a life of honor may sometimes suffer from shame through no moral faults of their own, but also may the morally irresponsible agents sometimes obtain honor through devious means. For further elucidation of the ethical significance of shame and honor, Xunzi provides us a pair of distinctions, between two sorts of honor or shame: (1) honor justly deserved *(yi-rong)* and honor obtained as a result of particular circumstances of life *(shi-rong)*, and (2) shame justly deserved *(yi-ru)* and shame derived from particular circumstances *(shi-ru)*. Alternatively, we may label the distinction as a distinction between intrinsic honor and extrinsic honor, on the one hand, and between intrinsic shame and extrinsic shame on the other. Xunzi states this pair of distinctions as a critical response to Songzi's thesis that "it is no shame to suffer insult *(jianwu buru)*." Says Xunzi:

In any argumentation one must first establish proper standards. Only then can we evaluate the claims of the participants. Without such standards, we cannot distinguish between acceptable and unacceptable claims.... [With regard to Songzi's thesis,] we must distinguish two different sorts of cases: intrinsic honor

---

121. Read *shen* as *shenming* in *jiebi* L488. Says Xunzi: "*Xin* (mind) is the ruler of the body and the host of godlike insights." The original reads: *"xin ze, xing zhi jun ye, er shenming zhi zhu."* I follow Machle by rendering *zhu* as "host," but differ from him on interpreting *shenming*. See Edward J. Machle, "The Mind and the 'Sheng-ming' in Xunzi," *Journal of Chinese Philosophy* 19, no. 4 (1992), 361–86. For discussion on this issue, see my "Ethical and Religious Dimensions of *Li*," Essay 7 of this volume.

(yi-rong) and extrinsic honor *(shi-rong)* as well as intrinsic shame *(yi-ru)* and extrinsic shame *(shi-ru)*. A cultivated will, wide-ranging virtuous conduct, wise and well-informed deliberation—this is the honor that comes from within a self-same person; this is what is meant by intrinsic honor *(yi-rong)*. High noble rank, great tribute or emoluments, and surpassing power—above these are emperor and the feudal nobles, and below there are the cabinet ministers, the prime minister, the officers, and the prefects—this is the honor which comes from without; this is what is meant by extrinsic honor *(shi-rong)*. Licentiousness, filthiness, transgression of duty, violation of law, and of the sense of what is right and reasonable, arrogance, oppression, and avarice—this is shame which comes from a self-same person—this is what is meant by intrinsic shame *(yi-ru)*. Reviling, insult, ... quartering, being led in chains, ... this is shame that comes from without; this is what is meant by extrinsic shame *(shi-ru)*. (*zhenglun* L410, D208*)

Note that intrinsic honor is basically the honor that one can rightfully claim because of one's virtuous conduct, thus it is labeled *yi-rong*, i.e., the *rong* (honor) that accords with *yi*, the standard of rightness. Similarly, intrinsic shame is the shame that one rightfully deserves, thus it is labeled *yi-ru*, i.e., the *ru* that accords with *yi*. In both cases, the honor and shame are self-wrought—an outcome of voluntary conduct for which moral responsibility may be properly ascribed and evaluated according to the standard of right conduct (*yi*). Nonetheless, the honor or shame that one experiences can come about through one's circumstance or station in life. Thus the honor or the shame one enjoys or suffers in society may not always reflect one's moral merits. Whether or not the person's condition is considered morally worthy depends on the standard of *yi*. The fact that a person enjoys honor conferred by others or lives in some shameful situation does not provide a necessary or sufficient justification for pronouncing the moral worth of the person's condition. For a person genuinely committed to *dao* as the ideal of the good human life as a whole, *yi-rong*, the honor bestowed by significant others or members of the community, if it truly reflects the person's virtues, is rightfully deserved (*quanxue* L5, W17), may be joyfully accepted, just as the shame derived from circumstances may be endured with equanimity.

Thus, given the fourfold distinction, it is possible for a man of intrinsic honor to have extrinsic shame, or to live in a shameful circumstance. For example, he may occupy a low social position or lead a life of poverty through no moral fault of his own. Likewise, a man of intrinsic shame may be honored in the extrinsic sense of honor. What situation a moral agent confronts by way of shame or honor thus depends essentially on moral desert, and not on the circumstances of his life in society. As Xunzi put it, "It is possible for a *junzi* to have extrinsic shame, but not intrinsic shame. On the other hand, it is possible for a small-minded man (*xi-*

aoren) to have extrinsic honor, but not intrinsic honor. There is nothing to hinder a man who has extrinsic shame from becoming a Yao; there is nothing to hinder a man of extrinsic honor from becoming a Jie." (*zhenglun* L411, D209*)[122]

In the ideal, fortunate case, an agent's experience of intrinsic honor coincides with extrinsic honor. But in actuality, the coincidence is a most uncommon occurrence of actual human life. For this reason, commitment to *dao* is a plunge into the unknown. It is a gamble for one who wants a morally satisfied life. Xunzi is confident that the commitment to *dao* as the supreme standard for evaluating desires and aversions will ultimately lead to fortune rather than misfortune. Xunzi proffers two arguments. For convenience we label these as passages E and F.

3.23

Xunzi presents the first argument:

E. If a man exchanges one object for another that is the same, then everyone will say that he has neither gained nor lost anything. If he exchanges one object for two that are the same, then everyone will say that he has lost nothing but in fact he has made a gain. But if he exchanges two objects for one, then everyone will agree that he has not gained but lost. . . . But to act in accordance with the Way *(dao)* is like exchanging one [kind of thing] for two [kinds of things]. How could it be a loss? . . . Any person who would actually exchange that which can gratify the desires of a hundred years for that which brings only a single moment of gratification simply does not know how to count. (*zhengming* L522, W153-54*)

At issue is the distinction and connection between two kinds of satisfaction, the satisfaction derived from one kind of desire and the satisfaction derived from another kind of desire. The argument points out that

---

122. The modern Chinese distinction between two notions of "saving face," *mianzi* and *lian*, somewhat reflects Xunzi's distinction between extrinsic honor *(shi-rong)* and intrinsic honor *(yi-rong)*. As Hu expounds it, the notion of *mianzi* pertains to social standing and does not necessarily have moral implications. The notion of *lian*, on the other hand, implies satisfaction of the moral standards of the society. A person concerned with *lian* is one who possesses a sense of decency and regard for moral virtues (Hu Hsien Chin, "The Chinese Concepts of 'Face,'" *American Anthropologist*, n.s., 46 (1944): 45–64). It is interesting to note also that Xunzi's distinction between extrinsic honor *(shi-rong)* and intrinsic *(yi-rong)* has its functional equivalents in two entries on "honour" in the *Oxford English Dictionary Online*. For *shi-rong*, we have "1. High respect, esteem, or reverence, accorded to exalted worth or rank; deferential admiration or approbation." For *yi-rong*, we have "2. a. Personal title to high respect or esteem; honourableness; elevation of character; 'nobleness of mind, scorn of meanness, magnanimity'; a fine sense of and strict allegiance to what is due or right." 2.a. continues with a parenthetical remark that echoes *shi-rong*: "also, to what is due according to some conventional or fashionable standard of conduct."

committing to and following the *dao* will yield two kinds of satisfaction. For explication, let us consider the background and context in Xunzi's theory of the problematic character of human desires.

First, a committed agent may derive satisfaction in fulfilling some of the naturally occurrent desires which are responses to our sensory and emotional nature *(qingxing)*:[123] "the eye's fondness for beautiful forms, the mouth's fondness for delicious flavor, the mind's fondness for profit, or the body's fondness for pleasure and ease" (*xing'e* L544, W160). He may also have desires that come about through self-cultivation and reflection. Significantly, these desires are mediated by reason and reflection, and yield satisfaction of a different kind. In Xunzi's words:

> A single desire which one receives from Heaven *(tian)* is regulated and directed by the mind in many different ways. Consequently, it may be difficult to assign it to the same category as the one received from Heaven.[124] (*zhengming* L527, W151*)

Although this text is difficult to render in a completely satisfactory way, my translation does display a crucial distinction elucidated by Liang Qixiong.[125] According to Liang, Xunzi is making a distinction between *tianxing yu* and *lixing yu*. The former pertains to naturally prereflective desire; the latter is a consequence of rational management of the human mind. Thus, they cannot be viewed as members of the same class or category *(lei)*.[126] More perspicuously, Xunzi's distinction pertains to the distinction between first-order and second-order desires.[127] Second-order desires are an outcome of reflective choice informed by reasoned judgment and self-cultivation. As earlier noted (3.21 above), the commitment to *dao* must be marked by sincerity of thought and abide by *ren* and the practice of *yi* (*shouren xingyi* [*bugou pian* L47]). More often, Xunzi emphasizes the role of *li* (rites) in regulating the pursuit of de-

---

123. This felicitous translation of *qingxing* owes to Chong Kim-chong, "Xunzi's Systematic Critique of Mencius," *Philosophy East and West* 53, no. 2 (2003). Note that for Xunzi, desires are responses to feelings, and feelings are constitutive elements of human nature *(xing)*: "*Xing* is a product of Heaven *(tian)*; feelings are the constitutive elements of *xing*; and desires are responses to the feelings" (*zhengming* L529).

124. Many commentators differ in interpreting this passage. Liang Qixiong has a survey of these views as noted by Knoblock. However, Knoblock thinks that none of the emendations proposed by the commentators are "well-founded or entirely satisfactory" (K3:343–44n97). As we shall see shortly, Liang Qixiong's explanation is quite plausible in the light of Xunzi's critique of the prevailing theories of desires. A recent commentator, Wang Zhonglin, also adopts Liang's explanation.

125. Liang, 321–22. Li Disheng gives a similar explanation (*zhengming* L528n7).

126. For an explication of Xunzi's notion of *lei*, see my *Ethical Argumentation*, 56–65.

127. For the distinction between first- and second-order desires or volition, see Harry G. Frankfurt, "Freedom of the Will and the Concept of Person," *Journal of Philosophy* 68, no. 1 (1971): 10.

sires, i.e., defining the boundaries of proper conduct. In addition to the delimiting function, *li* has also a supportive function, that is, to provide channels for satisfaction *(geren zhi qiu)*. More importantly, the function of *li* is to cultivate desires *(yangren zhi yu)*, that is, to transform the naturally occurrent desires in the light of cultural refinement *(lilun* L417).[128]

In light of the foregoing discussion, we can restate the argument in passage E. Given a choice informed by the distinction of first-order and second-order desires, the agent would adopt and follow *dao*, since it promises satisfaction of both naturally occurrent desires and morally reflective desires. In this way, committing to *dao* is like exchanging one kind of satisfaction for two kinds of satisfaction. Moreover, given the long-lasting satisfaction of moral desires, it would be foolish to depart from *dao* and seek episodic satisfaction of naturally occurrent desires.

Passage E may also be reconstructed by pondering the distinction between *yi* and *li**. It is a plausible presumption that a life committed to the realization of *dao* will bring about goods or benefits independently of *li** or acquisition of personal gain. This is especially the case when *li** is broadly construed to include both private *(sili*)* and public benefits *(gongli*)*, and the latter may be properly regarded as an instance of following *yi*, or in Xunzi's preferred term *gongyi*. Of course, in the event of conflict between *gongyi* and private desires *(siyu)*, as noted earlier (3.19 above), the agent must overcome the demands of the latter *(xiushen* L36). This view seems to be implicit in idea of *yi yi wei li**, i.e., one must "consider righteousness as a form of benefit."[129] Now following *dao* will bring not only public goods or benefits, but also private benefits. Goods that are enjoyed in common can also be enjoyed in privacy. Following *dao* will thus bring two kinds of benefits as compared to the one kind of benefit pursued by a self-serving person. Thus the paradigmatic person or *junzi* is "joyful in obtaining the guidance of *dao*, whereas the small-minded person is joyful in gratifying his desires" *(yuelun* L462).

3.24

Let us turn briefly to passage F.

F. Let us probe more deeply into the hidden aspects of the matter—those that are difficult to observe. No one who intentionally makes light of reason *(li)* can

---

128. For more discussion of the different dimensions of *li*, see *Moral Vision and Tradition,* Essay 13; and Essays 2 and 7 of this volume.

129. *Daxue,* chap. 10. The complete saying is this: *Guo bu yi li wei li, yi yi wei li ye* ("In a state, financial profit is not considered real profit whereas righteousness is considered real profit"). See Chan, *Source Book,* 94*.

fail to be led astray by undue attention to external objects. No one who pays undue attention to external objects can fail to feel anxiety *(you)*. No one whose behavior departs from the guidance of reason *(li)* can fail to be endangered by external objects. No one who is endangered by external objects can fail to feel dread *(kong)*. When the mind is in the state of anxiety and dread, even though the mouth is filled with delicious food, it will not be aware of its flavor. . . . In such a state, a person may encounter all the loveliest things in the world and yet be unable to feel any gratification. Even if he should feel a moment's gratification, he could never completely shake off his anxieties and fear. (*zhengming* L533, W154–55*)

Doing what conforms to *dao* will lead to peace and harmony within one's mind, instead of being seduced by the pursuit of external objects that satisfy the desires that arise from our sensory and emotional nature *(qingxing)*, which plausibly leads to anxiety and fear. For averting fear and anxiety, Xunzi would counsel the agent to engage in both learning and self-cultivation—the central themes of the first two books *(Quanxue pian* and *Xiushen pian)* in the *Xunzi*. Self-examination is specially stressed in the first book. Xunzi would agree with Confucius that a *junzi* is free from fear and anxiety, because on self-examination, he finds nothing with which to reproach himself (*Lunyu* 12.4). In the end the decision rests on the person who is contemplating commitment to *dao*. There is no warranty for happiness in *dao*-commitment, but the person must carefully consider the arguments in passages E and F.

3.25

The foregoing discussion highlights some of the features of Xunzi's conception of shame as compared with that of Confucius and Mencius. Unlike Confucius and Mencius, Xunzi does not assign any importance to the sense of shame as an internal monitor of conduct. What is stressed instead is *yi* as a standard for assessing the pursuit of profit, very much in the spirit of the teachings of Confucius and Mencius. While Confucius and Mencius seem to focus on the prospective significance of shame, Xunzi also draws our attention to its retrospective significance, as implied in the distinction between intrinsic and extrinsic shame. For Xunzi, as for Confucius, one major question about shame is this: Should I, as a sincere, committed moral agent, feel shame in doing or having performed such an action? For both, the answer depends on whether my action conforms to or violates the requirement of *yi*. By discussing the problem of choice between honor and shame as ideal ways of life and the crucial role of *lü* or deliberation in decision-making, Xunzi provides us a much richer conception of the role of *yi* in the moral life. However, Mencius's focus on the feeling and the sense of shame remains important in appreciating the experience of shame. Xunzi's fundamental contribution to the Confucian conception of the ethical significance of shame is his distinctive idea of shame as an ethical concept, as an opposite of the ethical concept of honor. Only intrinsic shame is ethically significant because it provides, so to speak, a contrast for appreciating intrinsic honor, which embodies the ideal of nobility or *junzi*. However, Xunzi admires and exalts Confucius as one who was humane *(ren)*, wise, and completely free from obsession *(bi)*.[130] For Confucians in general, even more important is Confucius's brilliant insight in divesting the established notion of *junzi* of its aristocratic connotations. For Confucius, as for Mencius and Xunzi, all ordinary persons are capable of becoming *junzi*, so long as their commitment to *dao* is genuine *(cheng)* and they earnestly engage in self-cultivation *(xiushen)* and self-examination *(zixing)* for purposes of correcting moral faults and/or reforming themselves in accord with the requirements of *ren* and *yi*. Notably, both Mencius and Xunzi go beyond Confucius in claiming that all humans are capable of becoming sages. Unlike Mencius, however, Xunzi does not think that cultivating this capacity *(keyi)* alone is sufficient for acquiring the ability *(neng)* of becoming a sage.[131]

3.26

Early in this essay we focused on three features of shame in Aristotle's works: shame as (1) a feeling or emotion that is experienced as a consequence of misconduct of a committed moral agent, i.e., a person committed to a morality or practical moral theory, (2) as a moral condition of the agent, and (3) the retrospective and prospective significance of a sense of shame. Xunzi's contribution to the study of the ethical significance of shame lies in offering two additional features: (4) the key role of honor in understanding shame as an ethical concept, and (5) the relation between the inner condition of moral agents and outward

130. For Xunzi, unlike such thinkers as Mozi, Songzi, and Zhuangzi, Confucius was benevolent, wise, and free from obsession or cognitive blindness *(bi)*. "This is why his study of methods that could produce order deserves to be considered equal to that of the Ancient Kings. His school alone had a holistic vision of the way of government *(zhoudao)* and could be adopted and put into practice. Moreover, his school was not obsessed *(bi)* with what it had completed and accumulated *(chengji)*. Thus the moral authority of Confucius was equal to that of the Duke of Zhou and his reputation was on an equal footing with that of the Three Kings. Such are the blessings of the freedom from obsession" *(jiebi* L478, K3: 103*).

131. For an excellent discussion of the distinction between *keyi* and *neng* in Xunzi's critique of Mencius's conception of human nature *(xing)*, see Chong, "Xunzi's Systematic Critique of Mencius."

circumstances in a society or community. These additional considerations are especially important to the question of ethical justification of judgment of the experience of shame in human life. Xunzi's fourfold distinction concerning honor and shame provides a basis for evaluating the opinion of significant others, much stressed by Aristotle in his analysis of shame. However, the emphasis in both Aristotle and Xunzi on the condition of moral agents paves the way toward a better appreciation of ethical shame, for what matters ultimately is not the feeling of pain or uneasiness, which is bound to be episodic anyway, but on the enduring state of moral character that is marked by the concern with intrinsic honor rather than extrinsic honor. For Xunzi, a morally healthy life must not only be noble, but also be complete *(quan*)* and pure *(cui)*. In Xunzi's words:

> The *junzi* knows that what lacks completeness and purity does not deserve to be called beautiful. Therefore he reads and listens to explanations in order to penetrate the Way, and ponders in order to understand it, associates with men who embody it in order to make it part of himself, and shuns those who impede it in order to sustain and nourish it. He trains his eyes, so that they desire to see only what is right, his ears so that they desire to hear only what is right, his mind so that it desires to think only what is right. When he has truly learned to love what is right, his eyes will take greater pleasure in it than in the fine color and ... when he has reached this stage, he cannot be subverted by power or the love of profit; he cannot be swayed by the masses; he cannot be moved by the world. This is what is meant by "moral integrity." (*quanxue* L19, W22-23*)[132]

In sum, the ethical significance of shame lies in its intrinsic rather than extrinsic character, and what is morally valuable is intrinsic honor rather than extrinsic honor. For Xunzi, what matters ultimately is neither shame nor honor, but moral integrity.[133]

---

132. Xunzi continues: "If a person has moral integrity, he can have settled aspiration [to attain *dao*]. With this aspiration, he can respond appropriately to things. With settled aspiration and ability to respond to things, he may be said to be a complete man (*chengren* [a man of complete ethical attainment]). The Heaven *(tian)* manifests brightness, the earth manifests breadth, the *junzi* values completeness" (*quanxue* L19, W23*).

133. I am grateful to Kim-chong Chong and an anonymous reader of *Philosophy East and West* for valuable suggestions. Sections 3.23 and 3.24 above owe primarily to their stimulating comments.

PART II
OTHER STUDIES IN CHINESE PHILOSOPHY

Essay 9

PRACTICAL CAUSATION AND CONFUCIAN ETHICS

There are times in which a reflective moral agent experiences a state of perplexity over his status or existence within the world. This perplexity may be occasioned by his lack of understanding of the course of natural events in relation to his needs, desires, ideals, and aspirations. This experience may give rise to a more general attitude toward the world. In the manner described by Dewey, the agent "may find himself living in an aleatory world, his existence involves, to put it baldly, a gamble." To him, "the world is a scene to risk; it is uncertain, unstable, uncannily unstable. Its dangers are irregular, inconstant, not to be counted upon as to their times and seasons."[1] The practical question of acting calls for a formulation of these uncertainties into some conceptually manageable form, into what Dewey terms "problematic situations." The function of reflection or inquiry is to transform the indeterminate situations into determinate ones.[2] This process, in part, depends upon the agent's ability to utilize the explanatory knowledge of nature at the service of satisfactorily resolving his problems. However, an agent, in moments detached from the necessity of acting, may acquire independent interest in the pursuit of the knowledge of nature. His reflective activity thereby takes a theoretical turn. The notion of causation plays a crucial role in the quest for knowledge. The understanding of nature as a causal order is tied to the theory that explains the relation between events and states of affairs. In this sense, the notion of causation becomes theory-dependent. In the words of R. G. Collingwood, the attempt is "made to consider natural events not practically as things to be produced or prevented by human agency, but theoretically, as things that happen independently of human will but not independently of each other: causation being the name by

---

1. John Dewey, *Experience and Nature,* 2nd ed. (New York: Dover Publication, 1958), 41.
2. See John Dewey, *Logic: Theory of Inquiry* (New York: Henry Holt, 1938), 79.

which this dependence is designated."³ However, if the agent, in assuming the perspective of the knower, remains dominated by the question of acting, his notion of causation of natural events may be viewed from the practical perspective. The notion of causation may be employed as referring "to a type of case in which natural events are considered from the human point of view, as events grouped in pairs, where one member in each pair C is immediately under human control, whereas the other, E, is not immediately under human control but can be indirectly controlled by man because of the relation in which it stands to C. This is the sense which the word 'cause' has in the practical sciences of nature, that is, the sciences of nature whose primary aim is not to achieve theoretical knowledge about nature but to enable man to enlarge his control of nature."⁴ Significantly this practical notion of causation is conceptually tied to the notion of action but is distinct from the Aristotelian notion of an agent as an efficient cause. In the recent words of Georg Heinrik von Wright, "to say that we cause effects is not to say that agents are causes. It means that we do things which then as causes produce effects, 'act' or 'operate' as causes."⁵

Given the legitimacy of the practical notion of causation, it is of prime interest to a Confucian agent to reflect upon its role in the context of his understanding of the world in relation to his actions. The Confucian agent who is committed to an ethics that purports to provide action-guides must also be interested in rendering intelligible and plausible his conception of the world in relation to his moral life. This essay concerns the role of practical causation in the Confucian conception of the world with respect to the notions of influence and response *(gan* and *ying)*. My aim is to sketch, in a tentative way, a landscape in which Confucian ethics involves consideration that may be of interest to moral philosophy. In the course of this journey, I shall assume the point of view of a reflective Confucian agent in search of a contemporary elucidation and assessment of his ethics.⁶

---

3. R. G. Collingwood, *An Essay on Metaphysics* (Oxford: Clarendon Press, 1962), 287.

4. Ibid., 286. More formally, "*p* is a cause relative to *q* and *q* an effect relative to *p* if and only if by doing *p* we could bring about *q* or by suppressing *p* we could remove *q* or prevent it from happening" (Henrik von Wright, *Explanation and Understanding* [Ithaca, N.Y.: Cornell University Press, 1971], 70). For a similar view, see also Douglas Gasking, "Causation and Recipes," *Mind* 64, no. 256 (1955): 479–87.

5. In this sense, "to think of a relation between events is to think of it under the aspect of (possible) action." See von Wright, *Explanation and Understanding*, 73–74.

6. Henceforth my use of the notion of agency is to be understood in the context of a Confucian morality. This is thus a Confucian essay rather than an essay in Confucian philosophy. For this purpose, I shall take some of my previous studies as a point of departure. See particularly my "Reflection on the Structure of Confucian Ethics," *Philosophy East and West* 21, no. 2 (1971): 125–40, and "Reflection on Methodology in Chinese Philosophy," *International Philosophical Quarterly* 11, no. 2 (1971): 236–38.

As it is familiar to students of Chinese philosophy, the Confucian conception of the world is embedded in a vision of the world as ultimately harmonious with man's experiences and doings in accordance with *dao* or certain moral requirements. In a classic expression, this vision is stated in terms of the central harmony of man, heaven *(tian)*, and earth *(di)*.[7] What a man does is, in this ideal sense, potentially productive of states of affairs that figure as ingredients in moral achievement. This vision of the harmony of man and his world is essentially a moral ideal rather than a theory that purports to explain the nature of the world.[8] It is a perspective, a point of orientation, rather than a theory to be applied to practice. However, for a perspective to be intelligible, the agent needs to understand the background conception of the actual world in relation to his actions. In the interest of intelligibility, a reflective Confucian agent may attempt to articulate his conception of the world in terms of the notion of *gan* and *ying*, or influence and response.[9] In this conception, the actual world of events is viewed as a set of influences to which the agent needs to respond in some morally effective way, to act in a manner that ultimately comports with his vision.

Depending on context, the notions of *gan* and *ying* may be rendered in various ways. A recent lexical guide indicates that *gan* may be used in the sense of influence, move, or affect; *ying* has two uses: (1) in the sense of reply, response, echo, or fulfill, and (2) in the sense that roughly corresponds to ought, should, must, suitable, right, proper, or necessary. For our present purpose, the relevant sense of the compound expression *ganying* is "influence and response" or more correctly, "responding to influence."[10] On my proposed Confucian conception of

---

7. *Zhong Yong (The Doctrine of the Mean)*, in *A Source Book in Chinese Philosophy*, trans. Wing-tsit Chan (Princeton, N.J.: Princeton University Press, 1963), chap. 22.

8. This Confucian vision is an ideal theme rather than an ideal norm that provides precepts for actions. See my "Confucian Vision and Experience of the World," *Philosophy East and West* 25, no. 3 (1975): 319–33; reprinted in my *Moral Vision and Tradition: Essays in Chinese Ethics* (Washington, D.C.: The Catholic University of America Press, 1998). For the distinction between ideal themes and ideal norms, see my *Dimensions of Moral Creativity: Paradigms, Principles, and Ideals* (University Park: Pennsylvania State University Press, 1978), chap. 8.

9. I here follow James Legge in rendering "*gan* and *ying*" as "influence and response." See the *Xiaojing (Hsiao Ching)* in The Sacred Books of the East, vol. 3 (Delhi: Motilal Banarsidass, 1966), chap. 16. This is a reprint edition originally published by the Clarendon Press, Oxford, 1879. Mary Lelia Makra prefers "evocation and response" in *The Hsiao Ching* (New York: St. John's University Press, 1961), 35. A. C. Graham proposes "stimulation and response" as translation and insightfully notes that "these concepts occupy much the same place in Sung philosophy as causation in the West." See A. C. Graham, *Two Chinese Philosophers: Ch'eng Ming-tao and Ch'eng Yi-ch'uan* (London: Lund Humphries, 1958), 38.

10. *A New Complete Chinese-English Dictionary* (Hong Kong: Zhongjian, 1964). See also H. G. Creel, Chang Tsung-ch'ien, and R. C. Rudolph, *Literary Chinese by Inductive Method*, 3

man and the world, natural events or states of affairs are to be viewed as an open set of influences that call for some sort of human responses or actions.

In order to appreciate the significance of this Confucian conception, it is important to note that the notion of *gan* as influence is conceptually distinct from the notion of determination. To regard natural events as influences is to regard them under the aspect of possible action.[11] In this way, natural events are viewed as actual or potential factors that affect the moral life. Quite obviously, much of our encounter with the natural world has no special bearing in the moral sense. It appears that only those events, from the moral point of view, that affect human life and are subject to some form of control by way of human action are considered as influences. In this view an implicit judgment of importance is involved. Confronted by a set of events, what event is to be regarded as an influence depends, in the final analysis, upon a sort of selective decision based on a normative judgment. In order for the judgment to be accepted as reasonable, the event in question must not be a mere isolated or episodic occurrence. What event constitutes actual influence presupposes a potential recurrence of the event. This does not imply that the agent has the necessary conceptual apparatus for the identification and description of events in general. For some events may appear to be novel occurrences unrelated to the agent's past experiences. The events as influences, so understood, call for some sort of engagement and response. To view events in this way is to view them as matters to be attended to rather than as determinants of action. An event as an influence may be compared to advice or exhortation. And as Reid insightfully shows, advice or exhortation does not deprive man of his freedom of action, "for in vain is advice given when there is not a power either to do, or to forebear, what it recommends."[12] It is man as agent that responds to events as influences. Whether these influences will become a constitutive factor in action depends on the agent's own determination. In a more activist terminology, we may construe these

---

vols. (Chicago: University of Chicago Press, 1960), 1:163. It should be noted that the Chinese phrase *ganying* has no exact English equivalent. Joseph Wu has kindly pointed out in written communication: "To translate *gan* as 'influence' is to emphasize the external or objective aspect of the *gan* process. If we translate it with English terms such as 'receptiveness,' 'being sensitive to,' or 'being moved,' our emphasis would be shifted to the subjective aspect. Furthermore, this phrase in ordinary Chinese is heavily loaded with religious tone, notably due to the influence of a Daoist religious text *The Gan Ying Pian*." For my present ethical purpose, I have rendered *"ganying"* as "responding to influence." I am grateful to Joseph Wu for this emendation.

11. See note 6 above.

12. Thomas Reid, *Essays on the Active Powers of the Human Mind* (Cambridge, Mass.: MIT Press, 1969), 283–84.

events as *challenges* to action. This conception is anthropocentric, but it need not commit a Confucian to animism as a world hypothesis.[13] The conception of influence and response is thus a practical rather than a theoretical conception. It pretends to offer no explanation on the nature of the world. It is more plausibly regarded as a *model*, that is, an imaginative schema for guiding actions toward the Confucian vision of central harmony.[14]

I have suggested that the model of influence and response forms the background conception for the Confucian vision of central harmony. This suggestion may be clarified by the following. The Confucian vision is an ideal that functions as a point of orientation, as a theme to be developed rather than as a norm with preceptive implications. An ideal is essentially an intellectual conception. Unless it is endowed with some sort of an actuating import for the life of the moral agents, the ideal remains an object of academic rather than practical interest. If we suppose that a moral agent is committed to the Confucian ideal, this commitment, in part, implies a belief in the possible realization of the ideal. The point of having an ideal is to alter circumstances or states of affairs in the actual world. This required some sort of model that can *mediate* between the ideal and the actual. This mediation is necessary because the ideal has no direct contact with the actual world. In its inception, it may simply be an intellectual expression of a desire to see the actual world in a different way. The ideal, if it is not to remain a mere abstract conception, must thus be coupled with some sort of an active will to see to its practical realization.[15] However, this active will may simply be a blind response to the actual world without some sort of a mediating conception. The model of influence and response may be viewed thus as a mediating conception in the sense of providing some sort of an imaginative schema that bridges the gap between the ideal and the actual worlds. In this sense, it forms an indispensable conception for the actuating import of the Confucian vision. However, this model of influ-

13. S. C. Pepper, *World Hypotheses* (Berkeley and Los Angeles: University of California Press, 1948), chap. 6.
14. This idea is suggested by Kant's notion of a "typic" of moral judgments in the *Critique of Practical Reason*. For a plausible rendering of Kant's notion, see Paul Dietrichson, "Kant's Criteria of Universalizability," in *Kant: Foundations of the Metaphysics of Morals: Text and Critical Essays,* ed. R. P. Wolff (Indianapolis, Ind.: Bobbs-Merrill Co., 1969), 163–207. Note that in using this Kantian notion of an imaginative schema, I do not mean to suggest any Kantian interpretation of Confucian ethics. For my own view, see note 6 and "Opposites as Complements: Reflections on the Significance of *Tao,*" *Philosophy East and West* 3, no. 2 (1981): 123–40; reprinted in *Moral Vision and Tradition*.
15. This discussion owes much to James's essay, "What Makes a Life Significant?" See William James, *Essays on Faith and Morals* (New York: Longmans, Green & Co., 1949), 304–7. For the distinction between ideal theme and ideal norm, see my *Dimensions of Moral Creativity*, chap. 8.

ence and response, by itself, embodies no principles or procedures for actuating the ideal vision. Given this background conception, the ideal may be developed in different ways by different moral agents. Much depends on factors that limit the possibility of practical causation.

The limiting factors on what one can do to mold his actual world closer to the ideal, by and large, are familiar to ordinary agents. Apart from the obvious material or physical limitation in terms of natural laws, other sorts of factors figure prominently in the conception of possible action. The limits of practical causation are significantly the moral limits that characterize the boundary of actions. The notion of an action, from the moral point of view, is thus to be construed as satisfying certain moral requirements. To a Confucian, these requirements relate to certain criteria deemed indispensable to preserving a communal form of life.

These moral requirements are expressed in terms of Confucian notions such as *li* (ritual propriety), *ren* (human-heartedness), *yi* (rightness, fittingness), and other moral notions, for example, *yong* (courage), *xin* (trustworthiness), and *zhi* (uprightness). Given the dominant concern with *ren*, *li*, and *yi*, all other virtue-words may be more plausibly conceived as being embedded in *ren*.[16] The notion of *li* indicates the agent's tie to his cultural tradition; *ren* expresses a more concrete conception of the vision of central harmony. In other words, the *li*-criterion may be regarded as a limit imposed by tradition. It is an acknowledgment of the agent's anchorage upon the historic and cultural aspect of his existence. To act in accordance with *li* is in part to reanimate a historic tradition.[17] The *li* provide the normative identification of actions as moral actions. They encapsulate conventional standards rooted in a historic past. But a mere normative identification of an action as moral may simply be a formal gesture. Without *ren*, *li* may degenerate into a mere requirement of formal conformity. For *li* to be morally significant, it must presuppose a moral intent expressed by *ren* and appropriate application in accord with *yi*. From the point of view of *ren*, the significance of *li* lies in its ideal focus, and in providing a concrete context for the successful execution of *ren*-actions. A reasonable action, in this view, must thus be characterized as a successful execution of a moral intention. The power of the agent is in this way radically limited by the moral requirements. However, the operative force of these moral requirements ultimately depends upon the agent's ability and capacity to effectuate his moral intent with due appre-

16. For an explication of basic Confucian notions and tradition, see *Moral Vision and Tradition,* Essays 1, 12, and 13.

17. For a discussion of the philosophical significance of this aspect of *li*, see Herbert Fingarette, *Confucius—the Secular as Sacred* (New York: Harper Torchbooks, 1972), chap. 4.

ciation of the concrete circumstance that affords the opportunity of successful performance.

For an agent to regard a natural occurrence as an influence that calls for a response, we must suppose that he is in an indeterminate situation of wondering what to do.[18] As D. G. Brown points out, "With respect to any question of what to do, the point of view of the agent is that of a person whose action is in question, and therefore also that of the person for whom the question arises."[19] His point of view "sees a limit on the questions that logically can arise."[20] What he does in response to his practical question in part depends on his conception of the situation as in some manner problematic, in the sense that he can, in principle, formulate his situation as a problem to which a satisfactory solution may be forthcoming. The resolution of his problem ultimately depends upon his ability to bring to bear considerations relevant to his problem. Given his point of view as one of moral concern, a Confucian agent would utilize his repertoire of moral notions in his deliberation. Since he is not equipped with precepts that are analogous to, say, the Christian "commandments," he must exercise judgment in applying the moral notions.

In normal situations that are unambiguously characterized by conventional standards embedded in *li*, what he does as a response to his situation would simply be a product of moral training.[21] The notion of *ren* need not be explicitly appealed to as long as he assumes that a *li*-action is performed in the light of *ren*. Actions as normal responses to occurrences, which the agent confronts, fall outside the scope of responses that can effect changes in the natural world. In these cases, the natural world is deemed, so to speak, a conventional world rather than a problematic influence that calls for response that causally changes the existing state of affairs. In this sense, what he does is distinct from what he brings about.[22] Since the practical notion of causation concerns the

---

18. For an empirical characterization of indeterminate situations, see Dewey, *Logic: Theory of Inquiry*, 105–7. For a conceptual characterization of this agent's predicament, see R. M. Hare's discussion of "practical question" and "ought-question" in *Freedom and Reason* (Oxford: Clarendon Press, 1963).

19. D. G. Brown, *Action* (Toronto, Ontario: University of Toronto Press, 1968), 18.

20. Ibid., 19.

21. For the distinction between normal and exigent situations, see my "The Concept of Paradigmatic Individuals in the Ethics of Confucius," *Inquiry* 14 (1971): 41–55; or *Dimensions of Moral Creativity*, chaps. 4 and 5. This distinction appears to be also implicit in A. E. Murphy's *Theory of Practical Reason* (La Salle, Ill.: Open Court, 1964).

22. "By doing certain things we bring about other things. For example, by opening a window we let fresh air into the room (bring about ventilation), or lower the temperature, or bring it about that someone in the room feels uncomfortable, starts to sneeze, and eventually catches a cold. What we thus bring about are the effects of our action. That which we do is the cause of those effects" (von Wright, *Explanation and Understanding*, 66).

notion of bringing about things, the Confucian view would be more plausible if it restricted the notion of response to cases that fall outside the scope of conventional actions, that is, to exigent situations. In this way the model of influence and response would be more significantly understood in terms of the cases of actions that, prima facie, are not subject to conventional description. If we choose the broader notion of response, then the natural event as an influence would become a determinant; but in this case, it would be pointless to stress the necessity of action in the causally productive sense. In terms of our interest in the role of practical causation in Confucian ethics, I suggest that we understand the model of influence and response in the restrictive sense.

In general there are two sorts of situation that call for action or response in this restricted sense. The situation, as the agent views it, is a novel one. The natural event embedded in his situation is deemed a potential influence upon his life. His repertoire of moral notions does not provide an appropriate "principle of discrimination," consequently the question of performance is at stake.[23] Given his central concern with *ren*, the Confucian agent may have to improvise, as best he can, a method of dealing with his situation.[24] However, what he does in this sort of situation must at least fall within the orbit of the way of life that he shares with others. Crucially, the moral question must, in part, address itself to a sense of common understanding of what the way of life involves. This overall context of communal living is more an implicit setting than a subject of propositional knowledge, in Wittgenstein's felicitous term, "a form of life." His improvised method must respect the moral ideal inherent in his form of life. He may be called upon to vindicate his actions whenever his actions are challenged or deemed suspect by fellow agents. Significantly what he can bring about by what he does must have some sort of effect upon his conception of the natural order. Whether he succeeds in practical causation depends upon his ability to "fit" his action to the situation that he confronts and also upon his action, considered in some manner as *paradigmatic* from the communal point of view. The agent himself cannot decide on the significance of his response from this communal point of view any more than he can decide for other agents what they must do in the face of novel situa-

---

23. For this distinction between discrimination and performance, see Immanuel Kant, *Lectures on Ethics* (New York: Harper Torchbooks, 1963), 36.

24. I owe the present characterization to Collingwood's *Autobiography* (Oxford: Clarendon Press, 1939), 102–4. Though Confucian ethics does not involve the notion of rules, except in the case of *li*, which consists of a set of rules of proper conduct, Collingwood's discussion applies to it. For a further discussion of this topic in relation to moral creativity, see my "Relevance of Moral Rules and Creative Agency," *The New Scholasticism* 47, no. 1 (1973): 1–21; incorporated in *Dimensions of Moral Creativity*, chap. 5.

tions. The agent can be mistaken about his situation; what he considers to be novel may simply be a normal situation from the standpoint of other agents. "Novel situation" is in this way more a term of art rather than a descriptive notion. At any rate, what the agent deems novel must in some way be an exigent situation, that is, a situation that presents to the agent urgency to respond. How he responds in such an exigent situation makes a difference in his world, if not to the common world, which he shares with other agents. As a Confucian agent, the important question relates to the possibility of "method" for dealing with exigent cases.

The other sort of novel situations that call for response pertains to cases in which the moral notions appear to be applicable, but the agent feels unable to bring himself to apply them. Here the situation appears to be subject to conventional classification and description, but the agent is not content with applying the existing conceptual apparatus. Unless his response is to be merely an arbitrary and unreflective one, the same question arises about the possibility of having an intelligent method of action. In classical Confucian philosophy, the doctrine of rectifying names *(zhengming)* comes in handy as an aid for dealing with exigent situations.[25]

A Confucian thinker such as Xunzi would regard this method as a way of restoring moral and political order. He appears to state, without plausible arguments, that this doctrine of linguistic legislation is a weapon for salvaging the chaotic state of moral language owing to the lack of sages and true kings. Xunzi saw his own time in this way: "Nowadays . . . the sages and true kings have all passed away. Men are careless in abiding by established names; strange words come into use; names and realities become confused; and the distinction between right and wrong has become unclear. . . . If a true king were to appear now, he would surely set about reviving the old names and creating new ones as they were needed."[26]

What is significant in our own contemporary setting is to construe this notion of rectifying names as a sort of diagnostic device for understanding the moral ills that beset humanity. The breakdown in agreement on the import of moral issues is symptomatically expressed in the breakdown of moral notions, typified by the variety of uses among intelligent speakers. For our immediate concern, the notion of rectifying names is more profitably construed as an action-guiding procedure to

---

25. For a reconstructed sketch of the general features and import of this doctrine of *zhengming (cheng-ming)*, see the essay cited in note 16.

26. Burton Watson, trans., *Hsün-Tzu: Basic Writings* (New York: Columbia University Press, 1963), 141.

which an agent may avail himself in dealing with the two kinds of exigent situation. It is, I suggest, plausibly regarded as a method for effecting moral change, thus a characteristic procedure for practical causation. I have called it a procedure rather than a substantive principle, for the method does not issue in substantive dictates for action.[27]

Few moral agents are equipped with the genius and capacity to effectuate creativity in appraisive language. Even if they can invent new names for exigent situations, the results of what they do in accordance with their linguistic legislation may have no effect upon the general employment of moral language, nor upon the natural order to which his actions may be viewed as a significant contribution. Perhaps this is the heart of Xunzi's conception of the sage-king. Without attributing some sort of authority, individual legislation would appear to be simply an intrusion upon the existing conceptual framework that functions quite intelligibly regardless of idiosyncratic moral speech. However, in a modest way, a Confucian agent can contribute to moral language by introducing changes on a smaller scale. For the individual agent, this can be accomplished by reconstituting the substantive content of existing moral notions. Although in a normal setting his actions are completely characterized in terms of *li*, *yi*, and *ren*, in non-normal cases, he can exercise his normative creativity in the application of existing notions to cases that fall outside the common understanding of their intended scope. When this is recognized as paradigmatic, his uses of moral notions would be accepted as part of the constitutive content of the common morality.[28] Rectifying names would then be a limited procedure that would enable the agent to effect change in the existing moral order without a radical revision of the accepted conceptual framework. The procedure does not provide assurance in practice, but it does seem to provide insurance against arbitrary or whimsical linguistic legislation.

The preceding discussion on rectifying names as a procedure for dealing with exigent situations and actions assumes that Confucian moral notions are, in Julius Kovesi's sense, *open* rather than *complete* terms. According to Kovesi, "When a type of act selected completely

---

27. Xunzi, in his conservative attitude toward the Confucian tradition, would certainly disapprove of my present appropriation. But it appears to me that the notion of rectifying names has significance for understanding moral agency and actions independent of the philosophical thesis formulated in terms of the notion. [For a later more positive, appreciative, and systematic discussion of Xunzi's theory of *zhengming*, from both the conceptual and pragmatic points of view, see my *Ethical Argumentation: A Study in Hsün Tzu's [Xunzi's] Moral Epistemology* (Honolulu: University of Hawaii Press, 1985), chaps. 3 and 4. Chapter 4 focuses on the diagnosis of erroneous ethical beliefs.]

28. For an illuminating discussion of appraisive creativity in general, see Karl Aschenbrenner, *The Concepts of Value: Foundations of Value Theory* (Dordrecht, Holland: D. Reidel Publishing Co., 1971), 28–32.

from the moral point of view receives its own term (e.g., 'murder') then the words 'right' and 'wrong' are used only as reminders; they remind us what was the point of forming such notions." These are complete terms. Open terms are those not completely formed from the moral point of view (for example, killing).[29] Judgments are required in using moral notions as discriminators rather than as reminders. For the agent reared in the tradition of the *Analects*, the moral notions, if they are deemed applicable to exigent cases, are open notions, that is, open to discriminating judgment. The procedure of rectifying names is a procedure for moral judgment in exigent cases. Actions, characterized in its terms, if deemed paradigmatic, may bring effects to the existing moral states of affairs without infecting the conceptual scheme. So construed, the notion of rectifying names may be regarded as a Confucian notion of practical causation. What sort of philosophically interesting thesis may be developed out of the use of this notion is worthy of further exploration. For the present inquiry, we are merely content with focusing upon the significance of this procedure as a procedure for practical causation within the context of Confucian ethics.

In this article I have freely availed myself of recent conceptual insights in this Confucian exploration of the influence-and-response model and practical causation. This model is by no means alien to recent philosophy. In understanding the historian's task, W. H. Walsh remarks that the historian employs "a fundamental set of judgments on which all of his thinking rests. These judgments concern human nature: they are judgments about the characteristic responses human beings make to the various challenges set before them in the course of their lives, whether by the natural conditions in which they live or by their fellow beings."[30] The challenge-and-response model suggested here appears to bear a close affinity to the Confucian model. Of particular interest to moral philosophy is Carl Wellman's employment of this model in his epistemology of ethics.[31] However, when we employ this model for

---

29. Julius Kovesi, *Moral Notions* (London: Routledge and Kegan Paul, 1967), 109. Note that if we regard "murder" as a legal rather than a moral notion, there appear to be very few "complete terms" in Kovesi's sense. Significantly the precept "killing is wrong" involves an open rather than a complete term. At any rate, Confucian notions appear to be open notions. This is a characteristic of its nonlegal model of moral actions to which terms such as "moral rules" and "principles" find an uneasy habitation.

30. W. H. Walsh, *An Introduction to Philosophy of History* (London: Hutchinson's University Library, 1951), 65. Contrast this with Toynbee's explanatory use of the model of challenge and response in his account of the genesis of civilizations. See Arnold Toynbee, *A Study in History,* abridged edition, 2 vols. (Oxford: Oxford University Press, 1956), vol. 1, chap. 5.

31. Carl Wellman, *Challenge and Response: Justification in Ethics* (Carbondale: Southern Illinois University Press, 1971).

philosophical and other theoretical purposes, the model, as I have tried to show, has a momentous significance for a reflective Confucian agent. What he can do to mold the actual world closer to his moral vision depends on his practical conception of the natural world as containing events as influences that engage his attention and response. This conception, being a nontheoretical one, may have no significance to theoretical inquiry and knowledge of the relation between natural events. In moral philosophy, however, it appears to have significance in providing a focal lens for understanding an aspect of committed agency. But it offers no clue to providing, even in a rudimentary way, a synoptic account of the nature of the moral life, though any such account may profit from the reminder that any adequate theory must do justice to certain features of moral agency if it is to acquire an actuating import for morally concerned persons.[32]

32. This paper was read at the joint meetings of the Association for Asian Studies and the Society for Asian and Comparative Philosophy, Boston, March 31, 1974.

Essay 10

MORAL THEORY AND THE QUALITY OF LIFE

In our world today we are faced with a difficult, multifaceted predicament regarding the character of our natural environment. Population growth; industrial waste; pollution of our soil, rivers, and lakes; extermination of wildlife pose a set of interrelated problems that have an important bearing on the quality of human life.[1] Thanks to the recent discussions on this ecological problem, we are beginning to realize that our "good earth" can no longer be viewed as a depository of unlimited resources to be irresponsibly exploited at the service of our increasing wants and expectations in improving our material well-being. If our present situation continues, it is not unrealistic to think that perhaps in a not-too-distant future humanity will confront a crisis of major proportions. Prudence alone calls for an informed reconsideration and reorientation of our attitudes toward nature. The young science of ecology has provided us invaluable findings concerning the interdependence of natural systems. In the succinct words of a recent writer: "Ecology—the study of organisms in environments—has made us aware of the interactions within natural systems: the complex cycles of chemical elements, the food chain linking diverse species, the delicate balances among organisms."[2] In light of these findings, we can ill afford to engage in activities heedless of their eventuality in the further deterioration of our natural environment. We are justly urged to adopt what is called "the ecological attitude"—an attitude that "embodies the explicit recognition that environmental changes will have repercussions and that environmental exploitation must be restricted."[3]

Quite apart from matters of prudence, from the moral point of view

---

1. William T. Blackstone, "Ethics and Ecology," in *Philosophy and Environmental Crisis* (Athens: University of Georgia Press, 1974), 16.
2. Ian G. Barbour, ed., *Western Man and Environmental Ethics* (Reading, Mass.: Addison-Wesley Publishing Co., 1973), 3.
3. Blackstone, 21.

it seems quite proper to claim that all human beings have a right to a livable environment. As Blackstone forcefully argued, such a right can be established by an appeal to the moral principles of utility and justice.[4] However, such a claim may appear dubious in view of the diversity of morals and ethical systems. Whether or not we accept Blackstone's argument, the claim to such a right is significant in the way in which it focuses upon the relation between the ecological problem and the quality of our moral life, however it is normatively conceived. This lecture is an exploration of this theme. Section 1 deals with the idea of the quality of human life. Section 2 focuses on the welfare dimension of the quality of life and the significance of the claim of a right to a livable environment, against the background of a general conception of moral theory that takes seriously into account the notion of the quality of life. For pursuing this task I shall give a brief sketch of moral theory that acknowledges the importance of such a notion. In light of this conception of moral theory I shall argue for the plausibility of the claim of the right to a livable environment construed as an emphasis on an important aspect of moral theory independently of one's substantive normative commitments. In Section 3, I offer some suggestions on the question of the quality of life in terms of the quest for ideals of ethical excellence. Here the basic task is to explicate the notion of excellence. A related task involves the more practical question of actualization of one's conception of excellence in the actual world. In section 4, I propose a Confucian vision of harmony of man and nature as having import for the ecological problem in conjunction with recognition of the historical and cultural aspects of human existence.

1. THE IDEA OF QUALITY OF LIFE

Initially the notion of quality of life presents a conceptual problem. Although the term has enjoyed wide currency in recent years, in the context of ecological discussion its meaning is not always as clear as one might expect. The term "quality" appears to be a context-dependent notion, i.e., its application depends on the field of discourse. The application of the term "quality" ranges over persons, things, and experiences. We feel at ease in speaking about qualities of character, character traits or dispositions displayed in a person's conduct, and use such epithets as courageous, timid, benevolent, or self-centered in conveying our judgments concerning moral agents. So also, we speak of qualities of things in terms of their nature or kinds. In this setting, one relevant

---

4. Ibid., 25–32.

lexical sense of "quality" is this: "The nature, kind, or character (*of* something). Now restricted to cases in which there is a comparison (expressed or implied) with other things of the same kind, hence the degree of excellence or grade, etc."[5] Or quite neutrally, we may simply want to describe the sorts of things we have in mind. An interesting application of the term "quality" pertains to our experiences in contexts where we speak of experiences as being narrow or broad, superficial or deep. Notably, in different fields of discourse we often shift our attention between the descriptive and evaluative senses of the term "quality." For the most part no clear or rigid line is drawn between description and evaluation.

A moral philosopher quite rightly insists on the importance of not confusing description and evaluation.[6] However, it seems more faithful to ordinary discourse to regard the distinction not as an exclusive disjunction, but as a distinction between two endpoints of a spectrum of uses. Away from the middle region, either description or evaluation may dominate the use in particular bits of discourse. Toward the endpoint of the evaluative use, we are bound to confront greater complexity, especially in the manner in which the descriptive content of discourse is embodied in our evaluation of performance. In many ordinary contexts, our description of the "quality of life" cannot be easily distinguished from evaluation. As Geoffrey Warnock points out, ordinary discourse neither is nor needs to be regimented, like legal proceedings. If I am telling someone, for instance, "about the career of Mussolini, it would be unrealistic to look for—to assume that there must be—a point at which description of his doings terminates, and evaluation of them begins." This is, of course, not a claim that rejects the distinction, but a claim that in ordinary discourse "one might expect to find description and evaluation so inextricably intermingled as to constitute, as it were, a seamless garment."[7]

However, if one decides to use the distinction between description and evaluation, it is more profitable not to construe that distinction as a categorical disjunction that precludes any connection within moral thinking itself. As a dichotomy, the distinction is bound to hamper the philosophical studies of non-Western moral thought, for example, Confucian ethics. In attending to a basic notion of *li*, rituals or rules of

---

5. This is entry 8 for "quality" in *The Compact Edition of the Oxford English Dictionary* (New York: Oxford University Press, 1971).

6. For this distinction in ecological context, see Storrs McCall, "Human Needs and the Quality of Life," 7–8; and Alex C. Michalos, "Measuring the Quality of Life," 25–26. Both of these articles appear in *Values and the Quality of Life,* ed. John King-Farlow and William R. Shea (New York: Science History Publications, 1976).

7. Geoffrey Warnock, *Contemporary Moral Philosophy* (New York: St. Martin's, 1967), 64.

proper conduct, both the descriptive and evaluative aspects are present as complementary rather than exclusive features of the statements of ritual rules.[8] The rules themselves and the statements of rules are complementary rather than opposed. One may go even further in remarking: "Descriptive statements ... are not opposed to ones which are normative, but in fact presuppose them; we could not do the things we call describing if language did not provide (we had not been taught) ways normative for describing."[9]

In Confucian ethics, for instance, within the normal setting of human affairs and relations governed by *li*, moral problems are in part a matter of descriptive classification and in part a matter of evaluation of actions. Moreover a description of an action as complying with *li* has a *point* in the evaluation of that action rather than a mere factual description intelligible apart from particular normative contexts. Also, to classify an action as belonging to a *li*-requirement does not by itself entail the latter's relevance.[10] For the description or classification of an action in accord with a rule of *li* to be meaningful, a judgment of appropriateness of the rule according to *yi* (rightness, righteousness) must be presupposed for the evaluation to have a practical force.[11] Detached from this judgment of relevance, a mere descriptive classification of the *li* or rules of proper conduct would be devoid of any moral import.

2. MORAL THEORY AND THE DIMENSION OF WELFARE

In the case of discourse on the quality of life, the distinction between description and evaluation seems to reflect our concern with two dimensions of our moral experience. I suggest that our concern with the

---

8. For fuller discussion of the Confucian notion of *li*, see my "Reflections on the Structure of Confucian Ethics," *Philosophy East and West* 21, no. 2 (1971): 125–40; "Dimensions of *Li* (Propriety): Reflections on an Aspect of Hsün Tzu's Ethics," *Philosophy East and West* 29, no. 4 (1979): 373–94, incorporated as Essay 2 of this volume. [For a later, more general discussion of *li*, see my *Moral Vision and Tradition: Essays in Chinese Ethics* (Washington, D.C.: The Catholic University of America Press, 1998), Essay 12; and "The Ethical and the Religious Dimensions *Li*," *Review of Metaphysics* 55, no. 3 (2002): 501–49, incorporated as Essay 7 in this volume.]

9. Stanley Cavell, "Must We Mean What We Say?" *Inquiry* 1 (1958), reprinted in *Ordinary Language: Essays in Philosophical Method*, ed. V. C. Chappell (Englewood Cliffs, N.J.: Prentice-Hall, 1964), 93–94.]

10. The view proposed above is opposed to Fingarette's interpretation, which fails to do justice to the basic features of Confucian ethics; see note 8 above. Cf. Herbert Fingarette, *Confucius—The Secular as Sacred* (New York: Harper Torchbooks, 1972), 35–36.

11. See my "Concept of Paradigmatic Individuals in the Ethics of Confucius," *Inquiry* 14 (1971), incorporated as chap. 4 in *Dimensions of Moral Creativity: Paradigms, Principles, and Ideals* (University Park: Pennsylvania State University Press, 1978). Cf. Chung-ying

quality of life expresses a basic concern with the evaluative aspect of our moral experiences. In this light, the ecological problem, though in itself a complex composite problem, may be construed as part of a larger moral concern that demands attention from moral philosophers.

In a recent work, Nicholas Rescher draws our attention to *excellence* and *welfare* as two dimensions of the quality of life. "The former—as the overtones of the very word *quality* suggest—relates to excellence; the latter relates to satisfactions in general, and in particular, to happiness. The evaluation of a mode or pattern of life turns on two central factors: its *merits* as these are to be assessed by others and its *satisfactions* as these are experienced by the subject himself."[12] Below I follow Rescher in construing "welfare" as essentially pertaining to the basic requisites of a person's well-being in general. In this dimension, we focus upon certain descriptive indicators such as health, wealth and prosperity, security, and self-esteem as depicting certain requisites for personal well-being. Another range of indicators derives from interpersonal intercourse, such as family relationship, love and affection, friendship and congeniality, and environmental characteristics that yield satisfaction derivative from freedom and mutual respect, privacy, pleasing or aesthetic surroundings, and satisfactory physical environment.[13]

Concern with these welfare-indicators expresses a concern with the descriptive core of the notion of the quality of life. Most of these welfare-indicators are amenable to empirical inquiry, though the personal sense of satisfaction belongs more to the realm of idiosyncratic response than to the relatively objective indicators. For moral theory, the concern with welfare-indicators is more a concern with the question of whether the welfare-indicators, construed as basic requisites for human happiness, are either necessary or sufficient, or both, to constituting the

---

Cheng, "*Yi* as a Universal Principle of Specific Application in Confucian Morality," *Philosophy East and West* 22, no. 3 (1972): 269–80. [For a later systematic explication of the notion of *yi*, see *Moral Vision and Tradition*, Essay 13.]

12. Nicholas Rescher, *Welfare: The Social Issues in Philosophical Perspective* (Pittsburgh, Pa.: University of Pittsburgh Press, 1972), 61. Rescher's more technical terms are "aristic" and "hedonic" quality of life.

13. For the purpose of our limited aim, I have centered on what Rescher calls "the consensus happiness requisites," i.e., "what people in general regard as the essential requisites for a happy life (be it simply for human life as such or life as a member of their own societal environment)." A complete discussion, as Rescher points out, must also account for the idiosyncratic happiness factors, i.e., a person's own perception of "what he needs" for happiness, and his appraisal of the extent to which he possesses these resources, and the hedonic mood or "the psychological feeling tone (of a potentially ephemeral character) of being happy." See Rescher, *Welfare*, 62–77. For a later study of Rescher's value theory, see my "Ideals and Values: A Study in Rescher's Moral Vision," in *Praxis and Reason: Studies in the Philosophy of Nicholas Rescher*, ed. Robert Almeder (Lanham, Md.: University Press of America, 1982).

quality of life. Part of the philosophical task relates to an assessment of claims to satisfaction of welfare-indicators. But such assessment in some sense presupposes that we understand why these claims are made in the first place. I shall now attend to this task of understanding. We want to ask not just how these claims may be justified, but *why* a particular claim is made in the first place, that is, against what moral background is a claim made as part of what it is for living a good life.

Moral theory may be understood as consisting of two different but complementary enterprises: (1) as an activity of assessment of moral judgments, and (2) as an activity of understanding. The former is commonly called "epistemology of morals" or "epistemology of ethics," the latter has no standard name but we may term it "explication of morals." In discussing our ecological theme I shall deal with this latter enterprise. I shall not deal with the complex theoretical issues involved in the epistemology of morals, but instead engage in an explication of morals. In particular, I would like to raise a question, independently of any commitment to a theory of moral justification or of normative ethics, concerning the understanding of a certain ecological claim that we have a right to a livable environment. I shall leave the final assessment of that claim as an open question. What I hope to do in this section is to provide a way of understanding this claim as a special case of a more general claim that may be made within a moral theory construed as an explication of morals. It is the more general claim that I wish to understand and assess. I believe that this general claim can be sustained if we regard it as an answer to an important question on the practical significance of moral theory. In order to accomplish this task, I shall briefly characterize the elements of morality that form the subject matter of explication. With this sketch, I hope to state the nature of the general claim and offer some reasons for its acceptance.

Moral theory, considered as an enterprise of explication, ideally should deal with at least five elements of a fully developed morality: (1) preconditions, (2) presuppositions, (3) components, (4) means of achievement, and (5) styles of performance and styles of life.[14]

Let us note at the outset that normative ethics may place its emphasis on some of these elements and relegate other elements to peripheral concern. Preconditions, I suggest, centrally deal with conditions that need to be present for the reasonable applicability and practical possibility of compliance with the requirements expressed in moral principles or rules and ideals, which figure as the basic *components* of a morali-

---

14. The last three elements, from the dynamic point of view, consist of three dimensions of the creativity of morally committed agents: exemplary, reconstitutive, and ideal dimensions. For further discussion, see my *Dimensions of Moral Creativity*.

ty. Typically certain *presuppositions* seem to underlie any functioning morality, e.g., those that pertain to moral agency in terms of autonomy or responsibility for a person's own choices, decisions, and actions. So also a background or form of life that renders intelligible moral discourse concerning assessment of character or conduct. An explication of the components as involving principles or rules should also deal with the nature of the agent's strategies in pursuing his interests and ideals within the operative scope of morality. And in attending to the agent's performance, particularly in understanding the personal sense of significance in moral compliance, the agent quite often exhibits a certain manner or *style* in performance, and in the larger sense, displays a style of life. The style of moral achievement indicates the experience of significance in the life of a moral agent. As we shall see in Section 3, the dimension of excellence of the quality of life focuses on the excellence of life that relates to the agent's ideal or vision of the good life as a whole. These five elements of morality and their interrelations pose a challenging task for philosophical explication. The variability of emphasis in current moral philosophy does not necessarily lead to theoretical frustration or practical abulia, for such a variability may be illuminating in pointing to different aspects of the moral life, particularly in focusing upon possibly irreducible questions that a moral agent may raise concerning the nature and significance of his moral life.

Practical questions in the context of interpersonal relations are more likely to receive light through discussion of appropriate moral principles or rules. Arguably principles such as benevolence and justice should loom large in such a discussion. However, questions that deal with the meaning or significance of a man's life seem better understood in terms of the discussion on style of performance and style of life.[15] In prosecuting his task of explication, the philosopher cannot be normatively neutral in the methodological sense, for the elements of morality singled out for attention and elaboration implicitly contain a judgment of importance or what may be termed decisions of selectivity.[16] These decisions need not be taken to be either substantive or universal theses, for each has grounding in ordinary moral experience. In the final analysis, all these decisions of selectivity may turn out to be complementary lenses for understanding the complexity of elements and their connections within ordinary moral life. Thus a philosopher's decisions of selectivity in explication should not be regarded as arbitrary except in

---

15. For discussion on this aspect of moral theory, see *Dimensions of Moral Creativity*, chaps. 7–8.
16. See my "Some Reflections on Methodology in Chinese Philosophy," *International Philosophical Quarterly* 11, no. 2 (1971): 236–48.

the truistic sense that there exist alternative approaches to morality, or in cases where one can offer reasons to doubt their grounding in ordinary moral experiences. An initial policy of accommodation is proper in order to appreciate particular efforts at explication. *Ideally* a complete moral theory of explication must deal with all the five elements of morality. However, for our present task I shall concentrate my discussion on the preconditions of morality as a background for understanding the claim that we have a right to a livable environment.

I shall treat the claim that we have a right to a livable environment as a claim grounded in a more general and basic one that pertains to the *preconditions* of morality. This general claim may be stated as a claim to the satisfaction of certain preconditions for the moral life. Note that this claim is a general one that can be specified in terms of the sorts of precondition deemed by a particular normative ethical theory to be necessary or essential to the applicability and fulfillment of its basic principles or ideals. In this sense, the claim to the satisfaction of preconditions of morality depends on specifications in terms of one's commitment to a substantive normative ethics. Thus a utilitarian, aiming at the greatest happiness of all sentient beings, would specify the claim to the satisfaction of preconditions of morality differently from a Kantian, who bases his ethics on the principle of the humanity or dignity of persons. For the utilitarian, concerned with the maximization of happiness, emphasis would be placed on the preconditions that belong to the domain of welfare indicators.

A Kantian, on the other hand, believing that morality is essentially a matter of respect for persons, would obviously assign lesser importance to welfare indicators. This is not to say that these indicators are irrelevant but only that the possibility of living a good moral life or a life of goodwill is quite independent of a concern with welfare. By virtue of its intrinsic nature, the purity of the moral will in the exercise of autonomous legislation suffices for constituting the significance of the moral life. In effect, a Kantian would not attend to preconditions in general, though he may stress perhaps the psychological one construed as a capacity to engage in rational and coherent willing. This stress, though it appears to be narrow, does throw light upon the nature of the claim to the satisfaction of preconditions of morality. For the claim to the satisfaction of preconditions of morality is plausible only because it implicitly embodies a version of the principle "I ought implies I can"—an important Kantian insight into an element of morality. That this principle is essential to understanding morality can be better seen in its contrapositive or logical equivalent, "I cannot implies I ought not." What a morality requires as acceptable conduct must be something that an ordinary human being is capable of fulfilling. My compliance with moral rules or principles depends in part on my *current* capacity to satisfy their requirements. The presence or absence of this capacity is what distinguishes responsible from nonresponsible persons. The preconditions claimed to be essential are in fact the conditions for the exercise of this capacity for moral compliance, and this capacity is what marks us as moral agents rather than as mere living things. The claim to the satisfaction of preconditions of morality is, in effect, a claim that follows from our notion of human beings as moral agents.

We may now restate the claim to the satisfaction of preconditions of morality as a *claim* to the satisfaction of preconditions that render moral agency possible and practically efficacious within the world of human beings. To make one's moral agency something of real efficacy is to attend to the world in terms of what preconditions need be present for one's moral life to be practically possible. The claim of a right to a livable environment can now be seen as an application of the claim to the satisfaction of preconditions of morality, i.e., as a claim to the necessity of satisfaction of preconditions to the exercise of moral agency, in the specific sense of preconditions that pertain to our natural environment. Construed in this way, this claim, along with claims such as the claim to a right to a decent standard of living, or of health care, expresses concern with the sorts of preconditions deemed essential to the exercise of moral agency. Specifications of these preconditions, of course, depend on one's normative ethics.

Although it is difficult to obtain consensus in specifying preconditions positively, certain negative preconditions seem uncontroversial. A claim to a right to a decent standard of living, for example, may be construed not so much as a claim to a certain level of living acceptable to both the individual and his society, but as a claim to freedom *from* poverty understood as "an absolute deprivation or insufficiency." Anyone in this condition "is condemned to live in a fashion that is inadequate from the *biomedical* point of view, lacking the means to sustain life itself properly."[17] Poverty in this sense, as contrasted with being underprivileged,[18] is objectionable also from the moral point of view, for it is a deprivation of opportunities for the exercise of moral agency. And in the absence of these opportunities, the requirement of moral compliance is hardly reasonable. Given the state of poverty, the person who violates a particular moral rule, arguably, is free from moral blame, because he does not possess the capacity necessary to fulfill the moral requirement. Consider the moral rule against stealing. If this rule is to

17. Rescher, *Welfare*, 95.
18. Ibid.

be reasonably applied, we must assume that the agent could have done other than what is required in the reasonable sense of being an ordinary agent. But if the agent were currently in the state of deprivation, our moral rule would seem inapplicable to him. And if we insist that the rule *must* apply anyway, even in the absence of requisite capacity for compliance, our presumption here far exceeds the pretension of fairness in moral regulation. For neglect of preconditions in the basic and negative sense expresses a lack of concern for the importance of moral capacity which connects with its preconditions for the exercise of moral agency. Moreover, excepting the indomitable committed moral agents, satisfaction of preconditions is necessary for ordinary persons to endure in fulfilling moral requirements.[19]

Thus in the case of an agent's predicament marked by an absence of requisite preconditions, it seems unreasonable to insist that he is subject to moral blame. Morality as a system of regulations cannot reasonably be preached to a starving man, for to do so is to impose much too great a burden on the deprived person, who does not possess the requisite moral capacity. I am not saying that the deprived is not a voluntary agent, but I do question, à la Aristotle, whether it is reasonable to regard the domain of voluntary conduct as coextensive with that of moral conduct. Moral action presupposes a current capacity to comply with rules or principles. Where this capacity is absent, imputation of moral responsibility is senseless and, in an important sense, "unfair" to the agent. Another way to put the same point is to say that moral notions have no meaningful application to persons who fail to obtain conditions requisite to moral compliance.

Since the demands for the satisfaction of preconditions are often denied by different societies, it is not surprising that these demands are often expressed in the language of "rights." In the words of Morris Ginsberg, "Rights are generalized claims to the conditions required for the realization of some good, e.g., the satisfaction of a need, the fulfillment of a capacity. They thus imply some conception of well-being."[20] Such claims may be regarded as moral claims in view of the tendency of many societies to neglect their role in the moral life. Claims to the satisfaction of basic welfare-indicators may thus be justly construed as claims to the protection of moral rights, though a theory of moral rights is con-

---

19. Mencius is emphatic on this condition of moral agency. See D. C. Lau, trans., *Mencius* (Middlesex, England: Penguin Books, 1970), 1A7. [For further later discussion, see my "*Xin* and Moral Failure: Notes on an Aspect of Mencius's Moral Psychology," in *Mencius: Contexts and Interpretations,* ed. Alan Chan (Honolulu: University of Hawaii Press, 2002), incorporated as Essay 15 of this volume.]

20. Morris Ginsberg, "Diversity of Goods," in *Essays in Sociology and Social Philosophy,* vol. 1 (Melbourne: William Heineman, 1956), 112.

cerned with the more difficult issues that transcend a mere concern with preconditions of moral agency. In an incisive recent work, however, such a concern is expressed in the stress on the stage setting essential to any exercise of rights. Melden states that:

> It would be incoherent to ascribe the right to pursue one's interests [as a moral right] to such persons while conceding that in the circumstances in which they live, the only interests they can acquire because of their poverty, disease, lack of education and training, and the discrimination they suffer at the hands of those who are more fortunate, are the interests of social outcasts, who are resentful of their degradation and determined, whatever the cost to others may be, to fend for themselves and without regard to others. . . . In such circumstances the deficiencies in the stage setting essential to the exercise of rights such persons have as human beings are of such a radical nature that it would be cruel mockery to tell them that they have rights. . . . A right that cannot play a role in the moral lives of persons is as empty as an office in an institutional arrangement, which carries with it no duties or entitlements.[21]

Moral rights have thus no reasonable application for those who do not possess the capacity for their exercise. The acknowledged rights in this way would remain empty gestures, devoid of moral content; they do not have any practical significance for those who are deprived of proper preconditions for their exercise. Rights thus belong to the domain of entitlements. The language of rights helps "to define and serve to protect those things concerning which one can make a very special kind of claim."[22]

In light of a moral theory that stresses preconditions for the exercise of moral agency, such claims are readily intelligible in view of their deprivation in many societies. It may be said that a society that systematically neglects the importance of basic preconditions expressed in economic and biomedical welfare-indicators is both counterproductive and subject to moral criticism. It is counterproductive because it enjoins practically impossible conduct, thus deviating from the aim of promoting desirable conduct implicit in its regulative system of institutions. It is subject to moral criticism because it expresses a disregard for our ordinary sense of injustice and reasonableness in the imposition of constraints at the service of social cooperative undertakings.

In some circumstances our demand for certain preconditions, from the social point of view, cannot be reasonably honored. Quite obviously when a society is faced with a situation of extreme urgency or emer-

---

21. A. I. Melden, *Rights and Persons* (Berkeley and Los Angeles: University of California Press, 1977), 248–49.
22. Richard Wasserstrom, "Rights, Human Rights, and Racial Discrimination," in *Moral Problems*, 2nd ed., ed. James Rachels (New York: Harper & Row, 1975), 111.

gency such as war or internally disruptive civil disturbance of a massive scale that threatens its survival, the demands for preconditions for the exercise of our moral agency may appear pointless. In such a situation, any form of a claim to the right to preconditions of its exercise is quite justly set aside, for the situation calls for a suspension rather than a legitimation of such claims. The application of moral notions is, so to speak, held in abeyance, pending the restoration of social order construed in a manner sufficient for the normal functioning of a morality or moral practice. In drawing our attention to such extreme situations, evolutionary ethics or ethics of survival makes an important point, not in endorsing survival value as a moral value, or human life itself as a moral value, but rather that whatever is deemed intrinsically valuable in human life truistically depends on the existence of such a life for it to have any practical import. Evolutionary ethics rightly stresses a precondition for moral valuing, though not on its constitutive content. Seen in these terms, it lays its emphasis upon an overriding precondition for our moral life and human life in general. Whether or not we want to claim a moral right to survival in the evolutionary sense, it remains the case that morality as a regulative system would be quite pointless when human survival is at stake. Our legitimate claims to satisfaction of preconditions may thus be overridden by claims to human survival.[23]

However, in normal situations, the concern with the quality of life, in its welfare dimension, quite reasonably reminds us of an important element of morality. The plausibility of any special form of the claim to the satisfaction of preconditions of morality thus depends on a narrow but important interpretation of the quality of moral life. The claim of a right to a livable environment in the ecological sense is thus a part of this larger concern with the dimension of welfare. It remains for us to turn to the dimension of excellence of the quality of life that represents a concern with the *ideal,* rather than the principled component of morality. Whereas the welfare dimension focuses upon the aspect of morality as a regulative system, the excellence dimension of the quality of life focuses upon the ideals of the moral life. In the following section, I shall offer some reflections on this dimension, which has not received much attention in recent moral philosophy.

---

23. For a sustained and plausible defense of this claim in terms of an empirical value theory, see S. C. Pepper, *Sources of Value* (Berkeley and Los Angeles: University of California Press, 1958), chaps. 20–21.

3. DIMENSION OF EXCELLENCE

Let us turn to the dimension of excellence of the quality of life. The question of quality of life from this point of view may be construed as a quest for a way or style of life in which human beings can harmoniously live together and individual aspirations can find expression and fulfillment. Our basic task is to explicate the notion of moral excellence and show how such a notion is amenable to two different interpretations for a committed agent in light of the transformative significance of moral ideals in the comprehensive sense of ideals of the good life as a whole.[24] A related task pertains to the more practical question of the realization of one's conception of moral ideal in the actual world. I shall map out some limiting factors for performance and capabilities for achievement.

As involving the notion of moral excellence, the question of the quality of human life implies some sort of dissatisfaction with present states of affairs. It is basically a reflective question that expresses a concern with doing in light of a state of human existence deemed desirable from an ideal perspective. In this sense, the question is a question of moral vision, of an excellent, good life deemed capable of realization in the actual world. Depending on the attitude of the questioner, the question of the quality of life in the sense of excellence may be construed in two different ways: (1) as a question aiming at finding an ideal standard for assessing solutions to problems, and (2) as a question that calls for an ideal answer that endows a quality or *significance* to human existence without providing solutions to problems. From the prospective point of view, the first is a quest for a standard or a *norm* that can function as a criterion for measuring moral achievement and for assessing the desirability of different ways of life. A way of life that satisfies this criterion would be considered an excellent way of life. The second question is more of a quest for a *theme* in which human beings can develop in different ways of life, in short, the quest for a style of life. Thus the notion of the quality of human life as expressive of moral ideals admits of two different conceptions of quality or ideal: *ideal norm* and *ideal theme*. We may regard the ideal norm as a telos or target for a way of life, and ideal theme as a telos for a style of life. This distinction between way of life and style of life is not a distinction of a difference in content, but a difference in moral perspectives. The distinction, of course, does not preclude their possible relation within the life of a moral agent. An individual person may be satisfied with one without the other. A large part of Western ethical literature focuses on ideal norms. Ideal themes, on the

---

24. For a fuller discussion of these two interpretations of moral ideals, see my *Dimensions of Moral Creativity*, chap. 8.

other hand, appear to be a more prominent concern of Eastern ethics, particularly those in Chinese philosophy inspired by the teachings of Confucius and Laozi.

In sum, the notion of quality in human life in the sense of excellence admits of two uses that constitute two different types of conception of moral excellence or ideals. I construe this notion as a moral notion, taking the term "moral" in a broad sense. In this broad sense, we have two different domains of morality: excellence and acceptability. What lies outside these domains are morally indifferent. But what is deemed morally acceptable conduct may or may not be admitted into the domain of excellence.

To be intelligible, a vision of a quality of human life must, in some sense, be related to human nature as we know it. We can quite easily imagine how this question of moral ideal can arise for ordinary reflective persons. As ordinary persons we often encounter frustrations in not getting what we want. More often in contemporary society we experience conflicts of desires within or outside our own persons. This experience of conflicting mental states in our private and public roles quite naturally gives rise to a conception of quality that can in some way eliminate the conflicts in question. Moral teachers and philosophers of the past have offered their vision in terms of some sort of *harmony* to ameliorate this predicament that infects our social life or life of interpersonal relations. Where this conflict is seen essentially as a conflict of self-interests or desires, it is suggested that the quality of our interests lies in the way in which they *ought* to be satisfied. Thus harmony in some way is an ideal in which conflicting interests and desires may be settled. The ideal state of affairs is one in which one attempts to accommodate a diversity of interests and desires in so far as this accommodation can be made with the least cost of individual dissatisfaction. In William James's words: "That act must be the best act, accordingly, which makes for the *best whole*, in the sense of awakening the least sum of dissatisfactions. In the casuistic scale, therefore, those ideals must be written highest which *prevail at the least cost*, or by whose realization the least possible number of other ideals are destroyed."[25] In this view of the human predicament, the quality or vision of moral excellence is an inclusive and comprehensive harmony of interests. The moral ideal, an ideal norm in this case, is a standard for measuring moral achievement. This conception of harmony is sometimes termed "integration."[26]

25. William James, "The Moral Philosopher and the Moral Life," in *Essays on Faith and Morals* (New York: Longmans, Green and Co., 1949), 205.
26. For further discussion, see Ralph Barton Perry, *General Theory of Value* (Cambridge, Mass.: Harvard University Press, 1950), chaps. 21 and 22.

In contrast with the ideal of inclusive harmony, one may construe harmony more like an ideal theme. The term "ideal theme" is an appropriation of the notion of theme familiar in various linguistic contexts. We talk of a theme as a topic of discourse or discussion, or of a theme as "an idea, point of view, or perception embodied or expanded upon in a work of art," or as "a melody forming the basis of variations or other development in a composition."[27] Unlike ideal norms, ideal themes do not provide precepts, rules, directives, or principles for action.[28] They are ideal points of orientation that have an import for committed agents. Such terms as development, clarification, and expansion are thus quite at home in discussing ideal themes. In the case of ideal norms, terms such as application, compliance, and extension are more appropriate. The object of an ideal theme is not to integrate desires or interests, but to see to it that a *quality* is present in any satisfaction of desires. The interests and desires need not be integrated at all.

The point of excellence lies in their *manner* or style of satisfaction. When these desires conflict, the reconciliation is done through joining these agents in friendship rather than through negotiating conflicting purposes. Harmony has to do with *persons* themselves and not with their purposive intentions or ends-in-view. Here the ideal theme of harmony provides a perspective in which conflicts may be resolved, but unlike the ideal norm of harmony, it does not provide a method of solution to the problems. The value here lies in its focus upon the easing of the tension experienced in conflicts. It is difficult to deny that sometimes this tension is what beclouds the issues in interpersonal relations. These two conceptions of harmony are not incompatible. Just as an ideal norm can guide our conduct in conflict, an ideal theme can also guide us in light of the quality of concern with persons as possessing idiosyncratic wants and desires. The one focuses on the necessity of solution to conflicts between interests, the other on the quality of mutual concern and respect in personal relation. A comprehensive and satisfactory conception of harmony must embrace both these concerns: resolution of conflict between individual interests and reconciliation of persons in relation.

4. THE CONFUCIAN VISION OF NATURE AND HUMANITY

I turn now to a discussion of a comprehensive Chinese moral vision that acknowledges the important role our environment plays in the re-

---

27. *American Heritage Dictionary of the English Language* (1969).
28. For the distinction between ideal norm and ideal theme, see my *Dimensions of Moral Creativity*, chap. 8.

alization of the vision. As an ideal theme, the Chinese notion of *dao* expresses an ideal of harmony and unity of man and nature. In this conception, the things in nature constitute parts of a holistic vision, though the *dao* remains an inarticulate inspirational rather than an aspirational standard. Any attempt to erect a supreme norm for the moral life would be regarded as a constitutive strategy for the realization of the vision rather than an exclusive concern with adjudication of conflicts between individual interests. In view of its relevance to our ecological concerns today, I would like to inquire into the question "How can human beings, in light of a commitment to this vision of harmony as an ideal theme, bring the actual world closer to the ideal?" I shall discuss a couple of limiting but overlapping factors, which indicate the sort of challenge to the realization of this Chinese vision within the actual world.[29]

Although there is much that we can do to mold our actual world closer to the ideal, the natural order of objects and events contains much that we cannot do positively to effectuate our vision of harmony. At a basic level, given that our economic and biomedical preconditions obtain, efforts should be directed toward the vision as having an actuating import in the way we live. Things in the natural world should be respected, not as objects of detached contemplation, but as having an intrinsic value status, which figure as constitutive elements in the achieved state of moral excellence. At times things in the natural world present obstacles to the solution of some of our recurrent problematic situations; these obstacles must be regarded, not as impediments to the realization of the vision, but as potential elements for harmonization. In this light the ecological attitude betrays a larger concern. Things in nature present a challenge to our narrow preoccupation with increasing demand for satisfaction of nonbasic welfare-indicators. Moderation of our wants and cultivation of a caring attitude toward nature are thus essential to the realization of the moral ideal. As a Classical Confucian essay, *The Doctrine of the Mean (Zhong Yong)*, points out, the task of *cheng*, i.e., a gen-

---

29. For an elaboration of this notion of practical causation, see my "Practical Causation and Confucian Ethics," *Philosophy East and West* 25, no. 1 (1975), incorporated in this volume as Essay 9. These reflections are offered with Confucian ethics in mind, and consequently are not always applicable to Daoist ethics. [For earlier and later studies of Confucian and Daoist versions of *dao*, see my "Confucian Vision and Experience of the World," *Philosophy East and West* 25, no. 3 (1975): 319–33; "Chinese Moral Vision, Responsive Agency, and Factual Beliefs," *Journal of Chinese Philosophy* 7, no. 1 (1980): 3–26; "Opposites as Complements: Reflections on the Significance of *Tao*," *Philosophy East and West* 31, no. 2 (1981): 123–40; "Harmony and the Neo-Confucian Sage," *Philosophical Inquiry: An International Quarterly* 5, nos. 2–3 (1983): 124–42; and "Between Commitment and Realization: Wang Yang-ming's Vision of the Universe as a Moral Community," *Philosophy East and West* 43, no. 4 (1993): 611–49. All these papers were incorporated in *Moral Vision and Tradition*, as Essays 2, 4, 5, 7, and 9.]

uine, serious, sincere commitment to the vision of the unity or harmony of humanity and nature or the triadic vision of humanity, Heaven, and Earth *(can tiandi)*, essentially consists in self-cultivation and the utmost development of human nature conceived as intrinsically complementary to humanity and the natural order. A striking passage reads:

> Only those who are absolutely sincere can fully develop their nature. If they can fully develop their nature, they can then fully develop the nature of others. If they can fully develop the nature of others, they can develop the nature of things. If they can develop the nature of things, they can then assist in the transforming and nourishing process of Heaven and Earth. If they can assist in the transforming and nourishing process of Heaven and Earth, they can thus form a trinity with Heaven and Earth *(can tiandi)*.[30]

A more common expression of this vision is "the unity of Heaven and Earth *(tianren heyi)*."[31] Notably the process of realization of the vision is envisaged as a progressive enlargement of one's ideal concern, embracing both humanity and nature. The emphasis on "assisting in the transforming and nourishing process of Heaven and Earth" indicates humanity as the dynamic, creative partner in changes and transformation of natural processes.

Implied in the adoption of this vision of creative harmony is an attitude not of manipulation, but of *genial assistance* to things in fulfilling their own nature, i.e., a caring concern for their existence as complementary to one's own. Among the Song and Ming Neo-Confucians, Wang Yangming's influential expansion of this vision as a vision of *ren* (humaneness, benevolence) is perhaps the most wide-ranging and persuasive:

Passage A:

The great man regards Heaven, Earth, and the myriad things as one body *(yiti)*. He regards the world as one family and the country as one person . . . Forming one body with Heaven, Earth, and the myriad things is not only true of the great man. Even the mind *(xin)* of the small man is no different. Only he makes it small. Therefore, when he sees a child about to fall into a well, he cannot help a feeling of alarm and commiseration [*Mencius*, 2A6]. This shows that his humanity *(ren)* forms one body with the child. Again, when he observes the pitiful cries and frightened appearance of the birds and animals about to be slaughtered, he cannot help feeling an inability to bear their suffering. This shows that his

---

30. *Doctrine of the Mean*, section 22, in W. T. Chan, ed., *A Source Book in Chinese Philosophy* (Princeton, N.J.: Princeton University Press, 1963), 107–8. See also my *Moral Vision and Tradition*, Essay 2.

31. For an informative collection of textual sources for the idea of *tianren heyi* from *Yijing* (Book of Changes) to Wang Yangming, see Chen Rongjie (Wing-tsit Chan), "*Tianren heyi,*" in *Zhongguo zhexue cidian daquan*, ed. Wei Zhengtong (Taipei: Shuiniu, 1983).

humanity forms one body with birds and animals. It may be objected that birds and animals are sentient beings as he is. But when he sees plants broken and destroyed, he cannot help a *feeling of pity*. It may be said that plants are living things as he is. Yet, even when he sees tiles and stones shattered and crushed, he cannot help a *feeling of regret*. This shows that his humanity forms one body with tiles and stones.[32]

Wang's reformulation of the Classical Confucian ideal of the harmony of man and nature clearly points to an ideal of the *universe as a moral community*. As Wang succinctly states: "At bottom Heaven and Earth and all things are my body *(wushen)*. Is there any suffering or bitterness of the great masses that is not disease or pain in my own body?"[33] Remarkably, whereas the statement in the *Doctrine of the Mean* emphasizes positive action in caring and helping the development of the well-being of all things in the universe, Wang focuses on the sympathetic union with the affairs of suffering of beings capable of feeling and perception as well as the destruction of both sentient and nonsentient beings. This sensitivity is epitomized in one of the pioneers of Neo-Confucian philosophy, Zhou Dunyi (Chou Tun i, 1017–1073). We learned that Zhou cherished living things "so strong that he would not cut the grass outside his window."[34]

Well aware that in practice the Confucian emphasis on filial love and concern may conflict with that of the animals and plants embraced in the vision of *ren*, Wang thinks that the conflict requires the exercise of our sense of the relative importance of things.

Passage B:

We love both our plants and animals, and yet we can tolerate feeding animals with plants. We love both animals and men and yet we can tolerate butchering animals to feed our parents, provide for religious sacrifices, and entertain guests. We love both parents and strangers. But suppose here are a small basket of rice and a platter of soup. With them one will survive and without them one will die. Since not both our parents and the stranger can be saved by this meager food, we will prefer to save our parents instead of the stranger. This we can tolerate. We can tolerate all these because it is reasonable *(daoli)* that these should be done. As to the relationship between ourselves and our parents, there

---

32. Wang Yangming, *Instructions for Practical Living and Other Neo-Confucian Writings of Wang Yang-ming*, trans. Wing-tsit Chan (New York: Columbia University Press, 1963), 179, emphasis added. [For further discussion, see my *The Unity of Knowledge and Action: A Study in Wang Yang-ming's Moral Psychology* (Honolulu: University Press of Hawaii, 1982), chap. 3. This caring concern for all existent things is grandly manifest in Wang Yangming's conception of the universe as a moral community. See my "Between Commitment and Realization: Wang Yang-ming's Vision of the Universe as a Moral Community," *Philosophy East and West* 43, no. 4 (1993): 611–49; or *Moral Vision and Tradition*, Essay 9.]

33. Wang, *Instructions*, 179.

34. Chan, *Source Book*, 462.

cannot be any distinction of this and that or of greater or lesser importance. For being humane to all people and feeling love for all comes from this affection toward parents.[35]

Wang is clear that, in practice the vision of *ren*, which calls for love and respect for all existent things as intrinsic values, cannot be realized *in toto*. The conflict of intrinsic values is a fact of the human condition.

More generally, sacrifice of one thing or another for the maintenance and promotion of human welfare for the sake of our quality of life is inevitable. Wang would have agreed with Nicolai Hartmann that there is an *antinomic* character of all values that poses difficulties for their realization, and thus in the real world, every human is "continually confronted with the necessity of settling conflicts of values, of doing so that he can be answerable for his obligation. It is his destiny not to be able to escape the obligation."[36] However, as indicated in Wang's statement of the Confucian vision in *Passage B*, the sacrifice of one value for another, particularly for the sake of maintaining the life of our parents, is not merely a matter of obligation, but a sensitivity to the loss of values, as shown in our feelings of pity and regret. Implied in these feelings is a judgment of comparative value. Such a judgment may be described as "regret without repudiation," a counterpart to "remorse without repudiation."[37] However, unlike the guilt-oriented remorse, which tends to be retrospective and self-centered, regret without repudiation is prospective and other-directed, for the focus is the self in relation to other persons and things. The regret is an expression of our concern for the loss of values of other persons and things.

Arguably, as Hartmann points out, there is an accompanying obligation. In the light of the vision of *ren*, the obligation involved is the restoration of the values lost. If that is not possible, one must direct appropriate effort to restoring their functional equivalents. Of course, Wang would insist on the primacy of filial obligation stressed by Confucius, for family is the foundation for the cultivation and development of the ideal of *ren*. For Confucius, filial piety and fraternal affection are the roots *(ben)* of *ren*.[38] Moreover, a dedicated scholar or a *junzi*, a Confu-

---

35. Wang, *Instructions*, 222–23. Here I replaced "principle" with "reasonable" for *daoli*. *Daoli* is often rendered as "moral principle." [For a later discussion of this concept and its cognates such as *tianli*, *yili*, and *tiaoli*, see my *The Unity of Knowledge and Action*, 28–48.]

36. Nicolai Hartmann, *Ethics*, vol. 2 (London: George Allen & Unwin, 1932), 76.

37. D. Z. Phillips and H. O. Mounce, *Moral Practices* (London: Routledge and Kegan Paul, 1969), 101. [For a later discussion of the Confucian view of the fundamental value of family in the light of *ren*, see my "Confucian Vision and the Human Community," *Journal of Chinese Philosophy* 11, no. 3 (1984): 226–38, incorporated in this volume as Essay 11.]

38. D. C. Lau, trans., *Confucius: The Analects* (Middlesex, England: Penguin Books, 1978), 1.1.

cian paradigmatic individual, wholeheartedly dedicated to the ideal of *ren*, would even sacrifice his life for the sake of *ren*. As Confucius reminds his pupils, a *junzi* would not seek to preserve his life at the expense *ren;* he would even sacrifice his life so that *ren* may be realized.[39] The *junzi* are exceptionable persons of *ren*. Ordinary humans concerned with excellence may well have to be content with the effort at the rectification of the values lost in the course of maintaining the welfare as a precondition for pursuing the ideal of *ren*.[40]

Somewhat parallel to the ideal of *ren* as embodied in the *junzi* or Confucian paradigmatic individuals, in the Christian tradition one can think of St. Francis of Assisi's life of humility that embraces the totality of all God's creatures. And in a recent ecological discussion, it was even suggested that St. Francis be regarded as an ecological saint.[41] This Confucian affinity with a Christian paradigmatic individual may be misleading, for the Confucian stresses active participation in the course of nature, rather than a passive acceptance. The genial assistance in the transformations and changes in the natural world requires activities that harmonize with nature. Negative actions are appropriate in some circumstances of life, but for the most part, the ecological concern reflects part of a larger concern that involves other limiting factors in practical causation, i.e., the capacity of humans to effect changes in the natural world. In the absence of a conception of a personal God and providential order, the Confucian love for things in nature is oriented toward this world rather than a transcendent, supernatural affective state, though it also possesses a spiritual quality. This anthropocentric orientation toward moral excellence, however, does not preclude the presence of a quasi-religious dimension of moral experience.[42] For the joy in attaining harmony of humanity and nature may appear as a joy experienced in the intimate affinity of all things in harmony. The success in our genial participation in the course of nature brings with it also a reverence for life—an experience of the blending of the human and the sublime akin to the religious experiences of some mystics. The implicit caring attitude in the commitment to the vision is incompatible with that of domination over nature. As Xunzi reminds us, the world of na-

---

39. Ibid., 15.9.

40. For humanity today, the most difficult problem in light of the ideal of *ren*, or *agape*, pertains to intercultural ethical conflict. From the point of view of moral theory, it is this problem in the pursuit of ideal quality of human life, in conjunction with the welfare dimension, that requires urgent attention. [For a later discussion of this problem, see my *Moral Vision and Tradition*, Essay 13.]

41. Lynn White, Jr., "The Historical Roots of Our Ecological Crisis," in Barbour, *Western Man and Environmental Ethics*, 28–30. For a contrary view, see Rene Dubos, "A Theology of the Earth," also in Barbour's anthology.

42. For later discussion, see Essay 7 of this volume.

ture provides resources not only for the satisfaction of our needs and desires, but also for the beautification of human nature.[43] Within the Confucian vision, man's special place lies in his assisting role, and not in the manipulation of things in nature. Man's privileged status pertains to his capacity to realize his vision of harmony with nature, not in the exploitation of nature for his wants and purposes.

Since the Confucian vision is basically a vision of *ren*, expressive of an affectionate concern for the well-being of humanity, its actualization inevitably involves a concern with human affairs, with activities performed within a cultural and historic setting in which a moral tradition is embedded. Respect for one's moral tradition and for the Confucian, the *li* or rules of propriety, is integral to the caring concern with all things. Notably, a less than critical attitude is displayed in the Confucian dealing with other men within the constraints imposed by social and political institutions. Critique of moral tradition is possible but in ideal terms the task is to embed the vision of excellence within an established tradition. To a moral philosopher, this conservative, more accurately a conservational, attitude is likely to perpetuate existing evils within an established moral order. I shall not pursue this difficult issue here, except to remark that not all traditional constraints on conduct disable us in actualizing the vision of harmony.

One may observe here that whenever a person engages in criticizing traditional morality, he must espouse criteria of justification that have at least some connection with the way of life in which human beings are related to one another and mindful of elementary rules of civility. The task of the Confucian is to mediate his vision of excellence by way of *li* (ritual rules of proper conduct) within the actual world. Wholesale critique of a tradition has a practical force only when the critic can propose a viable alternative setting for conduct. The wholesale critical reformer faces also a gigantic task, for the tradition to be replaced is more like an iceberg. For the most part he can only deal with items exposed on the surface. A larger part is submerged beneath the surface. For the Confucian the more reasonable way is to deal with problems posed by the tradition in a piecemeal way. The vision of moral excellence has a practical force within one's cultural and moral setting. Transformation of the existing milieu of action is a matter of harmonization of conflicting elements in human life within a community of mutual care. The existing moral order thus constitutes a limiting factor in the actualization of the vision of the harmony of man and nature.[44]

43. See my "Dimensions of *Li*," or Essay 2 of this volume.
44. For a later, more extensive discussion on the nature of Confucian tradition as a living tradition, see my "The Idea of Confucian Tradition," *Review of Metaphysics* 45, no. 4 (1992): 803–40; or *Moral Vision and Tradition*, Essay 12.

In terms of our current concern with the ecological problem and the quality of human life in general, the Confucian vision appears to be relevant, particularly in its emphasis upon the dimension of excellence in the moral life. This emphasis, in the manner in which it envisages an ideal theme appears to be complementary to the more standard Western concern with an ideal norm and claims to the satisfaction of welfare-indicators. I hope my general presentation of the Confucian vision may thus serve as an invitation to the careful study and consideration of Chinese moral philosophy as an integral part of a moral theory that focuses on the quality of human life in relation to the human and natural order.[45]

45. This essay was presented as a lecture before the Seminar on Environment and Intercultural Communication, State University of New York College at Oswego, April 13, 1978. I am grateful to Professor Peter Hertz, chairman of the symposium, for the invitation, and to the audience for helpful discussion.

Essay 11

CONFUCIAN VISION AND THE HUMAN COMMUNITY

The conception of the unity and harmony of man and nature *(tian-ren heyi)* has been a pervasive feature in the history of Chinese philosophy. Of special interest to the inquiry concerning the relation between the individual and the community is the Confucian preoccupation with the problem of realizing this vision within human society. It is a concern with the possibility of transforming an existing social order, which already has established cultural tradition, into an order invested with the ethical ideal of *ren*, or humanity. In more concrete terms, *ren* is an ideal of the good life on the whole that is deemed capable of realization in varying human relationships within the setting of institutional practice and social structure as consisting of roles and statuses. In the teachings of Confucius, the task of *ren*-realization has a twofold aspect. The first aspect is a transformation of the social structure and the functional institutions into an order of *li* (ritual propriety) or a condition of civility wherein individuals pay heed to each other's integrity through compliance with formal requirements for proper behavior. The second aspect is a transformation of all social relationships into personal relationships. The latter task is a step both necessary to and constitutive of the former, for lying at the center of *li*-performance, ideally, is the exemplification of moral virtues or qualities which are a product of self-cultivation and actual engagement in promoting *ren* as a form of diffusive affection.[1]

---

[1]. For this aspect of Confucian ethics, see my *Dimensions of Moral Creativity: Paradigms, Principles, and Ideals* (University Park: Pennsylvania State University Press, 1978), chaps. 4 and 5; "Dimensions of *Li* (Propriety): Reflections on an Aspect of Hsün Tzu's Ethics," *Philosophy East and West* 29, no. 4 (1979), incorporated in this volume as Essay 2; and "*Li* and Moral Justification: A Study in the *Li Chi*," *Philosophy East and West* 33, no. 1 (1983), excerpted in Appendixes 1 and 2 of Essay 2 in the volume. See also Herbert Fingarette, *Confucius—The Secular as Sacred* (New York: Harper Torchbooks, 1972); and Tu Wei-ming, "The Creative Tension Between *Jen* and *Li*" and "*Li* as a Process of Humanization," *Philosophy East and West* 18, no. 2 (1968) and 22, no. 2 (1972).

Confucius once remarked that to be a man of *ren* is to "love all men."[2] It is, in effect, an affectionate concern for the well-being of all humans regardless of their abilities and circumstances. But this condition is an outcome of gradually extending the ambience of direct personal relations between individuals, more particularly, the extension of familial relationships, e.g., between parents and children, husband and wife, brothers and sisters. The task of creating a human community, in the succinct words of Liang Chi-chao, is "to cultivate and to foster the commonest feelings of affection among men in order to extend them to build up a society based on '*ren.*'"[3] An ideal human community, apart from having the unity of a social structure, is also a community of extensive mutual concern and care among its members. This essay focuses on the nature and possibility of extensive concern in human relationships.

Let us first attend to *ren* as a moral ideal, that is, as an ideal of the good human life as a whole. Basically, it is a conception of equality of human beings, not in the sense that they possess the same empirical characteristics, but in the sense that they share the same *status* of being human. The ideal of *ren* is what confers this common status of humanity. In this light, we can endorse Mencius's saying that *"ren* is man. When we speak of the two together the result is the Way *(dao)."*[4] To be a man of *ren* is to be truly human, i.e., to live in a way of life inspired by *ren*. However, descriptively, humans possess a variety of similarities and differences. The problem of *ren*-realization in human life is in part a problem of focusing upon those similarities that can serve as a basis for extensive concern. The common characteristic of sociality may serve as this basis, since the point of having the ideal is to enable men to live together in unity and harmony.

In the words of Confucius, a *junzi*, or morally superior man, cultivates himself "so as to give people security and peace" (*Analects*, 14.45); "he is sociable but not a partisan" (*Analects*, 15.21). Taking sociality as a point of departure, one can by reflection be gradually led to appreciate human intercourse as displaying a network of relationships. Every viable human society imposes a set of constraints, duties and obligations, regulating interactions between people in various contexts. The world *"ren"* signifies an ideal relation between two men. Notably, every society has evolved its own rules of behavior and classification of status. *Li*, for the Confucian, in part pertains to the established tradition governing vari-

---

2. Unless indicated otherwise, all my references to the *Analects* are taken from Wing-tsit Chan, trans., *A Source Book in Chinese Philosophy* (Princeton, N.J.: Princeton University Press, 1963). Asterisks indicate emendations.
3. Liang Chi-chao, *History of Chinese Political Thought* (Taipei: Chengwen, 1968), 52.
4. See D. C. Lau, trans., *Mencius* (Middlesex, England: Penguin Books, 1970), 7B16.

ous human relationships. The problem of *ren*-realization is thus a problem of *equalizing* the status of humanity without obliterating existing social distinctions. More specifically, it is a problem of focusing upon the *root*-possibility of *ren*-realization.

What impresses Confucius and subsequent Confucian thinkers is the natural relationship between parents and their offspring. This natural relationship is considered both paradigmatic and normative, for in the family the behavior of parents and children is characteristically one of care and affectionate concern. The family is the home and the natural setting in which care and concern have a vital role in its preservation. It is the locus in which members learn to *see* one another as a being actuated by needs and desires, and the way in which their satisfaction depends on paying due regard to appropriate constraints, coupled with an appreciation of the importance of mutual aid and development for ensuring the unity and harmony and well-being of the family. One of Confucius's disciples succinctly notes: "A superior man is devoted to the fundamentals [the root]. When the root is firmly established, the Way [of life inspired by *ren*] will develop. Filial piety and brotherly respect are the root of *ren*" (*Analects*, 1.2). Filial piety and brotherly respect offer the root-possibility for *ren*-realization. They may be said to be the basis for extensive moral concern, i.e., as a sort of basis for what may be called an activity of analogical projection.[5] Analogy here does not purport to be an inference or an argument. It is an activity that aims at extending the orbit of one's moral concern. *Ren* as an ethical ideal indicates a culminating state of such an extension. What is the analogizing activity here? To answer this question, we need to attend to what is normatively implied in the notion of filiality *(xiao)* and brotherly respect *(di)*. Both these notions imply an acknowledgment of mutual regard and respect for activities that significantly affect the lives of the members of the family in carrying out expectations that are embedded in direct personal relationships.

A father, for example, has the duty to care for his children by providing resources for the satisfaction of their needs and education; and his children have the duty to care for their father when the latter is sick or disabled because of old age. Moreover, these reciprocal obligations are to be performed with an attitude of reverence or respect *(jing)* styled with an expression of affectionate concern. It is this caring attitude that lies at the heart of *ren* as an ideal of extensive moral concern. Other human beings, not of the status of being one's parent or brother, can also

---

5. Cua, *Ethical Argumentation: A Study in Hsün Tzu's Moral Epistemology* (Honolulu: University of Hawaii Press, 1985), chap. 3.

be cared for as one's parent or brother. This is possible because of the analogizing of one's affection and thought. The similarity of other people in terms of being members of families is crucially the basis for one's analogizing activity. In other words, the similarity of status serves as a basis for extensive moral concern. We can thus speak of extensive moral concern as essentially a form of analogical projection of familial relationship.

This kind of analogical projection, through thought and feelings, is preeminently a display of one's reflective capacity to recognize other human beings as enjoying similar family status. And in light of *ren,* a recognition of such a status makes possible the extension of one's own moral concern, and ultimately embraces all human beings, as envisioned by Zhang Zai and Wang Yangming. It is in effect an expansive horizon for viewing all human beings as eligible partners in personal relations. However, each analogizing extension carries its own quality or style of personal relationship.[6] The relations between persons, in this sense, have their own distinctive features, by virtue of the style or qualities of performance of the persons involved. Moreover, how one ought to act in a particular relationship cannot be dictated by a set of determinate formulas or principles that may serve, so to speak, as premises of practical syllogisms. The analogizing of status has nothing to do with universalization, for it is an activity that occurs within the setting of an actual relationship between persons.

Apart from the prescriptions of *li* (ritual propriety), or conventional rules of proper behavior, there are, for the Confucian, no additional action-guiding principles that can serve as a basis of conduct. This is not to say that individuals have no moral commitments in terms of principles,[7] for any such commitment is always subject to reconsideration in terms of the agent's actual encounter in particular circumstances which require *yi,* or an exercise of judgment. There are situations in human life that are exigent in character and have to be dealt with by an occasional judgment of the right thing to do *(yi).* Thus, for Confucius, "a superior man *(junzi)* in dealing with the world is not for anything or against anything. He follows what is right *(yi)*" *(Analects* 4.10). This involves a sense of appropriateness. His occasional judgment may be guided by his personal rules of conduct, but such rules are not to be used for the purpose of universalization, for they are more like signposts that suggest directions for where one wants to travel and not a priori prescriptions for proper behavior. The conventional rules of conduct en-

6. Cua, *Dimensions of Moral Creativity,* chap. 7.
7. Cua, *Moral Vision and Tradition: Essays in Chinese Ethics* (Washington, D.C.: The Catholic University of America Press, 1998), Essay 14.

capsulated in *li* are likewise subject to the determination by judgment of their relevance to particular cases. In this way, "the *junzi* is broad-minded but not partisan" (*Analects* 2.14). He is not to be an implement, i.e., "not [to] be like an implement which is intended only for a narrow and specific purpose." Rather, "he should have broad vision, wide interest, and sufficient ability to do many things."[8]

A question justly arises: What is the role of moral reflection with respect to the analogizing of status? Moral reflection is a form of thinking addressed to a particular situation that concerns the matters at hand. A disciple of Confucius put it this way: "To study extensively, to be steadfast in one's purpose, to inquire earnestly, and to reflect on what is at hand—*ren* consists in these" (*Analects* 16.6). Cheng Yi, the Song Neo-Confucian, points out that to reflect on things at hand *(jinsi)* is "to extend on the basis of similarity in kind." On this conception, Zhu Xi incisively remarked:

> This is well said. We must not skip over steps and aim too far. We must only proceed from what we understand in what is near to us and move from there. For instance, if one is thoroughly familiar with doing one thing, he can, on the basis of this extend his skill to doing another. It is the same with knowledge.... For instance, if one understands how to be affectionate to his parents, he will extend this feeling, on the basis of similarity in kind, to being humane *(ren)* to all people, for being humane to people and being affectionate to parents are similar in kind. When he understands how to be humane to people, he will extend this feeling, on the basis of similarity in kind, to loving all things, for being humane to people and loving all things are similar in kind.[9]

Thus, given a commitment to *ren*, the agent engages in this sort of moral reflection in extending his thoughts and feelings on the basis of similarity of status in an occurrent situation.[10] Here, the agent is not deducing consequences from a moral rule or principle but deciding whether or not such a rule or principle is relevant in the light of the ideal of *ren*. What one ought to do is a matter of one's appreciation of the concrete import of *ren*. In any case, one can err or fail to realize *ren* in a particular situation. Put in another way, my analogizing of status may fail to realize *ren*, that is, in giving rise to undesirable consequences. And this failure may be experienced as a shame emotion, but significantly, such an experience is an occasion or opportunity to reexamine

---

8. This citation owes to Chan's incisive commentary in *Analects* 2.12.
9. Wing-tsit Chan, trans., *Reflections on Things at Hand: The Neo-Confucian Anthology Compiled by Chu Hsi and Lü Tsu-ch'ien* (New York: Columbia University Press, 1967), 94.
10. For an extensive discussion of this notion of moral reflection, see my *The Unity of Knowledge and Action: A Study in Wang Yang-ming's Moral Psychology* (Honolulu: University of Hawaii Press, 1982), chap. 3.

one's decision and conduct in the light of *ren*.[11] In this way, the agent can and must rectify himself. As it is said in *The Doctrine of the Mean*, "In archery we have something resembling the way of the superior man. When the archer misses the center of the target, he turns around and seeks for the cause of failure within himself."[12] Moreover, reflection on things at hand does not preclude consideration of long-range consequences of one's contemplated actions. As Confucius reminds his pupils: "If a man neglects to consider what is distant, he will find troubles with what is near at hand" (*Analects* 15.11). The important thing to attend to is the current problem to be settled with a view to realizing *ren*. Consideration of distant consequences is a component of moral reflection, but such a consideration should not be regarded as a decisive solution to all future problematic situations. Every situation or human affair has, as it were, an integrity of its own, to be met as a distinct or individual situation, though this does not preclude an attention to its similarity with other situations, particularly the similarity of personal status which is the basis of our analogizing activity in moral reflection.

A focus on the particular occasion and judgment in moral reflection, however, is not totally without any methodic guide. For Confucius, there is a "method" for realizing *ren* expressed in *zhong* and *shu*, which can be rendered as conscientiousness and regard for others, much reminiscent of the Christian "golden rule" (*Analects* 4.15). *Zhong* expresses loyalty to and conscientious regard for the moral standard or the ideal of *ren*, i.e., an attitude of sincerity and seriousness in one's commitment to *ren*; *shu* more especially pertains to other-regarding conduct. A commitment to *ren* is a commitment to realizing *ren* in the personal relations between oneself and another. In other words, it is an adoption of an attitude of moral regard. *Shu* may be said to be "the golden rule" that governs the exemplification of the *ren* attitude, i.e., "what I do not want *(yu)* others to do to me, I do not want to do to them" (*Analects* 5.11). Alternatively expressed: "what I do not desire *(yu)*, I ought not do to another" (*Analects* 12.2). In both formulations, what is crucial is the notion of *yu* or desire.

It is misleading to say that *shu* concerns the nature of desire in the ordinary sense, for it has more to do with the manner of satisfaction than with the nature of occurrent desires. A plausible explication of *shu* thus requires a distinction between first-order and second-order desires, which may be explained in this way: "Someone has a desire of the second-order either when he wants simply to have a certain desire or

11. See my "Ethical Significance of Shame: Insights of Aristotle and Xunzi," *Philosophy East and West* 53, no. 2 (2003), reprinted in this volume as Essay 8.
12. Chan, *Source Book*, 102.

when he wants a certain desire to be his will." This presupposes a capacity of reflective self-evaluation.[13] In this sense, *shu* has to do primarily with second-order rather than first-order desires. *Zhong* and *shu* may be said to be a method of reflection on first-order desires, for an assessment of their appropriateness in the context of human relations. To pay heed to *shu* is to deal earnestly with the question: "Do I want my present desire to be satisfied as I want analogous desires of others to be satisfied in a way that comports with *ren*?" The wanting here is a second-order desire. Thus, a reflection on the character of one's first-order desires has consequences for the moral character of one's acts. *Shu* as moral regard has a practical import only when it becomes a moral desire of the second-order, i.e., a desire to pay heed to others' desires in light of one's second-order desire to realize *ren*.

It must be admitted that *shu* can also be construed as a concern for others in terms of personal standards. Following Marcus Singer, one may regard *shu* as functionally equivalent to the Golden Rule. Negatively expressed: "Do not do to others as you would not expect them to do to you," or positively, "Do unto others as you would have them do unto you."[14] Our interpretation of *shu* as pertaining to second-order desire is compatible with this general formulation of the Golden Rule. For at issue is the question of one's willingness or desire to be treated in a certain way rather than the content of first-order desires. The issue has to do with the standard governing the satisfaction of one's first-order desires. What I morally want to do is to subject my present desires to assessment by the standard that I adopt as a matter of commitment. For a Confucian, to be a man of *ren* is to engage in reflection, which brings the ideal of *ren* to bear in actual conduct, and this obviously implies a desire or willingness to make others' desires a relevant consideration in light of *ren*.

To pay heed to *shu* is to have an other-regarding attitude. Coupled with *zhong*, or one's own sincere commitment to *ren*, such an other-regarding attitude is an aspect of self-regard, i.e., a regard for one's own character and moral condition. According to Confucius, "a man of *ren* desiring to establish his own character, also establishes the character of others, and desiring to be prominent himself, also helps others to be prominent. To be able to judge others by what is near to ourselves may be called the method of realizing *ren*" (*Analects* 6.28*). In this way, the

---

13. Harry Frankfurt, "Freedom of the Will and the Concept of Person," *Journal of Philosophy* 68, no. 1 (1971): 10. For a similar distinction implicit in Xunzi, see my "Dimensions of *Li* (Propriety)," 380–81.

14. Singer, "Defense of the Golden Rule," in *Morals and Values*, ed. Marcus Singer (New York: Charles Scribner's Sons, 1977), 122.

moral agent's own conduct serves as a measure or standard for others. But this is possible because his own character is achieved by way of embracing others as an integral component of his own moral development. *Shu* as extensive concern for others is thus a component of one's preoccupation with moral attainment or moral condition on the whole. My extensive concern for others is a concern for their *moral being* or condition on the whole. Whether or not another person accepts this concern is not a relevant issue, nor is the reciprocal regard of another person important to my own moral development. In Confucian language, the acceptance and reciprocation of others is a matter of fate *(ming)*. So long as my other-regarding desire and conduct is exemplified in my own life, I have preserved my moral integrity. In establishing or developing my own moral character in light of *ren*, I am also engaged in establishing or developing others' moral character, not in the sense of directly urging others to do so nor of asserting myself to be a moral paradigm, but in the sense that my own case serves as an embodiment of the possibility and actuating import of *ren*-realization. In this way I indirectly contribute to the development of others' moral character. When *zhong* and *shu* are construed as a practical rule of conduct, it is a *procedural* rather than a *substantive* guide to *ren*-realization.

Given a commitment to *ren* and the procedural guide of *zhong* and *shu*, extensive concern for others as rooted in the analogizing of status is an extension of direct personal relationships. A direct personal relationship consists of two features: (1) an acknowledgment of reciprocal duties or obligations; (2) a display of those obligations in conduct imbued with affection.[15] What makes a relationship personal rather than impersonal is the presence of the affective component. In Confucian ethics, particularly in the Mencian tradition, emphasis on the role of *xin* brings out more clearly this aspect of extending moral concern. *Xin* can be rendered as mind and heart, i.e., as embracing both the cognitive and affective components of personal relationship. And since such a relationship can only be sustained by the desire and effort of the persons involved in conduct that displays mutual care and concern, the conative component is also present. The notion of *xin* is thus important in depicting, in the ideal sense, what it is to be a moral agent or a man of *ren*.[16] Notably, in terms of *shu*, extending personal relationship is ex-

---

15. For an incisive discussion of this distinction, see John Macmurray, *Persons in Relation* (London: Farber and Farber, 1961). For Confucian ethics in particular, see my "*Li* and Moral Justification," 1–16, or Appendix 1 of Essay 2.

16. For more discussion of *xin*, see my "*Xin* and Moral Failure: Notes on an Aspect of Mencius's Moral Psychology," in *Mencius: Contexts and Interpretations*, ed. Alan K. L. Chan (Honolulu: University of Hawaii Press, 2002), incorporated in this volume as Essay 15.

tending *xin* in terms of the second-order desire to share both one's moral outlook and affection. The character *shu* does suggest this view.[17] It is composed of two characters, *ru* meaning similar, and *xin* meaning mind and heart. This suggests that extending a personal relationship involves crucially the sharing of similar mind and heart. Imagination in the place of another who is affected by one's conduct is naturally involved, but such a sympathetic imagination assumes that the other, who is outside the ambience of one's personal relation, can share the same commitment and value the affection that sustains such a commitment.

Extending one's personal relationship is a *valuing* process in the sense of extending shared concern with the intrinsic value of the ideal of *ren* and the affection that this ideal entails. This is not merely an intellectual, but also a continuing practical task. A morally concerned and responsible agent in his dealing with others may not succeed in extending his personal relationships. Apart from failure in reciprocal acknowledgment and conduct, one may also experience dislike of others' defective character and misconduct. In this way, disliking people can be seen to be compatible with extensive concern for their moral well-being. In the words of Confucius, "only a man of *ren* is capable of liking and disliking people" in the sense of liking their good and disliking their bad conduct. However, "if a person has the will (or firm determination) to become a man of *ren*, to that extent, he can be free from dislike on account of his misconduct" (*Analects* 4.3).

To the extent that another person falls outside the ambience of a moral agent's personal relationships, he can be an eligible partner in such a relationship. Even in cases of failure, extensive concern for others remains a concern for their moral condition and development. A personal relationship in this way, though self-contained within its ambience, is always *open* to anyone who has the desire and the will to enter such a relation. Ideally, the human community is a community of personal relationships. The task of realizing *ren* is the task of creating such a community. Whether or not such a vision of the unity and harmony of persons in a community can be realized is a question that addresses a more detailed consideration of the complex factors involved in the extensive moral concern and its implications for dealing with recurrent problems in human intercourse. From the agent's point of view, the important factors are these: (1) a proper conception of the current situation or matter at hand, (2) the current capacity of the agent in actualizing the vision of *ren*, (3) the acknowledgment and acceptance of others

---

17. The following remarks are indebted to Liang, *History of Chinese Political Thought*, 39.

regarding one's own extensive concern, (4) the liability to erroneous judgment and decision to respond appropriately to what the situation requires, (5) the freedom from the "paralysis" or weakness of will, (6) the relevance of conventional moral requirements, (7) the needs and desires of other people as affected by one's own moral decision, (8) the possibility of conflict between moral requirements, (9) the element of *ming* ("fate"), i.e., the situation may be such that it is beyond one's ability to change, even if one tries, and lastly (10) willingness to assume the burden of response to the challenge of reasonable justification of one's decision and actions.[18] All such factors require a plausible construction of a Confucian theory of moral psychology.[19] From the interpersonal point of view, a just treatment of relevant factors inevitably involves an excursion into social philosophy that goes beyond the scope of the present essay. But we can get a picture of such a community from the Confucian classic *Liji (Book of Rites)* in the following:

When the great *Dao* (Way) prevails, all the people of the world will work in the light of public spirit *(gong)*. The men of talents, virtues, and ability will be selected, and faithfulness will be the constant practice and harmony the constant objective of self-cultivation. Consequently, mankind will not only have their parents and care only for their children. All the elderly will be provided for and all the young will be employed in work. Commiseration will be expressed toward the widows and the widowers, the orphans and the children, the disabled and the sick in such wise that all are properly cared for. Men have their work and women their homes. . . . In this way, selfish scheming will be repressed and find no room for expansion, and thievery and disorder will not appear. Therefore, the gates of the houses are never closed. This state is called *datong* (the grand unity and harmony).[20]

This vision of human community as extensive moral concern has its primary locus and focus in personal relationships, which project an expansive horizon for embracing the whole of humanity. This vision of the human community, I believe, is a fair representation of the concrete possibility and significance of the Confucian ideal of *ren*. However, Con-

18. For the last factor, see my "Reasonable Action and Confucian Argumentation" and "Uses of Dialogues and Moral Understanding," *Journal of Chinese Philosophy* 1, no. 1 (1973), and 2, no. 2 (1975); *Ethical Argumentation*, chaps. 1–2.

19. For some efforts on this topic, see Cua, *The Unity of Knowledge and Action;* and "*Xin* and Moral Failure" and "Ethical Significance of Shame," incorporated in this volume as Essays 15 and 8, respectively.

20. This is my own rendering of the passage from *Liji* (The Record of Rites), which consists of emendations of Legge's and L. T. Chen's translation of Liang's *History of Chinese Political Theory*. See James Legge, trans., *The Li Ki or Collection of Treatises on the Rules of Propriety or Ceremonial Usages* [1885], 2 vols. in the series The Sacred Books of the East, ed. Max Müller (Delhi: Motilal Banarsidass, 1966). The original Chinese edition I used is Wang Meng'ou's *Liji jinzhu jinyi*, 2 vols. (Taipei: Shangwu, 1977).

fucians today will want to modify the vision to embrace a recognition of the equality of men and women, in terms both of ability and opportunity to achieve their aspirations, consequently, a recognition of the integrity of individual styles of life as harmonious polymorphous actualization of the vision of *ren* as an ideal of human community. Ultimately, the question of *ren*-realization depends on the committed agent's effort and performance in expanding the ambience of personal relationships. We do not know whether all human beings are willing and capable of lending their hands in actualizing the vision, but a Confucian remains firm in his faith in the vision. As Confucius once said: "It is man that can make the Way *(dao)* great, and not the Way that can make man great" (*Analects* 15.28).[21]

21. Earlier versions of this paper were presented at meetings of the International Society for Metaphysics, King's College, London, on July 21, 1980, and the joint panel of the Society for the Advancement of American Philosophy and the International Society for Chinese Philosophy in Baltimore, Maryland, on December 29, 1982. I am indebted to Dan Dahlstrom for valuable suggestions in preparing the final version for publication.

Essay 12

ETHICAL SIGNIFICANCE OF THOMÉ H. FANG'S PHILOSOPHY

In *The Chinese View of Life,* Thomé H. Fang (Fang Dongmei) presents a highly original thesis on the unitary spirit of Chinese morality and moral thought.[1] A historian or textual scholar will probably find Fang's exposition unpersuasive, but a philosopher sympathetic with hermeneutical method may find Fang's thesis a promising experiment in creative hermeneutics, or in the familiar language of the *Yijing,* a deployment of *shengsheng zhi li,* i.e., an exhibition of the principle of creative vitality in philosophical reconstruction. However, from the analytical point of view, Fang's thesis is interesting mainly in suggesting an integrative approach to classical Chinese philosophy. While Fang, like many contemporary Chinese scholars, has not been impressed with the contributions of analytic philosophy, I believe that he would have endorsed a method combining hermeneutical insights with relatively clear and deep analysis, especially of the principles of the value-centered ontology in primordial Confucianism. In one of his addresses on Chinese philosophy, his complaint against analytic method has less to do with the method *per se* than with the tendency of the practitioners of the method toward aspect-obsession, that is, the tendency to engage in "superficial, partial" rather than "penetrative, exhaustive analysis."[2] In the case of metaethics, because of the influence of the scientific attitude of value-neutrality, there is an evident neglect of the genuine spirit of morality. According to Fang, what we have instead is a play with ethical words without regard to the value implicit in their intelligible uses.[3] Later, I shall say more about the nature of Fang's dissatisfaction with analytic method.

---

1. Thomé H. Fang, *The Chinese View of Life: The Philosophy of Comprehensive Harmony* (Taipei: Linking, 1980), chap. V.
2. See Fang, *Dongmei xiansheng yuanjiang ji* (Taipei: Liming, 1980), 56.
3. Fang, *Yuanshi Rujia Daojia zhexue* (Taipei: Liming, 1983), 164.

Fang's thesis on the unity of the spirit of Chinese morality and moral thought, to my knowledge, has not been subjected to systematic analysis. For this reason, we confront a difficulty in interpretation and evaluation. It is puzzling to me that despite his critique of a lack of logical acumen among most Song Confucians, with respect to, say, their careless use of *ji*, as in such expressions as *xing ji li* and *xin ji li*,[4] he makes no attempt to provide a holistic or penetrative analysis. In its place we have a general judgment: "As a matter of fact, the Neo-Confucians in the Sung [Song] dynasty were weak in logic; they often, if not always, committed a logical fallacy by saying A is B, thereby to express the analytic identity between two entities."[5] It is more plausible to construe the Neo-Confucian uses of *ji* as quasi-identity expressions, as related attempts to amplify the Confucian vision of the unity and harmony of man and nature *(tianren heyi)*, than as literary identities that offend the logical canon governing the uses of analytic distinctions. At any rate, in the case of such widespread use of *ji* in Wang Yang-ming, one can propose an interpretation consistent with Fang's emphasis on holistic or integrative analysis.[6]

Let me now focus on Fang's thesis on the unitary spirit of Chinese morality and moral theory as a thesis in axiological or ethical metaphysics. I use the term ethical metaphysics in order to distinguish it from Mou Zongsan's notion of a moral metaphysics, a notion invented as a critical contrast with Kant's notion of a metaphysics of morals. Unlike Kant's notion, which takes morality as a subject matter of metaphysics, Mou considers moral metaphysics (inclusive of ontology and cosmology) a subject matter to be approached through a conception of human moral nature.[7] Whitehead and Bergson, on the other hand, more markedly inspire Fang's ethical metaphysics, in his conception of organicism and flux in nature. It is quite evident, however, that both Fang and Mou are concerned with the basic issue of the metaphysical foundation of Chinese morality and moral theory. Unlike Mou, Fang is explicit on this issue, construed as one concerning the coherent inheritance of the insights of classical Confucianism, Daoism, and Mohism. The inclusion of Mohism is somewhat problematic, since we have no

4. Fang's renderings are "Nature is Reason" and "Mind is Reason." See *Chinese Philosophy: Its Spirit and Its Development* (Taipei: Linking, 1981), 397.

5. Ibid., 396–97.

6. For such an attempt, see A. S. Cua, *The Unity of Knowledge and Action: A Study in Wang Yang-ming's Moral Psychology* (Honolulu: University of Hawaii Press, 1982), 79–91.

7. See Mou Zongsan, *Xinti yu xingti* (Taipei: Zhengzhong, 1973), vol. 1, 136–40. For an assessment of Mou's term with a different interpretation, see my "Reflections on Moral Theory and Understanding Moral Traditions," in *Interpreting Across Boundaries: New Essays in Comparative Philosophy,* ed. Gerald James Larson and Eliot Deutsch (Princeton, N.J.: Princeton University Press, 1988).

such discussion in Fang's *Chinese Philosophy: Its Spirit and Its Development.* Even in the earlier *The Chinese View of Life,* we find few references to Mozi or to the later Mohists. At any rate, the issue, while not a live one in contemporary Western moral philosophy, is germane to understanding some recent works. I have in mind, for example, Paul Weiss's work entitled *Toward a Perfected State.*[8] Much of this work, in my view, presupposes a solution to the problem of axiological or ethical metaphysics.[9]

For understanding the metaphysical foundation of Chinese moral life and thought, Fang reminds us that we must have a grasp of the Chinese vision of the universe, not as a material and mechanical process, "but as a realm of vital impetus, . . . an all-pervasive and all-comprehensive concurrence of universal life, an appreciation of the good as inherent in our original endowment; and more importantly, an awareness that the illuminant minds of men are always accessible to any value that has been thrust in and are capable of developing it into other values of a higher type through their own creative efforts." Fang continues,

> Man and the Cosmos are harmoniously interrelated, individual human beings among themselves are systematically interlocked, and men and other things are set in well-balanced order: all of these tend to converge on one pivotal point, namely, the creation of value. . . . The Universe represents for us the perpetual augmentation of value. The universe and the human life are the concurrent processes of creative values.[10]

This passage offers a succinct statement on the metaphysical foundation of morality. In effect, it is Fang's interpretation of the Confucian vision of the unity and harmony of man and nature *(tianren heyi).* The statement is as profound as it is difficult to elaborate in a systematic way. In *The Chinese View of Life,* it is one of Fang's alternative expressions of his philosophy of comprehensive harmony, or as I would like to call it, a statement of the nature of an axiological metaphysics.[11] With respect to

---

8. Paul Weiss, *Toward a Perfected State* (Albany: State University of New York Press, 1986).

9. For a critical study of Weiss's book, see my "The Structure of Social Complexes," *Review of Metaphysics* 41, no. 2 (1987).

10. Fang, *The Chinese View of Life,* 95–96.

11. "The essential points pertaining to different systems of Chinese philosophy are these: (1) The world is not taken for what it is in natural regard; it waits to be transmuted into a moral universe for the Confucians, and especially for the Neo-Confucians, into an aesthetic realm for the Taoists, and into a religious domain for the Buddhists. All of these differentiating realms or domains ultimately go into the make-up of the integral universe or the world as a whole which, philosophically considered, should be a *transfigured* world. The task of Chinese metaphysics is an analysis of facts issuing in an understanding of destiny. The transfigured world is nothing less than a teleological system of axiological importance. (2) The human individual is a very complicated concept; its richness of meaning is not exhausted by a simplified unitary procedure of approach" (Fang, *Chinese Philosophy,* 35).

Chinese morality, it is a statement of the background vision that renders intelligible her thought and practice. In what follows, I shall inquire into the possibility of systematic elaboration of this vision.

For this purpose, we are fortunate to have two complementary guides in Fang's *Chinese Philosophy* and *The Chinese View of Life*. In the former, we find an approach in terms of his discussion of three ostensibly common features among primordial Confucianism, primordial Daoism, and Mahayana Buddhism, namely, (1) the doctrine of pervasive unity, (2) the doctrine of *dao*, and (3) the exaltation of the individual, along with an emphasis on a conception of the human individual in terms of observed actualities and idealized possibilities.[12] The doctrine of pervasive unity, according to Fang, is implicit in Confucius's saying that the *Dao* inherent in me is that of an all-pervading unity (*Lunyu*, 15.2). And significantly, in Confucianism this theme is diversified into the *dao* of Heaven *(tian zhi dao)*, the *dao* of the Earth *(di zhi dao)*, and the *dao* of man *(ren zhi dao)*, reminiscent of Xunzi's distinction, though it is the *dao* of man that occupies the center of Xunzi's ethical inquiry.[13] For my present purposes, it is on the *dao* of man that I shall focus, with a reminder, of course, of its interplay with the *dao* of Heaven and Earth. With the supposition that it is the *dao* of man that pervades Confucian thought, we can appreciate the different approaches to *dao* in Daoism and Chinese Buddhism as different yet complementary versions of the holistic character of the Confucian *dao*, made explicit in Xunzi and in Song-Ming Confucianism.

While Fang seems to reject this interpretation, it is quite consistent with his view that Confucianism is a constructive philosophy of comprehensive harmony invested with creative energies of life.[14] Indeed, the philosophy of comprehensive harmony expounded in Fang's *The Chinese View of Life* can hardly be rendered intelligible without such a presupposition. This means that the principal insights of primordial Daoism and Chinese Buddhism can be considered eligible candidates for absorption and integration within the framework of primordial Confucianism. The primary focus on the *dao* of man provides a criterion for determining the ethical contributions of classical Daoism and Chinese Buddhism, i.e., for testing their concrete significance for human life, and for assessing the claim that they may be considered different versions of *dao*. In this line of thinking, we may even include Mohism, as suggested by Fang's remark that Confucianism, Daoism, and Mohism are different versions of his philosophy of comprehensive harmony.[15] If

12. Ibid., 23–27.
13. Li Disheng, *Xunzi jishi* (Taipei: Xuesheng, 1979), Book 8, *Ruxiao pian*.
14. *Chinese Philosophy*, 33.   15. *The Chinese View of Life*, 115.

I am not far from the mark, the exaltation of the individual—Fang's third common feature—simply brings out the locus and point of departure for pursuing the realization of the *dao* of man, the thread *(kuan)* that runs through Confucius's teachings.

However, Fang's approach of ascribing three common features to major Chinese philosophical traditions is problematic. In the first place, particularly in light of Fang's devaluation of the contributions of Neo-Confucianism, with the possible exception of Wang Yangming's thought, it is difficult to lay out in a clear and convincing manner the view that these ways of thinking can be explicated in a co-equal and interdependent fashion without espousing in some sense the primacy of one over the other two. My own inclination to assign a preeminent status to classical Confucianism is probably not subject to the same critique. For however we conceive *dao*, for the Confucian, any pretended version must have a concrete significance for changing human life, a cash-value, so to speak, in terms of its relevance to actual thought and practice within a moral community. For the Confucian, while saying this is not altogether informative, it is an important truism, a reminder that the exaltation of the human individual is something to be done only within the setting of a moral community.[16] Any attempt to show the concrete significance of *dao* must pay heed to actual, living humans as members of a community of persons. The transformation of human actualities into idealized possibilities depends largely on the respect accorded to each human actuality as having potentialities for ideal transformation. Moreover, there is also the need to accept human limitations, particularly in relation to the constraints imposed by natural order. However we conceive this natural order, the very notion of transforming actual humanity into idealized possibility depends, in part but in a crucial way, on acknowledging the constraints of nature upon human thought and action.

Let me turn to another guide in *The Chinese View of Life*, a guide that is complementary to the one in *Chinese Philosophy*, and to a large extent adopted in the latter with little additional elaboration. I have in mind the chapter on cosmology. Before proceeding to this guide, let me offer a preface and also record my admiration upon reading Fang's brilliant and incisive use of what appears as a perplexing distinction—the *ti-yong*

---

16. For further discussion, see my "Confucian Vision and the Human Community," *Journal of Chinese Philosophy* 11, no. 3 (1984), incorporated in this volume as Essay 11. See also my "Between Commitment and Realization: Wang Yang-ming's Vision of the Universe as a Moral Community," *Philosophy East and West* 43, no. 4 (1993), or *Moral Vision and Tradition: Essays in Chinese Ethics* (Washington, D.C.: The Catholic University of America Press, 1998), Essay 9.

distinction, which is commonly rendered as substance and function.[17] At issue for Fang is the plausible articulation of the essential features of Chinese cosmology. Says Fang, "The Universe ... is a kind of well-balanced and harmonious system which is materially vacuous but spiritually opulent and unobstructed. Its physical form may be limited in extent, but its ideal function is infinite in essence." Here, Fang points out, we have a characterization of Chinese cosmology as a conception of "finite substance, which is, withal, a conception of infinite function."[18]

Fang urges us to think of "a lecture-hall as a vast expanse of hollow space scented with pure air," of a Chinese poem that contains "the line a silent lover before you is most charming," of Laozi's comparison of cosmic vacuity *(xu)* to bellows: "It is hollow, yet it loses not its power; being active, it sends forth air all the more" *(Daodejing,* chap. 5).[19] And we may add Zhuangzi's notion of the usefulness of the useless *(wuyong zhi yong).*[20] "The whole mystery lies in the attempt to transform what is substantially solid, to annul what is physically impenetrable and to realize what is ideally vacuous in spiritual function." For Fang, the possibility of such a transmutation lies in keeping our attention on the pivot of *Tao [Dao],* in "intending to be thoroughly impartial and sympathetic to the rest of the universe. And, therefore, we are in a moral position to enable all things in the universe to be in a state of essential relativity and mutual sympathy, acquiescing in the feeling that there is a sense of infinite joy and bliss permeating every form of existence."[21] Indeed in Chinese wisdom, the universe has attributes of both morality and art; it is "fundamentally the realm of value." For this reason, we can properly characterize Chinese cosmology as "essentially a value-centric philosophy."[22]

Fang goes on, in a more perspicuous way, to offer a set of principles, which is more a project for systematic exposition than a detailed explication of his theory of axiological or ethical metaphysics. My difficulty in embracing this project *in toto,* however, does not affect my appreciation of his insightful use of the *ti-yong* distinction, for so often Chinese philosophical distinctions such as *tiyong, liqi,* or *jinquan* have caused a great deal of Western misunderstanding owing to the predominant ten-

17. For further discussion, see my "On the Ethical Significance of *Ti-Yong* Distinction," *Journal of Chinese Philosophy* 29, no. 2 (2002): 163–70.
18. *The Chinese View of Life,* 35.
19. Ibid., 37–38.
20. Zhuangzi, *Renjian shi.* Burton Watson, trans., *The Complete Works of Chuang Tzu [Zhuangzi]* (New York: Columbia University Press, 1968), 63.
21. *The Chinese View of Life,* 38. My edition contains a misprint: "annual" instead of "annul."
22. Ibid., 40 and 43.

dency in the West toward bifurcation, as Fang repeatedly stresses. Perhaps, another reason lies in the traditional Western tendency to accept the logic of genus and species as having a fixed categorial reference and use independent of the context of discourse. So often, useful distinctions, e.g., mind and body, means and end, action and consequences, are readily transformed into dichotomies, thus precluding a serious inquiry into their interconnection. Instead, external relation is more the typical concern among Western philosophers, with Whitehead and Dewey as notable exceptions. Regardless of the truth inherent in this observation about Western philosophy in general, most useful philosophical distinctions among concepts, for Chinese philosophers, are contextual rather than categorial. This is unsurprising given the shared, common vision of the unity and harmony of man and nature *(tianren heyi)*, which encourages the exploration and establishment of interconnection rather than mere external connection. As Fang forcefully points out in his introductory lecture on primordial Confucianism and primordial Taoism:

> From her external appearance, Chinese thought seems to be defective, for it is quite different from recent Western philosophy's stress on analytic method. Actually, Chinese philosophy is not devoid of such an emphasis. For example, the School of Names and later Mohism have attained a high degree of development. But for later Chinese, to speak of analysis, it must be deep and thoroughgoing. Fragmentary analysis is faulty; it seizes on one or another aspect of the subject matter, resulting in the construction of one-sided views, and thus is incapable of penetrating into the holistic character *(quanti)* of the meaning of the universe and human life.... It is only the use of deep and thoroughgoing analysis that can assist us, through our reflective intuition, in grasping the holistic meaning, value, and reality of the universe. Only in such an inquiry can a philosophy be entitled the great and profound system of thought.[23]

These remarks on analysis provide us a clue to a systematic way of understanding Fang's set of principles for articulating his vision of comprehensive harmony. Fang lists and briefly explains six principles, earlier given in a Chinese article entitled "Three Types of Philosophic Wisdom *(Zhexue sanhui)*":[24]

P1. Life *(sheng zhi li)*.

P2. Love *(ai zhi li)*.

P3. Primordial unity *(yuanshi zhi tongyi li)*.

P4. Creative advance *(huayu zhi li)*.

---

23. *Yuanshi Rujia Daojia zhexue*, 19. My translation.
24. See Fang, *Shengsheng zhi de* (Taipei: Li-ming, 1982). 25. Ibid., 109.

P5. Equilibrium and harmony *(zhonghe zhi li)*.
P6. Extensive connection *(pangtong zhi li)*.

In *The Chinese View of Life*, these principles are proffered as a compendious statement. Only four principles are deemed relevant in his *Chinese Philosophy*. In his exposition of the second phase of primordial Confucianism for instance, P2 and P5 are ignored for the reason that he is mainly concerned with their bearing upon the philosophy of change *[Yijing]*. Notably, Fang reminds us that these principles are interrelated, for "from the viewpoint of organicism, no set of fundamental principles formulated in a system of metaphysics can be cut and thrust into an airtight compartment without interpenetration."[25] The exposition of the four principles quotes extensively from *The Chinese View of Life*. For a moral philosopher, this is quite surprising in view of Fang's recurrent emphasis on the value-centric character of Chinese ontology and metaphysics. The omission of P2 and P5 (principle of love and principle of equilibrium and harmony), in effect, relegates the Confucian ethical concern to a position subordinate to the metaphysical one.

P3 and P4 (primordial unity and creative advance) are not really two distinct principles of co-equal status, for the former, conceived as the principle of universal flux, already involves the idea of one special characteristic of emergent novelty, except that the principle of creative advance suggests progress toward the development and realization of *dao*. But this suggestion is misleading, for as Fang is wont to stress, creative novelties cannot always be regarded as emergent, assuming a character completely divested of its association with the source of emergence. To use Stephen Pepper's term, emergent novelties crucially depend on intrusive novelties, for how else can we identify the former without attending to the latter, novelties that have a historical past?[26] Process is not always progress or spontaneous exhibition of creative advance.

For developing a more viable conception based on Fang's insights, I suggest that we recast his concern with principles in a different set, incorporating some of his principles. Before I give such a list, I must warn you of its provisional character. In assembling my list, I have discarded more than two different versions. The present one represents nothing more than a proposal for further discussion and not a final formulation. For the present, the principles are offered as a point of departure for further inquiry, as an initial inkling toward a satisfactory solution to the current issue on the metaphysical foundation of Chinese morality.

26. For this distinction between intrusive and emergent novelties, see S. C. Pepper, *World Hypotheses* (Berkeley and Los Angeles: University of California Press, 1948), 256–57.
27. See my *Moral Vision and Tradition*, Essays 2, 4, 5, and 7.

The sketch includes some of Fang's principles and acknowledges one of his insights on Zhuangzi's notion of *qi-wu*, which he marvelously renders as "leveling up all things." And like Fang, I drop out the principle of love and the principle of equilibrium and harmony, not because of my desire to subordinate the ethical to the metaphysical perspective, but because of a presumption that these principles are best regarded as alternative, complementary expressions of the Confucian *dao*, which is basically an ethical vision.[27] In my view, at issue in providing a metaphysics as the foundation of morality or moral theory is the question of the employment of metaphysical inquiry in elucidating an ethical vision.[28] This assumption is indubitably open to challenge. However, it is an assumption implicit in Fang's characterization of Chinese cosmology. Recall his view that for the Chinese, the universe has the attributes of morality and art. Again, like Fang, I take it as unproblematic to think of this universe as a realm of flux, a concurrence of universal life. Against these background assumptions, here is my list of principles:

P1. Unceasing creative dynamics and interplay.

P2. Essential relativity and value transcendence.

P3. Extensive connection.

P4. Rectification.

P5. Reconciliation.

The limitation of both space and time, not to say of my present uncertainty in exposition, allows me only a few brief explanations. An alternative expression of P1 is Fang's *sheng zhi li*, which is a collapse of *sheng-sheng zhi li* in the *Yijing*. In one of his lectures, Fang thinks that this expression means "unceasing, continuous creativity."[29] I take this principle also as implicit in Xunzi's notion of using *yi* (sense of rightness) to cope with changing circumstances *(yiyi bianying)*.[30] I have added to Fang's principle of life a notion of interplay of the creative activities of different entities, for their activities do affect one another. Here we have an articulate aspect of Confucian ethical vision. For P2, the principle of essential relativity and transcendence, is a fundamental insight of Zhuangzi,[31] and involves an acknowledgment of the value perspective of

28. See my *The Unity of Knowledge and Action*, chap. 4; and *Moral Vision and Tradition*, Essay 7.

29. Fang, *Dongmei xiansheng yuanjiang ji*, 182.

30. See Xunzi, *Bugou pian* and *Zhishi pian*. For its significance in ethical justification, see my *Ethical Argumentation: A Study in Hsün Tzu's Moral Epistemology* (Honolulu: University of Hawaii Press, 1985), esp. 61–87.

31. See *Chinese Philosophy*, chap. 5, and my "Forgetting Morality: Reflections on a Theme in *Chuang Tzu*," *Journal of Chinese Philosophy* 4, no. 4 (1977), or *Moral Vision and*

each entity and yet at the same time makes explicit the nature of the ethical vision as an object of inspiration and aspiration toward the transcendence of such limited perspectives. Value-transcendence is what one can learn from Zhuangzi's reminder that it is *ming* (clarity, enlightenment) that enables us to level things up *(qi-wu)*.

However, such transcendence is possible because of our acceptance of P3, the principle of extensive connection. For it is such an acknowledgment of interconnectedness of all existent things that enables us to appreciate the limitation of individual value-perspectives. In this light, we may observe here that it is this acknowledgment in Chinese ethics that is incompatible with the Western notion of exclusive, atomic individuals, particularly in political liberalism. For the Chinese, the exaltation of the individual is not the exaltation of discrete, atomic individuals. On the contrary, the respect for the integrity of individual persons does not entail exclusiveness, because each is an embodiment of a limited good complementary to other limited goods in the light of the vision of comprehensive harmony. In my view, such a vision is essentially an ideal of ethical excellence. In this manner, P4 and P5 (the principle of rectification and the principle of reconciliation) are needed to articulate the concrete significance of the ideal of ethical excellence.[32]

After all, leveling things up *(qi-wu)* is not a matter of embracing every individual value-perspective, without qualification, with *dao*, the overarching, unifying perspective of ethical excellence. Rather, the appeal to the unifying perspective involves an intercalation of the diversity of individual, limited value-perspectives. Unlike Zhuangzi we do not regard *ming* (clarity, enlightenment) as a self-sufficient state of *dao*-achievement. *Ming*, for us as for Xunzi, is a precondition for rendering sound judgments concerning injustices incurred and values lost in the interplay of humans with limited perspectives. Such judgments, from the point of view of the vision of ethical excellence, must also be concerned, not only with impartial rectification of undesirable states of affairs, but also with restoring the values lost or their functional equivalents.

Value-transcendence thus involves value-restoration and rectification.

Tradition, Essay 3. Cf. Weiss, *Toward a Perfected State,* 353ff.

32. This use of ethical excellence differs from Weiss's. For him, it is a principle rather than an ideal theme. The mediating principles I have formulated for Weiss are quite different, since they have a status peculiar to Weiss's metaphysics. (See my "The Structure of Social Complexes.") For the notion of ideal theme as distinct from that of an ideal norm, see my *Dimensions of Moral Creativity: Paradigms, Principles, and Ideals* (University Park: Pennsylvania State University Press, 1978), chap. 8. For the use of ideal theme in connection with Wang Yang-ming's notion of *ren* or *dao*, see my *The Unity of Knowledge and Action.*

33. For further discussion of principles of intercultural adjudication, see my "Reason-

There are no fixed rules for leveling things up *(qi-wu)*. However, given the actuality of human conflict, the concrete significance of the ideal of ethical excellence, for the Confucian, lies in the possibility of reconciliation. Stated as a principle of reconciliation (P5), it urges individuals in conflict to view their disagreement as a subject for transformation into agreement, rather than as a set of insoluble and essentially contested issues. Moreover, given the omni-possibility of resentment, the principle of reconciliation redirects the attention of the parties in conflict toward the possibility of developing personal relationships where disagreements are deemed a subject for mediation or voluntary arbitration rather than for adjudication. Notably, this focus on the primacy of mediation over adjudication provides a concrete significance to Fang's notion of transforming human actualities into idealized possibilities in the light of his vision of comprehensive harmony.[33]

The foregoing sketch of principles contains brief pointers for further inquiry rather than a final, determinate solution to the difficult problem of the metaphysical foundation of Chinese morality. To forestall misunderstanding, the principles are not intended to have the status of normative principles of conduct. They are offered primarily with a view to elucidating the concrete significance of *dao* as a vision of ethical excellence. They are, so to speak, principles for mediating the ideal and the actual world of humanity. In Confucian ethical theory, the development of normative principles of conduct pertains to a different mode of inquiry.[34] I am confident, however, that such an endeavor will ultimately make use of these mediating principles.[35]

---

able Challenges and Preconditions of Adjudication," in *Tradition and Modernity: East-West Philosophical Perspectives,* ed. Eliot Deutsch (Honolulu: University of Hawaii Press, 1991). More extensive discussion is given in *Moral Vision and Tradition,* Essay 13.

34. For a preliminary discussion of this problem, see my "The Status of Principles in Confucian Ethics," *Journal of Chinese Philosophy* 16 (1989). More extensive discussion is given in *Moral Vision and Tradition,* Essay 13.

35. This paper is a revised version of the one presented at the International Symposium on Thomé H. Fang's Philosophy, Taipei, Taiwan, August 15–18, 1987.

Essay 13

REASON AND PRINCIPLE IN CHINESE PHILOSOPHY

Perhaps the best approach to the Chinese conception of reason is to focus on the concept of *li*, commonly translated as "principle," "pattern," or sometimes "reason." While these translations in context are perhaps the best, explicating the uses of *li* is desirable and instructive for understanding some of the main problems of Chinese philosophy. Because there is no literal English equivalent, one cannot assume that *li* has a single, easily comprehensible use in Chinese discourse. This assumption is especially problematic in appreciating the basic concerns of Confucian ethics. A closer examination of the uses of *li* and "principle" reveals a complexity that cannot be captured by a simple formula. Apart from the question whether *li* and "principle" are functionally equivalent, one may also ask whether *li* in Confucian ethics can be properly considered a context-independent notion in the way that "principle" can. For a contemporary Confucian moral philosopher, Confucian ethics is more plausibly viewed as a form of virtue ethics.[1] Absent an explanation of the uses of *li*, the translation of *li* as "principle" unavoidably leads to such misleading questions as: What are the principles of Chinese or Confucian ethics? If such principles exist, do they serve as premises for the derivation of moral rules? Are Confucian principles universal or relative? While these questions are fundamental in Western moral theory, their importance for Confucian ethics depends on a prior consideration of the status of principles in Confucian ethics.[2]

Difficulties also arise with the translation of *li* as "pattern." Again we need to have some clear answers to such questions as: What sort of pat-

---

1. See my "The Conceptual Framework of Confucian Ethical Thought," *Journal of Chinese Philosophy* 23, no. 2 (1996): 153–74. For a more extensive discussion, see my *Moral Vision and Tradition: Essays in Chinese Ethics* (Washington, D.C.: The Catholic University of America Press, 1998), Essay 13.

2. See my "The Status of Principles in Confucian Ethics," *Journal of Chinese Philosophy* 16, nos. 3–4 (1989): 273–96; or *Moral Vision and Tradition*, Essay 14.

tern? Are these patterns natural or artificial, that is, products of human invention? If they are natural, how do we go about finding them? More important, even if we regard "principle" or "pattern" as an acceptable rendering of *li*, we still need to explore its role in ethical argumentation.[3] Such an inquiry presupposes that we have some understanding of the uses of *li* in Chinese ethical discourse. This essay is a tentative, highly selective treatment of *li*. It is an attempt to provide an ideal explication or constructive interpretation of *li* from the perspective of Confucian moral philosophy. Section 1 deals with the basic uses of *li* as a generic term. Section 2 discusses the function of *li*-binomials and the significance of principled interpretation of some basic notions of Confucianism.

1. BASIC USES OF 'LI'

For pursuing the study of *li*, Tang Junyi's pioneering study is a most valuable guide, particularly for the place of *li* in the history of Chinese thought.[4] Also instructive is Wing-tsit Chan's essay on the conceptual evolution of the Neo-Confucian notion of *li*.[5] As a preliminary, following Xunzi,[6] let us distinguish between *li* as a single term, that is, a single Chinese character or graph *(danming)*, and *li* as a constituent element of a compound term *(jianming)*, say, a binomial term, for example, *wen-li*. For resolving problems of ambiguity and vagueness in single terms, it is a common practice of modern Chinese and Western Sinologists to appeal to relevant binomials. This method of interpretation is widely used by modern Chinese translators/annotators of classical Chinese texts. In section 2, we will say more about this procedure.

Among Pre-Qin Classical Confucian texts, only in *Xunzi* do we find extensive use of *li* as a single term or graph. In this text, we find about 85 occurrences of *li* with different uses. The descriptive use of *li* in the sense of pattern or orderly arrangement may be shown by using a *li*-binomial *wen-li*, as Xunzi sometimes does. Since *wen* pertains to "(cultural) refinement," *wen-li* can properly be rendered as "cultural pattern." Often, this descriptive use of *li* has normative import, that is, *wen-li* has not only *de facto* but also *de jure* status. Chan points out that there

---

3. See my *Ethical Argumentation: A Study in Hsün Tzu's Moral Epistemology* (Honolulu: University of Hawaii Press, 1985), chap. 2.

4. Tang Junyi, *Zhongguo zhexue yuanlun: Daolun pian* [Foundations of Chinese Philosophy: Introductory Volume] (Taipei: Xuesheng, 1978).

5. Wing-tsit Chan, "The Evolution of the Neo-Confucian *Li* as Principle," *Tsing Hua Journal of Chinese Studies*, n.s., 4 (1964): 123–49.

6. Li Disheng, *Xunzi jishi* (Taipei: Xuesheng, 1979), *Zhengming Pian*, Book 22. Unless indicated otherwise, this work is the basis for all references to *Xunzi*, hereafter cited by the title and book number of Xunzi's essay, followed by page numbers.

are also uses of *li* in ancient literature in the sense of "to put in order or distinguish."[7] Since the descriptive use of *li* frequently has an explanatory function, its occurrence is sometimes associated with *gu*, which can be rendered as "reason" or "cause." While the explanatory use of *li* sometimes has normative import, the distinction between its descriptive cum explanatory and normative uses remains philosophically and practically significant. This distinction seems implicit in Zhu Xi's explanation of the meaning of *li:*

> Regarding things in the world, if they exist, then *(ze)* we may say that each must have a reason or cause *(gu)* that accounts for its being what it is *(soyiran zhi gu).* Also, each must have a standard *(ze)* for [determining] what it ought to be *(dangran zhi ze).* This is what is meant by *li.*[8]

The first remark suggests that *li* has an explanatory use and that the reason or cause of a thing's being what it is *(soyiran zhi gu)*, in some sense, is derived from observation or experience. This seems implicit in the first occurrence of *ze* as a conclusion-indicator. In the Neo-Confucianism of the Song and Ming dynasties, however, we do not find any interest in natural causation akin to that of Western philosophy. Xunzi, perhaps the most "rationalistic" among Chinese philosophers, does acknowledge that participants in ethical argumentation must "exhaust the *gu* of things." The *gu* here pertains to reasons for supporting one's practical thesis, say, as a policy of action.[9] Instead of a theoretical conception of causal explanation, we are more likely to find the notion of *ganying* (stimulus or challenge and response).

In the Song Confucian metaphysics, every entity consists of *li* and *qi* (ether, energy, material/vital force). *Li* and *qi* are inseparable. The former is static, the latter dynamic. Thus the preferred explanation of the interaction between things makes use of the notion of *ganying* or "stimulus and response." As A. C. Graham points out, these concepts of *gan* and *ying*

> occupy the same place in Sung [Song] philosophy as causation in the West. . . . If it is assumed that things consist of inert matter, it is natural to think in terms of "effect" which passively allow themselves to be pushed by "causes." But if inert matter is only the essentially active ether *[qi]* in an impure state, this kind of action will only be of minor importance; in the purer ether, when A acts on B, B will not only be moved by it, but will respond actively.[10]

---

7. Chan, "The Evolution of the Neo-Confucian *Li* as Principle."
8. Rongjie Chen (Wing-tsit Chan), "Li," in *Zhongguo zhexue cidian daquan* [Comprehensive Dictionary of Chinese Philosophy], ed. Wei Zhengtong (Taipei: Shuiniu, 1983), 481.
9. See my *Ethical Argumentation*, chap. 1.
10. A. C. Graham, *Two Chinese Philosophers: Ch'eng Ming-tao and Ch'eng Yi-ch'uan* (London: Lund Humphries, 1958), 38.

With the notion of *ganying* in mind, if we render *gu* in Zhu Xi's first remark as "cause," we must employ the notion of practical rather than theoretical causation.[11] From the Confucian perspective, *ganying* conveys the idea of human sensitivity to natural things and events as having a decisive impact *(gan)* on human life. Humans must respond *(ying)* to these things and events by acting in a way that ultimately comports to the Confucian ethical vision or ideal of the unity and harmony of humanity and nature *(tianren heyi)*. Differently put, things and events in nature are challenges to human ingenuity in coping with problems in their lives.[12]

Zhu Xi's second remark that "each must have a standard *(ze)* for [determining] what it ought to be *(dangran zhi ze)*" stresses the normative sense of *li*. *Ze* can also be rendered as "rule" or "law." However, since we do not find any notion of natural law comparable to that of Western philosophy, *ze* is better construed as the standard that determines things as they *should* be.[13] Unlike compliance with rules, one can try to comport with standards according to one's conception of the best thing to do. There are, so to speak, degrees of perfection in individual efforts at attaining the ideal of the good human life.

While the *ze* of each thing is said to be inherent in it, it has ontological import. Nevertheless, if we are right that *ze* in Zhu Xi's first remark is a conclusion-indicator, understanding the *ze* of a thing is an outcome of study and reflection. For elucidation we may consider Zhu Xi's comment on the phrase "the extension of knowledge" in the *Great Learning* [*Daxue*]:

If we wish to extend our knowledge to the utmost, we must investigate exhaustively the *li* of things.... It is only because we have not exhausted the *li* of all things that our knowledge is still incomplete. In the education of the adult, the first step is to instruct the learner, about all things in the world, to proceed from what knowledge he has of *li* [of things], and investigate further until he reaches the limit. After exerting himself in this way for a long time, he will one day achieve a *wide and far-reaching penetration [guantong]*. Consequently, he can apprehend the qualities of things, whether internal or external, the refined or the coarse.[14]

11. R. G. Collingwood, *An Essay on Metaphysics* (Oxford: Clarendon Press, 1962).
12. A. C. Cua, "Practical Causation and Confucian Ethics," *Philosophy East and West* 25, no. 1 (1975): 1–10; incorporated in this volume as Essay 9.
13. Chun Zhun [Ch'en Ch'un], *Beixi xiansheng ziyi xiangjiang* [Neo-Confucian Terms Explained] (Taipei: Guangwen, 1979), 144–45. For English translation, see *Neo-Confucian Terms Explained: (The Pei-hsi tzu-i) by Ch'en Ch'un, 1159–1223* (New York: Columbia University Press, 1986).
14. Wing-tsit Chan, *A Source Book in Chinese Philosophy* (Princeton, N.J.: Princeton University Press, 1963), 89 (emended).

Guantong, rendered by Chan as "wide and far-reaching penetration," is an attainment of comprehensive understanding of things through *qiongli*—the exhaustive investigation of the *li* of things. More important, as a metaphor, *guantong* ("the thread that runs through things") intimates the idea that understanding consists in having an insight into the interconnection of all things. This idea of *guantong* echoes Xunzi's notion of *liguan* or *li* as the thread that runs through things, events, and human affairs. Implicit in the idea of *guantong* is a holistic ideal or unifying perspective.[15] Cheng Yi's famous apothegm *liyi er fenshu*, "*li* is one with diverse manifestations"—an idea he attributed to Zhang Zai's "Western Inscription"—is perhaps a good way of characterizing this Confucian ideal of the good human life.[16] As a component of *liyi er fenshu*, *li* is a generic term. On the other hand, the *li* in our citation from Zhu Xi is a specific term. This use of *li* as a specific term is clear in Zhu Xi's contrast between *dao* (the holistic, unifying ideal) and *li* is evident in a couple of terse sayings: (1) "*dao* is a unifying term *(tongming)*, *li* is [a term referring to its] detail items"; and (2) "*Dao* is a holistic word *(daozi hongda)*, *li* is a word for details *(lizi jingmi)*."[17] As a specific term, *li* has a plurality of uses that may be further specified in particular discursive context. Furthermore, Zhu Xi's remarks suggest that *li* is a generic term functionally equivalent to "reason," which can be contextually specified either as a descriptive/explanatory or normative term. This suggestion has a partial sanction in the modern Chinese notion of *liyu*, meaning "reason," "ground," or "rationale."

Before going further, a caveat is necessary. Because of their fundamental ethical orientation, for the most part Confucian thinkers, with Xunzi as a possible exception, do not clearly distinguish descriptive, explanatory, and normative uses of terms. Terms such as "father" and "son" are commonly used with implicit normative force. Differently put, factual statements made in ethical contexts are generally regarded as invested with moral import. Being a father or a son already implies certain obligations. In the Classical Confucian language of rectification of names, when a son does not live up to his obligations, the "name" *(ming)* of being a son requires ethical correction. Ideally, correction of misconduct must be accompanied by a transformation of the person's

---

15. See my "The Possibility of Ethical Knowledge: Reflections on a Theme in the *Hsün Tzu*," in *Epistemological Issues in Classical Chinese Philosophy*, ed. Hans Lenk and Gregor Paul (Albany: State University of New York Press, 1993), 159–180; incorporated as Essay 6 in this volume.

16. Chan, *Source Book*, 550. For an informative exposition, see Shu-hsien Liu, "*Liyi fenshu*" in *Encyclopedia of Chinese Philosophy*, ed. Antonio S. Cua (New York and London: Routledge, 2003).

17. Zhu Xi, *Zhuzi yulei* (Taipei: Zhengzhong, 1962), Book 6a.

character. In this sense, rectifying names *(zhengming)* is a procedure for rectifying misconduct.

This Confucian view finds a partial affinity with that of Arthur Murphy: The term "brother," in the statement of a ground of obligation, is not practically a noncommittal term. "To be a brother is not just to be a male sibling—it is a privilege, a burden and, whether we like it or not, a commitment."[18] While the doctrine of the exclusive disjunction of facts and values is questioned, the legitimacy of the distinction in appropriate context is acknowledged. In cases where a reasonable Confucian agent is unhappy with the connection of facts and values, he or she may appeal to the distinction. Say that a father makes an unethical demand; the filial son, who is expected to obey his father's wishes, may quite properly disobey. The virtue of filiality does not require unconditional obedience. Xunzi points out that there are circumstances in which a son should follow *yi* (rightness), his sense of what is right, rather than his father's commands, for example, when obedience to parental wishes may harm or disgrace the family, or require bestial behavior.[19] Accordingly, the Confucian may invoke the distinction between fact and value without adopting the doctrine of the dichotomy of facts and values. At issue is the problematic connection between fact and value. Doubt about the connection may result in divesting the factual content implied in one's moral attitude. The task of a Confucian moral philosopher is not to legislate on the connection between fact and value. The task is to provide an elucidation of the contexts in which questions about the connection may appositely arise for moral agents, and to map out possible answers that are consistent with an intelligent adherence to the Confucian ethical tradition.

If *li* is functionally equivalent to "reason," in relevant contexts we may regard the common Confucian expression of the form '*x zhi li*,' roughly 'the *li* of *x*,' as subject to specification in terms either of "reasons for belief" or of "reasons for action." Zhu Xi's remarks on the two basic uses of *li* are amenable to this procedure of explication. "The reason that a thing is what it is *(soyiran zhi gu)*" may be paraphrased as "the reason for believing that such and such a thing exists and/or has these characteristics," and "the norm for what a thing ought to be *(dangran zhi ze)*" as "the reason for acting in accord with the norm or standard of action." In both cases, we are concerned with the *rationales* for accepting factual beliefs and norms for conduct, though, as stated earlier, we must not assume the exclusive disjunction of facts and values.

18. Arthur Edward Murphy, *The Theory of Practical Reason* (La Salle, Ill.: Open Court, 1965), 109–10.
19. *Zidao pian,* Book 29.

From the Confucian point of view, concern with facts is important because they have implications for conduct. *Dangran zhi ze* may thus be rendered as the rationales for accepting the norm or standard of action. Such rationales for norm-acceptance presuppose an understanding of the idea of Confucian tradition *(daotong)*. This living ethical tradition, to borrow Josiah Royce's term, is "a community of interpretation."[20] Members of the community of interpretation are united by a sense of common good or well-being, informed by knowledge of its cultural history and respect for its relevance for dealing with problems of the present and the future. Moreover, like any ethical tradition today, for example, Daoist, Buddhist, Jewish, Christian, or Muslim, the tradition undergoes changes because of reasonable internal and external challenges.[21]

Since the two basic uses of *li* represent the exercise of reason in the generic sense, i.e., as a distinctive capacity of the human mind exemplified in such mental acts as thinking, deliberating, inferring, and judging, rendering *li* as a functional equivalent of "reason" is plausible. For a Confucian moral philosopher, the emphasis is placed on the practical and not the theoretical exercise of reason. However, this emphasis does not depreciate the importance of theoretical inquiry, especially in contexts where empirical knowledge is indispensable to ascertaining accurate grounds for ethical judgment. In *Xunzi*, for example, "accord with evidence *(fuyan)*" along with conceptual clarity and consistency are important requirements for participants in ethical argumentation. An ideal of rational coherence *(tonglei)* is presupposed as the basis for ethical justification.[22]

In one passage, Xunzi points out that the human mind can either fail *(shili)* or succeed *(zhongli)* in the exercise of reason.[23] The main obstacle lies in *bi* (obscuration/blindness of mind). A *bi* is any sort of factor that obstructs the mind's cognitive task. According to Xunzi, whenever we make distinctions among things, our minds are likely to be obscured or blinded *(bi)* by our tendency to attend to one thing rather than another. This tendency is a common human affliction. All distinctions owe their origin to comparison and analogy of different kinds of things. They are made according to our current purposes, and thus are relative to a par-

---

20. See my "The Idea of Confucian Tradition," *Review of Metaphysics* 45, no. 4 (1992): 803–40, an expanded version of which appeared as Essay 11 in *Moral Vision and Tradition*.
21. See my "Reasonable Challenges and Preconditions of Adjudication," in *Tradition and Modernity: East-West Philosophical Perspectives*, ed Eliot Deutsch (Honolulu: University of Hawaii Press, 1991). For a more elaborate discussion, see *Moral Vision and Tradition*, Essay 14.
22. See *Ethical Argumentation*, 61–65.
23. *Zhengming pian*, Book 22, 52.

ticular context of thought and discourse. Distinctions, while useful, are not dichotomies. In *bi*, a person attends exclusively to the significance of one item and disregards that of another. Both common people and philosophers are prone to exaggerate the significance of their favored views of things.

Since the state of *bi* is contrary to reason *(li)*, it is unreasonable to attend to the significance of one thing at the expense of a careful consideration of another. Well aware of the distinction between desire and aversion, for example, a person may pursue his current desire without thinking about its possible unwanted or harmful consequences. That person's mind may be said to be beset by *bi*. More generally, humans suffer because of their concern for acquisition of benefit and the avoidance of harm. When they see something beneficial, they do not consider carefully whether it may lead to harmful consequences. Moreover, even if consequences are considered, they may fail to attend to distant consequences *(yuan)* and simply concentrate on immediate ones *(jin)*, though well aware that distant consequences may have influence or relevance in their lives. Conversely, a person may be preoccupied with distant consequences, without attending to immediate ones that might bring disaster to his or her life.

When the mind is in the state of *bi*, reason is not functioning properly. The opposite of *bi* is clarity of mind *(ming)*. Says Xunzi, "If a person guides his or her mind with *li* (reason), nourishes it with the view of attaining clarity *(ming)*, and does not allow things to upset mental composure, then that person is adequately prepared to resolve perplexities concerning right and wrong."[24]

2. *Li*-BINOMIALS AND PRINCIPLED INTERPRETATION

While the previous section provides a guide to understanding the generic sense of *li*, exploring its concrete significance in particular contexts of discourse is also important. A useful line of inquiry is to ponder some uses of *li* as a component of *li*-binomials. Since this is largely an uncharted territory, our hypothesis concerning the function of *li*-binomials is proffered as a recommendation and not as an explanatory thesis.

Formally, our hypothesis may be stated by way of Xunzi's distinction between generic *(gongming)* and specific or differentiating terms *(bieming)*, namely, the *li*-binomials are specific terms for *li* as a single, generic

---

24. See *Jiebi pian*, Book 21, 490; Cua, *Ethical Argumentation*, chap. 4.

term.²⁵ A generic term is a formal, general, abstract term amenable to specification by other terms in different discursive contexts. These terms, used in practical or theoretical contexts, may be said to be specific terms in the sense that they specify the significance of the use of a generic term adapted to a current purpose of discourse.

Alternatively, a generic term may have various levels of abstraction differentiated by the use of specific terms. A specific term, in turn, may function as a generic term in a particular discursive context when the current purpose requires such further specification. In the language of concept and conceptions, a generic term designates a *concept* that can be used in developing various *conceptions*.²⁶ To avoid misunderstanding, our hypothesis on *li*-binomials is not intended to cover all the specific terms for *li* as a generic term. For the generic sense of *li* can have many specific terms *(bieming)*, say, as instantiations of the schema '*x zhi li'* (the *li* of *x*). For example, one can talk about the *li* of love *(ai zhi li)*, the *li* of filiality *(xiao zhi li)*, the *li* of rites *(li* zhi li)*, or the *li* of tables or chairs. In all these cases, we are talking about the rationales of our factual or normative beliefs about *x*.

In his study of the history of the idea of *li* in Chinese thought, Tang Junyi employs six *li*-binomials. This brilliant study is intricate, and difficult to appreciate if one does not have Tang's encyclopedic knowledge of the texts—an ability rarely exhibited in the works of Sinologists today. For philosophical scholars who have some knowledge of Chinese thought, Tang's study of *li* should be an exciting challenge. For those not so equipped, Liu Shu-hsien provides a valuable, succinct discussion of Tang's work on *li*.²⁷

Tang proposes the thesis that there are six different meanings of *li*, expressed in such *li*-binomials as *wenli, mingli, kongli, xingli, shili,* and *wuli,* exemplified in Chinese thought from the Pre-Qin to Qing times. Roughly, these *li*-binomials, according to Tang, pertain to highly articulated conceptions of *li* in different periods of Chinese thought. *Wenli* focuses on the ethical significance of cultural patterns inclusive of social and political orders in the Pre-Qin period; *mingli* on the use of "names" or language in quasi-theoretical speculations in the Wei-Jin period, often associated with "dark" or "profound" speculations *(xuanxue); kongli* on the Buddhistic notion of *sunyata* or emptiness; *xingli* on nature/human nature in Song-Ming periods; and *shili* on human affairs in the Qing period.

25. *Zhengming pian,* Book 22, 515–16.
26. John Rawls, *A Theory of Justice* (Cambridge, Mass.: Harvard University Press, 1971), 5.
27. Liu Shu-hsien, "*Li*: Principle, Pattern, Reason," in *Encyclopedia of Chinese Philosophy.*

Instead of stating his methodology, Tang stresses the pivotal role of *li* in Song-Ming and Qing Confucianism. Equally important is his reminder on the renewed attention to the significance of *li* after the introduction of Western philosophy and scientific thought in the late nineteenth and early twentieth centuries. He cites various examples of the use of *li* in Chinese translation of different Western concepts. In each case, he uses a *li*-binomial. For instance, "reason" was translated as *lixing*, "axiom" as *gongli*, "theorem" as *dingli*, and notably, "principle" as *yuanli*. More examples are familiar to educated Chinese today. Given *xue* as a familiar Chinese rendering of an academic discipline, "physics" is translated as *wuli xue*, "psychology" as *xinli xue*, and "ethics" as *lunli xue*. Significantly, "logic," which used to be translated by some scholars as *lize xue*, is now rejected by Chinese philosophers. The familiar Chinese term for "logic" today is a transliteration, *luoji*.

Since Tang gives no guide to the basis of his interpretive study of *li*, his use of *li*-binomials is possibly influenced by his knowledge of Western philosophy and modern science. The use of *li* as in the translation of "physics" may be a native linguistic adaptation of *wuli* (the *li* of things), a familiar term in Neo-Confucianism (Song and Ming Confucianism). Especially significant is Tang's example of *yuanli* as a translation of "principle." Among contemporary Chinese philosophers today, the use of *lize* as "principle" is also quite common.

A Confucian philosopher would ask about the *li* or rationales for Tang's examples. What is the rationale for using *li* in such translation of English terms? If "principle" is translated as *yuanli*, what does *yuanli* mean for an educated Chinese who does not know that *yuanli* is originally a translation of "principle"? It is also significant to note that "principle" is also commonly translated as *yuanze*. Recall our earlier discussion of the use of *ze* as a conclusion-indicator or a standard for determining what a thing ought-to-be in Zhu Xi's explanation of the meaning of *li* (section 1 above). The translation of "principle" as *yuanze* is probably the result of the influence of Western preoccupation with "laws of nature," "natural law," or "rules for conduct." As a conjecture, these Chinese translations of key terms in Western philosophical discourse reflect the influence of Western philosophical education. One also wonders whether the acceptance of the translation of *li* as "principle" is Western Sinologists' unconscious reading of *li* as *yuanli*, which is a standard Chinese translation of "principle."

Before we deal with the principled interpretation of *li*, to avoid misunderstanding we must note that our hypothesis on *li*-binomials does not prejudge the issue of the proper reading of Chinese philosophical texts. Implicit in our hypothesis on *li*-binomials is that these binomials express distinct notions, although they are specific terms *(bieming)* that differentiate the concrete significance of *li* as a generic term *(gongming)*. An alternative hypothesis is to regard these *li*-binomials as simply conjunctions of single terms or graphs. Our hypothesis does not reject this alternative, especially as an approach to the study of ancient Chinese philosophical texts. Absent a punctuation system, the scholar has to use his or her linguistic intuitions in resolving queries on reading texts and arrive at a reasoned decision. In *Xunzi*, this alternative approach is plausible in cases of co-occurrence of *li** (rites) and *yi* (rightness), i.e., '*li* yi*.' If one views the co-occurrence of *li** (rites) and *yi* (rightness) as a binomial, *li*yi*, the punctuation problem is resolved by rendering passages of co-occurrence of *li** (rites) and *yi* (rightness) as a compound term, expressing a single concept. This interpretive method of translation is sometimes used by Burton Watson, construing the co-occurrence of *li** (rites) and *yi* (rightness) as a binomial, thus "ritual principles."[28]

Arguably, a more plausible answer to the problem of co-occurrence of *li** and *yi* in *Xunzi* is to view the co-occurrence as a conjunction of single graphs.[29] Many crucial passages are hardly intelligible if we read the co-occurrence of *li** and *yi* as a binomial *li*yi*.[30] Perhaps the best way to deal with the plausibility of principled interpretation of *li* is to consider some common *li*-binomials in Song-Ming Confucianism. In Wang Yang-ming's case, we find four *li*-binomials: *tianli, daoli, yili,* and *tiaoli*. These *li*-binomials present a challenge to philosophical interpretation. As elaborated elsewhere, these *li*-binomials are unintelligible when construed as different sorts of principles.[31] As compound terms *(jianming)*, they function more like focal notions, expressing distinct ideas associated with *li* in different contexts of discourse. *Tianli* is often used to convey the Neo-Confucian notion of *ren*, the ideal of the universe as a moral community; *daoli*, the idea of the dynamic indeterminacy of the ideal *dao* (often used interchangeably with *tianli*); *yili*, the idea of the rightness or appropriateness of reason to an occurrent situation, which requires independent judgment or discretion; and *tiaoli*, the idea of an occasional achievement of a temporal, practical order.

Suppose we adopt the translation of *tianli* as "principle of nature," *yili* and *daoli* as "moral principle."[32] Apart from the questions we raised

28. *Xing'e pian*, Book 23; Burton Watson, trans., *Hsün Tzu [Xunzi]: Basic Writings* (New York: Columbia University Press, 1963), 160.
29. For example, Chan, *Source Book,* 130.
30. See my "The Problem of Conceptual Unity in Hsün Tzu and Li Kou's Solution," *Philosophy East and West* 39, no. 2 (1989): 115–34; incorporated in this volume as Essay 4.
31. See my *The Unity of Knowledge and Action: A Study in Wang Yang-ming's Moral Psychology* (Honolulu: University Press of Hawaii, 1982), chap. 2.
32. Chan, *Source Book*.

at the beginning of this article, we may ask for a clear statement of the sort of principle, say, implied in *tianli*. *Tianli* is often used in Song-Ming Confucianism as something (an ethical ideal) obscured *(bi)* by human desires. We do not find any statement comparable to Kant's Principle of the Law of Nature. To Cheng Hao and Wang Yangming, as an ethical ideal, *tianli* is a matter of personal realization and not a principle to be used for deriving moral rules or standards. Similar remarks apply to the translation of *daoli* and *yili* as "moral principle," suggesting that the Confucians have a principle analogous to Kant's Principle of Humanity. The Confucians do have an ideal of dignity or respect for persons, but this ideal pertains to the recognition of meritorious performance rather than a respect for person qua person independently of actual conduct.[33] Translation of *yili* as "moral principle" is especially questionable. In Wang Yangming's major works, this focal notion emphasizes reasoned judgment on an occurrent, problematic, exigent situation, that is, the situation that receives no guidance from established standards of conduct. In other words, in hard cases of the moral life, we must attend to the merits of particular situations independently of one's favored doctrines or beliefs about the proper application of established norms of conduct.

Ideally, disagreement and/or dispute concerning the current import of the Confucian tradition is subject to criticism. Thus, the notion of *li* has a key role to play in ethical argumentation conceived as cooperative enterprise in which participants attempt to arrive at an agreeable solution to a problem of common concern. In such a discourse, *li* has both explanatory and justificatory uses in proffering and evaluating normative claims.[34] Thus, the construal of *li* as "reason" or "rationale," in the light of its argumentative functions, is more plausible and philosophically significant. Accordingly, we can ask questions amenable to reasoned answers, though these answers are matters of philosophical reconstruction. However, such scholarly efforts in reconstruction also contribute to the development of Confucianism. For example, with respect to *tianli*, we can now ask: What is the *li* or rationale for espousing the notion of *tianli*? If *tianli* is alleged to be opposed to the pursuit of human desires, as in Song-Ming Confucianism, then one must have some reasons for accepting their thesis. This was a momentous issue for Qing Confucians.

Also, questions can be raised about the *li* of *yili*, or of *daoli*. Even if both *li*-binomials convey the idea of changes and indeterminacy of nat-

---

33. See *Dimensions of Moral Creativity*, chap. 7.
34. See *Ethical Argumentation*, chap. 2.

ural events and human affairs, one can still ask about the *li* or rationale for characterizing such matters in particular situations as falling outside the scope of the application of normal, established standards of human conduct. As to *tiaoli*, which clearly expresses the idea of pattern or order, questions about the translation of *li* as "pattern" may be asked, as suggested at the beginning of this essay. Our questions, say, concerning the nature of pattern or order are best formulated as questions about the *li* or rationales for taking certain order as normative rather than as merely descriptive.

Although the translation of *li* as "principle" is misleading, the question concerning the role of principles in Confucian ethics or in Chinese philosophy is an important question. Presumably, it is the concern with this question that underlies the principled interpretation of *li*. Three different, yet complementary ways of exploring answers to this question must be considered. First, one may acknowledge that the occasional use of the concept of principle in contemporary Chinese philosophy or ethics is significant. "Principle" has a role in articulating preceptive principles, that is, "first-personal precepts adopted by particular persons and dependent for their authority entirely upon such persons' loyalty to them."[35] In this sense, principles represent the agent's understanding of the preceptive guidance of Confucian ethics. Second, as statements of belief and/or theses in argumentative discourse, principles can function as means for internal or external critiques of the established Confucian tradition. These principles are not mere instruments of criticism, but proposals for reconstituting the tradition. As argumentative topics, they are not fixed rules for ethical deliberation. Third, perhaps the most important, the use of the language of principle, in the light of wide intercultural contact today, is an attempt to reformulate the relevance of some basic Confucian concepts of virtue in order to set forth certain ground rules or procedures as preconditions of adjudication for intercultural, ethical conflict. (This function of principle is perhaps the point of translating "principle" as *yuanze*, since *ze* can be used as a Chinese translation of "rule" or "procedure," and *yuan* for "fundamental" or "essential.") The presumption, though defeasible, is that external challenges to a particular tradition are reasonable only from the internal point of view of the tradition in question.[36]

35. Henry D. Aiken, "On the Concept of a Moral Principle," in *Isenberg Memorial Lecture Series, 1965–1966* (East Lansing: Michigan State University Press, 1969), 113.
36. See my "The Status of Principles in Confucian Ethics," *Journal of Chinese Philosophy* 16 (1989): 273–96; "Reasonable Challenges and Preconditions of Adjudication," in Deutsch, *Tradition and Modernity*, 279–98. For an expanded version of these papers, see *Moral Vision and Tradition*, Essay 14.

The preceding uses of the language of principle may be adopted in Confucian discourse and dialogue with other ethical traditions. Notably, the use of "principle" contextually implies that the claims at issue are in some sense fundamental, the *principia*, the originating sources of ethical discourse. (Perhaps this is the motivation for writers who adopt the translation of "principle" as *yuanli*, as *yuan* may be regarded as a functional equivalent of *principium*.) In other words, the professed claims formulated in the language of principles express convictions about the foundation or the core basic ethical beliefs deemed inherent in the ethical tradition. Arguably tradition is an interpretive concept.[37] Principles, as claims about the *principia* of ethical discourse, are defeasible, and therefore cannot be considered as final or absolute norms. As a focus on *principium*, one can appreciate the translation of "principle" as *yuanli*, for it suggests the idea that it is the ethical foundation of the tradition that provides the point of departure for intellectual discourse.

This essay presents some aspects of the Chinese conception of reason. As a single, generic term, *li* is functionally equivalent to "reason" in the sense of our capacity for thinking, imagining, or reasoning. Obviously, one may ask with respect to Confucianism familiar philosophical questions concerning the relation of reason and experience, reason and passion, and reason and insight. An exploration of these questions will undoubtedly contribute to further understanding and just evaluation of certain pivotal aspects of Chinese philosophy. In another sense, the essay deals with the Chinese, Confucian conception of rationality, provided that rationality is not so narrowly conceived as to be exclusive of reasonableness as an intelligent way to cope with exigent, rule-indeterminate situations of human life.[38] It is hoped that this essay provides some useful guides for further study.

37. See my "The Idea of Confucian Tradition," or *Moral Vision and Tradition*, Essay 12.
38. See my *The Unity of Knowledge and Action*, chap. 4.

Essay 14

EMERGENCE OF THE HISTORY OF CHINESE PHILOSOPHY

This essay is an inquiry into the constructive challenge of Western philosophy to the development of the history of Chinese philosophy. The discussion focuses on the methodological aspects of three major works that appeared from 1919 to 1982. These works are remarkable, not only for illustrating the different Western philosophical assumptions and backgrounds of these writers, but also for their importance in Chinese philosophical education and discourse. As preliminaries, in section 1, I consider the idea of Chinese philosophy and samples of the critical-historical spirit of ancient Chinese thought. In section 2, I turn to three major works on the history of Chinese philosophy, that is, the works of Hu Shih (Hu Shi), Fung Yu-lan (Feng Yulan), and Lao Sze-kwang (Lao Siguang), and conclude with some remarks on the contributions of a few recent works to the study of the history of Chinese philosophy.

1. PRELIMINARIES

A. *The Idea of Chinese Philosophy*

It is common today for a teacher or scholar in Chinese philosophy to encounter the query, "What is Chinese philosophy?" Sometimes this query is a disguise for expressing doubt as to whether there could even be such a thing as Chinese philosophy. There is a terse answer to the question: "Since philosophy is a Western term, Chinese philosophy is an invention of Western-trained Chinese scholars." This answer, however, is not helpful. A better answer would be a reminder that, from ancient times to the present, ethics has been a recognized branch of Western philosophical inquiry. And ethics has its counterpart in ancient Chinese thought. Both Socrates and Confucius were preoccupied with basic questions of normative ethics, questions about the manner of life that best befits humanity, about the ideals of human excellence and wellbeing. Plato and Aristotle brilliantly pursued these questions. We find comparable achievements in the works of Mencius and Xunzi (Hsün Tzu). Xunzi's writings, moreover, reveal significant interest and insights into some basic problems of moral epistemology, e.g., the problems of ethical language and justification as a form of argumentative discourse.[1]

Of course, the word "philosophy" has no equivalent in Chinese before translations of Western philosophical works in the nineteenth century. Yan Fu (1823–1921) was the first to translate into Chinese Thomas Huxley's *Evolution and Ethics* in 1898.[2] Later Yan Fu translated some works of John Stuart Mill, Herbert Spencer, and Montesquieu. In the early 1960s, Wing-tsit Chan wrote:

At the turn of the century, ideas of Schopenhauer, Kant, Nietzsche, Rousseau, Tolstoy, and Kropotkin were imported. After the intellectual renaissance of 1917, the movement advanced at a rapid pace. In the following decade, important works of Descartes, Spinoza, Hume, James, Bergson, and Marx, and others became available in Chinese. Dewey, Russell, and Dreisch came to China to lecture, and special numbers of journals were devoted to Nietzsche and Bergson.... Almost every trend of thought had its exponent. James, Bergson, Eucken, Whitehead, Hocking, Schiller, T. H. Green, Carnap, and C. I. Lewis had their own following. For a time it seemed Chinese thought was to be completely Westernized.[3]

In Taiwan and Hong Kong today, we also find followers of Kant, Husserl, Heidegger, Wittgenstein, Maritain, Gilson, Quine, Pepper, Gadamer, Derrida, and different philosophical schools of thought. If one visits any Taiwan or Hong Kong university today, he is likely to find a department of philosophy with a wide offering of standard subjects and also courses such as Chinese Philosophy, Indian Philosophy, Buddhistic Philosophy, and Comparative Philosophy. In the People's Republic of China, there are still followers of Marx and Lenin, as well as specialists in logic, philosophy of science, and aesthetics.[4]

The translation of Western philosophical concepts and doctrines

---

1. See A. S. Cua, *Ethical Argumentation: A Study of Hsün Tzu's Moral Epistemology* (Honolulu: University of Hawaii Press, 1985), and *Moral Vision and Tradition: Essays in Chinese Ethics* (Washington, D.C.: The Catholic University of America Press, 1998), Essay 10.

2. For an informative study, see Benjamin Schwartz, *In Search of Power: Yen Fu and the West* (Cambridge, Mass.: Harvard University Press, 1964).

3. Wing-tsit Chan, trans., *A Source Book in Chinese Philosophy* (Princeton, N.J.: Princeton University Press, 1963), 743.

4. For a survey of Chinese philosophy in post-Mao China, Taiwan, and the overseas diaspora, see Lin Tongqi, "Recent Trends in Post-Mao China"; Vincent Shen, "Recent Trends in Taiwan"; and Chung-ying Cheng, "Recent Trends in Overseas Chinese Philosophy" and "Confucianism: Twentieth Century," in *Encyclopedia of Chinese Philosophy*, ed. A. S. Cua (New York and London: Routledge, 2003).

provided an impetus to the development of Chinese philosophical discourse. In perusing a Chinese dictionary of philosophy, first published in 1925 *(Zhexue cidian)*,[5] we find a few Chinese translations of philosophical subjects and terms, e.g., ethics, logic, ontology, essence, accident, substance, attributes, and reason. These terms still have currency today. In fact "logic" appears as a transliteration that becomes part of modern Chinese. It is instructive to note how some translations of standard Western philosophical terms represent an effort of Chinese and Japanese scholars to find functional equivalents in Chinese. Consider the word "philosophy." An ingenious Japanese scholar's translation of "philosophy" as *zhexue* is a good example. Nishi Amane, in his *Hyakuichi shimron [Baiyi xinlun]* (1874), appeared to be the first scholar to use *zhexue* as a translation for the Greek *philosophia* and "philosophy." For justification of this translation of "philosophy" as *zhexue*, Nishi Amane appealed to Zhou Dunyi's notion of *xi xianxue* or *xi zhexue*, that is, "to aspire to the learning of a worthy person" or "to aspire to the learning of an intelligent, knowledgeable person." This is an interpretive translation, for Nishi explicitly appealed to a brief remark of Zhou Dunyi (Zhou Lianxi, 1017–73) in *Tongshu* (Chapter 10): "The sage aspires to become Heaven, the worthy aspires to become a sage, and the gentleman *[junzi]* aspires to become a worthy." Zhou's remark was interpreted as "to aspire and pursue, through learning, in order to acquire the wisdom of the worthy and the intelligent, knowledgeable person."[6]

In Chinese the first character or graph *zhe* means wisdom. An alternative term for wisdom is *zhi*, often used interchangeably with its homophone, meaning "knowledge" and/or "capacity to acquire knowledge."[7]

---

5. *Zhexue cidian*, 4th ed. (Taipei: Shangwu, 1976). While the publisher did not give any date of publication, the first Preface by Cai Yuanbei, an eminent philosopher of education and promoter of Western philosophy, was dated 1925. The second Preface in my 1976 edition was dated 1927.

6. My former graduate student Kazuaki Ohashi informed me that Nishi Amane, in his *Hyakuichi shimron [Baiyi xinlun]* (1874) appeared to be the first scholar to use *zhexue* as a translation for the Greek *philosophia* and "philosophy." For detailed discussion, see Zhong Shaohua, "Qingmo zhongguo ren duiyi <<zhexue>> de zhuiqiu," *Newsletter of the Institute of Chinese Literature and Philosophy* 2, no. 2 (Taipei: Academia Sinica, 1992), esp. 162–67. I owe this reference and a copy of this article to Professor Nicolas Standaert of the Katholieke Universiteit Leuven. See Zhong, 163. (For translation of Zhou's remark, see Chan, *A Source Book in Chinese Philosophy*, 471.) As for the currency of *zhexue* in Chinese education, Lao Sze-kwang remarks: "Although it is impossible to identify who first introduced this Japanese translation of 'philosophy' into China, it is quite certain that when the Capital University in Peking, in the first decade of the twentieth century, did adopt this term *che-hsüeh (zhexue)* as a title for courses, this should indicate the official acceptance of this translation" (Lao Sze-kwang, "On Understanding Chinese Philosophy: An Inquiry and a Proposal," in *Understanding the Chinese Thought: The Philosophical Roots*, ed. Robert E. Allinson [Hong Kong: Oxford University Press, 1989], 291n1).

7. In the *Analects*, *zhi* in the verbal form is sometimes used in the sense of "to realize."

Given its primarily practical orientation, ancient Chinese thinkers were, for the most part, preoccupied with ethical questions about right conduct and the best conception of human life. The good human life is commonly envisaged by the Confucians as a life of *ren*, an affectionate concern for the well-being of one's fellows in a community, society, or state governed by a wise and virtuous ruler.[8] *Xue* is learning. "Philosophy" translated as *zhexu* means in Chinese "learning to become a wise and knowledgeable person." As learning and practice can be a delightful experience, the student may come to love the subject.

Interpreting philosophy as the love of wisdom reflects the Confucian concern with practice or application of learning. Confucius once remarked: "Is it not a delight to apply one's learning at an appropriate time?"[9] For the Confucian, learning is important because of its relevance to resolving problems of human life. It is the acquisition of practical and not theoretical knowledge. This translation of "philosophy" as *zhexue* seems to be a very good attempt to find a functional equivalent in Chinese language prior to the careful study of Western philosophy. Indeed, the translation of "philosophy" from the Greek, in one interpretation, is closer to the ancient Chinese conception. John Passmore remarks:

> The Greek word *sophia* is ordinarily translated into English as "wisdom," and the compound *philosophia*, from which "philosophy" derives, is translated as "the love of wisdom." But *sophia* has a much wider range of application than the modern English "wisdom." Wherever intelligence can be exercised—in practical affairs, in the mechanical arts, in business—there is room for *sophia*.[10]

Such a use, however, reflects the retrospective sense of knowledge, i.e., knowledge derived from realizing the import of learning. Such knowledge, however, also involves use of *zhi* in the sense of acquiring information. There are also uses of *zhi* in the senses of acknowledgment, understanding or appreciation, and knowing-how. For the informational sense, see, for example, 2.11, 2.23, 5.9, 7.31; for the sense of understanding and appreciation, see, for example, 2.4, 4.14, 11.12; for knowing-how, 12.22. No doubt, these sample uses of *zhi* are subject to interpretation. For the distinction between prospective and retrospective senses of knowledge, see A. S. Cua, *The Unity of Knowledge and Action: A Study in Wang Yang-ming's Moral Psychology* (Honolulu: University Press of Hawaii, 1982), chap. 1; and "The Possibility of Ethical Knowledge: Reflections on a Theme in the *Hsün Tzu*," in *Epistemological Issues in Ancient Chinese Philosophy*, ed. Hans Lenk and Gregor Paul (Albany: State University of New York Press, 1993); incorporated in this volume as Essay 6. Cf. Roger T. Ames, "Confucius and the Ontology of Knowing," in *Interpreting Across Boundaries: New Essays in Comparative Philosophy*, ed. Eliot Deutsch and Gerald James Larson (Princeton, N.J.: Princeton University Press, 1988).

8. A. S. Cua, *Dimensions of Moral Creativity: Paradigms, Principles, and Ideals* (University Park: Pennsylvania State University Press, 1978), chap. 4.

9. D. C. Lau, *Confucius: The Analects (Lun Yü)* (Middlesex, England: Penguin Books, 1979), 1.1.

10. John Passmore, "Philosophy," in *Encyclopedia of Philosophy*, ed. Paul Edwards, vol. 6 (New York: Macmillan & Free Press, 1967).

Passmore goes on to discuss different conceptions of philosophy—a topic familiar to philosophy majors today. The Chinese translation, though an interpretive adaptation, at least captures part of the meaning of *philosophia*. The term *zhexue* is now a standard Chinese term.

However, if one thinks of philosophy as the construction of grand systems of thought as exemplified in Aristotle, Aquinas, Hobbes, Kant, or Hegel, a person may find the idea of Chinese philosophy problematic. Arguably the works of Zhu Xi may be considered an embodiment of a grand system. Setting aside this essentially contestable issue and focusing on ethics as a basic, or even *the* basic, subject of philosophical inquiry, the history of Chinese thought is replete with examples. Since translation is an interpretive task, the Chinese translation of "ethics" as *lunli xue* perhaps illustrates best the concern of the Confucian tradition. Read independently of its being a translated term, *lunli xue* may be explained as an inquiry concerning the rationales of human relationships—one principal concern of Confucian ethics. Those impressed with the recent Western emphasis on personal relationships will find an ancient Confucian precursor for their ethical and/or political theory.[11]

Since a translation is an interpretive adaptation of an idea in a foreign language, it should not be a surprise for a Western philosophy student or scholar to have difficulties with the existing translations of some Chinese texts. For many Western philosophers, Wing-tsit Chan's *A Source Book in Chinese Philosophy* is not a very helpful introduction. While it is an impressive contribution to Sinological scholarship, his use of English words for translating key Chinese concepts is not always perspicuous to Western philosophers, in spite of Chan's painstaking effort to explain them. For example, when *li, yili,* and *tianli* are rendered as "principle," "moral principle," and "principle of nature," one can be puzzled about what these English terms mean. Absent an explanation of the uses of *li*, the translation of *li* as "principle" unavoidably leads to such misleading questions as: What are the principles of Chinese or Confucian ethics? If such principles exist, do they serve as premises for derivation of moral rules? Are Confucian principles universal or relative? The selected texts do not provide clear answers to the question of how one goes about formulating the so-called principles.[12]

---

11. For more discussion, see A. S. Cua, "Confucian Philosophy, Chinese," in *Encyclopedia of Philosophy* (London: Routledge, 1998), vol. 1, 536–49.

12. For two specialized discussions of the concept of *li* (reason/principle), see my *Ethical Argumentation*, 20–29; and *The Unity of Knowledge and Action*, 26–50. A more general discussion is given in my "Reason and Principle in Chinese Philosophy: An Interpretation of *Li*," in *A Companion to World Philosophy*, ed. Eliot Deutsch and Ron Bontekoe (Oxford: Blackwell, 1997); incorporated in this volume as Essay 13. For a conceptual history of *li* in Neo-Confucianism, see W. T. Chan, "The Evolution of the Neo-Confucian Concept *Li* as

Moreover, though perhaps unavoidable, use of such labels as "idealistic," "naturalistic," "rationalistic" for certain tendencies of Chinese thought maybe misleading in implying that these tendencies are the Chinese counterparts of those in Western philosophy.[13] Unless they are carefully defined, even in Western philosophy today, these labels are useful largely as convenient pedagogical and/or mnemonic devices. I must note that, to a certain degree, a philosophical bilingual would face similar difficulties in reading Chan's book, while admiring his marvelous achievement.

B. Ancient History of Chinese Thought

While the idea of the history of Chinese philosophy is a Western importation, the importance of critical exposition of prevailing "winds of doctrine" is recognized in some works in ancient Chinese thought. Somewhat reminiscent of book alpha of Aristotle's *Metaphysics*, Chapter 33 of the *Zhuangzi* gives a critical account of Zhuangzi's contemporaries or predecessors.[14] While acknowledging that there are many thoughtful persons in the world concerned with *dao* (Way), the writer asks: "Where do we find what the ancients called 'the arts of *dao (daoshu)*,' the arts for pursuing *dao* [or the ideal of the good human life]? I say that *dao* pervades everything that exists in the universe." In this essay we find an extant, critical statement of Mozi, Shen Dao, and Hui Shi, a famous proponent of such logical paradoxes as "I set off for Yüeh today and came there yesterday," "The southern region has no limit and yet has a limit," and "Fire is not hot." This chapter in *Zhuangzi* praises Laozi and Zhuang Zhou (i.e., Zhuangzi), showing the author's ethical commitment. Notably, Zhuangzi has a holistic moral vision of the unity of humans and other things in the universe: "Heaven and earth were born at

---

Principle," *Tsing Hua Journal of Chinese Studies*, n.s., 4, no. 2 (1964): 123–49; and Shu-hsien Liu, "*Li* (Principle, Pattern, Reason)," in the *Encyclopedia of Chinese Philosophy*, ed. A. S. Cua (New York and London: Routledge, 2003).

13. This remark also applies to the standard Marxist texts' classification of Chinese philosophy into "materialism" and "idealism." See for example, Ren Jiyu, editor-in-chief, *Zhongguo zhexue shi* (Beijing: Renmin, 1979).

14. For a brief informative account of later works, inclusive of classification of ancient schools of thought, see Y. P. Mei, "Ancient Chinese Philosophy according to the *Chuang Tzu*, Chapter 33, The World of Thought, with an English Translation of the Chapter," *Tsing Hua Journal of Chinese Studies*, n.s., 4, no. 2 (1964). A good interpretive study in the intellectual history in the Ming dynasty is Huang Zongxi's *Ming Ru xue'an*. For a selected translation, see Julia Ching and Chaoying Fang, *The Records of Ming Scholars* (Honolulu: University of Hawaii Press, 1987). See also *The Complete Works of Chuang Tzu*, trans. Burton Watson (New York: Columbia University Press, 1968), chap. 33.

the same time as I was, and the ten thousand things are one with me."[15] In Chapter 2, Zhuangzi offers a brilliant critique of the Mohists and the Confucians. Among other things, Zhuangzi maintains that there are neither fixed meanings of words nor neutral, external standards for deciding the correctness or incorrectness, truth or falsity of their claims. The best course is to transcend the dispute and maintain clarity of mind *(ming)*. Says Zhuangzi, "The torch of chaos and doubt—this is what the sage steers by. So he does not use things but relegates all to the constant. This is what it means to use clarity."[16]

In the same holistic spirit, but appreciative of the value of argumentative discourse, Xunzi gives an insightful critique of influential thinkers in his time. Also, echoing Zhuangzi, Xunzi acknowledges the merits of the doctrines of various Confucian and non-Confucian thinkers, for their doctrines were plausible, that is, they had good reasons for espousing their doctrines. Regrettably, they grasp only "one corner" of *dao* and mistake it as characteristic of the whole. For example, Mozi exaggerated the importance of benefit or utility without appreciating the beauty of form or cultural refinement in human life. Zhuangzi was too preoccupied with the thought of Heaven and paid hardly any attention to the needs of humanity. Says Xunzi: "*Dao* embodies the constant, yet exhausts all changes. One corner is insufficient to characterize it."[17] These thinkers were victims of *bi* (obscuration, blindness), that is, their minds were so dominated by one persistent idea of *dao* that, as a consequence, they failed to take account of other equally important aspects of *dao*. Like Zhuangzi, Xunzi emphasizes clarity of mind. But for Xunzi, clarity of mind is a mental state free from cognitive blindness or obsession with doctrines, a preparation for the acquisition of knowledge and sagely wisdom, and not a characteristic of sagely attainment. It is noteworthy that, apart from being the defender of the Confucian tradition against external challenges, Xunzi is also an internal critic of the Confucian thought and practice of his time. He reminds the learned Confucians that they must not confuse different sorts of Confucians *(Ru)*: the great

---

15. Watson, *The Complete Works of Chuang Tzu*, 43.

16. Ibid., 42. Zhuangzi's skepticism of the existence of neutral standards for evaluating philosophical, ethical claims has some affinity with MacIntyre's thesis that there are no tradition-independent standards of rationality. However, unlike MacIntyre, who endorses a sort of rationalistic version of Thomism, Zhuangzi would not endorse any particular system of thought. See Alasdair MacIntyre, *Whose Justice? Which Rationality?* (Notre Dame, Ind.: University of Notre Dame Press, 1988).

17. Li Disheng, *Xunzi jishi* (Taipei: Xuesheng, 1979), 478. Cf. Burton Watson, trans., *Hsün Tzu: Basic Writings* (New York: Columbia University Press, 1963), 125. For other critical remarks, see *Xunzi*, Books 8 and 17; John Knoblock, *Xunzi: A Translation and Study of the Complete Works*, vols. 1 and 3 (Stanford, Calif.: Stanford University Press, 1989, 1994).

and sagacious, the refined, and the vulgar.[18] The value and integrity of Confucian teachings should not be perfunctorily identified with those in common practice.

In this connection, let us note the ancient Confucian doctrine of rectifying names or terms *(zhengming)* as a method for dealing with internal and external critiques of Confucian thought. Part of the purport of this classical doctrine of rectifying the uses of names or terms is to insure that persons carry out their tasks in accord with the responsibility implicit in the names and titles. Hu Shih aptly states that for Confucius, rectification of names is not a task for the grammarian or lexicographer, for it is primarily an ethical task of intellectual reorganization.

> Its object is, first, to make the names stand for what they ought to stand for, and then to so reorganize the social and political relations and institutions as to make them what their names indicate they ought to be. The rectification of names thus consists in making real relationships and duties and institutions conform as far as possible to the *ideal* meanings, which, however obscured and neglected they may now become, can still be re-discovered and re-established by proper study and, literally "judicious" use of the names.[19]

Influenced especially by Later Mohist logic, Xunzi expands the scope of the doctrine of rectifying names to embrace more extensive linguistic, conceptual, and pragmatic concerns.[20] The Confucian task of intellectual reorganization may also be ascribed to Zhu Xi's (1130–1200) concern with the idea of Confucian tradition *(daotong)* as a way of meeting the internal and external challenges of non-Confucian thought, such as Buddhism and Daoism.[21]

In the twentieth century the challenge for rewriting the history of Chinese thought comes from Western philosophy. Some Western-trained philosophy scholars of "Han learning" or Chinese studies must have experienced what Alasdair MacIntyre calls "epistemological crisis," that is, the realization that the development of Chinese thought had for some time been stagnant. To these thinkers, issues in discourse must have appeared sterile, as they could no longer be resolved through the employment of current internal standards of reasoned discourse. Mac-

---

18. *Xunzi*, Book 8.
19. Hu Shih, *The Development of the Logical Method in Ancient China* (New York: Paragon Book Reprint Corp., 1963), 26. (This is a reprint of the 1922 Shanghai edition.) Note that this doctrine of rectifying names may be plausibly viewed as an intellectual formulation of Confucius's recurrent emphasis on the unity of words and action. For more discussion, see my *Dimensions of Moral Creativity*, chap. 5.
20. See Cua, *Ethical Argumentation*, chaps. 3–4.
21. See my "The Idea of Confucian Tradition," *Review of Metaphysics* 45, no. 4 (1992). A revised, expanded version is given in Essay 12 of my *Moral Vision and Tradition*.

Intyre insightfully remarks: "The solution to a genuine epistemological crisis requires the invention or discovery of new concepts and the framing of some new type or types of theory."[22]

In the older spirit of the Confucian doctrine of rectifying names, the epistemological crisis is a crisis of "intellectual reorganization." The challenge of Western philosophy involves nothing less than a wholesale reconsideration of the philosophical significance of the history of Chinese thought. The task involves adaptation of alien Western philosophical concepts and/or doctrines in interpreting the significance of classical texts—a hermeneutical problem. In Ronald Dworkin's felicitous term, the task is "constructive interpretation." The aim of constructive interpretation, as a species of the enterprise of creative interpretation, aims to present in the best light a coherent explanatory account of an object or an existing practice, and more significantly a sound or adequate justification of the practice.[23] The key issues involved in constructive interpretation remain a continuing concern of Chinese philosophers today. Below I focus on some of these issues in three outstanding works of Hu Shih, Fung Yu-lan (Feng Yulan), and Lao Sze-kwang (Lao Siguang) on the history of Chinese philosophy.

2. HISTORY OF CHINESE PHILOSOPHY

A. Hu Shih (1891–1962)

It is a plausible presumption that a writer of the history of Chinese philosophy must have extensive training in Western philosophy and some familiarity with works on the history of Western philosophy. Indeed, the subject of the history of Chinese philosophy is a philosophical transformation of the history of Chinese thought. To my knowledge, the pioneering work is Hu Shih's *An Outline of the History of Chinese Philosophy, Part I* (in Chinese), published in 1919, two years after the submission of his brilliant doctoral dissertation to Columbia University. (Earlier I cited this work in connection with the Confucian doctrine of rectifying names.) Hu did not complete his three-part project on the history of Chinese philosophy. The last two parts were intended to be an account of "medieval" and contemporary Chinese philosophy. While Hu's work pretends to be no more than an outline, in some respects it is still a useful work of reference. One finds insightful discussion of the evolution of the Confucian concept of *li* or rules of proper conduct as

---

22. MacIntyre, *Whose Justice? Which Rationality?* 362.
23. Ronald Dworkin, *Law's Empire* (Cambridge, Mass.: Harvard University Press, 1986), 52.

well as logical-conceptual issues involved in interpreting, say, Xunzi's conception of empirical knowledge.[24]

Cai Yuanbei's Foreword (dated August 3, 1918) singles out four special qualities of Hu's book: (1) the use of the methods of evidence, (2) the skill in distinguishing the "pure" elements of philosophical thought from those of the mythological and political history of the Chinese people, (3) ability to render impartial evaluation of the merits and demerits of different philosophies, and finally (4) the systematic character of the work. Cai reminds the reader that Hu is among the very few scholars trained in Western philosophy who also has a mastery of "Han Learning."[25]

Hu's long introductory chapter explains his aims and methodology. At the outset, Hu points out that there is no fixed definition of "philosophy." However, Hu proposes a broad conception: Any kind of study and research that deals with the most important and fundamental questions may be called "philosophy," for example, the question concerning the goodness or badness of human conduct. Hu delineates six different sorts of philosophical inquiry, familiar to students of Western philosophy: cosmology, epistemology, ethics, philosophy of education, political philosophy, and philosophy of religion. Says Hu, "These kinds of inquiry, from the ancient times to the present, have passed through many philosophers' investigations. Continually, since the inception of the formulation of a question, different interpretations and methods of solution have been proposed and contested in argumentation. Sometimes, one question, after a few thousand years, still has received no definitive method of resolution."[26] Hu cites the example of the ancient Chinese dispute on human nature *(xing)* in the doctrines of Gaozi, Mencius, and Xunzi, and in subsequent views in the history of Chinese thought.

Hu focuses on three objectives of a history of philosophy: (1) understanding changes or transformations of a particular school of thought,

---

24. See my "The Concept of *Li* in Confucian Moral Theory" in *Understanding the Chinese Mind: The Philosophical Roots*, ed. Robert Allinson (Hong Kong: Oxford University Press, 1989). For more discussion, see "The Ethical and the Religious Dimensions *Li* (Rites)," *Review of Metaphysics* 55, no. 3 (2002): 501–49, incorporated in this volume as Essay 7. For Xunzi's conception of knowledge, see my *Ethical Argumentation*, chap. 2, and "The Possibility of Ethical Knowledge," or Essay 6 in this volume.

25. Hu's work is a notable achievement, especially when we compare the philosophical quality of his work with most works of Late Qing promoters and writers on Western philosophy. For an informative survey, see Zhong's article cited in note 6.

26. Hu Shih, *Zhongguo zhexue shi dagang* (Taipei: Shangwu, 1947), 1–2. Please note that, except for occasional translations of the Chinese texts of Hu Shih, Fung Yu-lan, and Lao Sze-kwang, I have freely presented their views as I understand them. As indicated earlier, translation is in part an interpretive adaptation.

(2) the reasons and causes for such transformations, and (3) objective, critical evaluation. Hu pays a great deal of attention to the method for evaluating sources, modeled after the Western method of writing history. Perhaps, as Lao Sze-kwang later complains, he spends too much time with the problem of distinguishing genuine materials from forgeries. Hu briefly discusses five kinds of evidence: historical events, linguistic usages of the time, literary styles, the coherent or systematic character of thought, and secondary, collaborative evidence. In the last section of the Introduction, Hu stresses a deeper level of the method of *guantong*, the orderly, sequential presentation of the development of a school of thought. In the bibliographic notes to the introductory chapter, Hu lists mostly Western sources such as the German Wilhelm Windelband (1848–1915), *A History of Western Philosophy*, translated into English by J. H. Tufts and published in 1893. Our sketch of Hu's concerns is familiar to teachers of Western philosophy. Noteworthy is Hu's use of the notions of syllogism, proposition, and judgment in his discussion of the Later Mohist logic.

In 1919, just eight years after the founding of the Republic of China, a Chinese scholar or university student of "Han Learning" would have found Hu's book to be important, as it presents a new point of view on the history of Chinese thought. A fellow Chinese with a graduate education in Western philosophy would find Hu's *History* an inspiring and enlightening work of Chinese scholarship in the 1920s. For philosophers interested in the informal, pragmatic, logical aspect of ancient Chinese thought, he or she will find another pioneering study in Hu's *The Development of the Logical Method in Ancient China*. Influenced by Dewey's "experimental logic," Hu critically expounds the logical aspects of the *Analects of Confucius*, works of Mozi and his school, and Xunzi. The impressive attempt at a comprehensive, reconstructive study of the later Mohists' fragmentary, discursive texts appears almost a half-century after Hu's doctoral dissertation.[27]

This work on logical method also expresses Hu's attitude toward the history of Chinese thought, his solution, so to speak, to the "epistemological crisis." Hu writes: "How can we [Chinese] best assimilate modern civilization in such a manner as to make it congenial and congruous and continuous with the civilization of our own making?" The more specific problem is to find "a congenial stock with which we may organically link with the thought-systems of modern Europe and America, so that we may further build up our own science and philosophy on the

---

27. A. C. Graham, *Later Mohist Logic, Ethics and Science* (Hong Kong and London: Chinese University of Hong Kong Press, 1978).

new foundation of an internal assimilation of the old and the new." Critical of Song-Ming Confucianism, or what is commonly known in the West as Neo-Confucianism, as represented by major works of Zhu Xi and Wang Yangming, Hu thinks that these thinkers "rejuvenated the long-dead Confucianism by reading into it two logical methods which never belonged to it," i.e., "the theory of investigating into the reason in everything for the purpose of extending one's knowledge to the utmost, which is the method of Sung [Song] School; and the theory of intuitive knowledge, which is the method of the School of Wang Yang-ming." While appreciative of Wang's merits, Hu expresses his judgment that the method is "wholly incompatible with the method of science." As to the Song method of the investigation of things, it is a fruitless method in three different ways: "(1) by the lack of an experimental procedure, (2) by its failure to recognize the active and directing role played by the mind in the investigation of things, and (3) most unfortunate of all, by its construction of 'thing' to mean 'affairs.'" Hu has no doubt that the future of Chinese philosophy depends on "emancipation from the moralistic and rationalistic fetters of Confucianism."[28]

Hu's view raises important issues concerning his reading of Song-Ming Confucianism. One wonders, however, whether he has neglected a principal concern with ethical methodology in the works of Cheng Yi and Zhu Xi, and Wang Yangming. Significantly, their different conceptions of ethical methodology deploy the Confucian classic, the *Great Learning (Daxue)*, which emphasizes self-cultivation as the root or basis for the attainment of the Confucian ideal of human excellence. This emphasis on self-cultivation crucially involves not only the development of moral character, but also empirical inquiry, for example, Zhu Xi's interpretation of "investigation of things" as an activity of exhausting the *li* (rationales) for the existence of things and our conception of what things ought-to-be. More important, without a constructive, philosophical interpretation of Song-Ming Confucianism, it seems arbitrary to counsel Chinese thinkers to "build up our own science and philosophy on the new foundation of an internal assimilation of the old and the new."

28. Hu Shih, *The Development of the Logical Method in Ancient China*, 7–9. For my view on some of these issues on Wang Yang-ming and Confucian tradition, see my *The Unity of Knowledge and Action*, and *Moral Vision and Tradition*, Essays 9 and 11.

B. Fung Yu-lan (Feng Yulan 1895–1990)

The first volume of Fung's *History of Chinese Philosophy* (in Chinese) was published in 1931 and the second volume in 1934. Derk Bodde's English translation is an outstanding achievement, particularly in introducing Fung's work to English-speaking philosophers. The coverage of the first volume, from the beginnings to about 100 B.C., is more extensive than Hu Shih's *Outline*. All major thinkers and schools discussed by Hu reappear in Fung's first volume. Since both Hu and Fung obtained their doctoral degrees in philosophy from Columbia University, it is not surprising that they shared a similar judgment of the philosophical significance of the literature of ancient Chinese thought. However, the difference in time makes a noticeable difference in influence. Hu was largely influenced by John Dewey in the 1910s, Fung by William P. Montague in the 1920s. However, as we will later note, Fung was also appreciative of William James's and other philosophers' insights.

In the Introduction, reminiscent of but more explicit than Hu Shih's, Fung points out that originally "philosophy" was a Western term. According to Fung, one main task of the history of Chinese philosophy consists in selecting works that are amenable to philosophical treatment. The pursuit of this task presupposes that one has some understanding of the term "Western philosophy." Fung remarks: "In the West, the use of 'philosophy' has a long history. Different philosophers have their own definitions. However, for purposes of convenience, let us attend to its content. If we know the content of philosophy, we can know what sort of thing philosophy is."[29]

Again, much in the spirit of Hu Shih, Fung proceeds to mention the threefold Greek division of philosophy into physics, ethics, and logic, alternatively, "A Theory of World," "A Theory of Life," and "A Theory of Knowledge." Fung maintains that philosophy is a product of reason. "[Thus,] if philosophers want to establish the reasoned foundation of their theses, they must provide arguments, proofs or demonstrations.

---

29. Fung Yu-lan, *Zhongguo zhexue shi, fupu pian* (Hong Kong: Taipingyang, 1975), 1. Unless indicated otherwise, the following exposition is an interpretive reading of the Chinese text, 1–27. The Preface was dated 1962. Bodde's Introductory Chapter is a selected translation of Fung's Introduction to the Chinese edition. See Fung Yu-lan, *History of Chinese Philosophy*, 2 vols., trans. Derk Bodde (Princeton, N.J.: Princeton University Press, 1953). Shortly before his death in 1990, Fung completed a seven-volume comprehensive history of Chinese philosophy from the Marxist point of view. For a discussion of some salient features of this work, see Nicolas Standaert, "The Discovery of the Center through the Periphery: A Preliminary Study of Feng Youlan's *History of Chinese Philosophy* (New Version)," *Philosophy East and West* 45, no. 4 (1995): 569–90; and Nicolas Standaert and Bie Geivers, "Fung Yu-lan: Works on the History of Chinese Philosophy," in *Encyclopedia of Chinese Philosophy*.

This is the purport of Xunzi's saying, 'they [the thinkers criticized] have reasons for supporting their views and thus their words appear plausible,'[30] and Mencius's saying, 'Do I love to argue? I have no other alternative' [*Mencius*, 3B9][31])."[32]

Possibly addressing the audience of Western-trained Chinese thinkers who have no special interest in the philosophical study of Chinese thought or those skeptical of the intelligibility of talk about Chinese philosophy, Fung remarks: "There are three questions that most often occur to all persons interested in the history of Chinese thought. First, what is the nature of Chinese philosophy, and what contribution has it to make to the world? Secondly, is it true, as is often said, that Chinese philosophy lacks system? And thirdly, is it true that there is no such thing as growth in Chinese philosophy?"[33] Regarding the first question, Fung points out that we do find ethical and metaphysical concerns, but very little attention to logic or methodology and epistemology. For the most part Chinese philosophers do not think that knowledge has intrinsic value. Even in the case of knowledge of the practical sort, Chinese philosophers would stress its application to actual conduct rather than approve of empty discourse. Lack of Chinese contribution to epistemology can be explained partly by the widely shared ideal of "inner sageliness and outer kingliness" *(neisheng waiwang)* and partly by their lack of clear demarcation of "the distinction between the individual and the universe," alternatively put, the lack of the Western conception of the "ego." As to methodology, what the Chinese thinkers have emphasized, given their ideal of "inner sageliness and outer kingliness," are methods of self-cultivation. In this regard, China has "a great contribution to offer."

The foregoing contains a partial answer to the second question, "Is it true, as is often said, that Chinese philosophy lacks system?" Fung maintains that we must distinguish "formal *(xingshi)*" from "real" systems *(shizhi xitong)*. Says Fung:

> It may be admitted that Chinese philosophy lacks formal system; but if one were to say that it therefore lacks any real system, meaning that there is no organic unity of ideas to be found in Chinese philosophy, it would be equivalent to saying that Chinese philosophy is not philosophy, and that China has no philosophy. The earlier Greek philosophy also lacked formal system. Thus Socrates

---

30. This saying appears frequently in Xunzi's essay "Against Twelve Thinkers *(fei shi'erzi pian)*." See *Xunzi*, Book 6, 93–97.
31. D. C. Lau, trans., *Mencius* (Middlesex, England: Penguin Books, 1970), 3B9. Lau's translation is amended to reflect Fung's different punctuation of the Chinese text.
32. Fung, *Zhongguo zhexue shi*, 6–7.
33. Fung, *A History of Chinese Philosophy*, vol. 1, 1.

wrote no books himself, Plato used the dialogue form in his writings, and it was not until Aristotle that a clear and ordered exposition was given on every problem. Hence if we judge from the point of view of formal system, Aristotle's philosophy is comparatively systematic, yet insofar as the actual content of the philosophy is concerned, Plato's philosophy is equally systematic.... Although Chinese philosophy, formally speaking, is less systematic than that of the West, in its actual content it has as much system as does Western philosophy. This being so, the important duty of the historian of philosophy is to find within a philosophy that lacks *formal* system, its underlying *real* system.[34]

Perhaps Fung's distinction of formal and real systems is more plausibly rendered as a distinction between explicit or articulate and implicit or inchoate systems of philosophy. The idea of a formal system of philosophy sometimes has as its paradigm a logical, deductive, or quasi-deductive system as exemplified in Spinoza and Kant. Fung's use of "organic unity" suggests his adoption of the Hegelian terminology—an apt adaptation consistent with the holistic vision of *dao* in Zhuangzi and Xunzi, noted in section 1B above.

If one accepts Fung's thesis that Chinese thought has "real" systems though it lacks "formal systems," this thesis must be qualified by saying that so-called "real" systems are products of philosophical reconstruction or constructive interpretation. In this task, one must preserve the holistic spirit of Chinese philosophy. In a section entitled "The Unity of Philosophy," Fung cites Confucius's remark, "There is one thread that runs through my teachings."[35] More informative is Fung's citation of Xunzi's critique of different influential thinkers, that their minds have been "obscured *(bi)*" because they were so preoccupied with one thing and neglected the importance of other things. (Xunzi's comments on Mo Tzu and Zhuangzi were given in section 1B above.) Notably, Fung also reminds his reader of William James's view in *A Pluralistic Universe*: "If one aspect of the universe attracts the special attention of a philosopher, he would hold to it as if it were characteristic of the whole."[36]

34. Ibid., 4.
35. *Analects* 4.15.
36. Fung seems to have this passage in mind: "No philosophy can ever be anything but a summary sketch, a picture of the world in abridgement, a foreshortened bird's-eye view of the perspective of events. And the first thing to notice is this, that the only material we have at our disposal for making a picture of the whole world is supplied by the various portions of that world of which we have already had experience. We can invent new forms of conception, applicable to the whole exclusively, and not suggested originally by parts. All philosophers, accordingly, have conceived of the whole world after the analogy of some particular feature of it has particularly captivated their attention" (William James, *Essays in Radical Empiricism and A Pluralistic Universe* [New York: Dutton, 1971], 125–26). Recall Francis Bacon's remark: "The dispositions for philosophy and the sciences is this: that some are more vigorous and active in observing differences of things, others in observing their resemblances.... [Each carries the liability of] catching either at nice dis-

We find a similar view in a succinct remark of Wittgenstein, reminiscent of Xunzi's view of philosophers as victims of *bi* (obscuration/blindness) or aspect-obsession: "A main cause of philosophical disease—a one-sided diet: one nourishes one's thinking with only one kind of example."[37] This sort of preoccupation easily leads to overlooking other kinds of examples that may be even more important in formulating an adequate view of things. Like ordinary persons, great thinkers of the East or the West have a proclivity to exaggerate the significance of their insights as embodying "the whole truth and nothing but the truth." They tend to regard their partial views as representing the whole, presuming that they have the best understanding of the subject matter of inquiry. In the spirit of Zhuangzi, they are prompt to overstate the scope of their insights, "forgetful *(wang)*" of the limits of the exercise of our intellectual capacity.[38]

Let us turn to the third question: "Is it true that there is no such thing as progressive growth in Chinese philosophy?" Fung answers: "The problems and scope of Chinese philosophy from the Han dynasty onward are not so numerous and comprehensive as those of the philosophy that preceded it, and yet the later philosophy is certainly more clearly expounded than the earlier one."[39] (This judgment seems implicit in Hu Shih's critique of Song-Ming Confucianism.) Invoking Aristotle's distinction between potentiality and actuality, Fung maintains, in this Introduction to the first volume, that "movement from such potentiality to actuality constitutes progress."

However, as evident in Fung's division of the history of Chinese philosophy into two periods, progress does not mean advancement or development of new philosophical perspectives in the modern Western sense. The two periods are the Period of the Philosophers *(zixue shidai)*, from Confucius (551–479 b.c.) to Huainanzi (died 122 B.C.), and the Period of Classical Learning *(jingxue shidai)*, from Dong Zhongshu (195–105 B.C.) to Kang Youwei (1858–1927). The Period of Philosophers is characterized by "the simultaneous flourishing of many schools." This explains the scope of Fung's first volume, covering "only

---

tinctions or shadows of resemblance" (Francis Bacon, *Novum Organum*, Aphorism 55, in the *Works of Francis Bacon*, vol. 3 [Philadelphia, 1856], 349).

37. Ludwig Wittgenstein, *Philosophical Investigation*, trans. G. E. M. Anscombe, 3rd ed. (New York: Macmillan, 1958), #595.

38. This seems to be the purport of Zhuangzi's notion of "equalizing all things *(qiwu)*" in his critique of the disputes between the Confucians and the Mohists. See Watson, *The Complete Works of Chuang Tzu*, chap. 2. For the notion of "forgetting *(wang)*," see my "Forgetting Morality: Reflections on a Theme in *Chuang Tzu*," *Journal of Chinese Philosophy* 4, no. 4 (1977); or *Moral Vision and Tradition*, Essay 3.

39. Fung, *A History of Chinese Philosophy*, 1:5; *Zhongguo zhexue shi*, 22–25.

some four hundred odd years." For any philosophy student today, this is the most exciting period of Chinese thought. Perhaps for this reason, since the 1960s many philosophical scholars and historians of Chinese thought have devoted their time and energy to the ancient literature. This is a period when many original thinkers confronted each other in a free arena of argumentative discourse.

The Period of Classical Learning, on the other hand, is for the most part a period of Confucian Classicism or "scholasticism." According to Fung, if one follows the usual division of Western philosophy into ancient, medieval, and modern, "it may be said that China has actually had only an ancient and a medieval philosophy but still lacks a modern philosophy." Says Fung in 1934: "China, until very recent times, regardless of how we view it, has remained essentially medieval, with the result that in many respects it has failed to keep pace with the West. A modern age, indeed, has been lacking in Chinese history, and philosophy is but one particular aspect of this general situation."[40] Fung's view of the problem of Chinese philosophy raises an important issue of "the development of Chinese philosophy," alternatively, the evolution of the history of Chinese thought into a history of philosophy.

For Fung, philosophy must be distinguished from philosophers. A philosopher's philosophy reflects his character *(renge)*, that is, an individual temperament and experience. Following James, Fung distinguishes between tender-minded and tough-minded philosophers. "The tender-minded philosophers, because of tenderness of mind, cannot bear to sum up *(guina)* things, events, or states of affairs as the sphere of things that have no value whatever. Thus, their philosophies are idealistic, religious, free-willist, and monistic. The tough-minded philosophers, on the other hand, will have no qualms in ruthlessly summing up things, events, or states of affairs as the sphere of things that have no value whatever. Thus, their philosophies are materialistic, irreligious, fatalistic, and pluralistic."[41] Fung also cites Höffding's reminder, much in James's spirit, of the importance of "personal equation." Common to philosophical problems (e.g., problems of knowledge, existence, estimation or worth, and consciousness) is "that they lie on the borders of our knowledge, where exact methods can no longer help us; hence it is impossible but that the personality of the inquirer should determine

---

40. *Zhongguo zhexue shi,* 2:1–5.
41. Fung mistakenly refers to James's *A Pluralistic Universe* (*Zhongguo zhexue shi,* 15). His remark is almost a verbatim report of James's two-column table for contrasting tender-minded and tough-minded philosophers in *Pragmatism.* See William James, *Pragmatism and Four Essays from the Meaning of Truth* (Cleveland and New York: Meridian Books, 1955), Lecture 1, 22.

the course of his thought, although he himself may be unaware of the fact.... We must also take account, especially with regard to the problem of the estimation of worth, historical circumstances, and intellectual movements in other spheres."[42]

Therefore, when we take a person's philosophy as a subject of historical inquiry, we must pay attention to the circumstances and trends of events, as well as the different aspects of the intellectual situation of the time. Fung informs the readers that Mencius has a similar emphasis: "When one reads the poems and writings of the ancients, can it be right not to know something about them as men? Hence one tries to understand the age in which they lived."[43] Says Fung, "Although their motivation lies in their interest in the aspect of self-cultivation, the Song Confucians are specially attentive to *qixiang*, the prevailing spirit and atmosphere of the ancient sages. Thus the researcher of the history of philosophy must also have the same attitude toward a man's philosophy, that is, attentive to his *qixiang*."[44]

Fung also discusses the relation between history and the history of philosophy. Just as the circumstances, events, and intellectual situation of the time influence a philosopher's thought, the philosopher can also influence his age and the different aspects of thought. Alternatively put: "History can influence philosophy, philosophy can also influence history."[45] Next Fung takes up the problems of writing history. Among his contemporaries, a common saying is that in writing history, one must inquire into the antecedents and consequents of events. However, because of the surfeit of materials, it is impossible to have a complete or exhaustive narrative. Inevitably, selective decision is involved in studying the documents that constitute both the primary and secondary sources. It is doubtful that a sincere and dedicated historian, in relying upon his selective materials, can write a completely "faithful *(xin)*" or reliable history.

There are three major difficulties.[46] For clarifying the first difficulty, Fung cites a couple of passages from classical texts. In the Great Appendix of the *Yijing*, we find a saying attributed to Confucius: "Just as writing is a poor vehicle of speech, speech is a poor vehicle of thought."[47] In

42. Fung, *Zhongguo zhexue shi*, 15. Note that I have replaced Fung's paraphrase with the clearer English translation he cites. See Harold Höffding's *History of Modern Philosophy*, trans. B. E. Meyer (New York: Humanities Press, 1924), xvi.
43. Translation adopted from Lau, *Mencius*, 5B8, 158.
44. Fung, *Zhongguo zhexue shi*, 15–16.
45. Ibid., 16.
46. Ibid., 19–21. Below is a concise paraphrase of Fung's discussion of the difficulties of fidelity to history.
47. My translation. Cf. James Legge, trans., *I Ching: Book of Changes*, ed. Ch'u Chai and Winberg Chai (New York: University Books, 1964), 376–77.

the same spirit, Zhuangzi says: "When men of old died, they took with them the things that cannot be transmitted. So what you are reading there must be nothing but the chaff and dregs of the men of old."[48] Fung, therefore, contends that the researchers of history can only rely upon these "dregs" which they cannot completely comprehend.

The second difficulty is this. Even for a dedicated and profoundly reflective scholar who understands the writers' intention, ancient texts are not completely credible. Mencius remarks: "In the *Wu Qing* chapter [of the *Book of History*] I accept only two or three strips."[49] The historian can employ scientific method in weighing the reliability of sources and engage in the task of analysis. Afterward, the work of synthesis follows, tying the materials together through the exercise of imagination. Presumably, Fung has this point in mind. In order to establish continuity of texts, the historian may need to envisage appropriate hypotheses and supply the lacuna, especially those of the ancient texts, as well as to engage in constructive interpretation of central concepts of a philosopher's thought. All these tasks require the exercise of imagination. Historical claims, like Kant's "maxims," inevitably embody "subjective principles of volition" rather than "objective principles."[50] Consequently, we have no assurance that the historian's claims about his subject matter completely accord with the requirements of objective history. Moreover, unlike scientists who can set up experiments to test the adequacy of hypotheses, the historians cannot set up analogous experiments for testing historical hypotheses. This is the third difficulty.

At the time Fung published his work, in the early 1930s, Chinese philosophy and its history must have been an established subject of study. His lengthy introduction could have in mind a particular audience of philosophy students and perhaps skeptics. At that time Fung's work was the first full-scale effort at presenting a history of Chinese philosophy. Until today, Derk Bodde's translation is the only one available in English. Before he died in 1990, at the age of ninety-five, Fung completed a comprehensive, seven-volume, new history of Chinese philosophy. It

---

48. Translation adopted from Watson, *The Complete Works of Chuang Tzu*, 153. In the Ming dynasty, Wang Yang-ming is quite explicit about this aspect of teaching. Says Wang, "Sages and worthies wrote about them very much like a portrait painter painting the true likeness and transmitting the spirit. He shows only an outline of the appearance to serve as a basis for people to seek and find the true personality. Among one's spirit, feelings, expressions, and behavior, there is that which cannot be transmitted. Later writers have imitated and copied what the sages have drawn." (This is an emended translation based on Wang Yang-ming, *Instructions for Practical Living and Other Neo-Confucian Writings*, trans. Wing-tsit Chan [New York: Columbia University Press, 1963], section 20.)

49. Lau, *Mencius*, 7B3, 194.

50. Immanuel Kant, *Foundations of the Metaphysics of Morals*, trans. Lewis White Beck (Indianapolis, Ind.: Bobbs-Merrill, 1959), 17n.

was written from a single-minded Marxist point of view. His earlier work presented here, though more limited in scope, is informed by a liberty of spirit absent in much of Chinese Marxist histories of Chinese philosophy, thus open to greater independent, constructive philosophical interpretation of Chinese thought.[51]

C. Lao Sze-kwang (1927–)

The third and final volume of Lao's *History of Chinese Philosophy* (in Chinese) was completed and published in 1982. As compared to Fung's history, it has a narrower scope. The last chapter deals with Dai Zhen (1723–77). As any recent Western-trained Chinese philosopher would expect, Lao must provide some justification for his renewed attempt to write a history of Chinese philosophy, given the widespread familiarity with Fung Yu-lan's work. As compared with Fung's, Lao's is a more philosophically sophisticated work and is addressed to an audience familiar with works of Western philosophy published since the 1930s. Since World War II, many Chinese have studied philosophy in the United States and Europe. Given these writers' background in Chinese philosophy education, writings in Chinese on Western philosophy and Chinese philosophy are a familiar phenomenon. For philosophers and scholars in Taiwan and Hong Kong, and other Chinese in the diaspora, Chinese philosophy is a subject worthy of serious scholarly and/or philosophical pursuit. Except for an encounter with Western skeptics ignorant of the extensive works in Chinese philosophy since the 1960s, a Chinese philosopher or historian of philosophy is no longer beset with the question about the existence of Chinese philosophy. Of course, what is supposed is a contemporary Chinese philosophy audience. This is Lao's implicit audience in his long Preface in the first volume and Postscript in the third volume.

In his Preface, Lao points out that the course "History of Chinese Philosophy" had been an established offering in Chinese universities prior to Hu Shih's lectures (at the University of Peking in the late 1910s). Until the time he completed his first volume in 1967, Lao claims that on the history of Chinese philosophy there has been no "acceptable" work that conforms to "proper [Western] standards." Lao as-

---

51. Some Marxist histories of Chinese philosophy are valuable in presenting extensive expositions and selections from original sources. See, for example, Hou Wailou, editor-in-chief, *Zhongguo sixiang tongshi*, 5 vols. (Beijing: Renmin, 1959); and Ren Jiyu, editor-in-chief, *Zhongguo zhexue shi*, 4 vols. (Beijing: Renmin, 1979). For accounts of Fung's philosophy, see Lujun Yin, "Fung Yu-lan," in *Encyclopedia of Chinese Philosophy*. For Fung's histories of Chinese philosophy, see Standaert's paper cited in note 29.

sumes that there are general standards of competence for Western philosophical writings. Lao remarks that there are philosophy textbooks in Chinese, arbitrarily and conveniently composed by instructors for lecture purposes. With the exception of Fung Yu-lan's *History of Chinese Philosophy*, there are no competently written works on the history of Chinese philosophy. Hu Shih's incomplete *Outline of the History of Chinese Philosophy* is said to be a subject of ridicule, presumably by Lao's audience of colleagues and graduate students in Chinese universities. For Lao, the defect of Hu's *Outline* does not lie in its incompleteness, but in its lack of "philosophical" elements. To Lao a history of philosophy must be a "philosophy" and a "history." The historian of philosophy must not only present a narrative account of actual thought and related events but also have an "explanatory theory." The former is the task of historians, and the latter requires "theoretical foundation and analytical method." If these two requirements are not satisfied, what is written can only be considered "history" and not "history of philosophy." While Hu's history is a pioneering work, "strictly speaking, it can only be viewed as an unsuccessful experiment." Hu spends too much time on questions of dating and authenticity of texts. Although these questions may be considered a part of the historian of philosophy's task, they are not the most important. Moreover, Hu Shih's use of *changshi* (common sense or common knowledge) as a basis of explanation is problematic. Says Lao, "In any case, using *changshi* to interpret philosophy cannot make any contact with the real questions [of philosophy]."[52]

As regards Fung's *History*, it is definitely superior to Hu's. According to Lao, while Fung's is a history of philosophy, it is not a successful piece of work. For Fung does not show much depth in his command of Western philosophical literature. Fung's use of "concepts and theories is limited to early Plato's theory and New Realism." Fung hardly shows a firm grasp of Western philosophical theories. Moreover, lacking understanding of the special characteristics of Chinese philosophy, Fung could handle simple theories. "But as soon as he confronts Song-Ming *lixue* [Neo-Confucianism], he displays his weaknesses. From the very beginning, he could not deal with the concept of moral subjectivity. Though it may seem improbable, he was unaware of his deficient understanding [of the concept of] subjectivity itself. Consequently, he could only give an account, in a forced manner, of the Confucian doctrine of perfect virtue *(chengde zhixue)* as a mere metaphysical theory and failed to understand its essential aspects."[53] Lao goes on to claim that there is a

---

52. Lao Sze-kwang, *Xinbian Zhongguo zhexue shi*, vol. 1 (Taipei: Sanmin, 1984, 1st ed., 1982), 1–2.
53. Ibid., 1:3.

"great distance" between Fung's later *Xin lixue* (A New Doctrine of *Li*) and Song-Ming *lixue* (study of *li* or principle/rationale), as only early Plato's works and New Realism inform Fung's work.

Lao expounds at greater length his own conception of the history of philosophy, stressing the importance of methodology. Four methods of inquiry are discussed: systematic, developmental, analytic, and inquiry into fundamental questions of philosophic thought. The systematic method must also pay attention to the original contexts of theoretical thought. However, because of the writer's own philosophical interest, frequently he or she is liable to focus on philosophical questions and neglect the actual contexts of discourse. While the method of systematic inquiry has its pitfalls, from the holistic point of view, it has merits when it is employed with care. The developmental method raises complex questions. If the use of the method of systematic inquiry tends to err easily on the subjective side, the use of developmental method often results in a partial grasp of segments of actuality with no appreciation of the holistic character *(quanti)* of theories. As a result, what we get is a narrative of fragments. (Recall Xunzi's doctrine of *bi* or aspect-obsession.) For Lao, from the philosophical point of view, this is a serious defect, because it is contrary to the basic objectives of philosophy.

On the analytical method of inquiry, Lao stresses the importance of "philosophical analysis," which gives rise to syntactical and semantical analyses. Particularly worthy of attention and also influential is the emergence of the theory of "meaning criteria" and the use of this kind of theory in the critique of traditional philosophy. While it is not expected of a historian of philosophy, training in the skills of philosophical analysis can be useful in carrying out the tasks. Nevertheless, philosophical analysis cannot be a substitute for the historian's task of synthesis, for it can deal only with existing materials, and cannot propose new materials, in particular, an overall judgment of the history of philosophy as a whole. In sum, the three conditions for a history of philosophy are truth, system, and unity. The first requires that the narrative be faithful to the actual texts and circumstances; the second, the systematic exposition of theory; and the third, the unifying character of the judgment of the whole history of philosophy.

How is it possible for a historian to satisfy these requirements? Lao proposes his fourth method, embracing the other three methods. Lao says that for some time he has devoted much thought and energy to this question and arrived at the conclusion that, comparatively speaking, the fourth method is a good method. There are three steps in this method of inquiry into fundamental questions of philosophy. The first step consists in having a good understanding of the foundation of Chinese thought. Every individual thinker or school has, as its basis, an *ideal theory* for resolving certain fundamental problems. Although explanation is central to this task, one must also deal with the question of textual analysis. As regards the second step, after having a handle on fundamental questions, we can then proceed to an explication of the relevant theory. In the process, secondary questions may emerge. Each of these questions has its own answer, forming a section of the theory. Finally, organize all the levels of the theory, thus completing the task of explicating an individual theory. In doing so, we adequately satisfy the first two conditions, i.e., "truth," and "system."

The last step, corresponding to the third requirement of unity, lies in coherently organizing the materials into a series of the fundamental questions of different historical periods before rendering a holistic judgment on a theoretical basis. However, one must acknowledge certain "presuppositions *(shezhun)*," reflecting the writer's "own knowledge and experience *(shezhun)* as well as his philosophic wisdom." Finally, the method of inquiring into fundamental questions must be consonant with the writer's presuppositions.

In the concluding section of "Prefatory Remarks," Lao takes up some distinctive problems of the history of Chinese philosophy. The first problem, as Hu and Fung have noted, lies in managing the extant ancient textual materials. As an excuse for not engaging in argumentation, many Pre-Qin thinkers were fond of appealing to the past.[54] Also problematic is the tendency of some Post-Qin and Post-Han writers to forge documents. Secondly, hitherto Chinese philosophy has paid no attention to analysis. It has neither logic nor epistemology. Says Lao, "We must admit that what China lacks is analytical skills. Naturally, we have to adopt most of these skills derived from Western achievements." Thirdly, the fundamental questions of Chinese philosophy differ from those of Western philosophy. In the course of exposition, it is inevitable that the writer will employ his theoretical presuppositions, hoping to encompass both Chinese and Western philosophy. In a somewhat modest tone, Lao reminds his reader that his *History of Chinese Philosophy* is but one attempt to use the method of probing fundamental philosophical questions. When the draft for the whole project is completed, he ex-

---

54. The illegitimate use of the "appeal to the ancients" has often been unjustly ascribed to all Chinese thinkers of the Classical period. A careful examination of the works of Xunzi demonstrates the reasonableness of this appeal. See my "Ethical Uses of History in Early Confucianism: The Case of Hsün Tzu [Xunzi]," *Philosophy East and West* 35, no. 2 (1985): 133–56; incorporated in this volume as Essay 3. For a pinyin version, see essay of the same title in *Virtue, Nature, and Moral Agency in the Xunzi*, ed. T. C. Kline and Philip Ivanhoe (Indianapolis, Ind.: Hackett, 2000).

presses the hope that others may write a more successful history of Chinese philosophy. (The third and last volume of his *History* was published in 1982.)

Lao's critique of the works of Hu and Fung on the history of Chinese philosophy is hardly fair-minded. Lao's work is a philosophical, analytic reconstruction of the history of Chinese thought. It is distinguished by its conceptual analysis, emphasis on arguments and reasoned justification of interpretation, and a much greater command of Western philosophy and recent Confucianism that flourished in Hong Kong and Taiwan. Lao's critique of Hu Shih and Fung Yu-lan, however, makes no allowance for the nature of a particular audience.[55] Lao seems to regard his audience as a universal audience, a presumption of most Western philosophers since Plato. Like many philosophers of our age, with a penchant for objectivity or "the view from nowhere," Lao is a child of those Western philosophers beset by the fear of relativism and subjectivism. He does not seem to be worried about the problems recently presented by Richard Rorty, Alasdair MacIntyre, Derrida and his fellow deconstructionists. Indeed, the late distinguished philosophical Sinologist Angus Graham, in his book on ancient Chinese philosophy, proposed a novel deconstructionist interpretation of Lao Tzu.[56] Incidentally, Graham's philosophical history of ancient Chinese thought is based largely on his philological research in Classical Chinese and works of Benjamin Whorf and Gilbert Ryle. Notably absent are insights, say, derived from the works of Wittgenstein or J. L. Austin.

Were Hu Shih alive today, he would have pragmatically responded to Lao's or Graham's work by appealing to the middle and later works of Dewey such as *Experience and Nature* (1925, 2nd ed. 1929), *Art as Experience* (1934), and *Logic: The Theory of Inquiry* (1938), or perhaps to the more recent methodological pragmatism of Nicholas Rescher.[57] Perhaps out of courtesy, Lao acknowledges Hu's *Outline* as a pioneering work, but he pays no attention to Hu's introductory chapter, especially those sections devoted to articulating his conception of the subject. While there is a terminological difference, would Lao disagree with Hu's three objectives: understanding the changes or transformation of a particular school of thought, the reasons and causes for such transfor-

---

55. For the distinction between a universal audience and a particular audience, see Chaim Perelman and Anna Olbrechts-Tyteca, *The New Rhetoric: A Treatise on Argumentation* (Notre Dame, Ind.: University of Notre Dame Press, 1969), 31–35.

56. A. C. Graham, *Disputers of the Tao: Philosophical Argument in Ancient China* (La Salle, Ill.: Open Court, 1989).

57. Nicholas Rescher, *Methodological Pragmatism* (New York: New York University Press, 1977.)

mation, and objective, critical evaluation? As to Lao's complaint that Hu's is not a "philosophical" book, presumably because Hu spent too much time on textual analysis, it must be noted that at the time Hu wrote his book, in 1918, ancient Chinese texts, as Lao is well aware, were in a state of confusion. Hu has a pragmatic rather than analytic conception of philosophical scholarship. While textual scholarship has no essential connection with philosophy, it is still important for a philosophical historian to use the state of the art as a springboard for determining the development of a school of thought. Textual scholarship was more advanced at the time Lao wrote his first volume. However, there was still much uncertainty about the background, current circumstances, climates of opinion, and contexts of discourse.[58]

Instead of a sweeping rejection of Hu's book as non-philosophical, Lao should have examined Hu's objectives and shown the ways in which Hu failed to accomplish his objectives. We must agree that Hu's methodological remarks in his *Development* are, in the light of Fung or Lao or any later writer's philosophical training and commitments, much too biased toward Dewey's instrumentalism. For instance, Hu's unqualified condemnation of Song-Ming Confucianism was based on an implausible assumption that Zhu Xi and Wang Yangming were concerned with the application of inductive, deductive, or intuitive scientific methods to human affairs. Even a cursory reading of some of Zhu's and Wang's works would lead to an appreciation of the different ways they tried to preserve what they considered the "Confucian tradition" and their concern with ways in which the Confucian tradition was misinterpreted, abused, and misused, particularly in the hands of irresponsible scholars and/or officials. As I have shown elsewhere, a living tradition, as distinct from traditionalism or blind adherence to tradition, is amenable to quite different constructions, especially with regard to its concrete, temporal significance.[59] In passing, a contemporary Confucian appreciative

---

58. On textual uncertainty, recently Knoblock, an excellent translator and scholar of Xunzi's works, remarked: "Until we can establish a firm chronology of debates, determine with assurance the relative dates of texts, resolve problems of the authenticity of some texts, and explore the broader range of Chinese thinking, leaving behind the theological and imperial imperatives of orthodox *Ru* [*Ju*, 'Confucian'] thinkers, we shall not succeed in beginning the task of 'reconstructing' Chinese philosophy, however consistent and coherent the game we play." One may not agree with Knoblock's attitude toward "reconstruction" if that term put within quotation marks is meant to express a negative attitude toward philosophical reconstruction. The remark seems a good reminder of the utility of textual scholarship to the philosophical enterprise. See John Knoblock, *Xunzi: A Translation and Study of the Complete Works*, vol. 1 (Stanford, Calif.: Stanford University Press, 1988), xi.

59. For further discussion, see my "The Idea of Confucian Tradition," or *Moral Vision and Tradition,* Essay 12.

of the insights of Zhu Xi and Wang Yangming might even welcome Dewey's version of pragmatism, as a supplement to explicating the nature of Confucian ethics, since it provides a fairly effective way of clarifying its practical orientation. Let me explain.

Two salient features of Confucian ethics are the primacy of practice and the legitimate use of plausible presumption. The former admits of a pragmatic interpretation, because of the Confucian preoccupation with problematic situations and their ethical solutions. Although Confucians do not explicitly reject the doctrine of "fixed" or absolute ends, their emphasis on *yi* (rightness) suggests that ethically acceptable conduct in problematic situations must in some way be based on reasoned judgment appropriate to the case at hand. In Xunzi's words, in coping with changing and exigent situations of human life, one must employ *yi* or one's sense of rightness *(yiyi bianying)*. Redolent of Dewey's conception of deliberation in *Human Conduct,* Xunzi insists on clarity of mind as a prerequisite to wise and informed deliberation *(zhilü)*, in dealing with problematic situations of human life.[60] Xunzi would have agreed with Dewey that, in the final analysis, the really important matter pertains to the resolution of problematic situations through the use of means derived from past experience. A propensity to rely on common knowledge of the day without regard to the relevance of past experiences or the wisdom of tradition is a ubiquitous, human affliction. An appeal to the wisdom of the past should not be rejected outright, because it is an appeal to the past deemed as a repository of insights or plausible presumptions. Xunzi would also urge that just as we must employ the wisdom of the past to deal with the present perplexities *(yigu chijin)*, we must employ our knowledge of the present to evaluate any claims based on our knowledge of the past and/or past experience *(yijin chigu)*.[61] Moreover, the Confucian insistence on the unity of moral knowledge and action, words and actions has affinity with Dewey's thesis on the intrinsic connection between theory and practice.[62]

Lao's critique of Fung's *History* is especially revealing of his own conception of philosophy and the history of philosophy. Lao is not satisfied with Fung's limited knowledge and use of Western philosophy. Lao cites Fung's inability to appreciate the character of Song-Ming Confucianism, for he has no conception of "moral metaphysics." Lao has a more extensive knowledge of Western philosophy. But his appeal to "moral

---

60. See my "The Possibility of Ethical Knowledge," or Essay 6 in this volume.

61. These are the elucidative and evaluative functions of the appeal to established historical knowledge in argumentative discourse. For further discussion, see my "Ethical Uses of History in Early Confucianism," or Essay 3 in this volume.

62. See my *The Unity of Knowledge and Action*.

metaphysics" is an anachronism, for it is a Chinese/English term coined in the 1960s by Mou Zongsan, then a senior colleague of Lao's at the Chinese University of Hong Kong. Mou, an encyclopedic and original Chinese philosopher, expounds his thesis against the background of Kant's conception of "metaphysics of morals." For a student of Western philosophy with no knowledge of Chinese philosophy, "moral metaphysics" is an unfamiliar term. As far as I know, it is a technical term used by Mou Zongsan to distinguish his Confucian metaphysical theory of morals from Kant's metaphysics of morals. The term "moral metaphysics" is valuable in suggesting an important enterprise for Chinese moral philosophy. According to Mou, Kant has only metaphysics of morals but no moral metaphysics. Kant's conception is no more than a "metaphysical exposition of morals" or a "metaphysical deduction of morals." Metaphysics of morals takes morality as a subject matter. It borrows from the fruits of metaphysical inquiry in order to discover and establish the fundamental principles of morality. Moral metaphysics (inclusive of ontology and cosmology) considers metaphysics as a subject matter and approaches it through the human moral nature. In other words, for Mou, moral practice, in the sense of authentic attainment of Confucian sagehood, is the basis for conferring metaphysical significance on all things.[63]

Whether Mou is right about Kant or about mainline Confucianism, the distinction between moral metaphysics and metaphysics of morals is a useful approach for studying Song-Ming Confucianism. This distinction raises an important question on the interpretation of Chinese Confucian ethics as normative ethics, metaethics, or metaphysical ethics. I wonder whether Lao's use of Mou's interpretive thesis and such terms as *zhuti* (subjectivity) in criticizing Fung's work is an example of the fallacious use of "appeal to authority." If we deem moral theory as a relatively autonomous discipline, we can appropriate Mou's distinction for delineating an important aspect of philosophical inquiry without depreciating Fung's history.

Underlying Lao's dissatisfactions with Hu's and Fung's works is the extent to which his philosophical presuppositions are informed by a greater knowledge of recent Western and Chinese philosophy. It is unsurprising that Hu's and Fung's presuppositions were informed by philosophical movements that prevailed in their own times. Philosophi-

---

63. For a different view of Confucian ethics, see my "Reflections on Moral Theory and Understanding Moral Tradition" in *Interpreting Across Boundaries: New Essays in Comparative Philosophy*, ed. Gerald James Larson and Eliot Deutsch (Princeton, N.J.: Princeton University Press, 1988), and "Problems of Chinese Moral Philosophy," *Journal of Chinese Philosophy* 27, no. 3 (2000): 269–85.

cal presuppositions in a history of Chinese or of Western philosophy reflect the influence of current philosophical concerns, as evident in Western as well as Chinese graduate philosophy education. Hu was influenced by John Dewey, perhaps not sensitive to the Hegelian elements in Dewey's philosophy. Fung was influenced by his studies of early Plato, James, and Neo-realism. How could Hu and Fung be faulted for not knowing analytic philosophy or Mou Tsung-san? Fung seemed to be familiar with some works of the Vienna Circle. Fung said of his *Xin lixue*, one target of Lao's critique: "The work of New *Lixue* is to *re-establish* metaphysics by going through the empiricism of the Vienna Circle."[64] He could not be expected to know Wittgenstein's *Philosophical Investigations*.

Nevertheless, Lao's efforts at writing a philosophical history of Chinese thought merit approval, for a mastery of the literature of the history of Chinese thought and analytical method is an enormous undertaking. Most Chinese and Western scholars of Chinese thought are specialists in a historical period or in specific works of individual thinkers. Many of them do not have extensive philosophical training. Lao's emphasis on philosophical and argumentative analysis, as contrasted with Hu's on textual analysis, is a valuable contribution. From the standpoint of philosophical analysis, Lao's history is superior to Fung's. For a philosophical reader of Chinese classics, Lao's *History* provides an excellent guide to the rich repertoire of resources for philosophical thought, while he or she may demur on Lao's rash judgment on the worth of the works of Hu and Fung. Setting aside questions of textual fidelity and acceptability of his philosophical interpretations, Lao has performed a great service in providing a most useful resource for the development of the history of Chinese philosophy. Regrettably, Lao does not have a Derk Bodde for an English translation of his history. While Lao's requirements for writing a history of Chinese philosophy may appear too exacting, a Western-trained Chinese philosopher or a Sinicized Western philosopher would find Lao's *History* an invaluable guide to research.

While textual scholarship is an important enterprise, philosophical interpretation of Chinese thought has integrity of its own, independently of the question of contribution to textual scholarship. Apart from philosophical interpretation, there are also legitimate philological, intellectual, religious, and political interpretations. Admittedly, the history of Chinese thought maybe interpreted in these different, and possibly complementary, ways. Especially illuminating is a commingling of

64. Quoted in Wang Shouchang, "Feng Youlan and the Vienna Circle (A Synopsis)," *Journal of Chinese Philosophy* 21, nos. 3/4 (1994): 265.

philosophical and historical studies of ideas, as in Lovejoy's *Great Chain of Being*. However, absent the knowledge of and sensitivity to philosophical problems and issues, a confusion of these interpretive approaches will impede not only efforts at any wholesale philosophical transformation of the history of Chinese thought, but also the development of Chinese philosophy.[65]

While Lao's requirements for writing the history of Chinese philosophy may appear too exacting, he is right that a historian of Chinese philosophy must to some extent be a philosopher. Ideally, an understanding of basic philosophical questions in different branches of philosophy is a prerequisite to any serious philosophical inquiry into the thought of a historical period or of a major philosopher. A coherent statement of presuppositions in writing a history of philosophy, as Lao rightly insists, would provide the reader a unifying perspective of the writer's philosophical convictions. Nevertheless, in the Postscript to the third volume, Lao expresses his belief that Chinese philosophy has "universal significance" if we distinguish between "open and closed concepts" of philosophy. The terminology is reminiscent of Karl Popper's *Open Society and Its Enemies*. In a later English article, Lao explains that an "open concept" of philosophy would "enable people of different philosophical traditions to communicate with each other." In this conception, philosophy is a reflective enterprise. Understanding Chinese philosophy rests on appreciating its primary, "orientative" character, that is, that Chinese "intends to effect some change in the self or in the world." Alternative terms are "self-transformation" and "transformation of the world." Such a philosophy would give a statement of purpose, justification, and pragmatic maxims. Lao cites Zhuangzi and Mencius as examples. It is noteworthy that Lao shows concern with intercultural communication. Presumably he would also agree that this concern must be followed with an endeavor to provide some guidelines for resolving problems of intercultural conflict.[66]

---

65. Admittedly, the linguistic, religious, social anthropological, political, and other approaches may furnish valuable perspectives for the philosophical interpretation of Chinese thought. A singular example is the concept of *li* (rites) in Confucian ethics. See, for example, Herbert Fingarette, *Confucius—The Secular as Sacred* (New York: Harper Torchbooks, 1972); A. S. Cua, "Dimensions of *Li* (Propriety): Reflections on an Aspect of Hsün Tzu's Ethics," *Philosophy East and West* 29, no. 4 (1979), Essay 2 in this volume; and *"Li* and Moral Justification: A Study in the *Li Chi,"* *Philosophy East and West* 33, no. 1 (1983). See also "The Ethical and the Religious Dimensions of *Li* (Rites)," *Review of Metaphysics* 55, no. 3 (2002): 501–49, incorporated as Essay 7 in this volume.

66. Lao, "Understanding Chinese Philosophy," 265–91. For an attempt to state a set of Confucian principles as ground rules for adjudicating intercultural, ethical conflict, see my "Reasonable Challenges and Preconditions of Adjudication" in *Tradition and Modernity: East-West Philosophical Perspectives,* ed. Eliot Deutsch (Honolulu: University of Hawaii Press, 1991); expanded in Essay 14 of my *Moral Vision and Tradition*. Before concluding, I

The foregoing account of the works of Hu Shih, Fung Yu-lan, and Lao Sze-kwang presents illustrative samples of the positive influence of Western philosophy in the development of the history of Chinese philosophy. I should be remiss not to mention the massive work of Archbishop Luo Guang's *History of Chinese Philosophical Thought*. The seventh and presumably the last volume, published in 1986, deals with the period since the founding of the Republic of China in 1911. Separate chapters are devoted to major nonhistorical, philosophical works of Hu Shih and Fung Yu-lan as well as important contributions of the recent past, e.g., works of Xiong Shili, Tang Junyi, Thomé H. Fang (Fang Dongmei), and Lo Guang's own philosophy of life. Today, philosophical writings in Chinese are quite extensive, covering topics in Western philosophy, Chinese philosophy, Indian, Buddhistic, and comparative East-West philosophy. Philosophy journals in Taiwan, for example, are pretty much modeled after those in English. Unfortunately, except for some works of Thomé H. Fang, many original works of such influential philosophers as Mou Zongsan and Tang Junyi are not available in English.[67] Worthy of note is Fang's attempt in English to portray the holistic spirit of the history of Chinese philosophy. In *Chinese Philosophy: Its Spirit and Its Development,* Fang discusses the unitary spirit of Chinese philosophy by focusing on three ostensibly common features among primordial Confucianism, primordial Daoism, and Mahayana Buddhism, namely, (1) the doctrine of pervasive unity, (2) the doctrine of *dao,* and (3) the exaltation of the individual, along with an emphasis on a conception of the human individual "in terms of observed actualities and idealized possibilities." This large book complements his earlier English work on the Chinese philosophy of comprehensive harmony.[68] Perhaps, when translations of the principal writings of other major contemporary Chinese thinkers are available in English, there will be a beginning of creative and fruitful Chinese-Western philosophical dialogue on the history of philosophy, or East-West philosophy.

Apart from the importance of Chinese-Western philosophical dialogue, the study of Chinese philosophy should interest anyone con-

---

must draw attention to Lao Sze-kwang's ongoing Internet project *Lexicon of Confucianism* (in Chinese). The project is divided into texts, commentaries, personalities, and concepts. I have looked up some entries on fundamental concepts of Confucianism, such as *dao/tao, ren/jen* (humanity, benevolence), *yi/i* (rightness, righteousness), and *li/li* (rites). All are quite informative, particularly as a guide to the conceptual history of these notions. Doctrines pertaining to such problems as *xing/hsing* (human nature) provide an excellent guide to the issues and the historical, philosophical scholarship.

67. Tang's English papers entitled *Essays on Chinese Philosophy and Culture* were published as volume 19 of the *Collected Works of Tang Junyi* (Taipei: Student Book Co., 1987).

68. Thomé H. Fang, *The Chinese View of Life: The Philosophy of Comprehensive Harmony* (Taipei: Linking, 1980).

cerned with exploring the possibility of discovering fresh resources for dealing with philosophical questions, especially those of moral philosophy. Knowledge of Classical and Neo-Confucianism and Classical Daoism is especially germane to the pursuit of normative ethics, metaethics, and philosophy of morals. Questions of other branches of philosophy may also receive some light from the study of Chinese classics. I also hope that the last hundred years of endeavor by Chinese philosophical scholars may pave the way toward developing Chinese philosophy as a component of a world-philosophical inquiry. At the beginning of the twenty-first century, this should be an exciting prospect for young philosophers trained in both Chinese and Western philosophy.[69]

69. An early version of this paper was presented at the centenary celebration of the School of Philosophy at the Catholic University of America in the fall of 1996.

Essay 15

XIN (MIND/HEART) AND MORAL FAILURE: NOTES ON AN ASPECT OF MENCIUS'S MORAL PSYCHOLOGY

The following is a study of an aspect of Mencius's moral psychology. The first section deals with *xin* (mind-heart) as the seat of the "four beginnings" *(siduan)* of the four Confucian cardinal virtues, e.g., *ren* (benevolence, human-heartedness), *yi* (rightness, righteousness), *li* (rites, ritual propriety), and *zhi* (wisdom). This discussion presupposes the vision of the Confucian *dao*, an ethical ideal of the unity and harmony of Heaven and humanity *(tianren heyi)*. The second section examines Mencius's account of moral failure with a Xunzian supplement. The essay concludes with some remarks on Mencius's contributions to Confucian ethical theory.

1. 'XIN' AS THE SEAT OF VIRTUES

In an earlier paper, I proposed that the contrasting positions of Mencius and Xunzi on human nature are versions of internalism and externalism.[1] At issue is the question of the connection between morality and human nature. For Mencius, an internalist, the connection is intrinsic, for the intelligibility of moral achievement depends on certain inherent moral capacities. For Xunzi, an externalist, the connection is extrinsic. When we focus on the regulative aspect of morality, we readily think of morality as a system of rules, which aims to counteract a certain problematic basic motivational structure, particularly the native tendency of humans to create problems for one another. However, if we focus on the ideal aspect of morality, or *ren* (in the broad sense), as an ideal of

---

1. A. S. Cua, "Morality and Human Nature," *Philosophy East and West* 32, no. 3 (1982): 279–94; also in Cua, *Moral Vision and Tradition: Essays in Chinese Ethics* (Washington, D.C.: The Catholic University of America Press, 1998), Essay 6.

the good human life as a whole, it is an object of sentiment as well as an object of volition for a committed agent. This moral ideal furnishes a way of seeing persons as having moral import. It is a perspective, a point of orientation, an *ideal theme* rather than a norm for assessing conduct.[2] Given the commitment to the ideal, compliance with rules and principles of morality has ethical significance only when these rules and principles are invested with the ideal of humanity. For this sort of moral achievement, morality can have nothing to do with benefits extrinsic to personal commitment. Perhaps this is the basis for the familiar characterization of the difference between Mencius and Xunzi as located in their respective emphasis on *ren-and-yi* and *li-and-yi*. Mencius's doctrine of *siduan*, four seeds or sprouts of Confucian virtues, makes an important contribution to the problem of the connection between morality and human nature.

If we look at the four cardinal virtues as general specifications of the Confucian ideal of *dao*, Mencius's doctrine of *siduan* provides an insightful account of the possibility of realizing this holistic ideal of the good human life. Consider Mencius's doctrine as an answer to the question, "How can I become a Confucian agent?" In some ways, this is reminiscent of Kierkegaard's "How can I be a Christian?" Notably, this is a question of self-transformation, of the actuating import of the Confucian ideal of *dao* or *ren* in a broad sense. However, in Classical Confucian ethics, *ren* is often used in a narrow sense.[3] The distinction between the broad and the narrow senses of *ren* is clear, for example, in Zhu Xi's view that *ren* embraces the four virtues, which include *ren* in the narrow sense *(ren bao side)*.[4] *Xin* is the seat of *siduan*. The proper development of *siduan* into virtues or ethical attributes depends on perseverance or preserving the constancy of *xin (hengxin)*.[5]

Recall that the *siduan* are the *xin* of (1) compassion *(ceyin zhi xin)*, (2) aversion to shame *(xiuwu zhi xin)*, (3) courtesy and modesty *(cirang zhi xin)*, and (4) right and wrong *(shifei zhi xin)*. If we regard the *siduan* as sentiments, we can say that *xin*, while expressive of a feeling, has both cognitive and emotive aspects. The adoption by many Sinologists of

---

2. See my *Dimensions of Moral Creativity: Paradigms, Principles, and Ideals* (University Park: Pennsylvania State University Press, 1978), chap. 8.

3. See Wing-tsit Chan, "The Evolution of the Confucian Concept *Jen [Ren]*," *Philosophy East and West* 4, no. 4 (1955): 295–319; Cua, *Dimensions of Moral Creativity;* and Kwong-loi Shun, *Mencius and Early Chinese Thought* (Stanford, Calif.: Stanford University Press, 1997).

4. See *Renshuo,* translated in W. T. Chan, *A Source Book in Chinese Philosophy* (Princeton, N.J.: Princeton University Press, 1963), 394; Zhu Xi, *Zhuzi yulei,* 8 vols. (Taipei: Zhengzhong, 1962), 6.10a.

5. On *siduan* as "ethical attributes," see Shun, *Mencius,* 48.

"mind-heart" as a translation of *xin* rightly presumes a Mencian rejection of an exclusive disjunction between "reason/judgment" and the "passions/emotions." This notion of sentiment captures the sense of Butler's apt characterization of "moral faculty" as "a sentiment of the understanding or perception of the heart."[6] More importantly, implicit in the notion of sentiment is prereflective judgment. As Reid points out,

> Our moral determinations may, with propriety, be called *moral sentiments*. For the word *sentiment*, in the English language, never, as I conceive, signifies mere feeling, but judgment accompanied with feelings. . . . So we speak of sentiments of respect, of esteem, of gratitude. But I have never heard the pain of the gout, or any other mere feeling, called a sentiment.[7]

Plausibly, these sentiments embody *prereflective* judgments subject to reasoned refinement.[8] In this light, Mencius's doctrine of *siduan* is a doctrine of moral sentiments.

More formally, the *xin* of compassion, for instance, is expressed as a *qing* or feeling, which pragmatically implies an epistemic attitude, i.e., belief, thought, or judgment.[9] Thus, the *xin* of compassion involves the

---

6. In "A Dissertation Upon the Nature of Virtue," Butler writes: "It is manifest great part of common language, and of common behavior over the world, is formed upon the supposition of such a moral faculty, whether called conscience, moral reason, moral sense, or divine reason; whether considered as a *sentiment of the understanding or perception of the heart*, or, which seems the truth, as including both" (Joseph Butler, *Five Sermons* [Indianapolis, Ind.: Bobbs-Merrill, 1950], 82; my emphasis). James Legge quotes extensively from Butler's first three sermons in discussing Mencius's *siduan* with emphasis on "conscience" or "the principle of reflection," and maintains that the substance of Butler's reasoning "is to be found in Mencius." See James Legge, trans., *The Works of Mencius*, in *Chinese Classics*, vol. 1 (Oxford: Oxford University Press, 1893), 58–62; see also D. C. Lau, trans., *Mencius* (Middlesex, England: Penguin Books, 1970), Introduction, 12.

7. Thomas Reid, *Essays on the Active Powers of the Human Mind* (Cambridge, Mass.: MIT Press, 1969), 468–69.

8. This is a qualification of Reid's notion of moral sentiments. Similar qualification would apply to Solomon's claim: "The heart of every emotion is its value judgments, its appraisals of gain and loss, its indictments of offences and its praise of virtue, its often Manichean judgments of 'good' and 'evil,' 'right' and 'wrong'" (see Robert Solomon, *The Passions: The Myth and Nature of Human Emotion* [New York: Anchor Books, 1977], 267). More concisely, Solomon writes, "Emotions are judgments—normative and often moral judgments" (see Cheshire Calhoun and Robert Solomon, eds., *What Is an Emotion? Classic Readings in Philosophical Psychology* [New York: Oxford University Press, 1984], 312). Arguably, one of the difficulties of such a thesis is that it fails to acknowledge the "conceptual gulf between 'emotion' and 'belief'" (Calhoun and Solomon, 330–31). For linguistic facility, perhaps it is better to regard Mencius's doctrine as a doctrine of moral senses. In this way, we can simply speak of the *xin* of compassion as "the sense of compassion," the *xin* of modesty and courtesy as "the sense of modesty," the *xin* of aversion to shame as "the sense of shame," and the *xin* of right and wrong as "the sense of right and wrong."

9. In Xunzi, we find a sharper distinction between *xin* and *qing* (passions/feelings). *Xin* has a primary cognitive function that is distinct from *qing*. When this function is guided by *li** (reason), *xin* can provide a reliable ethical guide to the expression of *qing*. This

following: (a) a feeling of alarm and distress, (b) an implicit belief, thought, or judgment that one ought to help the person in distress, and (c) a disposition to act accordingly. Since the *siduan*, the germs of virtue, are spontaneously expressed, these epistemic attitudes are subject to reasoned evaluation. I take this to be the purport of Mencius's remark that reason and rightness *(li* yi)* are common to all *xin*. Says Mencius, "The sage is simply the man first to discover this common element in my heart *(xin)*. Thus reason and rightness please my heart in the same way as meat pleases my palate" (6A7).[10] In this interpretation, *ren* (in the narrow sense of benevolence), for example, is a fruition of the *xin* of compassion, presuming that it is properly expressed and that the epistemic attitude is reasonably justified. If this point is acceptable, we can say that for Mencius, expressing the four *xin* does not automatically lead to the acquisition of the four virtues *(ren, yi, li, and zhi)*, unless the expression is mediated by reason *(li*)*.

As germs of the cardinal virtues, the *siduan* are capacities for ethical achievement. Basically, they are capacities of agency (e.g., capacities to initiate and bring about changes in current states of affairs, changes that are explainable by the notion of practical, rather than theoretical, causation).[11] The Confucian cardinal virtues are achievements. This interpretation is based on a retrospective view of Confucian virtues as the successful development of the *siduan*. In this way, moral virtues are qualities of character. Consequently, we can depict the Mencian cardinal

---

notion of *xin* is best rendered as "mind" in the sense of the mental capacity of remembering, thinking, judging, and reasoning, rather than a sort of mental feeling or affection, as seems to be implicit in Mencius's doctrine of *siduan*. It must be noted that Xunzi's conception of *xin* also embraces a volitional function, which may counter its intellectual or cognitive function, resulting in different sorts of cognitive delusion *(huo)*. However, when it approves of *dao* and is guided by *li**, *xin* can provide a reliable ethical guide to conduct. For a fuller discussion, see Cua, *Ethical Argumentation: A Study in Hsün Tzu's Moral Epistemology* (Honolulu: University of Hawaii Press, 1985), chap. 4; and "The Possibility of Ethical Knowledge: Reflections on a Theme in the *Hsün Tzu*," in *Epistemological Issues in Ancient Chinese Philosophy*, ed. Hans Lenk and Gregor Paul (Albany: State University of New York Press, 1993); incorporated in this volume as Essay 6.

10. Translations from the *Mencius* are based on Lau (1970), with modification in some cases. For the Chinese original, see Shi Ciyun, *Mengzi jinzhu jinyi* (Taipei: Shangwu, 1974).

11. For the distinction between theoretical and practical causation, see R. G. Collingwood, *An Essay on Metaphysics* (Oxford: Clarendon Press, 1962), 287. For the role of practical causation in Confucian ethics, see Cua, "Practical Causation and Confucian Ethics," *Philosophy East and West* 25, no. 1 (1975): 1–10; reprinted in this volume as Essay 9. In this connection, ethical capacities may also be called "active powers" in Reid's sense (Reid, *Essays*, 11): "The term *active power* is used ... to distinguish it from speculative powers, the same distinction is applied to the powers by which they are produced. The powers of seeing, hearing, remembering, distinguishing, judging, reasoning, are speculative powers; the power of executing any work of art or labour is active power. The exertion of active power is called *action;* and as every action produces some change, so every change must be caused by some exertion, or by the cessation of some exertion of power."

virtues as ethical attributes or qualities of persons.[12] This is consistent with a prospective view of virtues as goals of action. These two conceptions are complementary, since the former depends on learning the moral significance of the virtues as having actuating or transformative import in human life.[13]

In sum, for Mencius, expressing the four *xin* does not automatically lead to the ethical virtues of *ren, yi, li, and zhi,* unless their expression is mediated by reason and a sense of rightness *(li* and yi).* Among other factors, the exercise of *quan* (weighing of circumstance) in exigent situations plays a crucial role. In the next section, we will discuss the other factors.

In normal situations, informed by Confucian culture and in the absence of the interfering factors to be explored later, one would expect, say, compassion to be expressed fairly spontaneously. Mencius stresses *quan* as a standard: "It is by weighing a thing that its weight can be known and by measuring it that its length can be ascertained. It is so with all things, but particularly with the heart *(xin)*" (1A7). Consider the exercise of *quan* in, for example, the case of the drowning sister-in-law (4A17). Implicit is a reasonable prereflective judgment of rightness in an exigent situation.[14] Moreover, the proper exercise of *quan* presupposes that the agent has an open mind. As Mencius (7A26) reminds the Confucian agent, he must not hold on to any one particular moral doctrine even if it represents a moderate position between extremes *(buzhiyi).* Apart from the case of the drowning sister-in-law, we find suggestions of other features; for example, Mencius's characterization of Confucius (5B1) as a sage of timeliness *(sheng zhi shizhe),* and his saying

---

12. Shun, *Mencius,* 48.
13. Cua, *Dimensions of Moral Creativity,* chap. 2, and *The Unity of Knowledge and Action: A Study in Wang Yang-ming's Moral Psychology* (Honolulu: University Press of Hawaii, 1982), chap. 1.
14. A study of the notion of *quan* in *Zhuzi yulei* discloses some salient features. Concisely put: (a) As a metaphorical extension of the basic sense of a steel yard for measuring weight, *quan* pertains to assessment of the importance of moral considerations to a current matter of concern. Alternatively, the exercise of *quan* consists in a judgment of the comparative importance of competing options answering to a current problematic situation. (b) The situation is such that it presents a *hard case,* that is, a case falling outside the scope of operation of normal standards of conduct *(jing).* These standards of conduct provide insufficient guidance for the situation at hand. (c) *Quan* is an exercise of moral discretion and must conform to the requirement of *yi* (rightness, righteousness). (d) The judgment must accord with *li** (reason, principle), that is, be a principled or reasoned judgment. (e) The immediate objective of *quan* is to attain timely equilibrium *(shizhong),* namely, to do the right thing *(yi)* as appropriate to the demand of the current situation. (f) The ultimate objective of *quan* is to further the realization of *dao* or *ren* as the holistic ideal of the good human life. See Chan, *Source Book;* and Cua, *Dimensions of Moral Creativity.* For more extensive discussion, see Cua, "The Idea of Confucian Tradition," *Review of Metaphysics* 45, no. 4 (1992): 803–40; or Cua, *Moral Vision and Tradition,* Essay 12.

that reason and rightness *(li* yi)* are common to all *xin* (6A7). These remarks provide partial support for our interpretation of the cognitive-emotive nature of *siduan*. If this interpretation is correct, we must reject the philosophical attribution of ethical intuitionism to Mencius.[15]

I assume that Mencius's ethical ideal of *ren* in the broad sense is an ideal theme, an ideal of the good human life that has a concrete specification in particular human lives, regardless of their stations in society. The rich and the poor, the eminent and the mean, must have the same opportunity for realizing *ren*. The actuating force of Confucian aretaic notions presupposes a reflective capacity of the committed Confucian agent to make reasonable judgments in particular circumstances. I take this to be the force of Mencius's remark on *buzhiyi* (not holding to one thing): "Holding on to the middle *(zhong)* is closer to being right, but to do this without moral discretion *(quan)* is no different from holding to one extreme. The reason for disliking those who hold to one extreme is that they cripple the Way *[dao]*. One thing is singled out to the neglect of a hundred others" (7A26).[16] Mencius, as mentioned, admired Confucius as a timely sage (5B1). This stress on timeliness underlies Mencius's example of the drowning sister-in-law, where *quan* is exercised. In contrast, where a situation permits time for reflection and decision, Xunzi would say that this is a case for using *yi* to cope with changing circumstances *(yiyi bianying)*.[17]

The development of *xin* presupposes an extension of *ren*, an affectionate concern for human beings and ultimately for all things in the world. Says Mencius,

> If a man is able to develop all these four germs that he possesses, it will be like a fire starting up or a spring coming through. When these are fully developed, he can take under his protection the whole realm within the Four Seas, but if he fails to develop them, he will not be able even to serve his parents. (2A6)

The realization of this vision presupposes the "constancy of *xin (hengxin)*." For example, "Am I willing, as a Confucian committed to *ren* as an

---

15. Appeal to *liangzhi* and *liangneng* (7A15) does not support an intuitionist interpretation. "Intuition" in Western ethical theory is a technical term with various philosophical uses. Unless one clearly stipulates its use, the attribution of ethical intuitionism to Mencius is uninformative and highly misleading. My emphasis on the cognitive aspect of *siduan* does not imply acceptance of any version of ethical intuitionism. For the uses of "intuition" in ethical theory, see Cua, "The Concept of Moral Intuition," *Reason and Virtue: A Study in the Ethics of Richard Price* (Athens: Ohio University Press, 1966), Appendix.

16. For an insightful discussion of *buzhiyi*, see Chen Daqi, *Mengzi de mingli sixiang ji qi bianshuo shikuang* (Taipei: Shangwu, 1968), chap. 2. Lau translates *quan* as "proper measure" in this instance.

17. See *Bugou pian* 43; *Zhishi pian* 306. The Chinese text I used is Li Disheng, *Xunzi jishi* (Taipei: Xuesheng, 1979).

ideal of the good human life, in the current difficult case, to forego self-interest?" An affirmative answer to this question requires the Confucian agent to harmonize his or her thought, feeling, words, and deeds. In this light, the realization of the Confucian ideal of the good human life is a personal achievement.

2. MORAL ACHIEVEMENT AND FAILURE

For Mencius's conception of moral achievement, i.e., the full development of the four germs *(siduan)* into four cardinal virtues *(ren, li, yi, zhi)*, we present the following schema for explication:

The *xin* of X (for example, compassion) is the capacity to feel X and be mindful of the situation that calls for performing X-act. If X is appropriately expressed in the current case and certain deficiencies are not present, then the Confucian agent may be ascribed the virtue V. Alternatively, an act cannot be properly described as a V-act, unless it is an exercise of X as an inherent human capacity.

Failure to develop *xin* is due to failure to overcome certain deficiencies of moral agency. I distinguish six such deficiencies in this context:

D1. Lack of will. The agent may be unwilling to subject his/her desires to reasoned assessment, or does not appreciate the import of extending *xin* (e.g., in the case of extending beneficence *[tui'en]*).

D2. Lack of a constant *xin (hengxin)*. This may be due to the enticement of personal gain at the expense of *yi*, or failure in preserving moral integrity.

D3. Lack of a sense of moral priority or importance, especially when there is a conflict of goods.

D4. Lack of constant self-examination, leading to failure in correcting moral faults.

D5. Lack of means to support a constant *xin*.

D6. Lack of appreciation of the nature of the current situation.

In the proposed schema, we assume a negative approach to understanding moral achievement, i.e., the full development of *xin*, through an inquiry into the possibility of moral failure. This approach makes no claim to completeness or adequacy, for it gives only the principal and necessary and not the sufficient conditions for understanding Mencius's conception of moral achievement as a full development of *xin* as the seat of the cardinal virtues.

(D1) Lack of Will

When King Xuan of Qi inquired about a virtuous person becoming a true king, Mencius cited the incident when the King could not bear to see the blood of an ox in a sacrifice and suggested the use of a lamb instead. Mencius remarks: "The heart *(xin)* behind your action is sufficient to enable you to become a true king. . . . Your failure to become a true king is due to a refusal to act *(buwei)*, not to an inability to act *(buneng)*." Mencius explains the difference between refusal to act and inability to act as follows:

If you say to someone, "I am unable to do it," when the task is one of striding over the North Sea with Mount T'ai under your arm, then this is a genuine case of inability to act. But if you say, "I am unable to do it," when it is one of massaging an elder's joints for him, then this is a case of refusal to act, not of inability. Hence your failure to become a true king is not the same in kind as "striding over the North Sea," but the same as "massaging an elder's joints for him."

. . . In other words, all you have to do is take this very heart here and apply it to what is over there. Hence one who extends his bounty *(tui'en)* can bring peace to the Four Seas; one who does not cannot bring peace even to his own family. (1A7)

The foregoing passage provides a basis for discussing the sources of moral failure. Moral failure may be a failure owing to lack of willingness to extend *xin*, which reflects a failure to appreciate the distinction between *buneng* and *buwei*. *Buneng*, the inability to act in an appropriate way, construed as incapacity, may be an exculpating circumstance for excuse or justification of moral failure. *Buwei*, the refusal to act, however, is an expression of resolve. Because it manifests the agent's character, it is subject to ascription of ethical responsibility, even though the agent may not be conscious of the nature of his act. Given the native moral capacity, the agent, King Xuan of Qi, can extend beneficence *(tui'en)* to the people, thus bringing peace to the realm. More fundamentally, every sincere committed Confucian must extend *ren* and *yi* (7B31). With Xunzi, we may want to make a related distinction between *neng* (actual capacity) and *ke* (theoretical possibility). It is theoretically possible that everyone can become *(ke yi wei)* a sage, yet as a matter of actuality, some cannot *(buneng)* become one. "Thus, there is a wide distance between *neng bu neng* and *ke bu ke*. We must not confuse the distinction."[18] Mencius's case of *buwei* (not doing) is perhaps more clearly

---

18. *Xingwu pian* 554; cf. Burton Watson, trans., *Hsün Tzu: Basic Writings* (New York: Columbia University Press, 1963), 167–68, and John Knoblock, *Xunzi: A Translation and*

read as *buken*, unwillingness, implying deliberate intention not to do something or a deliberate negative action as the Daoist *wuwei*.

(D2) Lack of Hengxin

At issue then is the importance of preserving *hengxin* (a constant *xin*).[19] For if a person does not do *(buwei)* the right or good thing in a particular situation, it may be that he or she was unwilling *(buken)* to do so. Following Confucius, Mencius draws a fairly sharp contrast between *yi* (rightness) and profit or personal gain (1A1). The envisaged conflict between *yi* and concern with personal gain provides a partial ground for construing *yi* as reflecting the Confucian moral point of view as contrasted with the point of view of self-interest.[20] For Mencius, an agent's lack of *hengxin*, the constant or persevering *xin*, may well be a result of preoccupation with personal gain without attending to the relevance of *yi* as a basis for assessment, or the exercise of *quan* particularly when the situation is one that promises personal gain.

Alternatively, lack of *hengxin* is a failure to appreciate *xin* as a weighing standard for determining the ethically proper course of action. Moreover, the failure may also be a result of the corruption of moral integrity. Mencius once said that a great man "cannot be led into excesses when wealthy and honoured or deflected from his purpose when poor and obscure, nor can he be made to bow before superior force" (3B2). On another occasion, Mencius was insistent on the ethical integrity of the sages: "The conduct of the sages is not always the same. Some live in retirement, others enter the world; some withdraw, others stay on; but it all comes to keeping their integrity intact *(guijie qishen)*" (5A7). Indeed, integrity is not limited to the sages: No self-respecting villager would sell himself into slavery "in order to help one's prince towards achievement" (5A9). More important, a wayfarer, or even a beggar, would not accept a basket of rice or a bowl of soup if it were tendered in an abusive manner, particularly when the behavior violates the requirements of *li* and *yi* (6A10).

Ordinarily, failure to preserve one's ethical integrity is a failure of *cheng* (being true to oneself). Says Mencius, "Being true *(cheng)* is the

---

Study of the Complete Works, 3 vols. (Stanford, Calif.: Stanford University Press, 1989–1994), 3:159–60. For an excellent study of the distinction between *keyi* and *neng* in the *Xunzi*, see Kim-chong Chong, "Xunzi's Systematic Critique of Mencius," *Philosophy East and West* 53, no. 2 (2003).

19. I construe *hengxin* as an agent's commitment to Confucian *dao* or *ren*. For a discussion of the creative aspect of Confucian agency focusing on Wang Yangming, see Cua, *Unity of Knowledge and Action*.

20. Cua, *Dimensions of Moral Creativity*, 67–68.

Way of Heaven; to reflect upon this is the Way of man. There has never been a man totally true to himself who fails to move others. On the other hand, one who is not true to himself can never hope to move others" (4A12). Indeed, the utmost development of *xin (jinxin)* presupposes knowing one's nature *(xing)*. Elsewhere, Mencius states:

> For a man to give full realization to his heart *(jin qixin)* is for him to understand his own nature and a man who knows his own nature will know Heaven *(tian)*. By retaining his heart *(cun qixin)* and nurturing his own nature *(yang ci xing)* he is serving Heaven. Whether he is going to die young or live to a ripe old age makes no difference to his steadfastness of purpose. It is through awaiting whatever is to befall him with a perfected character that he stands firm on his proper destiny. (7A1)

Since moral integrity lies in a genuine commitment to the actuating force of *ren* and *yi*, the agent must be prepared to sacrifice his or her life for the sake of that commitment. Recall Confucius's saying: "A scholar dedicated to *dao* or a *ren*-person would not seek to stay alive at the expense of *ren*. He would accept death in order to have *ren* actualized."[21] Mencius is more elaborate on this spirit of sacrifice as depicted in his well-known statement of inner moral conflict:

> Fish is what I want; bear's palm is also what I want. If I cannot have both, I would rather take bear's palm than fish. Life is what I want; doing what accords with *yi* is also what I want. If I cannot have both, I would rather take *yi* than life. On the other hand, though death is what I loathe, there is something I loathe more than death. That is why there are troubles I do not avoid. If there is nothing a man wants more than life, then why should he have scruples about any means, so long as it helps him to avoid troubles? Yet there are ways of remaining alive and ways of avoiding death to which a man will not resort. In other words, there are things a man wants more than life and there are also things he loathes more than death. This is an attitude not confined to the good person but common to all men. The good person simply never loses it. (6A10)

Here we have the familiar Confucian emphasis on *yi* as a guide to one's moral life: "The ethically paradigmatic individual *(junzi)* considers *yi* as the most important thing in life" *(Lunyu* 17.23). Mencius's remark is especially noteworthy, because it draws attention to the importance of making an autonomous choice when the agent confronts, so to speak, the ultimate predicament, whether to sacrifice life or *yi*. Notably, the ethical attitude depicted in 6A10 refers to a natural innate ethical capacity of all humans. Sagehood is simply the culmination of the devel-

---

21. *Lunyu* 15.9. Translations from the *Lunyu* are based on D. C. Lau, trans., *Confucius: The Analects* (Middlesex, England: Penguin Books, 1979), with modification when necessary. For the Chinese text, see Mao Zishui, *Lunyu jinzhu jinyi* (Taipei: Shangwu, 1975).

opment of *xin* of common humanity (4A2), not the exclusive attainment of a few elites who have dedicated their lives to the actualization of *siduan*.

(D3) Lack of a Sense of Moral Priority

The lack of a sense of moral priority or importance is connected with (D2) in the sense that it may be influenced by the factors that interfere with the preservation of *hengxin*. However, for Mencius, given his view on the inherent goodness of human nature, (D3) is a fairly typical human experience. According to Mencius, one can distinguish the degrees of ethical worth of persons by observing their choices, since they reflect concern with the greater or smaller import of the different aspects of personhood *(dati* and *xiaoti)*. Human beings are creatures of the same kind, but some are greater than others because of the choices they make. Those who follow and nurture *dati* (the more important and more valuable aspects of personhood) become great men, and those who follow *xiaoti* (the less important and less valuable aspects of personhood) become small men.

Now consider a gardener. If he tends the common trees while neglecting the valuable ones, then he is a bad gardener. A man who takes care of one finger to the detriment of his shoulder and back without realizing his mistake is a muddled man. A man who cares only about food and drink is despised by others because he takes care of the less important and less valuable aspects of himself *(xiaoti)* to the detriment of the more valuable aspects *(dati)*. If a man who cares about food and drink can do so without neglecting any other aspects of his person, then his mouth and belly are much more than just a foot or an inch of his skin. (6A14)

What explains the difference between great and small persons? Mencius replies that though equally human, some are guided by *dati* and some by *xiaoti*.

The organs of hearing and sight are unable to think and can be misled by external things. When they interact, they merely attract one another. The organ of *xin* can think. But it *(xin)* will succeed in performing its function only if it thinks. If it does not, it will not function properly. This is what Heaven has given me. If one makes one's stand on what is of greater importance in the first instance, what is of smaller importance cannot displace it. In this way, one cannot but be a great man. (6A15)

The above passages from 6A14 and 6A15 contain invaluable insights when we reflect on the task of moral theory and agency. First, Mencius's conception of agency presupposes the idea of the freedom of choice.

Indeed, it is difficult for moral theorists to make sense of their subject matter unless moral agents are presumed to have freedom of choice and their choices are subject to reasoned evaluation. Mencius is emphatic that *xin* is a standard of evaluation (1A7). Thus Mencius's use of *xin*, in the light of 6A15 and 1A7, pertains to *xin* as an "evaluative mind."[22] This use supports our earlier interpretation that *xin* has a cognitive aspect, which appertains primarily to evaluation. An elaboration of the *xin* of aversion to shame *(xiuwu zhi xin)* and the *xin* of right and wrong *(shifei zhi xin)* is hardly intelligible without the cognitive aspect of *xin*. The former as the root of the virtue *yi* implies that the agent can know and appreciate the distinction between shame and honor and can identify the sorts of situation to which the distinction applies. The latter, the *xin* of right and wrong, is the rudimentary capacity to distinguish right from wrong conduct, though the agent may make mistakes in such an identification. Indeed, Mencius's *liangzhi*, however it is rendered, implies *liangneng*, which, as Wang Yangming points out, is the innate capacity to appreciate moral distinctions or an expression of *shifei zhi xin*.[23] More generally, we may say that for Mencius, the successful actualization of the four *xin* or *siduan* depends crucially on reflective mediation.

Pondering Mencius's notion of freedom of choice, one may ask whether this notion conveys the idea of autonomy. If one proffers an affirmative answer, the autonomy must be understood in the value-neutral sense of self-government, a notion that has nothing to do with issues of the validity of Kantian and post-Kantian conceptions of moral autonomy.[24] This sense of autonomy of *xin* is explicit in *Xunzi:*

22. Donald J. Munro, *The Concept of Man in Ancient China* (Stanford, Calif.: Stanford University Press, 1969).

23. See, for example, Wang Yangming, *Instructions for Practical Living and Other Neo-Confucian Writings,* trans. Wing-tsit Chan (New York: Columbia University Press, 1963), section 162; and Cua, *Moral Vision and Tradition,* Essay 9.

24. Perhaps to avoid misleading association with the ideal of moral autonomy, it may be better to adopt the term "autarchy," as suggested by Benn. Among other things, ascription of autarchy to any person depends on whether the agent is capable of recognizing the evidential and inferential grounds for justifying changes in belief, capable of making decisions in the light of preferences, and capable of formulating policies that will actualize present preferences. See S. I. Benn, "Freedom, Autonomy, and the Concept of a Person," *Proceedings of the Aristotelian Society,* 76 (1976), 116. Though a matter of constructive interpretation, Benn's notion of autarchy may be ascribed to Mencius in an inchoate form. Most of Benn's requirements for autarchy are much more explicit in Xunzi; see, for example, Cua, *Ethical Argumentation* and "The Possibility of Ethical Knowledge," Essay 6 in this volume. For the notion of constructive interpretation as one of finding the best explanation and justification of a topic for explication, see Ronald Dworkin, *Law's Empire* (Cambridge, Mass.: Harvard University Press, 1986).

Xin is the ruler of the body and the host of godlike insights *(shenming zhi zhu)*. It gives commands but does not receive commands. [Of its own volition] it prohibits or permits, renounces or selects, initiates or stops. Thus the mouth can be forced to speak or to be silent; the body can be forced to crouch down or to stretch out. But *xin* cannot be forced to change its opinions. What it considers right it will accept; what it considers wrong it will reject. Hence, we have the saying: "The salient features of *xin (xinrong)* are these: Its choices are not subject to any external control. Inevitably it manifests its own choices."[25]

Here we have a statement of *xin*'s freedom of volition. Thus *xin* must be guided by reason *(li*)*. Without such guidance, it would be incapable of resolving doubts concerning right or wrong conduct. Because of its volitional freedom, without knowing and accepting the ideal of *dao* as the ethical standard for evaluating conduct, *xin* may even reject *dao* as a guide to right conduct. Xunzi agrees with Mencius that all human beings can become sages.

The sage follows his desires, satisfies all his emotions and at the same time is restrained, because he possesses reason *(li*)*. What has he to do with strength of will, endurance, or fearlessness? The man of *ren* practices *dao* through inaction; the sage practices *dao* through non-striving. The thoughts of a benevolent man are reverent; the thoughts of the sage are joyous. This is the way to govern *xin*.[26]

Given its autonomy, from Xunzi's standpoint, the problem is the unity of *xin*, that is, coordination of its intellectual and volitional functions by way of the ethical ideal of *dao*.[27] This is a problem of self-transformation. In Confucius's view *(Lunyu* 12.1), the agent must have self-discipline and pay heed to the requirements of the rules of proper conduct *(li)*.

Let us now focus again on Mencius's distinction between *dati* and *xiaoti*, the greater and the lesser aspects of personhood. Without a *xin* informed by reflection and the ideal of *dao* or *ren*, the person would be unable to make proper ethical choices. The distinction between *dati* and *xiaoti* supposes that the situation an agent confronts is one of conflict between goods that are deemed desirable, i.e., the available options seem to the agent to be benefit-producing. Recall our earlier citation of 6A10 involving the choice between fish and bear's palm, and in the

---

25. *Jiebi pian* 488. This translation is an emendation of Watson, 129; and Knoblock, 3:105. My translation differs from both with respect to the italicized expressions, which is a critical interpretation of Machle's discussion of the beginning of the passage, but it differs from him on the interpretation of *shenming*. See Edward Machle, "The Mind and the 'Shen-ming' in Xunzi," *Journal of Chinese Philosophy* 19, no. 4 (1992): 361–86. For justification of my rendering of *shenming zhi zhu*, see Cua, "The Ethical and the Religious Dimensions of *Li*," *Review of Metaphysics* 55, no. 3 (2002): 501–49; incorporated in this volume as Essay 7.

26. *Jiebi pian* 494; Watson, 133; modified.

27. Cua, *Ethical Argumentation*, 138–41.

more extreme case the choice between *yi* and life. More generally, in any situation that presents live options between desirable states of affairs, Confucian agents may make the wrong choice, because of failure to weigh adequately the comparative value of options in the light of their ethical commitments. Among other things, moral theory should be concerned with this sort of ordinary human experience of a conflict of goods or values rather than with conflict between goods and evils.[28] Moreover, in the light of the role of reflection guided by an ethical ideal, the proper evaluation of the degree of importance among competing options would require reasoned judgment. Since this judgment may differ from that imposed by established rules of conduct, it acknowledges implicitly the distinction between the customary and reflective morality.[29] We may also add that moral theory must also deal with exigent cases that call for the exercise of *quan* discussed in section 1 above.

Before proceeding further, we must note a profound difference in attitude between Mencius and Xunzi toward human desires, quite apart from their different conceptions of human nature *(xing)*. While both recognize the problematic tendency of some of our desires and the importance of distinguishing ethical from non-ethical desires (7B25), Mencius would advocate a reduction of desires in self-cultivation. Says Mencius,

> There is nothing better in nourishing *xin* than to reduce the number of one's desires. When a man has but few desires *(guayu)*, even if there is anything he fails to retain in himself, it cannot be much; but when he has a great many desires, then even if there is anything he manages to retain in himself, it cannot be much. (7B35)

Compare this attitude with Xunzi's critique of two prevailing theories of desires:

> Those who advocate the elimination of desires before there can be orderly government fail to consider whether the desires can be guided, but merely deplore the fact that they exist at all. All those who advocate the reduction of desires *(guayu)* before there can be orderly government fail to consider whether desires

---

28. John Dewey, *Theory of the Moral Life*, ed. Arnold Isenberg (New York: Holt, Rinehart and Winston, 1963), 3–7. This is a redaction of Part II of Dewey and James Tufts, *Ethics*, rev. ed. (New York: Holt, Rinehart and Winston, 1932).

29. Dewey argues that moral theory "emerges when men are confronted with situations in which different desires promise opposed goods and in which incompatible courses of action seem to be morally justified. Only such a conflict of good ends and of standards and rules of right and wrong calls for personal inquiry into the bases of morals. . . . For what is called moral theory is but a more conscious and systematic raising of the question which occupies the mind of any one who in the face of moral conflict and doubt seeks a way out through reflection" (Dewey, *Theory of the Moral Life*, 5).

can be regulated, but merely deplore the fact that they are so numerous. Beings that possess desires and those that do not possess desires belong to two different categories—the categories of the living and the dead. But the possession or non-possession of desires has nothing to do with good government or bad.[30]

Here perhaps lies Xunzi's greater emphasis on *li* as rules of proper conduct, for in addition to their regulative and ennobling functions, crucially *li* have also a supportive function. In Xunzi's view, *li* also provide channels for the satisfaction of desires *(geiren zhi qiu)*. As suggested in his remark on the good *(shan)* as that which is (ethically) desirable (7B25), Mencius would agree with Xunzi that those desires that counter the realization of the Confucian *dao* must be transformed into ethically desirable ones.[31] In other words, one must distinguish between natural, occurrent desires and reflective desires. Indeed, this distinction is implicit in Mencius's statement of moral conflict (6A10). Yet he does not seem to appreciate fully the supportive function of *li*. One might object that Mencius advocated the reduction of desires because of his concern with "distorted desires."[32] To this rejoinder, Xunzi would point out that at issue is the development of reflective desires in accord with the guidance of reason and invested with a concern with *li* and *yi*.[33] Again, we find grounds for the common distinction of emphasis on government by *ren* in Mencius and government by *li* in Xunzi. A reasonable solution may lie in reconciling internalism and externalism on the connection between morality as a regulative system and human nature. This issue in Confucian ethical theory has its counterpart in Western

---

30. *Zhengming pian* 527, Watson, 151; modified. Elimination of desires is advocated in the *Laozi*, chap. 37; and by Song Xing, criticized by Xunzi in the *Zhengming pian*. For further discussion of Xunzi's view on this issue, see Cua, "Dimensions of *Li* (Propriety): Reflections on an Aspect of Hsün Tzu's Ethics," *Philosophy East and West* 29, no. 4 (1979): 373–94, incorporated in this volume as Essay 2; and *Moral Vision and Tradition*, Essay 13.

31. Cua, *Moral Vision and Tradition*, Essay 13.

32. Shun, *Mencius*, 174–75.

33. The distinction between natural and reflective desires seems implicit in the following perplexing passage in *Xunzi*: "A single desire which one receives from nature *(tian)* is regulated and directed by the mind in many different ways, consequently, it may be difficult to identify and distinguish it from its original appearance.... If the guidance of the mind accords with reason *(zhongli)*, although desires are many, what harm will this be to good government?" (*Zhengming pian* 527; Watson, 151, modified). This interpretation by way of Frankfurt's distinction between first-order and second-order desires (Harry G. Frankfurt, "Freedom of the Will and the Concept of Person," *Journal of Philosophy* 68, no. 1 [1971]), corresponding to the distinction between natural and reflective desires, was proposed in my "Dimensions of *Li*" (1979): 380–81. After publication, I discovered a similar interpretation of this problematic passage in Liang Qixiong's annotated text. Liang remarks that the contrast lies in the distinction between *tianxing yu* (desires as endowed by nature or natural desires) and *lixing yu* (desires as guided by reason or reflective desires). Because of this distinction, it is difficult to classify all desires in the same way. See Liang Qixiong, *Xunzi jianshi* (Taipei: Shangwu, 1978), 323.

ethical theory, in the debate between Kantianism and Utilitarianism, though the Confucian issue is more complex, as it involves questions concerning the viability of a moral tradition *(daotong)*. With few exceptions, post-Kantian Western ethical theory rejects moral tradition as being an uncritical guide to conduct, although pre-Kantians like Shaftesbury and Reid would emphasize *sensus communis,* the sense of common interest in a moral community.[34] The anti-tradition moral theory fails to distinguish intelligent, critical adherence to tradition from blind adherence to the prevailing understanding of the living significance of tradition. As Pelikan succinctly states: "Tradition is the living faith of the dead, traditionalism is the dead faith of the living."[35]

Before we take up (D4), let us also observe that value conflict does not pertain only to the conflict between moral and nonmoral values. Perhaps the more difficult cases involve conflict between moral goods. Notably our *xin* of compassion *(ceyin zhi xin)* may conflict with our sense of honor or aversion to shame *(xiuwu zhi xin)*. Such cases give rise to the question of the unity of *siduan* and consequently, the unity of the four cardinal virtues. Zhu Xi's doctrine of *ren* (in the broad sense) as the virtue of *xin (xin zhi de)* and as embracing the four virtues is one attempt worthy of further inquiry. At any rate, without a doctrine of the hierarchy of values, the burden is placed upon the Confucian agent to exercise *quan* carefully. For one committed to *ren,* the task involved is the burden of *ren* (*Lunyu* 8.7), a burden of moral creativity.

(D4) Lack of Self-Examination

Obviously the exercise of moral creativity depends on self-cultivation, which involves constant self-examination, so that the agent can correct his/her character faults and misconduct. Thus (D4) is a familiar Confucian concern. In the *Lunyu*, we have this remark of Zengzi's: "Everyday I examine myself on three counts. In what I have undertaken on another's behalf, have I failed to do my best? In my dealing with my friends have I failed to be trustworthy? Have I passed on to others anything that I have not tried out myself?" (*Lunyu* 1.4).

Self-examination may also be described, following the *Great Learning (Daxue),* as a process of attaining *chengyi* or sincerity of thought, which significantly requires avoidance of self-deception. Ideally the result of

---

34. Cua, *Moral Vision and Tradition,* Essay 12.
35. Jaroslav Pelikan, *The Vindication of Tradition* (New Haven, Conn.: Yale University Press, 1982), 65. The most important exception is Alasdair MacIntyre, *After Virtue* (Notre Dame, Ind.: University of Notre Dame Press, 1984, and *Whose Justice? Which Rationality?* (Notre Dame, Ind.: University of Notre Dame Press, 1988).

self-examination is freedom from self-reproach. As Confucius reminds his pupils, "If, on examining himself, a man finds nothing to reproach himself for, what worries or fear can he have?" (*Lunyu* 12.4). Mencius concurs: "A *junzi* (paradigmatic individual) differs from other men because he examines his heart *(xin)*. He examines his heart by means of *ren* and *li*."[36] Suppose someone treats him in an outrageous manner. He will turn around and examine himself *(zifan)*, and say to himself "I must be lacking in *ren* and *li*, or how could such a thing happen to me?" When self-examination discloses that he has done nothing contrary to *ren* and *li*, and yet the outrageous treatment continues, he will say to himself, "I must have failed to do my best for him" (4B28). It must be noted that the possibility of others' reproach or the concern with honor or one's "face" *(mienzi)* is also a proper subject of self-examination. We find this point in an apt comment on *chengyi* in *Daxue* (section 6):

Therefore the *junzi* must be watchful when he is alone. Tseng Tzu [Zengzi] said, "What ten eyes are beholding and what ten hands are pointing to—isn't it frightening?" Wealth makes a house shining and virtue makes a person shining. When one's mind is broad and his heart generous, his body becomes big and is at ease. Therefore a *junzi* always makes his thought sincere.[37]

Ideally, intrinsic honor *(yirong)* coincides with circumstantial honor *(shirong)*.[38] In the end, if frequent self-examination is successful, one can

---

36. *Mencius* 4B28. My translation here reads *cun* as *cha* (examine) in accordance with Jiao Xun's gloss. See Shi Ciyun, *Mengzi jinzhu jinyi*, 233n.

37. Chan, *Source Book,* 90; modified.

38. It is often said that modern Chinese are concerned with "face." But as Hu Hsien Chin points out, there is a distinction between *mianzi* and *lian*. The former pertains to social standing and does not necessarily have moral implications. The latter implies satisfaction of the moral standards of the society. A person concerned with *lian* is one who possesses a sense of decency and regard for moral virtues. See Hu Hsien Chin, "The Chinese Concepts of 'Face,'" *American Anthropologist*, n.s., 46 (1944): 45–64. This distinction between social and ethical standards is implicit in Mencius's conception of shame (see Shun, *Mencius,* 58–53). More explicit is Xunzi's distinction between intrinsic shame *(yiru)*, i.e., shame justly deserved because of the agent's misconduct, and circumstantial shame *(shiru)*, i.e., shame experienced as a result of external circumstances, e.g., poverty, lowly social position, and the like. Also, for the Confucian, concern for one's name *(ming)* or reputation is always a reasonable concern except, according to Xunzi, in the case of circumstantial shame, i.e., when one is in a shameful situation that has nothing to do with one's moral fault. In this way, Xunzi may concur with Hume's insightful remark on the love of fame: "By our continual and earnest pursuit of a character, a name, a reputation in the world, we bring our own deportment and character frequently in review and consider how they appear in the eyes of those who approach and regard us. This constant habit of surveying ourselves, as it were, in reflection, keeps alive all the sentiments of right and wrong, and begets in noble natures a certain reverence for themselves as well as others, which is the surest guardian of every virtue" (David Hume, *An Inquiry Concerning the Principles of Morals* [Indianapolis, Ind.: Bobbs-Merrill, 1957], 96). For a study of the Confucian conception of shame, see note 49 below.

claim with justification to have a modicum of self-knowledge *(zizhi)*. One hopes the process of self-examination, in conjunction with the constant practice of *ren, li,* and *yi,* will culminate in personal attainment or realization of *dao (zide).*

However, this process requires the person to engage in reflection detached from preoccupation with personal gain, especially in a context in which one is predisposed to violate the requirement of *yi* (rightness). Earlier we cited Confucius's reminder that a *junzi* considers *yi* to be of the highest importance *(Lunyu* 17.23). The aim of self-examination is self-knowledge. At a minimum, self-knowledge consists in acknowledging one's knowledge and ignorance. This is perhaps the force of Confucius's saying: "To say you know when you know, and to say you do not when you do not, that is knowledge *(zhi)*" *(Lunyu* 12.17). Self-knowledge enables the moral agent to prevent the recurrence of misconduct, and in so doing to preserve his *xin (cunxin).*

(D5) Lack of Means to Support a Constant Xin (Hengxin)

We must note the frequent interplay of the above conditions of deficiency (D1–D4). Take, for example, the lack of concern with moral priority. Crucially this depends on circumstances occasioned by the presence of things cherished by the agent. Failure to preserve constant *xin (hengxin)*, despite the agent's sincere efforts, may simply be a result of inaccessible and/or unavailable means to support it. Says Mencius,

> Only a *junzi* can have a constant heart *(hengxin)* in spite of a lack of constant means of support. The people, on the other hand, will not have constant hearts if they are without constant means. Lacking constant hearts, they will go astray and fall into excesses, stopping at nothing. To punish them after they have fallen foul of the law is to set a trap for the people. How can a benevolent man in authority allow himself to set a trap for the people? Hence when determining what means of support the people should have, a clear-sighted ruler ensures that these are sufficient, on the one hand, for the care of parents, and, on the other, for the support of wife and children, so that the people always have sufficient food in good years and escape starvation in bad; only then does he drive them toward goodness; in this way the people find it easy to follow him. (1A7)

Mencius's concern for human welfare as a prerequisite for the pursuit of the Confucian *dao* is an important insight for moral theory. It is unreasonable for any moral theory to require compliance with its principles or ideals without a clear understanding of the defeasible conditions. What is the point of asking ordinary people to follow the commands of the presumably *ren* ruler unless they are provided with the necessary means to do so? Even if one wants to do the good and the right thing as required by the Confucian cardinal virtues, one must have adequate means for sustaining at least a decent standard of living. Confucius's attitude in *Lunyu* (12.7) does not fully appreciate this point about good government. He seems to advocate trust of the people over providing sufficient food for them, though subsuming arms to these concerns. Admittedly a *junzi* would sacrifice his life for the sake of *ren* (*Lunyu* 15.9). For ordinary people, on the contrary, the lack of constant means of support is one major source of moral failure.

I think Mencius would agree with Xunzi that handicapped or incapacitated persons such as the dumb, the deaf, and the crippled deserve special consideration and protection for welfare. "The government should gather them together, look after them, and give them whatever work they are able to do. Employ them, provide them with food and clothing, and take care to see that none are left out."[39] Claims of disability must be demonstrated, for those who are capable of working even in menial tasks must assume some responsibility. Economic goods for maintaining a morally decent life need not be extensive in quantity; but minimal economic sustenance and accessibility to goods are preconditions of moral conduct. Were these goods unavailable or inaccessible, anticipation of virtuous and/or right conduct is hardly reasonable. Moral requirements for action are thus subject to defeat by the absence of resources, the necessary means to moral performance. Although a few laudable moral agents are capable of self-sacrifice and even giving up their life for the sake of *ren*, we cannot reasonably expect ordinary humans to do the same. In my youth I was impressed by someone saying, "You cannot preach morality to a starving man." This serves as a constant reminder in my decades of teaching ethics: Ethics is empty of moral significance unless it acknowledges the intimate connection between scarcity and moral evils. Today when we ponder the woeful poverty of millions of people throughout the world, it is difficult not to acknowledge our responsibility to ameliorate their predicament.[40]

---

39. *Wangzhi pian* 161; Watson, 34.

40. In James's suasive words: "Whether we are empiricists or rationalists, we are ourselves parts of the universe and share the same one deep concern in its destinies. We crave alike to feel more truly at home with it, and to contribute our mite to its amelioration" (William James, *Essays in Radical Empiricism and A Pluralistic Universe* [New York: E. P. Dutton, 1971], 128). [For more discussion of the significance of welfare considerations for moral theory, see "Moral Theory and the Quality of Life," Essay 10 in this volume.]

(D6) Lack of Appreciation of the Situation

The lack of appreciation of the nature of the situation at hand is a common human failing. One reason for this failure is the tendency of most human beings to adhere to fixed ideas. Because of this tendency, many rigid adherents of Confucian orthodoxy often fail to appreciate the importance of *quan* and the exercise of *yi* in exigent circumstances.[41] These Confucians seem oblivious to Mencius's reminder that persons dedicated to the fulfillment of *ren* do not always traverse the same paths. "All that is expected of a *junzi* is *ren*. Why must he be exactly like other *junzi*?" (6B6). In the pursuit of *ren* or the ideal of the good human life, sincere and thoughtful persons *(chengzhe)* would pursue different paths to realize the ideal. After all, *ren* (in the broad sense) is an abstract ideal of the good human life that requires concrete specification in the lives of ordinary humans. Because of differences in temperament, experience, and stations in society, persons devoted to *ren* will respond to changing circumstances in quite different ways. Since *ren* is an ideal theme, it has polymorphous actualization in the human world. If my interpretation of this aspect of Mencius's thought is disputed, consider my reading as a response to those Kantian interpreters of Mencius.[42] Issues of universality of moral principles or moral autonomy are alien to Confucian ethics, though I do not deny that Kantian ethics can contribute to the development of Confucian ethics. In Mencius and Xunzi, and later Song-Ming Confucianism, we find a predominant idea of reason *(li*)* as reasonableness rather than rationality.[43]

One aspect of reasonableness is the ability to size up the situation, to consider whether moral notions have appropriate application in a current situation. I take this to be the point of Zixia's remark in *Lunyu* (19.6): "Learn widely and be steadfast in your purpose, inquire earnestly and reflect on what is at hand *(jinsi)*, and there is no need for you to look for *ren* elsewhere."[44] Among Confucians influenced by Mencius,

---

41. For an informative study of Song-Ming orthodoxy in Confucianism, see Wm. Theodore de Bary, *Neo-Confucian Orthodoxy and the Learning of Mind-and-Heart* (New York: Columbia University Press, 1981).

42. Li Minghui, *Kangde lunli xue yu Mengzi daode sikao zhi chongjian* (Taipei: Zhongyang yanjiu yuan, 1994).

43. For further discussion of *li**, see Cua, *Dimensions of Moral Creativity*, 96–98; *Unity of Knowledge and Action*, 91–100; and "Reason and Principle in Chinese Philosophy," in *A Companion to World Philosophies*, ed. Eliot Deutsch and Ron Bontekoe (Oxford: Blackwell, 1997); incorporated in this volume as Essay 13.

44. This remark inspired the title of Zhu Xi and Lü Zuqian's anthology of Song Confucianism, *Jinsi lu*. See W. T. Chan, trans., *Reflections on Things at Hand: The Neo-Confucian Anthology Compiled by Chu Hsi and Lü Tsu-ch'ien* (New York: Columbia University Press, 1967).

Wang Yangming especially stresses the importance of reflection of things at hand. "The sage does a thing when the time comes.... The study of changing conditions and events is to be done at the time of response. The thing to do is to keep the mind clear as a mirror and engage in moral reflection."[45] Note that this Confucian notion of reasonableness does not deny the use of reason (li*) in deductive or inductive inferences, though it favors informal, practical reasoning that employs a variety of plausible considerations in support of a conclusion.[46] If this Confucian theory of argumentation is deemed plausible, the study of the logic of *quan* is one important task of contemporary Confucian philosophy.[47]

Conclusion

This essay on Mencius's conception of moral failure is a prolegomenon to a larger project on Confucian moral psychology. Among other things, we need a more elaborate treatment of *siduan* and the factors or sources of moral failure,[48] correction of character flaws and misconduct *(gaiguo)*, and shame as an internal monitor of moral thought and action.[49] Perhaps more important is the Confucian problem of conflict of values.[50] This essay articulates some of Mencius's insights concerning creative moral agency. Morality, in its ideal aspect, is a personal creative achievement. For this reason, Confucian paradigmatic individuals *(junzi)*, committed to *dao* or *ren*, will always have a role to play in character education and self-cultivation.[51]

Moreover, it is difficult to make sense of moral achievement unless something like the *siduan* provides the roots for moral growth. The interfering factors in the successful exercise of moral agency will always be a source of concern. One thing perhaps stands out: Unless our mind *(xin)* is free from obscurations *(bi)* and attendant delusions *(huo)*, as Xunzi points out, it is unlikely that our *siduan* will flourish into the Con-

45. Wang, *Instructions for Practical Living*, section 21; modified.
46. Cua, *Ethical Argumentation*, chap. 2; *Moral Vision and Tradition*, Essays 1 and 10.
47. For a discussion of this concept, see Cua, "*Quan (Ch'üan):* Moral Discretion," in *Encyclopedia of Chinese Philosophy*, ed. Antonio S. Cua (New York and London: Routledge, 2003).
48. Shun, *Mencius*, 173–79.
49. For the Confucian conception of shame, see my "Ethical Significance of Shame: Insights of Aristotle and Xunzi," *Philosophy East and West* 53, no. 2 (2003); incorporated in this volume as Essay 8.
50. Tang Junyi, *Renwen jingshen zhi chongjian* (Taipei: Xuesheng, 1977).
51. See my "Competence, Concern, and the Role of Paradigmatic Individuals *(Chüntzu)* in Moral Education," *Philosophy East and West* 42, no. 2 (1992): 215–27; or *Moral Vision and Tradition*, Essay 8.

fucian cardinal virtues. Without a clear mind guided by reason *(li*)*, our *siduan* are easily subverted and misdirected, leading to a life contrary to *ren*. In addition to desires and aversion, there are other sources of *bi* that lead to moral failure, for example, inordinate concern with the beginning or end, distant and immediate consequences of action, the breadth or shallowness of knowledge, the authority of the past or the present.[52] When our mind is not functioning properly, we make distinctions among myriad things and unreasonably place more value on one thing than another, thus leading to misconduct. This is a common human affliction, according to Xunzi. Even reflective moral desires, modified by varieties of satisfaction provided by popular culture, may become a source of moral failure. This is the human condition. No moral theory can provide an assurance of the success of its guidance. For Confucius and Mencius, this is a matter of fate *(ming)*, a consequence of one's ethical commitment to *ren, yi,* and *li*. Confucian ethics does not provide a definitive guidance to the good human life. What really matters for a committed Confucian is *cheng,* a sincere, serious, and unwavering concern for *dao* or *ren,* and overcoming the deficiencies of moral agency.

Issues of universality of moral principles or universalizability of personal moral decisions have little relevance to Confucian ethics. As a Confucian moral philosopher, I wonder whether these issues, rooted in Western philosophical traditions inspired by Plato, are an example of *bi* or obsession with a Western philosophical tradition. If one is committed to something like the Confucian or the Daoist *dao,* why must the person insist that there is only one way to understand moral concepts and their application to human life? Without a serious study of other moral traditions, the search for one philosophical moral theory that applies to all moral traditions, as Xunzi would say, is a delusion, a result of *bi,* a darkening or blindness of *xin* to the ethical significance of other moral traditions and moral theories. Of course, for a genuine understanding and interaction of philosophical traditions rooted in different cultures, as Xunzi reminds us, one must deploy the art and skill of accommodation *(jianshu);* that is to say, parties in disputation must have a spirit of accommodation and mutual respect, for self-respect and respect for others are complementary qualities of participants in ethical argumentation, which is a form of reasoned discourse aiming at resolving

---

52. For a study of Xunzi's view on the distinction between past and present in ethical argumentation, see Cua, "Ethical Uses of the Past in Early Confucianism," *Philosophy East and West* 35, no. 2 (1985): 133–56; incorporated in this volume as Essay 3. The paper appears also in *Virtue, Nature, and Moral Agency in the Xunzi,* ed. T. C. Kline and Philip J. Ivanhoe (Indianapolis, Ind.: Hackett, 2000).

problems of common concern. For Xunzi a *junzi* practices the art of accommodation: "He is talented but can embrace those who are incapable of assuming duties; he is intelligent, but can embrace the stupid; he has extensive learning but can embrace those with limited learning; he is pure in dedication to his task, but can embrace those with diverse purposes."[53] Recall again Mencius's remark (6B6), "All that is expected of a *junzi* is *ren*. Why must he be exactly the same as other *junzi*?" For ideals of the good human life are basically abstract notions or ideal themes that call for concrete, individual specification and realization.[54]

53. *Feixiang pian* 86; Cua, *Ethical Argumentation*, 10.
54. I am grateful to Professor Alan Chan for helpful suggestions and his invitation to present this paper at the Mencius Workshop at the University of Singapore in January 2000.

Bibliography

Aiken, Henry D. "The Aesthetic Relevance of Artists' Intention." In *Art and Philosophy: Readings in Aesthetics,* edited by W. E. Kennick. New York: St. Martin's Press, 1964.
———. "On the Concept of a Moral Principle." In *Isenberg Memorial Lecture Series, 1965–1966.* East Lansing: Michigan State University Press, 1969.
Allinson, Robert E. "The Confucian Golden Rule: A Negative Formulation." *Journal of Chinese Philosophy* 12, no. 3 (1985): 305–15.
Almeder, Robert, ed. *Praxis and Reason: Studies in the Philosophy of Nicholas Rescher.* Lanham, Md.: University Press of America, 1982.
Ames, Roger T. *The Art of Rulership: A Study in Ancient Chinese Political Thought.* Honolulu: University of Hawaii Press, 1983.
———. "Confucius and the Ontology of Knowing." In *Interpreting Across Boundaries: New Essays in Comparative Philosophy,* edited by Eliot Deutsch and Gerald James Larson. Princeton, N.J.: Princeton University Press, 1988.
———. "Meaning as Imaging: Prolegomena to a Confucian Epistemology." In *Culture and Modernity: East-West Philosophical Perspectives,* edited by Eliot Deutsch. Honolulu: University of Hawaii Press, 1991.
Aquinas, Thomas. *A Treatise on Law.* Chicago: Henry Regnery Co., 1967.
Aristotle. *Rhetorica.* Translated by Rhys Roberts. In *The Works of Aristotle,* vol. 11. Oxford: Clarendon Press, 1952.
———. *Nicomachean Ethics.* Translated by Martin Ostwald. Indianapolis, Ind.: Bobbs-Merrill, 1962.
———. *On Rhetoric: A Theory of Civic Discourse.* Translated by George A. Kennedy. New York: Oxford University Press, 1991.
Ashenbrenner, Karl. *The Concepts of Value: Foundations of Value Theory.* Dordrecht, Holland. D. Reidel Publishing Co., 1971.
Attfield, Robin. "On Being Human." *Inquiry* 14 (1974).
Austin, J. L. *Philosophical Papers.* Oxford: Clarendon Press, 1961.
———. *How to Do Things with Words.* Cambridge, Mass.: Harvard University Press, 1962.
———. *Sense and Sensibilia.* Oxford: Clarendon Press, 1962.
Bacon, Francis. *Novum Organum.* In the *Works of Francis Bacon,* vol. 3. Philadelphia: Perry and MacMillan, 1856.
Baier, Kurt. *The Moral Point of View.* Ithaca, N.Y.: Cornell University Press, 1958.
Barbour, Ian G., ed. *Western Man and Environmental Ethics.* Reading, Mass.: Addison-Wesley Publishing Co., 1973.
Beardsmore, R. W. *Moral Reasoning.* London: Routledge and Kegan Paul, 1969.
Beijing University Philosophy Department. *Xunzi xinzhu.* Taipei: Liren, 1983.
Benedict, Ruth. *The Chrysanthemum and the Sword: Patterns of Japanese Culture.* New York: Houghton Mifflin, 1946.

Benn, S. I. "Freedom, Autonomy, and the Concept of a Person." *Proceedings of the Aristotelian Society* 76 (1976).
Berger, Peter. "On the Obsolescence of the Concept of Honour." *Archives européennes de sociologie* 11 (1970). Reprinted in *Revisions: Changing Perspectives in Moral Philosophy*, edited by Stanley Hauerwas and Alasdair MacIntyre. Notre Dame, Ind.: University of Notre Dame Press, 1983.
Berkeley, George. *The Works of George Berkeley*. 9 vols. Edited by A. A. Luce and T. E. Jessop. London: Thomas Nelson & Sons, 1953.
Black, Max. *Models and Metaphors*. Ithaca, N.Y.: Cornell University Press, 1962.
Blackstone, William T. "Ethics and Ecology." In *Philosophy and Environmental Crisis*. Athens: University of Georgia Press, 1974.
Bowsma, O. K. "The Expression Theory of Art." In *Aesthetics and Language*, edited by W. Elton. Oxford: Blackwell, 1954.
Brown, D. G. *Action*. Toronto, Ontario: University of Toronto Press, 1968.
———. "Knowing How and Knowing That, What." In *Ryle: A Collection of Critical Essays*, edited by O. P. Wood and George Pitchers. New York: Anchor Books, 1970.
Butler, Joseph. *Five Sermons*. Indianapolis, Ind.: Bobbs-Merrill, 1950.
Butterfield, Herbert. "Historiography." In *Dictionary of the History of Ideas*, vol. 2, edited by Philip P. Wiener. New York: Charles Scribner's Sons, 1973.
Cai, Renhou. *Kong Meng Xun zhexue*. Taipei: Xuesheng, 1984.
Calhoun, Cheshire, and Robert Solomon, eds. *What Is an Emotion? Classic Readings in Philosophical Psychology*. New York: Oxford University Press, 1984.
Campbell, J. K. *Honour, Family, and Patronage*. Oxford: Oxford University Press, 1964.
Cavell, Stanley. "Must We Mean What We Say?" *Inquiry* 1 (1958). Reprinted in *Ordinary Language: Essays in Philosophical Method*, edited by V. C. Chappell. Englewood Cliffs, N.J.: Prentice-Hall, 1964.
Chan, Alan K. L., ed. *Mencius: Contexts and Interpretations*. Honolulu: University of Hawaii Press, 2002.
Chan, Wing-tsit. "The Evolution of the Confucian Concept *Jen [Ren]*." *Philosophy East and West* 4, no. 4 (1955).
———. "Chinese Theory and Practice." In *Philosophy and Culture: East and West*, edited by C. A. Moore. Honolulu: University of Hawaii Press, 1962.
———, trans. *Instructions for Practical Living and Other Neo-Confucian Writings of Wang Yang-ming*. New York: Columbia University Press, 1963.
———, trans. *A Source Book in Chinese Philosophy*. Princeton, N.J.: Princeton University Press, 1963.
———. "The Evolution of the Neo-Confucian *Li* as Principle." *Tsing Hua Journal of Chinese Studies*, n.s., 4 (1964).
———, trans. *Reflections on Things at Hand: The Neo-Confucian Anthology Compiled by Chu Hsi [Zhu Xi] and Lü Tsu-ch'ien*. New York: Columbia University Press, 1967.
———. "Chinese and Western Interpretations of *Jen*." *Journal of Chinese Philosophy* 2, no. 2 (1975): 107–29.
———. "*Li*." In *Zhongguo zhexue cidian daquan* [Comprehensive Dictionary of Chinese Philosophy], edited by Wei Zhengtong. Taipei: Shuiniu, 1983.
———, ed. *Chu Hsi and Neo-Confucianism*. Honolulu: University of Hawaii Press, 1986.
———, trans. *Neo-Confucian Terms Explained: (The Pei-hsi tzu-i) by Ch'en Ch'un, 1159–1223*. New York: Columbia University Press, 1986.

Chen, Daqi. *Xunzi xueshuo*. Taipei: Zhonghua wenhua she, 1954.
———. *Kongzi xueshuo lunji*. Taipei: Zhengzhong, 1958.
———. *Mingli luncong*. Taipei: Zhengzhong, 1960.
———. *Kongzi xueshuo*. Taipei: Zhengzhong, 1976; 1st ed. 1964.
———. *Mengzi de mingli sixiang ji qi bianshuo shikuang*. Taipei: Shangwu, 1968.
———. *Qianjian ji*. Taipei: Zhonghua, 1968.
———. *Pingfan de daode guan*. 2nd ed. Taipei: Zhonghua, 1977.
———. *Mengzi daijie lu*. Taipei: Shangwu, 1980.
———. *Kongzi yanlun guantong ji*. Taipei: Shangwu, 1982.
———. *Chen Bainian xiansheng wenji*. Vol. 3. Taipei: Shangwu, 1994.
Chen, Daqi, et al. *Kongzi sixiang yanjiu lunji*. Vol. 2. Taipei: Liming, 1983.
Chen, Qiyou. *Han Feizi jishi*. 2 vols. Taipei: World Publishing Co., 1963.
Chen, Zhun [Ch'en Ch'un]. *Beixi xiansheng ziyi xiangjiang* (Neo-Confucian Terms Explained). Taipei: Guangwen, 1979.
Cheng, Andrew. *Hsün Tzu's Theory of Human Nature and Its Influence on Chinese Thought*. Peking: privately published, 1928.
Cheng, Chung-ying. "*Yi* as a Universal Principle of Specific Application in Confucian Morality." *Philosophy East and West* 22, no. 3 (1972): 269–80.
———. "Conscience, Mind and Individual in Chinese Philosophy." *Journal of Chinese Philosophy* 2, no. 1 (1974): 79–86.
———. "Harmony and Conflict in Chinese Philosophy." *Journal of Chinese Philosophy* 4, no. 3 (1977).
———. "Recent Trends in Overseas Chinese Philosophy." In *Encyclopedia of Chinese Philosophy*, edited by Antonio S. Cua. New York and London: Routledge, 2003.
Ching, Julia, and Chaoying Fang, trans. *The Records of Ming Scholars*. Honolulu: University of Hawaii Press, 1987.
Chong, Kim-chong. "Xunzi's Systematic Critique of Mencius." *Philosophy East and West* 53, no. 2 (2003).
Collingwood, R. G. *An Autobiography*. Oxford: Clarendon Press, 1939.
———. *An Essay on Metaphysics*. Oxford: Clarendon Press, 1962.
The Compact Edition of the Oxford English Dictionary. New York: Oxford University Press, 1971.
A Concordance to the Analects. Harvard-Yenching Institute Sinological Index Series, supplement no. 16. Taipei: Chinese Materials and Research Aids Service Center, 1972.
A Concordance to Hsün Tzu. Harvard-Yenching Institute Sinological Index Series, supplement no. 22. Taipei: Chinese Materials and Research Center, 1966.
A Concordance to Meng Tzu. Harvard-Yenching Institute Sinological Index Series, supplement no. 17. Taipei: Chengwen, 1973.
Copp, David, and David Zimmerman, eds. *Morality, Reason, and Truth*. Totowa, N.J.: Rowman and Allanheld, 1985.
Creel, H. G. *Chinese Thought from Confucius to Mao Tse-tung*. Chicago: University of Chicago Press, 1953.
———. *Confucius and the Chinese Way*. New York and Evanston: John Day, 1960.
Creel, H. G., Chang Tsung-ch'ien, and R. C. Rudolph. *Literary Chinese by Inductive Method*. 3 vols. Chicago: University of Chicago Press, 1960.
Cua, A. S. *Reason and Virtue: A Study in the Ethics of Richard Price*. Athens: Ohio University Press, 1966.
———. "Toward an Ethics of Moral Agents." *Philosophy and Phenomenological Research* 28, no. 2 (1967): 163–74.

———. "The Logic of Confucian Dialogues." In *Studies in Philosophy and the History of Philosophy* 4, edited by J. K. Ryan. Washington, D.C.: The Catholic University of America Press, 1969, 18–33.

———. "Morality and Paradigmatic Individuals." *American Philosophical Quarterly* 6, no. 4 (1969): 324–29. Incorporated in A. S. Cua, *Dimensions of Moral Creativity: Paradigms, Principles, and Ideals.* University Park: Pennsylvania State University Press, 1978.

———. "Problem of Moral Actuation." *Man and World* 3, nos. 3–4 (1970): 338–50. Incorporated in A. S. Cua, *Dimensions of Moral Creativity: Paradigms, Principles, and Ideals.* University Park: Pennsylvania State University Press, 1978.

———. "The Concept of Paradigmatic Individuals in the Ethics of Confucius." *Inquiry* 14 (1971): 41–55. Incorporated in A. S. Cua, *Dimensions of Moral Creativity: Paradigms, Principles, and Ideals.* University Park: Pennsylvania State University Press, 1978.

———. "Dignity of Persons and Styles of Life." *Proceedings of the American Catholic Philosophical Association* 45 (1971): 120–29. Reprinted in *New Dynamics in Ethical Thinking*, edited by George F. McLean. Lancaster, Pa.: Concorde Publishing House, 1975.

———. "Reflections on the Structure of Confucian Ethics." *Philosophy East and West* 21, no. 2 (1971): 125–40. Incorporated in A. S. Cua, *Dimensions of Moral Creativity: Paradigms, Principles, and Ideals.* University Park: Pennsylvania State University Press, 1978.

———. "Some Reflections on Methodology in Chinese Philosophy." *International Philosophical Quarterly* 11, no. 2 (1971): 236–38.

———. "Reasonable Action and Confucian Argumentation." *Journal of Chinese Philosophy* 1, no. 1 (1973): 57–75. Incorporated in A. S. Cua, *Moral Vision and Tradition: Essays in Chinese Ethics.* Washington, D.C.: The Catholic University of America Press, 1998.

———. "Relevance of Moral Rules and Creative Agency." *The New Scholasticism* 47, no. 1 (1973): 1–21. Incorporated in A. S. Cua, *Dimensions of Moral Creativity: Paradigms, Principles, and Ideals.* University Park: Pennsylvania State University Press, 1978.

———. "Ethics, Contemporary Analytic Theories of." In *New Catholic Encyclopedia*, supplementary vol. 16 (1967–1974).

———. "Confucian Vision and Experience of the World." *Philosophy East and West* 25, no. 3 (1975): 123–40. Incorporated in A. S. Cua, *Moral Vision and Tradition: Essays in Chinese Ethics.* Washington, D.C.: The Catholic University of America Press, 1998.

———. "Uses of Dialogues and Moral Understanding." *Journal of Chinese Philosophy* 2, no. 2 (1975): 131–48.

———. "Forgetting Morality: Reflections on a Theme in *Chuang Tzu*." *Journal of Chinese Philosophy* 4, no. 4 (1977). Incorporated in *Moral Vision and Tradition: Essays in Chinese Ethics.* Washington, D.C.: The Catholic University of America Press, 1998.

———. *Dimensions of Moral Creativity: Paradigms, Principles, and Ideals.* University Park: Pennsylvania State University Press, 1978.

———. "Tasks for Confucian Ethics." *Journal of Chinese Philosophy* 6, no. 1 (1979): 55–67.

———. "Chinese Moral Vision, Responsive Agency, and Factual Beliefs." *Journal of Chinese Philosophy* 7, no. 1 (1980): 3–26. Incorporated in A. S. Cua, *Moral Vision and Tradition: Essays in Chinese Ethics*. Washington, D.C.: The Catholic University of America Press, 1998.

———. "Opposites as Complements: Reflections on the Significance of *Tao*." *Philosophy East and West* 3, no. 2 (1981): 123–140. Incorporated in A. S. Cua, *Moral Vision and Tradition: Essays in Chinese Ethics*. Washington, D.C.: The Catholic University of America Press, 1998.

———. "Basic Metaphors and the Emergence of Root Metaphors." *Journal of Mind and Behavior* 3 (1982): 251–58.

———. "Ideals and Values: A Study in Rescher's Moral Vision." In *Praxis and Reason: Studies in the Philosophy of Nicholas Rescher*, edited by Robert Almeder. Lanham, Md.: University Press of America, 1982.

———. "Morality and Human Nature." *Philosophy East and West* 32, no. 3 (1982): 279–94. Incorporated in A. S. Cua, *Moral Vision and Tradition: Essays in Chinese Ethics*. Washington, D.C.: The Catholic University of America Press, 1998.

———. *The Unity of Knowledge and Action: A Study in Wang Yang-ming's Moral Psychology*. Honolulu: University Press of Hawaii, 1982.

———. "Hsün Tzu's Theory of Argumentation: A Reconstruction," *Review of Metaphysics* 36, no. 4 (1983): 867–92.

———. *Ethical Argumentation: A Study in Hsün Tzu's* [Xunzi's] *Moral Epistemology*. Honolulu: University of Hawaii Press, 1985.

———. "Some Aspects of Ethical Argumentation: A Reply to Daniel Dahlstrom and John Marshall." *Journal of Chinese Philosophy* 14, no. 4 (1987): 501–16.

———. "The Structure of Social Complexes." *Review of Metaphysics* 41, no. 2 (1987): 335–53.

———. "Reflections on Moral Theory and Understanding Moral Tradition." In *Interpreting Across Boundaries: New Essays in Comparative Philosophy*, edited by Gerald James Larson and Eliot Deutsch. Princeton, N.J.: Princeton University Press, 1988.

———. "The Concept of *Li* in Confucian Moral Theory." In *Understanding the Chinese Mind: The Philosophical Roots*, edited by Robert Allinson. Hong Kong: Oxford University Press, 1989.

———. "The Status of Principles in Confucian Ethics." *Journal of Chinese Philosophy* 16, nos. 3–4 (1989): 273–96. Incorporated in *Moral Vision and Tradition: Essays in Chinese Ethics*. Washington, D.C.: The Catholic University of America Press, 1998.

———. "Feature Review: John Knoblock, *Xunzi: A Translation and Study of the Complete Works*, Volume I, Books 1–6." *Philosophy East and West* 41, no. 2 (1991): 215–27.

———. "Reasonable Challenges and Preconditions of Adjudication." In *Tradition and Modernity: East-West Philosophical Perspectives*, edited by Eliot Deutsch. Honolulu: University of Hawaii Press, 1991. Incorporated in *Moral Vision and Tradition: Essays in Chinese Ethics*. Washington, D.C.: The Catholic University of America Press, 1998.

———. "The Idea of Confucian Tradition." *Review of Metaphysics* 45, no. 4 (1992): 803–40. Incorporated in *Moral Vision and Tradition: Essays in Chinese Ethics*. Washington, D.C.: The Catholic University of America Press, 1998.

———. "Reasonable Persons and the Good: Reflections on an Aspect of Weiss' Ethical Thought." In *Philosophy of Paul Weiss*, edited by Lewis E. Hahn, Library of Living Philosophers. La Salle, Ill.: Open Court, 1995.

———. "Confucian Philosophy, Chinese." In *Encyclopedia of Philosophy*. London: Routledge, 1998.
———. *Moral Vision and Tradition: Essays in Chinese Ethics*. Washington, D.C.: The Catholic University of America Press, 1998.
———. "Problems of Chinese Moral Philosophy." *Journal of Chinese Philosophy* 27, no. 3 (2000): 269–85.
———. "On the Ethical Significance of *Ti-Yong* Distinction." *Journal of Chinese Philosophy* 29, no. 2 (2002): 163–70.
———, ed. *Encyclopedia of Chinese Philosophy*. New York and London: Routledge, 2003.
Dahlstrom, Daniel. "The *Tao* of Ethical Argumentation." *Journal of Chinese Philosophy* 14, no. 4 (1987): 475–85.
Dawson, Raymond, trans. *Confucius: The Analects*. Oxford: Oxford University Press, 1993.
de Bary, Wm. Theodore. *Neo-Confucian Orthodoxy and the Learning of Mind-and-Heart*. New York: Columbia University Press, 1981.
———. *The Liberal Tradition in China*. Hong Kong: Chinese University of Hong Kong Press, 1983.
Deigh, John. "Shame and Self-Esteem: A Critique." *Ethics* 93 (1983): 225–45.
Deutsch, Eliot. *Studies in Comparative Aesthetics*. Monograph no. 2 of The Society for Asian and Comparative Philosophy. Honolulu: University of Hawaii Press, 1975.
———, ed. *Tradition and Modernity: East-West Philosophic Perspectives*. Honolulu: University of Hawaii Press, 1991.
Deutsch, Eliot, and Ron Bontekoe, eds. *A Companion to World Philosophy*. Oxford: Blackwell, 1997.
Dewey, John. *Human Nature and Conduct*. New York: The Modern Library, 1922.
———. *Logic: Theory of Inquiry*. New York: Henry Holt, 1938.
———. *Experience and Nature*. 2d ed. New York: Dover Publication, 1958.
———. *Theory of the Moral Life*. Edited by Arnold Isenberg. New York: Holt, Rinehart and Winston, 1963.
Dewey, John, and James Tufts. *Ethics*. Rev. ed. New York: Holt, Rinehart and Winston, 1932.
Dietrichson, Paul. "Kant's Criteria of Universalizability." In *Kant: Foundations of the Metaphysics of Morals: Text and Critical Essays*, edited by R. P. Wolff. Indianapolis, Ind.: Bobbs-Merrill, 1969.
Dobson, W. A. C. H. *Mencius: A New Translation arranged and annotated for the General Reader*. Toronto, Ontario: University of Toronto Press, 1963.
Dover, K. J. *Greek Popular Morality in the Time of Plato and Aristotle*. Berkeley: University of California Press, 1974.
Downie, R. S. *Roles and Values*. London: Methuen & Co., 1971.
Dray, William H. *Philosophy of History*. Englewood Cliffs, N.J.: Prentice-Hall, 1964.
———. *Perspective on History*. London: Routledge and Kegan Paul, 1980.
Du Boulay, Juliet. *Portrait of a Greek Mountain Village*. Oxford: Oxford University Press, 1974.
Duan, Yucai. *Shuowen jiezi zhu*. Shanghai: Guji, 1981.
Dubos, Rene. "A Theology of the Earth." In *Western Man and Environmental Ethics*, edited by Ian G. Barbour. Reading, Mass.: Addison-Wesley Publishing Co., 1973.

Dubs, Homer H. *Hsüntze: The Moulder of Ancient Confucianism.* London: Arthur Probsthain, 1927.
———. "Mencius and Sün-dz on Human Nature." *Philosophy East and West* 6, no. 3 (1956): 213–22.
———, trans. *The Works of Hsüntze.* Taipei: Chengwen, 1966.
Dworkin, Gerald. *The Theory and Practice of Autonomy.* Cambridge: Cambridge University Press, 1988.
Dworkin, Ronald. *Law's Empire.* Cambridge, Mass.: Harvard University Press, 1986.
Eberhard, Wolfram. *Guilt and Sin in Traditional China.* Berkeley: University of California Press, 1967.
Edel, May, and Abraham Edel. *Anthropology and Ethics.* Springfield, Ill.: Charles C. Thomas, 1959.
Fang, Thomé [Fang, Dongmei]. *Dongmei xiansheng yuanjiang ji.* Taipei: Liming, 1980.
———. *Chinese Philosophy: Its Spirit and Its Development.* Taipei: Linking, 1981.
———. *The Chinese View of Life: The Philosophy of Comprehensive Harmony.* Taipei: Linking, 1980.
———. *Shengsheng zhi de.* Taipei: Liming, 1982.
———. *Yuanshi Rujia Daojia zhexue.* Taipei: Liming, 1983.
Fehl, Noah. *Li: Rites and Propriety in Literature and Life—A Perspective for a Cultural History of Ancient China.* Hong Kong: Chinese University of Hong Kong Press, 1971.
Field, G. C., *Moral Theory.* London: Methuen, 1966.
Findlay, J. N. *Axiological Ethics.* New York: St. Martin's Press, 1970.
Fingarette, Herbert. *On Responsibility.* New York: Basic Books, 1967.
———. *Confucius—the Secular as Sacred.* New York: Harper Torchbooks, 1972.
———. "Following the 'One Thread' of the *Analects.*" *Journal of the American Academy of Religion* 47, no. 35 (1979).
Fogelin, Robert J. *Understanding Arguments: An Introduction to Informal Logic.* New York: Harcourt Brace Jovanovich, 1978.
———. *Figuratively Speaking.* New Haven, Conn.: Yale University Press, 1988.
Frankena, William K. *Ethics.* 2nd ed. Englewood Cliffs, N.J.: Prentice-Hall, 1973.
Frankfurt, Harry. "Freedom of the Will and the Concept of Person." *Journal of Philosophy* 68, no. 1 (1971). Reprinted in *The Importance of What We Care About.* Cambridge: Cambridge University Press, 1988.
Fu, Wei-hsun, and Wing-tsit Chan. *Guide to Chinese Philosophy.* Boston: G. K. Hall, 1978.
Fung, Yu-lan (Feng Youlan). *The Spirit of Chinese Philosophy.* Translated by E. R. Hughes. London: Routledge and Kegan Paul, 1947.
———. *A Short History of Chinese Philosophy.* New York: Macmillan, 1950.
———. *History of Chinese Philosophy.* 2 vols. Translated by Derk Bodde. Princeton, N.J.: Princeton University Press, 1953.
———. *Zhongguo zhexue shi xinbian.* Beijing: Renmin, 1964.
———. *Zhongguo zhexue shi, fupu pian.* Hong Kong: Taipingyang, 1975.
Gardner, Daniel K. *Chu Hsi [Zhuxi]: Learning to be a Sage.* Berkeley: University of California Press, 1990.
Gasking, Douglas. "Causation and Recipes." *Mind* 64, no. 256 (1955): 479–87.
Giles, Lionel. *The Sayings of Confucius.* London: John Murray. Reprinted by Charles Tuttle, 1907.

Ginsberg, Morris. *Essays in Sociology and Social Philosophy*. Vol. 1. Melbourne: William Heineman Ltd., 1956.
Goodman, Nelson. *The Languages of Art*. Indianapolis, Ind.: Bobbs-Merrill, 1968.
Graham, A. C. *Two Chinese Philosophers: Ch'eng Ming-tao and Ch'eng Yi-ch'uan*. London: Lund Humphries, 1958.
———. "The Background of the Mencian Theory of Human Nature." *Tsing Hua Journal of Chinese Studies*, n.s., 7, nos. 1-2 (1967).
———. *Later Mohist Logic, Ethics and Science*. Hong Kong and London: Chinese University of Hong Kong Press, 1978.
———. *Disputers of the Tao: Philosophical Argument in Ancient China*. La Salle, Ill.: Open Court, 1989.
Grimaldi, William M. *Studies in the Philosophy of Aristotle's Rhetoric*. Wiesbaden: Franz Steiner Verlag, 1972.
Hall, David L., and Roger T. Ames. *Thinking Through Confucius*. Albany: State University of New York Press, 1987.
Hamburger, Max. "Aristotle and Confucius: A Study in Comparative Philosophy." *Philosophy* 31 (1956): 324–57.
Hansen, Chad. "Freedom and Moral Responsibility in Confucian Ethics." *Philosophy East and West* 22, no. 2 (1972).
———. "*Qing*: Reality or Feeling." In *Encyclopedia of Chinese Philosophy*, edited by Antonio S. Cua. New York and London: Routledge, 2003.
Hare, R. M. *Freedom and Reason*. Oxford: Clarendon Press, 1963.
Hart, H. L. A. *The Concept of Law*. Oxford: Clarendon Press, 1961.
Hartmann, Nicolai. *Ethics*. Vol. 2. London: George Allen & Unwin, 1932.
Hauerwas, Stanley, and Alasdair MacIntyre, eds. *Revisions: Changing Perspectives in Moral Philosophy*. Notre Dame, Ind.: University of Notre Dame Press, 1983.
Hepburn, R. W. "Emotions and Emotional Qualities: Some Attempts at Analysis." In *Aesthetics in the Modern World*, edited by Harold Osborne. New York: Weybright and Talley, 1960.
Hobbes, Thomas. *Leviathan*. Oxford: Clarendon Press, 1952.
Höffding, Harold. *History of Modern Philosophy*. Translated by B. E. Meyer. New York: Humanities Press, 1924.
Holzman, Donald. "The Conversational Tradition in Chinese Philosophy." *Philosophy East and West* 6, no. 3 (1956).
Hou, Wailou, editor-in-chief. *Zhongguo sixiang tongshi*. 5 vols. Beijing: Renmin, 1959.
Hsieh, Shan-yuan. *The Life and Thought of Li Kou, 1009–1059*. San Francisco: Chinese Materials Center, 1979.
Hsieh, Yu-wei. "Filial Piety and Chinese Society." In *Philosophy and Culture: East and West*, edited by C. A. Moore. Honolulu: University of Hawaii Press, 1962.
———. "The Status of the Individual in Chinese Ethics." In *The Chinese Mind: Essentials of Chinese Philosophy and Culture*, edited by Charles Moore. Honolulu, Hawaii: East-West Center Press, 1967.
Hu, Hsien Chin. "The Chinese Concepts of 'Face.'" *American Anthropologist*, n.s., 46 (1944): 45–64.
Hu, Shih [Hu Shi]. *Zhongguo zhexue shi dagang*. Part 1. Taipei: Shangwu, 1947. Reprint of 1918 edition.
———. *The Development of the Logical Method in Ancient China*. Shanghai, 1922; New York: Paragon Reprint Corp., 1963.
———. "Ji Li Gou de xueshuo." In *Hu Shih wencun*, vol. 2. Taipei: Yuandong, n.d.
Hua, Zhonglin, et al. *Rujia sixiang yanjiu lunji*. Vol. 2. Taipei: Liming, 1983.

Hughes, E. R. *Chinese Philosophy in the Classical Times.* New York: E. P. Dutton, 1942.
Hume, David. *A Treatise of Human Nature.* Edited by L. A. Selby-Bigge. Oxford: Clarendon Press, 1951.
———. *An Inquiry Concerning the Principles of Morals.* Indianapolis, Ind.: Bobbs-Merrill, 1957.
———. "Of the Delicacy of Taste and Passion." In *Essays: Moral, Political and Literary.* Oxford: Oxford University Press, 1963.
Hummel, Arthur. "Some Basic Moral Principles in Chinese Culture." In *Moral Principles of Action,* edited by Ruth Nanda Ashen. New York and London: Harper, 1952.
Hutcheson, Francis. *Illustrations on Moral Sense.* Cambridge, Mass.: Harvard University Press, 1971.
Isenberg, Arnold. "Natural Pride and Natural Shame." *Philosophy and Phenomenological Research* 10, no. 1 (1949).
James, William. *The Varieties of Religious Experience.* New York: Longmans, Green and Co., 1902.
———. *Essays on Faith and Morals.* New York: Longmans, Green and Co., 1949.
———. *Pragmatism and Four Essays from the Meaning of Truth.* Cleveland and New York: Meridian Books, 1955.
———. *Essays in Radical Empiricism and A Pluralistic Universe.* New York: E. P. Dutton, 1971.
Jen, Chuo-hsuan. "The Philosophical System of Hsün Tzu." In *Zhexue lunwen ji,* vol. 1. Taipei: Shangwu, 1967.
Joachim, Harold H. *Descartes' Rules for the Direction of the Mind.* London: George Allen & Unwin, 1957.
Kant, Immanuel. *Critique of Practical Reason.* Translated by Lewis White Beck. New York: The Liberal Arts Press, 1956.
———. *Foundations of the Metaphysics of Morals.* Translated by Lewis White Beck. Indianapolis, Ind.: Bobbs-Merrill, 1959.
———. *Lectures on Ethics.* New York: Harper Torchbooks, 1963.
———. *The Metaphysical Principles of Virtue.* Indianapolis, Ind.: Bobbs-Merrill, 1964.
Kao, Ming [Gao Ming]. *Sanli yanjiu.* Taipei: Liming, 1981.
———. "Chu Hsi and the Discipline of Propriety." In *Chu Hsi and Neo-Confucianism,* edited by Wing-tsit Chan. Honolulu: University of Hawaii Press, 1986.
Karlgren, Bernard. *Grammata Serica.* Taipei: Chengwen, 1966. Reprinted from *The Bulletin of the Museum of Far Eastern Antiquities* (Stockholm) 12 (1940).
———. *Analytic Dictionary of Chinese and Sino-Japanese.* Taipei: Chengwen, 1975. First published in 1923 by Librairie Orientaliste Paul Geuthner.
Kato, Joken. "The Meaning of *Li.*" *Philosophical Studies of Japan* 4 (1963).
Kekes, John. "Shame and Moral Progress." *Midwest Studies in Philosophy* 13 (1988).
Kevy, Peter. "The Logic of Taste." In *Thomas Reid: Critical Interpretations,* edited by S. F. Barker and T. L. Beauchamp. Philadelphia: Philosophical Monographs, 1976.
King-Farlow, John, and William R. Shea, eds. *Values and the Quality of Life.* New York: Science History Publications, 1976.
Kline, T. C., and Philip Ivanhoe, eds. *Virtue, Nature, and Moral Agency in the Xunzi.* Indianapolis, Ind.: Hackett, 2000.

Knoblock, John. *Xunzi: A Translation and Study of the Complete Works.* Vols. 1–3. Stanford, Calif.: Stanford University Press, 1988, 1990, 1994.
Kolnai, Aurel. *Ethics, Value, and Reality.* Indianapolis, Ind.: Hackett, 1978.
Kovesi, Julius. *Moral Notions.* London: Routledge and Kegan Paul, 1967.
Ku, Hung-ming, trans. *The Analects.* Taipei: Xinsheng Daily News, 1984.
Lao, Sze-kwang [Lao Siquang]. *Xinbian Zhongguo zhexue shi.* 3 vols. Taipei: Sanmin, 1984, 1st ed., 1982.
———. "On Understanding Chinese Philosophy: An Inquiry and a Proposal." In *Understanding the Chinese Mind: The Philosophical Roots,* edited by Robert E. Allinson. Hong Kong: Oxford University Press, 1989.
Larson, Gerald James, and Eliot Deutsch, eds. *Interpreting Across Boundaries: New Essays in Comparative Philosophy.* Princeton, N.J.: Princeton University Press, 1988.
Lau, D. C. "Theories of Human Nature in *Mencius* and *Shyuntzyy.*" *Bulletin of the School of Oriental and African Studies* 15 (1953).
———, trans. *Mencius.* Middlesex, England: Penguin Books, 1970.
———. *Confucius: The Analects.* Middlesex, England: Penguin Books, 1979.
Lee, S. T., comp. *A New Complete Chinese-English Dictionary.* Hong Kong: Zhongjian, 1964.
Legge, James, trans. *The Chinese Classics.* Vol. 1. Oxford: Clarendon Press, 1893.
———, trans. *The Works of Mencius.* In *Chinese Classics,* vol. 1. Oxford: Oxford University Press, 1893.
———, trans. *I Ching: Book of Changes.* Edited by Ch'u Chai and Winberg Chai. New York: University Books, 1964.
———, trans. *The Hsiao Ching.* In The Sacred Books of the East, vol. 3. Edited by Max Müller. Delhi: Motilal Banarsidass, 1966.
———, trans. *The Li Ki or Collection of Treatises on the Rules of Propriety or Ceremonial Usages.* In The Sacred Books of the East, vols. 27–28. Edited by Max Müller. Delhi: Motilal Banarsidass, 1966.
Lewis, C. I. *An Analysis of Knowledge and Valuation.* La Salle, Ill.: Open Court, 1946.
Lewis, Helen B. *Shame and Guilt in Neurosis.* New York: International Universities Press, 1971.
Li, Disheng. *Xunzi jishi* [An Annotated Edition of *Xunzi*]. Taipei: Xuesheng, 1979.
Li, Gou. *Li Taibo xiansheng quanji.* Vol. 1. Taipei: Wenhai, 1971.
Li, Minghui. *Kangde lunli xue yu Mengzi daode sikao zhi zhongjian.* Taipei: Zhongyang yanjiu yuan, 1994.
Liang, Chi-chao. *History of Chinese Political Thought.* Taipei: Chengwen, 1968.
Liang, Ch'i-hsiung [Liang Qixiong]. "A Descriptive Review of Hsün Tzu's Thought." *Chinese Studies in Philosophy* 6, no. 1 (1974).
Liang, Qixiong [Liang Ch'i-hsiung]. *Xunzi jianshi.* Taipei: Shangwu, 1978.
Liang, Shiqiu. *A New Practical Chinese-English Dictionary.* Taipei: Far East, 1972.
Liao, W. K., trans. *The Complete Works of Han Fei Tzu.* 2 vols. London: Arthur Probsthain, 1959.
Lin, Tongqi. "Recent Trends in Post-Mao China." In *Encyclopedia of Chinese Philosophy,* edited by Antonio S. Cua. New York and London: Routledge, 2003.
Lin, Yutang, ed. and trans. *The Wisdom of Confucius.* New York: Modern Library, 1938.
———. *The Pleasures of a Nonconformist.* London: Heineman, 1962.

———. *Chinese-English Dictionary of Modern Usage*. Hong Kong: Chinese University of Hong Kong Press, 1972.
Liu, Shu-hsien. "*Li:* Principle, Pattern, Reason." In *Encyclopedia of Chinese Philosophy*, edited by Antonio S. Cua. New York and London: Routledge, 2003.
Liu, Wu-chi. *A Short History of Confucian Philosophy*. New York: Dell, 1964.
Long, Yuchun. *Xunzi lunji*. Taipei: Xuesheng, 1987.
Lorenz, K. Z. "Ritualization in the Psycho-social Evolution of Human Culture." In *A Discussion of Ritualization of Behaviour in Animals and Man*, Philosophical Transactions of The Royal Society of London, series B, no. 772, vol. 251.
Lynd, Helen Merrell. *On Shame and the Search for Identity*. New York: Harcourt, Brace, & World, 1958.
Machle, Edward J. "Hsün Tzu As Religious Philosopher." *Philosophy East and West* 26, no. 4 (1976).
———. "The Mind and the *'Shen-ming'* in Xunzi." *Journal of Chinese Philosophy* 19, no. 4 (1992): 361–86.
———. *Nature and Heaven in the Xunzi: A Study of the Tian Lun*. Albany: State University of New York Press, 1993.
MacIntyre, Alasdair. *After Virtue*. Notre Dame, Ind.: University of Notre Dame Press, 1984.
———. *Whose Justice? Which Rationality?* Notre Dame, Ind.: University of Notre Dame Press, 1988.
———. "Incommensurability, Truth and the Conversation Between Confucians and Aristotelians about the Virtues." In *Tradition and Modernity: East-West Philosophical Perspectives*, edited by Eliot Deutsch. Honolulu: University of Hawaii Press, 1991.
Macmurray, John. *Persons in Relation*. London: Farber and Farber, 1961.
Mair, Victor H., ed. *Experimental Essays on Chuang Tzu*. Honolulu: University of Hawaii Press, 1983.
Makra, Mary Lelia. *The Hsiao Ching*. New York: St. John's University Press, 1961.
Mao, Zishui. *Lunyu jinzhu jinyi*. Taipei: Shangwu, 1975.
Marshall, John. "Hsün Tzu's Moral Epistemology." *Journal of Chinese Philosophy* 14, no. 4 (1987): 487–500.
Mead, G. H. *Mind, Self, and Society*. Chicago: University of Chicago Press, 1952.
Mei, Y. P. "Hsün Tzu's Theory of Education with An English Translation of the *Hsün Tzu*, Chapter I, An Exhortation to Learning." *Tsing Hua Journal of Chinese Studies*, n.s., 2, no. 2 (1961).
———. "Ancient Chinese Philosophy according to the *Chuang Tzu*, Chapter 33, The World of Thought, with an English Translation of the Chapter." *Tsing Hua Journal of Chinese Studies*, n.s., 4, no. 2 (1964).
Melden, A. I. *Rights and Persons*. Berkeley and Los Angeles: University of California Press, 1977.
Michalos, Alex C. "Measuring the Quality of Life." In *Values and the Quality of Life*, edited by John King-Farlow and William R. Shea. New York: Science History Publications, 1976.
Moore, G. E. *Principia Ethica*. Cambridge: Cambridge University Press, 1969, 1st ed., 1903.
Morris, Herbert, ed. *Guilt and Shame*. Belmont, Calif.: Wadsworth, 1971.
———. *On Guilt and Innocence: Essays in Legal Philosophy and Moral Psychology*. Berkeley and Los Angeles: University of California Press, 1976.
Mote, Frederick. *Intellectual Foundations of China*. New York: Alfred A. Knopf, 1971.

Mou, Zongsan. *Xunzi dalüe.* Taipei: Zhongyang wenwu gongying she, 1953.
——. *Xinti yu xingti.* Vol. 1. Taipei: Zhengzhong, 1973.
——. *Ming Jia yu Xunzi.* Taipei: Xuesheng, 1979.
Munro, Donald J. *The Concept of Man in Ancient China.* Stanford, Calif.: Stanford University Press, 1969.
——. *The Concept of Man in Contemporary China.* Ann Arbor: University of Michigan Press, 1977.
Murphy, A. E. *The Theory of Practical Reason.* La Salle, Ill.: Open Court, 1964.
Nakamura, Hajime. *Ways of Thinking of Eastern Peoples: India, China, Tibet, and Japan.* Honolulu: East-West Center Press, 1964.
Nan, Huaijin and Xu Qinting. *Zhouyi jinzhu jinyi.* Taipei: Shangwu, 1979.
Needham, Joseph. *Time and the Eastern Man.* The Henry Myers Lecture, 1964. *Royal Anthropological Institute Occasional Paper,* no. 21, 1965.
A New Complete Chinese-English Dictionary. Hong Kong: Zhonghong jian, 1964.
Ng, Margaret. "Shame as a Moral Sanction." *Journal of Chinese Philosophy* 8, no. 1 (1981).
Nivision, David S. *"Zhong* and *Shu."* In *Encyclopedia of Chinese Philosophy,* edited by Antonio S. Cua. New York and London: Routledge, 2003.
O'Hear, Anthony. "Guilt and Shame as Moral Concepts." *Proceedings of the Aristotelian Society,* n.s., 77 (1976/77).
Olafson, Frederick. *Principles and Persons: An Ethical Interpretation of Existentialism.* Baltimore: Johns Hopkins University Press, 1967.
Osborne, Harold. "The Quality of Feeling in Art." In *Aesthetics in the Modern World,* edited by Harold Osborne. New York: Weybright and Talley, 1960.
——. *Aesthetics and Art Theory.* New York: E. P. Dutton, 1970.
Passmore, John. *Philosophical Reasoning.* London: Gerald Duckworth, 1961.
——. "Philosophy." In *Encyclopedia of Philosophy,* edited by Paul Edwards, vol. 6. New York: Macmillan & Free Press, 1967.
Pelikan, Jaroslav. *The Vindication of Tradition.* New Haven, Conn.: Yale University Press, 1982.
Pepper, S. C. *World Hypotheses.* Berkeley and Los Angeles: University of California Press, 1948.
——. *Sources of Value.* Berkeley and Los Angeles: University of California Press, 1958.
——. "Metaphor in Philosophy." In *Dictionary of the History of Ideas,* vol. 3. New York: Charles Scribner's Sons, 1973.
Perelman, Chaim, and Anna Olbrechts-Tyteca. *The New Rhetoric: A Treatise on Argumentation,* translated by John Wilkinson and Purcell Weaver. Notre Dame, Ind.: University of Notre Dame Press, 1969.
Peristiany, J. G., ed. *Honour and Shame: The Values of Mediterranean Society.* Chicago: University of Chicago Press, 1966.
Phillips, D. Z., and H. O. Mounce. *Moral Practices.* London: Routledge and Kegan Paul, 1969.
Pier, Gerhart, and Milton B. Singer. *Shame and Guilt.* New York: W. W. Norton, 1971.
Price, Richard. *A Review of the Principal Questions in Morals.* Edited by D. D. Raphael. Oxford: Clarendon Press, 1948.
Qian, Mu. *Sishu duben.* 2 vols. Taipei: Liming, 1992.
Rachels, James, ed. *Moral Problems.* 2nd ed. New York: Harper & Row, 1975.
Radcliff-Brown, A. R. "Taboo." In *Reader in Comparative Religion: An Anthropologi-*

cal Approach, 2d ed., edited by W. A. Lessa and E. Z. Vogt. New York: Harper & Row, 1965.
Raphael, D. D., ed. *British Moralists: 1650–1800*. 2 vols. Oxford: Clarendon Press, 1969.
Rawls, John. "Two Concepts of Rules." *Philosophical Review* 64 (1955).
———. *A Theory of Justice*. Cambridge, Mass.: Harvard University Press, 1971.
Reid, Thomas. *Essays on the Intellectual Powers of Man*. Cambridge, Mass.: MIT Press, 1969.
———. *Essays on the Active Powers of the Human Mind*. Cambridge, Mass.: MIT Press, 1969.
Ren, Jiyu, editor-in-chief. *Zhongguo zhexue shi*. 4 vols. Beijing: Renmin, 1979.
Rescher, Nicholas. *Welfare: The Social Issues in Philosophical Perspective*. Pittsburgh, Pa.: University of Pittsburgh Press, 1972.
———. *Conceptual Idealism*. Oxford: Blackwell, 1973.
———. *Dialectics*. Albany: State University of New York Press, 1977.
———. *Methodological Pragmatism*. New York: New York University Press, 1977.
———. *Skepticism*. Totowa, N.J.: Rowman and Littlefield, 1980.
Resnik, M. D. "Logic and Methodology in the Writings of Mencius." *International Philosophical Quarterly* 8, no. 2 (1968): 212–30.
Richards, I. A. *Mencius on the Mind*. London: Routledge and Kegan Paul, 1932.
Riezler, Kurt. *Man: Mutable and Immutable*. New York: Henry Regnery, 1951.
Rosemont, Henry, Jr. "State and Society in the *Hsün Tzu:* A Philosophical Commentary." *Monumenta Serica* 29 (1970–1971): 38–78.
———. "Notes from a Confucian Perspective: Which Human Acts Are Moral Acts?" *International Philosophical Quarterly* 16, no. 1 (1976): 49–61.
Ross, W. D. *The Right and the Good*. Oxford: Oxford University Press, 1930.
Rotenstreich, N. "On Shame." *Review of Metaphysics* 19, no. 1 (1965): 54–86.
Royce, Josiah. *The Problem of Christianity*. Chicago: University of Chicago Press, 1969.
Ryle, Gilbert. "Conscience and Moral Convictions." *Analysis* 7, no. 2 (1940). Reprinted in *Philosophy and Analysis*, edited by M. MacDonald. Oxford: Blackwell, 1954.
———. *The Concept of Mind*. New York: Barnes and Noble, 1949.
———. "Systematically Misleading Expressions." In *Logic and Language*, 1st ser., edited by A. G. N. Flew. Oxford: Blackwell, 1951.
Schilpp, Paul Arthur. *Kant's Pre-Critical Ethics*. 2nd ed. Evanston, Ill.: Northwestern University Press, 1960.
Schneider, Carl D. *Shame, Exposure, & Privacy*. Boston: Beacon Press, 1977.
Schwartz, Benjamin. *In Search of Power: Yen Fu and the West*. Cambridge, Mass.: Harvard University Press, 1964.
———. *The World of Thought in Ancient China*. Cambridge, Mass.: Harvard University Press, 1985.
Schwartz, Stephen P., ed. *Naming, Necessity, and Natural Kinds*. Ithaca, N.Y.: Cornell University Press, 1977.
Searle, John. "How to Derive 'Ought' from 'Is'" *Philosophical Review* 73, no. 1 (1964).
Selby-Bigge, L. A., ed. *British Moralists*. 2 vols. Indianapolis, Ind.: Bobbs-Merrill, 1964.
Shen, Vincent. "Chen Daqi (Ch'en Ta-ch'i)." In *Encyclopedia of Chinese Philosophy*, edited by Antonio S. Cua. New York and London: Routledge, 2003.

———. "Recent Trends in Taiwan." In *Encyclopedia of Chinese Philosophy*, edited by Antonio S. Cua. New York and London: Routledge, 2003.
Shi, Ciyun. *Mengzi jinzhu jinyi*. Taipei: Shangwu, 1974.
Shih, Vincent Y. C. "Hsün Tzu's Positivism." *Tsing Hua Journal of Chinese Studies*, n.s., 4, no. 2 (1964): 162–74.
Shun, Kwong-loi. *Mencius and Early Chinese Thought*. Stanford, Calif.: Stanford University Press, 1997.
———. "Xiao (hsiao): Filial Piety." In *Encyclopedia of Chinese Philosophy*, edited by Antonio S. Cua. New York and London: Routledge, 2003.
Singer, Marcus. *Generalizations in Ethics*. New York: Alfred A. Knopf, 1961.
———. "Defense of the Golden Rule." In *Morals and Values*, edited by Marcus Singer. New York: Charles Scribner's Sons, 1977.
Solomon, Robert. *The Passions: The Myth and Nature of Human Emotion*. New York: Anchor Books, 1977.
Song, Tianzheng. *Daxue jinzhu jinyi*. Taipei: Shangwu, 1977.
Standaert, Nicolas. "The Discovery of the Center through the Periphery: A Preliminary Study of Feng Youlan's *History of Chinese Philosophy* (New Version)." *Philosophy East and West* 45, no. 4 (1995): 569–90.
Standaert, Nicolas, and Bie Geivers. "Fung Yu-lan: Works on the History of Chinese Philosophy." In *Encyclopedia of Chinese Philosophy*, edited by Antonio S. Cua. New York and London: Routledge, 2003.
Stevenson, Charles, L. *Ethics and Language*. New Haven, Conn.: Yale University Press, 1944.
Stevenson, Leslie. *Seven Theories of Human Nature*. Oxford: Clarendon Press, 1974.
Strawson, P. F. "Social Morality and Individual Ideal." *Philosophy* 36 (1961).
Takehiko, Okada. "Chu Hsi and Wisdom as Hidden and Stored." In *Chu Hsi and Neo-Confucianism*, edited by Wing-tsit Chan. Honolulu: University of Hawaii Press, 1986.
Tang, Junyi (T'ang Chün-i). *Renwen jingshen zhi zhongjian*. Taipei: Xuesheng, 1977.
———. *Zhongguo zhexue yuanlun: Daolun pian* [Foundations of Chinese Philosophy: Introductory Volume]. Taipei: Xuesheng, 1978.
———. *Zhongguo zhexue yuanlun: Yuandao pian*. Taipei: Xuesheng, 1978.
———. *Essays on Chinese Philosophy and Culture*. In *Collected Works of Tang Junyi*, vol. 19. Taipei: Student Book Co., 1987.
Taylor, Charles. "Responsibility for Self." In *The Identities of Persons*, edited by Amelie Rorty. Berkeley and Los Angeles: University of California Press, 1976.
Taylor, Gabriele. *Pride, Shame, and Guilt: Emotions of Self-Assessment*. Oxford: Clarendon Press, 1985.
Toulmin, Stephen. *The Place of Reason in Ethics*. Cambridge: Cambridge University Press, 1950.
Toynbee, Arnold. *A Study in History*. Abridged edition, 2 vols. Oxford: Oxford University Press, 1956.
Tu, Wei-ming. "The Creative Tension between *Jen* and *Li*." *Philosophy East and West* 18, no. 2 (1968).
———. "*Li* as a Process of Humanization." *Philosophy East and West* 22, no. 2 (1972).
———. *Humanity and Self-Cultivation: Essays in Confucian Thought*. Berkeley, Calif.: Asian Humanities Press, 1979.

———. *Centrality and Commonality: An Essay on Confucian Religiosity*. Albany: State University of New York Press, 1989.
Tu, Weiming, and Mary Ellen Tucker, eds. *Confucian Spirituality*, vol. 1. New York: Crossroads, 2003.
Turbayne, C. M. *The Myth of Metaphor*. New Haven, Conn.: Yale University Press, 1962.
Turner, Victor. *Dramas, Fields, and Metaphors*. Ithaca, N.Y.: Cornell University Press, 1974.
Urmson, J. O. *The Emotive Theory of Ethics*. London: Hutcheson University Library, 1968.
Vlastos, Gregory, ed. *Socrates: A Collection of Critical Essays*. New York: Anchor Books, 1969.
von Wright, Henrik. *Explanation and Understanding*. Ithaca, N.Y.: Cornell University Press, 1971.
Waley, Arthur, trans. *The Analects of Confucius*. New York: Random House, 1938.
Wall, George B. *Introduction to Ethics*. Columbus, Ohio: Charles E. Merrill Publishing Co., 1974.
Wallace, G., and A. D. M. Walker, eds. *The Definition of Morality*. London: Methuen & Co., 1970.
Walsh, Vivian Charles. *Scarcity and Evil*. Englewood Cliffs, N.J.: Prentice-Hall, 1961.
Walsh, W. H. *An Introduction to Philosophy of History*. London: Hutchinson University Library, 1951.
Wang, Ch'ung. *Lun Heng*. 2 vols. Translated by Alfred Forke. New York: Paragon Book Gallery, 1962.
Wang, Meng'ou. *Liji jinzhu jinyi*. 2 vols. Taipei: Shangwu, 1977.
Wang, Shouchang. "Feng Youlan and the Vienna Circle (A Synopsis)." *Journal of Chinese Philosophy* 21, nos. 3/4 (1994).
Wang, Tianji. *Zhongguo luoqi sixiang shi*. Shanghai: Renwen, 1979.
Wang, Xianqian. *Xunzi jijie*. Taipei: World Publishing, 1961.
Wang, Yang-ming. *Instructions for Practical Living and Other Neo-Confucian Writings*. Translated by Wing-tsit Chan. New York: Columbia University Press, 1963.
Wang, Zhonglin. *Xinyi Xunzi doupen*. 3rd ed. Taipei: Sanmin, 1977.
Ware, James R., trans. *The Sayings of Confucius*. New York: Mentor Books, 1955.
Warnock, G. J. *Contemporary Moral Philosophy*. New York: St. Martin's Press, 1967.
———. *The Object of Morality*. London: Methuen & Co., 1971.
Wasserstrom, Richard. "Rights, Human Rights, and Racial Discrimination." In *Moral Problems*, 2nd ed., edited by James Rachels. New York: Harper & Row, 1975.
Watson, Burton, trans. *Hsün Tzu [Xunzi]: Basic Writings*. New York: Columbia University Press, 1963.
———, trans. *Mo Tzu [Mozi]: Basic Writings*. New York: Columbia University Press, 1963.
———, trans. *The Complete Works of Chuang Tzu [Zhuangzi]*. New York: Columbia University Press, 1968.
Wei, Zhengtong. *Xunzi yu gudai zhexue*. Taipei: Shangwu, 1974.
———. *Zhongguo zhexue sixiang shi*. Taipei: Dalin, 1980.
———. *Zhongguo zhexue cidian*. Taipei: Dalin, 1980.
———. *Zhongguo zhexue sixiang pipan*. Taipei: Buffalo Book, 1981.

———. *Zhongguo zhexue cidian daquan*. Taipei: Shuiniu, 1983.
Weiger, D. L., S.J. *Chinese Characters: Their Origins, Etymology, History, Classification and Signification*. New York: Paragon Book Reprint & Dover, 1965.
Weiss, Paul. *Toward a Perfected State*. Albany: State University of New York Press, 1986.
Wellman, Carl. *Challenge and Response: Justification in Ethics*. Carbondale: Southern Illinois University Press, 1971.
Wheelwright, Philip. *Metaphor and Reality*. Bloomington: Indiana University Press, 1962.
———. *The Burning Fountain: A Study in the Language of Symbolism*. Bloomington: Indiana University Press, 1968.
White, Lynn, Jr. "The Historical Roots of Our Ecological Crisis." In *Western Man and Environmental Ethics*, edited by Ian G. Barbour. Reading, Mass.: Addison-Wesley Publishing Co., 1973.
Williams, Bernard. *Morality: An Introduction*. New York: Harper Torchbooks, 1972.
———. *Shame and Necessity*. Berkeley: University of California Press, 1993.
Winch, Peter. "Nature and Convention." *Proceedings of the Aristotelean Society* 60 (1959–1960).
———. *Ethics and Action*. London: Routledge and Kegan Paul, 1972.
Wisdom, John. *Philosophy and Psychoanalysis*. Oxford: Blackwell, 1953.
———. *Paradox and Discovery*. Oxford: Blackwell, 1965.
Wittenborn, Allen, trans. *Further Reflections on Things at Hand: A Chu Hsi Reader*. Lanham, Md.: University Press of America, 1991.
Wittgenstein, Ludwig. *Philosophical Investigation*. Translated by G. E. M. Anscombe. 3rd ed. New York: Macmillan, 1958.
Woo, Peter K. Y. "A Metaphysical Approach to Human Rights from a Chinese Point of View." In *The Philosophy of Human Rights*, edited by Alan S. Rosenbaum. Westport, Conn.: Greenwood Press, 1980.
Xia, Zhentao. *Lun Xunzi de zhexue sixiang*. Shanghai: Renwen, 1979.
Xiong, Gongzhe. *Xunzi jinzhu jinyi*. Taipei: Shangwu, 1975.
Xu, Fuguan. *Zhongguo sixiang shi lunji*. Taipei: Xuesheng, 1975.
Xu, Shen. *Shuowen jiezi zhenben*. 2 vols. Taipei: Zhonghua, 1966.
Xue, Songliu, chief editor. *Xinbian Zhongguo cidian*. Rev. ed. Taipei: Da Zhongguo guoshu, 1998.
Yang, Huijie. *Tianren guanxi lun*. Taipei: Talin, 1981.
Yang, Liang. *Xunzi*. Taipei: Zhonghua, 1976.
Yang, Liuqiao. *Xunzi guyi*. Taipei: Yangzhe, 1987.
Yang, Yunru. *Xunzi yanjiu*. Taipei: Shangwu, 1974.
Ye, Jinggui. *Kongzi de daode zhexue*. Taipei: Zhengzhong, 1977.
Yearley, Lee H. "Hsün Tzu on the Mind: His Attempted Synthesis of Confucianism and Taoism." *Journal of Asian Studies* 36, no. 3 (1980).
Yin, Lujun. "Fung Yu-lan." In *Encyclopedia of Chinese Philosophy*, edited by Antonio S. Cua. New York and London: Routledge, 2003.
You, You. *Zhongguo mingxue*. Taipei: Zhengzhong, 1959.
Yü, Ying-shih. "Morality and Knowledge in Chu Hsi's Philosophical System." In *Chu Hsi and Neo-Confucianism*, edited by Wing-tsit Chan. Honolulu: University of Hawaii Press, 1986.
Zhang, Liwen. *Li* [An Anthology in Chinese]. Taipei: Hanxing, 1994.
Zhang, Xuan. *Wenzi xingyi liubian shidian*. Taipei: Xinan, 1980.

Zhao, Zehou. *Daxue yanjiu*. Taipei: Zhonghua, 1972.
Zeng, Chunhai. "Xunzi sixiang zhong de 'tong lei' yu 'li fa.'" *Fu Jen Philosophical Studies* 13 (1981): 71–85.
Zhexue cidian [Dictionary of Philosophy], 4th ed. Taipei: Shangwu, 1976.
Zhong, Shaohua. "Qingmo zhongguo ren duiyi <<zhexue>> de zhuiqiu." *Newsletter of the Institute of Chinese Literature and Philosophy* 2, no. 2, Academia Sinica, Taipei, 1992.
Zhong Yong [The Doctrine of the Mean]. In *A Source Book in Chinese Philosophy*, translated by Wing-tsit Chan. Princeton, N.J.: Princeton University Press, 1963.
Zhongwen da cidian (The Encyclopedic Dictionary of Chinese Language). 10 vols. 4th ed. Taipei: China Academy, 1979.
Zhou, Hongran. "*Yi zhi biaoxian neirong ji qi shijian.*" *Annals of Philosophy* 3 (1965).
Zhou, Shaoxian. *Xunzi yaoyi*. Taipei: Sanmin, 1976.
Zhu, Xi. *Zhuzi yulei* [Classified Conversations of Master Zhu]. Edited by Li Jingde. Taipei: Zhengzhong, 1962.
———. *Sishu jizhu* [Collected Commentaries on the Four Books]. Hong Kong: Taiping, 1980.

Index of Names

Aiken, H. D., 315n35
Allinson, R., 30n70
Almeder, R., 105n29, 263n13
Ames, R. T., 53, 74n9, 139n4, 149n50, 151n57, 157n73, 211n62, 319n7
Aquinas, T., 23n55, 105, 321
Aristotle, 41, 47, 105, 153n64, 171, 180n49, 192, 194–204, 209, 214, 222, 234–35, 242–43, 318, 321, 322, 331, 332
Attfield, R., 138n1, 192n24
Austin, J. L., 52n32, 85, 117n57, 156n72, 185, 340

Bacon, F., 331n36
Baier, K., 6n10, 12n11, 44n14
Barbour, I. G., 259n2
Barker, S. F., 54n37
Beardsmore, E. W., 32n79
Beauchamp, T. L., 54n37
Benn, S., 150n53, 359n24
Bergson, H., 293, 318
Berkeley, G., 52n34, 178
Blackstone, W. T., 259, 260
Bodde, D., 48n24, 329, 335, 344
Bontekoe, R., 163n13, 321n12, 367n43
Bowsma, O. K., 52n33
Brown, D. G., 253
Brown, J., 61n48
Butler, J., 29, 41, 142, 219, 250n6, 350
Butterfield, H., 73n1

Cai, Renhou, 142n23, 150n5, 157
Cai, Yuanbei, 319n5, 326
Calhoun, C., 350n8
Carnap, R., 318
Cavell, S., 262n9
Chan, A., 36n94, 216n77, 269n19, 270
Chan, W. T., x, 10n20, 13, 19n47, 77n19, 101n28, 104n28, 133n40, 180n77, 209n55, 265n31, 275n30–31, 285n8, 304–5, 307, 318, 321–22, 335n48, 367n44
Chang, Tsung-ch'ien, 249n10

Chappell, V. C., 262n9
Chen, Daqi, 100n8, 101n10, 103, 105n31, 106–7, 121, 122, 128, 138n3, 139, 141, 142n23, 143n28, 146n41, 151n56, 154n58, 164n15, 171n31, 217n80, 224
Chen, Qiyou, 149n51
Chen, Xiao, 92
Chen, Zhun, 306n13
Cheng, Chung-ying, 19n44, 34n86, 42n11, 262n11, 318n4
Cheng, Hao, 119, 172, 188, 314
Cheng, King, 89
Cheng, Yi, 77, 119, 134, 285, 307, 328
Chin, J., 322n14
Chong, Kim-chong, 239n123, 242n131
Collingwood, R. G., 203n34, 247, 248n3, 254n24, 301n11, 351n11
Confucius (Kongzi), 12, 17, 64, 69, 70, 74, 74n9, 75, 99, 100–101, 121, 128, 134–36, 145, 149, 169, 172, 174, 180, 181, 185–86, 191, 206–16, 218, 221, 222, 225, 241–42, 242n130, 272, 277–78, 281–87, 286, 289, 291, 295, 296, 317, 320, 324, 327, 331, 332, 334, 352–53, 356–57, 360, 364–66, 369
Creel, H. G., 75n12, 93n61, 249n10

Dahlstrom, D., 153n61, 230n113, 291n21
Dai, Master, 84
Dai, Zhen, 336
de Bary, W. T., 146n39, 367n41
Derrida, J., 318, 340
Descartes, R., 182, 318
Deutsch, E., 42n11, 151n57, 163n13, 293n7, 319n7, 344n63, 345n66, 367n43
Dewey, J., 23n55, 24, 62, 153, 233n118, 247, 298, 318, 327, 329, 340, 341, 342, 344, 361n29
Dietrichson, P., 89n52, 150n14
Disanayaki, W., 53n36, 211n63

389

Dobson, W. A. C. H., 220n88
Dong, Zhongshu, 332
Dover, K. J., 195
Downie, R. S., 23n55
Dray, W. H., 96n66
Dreisch, H., 318
Duan, Yucai, 162n10, 207n45
Dubs, H. H., x, 5n9, 10n20, 13, 17n38, 18–19, 33n87, 34, 39n3, 46, 49n28, 75, 87n49, 93n61, 102n20, 103, 109–13, 114, 119, 125, 148n46, 149n49, 150n52, 161n2, 162, 179n47, 191, 224
Duke Huan, 89
Duke of Zhou, 89, 242n130
Dworkin, G., 138n1, 150n53
Dworkin, R., 138n1, 192n4, 325, 359n24

Eberhard, W., 211n61
Edel, A. and M., 64n4
Edwards, P., 320n10
Elton, W., 52n33
Eucken, R. C., 318

Fang, C. 322n14
Fang, T. H., 143, 292–302, 346
Fehl, N. E., 39n2, 52n31
Field, G. C., 16n34
Findlay, J. N., 40n10
Fingarette, H., 32n80, 39n1, 46n18, 59–60, 99n4, 100n10, 101n19, 168, 210–12, 213n69, 218, 252n17, 262n10, 281n1, 345n65
Fisch, M., 96n66
Flew, A. G. N., 174-39
Fogelin, R. J., 83n39, 141, 180n49
Forke, A., 34n86
Francis, St. of Assisi, 278
Frankena, W. K., 41n8, 129
Frankfurt, H. G., 50n29, 152n58, 239n127, 287n13, 362n33
Fu, Cha, 89
Fung, Yu-lan (Feng Yulan), 33n82, 48n24, 71, 75n12, 140n8, 143n28, 317, 326n26, 329–36, 337–38, 339, 340, 342–44, 346

Gadamer, H–G., 318
Gaozi, 326
Geivers, B., 329n29
Giles, L., 168, 204n36, 209
Gilson, E., 318
Ginsberg, M., 268
Gong, Gong, 92
Graham, A. C., 4, 5n7, 14, 25n60, 33n83, 45n83, 139n4, 143, 146n41, 148n46, 152n60, 182, 213n67, 230n110, 249n9, 302, 327n27, 340
Green, T. H., 318
Grimaldi, W. M., 199n26
Guan, Zhong, 89

Hall, D. L., 139n4, 151n57, 157n73
Hamburger, M., 204n36
Han, Feizi, 149n50, 211
Hansen, C., 7n1
Hao, Yixing, 13n26
Hart, H. L. A., 23n55, 31, 194n4
Hartmann, N., 277
Hegel, G. W. F., 321
Heidegger, M., 318
Hepburn, R. W., 52n33
Hertz, P., 280n45
Hobbes, T., 23n55, 28, 184–85, 321
Hocking, W. E., 318
Höffding, H., 333
Holzman, D., 100n6
Homer, 196
Hou, Wailou, 336n51
Hsia (Xia), 74
Hsieh, Shan–yuan, 116n54
Hsieh, Yu–wei, 66n8
Hsu, C., 39n1
Hsu, F. L. K., 188n74
Hu, Hsien Chin, 238n122
Hu, Shih (Hu Shi), 105, 116n54, 162, 317, 325–28, 329, 332, 336, 337, 339, 340–44, 346
Huainanzi, 332
Huan, Dou, 92
Huang, Zongxi, 322n14
Hughes, E. R., 75n12
Hui, Shi, 322
Hume, D., 11n23, 17n35, 23n55, 28n65, 19, 29n66, 31, 54–55, 82n36, 170, 174n30, 318, 364n38
Husserl, E., 318
Hutcheson, F., 11n23, 27n62, 54n38, 61n48
Huxley, T., 318

Irwin, T., 198n23
Isenberg, A., 65, 361
Ivanhoe, P. J., 339n54

James, W., 58, 151n15, 177, 251n15, 272, 318, 329, 331, 333, 334, 366n40
Jessop, T. E., 52n34, 178n44
Jie, 77, 80–81, 88, 95, 96n65, 238
Joachim, H. H., 182n55

INDEX OF NAMES

Kang, Youwei, 332
Kant, I., 34, 89n52, 144, 157, 199n24, 251n14, 254n23, 266, 293, 314, 318, 321, 331, 335, 343
Kao, Ming (Gao Ming), 162n7
Karlgren, B., 206n45
Kato, J., 162n8
Kekes, J., 193n9
Kevy, P., 54n37
Kierkegaard, S., 349
King-Farlow, J., 261n6
Kline, T. C., 339n54
Knoblock, J., x, 5n9, 100n11, 146n41, 148n46, 154, 162n22, 179n47, 180n50, 182, 191n1, 206n44, 232, 239n124, 341n58, 360n25
Kolnai, A., 62
Kovesi, J., 11n22, 24, 75n10, 256–57
Kropotkin, P. A., 318
Ku, Hung-ming, 209n55

Lao, Sze-kwang (Lao Siguang), 317, 319n6, 326n26, 327, 336–46
Laozi (Lao Yzu), 149n51, 173, 231–32, 272, 297, 322, 362n30
Larsen, J., 151n57, 293n7, 319n7, 344n63
Lau, D. C., 4, 9n17, 13, 14, 19n47, 31, 33n83, 33n87, 35, 36, 44n86, 74n4, 114n52, 146n41, 157n74, 209n55, 225n92, 253n16, 350n6
Legge, J., 65n6, 67n1, 145, 161n3, 162, 209, 249n9, 290n20, 334n47, 350n6
Lenin, V. L., 318
Lenk, H., 164n16, 230n110, 307n15, 309n7
Lessa, W. A., 32n78
Lewis, B., 197n22
Lewis, C. I., 19n47, 114n52, 318
Lewis, H. B., 193n9
Li, Disheng, x, 5n9, 111n47, 141–42, 222n93, 239n125
Li, Gou, 103, 110, 113, 116–20, 122, 224n95
Li, Minghui, 367n42
Liang, Chi-chao, 282, 289n17
Liang, Qixiong (Liang Ch'i-hsiung), 49n28, 110n25, 139n6, 152n58, 154, 155n68, 222n93, 239, 362n33
Liao, W. K., 149n51
Lin, Tongqi, 318n4
Liu, Shu-hsien, 311, 321
Liu, Wu-chi, 75n12
Long, Yuchun, 230n110
Lorenz, K. Z., 49n25

Lovejoy, A., 345
Lü, Zuqian, 367n44
Luce, A. A., 52n34, 178n44
Luo, Guang, 346
Lynd, H., 201n31

Machalos, A. C., 261n6
Machle, E. J., 42n12, 174n37, 176n41, 182, 183, 232n121, 360n25
MacIntyre, A., 144n30, 195, 323n16, 324–25, 340, 365n35
Maier, V., 83n37
Makra, M. L., 249n9
Mao, Zishui, 40n5, 163n13, 357n21
Maritain, J., 318
Marx, K., 318
McCall, S., 261n6
McLean, G., 12n24
Mead, G. H., 204
Mei, Y. P., 80n29, 322n14
Melden, A. I., 67n9, 269
Mencius, 33–38, 56n42, 75, 83, 101–2, 108, 121, 128, 134, 145, 146, 148, 169, 170, 171, 174, 181, 183, 206, 207, 216–22, 226, 241–42, 268n19, 282, 318, 326, 336, 345, 348–70
Mill, J. S., 318
Montague, W. P., 329
Montesquieu, C. L., 318
Moore, C., 66n8
Moore, G. E., 142
Morris, H., 201n31, 203n34
Mote, F., 75n12
Mou Zongsan, 101n13, 142n23, 145, 293, 343–44, 346
Mounce, H. O., 32n79, 277n37
Mozi (Mo Tzu), 83, 83n37, 123n11, 143n23, 173, 176n40, 217, 231, 232, 294, 322, 323, 327
Müller, M., 63n1
Munro, D., 5n8, 15n32, 33n83, 37n95, 39n1, 73n2, 139n4, 143n28, 203n34, 359n22
Murphy, A. E., 32n79, 69, 253n21, 308

Nan, Huaijin, 223n94
Needham, J., 73n1
Ng, M., 211n61
Nietzsche, F. W., 318
Niphus, A., 178n44
Nishi, Amane, 319

Olbrechts-Tyteca, A., 199n27, 340n55
Osborn, H., 52n33

INDEX OF NAMES

Ostwald, M., 47n22, 196n19, 203, 204n35

Passmore, J., 83n88, 320–21
Paul, G., 164n16, 230n110, 307n15, 309n7
Pelikan, J., 146, 147, 363
Pepper, S. C., 21n51, 147, 188n72, 251n13, 270n23, 299, 318
Perelman, C., 199n27, 340n55
Perry, R. B., 272n26
Phillips, D. Z., 32n79, 277n37
Plato, 28n65, 195, 318, 331, 337, 338, 340, 344, 369
Price, R., 11n23, 54n38, 55

Qian, Mu, 172
Quine, W. V., 112n48, 318

Rachels, J., 269n22
Radcliff–Brown, A. R., 32n78, 39n25
Raphael, D. D., 11n23, 54n38
Rawls, J., 23n55, 93, 135, 138n2, 192n4, 311n26
Reid, T., 53n35, 54n37, 250, 250n12, 350, 350n11, 363
Ren, Jiyu, 322, 326n51
Rescher, N., 86, 105n29, 125n20, 144n31, 263, 267n17, 340n56
Richards, I. A., 35n92
Riezler, K., 198n23
Roberts, R., 197n21
Rorty, A., 50n29
Rorty, R., 340
Rosemont, H., 17n37, 31n75, 40–41, 46n18, 48n23, 109n43, 224n95
Rosenbaum, A. S., 67n10
Rotenstreich, N., 198n23, 201n32
Rousseau, J. J., 318
Royce, J., 309
Rudolf, R. G., 249n10
Russell, B., 318
Ryle, G., 154n68, 174n3, 199n24, 340

Schiller, F., 318
Schilpp, P. A., 199n24
Schneider, C. D., 194n10, 198n23
Schopenhauer, A., 318
Schwartz, B., 38n94, 168, 318n2
Searle, J., 13, 147n45
Selby–Bigge, L. A., 17n35, 61n48
Shaftesbury, Third Earl of, 11n23, 54n38, 363
Shea, W. R., 261n6
Shen, Buhai, 143n28
Shen, Dao, 322

Shen, V., 121n1, 318n4
Shensheng, 84
Shenzi (Shen Dao), 143n28
Shi, Ciyun, 351n10
Shih, V., 25n60
Shun, 77, 81, 92, 220n88, 367n48
Shun, Kwong–loi, 171n29, 206n45, 210n56, 220, 222, 349n3, 352n12, 362n32, 364n37, 368n48
Singer, M., 28n65, 287
Smith, A., 11n29
Socrates, 199n27, 317, 330–31
Solomon, R., 350n8
Songzi, 231–32
Spencer, H., 318
Spinoza, B., 318, 331
Standaert, N., 319n6, 329n29, 336n50
Stevenson, C., 35, 86n47
Stevenson, L., 3n1
Strawson, P. F., 3n1

Takehito, O., 132–33
Tang, 77, 92, 95, 96, 96n65, 304, 311–12
Tang, Junyi, 142n23, 188, 304, 311, 346, 368n50
Tang, Yang, 84
Taylor, C., 50n29
Taylor, G., 194n10, 202n33
Tolstoy, L. N., 318
Toulmin, S., 31n71, 44n15
Toynbee, A., 257n30
Tu, Wei–ming, 39n1, 146n39, 190, 281n1
Tufts, H., 327
Turbayne, C. M., 52n34, 185n62

Urmson, J. O., 93n59

Vogt, E. Z., 32n78
Von Wright, G. H., 248, 253n22

Waley, A., 40, 163, 207n46, 298n48, 210, 225
Walker, A. D. M., 40n7
Wall, G. B., 44n16
Wallace, G., 40n7
Walsh, V. G., 176n40
Walsh, W. H., 257
Wang, Chung (Wang Chong), 34n86
Wang, Meng'ou, 63n1, 145n33, 161n6, 290n20
Wang, Shouchang, 344n64
Wang, Tianyi, 109n42
Wang, Xianqian, x, 5n9
Wang, Yangming, 77n19, 120, 134, 136–37, 143, 156, 157n73, 172, 188, 189, 275–78, 284, 293, 296, 313, 314,

INDEX OF NAMES 393

319n7, 328, 336n48, 341, 342, 356n19, 359, 368
Wang, Zhonglin, 139n6, 148n18, 154n68, 239n19
Warnock, G. A., 23n55, 31n71, 261
Wasserstrom, R., 269n22
Watson, B., x, 5n9, 10n20, 13, 19n47, 49n28, 70n6, 77n20, 81n31, 83, 87n49, 102n20, 112, 148n46, 155n71, 174, 179n42, 182, 206n43, 221n91, 232, 297n20, 313, 322n38, 335n48, 360n25, 362n30
Wei, Zhengtong, 76n16, 101n13, 103, 107–9, 114, 116n54, 128, 143n23, 150n54, 214n70, 275n31, 305n8
Weiner, P. P., 73n1
Weiss, P., 294, 301n32
Wellman, C., 257
Wen, King, 77, 89, 92, 186, 221
Wheelwright, P., 30n9, 41, 127n30, 174n39, 187
White, A., 15
White, L., 278n41
Whitehead, A. N., 293, 318
Whorf, B., 340
Williams, B., 27n23, 194, 196, 198n23, 202n33, 204
Winch, P., 25n59, 32n79
Windleband, W., 327
Wisdom, J., 35
Wittgenstein, L., 25, 47, 254, 318, 332, 340, 344
Wollf, R. P., 89n52, 251n14
Woo, K. Y., 67n10
Wu, J., 249n10
Wu, King, 77, 92, 95, 96n65

Xia, Zhentao, 109n42
Xiong, Shili, 346
Xiqi, 84
Xu, Fuguan, 99n4
Xu, Qinting, 223n94

Xu, Xin, 206n45
Xuan of Qi, King, 355
Xue, Songliu, 205n40–41
Xunzi, 3–243, 255–56, 278, 295, 300, 301, 304, 305, 307, 308–9, 310, 313, 318, 323–24, 326, 327, 330–32, 338, 342, 348–49, 353, 355, 360–62, 364, 366–68, 370

Yan, Fu, 318
Yan, Yuan, 99–100
Yang, Liang, 13n26, 141, 232
Yang, Tzu (Yangzi), 217
Yang, Yunru, 75n10, 101n11
Yao, 77, 81, 92, 238
Ye, Jinggui, 100n9
Yin, Lujin, 336n51
You, You, 109n42
Yu, 30, 77, 80–81, 88, 92
Yü, Ying-shih, 133n40

Zeng, Chunhai, 142n23
Zhang, Xuan, 206n45
Zhang, Zai, 284, 307
Zhenzi, 99, 207n46, 363
Zhi, 81
Zhong, Shaohua, 319n6, 326n25
Zhou, 77, 92, 95, 96n65
Zhou, Dunyi, 276, 319
Zhou, Shaoxian, 103, 114–16
Zhu, Xi, 119, 120, 146, 157, 162, 168, 183, 191, 132–38, 194, 220, 285, 305–8, 312, 321, 324, 328, 341, 342, 349, 352n14, 363, 367n44
Zhuangzi, 83, 123n11, 173, 182n52, 242n130, 297, 299–300, 301, 322–23, 331, 332, 335, 345
Zi, Xu, 89
Zigong, 99, 215
Zilu, 69
Zimo (Tzu–mo), 217
Zixia, 367

Index of Subjects

accommodation, 171, 266, 269, 270, 272, 369–70
accord with evidence (*fuyan*), 5–6, 20, 23, 94, 101, 139, 149, 155–56, 309
accumulation (*ji*), 79, 81, 132, 148, 181–82, 235
analogical projection, 147, 183–84
analysis, 4, 11, 19, 21n25, 24n57, 31, 41, 53n35, 77, 87, 88n50, 104n28, 112, 119n52, 122, 126, 143, 191, 194, 199, 206n45, 292–93, 294n11, 298, 335, 338–41, 344; cost-benefit, 153, 229; of emotions, 200; of *li* (ritual), 39–62, 163–73; of means of persuasion, 199; of shame, 200–202; of *yi* (rightness), 126–32; textual, 339, 341, 344
argument, 5, 75, 85, 227
argumentation, 64, 74–76, 81, 83, 86–91, 94, 109, 117–18, 122, 131, 140n10, 142, 146, 148n46, 151n56, 155, 191–92, 212, 236–37, 305, 309, 314, 326, 339, 368, 369
autonomy, 46, 78, 138n1, 150n53, 152, 158, 172, 177, 182, 172, 226, 265, 357, 359–60, 367
axiological metaphysics, 294–302

bi (obscuration), 84–85, 97, 182, 231–35, 309–10, 323, 331–32, 338, 368
bieming (specific terms). *See* terms, generic and specific

can tiandi (forming a triad with Heaven and earth), 148, 160, 173–74, 177–78, 180–81, 189–90, 275. *See also* harmony
chang (constant, ordinary), 123–24, 126, 174–75, 223n94, 227
cheng (sincerity, truthfulness), 48, 56, 88, 118, 168–69, 180–81, 215, 218, 234, 236, 239, 274–75, 286, 356–57, 363, 369

choice, 36, 45, 46, 65, 81, 91, 148, 150–54, 149–53, 201, 213n64, 221, 223, 225–30, 233–35, 239–40, 241, 242, 265, 357–61; freedom of, 359–61
community, 25, 45, 49, 57, 70, 134, 165, 169, 177–78, 196, 204, 207, 222, 227–28, 237, 243, 254, 276, 279–91, 296, 309, 313, 320, 363. *See also* moral vision, relationships
compound term (*jianming*), 10, 102, 102n20, 205, 304, 313
comprehensive harmony, 272, 294–302, 346. *See also* harmony
conceptual distinction, 6, 21, 44, 89, 108, 148n46
conceptual reminders, 35–37
conflict, 24, 34, 36–37, 43–44, 48, 57–58, 65, 68–72, 104n28, 134, 143, 164–65, 167, 201n30, 214, 216, 224, 240, 272–74, 276–79, 290, 302, 315, 345, 354, 356–57, 361–63
consequences, 8–9, 17, 21, 24, 29n66, 30, 33–34, 36, 49, 55, 61, 81–82, 85, 88–89, 152–54, 157, 171, 198, 202, 214, 218, 225, 228, 233–34, 239, 242, 285–89, 298, 310, 323, 369
conservation, 68n1, 144–45, 279
constructive interpretation, 141, 150n52, 191, 304, 325, 331, 335–37
cost–benefit analysis, 153, 228–29

dao, 3n1, 12–13, 17–20, 37, 41, 57, 77–80, 82n32, 84, 90–92, 93n59, 95, 97, 99–101, 102n15, 106, 121–37, 138–47, 149, 150, 151n56, 152, 154n67, 158, 160, 168–70, 172, 174, 179, 181, 183–84, 190, 194, 217–18, 213, 218, 226, 228, 231–34, 236–342, 282, 291, 295–97, 299, 300–302, 307, 313, 322–23, 348–49, 352n14, 353, 357, 360, 362, 365, 368–69; as moral vision, 152–54, 169, 249, 274–80,

395

dao (*Continued*)
301, 331; constitutive means for, 114–16; *daoguan* (the thread of *dao*), 76, 147, 183, 231; *daotong* (transmission of *dao*), 146; doctrine of, 295; *zhidao* (knowing or understanding *dao*), 150, 156–57, 183, 184

deficiencies of moral agency, 354–68

deliberation *(lü)*, 52, 81, 85, 90–91, 104, 129–30, 136, 138, 146n41, 147n43, 148–59, 151–54, 154n64, 156–58, 175, 183, 189, 192, 225–26, 228–36, 241, 253, 315, 342; method of, 152–55, 228–29

delusion *(huo)*, 123, 156, 177, 219n83, 350n9, 368

description and evaluation, distinction between, 217, 261–62, 307–8

desires *(yu)*, 7–9, 11–16, 16–17, 21–33, 36–37, 41–44, 48–52, 68, 77, 78, 80, 82–85, 88–89, 93, 96, 124–25, 127, 129, 131, 135, 145, 150n52, 152–53, 157, 164–67, 160–71, 173, 177, 184, 200–208, 222, 228–34, 238–40, 243, 247, 272–73, 279, 283, 286–90, 300, 315–15, 319, 314–15, 354, 360–63, 369; second-order/reflective, 49–51, 68, 82, 152, 166, 286–87, 262

discrimination *(pian)*, 5–6, 20, 32, 151n56, 155, 217, 254, 269

emotions, 11, 14n31, 15–17, 49, 51–53, 55, 57, 59, 60, 68–71, 82, 167–68, 171, 186, 189, 199–200, 349–50, 356, 360. *See also* feelings

enjoyment, 16, 24, 70, 237, 238, 240. *See also* joy

ethical judgment. *See* judgments

ethical justification. *See* justification

ethical knowledge, 78, 138–59, 191–92. *See also* moral knowledge

ethics, 6, 31, 41, 44, 46, 57, 66, 119, 248, 257, 264, 266, 267, 270, 317–18, 326, 329, 332; axiological, 41; Confucian, 20, 40, 49, 52, 62, 64–66, 92, 116, 118–19, 121, 129, 140, 161, 167, 192, 194, 234, 248, 254, 257, 261–62, 288, 315, 342, 332, 343, 349, 367, 369; of speech, 212, 321

excellence. *See* ideal themes, moral excellence

explication, 4, 264–65

fact and value, 308. *See also* description and evaluation

family, 66, 146, 162, 177, 189, 195, 263, 275, 277, 283–84, 308, 355

fang (dykes), 68, 145–46

feelings/passions *(qing)*, 7–9, 11–16, 21, 24, 27, 29, 36–37, 48, 50–51, 55, 68, 71, 78, 145, 150, 152, 166–67, 186, 196, 200, 202, 219–20, 229, 277, 282, 284–85, 350. *See also* emotions; motivational structure

filial piety *(xiao)*, 11, 63, 65, 121, 171, 183–84, 276, 277, 283, 308, 311

focal notions, 103–4, 108, 114, 124–25, 132, 140, 313

former kings *(xianwang)*, 75–77, 81, 94–95, 101, 102n15, 145, 235n120

gan and *ying*, 305. *See also* practical causation

gong (impartiality, public spirit). *See* impartiality

gongming. *See* terms, generic and specific

good/goodness *(shan)*, 4, 7–13, 21–22, 27–28, 32, 51, 58–59, 61, 78–79, 92, 134, 148, 158, 168–70, 175, 177, 179, 181–82, 194–95, 197, 199; accumulation of, 132; and bad *(e)*, 4, 7–13, 21–22, 27–28, 33–37, 57, 78, 91–92, 166, 326

good life, the, 43, 55, 60, 100, 114, 122, 168, 170, 172–73, 185, 189–90, 213, 227–28, 231, 237, 264–66, 271, 281–82, 306–7, 322, 348–49, 352n14, 353–54, 367, 369–70. *See also* harmony

gu (cause, reason), 305–6

gu and *jin* (past and present), 73–98, 233

guan (thread), 123, 140–42, 231

guantong (comprehensive understanding), 141–42, 164, 184–85, 188, 306–7, 327

harmony, ideal of ix, 36, 45, 57, 60, 70–71, 79, 115, 124, 168, 172–76, 187–89, 211, 234, 241, 249, 251–52, 260, 272–79, 281–83, 289–95, 298, 306, 346, 348, 306. *See also* good life

hengxin (constant heart/mind), 218, 221, 327, 349, 352–54, 356–58, 365

history: elucidative use of, 88–90, 342; evaluative use of, 91–98, 342; pedagogical use of, 77–82; rhetorical use of, 83–88; writing, 335–36

history of philosophy, methods of, 338–39

honor, 12, 46–47, 56, 58–60, 70, 81–82, 170, 192, 196–97, 199, 206–9, 211, 222–23, 236–38, 242, 255, 259, 363–64; and shame, *see* shame and honor; and virtues, 197; intrinsic and extrinsic, 170–71, 237–38, 242–43, 364

human action, 17, 56–57, 176, 250
human nature *(xing, qingxing, xingqing)*,
  3–38, 49–50, 134, 152, 167, 175,
  191–92, 240, 257, 271–72, 275, 311,
  326, 348,–49, 358, 361–61; beautification of, 49–50, 167, 279; conceptual aspect, 3–20; definitions, 14n27; quasi-empirical aspect, 20–27
humility, 65–66, 71, 159, 177, 187, 278
huo (delusion), 123, 219n81, 233, 350n9, 368

ideal themes, 19, 59, 170, 249n8, 251, 271, 273–74, 280, 301n32, 349, 353, 367, 370. *See also dao*
impartiality *(gong)*, 10n20, 44, 85–86, 88–89, 96n66, 104, 109, 129, 213, 230
insight *(ming)*, 78, 182–83
integrity, 48, 54, 70, 80, 121, 129, 145, 164, 166, 172, 175, 177–78, 184, 190, 218, 243, 281, 286, 288, 291, 301, 324, 342, 356–57

jianquan (thoughtful consideration of all relevant factors), 152–53, 156, 228
joy, 8, 14–16, 49, 50–52, 56–58, 60, 68, 70–71, 151, 168, 171–72, 188, 208, 224, 227, 229, 240, 278, 284, 279, 360
judgments, ethical/moral, 55, 93–97, 109, 130, 131, 135, 138, 144, 146–47, 149, 154–58, 163, 166, 169, 212–13, 252, 260, 264, 301, 353; perceptual, 155–56; prereflective, 219, 350; value, 213, 257, 350
junzi (superior men, paradigmatic individuals), 12–13, 18, 44–46, 48, 51, 68–69, 79, 81–82, 84, 88–92, 107, 115, 123–24, 131, 135–36, 139, 141–42, 145, 163–64, 166–69, 172, 176, 180, 183–84, 204, 208–9, 211–15, 221, 223, 230, 235–37, 240–43, 208–9, 211–15, 221, 223, 230, 235–37, 240–43, 277–78, 282, 284–85, 319, 357, 364–68, 370. *See also* paradigmatic individuals
justification, 25, 40–44, 63, 86, 91–94, 97, 107, 119, 127, 130, 149, 154–55, 163, 177, 190, 204, 207, 223, 227, 243, 264, 279, 290, 310, 318–19, 325, 336, 340, 345, 355, 365

knowledge, 12, 35, 61, 69, 74n9, 79–80, 85, 90–94, 105–7, 132, 136, 166, 169–70, 177–79, 182–84, 189, 201, 230, 232–35, 247–48, 250, 285, 306,
  309, 319, 320n7, 323, 326, 328, 333, 337, 339, 342, 345, 365; ethical, 138–59, 191–92

later kings, 76–94
lei (kind, class), 90, 152, 155, 239
li (ritual, rites, propriety, rules of proper conduct), 6n11, 7, 11, 12, 17–20, 25, 30–32, 39–62, 63–72, 74, 76–78, 90, 92, 94–95, 97, 153–54, 156, 160–90, 209, 235n120, 261–62, 281, 325–26; aesthetic dimension, 11, 49–57, 61–62; and moral justification, 63–67; and moral virtues, 46–47; and music, 57, 68–72, 187; and personal relationship, 52, 63–67; and reason, 163–64; and *ren*, 48, 51, 59, 65, 68, 72, 93–95, 99–120, 125–26, 153, 161, 167–69, 189, 207–8, 217, 252; and social distinctions, 45; and *yi* (rightness, righteousness), 17–20, 28, 36, 48, 56, 65, 68–69, 72, 93–95, 97, 99–120, 127–32, 145, 167–69, 189, 206–8, 211, 213, 220–21, 224–25, 252, 262, 279, 282, 313, 349, 352, 356, 362, 365; bases of, 177–78; as constitutive means of *ren* or *dao*, 45, 55, 69, 114, 221; as dykes, 165–66; as a focal notion, 104–5; as religious rites, 58–60; deep significance of, 58; foundation, inner aspect, 172–85; foundation, outer aspect, 172–85; functions of, 164–68, 239–40; moral/ethical dimension, 43–49, 168–72; of mourning and sacrifice, 58–59 (*see also* religious sacrifices); origin, 164–65; religious dimension, 57–61; scope and evolution, 162–64; translation, 160–61
li (reason, rationale, principle, pattern), 40, 46, 49n28, 57, 79, 104, 107, 115, 124, 126, 142, 146, 151, 152, 163–64, 177, 181, 183, 186, 219n83, 226, 226n100, 231–34, 239, 241, 303–17, 319, 329–30, 350–53, 362, 368–69; as generic and specific terms, 307, 311, 351
li (advantage, personal gain, profit), 213–14, 218, 224, 236, 356
loyalty, 7, 48, 63, 121, 171, 186, 315; grades of, 89
lü (deliberation). *See* deliberation

metaphysics of morals, 293, 342–43
mind *(xin)*, 9, 9n17, 12, 14, 39, 46, 48–49, 54, 57, 71, 78–79, 84–85, 88–89, 91, 104, 133–34, 138, 149–52,

mind (xin) (Continued)
  155, 169, 170, 177, 180–82, 182, 187, 189, 194, 215, 219, 225–26, 229–30, 232–36, 239, 241, 243, 265, 288–89, 323, 331, 342, 348, 350, 362n33, 388; constant (hengxin), 218, 221, 249, 252, 254, 356–58, 365–66
ming (insight, clarity), 142, 180–81, 301
ming (name, term), 364. See also terms
model, 18, 20, 79–80, 82, 107, 164, 202–3, 251; of influence and response, 251–54, 257–58
modesty, 36, 48, 54, 169–70, 177, 192–93, 221n63, 212, 219, 349, 350n8
moral agency, deficiencies of, 354–68
moral agents, 6, 36–37, 37n95, 50, 53, 57–58, 66–70, 93, 201, 203, 236–38, 241–43, 247, 251–52, 256, 261, 265, 267, 287–89, 308, 358–59, 365–66
moral commitment, 235–36, 284
moral conduct, 6, 78, 105n25, 132, 198–99, 201, 209, 222, 268, 366
moral creativity, 256, 264n14, 300, 363
moral cultivation, 71, 182, 274, 277; and music, 68–72. See also self-cultivation
moral discourse, 6, 10, 12, 222, 265
moral distinctions, 9–13, 25, 27, 45–47, 70, 127–28, 130–31, 236, 359
moral education, 49, 71, 77–80, 90
moral excellence, 12, 18–19, 37, 91, 263, 271–74, 278–80, 301–2, 318. See also ideal themes
moral faults, 212, 214–15, 236, 242, 344, 363–65
moral ideals, two interpretations, 271–73. See also ideal themes
moral knowledge, 78n21, 191, 342. See also ethical knowledge; zhi (knowledge, understanding, acknowledgment)
moral learning, 78–80, 82, 93, 148, 164, 172, 181, 208
moral metaphysics, 342–43
moral point of view, the, 10–13, 16–21, 23, 25–27, 29–30, 36, 44, 216, 224, 250, 252, 256–59, 267, 356
moral priority, 354, 358–63, 365
moral reflection, 285–86, 368
moral rights, 268–70
moral sacrifice, 172, 221, 271, 357, 366. See also self-sacrifice
moral teachers, 79, 272
moral theory, 21, 32, 39, 66, 132, 242, 262–66, 269, 280, 293, 300, 303, 343, 358, 361, 363, 365–69
moral tradition, 32, 195, 201n31, 204, 207, 279, 308, 309, 342, 262–63, 363, 369

moral vision, 3, 17, 168–69, 172–78, 189–90, 274–80, 322
morality, 6n11, 9, 11, 17, 20, 23n55, 24, 27–28, 30–41, 44, 46, 61, 64, 73n3, 129, 161, 202, 210–11, 221, 224n95, 232, 256, 264–68, 270, 272, 279, 292–95, 297, 299–300, 302, 343, 349, 361–62, 366, 368; and human nature, 3–4, 14, 30–32, 37, 348–49; customary and reflective, 361; preconditions of, 264–70, 274, 315, 366
mortality, 57–60
motivational structure, basic (qingxing, xingqing), 9, 11–17, 20–21, 23, 30, 33, 36, 48–51, 68, 78, 160, 175, 152, 348

nobility, 47, 197, 199–200, 208, 222, 242

paradigmatic individuals, 18, 68–70, 74, 82, 101, 136, 164, 166, 168–69, 171–72, 180, 184, 203–4, 235, 278, 357, 364, 368. See also junzi
partiality (pian), 10–11, 29, 31, 88–89, 164, 229–335
past (gu) and present (jin), 73, 76, 81, 85, 91–92, 94, 233
pian (partiality). See partiality
plausible presumptions, 86, 92, 144, 158, 240, 335, 342
poverty, 43, 46, 68, 164, 208, 213, 237, 267–69, 366
practical causation, 247–58
practical coherentism, 144–47, 150, 157–59
preconditions of morality, 264–70, 274, 278, 315, 366
principles, 12–13, 32, 34, 103, 110, 119, 158, 174, 203, 206, 251–52, 260, 264–68, 273, 284–85, 292, 303, 131, 315–16, 335, 343, 349, 365, 367, 369; of comprehensive harmony, 298–302
prudence, 82, 104, 259–60

qing, 7–8, 11, 14–16, 68n2, 151–52, 219, 229, 350. See also feelings, emotion
quality of life, 260–69
quan (weighing circumstance/discretion), 85, 135–36, 146, 152, 170, 217–18, 228, 352, 352n14, 353, 356, 361, 364, 367–68; method of, 152–54, 352
quan (completeness), 80, 123–24, 141, 175, 243

rang (yielding, humility), 65–66
reason, 40, 46, 57, 79, 83, 104, 107, 115, 124, 126, 151–52, 158, 163, 177, 219, 226, 228, 231–32, 234, 239–41, 319,

329, 350–53, 360, 362, 367–69; and principle, 303–16
reasonableness, 48, 176–77, 203, 233n118, 269, 316, 367–68
reasons, 84, 86–88, 91, 97, 142, 149, 179–80, 216, 302, 323, 327, 330, 340–41; for actions, 130, 302, 308; for things, 179–80
reconciliation, 300, 302
rectification of lost values, 300–301
rectifying names/terms (*zhengming*), 6, 17, 33, 64, 100, 109, 145, 184, 255–58, 286, 308, 324–25
reflective desirability, 81–82, 85
relationships, human, 79–80; personal, 45, 49, 52, 63–67, 69, 72, 201, 281–84, 288–91, 302, 321. *See also* community
religious sacrifices, 43, 58–59, 63, 160–62, 164, 168, 176–78, 185–88, 276, 355
ren (benevolence, humanness, ideal humanity), 6n11, 12, 17–20, 36, 37, 41, 42, 42n11, 43, 45, 47–49, 51, 59, 62, 63, 66–69, 72, 77–79, 82, 90, 92, 100–101, 103–4, 104n28, 105, 116, 118–19, 125, 129, 131, 133–35, 167–73, 177, 188–89, 192, 194, 207, 212, 214, 216–17, 221–22, 225, 227, 242, 252–53, 256, 313, 320, 348–49, 351–54, 360, 362–63, 367–70; and humility, 169–70; and joy, 172, 188; and *li*, *see li* and *ren*; and *yi*, 17, 65, 67, 69, 78–79, 90, 92, 99–102, 118–20, 139, 148, 161, 167, 172, 180, 207–8, 212, 217, 220n88, 221, 235–36, 238–39, 242, 252, 357, 364; as a focal notion, 104–5, 124–25; method of, 286–89; vision of, 7, 207, 275–91, 367. *See also dao*, moral vision
ren, *li*, and *yi*, 18, 102, 115, 132, 136, 172n1, 189, 208, 228, 369, passim
respect for others, 58, 177, 314, 369
reverence, 48, 59–60, 65, 70–71, 169, 182n53, 185–87, 283, 364n38
rhetoric, 199–200, 222
rights, 19, 66–67, 73n1, 268–69
rules, 13, 18–19, 24–25, 28–32, 39, 67, 72n3, 85–86, 93, 97, 115, 117–19, 125, 128–31, 135, 262, 264–68, 273, 282, 284–86, 302–3, 306, 312, 314–15, 321, 348–49; of proper conduct, *see li* (ritual, rites, propriety, rules of proper conduct)

sage (*sheng, shengren*), 9n17, 13–14, 18, 27, 30, 33, 46, 50–51, 77, 89–91, 94–95, 97, 136, 139, 142, 144, 148n46, 149, 166–67, 174–75, 178–79, 180–84, 218, 242, 255–56, 319, 323, 330, 334, 343, 351–53, 355, 357–58, 360, 368
self-cultivation, 46, 81–82, 95, 106, 158, 181, 183, 236, 239, 241–42, 275, 281–82, 290, 328, 330, 334, 361, 363, 368
self-deception, 53, 59, 168, 215, 363–64
self-determination, 142, 149–50, 152
self-examination, 53–54, 79, 183, 214–17, 241, 285–86, 363–65
self-reproach, 193, 214–15, 241, 363–64
self-respect, 58, 79, 183, 215, 216, 217–218, 241, 269
self-sacrifice, 172, 221, 271, 277–78, 357, 366
self-transformation, 50, 190, 215, 235, 245, 349, 360
sensus communis, 363
sentiment, 54, 196, 219, 248–49, 349
shame, 12, 36, 47n20, 70, 81, 84, 89, 170–71, 191–246, 285–86, 359, 363, 364n38, 368; and guilt, 210–11; and honor, 195–97, 222–223, 236–38; and *li* (ritual), 210, 216; and virtues, 192, 201; and *yi* (rightness), 213–16, 220–21; Chinese terms (*chi, xiu,* and *ru*) for, 205–6, 209–10; defined, 192–94, 200; generic and specific terms of, 192–93, 295; in the *Analects*, 207–16; in the *Mengzi* (Works of Mencius), 214–22; in the *Xunzi*, 222–43; sense of shame (*chi*), 209–10, 214, 217; justly deserved (*shi-ru*) and circumstantial (*yi-ru*),194, 236–37
shan (goodness, excellence), 7–8, 9–13, 37, 92–93, 168, 172, 175, 177–78. *See also* good/goodness
shen (spirit, god), 88, 148n46, 162, 176, 178–82, 182n53, 184–85, 189, 223n94; *shenming*, 180–81, 236n121; *rushen* (like a god), 179–80
shu (consideration of others), 99, 169–70, 177–78, 286–89
siduan (four beginnings of virtues), 348–54
significant others, 202–4, 220, 222, 237, 243
sincerity. *See cheng* (sincerity, truthfulness)
situation, 24–25; boundary, 185; human, 23–29, 78, 127, 229n108; lack of appreciation of, 84–85, 367–68; normal/exigent or indeterminate, 126, 131–32, 134, 153, 221, 247, 253–56, 269–70, 274, 314, 316, 342, 352; par-

ticular, 16, 42–43, 70, 71, 73, 88, 104, 118, 127–30, 150–53, 221, 230–33, 255, 285, 289–90, 313, 315, 353–54, 356, 359, 360–66, 367; problematic, 26, 43–44, 69, 232, 234, 247, 253, 274, 286, 342 (*see also* conflict)
spoudaios, 203–4, 209. *See also* paradigmatic individuals

teaching, 20n48, 69, 82, 100, 179, 241, 335n48, 366
terms, generic *(gongming)* and specific *(bieming)*, 42–43, 76–77, 95, 110–13, 117–18, 122, 124, 138–39, 161, 171, 174, 192–94, 205, 304, 307, 309, 318, 311, 313, 316; single *(danming)* and compound *(jianming)*, 102–3, 107, 205–6, 304
testimony, 82, 85–86
thought–experiment, 20–27, 29, 33, 82
ti and *yong* (substance and function), 77, 123, 296–97
tian (Heaven, Nature), 25n60, 34, 58, 110n45, 168, 173–78, 185–86, 189, 223n34
tianren heyi (unity and harmony of *tian* and humanity), 172–73, 190, 275, 281, 293, 294, 298, 306, 348. *See also* harmony
timeliness, 169, 218, 352–53
tong (unity), 101–2, 108, 115, 124n17, 145
tonglei (unity of classes or kinds), 76, 102, 140, 142–45, 149, 307
tradition, 24, 32, 51–52, 59, 125, 135–36, 144–45, 146–47, 149, 157–58, 166, 211, 218, 252, 257, 279, 281–83, 308–9, 314–16, 321, 323–24, 341–45, 363, 369. *See also* community
translation, 319, 321
trustworthiness, 48, 88, 100, 117, 118, 121, 212, 252

value–transcendence, 301–2
virtues, 11, 17–18, 32, 37, 41, 47–49, 50–57, 59, 61, 63–67, 68, 92, 96, 100–102, 105, 110, 113–14, 119, 121–37, 145, 149, 166–68, 171, 173, 175, 185, 196–97, 199–200, 201–2, 218–21, 223–24, 227, 281, 290, 360; as achievements, 351–52; beauty of, 11, 54–56, 61–62; cardinal and dependent, 171, 348–49; *siduan* (four beginnings) of, 348–54; unity of, 121–37, 153–54. *See also li* and *yi*; *li* and *ren*; *yi* and *ren*
vision, Confucian, 3, 60, 136, 168–69, 172–73, 178, 180, 188–89, 190, 251–52, 260, 273–80, 281–91, 293–94. *See also* moral vision

wei (activity, productive activity, artifice), 7–8, 13–16, 13n26, 14, 167, 175, 189, 229
welfare, 18, 61, 125, 176, 221–22, 262–70, 274, 277–78, 280, 365–66
wen (refinement, elegant form, cultural style of life), 51–52, 167–69, 176–78, 304
wisdom, 16, 36, 72–74, 100, 105, 117–18, 132–38, 154, 157–58, 182–83, 157, 182–83, 186–87, 194, 207, 216, 221, 235, 297, 319–29, 324, 339, 242, 348
words and deeds, 59, 211–12, 354

xin (mind, mind/heart), 78, 134, 138, 149, 150–52, 154–55, 157–58, 170, 177, 180, 182–83, 189, 206, 216, 218–19, 220–22, 225–26, 229–30, 234, 236, 275, 288–89, 293, 348–70

yi (right, rightness, righteousness), 6n11, 7, 17–20, 28, 36, 40, 42, 42n1136, 77–79, 82, 90, 92, 95, 100, 121, 139, 153, 161, 163, 194, 205, 212, 218, 236, 252, 262, 284, 300, 308, 313, 342, 348, 351, 356–57, 359, 365; analysis of, 126–32; and *li* (rites), 99–120 (*see also li* and *yi*); and *li* (profit), 218, 223–28, 240, 356; and *ren*, 134–35, 348 (*see also ren* and *yi*); as a focal notion, 104–5; as a standard for honors and wealth, 208; as a standard for honor and shame, 236–38, 241–42
yu (desires). *See* desires

zhengming. *See* rectifying names/terms
zhexue (philosophy), 319–21
zhi (knowledge, understanding, acknowledgment), 151, 154, 156, 319, 319n7
zhi (wisdom), 36, 194, 348. *See also* wisdom
zhilü (wise and well–informed deliberation), 91, 104, 130, 151–58, 230
zhong (loyalty, conscientiousness), 89, 99, 169, 286–88
zhong (fitting, appropriate, center, middle), 77, 139, 353

Glossary

an 安
anwei lihai changti 安危利害常體
ba 霸
ben 本
benneng zhi zhi 本能之知
benti 本體
bi 蔽
bian 辨
bian 辯
bianhe 辨合
bianze jin gu 辨者盡故
bieming 別名
bu zhiquan bu zhi yingbian 不知權不知應變
buken 不肯
buneng 不能
buwei 不為
buzhiyi 不執一
cai 材
Cai Renhou 蔡仁厚
Cai Yuanbei 蔡元培
caizhi 材質
can 參
can tiandi 參天地
ceyin zhi xin 惻隱之心
chang 常
changlü guhou 長慮顧後
changshi 常識
changti 常體
changtong 常通
Chen Daqi 陳大齊
Chen Qiyou 陳奇猷
Chen Rongjie 陳榮捷
Chen Xiao 陳囂
Chen Zhun 陳淳
Cheng 誠
Cheng Chung-ying 成中英
Cheng Hao 陳顥
Cheng Wang 成王
Cheng Yi 陳頤
chengde zhi xue 成德之學
chenggong zhi zhi 成功之知
chengyi 誠意
chengze 誠者
chi 恥
chiru 恥辱
cirang zhi xin 辭讓之心
cui 粹
cun xin 存心
da qingming 大清明
da Ru 大儒
Dai Chen 戴震
dali 大理
dangran zhi ze 當然之則
danming 單名
dao wu zhongqiong 道無終窮
daoguan 道貫
Daojia 道家

daoli 道理
daotong 道統
dati 大體
de 德
Dong Zhongshu 董仲舒
du 度
Duan Yucai 段玉裁
e'de 惡德
fa zhi shu 法之數
fa zhi yi 法之義
fang 坊
Fang Dongmei 方東美
fangde 坊德
fen 分
Fu Cha 夫差
fu dao zhe tichang er jinbian
　　夫道者體常而盡變
Fung Yu-lan 馮友蘭
fuyan 符驗
gaiguo 改過
gan 感
Gao Ming 高明
Gaozi 告子
geiren zhi qiu 給人之求
gong 恭
gong 公
gong sheng ming 公生明
gongfu 功夫
gongming 共名
gongxin 公心
gongyi 公義
gu 故
gu 古
guai 怪
guan 貫
Guan Zhong 管仲

guanchuan 貫串
guanchuan 貫穿
guantong 貫通
guayu 寡欲
guijian 貴賤
guina 歸納
guishen 鬼神
gujin yiye 古今一也
gujin zhi zhengquan 古今之正權
Han Feizi 韓非子
haoli 好利
heng 亨
heng 衡
hengxin 恒心
Hou Wailu 侯外廬
Hu Shi 胡適
Huainanzi 淮南子
Huan Dou 驩兜
Huan Gong 桓公
Huang Zongxi 黃宗羲
Hui Shi 惠施
huo 惑
huowang 後王
ji 即
ji 積
jiande siyi 見得思義
jianming 兼名
jianquan 兼權
jianshu 兼術
jianwu 兼物
Jie 桀
jie 節
jin qi xin 盡其心
jin 今
jing 敬
jing 經

GLOSSARY

jingxue shidai　經學時代
jinsi　近思
junzi　君子
Kang Youwei　康有為
ke　可
kewei　可謂
kong　恐
Ku Hung-ming　辜鴻銘
kun　坤
Lao Sze-kwang　勞思光
Laozi　老子
le　樂
lei　類
li　利
li　理
li　禮
Li Disheng　李滌生
Li Gou　李覯
Li Minghui　李明輝
li yi zhi tong　禮義之統
li zhi gongxiao　禮之功效
li zhi zhengli　禮之證立
lian　臉
Liang Chi-chao　梁啟超
Liang Qixiong　梁啟雄
liangneng　良能
liangzhi　良知
lide　立德
ligong　立功
liguan　理貫
Liu Shu-hsien　劉述先
Liu Zongzhou　劉宗周
lixian　禮憲
lixingyu　理性欲
lixue　理學
liyan　立言

liyi zhi tong　禮義之統
lizhiben　禮之本
lizhili　禮之理
lizhishu　禮之數
lizhiyi　禮之義
Long Yuchun　龍宇純
long　隆
longli　隆禮
Lü Zuqian　呂祖謙
lü　慮
lun　倫
lunli xue　倫理學
Luo Guang　羅光
mei　美
mei qishen　美其身
meide　美德
Mengzi　孟子
mianzi　面子
ming　名
ming　命
ming　明
Mingjia　名家
mingjun　明君
Mou Zongsan　牟宗三
Mozi　墨子
Nan Huaijin　南懷謹
nei　內
neisheng waiwang　內聖外王
neng　能
Nishi Amane　西周
pian　偏
pian sheng an　偏生闇
pianshang zhi huan　偏傷之患
qi　期
qi　氣
qi yan zhi chengli　其言之成理

qian 乾
Qian Mu 錢穆
qing 情
qingxing 情性
qiongli 窮理
qiwu 欺侮
qiwu 齊物
qixiang 氣象
quan 權
quan 全
quancui 全粹
quanti 全體
rang 讓
ren 仁
ren bao side 仁包四德
Ren Jiyu 任繼愈
ren zhi longye 仁之隆也
renge 人格
renshi 人事
renxin 仁心
Ru 儒
ru 如
ru 辱
rushen 如神
shan 善
Shen Buhai 申不害
Shen Dao 慎道
shen 神
sheng sheng zhi li 生生之理
sheng zhi li 生之理
sheng 聖
shenming 神明
shenming zhi zhu 神明之主
shezhun 設準
shi 事
shi 士
shi 實
shi 時
Shi Ciyun 史次耘
shifei zhi xin 是非之心
shijian 識見
shirong 勢榮
shiru 勢辱
shizhi xitong 實質系統
shizhong 時中
shoulian 收斂
shouren xingyi 守仁行義
shu 恕
shuda 疏達
shuo 説
shutong 疏通
si er buxiu 死而不朽
siduan 四端
siyu 私欲
Songzi 宋子
sowei 所謂
soyiran zhi gu 所以然之故
suijiu tongli 雖久同理
Tang Junyi 唐君毅
tian 天
tianli 天理
tianren ganying 天人感應
tianren hede 天人合德
tianren heyi 天人合一
tianren zhi fen 天人之分
tiansheng rencheng 天生人成
tianxingyu 天性欲
tiaoli 條理
tiyong 體用
tiyong yiyuan 體用一源
tong 統
tong yu shenming 通於神明

tongchang de qingkuang 通常的情況	xing 形
tongchang de qingxing 通常的情形	xing zhi jun 形之君
tonglei 統類	xingqing 性情
tongming 統名	xingshi xitong 形式系統
Tsudo Shindo 津田真道	Xiong Gongzhe 熊公哲
tui 推	Xiong Shili 熊十力
tui'en 推恩	xiu 羞
wai 外	xiuchi 羞恥
wang 妄	xiukui 羞愧
wang 忘	xiuwu zhi xin 羞惡之心
wang 王	xu cheng 虛稱
Wang Chong 王充	Xu Fuguan 徐復觀
Wang Meng'ou 王夢鷗	Xu Qinting 徐芹庭
Wang Xianqian 王先謙	Xu Shen 許慎
Wang Yangming 王陽明	Xue Songliu 學頌留
Wang Zhonglin 王忠林	xuexin 學心
wei 偽	Xun 舜
Wei Zhengtong 韋政通	Xunzi 荀子
weizhi 謂之	Yan Fu 嚴復
wen 文	yang 養
Wen Wang 文王	Yang Liang 楊倞
Wu Wang 武王	yang qi xing 養其性
wuru 侮辱	Yang Yunru 楊筠如
wuwei 無為	Yangzi 楊子
xi xianxue 希賢學	Yao 堯
xi zhexue 希哲學	Ye Jinggui 葉經桂
Xia Zhendao 夏甄陶	yi 義
xianwang 先王	yigu chijin 以古持今
xiao 孝	yijin chigu 以今持古
xiaoren 小人	yili 義理
xiaoti 小體	ying 應
xin 信	yinren ziran 因任自然
xin 心	yirong 義榮
xin zhi de 心之德	yiru 義辱
xing 性	yiti 一體
xing 行	yiyi bianying 以一變應

yiyi wei li 以義為利
you 憂
Yu 禹
yu 欲
Yü Ying-shih 余英時
yuan 元
yuanjin 遠近
yue 樂
yumin 裕民
yuwu qushe zhi quan 欲惡取舍之權
ze 則
ze 擇
Zeng Chunhai 曾春海
zeshu 擇術
Zhang Xuan 張喧
Zhang Zai 張載
zhe 哲
zhen 貞
zheng 爭
zhengming 正名
zhengzhi 徵知
zhenshi wu wang 真實無妄
Zhenzi 曾子
zhexue 哲學
Zhi 跖
zhi 志
zhi 知
zhi 智
zhicang 智藏
zhi you sohe weizhi zhi 知有所合謂之智

zhidao 知道
zhilü 知慮
zhitong tonglei 知通統類
zhiwei 之謂
zhiwei er lun 知微而論
zhixing heyi 知行合一
zhizhong wuquan 執中無權
zhong 中
zhong 忠
Zhong Shaohua 鐘少華
Zhou 紂
Zhou Dunyi 周敦頤
Zhou Gong 周公
Zhou Shaoxian 周紹賢
zhu 主
Zhu Xi 朱熹
Zhuang Zhou 莊周
Zhuangzi 莊子
zhuti 主體
Zi Xu 子胥
zide 自得
zifan 自反
Zigong 子貢
zigu ji jin 自古及今
Zilu 子路
Zimo 子莫
Zixia 子夏
zixue shidai 子學時代
zizhi 自知
zongming 總名

www.ingramcontent.com/pod-product-compliance
Lightning Source LLC
Chambersburg PA
CBHW032023290426
44110CB00012B/648